Introducing Romans

Introducing Romans

Critical Issues in
Paul's Most Famous Letter

Richard N. Longenecker

WILLIAM B. EERDMANS PUBLISHING COMPANY
GRAND RAPIDS, MICHIGAN / CAMBRIDGE, U.K.

Published 2011 by
Wm. B. Eerdmans Publishing Co.
2140 Oak Industrial Drive N.E., Grand Rapids, Michigan 49505 /
P.O. Box 163, Cambridge CB3 9PU U.K.

Printed in the United States of America

17 16 15 14 13 12 11   7 6 5 4 3 2 1

Library of Congress Cataloging-in-Publication Data

Longenecker, Richard N.
Introducing Romans: critical issues in Paul's most famous letter /
Richard N. Longenecker.
p.   cm.
Includes bibliographical references and index.
ISBN 978-0-8028-6619-6 (pbk.: alk. paper)
1. Bible. N.T. Romans — Criticism, interpretation, etc.   I. Title.

BS2665.52.L66   2011
227′.106 — dc22
2010044282

www.eerdmans.com

Contents

Preface

The study of Romans has had a long history, with many matters of importance treated fruitfully in the past. There have also been, however, many rather tortuous convolutions and some "dead ends" in the understanding of the letter. Further, during the past century and a half a number of highly significant interpretive issues have arisen and various methods of interpretation have been proposed. It is impossible in short compass to deal with everything that has to do with the study of so important a writing as Paul's letter to the Christians at Rome. Nonetheless, particularly in light of the great amount of scholarly study and the diverse opinions that exist today, some overall account and evaluation of the major critical issues in the contemporary study of Romans seems appropriate — which is what we propose to do in what follows.

Our Present Procedures and Purposes

For pedagogical purposes, our introduction to Paul's most famous letter will be set out in terms of five sets of critical issues. Part One, "Important Matters Largely Uncontested Today," will deal with issues regarding the authorship, integrity, occasion, and date of the letter. Part Two, "Two Pivotal Issues," will highlight two key issues in the scholarly study of Romans, that is, (1) the identity, character, circumstances, and concerns of the letter's addressees, and (2) Paul's purpose or purposes in writing them. Part Three will treat a number of conventions, procedures, and themes of importance in the ancient world, both Greco-Roman oral, rhetorical, and epistolary conventions and Jewish (including Jewish Christian) procedures and themes — which conventions, procedures, and themes appear at various places in the letter and are used by its author to carry forward his argument. Part Four, "Textual and Interpretive Concerns," will focus on present-day endeavors to "establish" the Greek text of Romans and major interpretive approaches of prominence that are to the fore in its interpretation. And Part Five will sketch out matters pertaining to the focus or central thrust, structure, and argument of Paul's most famous letter. Not all of these topics are of equal concern in current NT scholarship. Nor need equal space be devoted to all of them alike. Nonetheless, all of them are significant and have critical importance for any contemporary study of Paul's letter to the Christians at Rome.

Much of what will be presented has to do with what NT scholars today believe regarding how Romans should be understood — that is, with the "state of the question" regarding the letter's important introductory issues. At some points a seeming convergence of scholarly opinion will need to be challenged by (1) better data that is available today on the question at hand, (2) better evaluations of the presently available and newly arising data, (3) better statements regarding the issues and implications involved, and/or (4) better solutions to the issues proposed. In every case, additional data on any particular matter may very well come to the fore, more perceptive evaluations might be given, more adequate statements of the issues and implications involved might be made, and better solutions to each of these concerns could be proposed. As is the case with any finite human endeavor, NT scholarship is always "a work in progress." Yet some sketch of the major critical issues involved in the current study of Paul's letter to Rome needs to be set out, and this is what will be attempted in what follows.

Our use of the adjective "critical," therefore, is not meant to suggest unfavorable or faultfinding comments. Rather, it is used to signal two much more positive things. First, to connote a careful and informed treatment of vital and indispensable issues that will result in a judicious evaluation of the data of pertinence that is available for a scholarly study of Romans. Second, to indicate that the focus of our treatment will be on matters that are usually considered introductory to any serious study of Romans — that is, on such matters as authorship; integrity; occasion; date; addressees; purpose; Greco-Roman oral, rhetorical, and epistolary conventions; Jewish and Jewish Christian thematic and rhetorical features; the establishing of the letter's Greek text; some recent interpretive approaches of importance; the focus or central thrust of the letter; and the structure and argument of the letter — rather than on strictly exegetical matters. And by the use of the noun "issues" we mean simply important matters for consideration that necessarily belong to any scholarly study of Romans.

Romans as a Particular Challenge for Interpretation

Paul's letter to the Christians at Rome has proven to be a particular challenge for commentators. This has largely been due to uncertainties regarding (1) the identity, character, circumstances, and concerns of its addressees, and (2) Paul's purpose or purposes in writing. It has also been, however, because of conflicting proposals with respect to (3) the nature of Paul's rhetoric in the development of his argument, (4) his use of Jewish and Jewish Christian procedures and themes in the unfolding of his various presentations, and (5) what exactly should be considered dominant among the various interpretive approaches that have been put forward and continue to be espoused today. Further, suggestions are rampant as to (6) how the letter is structured, (7) what constitutes its focus or central thrust, and (8) how its argument should be seen as developing.

All of these critical issues, and more, are matters that will be discussed in what follows, with rather distinctive conclusions being often proposed. For Romans, though the most famous of Paul's letters, is in many ways not like his other NT letters. So while in past times it was often asked, Why are Paul's other letters not like Romans?, today it is most often asked, Why is Romans not like Paul's other letters? And it is this question, in its various forms, that our treatments of these various critical issues in Paul's letter to Rome will attempt to answer — with the answers to that question providing guidance for an appreciation of Paul's teaching and an understanding of the rise of Christian doctrine.

Romans as a Particular Challenge for Contextualization

Romans is not only a highly significant NT letter for the knowledge of Christian doctrine that it offers its readers (i.e., what it teaches); it is also an important NT letter for an appreciation of how the Christian message was contextualized among various groups of people in Paul's day (i.e., how the "Good News" of the Christian gospel was variously expressed) and as a template for an understanding of how the Christian gospel may be effectively contextualized today (i.e., how the Christian gospel may be variously expressed in our day in various cultures and to somewhat differing mindsets). Most of the other NT writings — not only the letters, but also the Gospels, Acts, and Apocalypse — reveal how early Christian authors contextualized the Christian message to various people in their own particular circumstances and within their own rather distinctive understandings. Paul in his letter to the Christians at Rome does this as well — revealing to us (1) something of how the Christians at Rome (who were dominantly Gentile believers in Jesus but had come to Christ through the witness of traveling Jewish Christians, and so had been influenced by the theology and language of Jewish Christianity; see Chapter IV: "Addressees") understood and expressed their Christian faith, as those matters are reflected in much of what Paul writes in 1:16–4:25 and 9–11, and (2) how he clarified some of the basic Jewish Christian teachings and concerns that he shared with his addressees in his denunciations of 1:18–3:20, and then went on to sharpen certain basic Christian commitments and "forensic" language in his positive affirmations of 1:16-17; 3:21-23, 27-31; and chapter 4.

Paul's letter to the Christians at Rome, however, does even more than all of that. For it also reveals (3) how he contextualized the Christian gospel in his own ministry to pagan Gentiles who had little or no knowledge of the Jewish (OT) Scriptures and had not been influenced by either Judaism or Jewish Christianity — as can be seen in his more "personal," "relational," and "participationistic" message that he sets out in 5–8, together with his "christocentric" ethical exhortations in chapter 12 and 13:8-14. Further, (4) it gives insight into some of the central tenets of early Jewish Christianity, which looked to the Jerusalem Church as the Mother Church of Christendom and sought to reproduce its preaching, piety, and lifestyle — with such insight being provided particularly by the early Christian confessional material that Paul quotes in 3:24-26, but also by the various smaller portions of Christian confessional material that he cites elsewhere at various places in the letter.

Thus while all of the writers of the NT evidence a bipolar relationship between the various circumstances, orientations, and needs of the people being addressed *vis-à-vis* the Christian gospel as proclaimed and contextualized by each of those authors for the particular people they addressed, Paul's letter to the Christians at Rome reveals four such polarities:

(1) that of the mixed group of Gentile and Jewish believers in Jesus in the various Christian congregations at Rome, as Paul speaks to them in a manner that he believed they would understand and appreciate in 1:16–4:25 and then again in 9–11;

(2) that of early Jewish Christianity, which was centered in the Mother Church at Jerusalem, a portion of whose confessional material Paul quotes in 3:24-26 and at various other strategic places in his letter to Rome.

(3) that of Paul himself, as expressed in the body opening and body closing sections of the letter, as well as in the "spin" that he gives to all that he writes throughout the letter; and,

(4) that of the apostle's own contextualization of the Christian gospel to pagan Gentiles in the Greco-Roman world of his day, as he sets out before his Roman addressees a portrayal of the essential features of his Christian proclamation to Gentiles in the central theological section of 5–8 and then applies that contextualized proclamation in the christocentric ethical section of 12:1–15:13, both generally and specifically — which contextualized understanding of the Christian gospel his Gentile converts had accepted apart from any Jewish understanding or direct Jewish Christian influence;

All of these factors raise important critical issues that present particular challenges not only for the interpretation of Paul's letter to Christians at Rome in that early Christian first century but also for the contextualization of the Christian gospel (i.e., the message of "Good News") today.

Abbreviations

General

ad loc.	*ad locum* (at the passage)
c.	*circa* (about)
cf.	*confer* (compare)
contra	in contrast to
ed.	edited, edition, editor
e.g.	*exempli gratia* (for example)
Ep(p)	Letter(s)
ET	English Translation
et al.	*et alii* (and others)
ff.	following (verses, pages)
fl.	*floruit* (flourished)
GT	German Translation
idem	*idem* (something previously mentioned)
i.e.	*id est* (that is)
LXX	Septuagint
mg.	margin
MS(S)	Manuscript(s)
MT	Masoretic Text
n.	note
n.d.	no date
NT	New Testament
OT	Old Testament
passim	*passim* (here and there)
p., pp.	page, pages
par	parallel passage
TR	Textus Receptus

trans.	translation, translator, translate
v., vv.	verse, verses
vid	*videtur* (it seems or apparently; used to indicate that the reading is not certain, especially in a damaged manuscript)
viz.	*videlicet* (namely)
vol.	volume

Bible Translations: Contemporary English Versions

ASV	*American Standard Version*
AV	Authorized Version
BV	*The New Testament: Berkeley Version* (Gerrit Verkuyl)
CEV	*Contemporary English Version*
Goodspeed	*An American Translation* (Edgar J. Goodspeed)
JB	*The Jerusalem Bible*
KJV	*The Holy Bible: King James Version*
Knox	*The New Testament of Our Lord and Saviour Jesus Christ, Newly Translated from the Vulgate Latin* (John Knox)
LB	*The Living Bible*
Moffatt	*The Holy Bible: A New Translation* (James Moffatt)
NABRNT	*New American Bible, Revised New Testament*
NASB	*New American Standard Bible*
NEB	*New English Bible*
NET	*New English Translation*
NIV	*New International Version*
NJB	*New Jerusalem Bible*
NKJV	*New King James Version*
NLT	*New Living Translation* (revision of *The Living Bible*)
NRSV	*New Revised Standard Version*
Phillips	*The New Testament in Modern English/Letters to Young Churches* (J. B. Phillips)
REB	*Revised English Bible*
RSV	*Revised Standard Version*
TEV	*Today's English Version/Good News for Modern Man*
TNIV	*Today's New International Version*
Weymouth	*The New Testament in Modern Speech* (Richard F. Weymouth)
Williams	*The New Testament: A Private Translation in the Language of the People* (Charles B. Williams)

Texts

GNT[4]	*The Greek New Testament.* 4th rev. ed. Stuttgart: Deutsche Bibelgesellschaft/United Bible Societies, 1993.
Kittel	*Biblia Hebraica,* ed. R. Kittel. Stuttgart: Privilegierte Württembergische Bibelanstalt, 1929.
NA[27]	Nestle-Aland, *Novum Testamentum Graece post Eberhard Nestle et Erwin Nestle.* 27th ed. Stuttgart: Deutsche Bibelgesellschaft, 1993.
Rahlfs	*Septuaginta,* 2 vols., ed. A. Rahlfs. Stuttgart: Privilegierte Württembergische Bibelanstalt, 1935.
W-H	*The New Testament in the Original Greek,* with *Introduction* and *Appendix,* 2 vols., B. F. Westcott and F. J. A. Hort. Cambridge — London, 1881; 2nd ed. 1896.

Grammatical, Syntactical and Lexical Aids

BAG	*A Greek-English Lexicon of the New Testament and Other Early Christian Literature,* by W. Bauer, W. F. Arndt, and F. W. Gingrich. Chicago: University of Chicago Press, 1957.
BDB	*A Hebrew and English Lexicon of the Old Testament, with an Appendix containing the Biblical Aramaic,* by F. Brown, S. R. Driver, and C. A. Briggs. Oxford: Clarendon, 1907; corrected 1952.
BDF	*A Greek Grammar of the New Testament and Other Early Christian Literature,* by F. Blass, A. Debrunner, and R. W. Funk. Chicago: University of Chicago Press, 1961 (ET from 1913 German 4th ed.).
Burton	*Syntax of the Moods and Tenses in New Testament Greek,* by E. D. Burton, 3rd ed. Chicago: University of Chicago Press, 1898.
D-M	*A Manual Grammar of the Greek New Testament,* by H. E. Dana and J. R. Mantey. Toronto: Macmillan, 1927.
LSJM	*A Greek-English Lexicon,* by H. G. Liddell and R. Scott; revised by H. S. Jones and R. McKenzie. Oxford: Clarendon, 1968.
M-G	*A Concordance of the Greek Testament,* ed. W. F. Moulton and A. S. Geden. Edinburgh: T&T Clark, 1897; 4th ed. revised by H. K. Moulton, 1963.
M-M	*The Vocabulary of the Greek Testament, Illustrated from the Papyri and Other Non-Literary Sources,* by J. H. Moulton and G. Milligan. London: Hodder and Stoughton, 1930.
Moule	*An Idiom-Book of New Testament Greek,* by C. F. D. Moule. Cambridge: Cambridge University Press, 2nd ed. 1959.
M-T	*A Grammar of New Testament Greek,* by J. H. Moulton and N. Turner. Edinburgh: T&T Clark: Vol. 1, *Prolegomena* (3rd ed., 1908); Vol. 2, *Accidence and Word-Formation with an Appendix on Semitisms in the New Testament,* by J. H. Moulton and W. F. Howard

(1919, 1929); Vol. 3, *Syntax*, by N. Turner (1963); Vol. 4, *Style*, by N. Turner (1976).

ATRob   *A Grammar of the Greek New Testament in the Light of Historical Research*, by A. T. Robertson. London: Hodder & Stoughton; New York: Doran, 2nd ed. revised and enlarged, 1915; repr. Nashville: Broadman, 1934.

Thrall   *Greek Particles in the New Testament. Linguistic and Exegetical Studies*, by M. E. Thrall. Leiden: Brill, 1962.

Reference Works

ANF   *Ante-Nicene Fathers*, ed. A. Roberts and J. Donaldson; American edition, 10 vols., ed. A. C. Coxe. Grand Rapids: Eerdmans, 1987.

APOT   *Apocrypha and Pseudepigrapha of the Old Testament*, ed. R. H. Charles (1913, repr. 1963).

CCLat   *Corpus christianorum, series latina*

CIJ   *Corpus inscriptionum Judaicarum*, 2 vols., ed. J. B. Frey (1936-52).

CSEL   *Corpus scriptorum ecclesiasticorum latinorum*, Vienna Academy (1866ff.).

JE   *Jewish Encyclopedia*, 12 vols., ed. I. Singer. New York: Ktav, 1901-1906.

NTA   *New Testament Apocrypha*, 2 vols., ed. W. Schneemelcher, trans. R. McL. Wilson. London: Lutterworth, 1963, 1965.

OTP   *Old Testament Pseudepigrapha*, 2 vols., ed. J. H. Charlesworth (1983, 1985).

PG   *Patrologia graeca*, 162 vols., ed. Jacques-Paul Migne (1857-86).

PL   *Patrologia latina*, 221 vols., ed. Jacques-Paul Migne (1844-66).

Statistik   *Statistik des neutestamentlichen Wortschatzes*, by R. Morgenthaler. Zurich and Frankfurt-am-Main: Gotthelf Verlag, 1958.

Str-Bil   *Kommentar zum Neuen Testament aus Talmud und Midrasch*, 5 vols., by H. L. Strack and P. Billerbeck. Munich: Beck, 1922-1961.

TDNT   *Theological Dictionary of the New Testament*, 10 vols., ed. G. Kittel and G. Friedrich, trans. G. W. Bromiley. Grand Rapids: Eerdmans, 1964-74 (ET of *TWNT*).

TWNT   *Theologisches Wörterbuch zum Neuen Testament*, 10 vols., ed. G. Kittel (vols. 1-4) and G. Friedrich (vols. 5-10). Stuttgart: Kohlhammer, 1933-1978.

Series (Commentaries, Texts and Studies)

AB   Anchor Bible

ACNT   Augsburg Commentary on the New Testament

ANRW   Aufstieg und Niedergang der Römischen Welt

ANTF   Arbeiten zur neutestamentlichen Textforschung

ATANT	Abhandlungen zur Theologie des Alten und Neuen Testaments
BEvT	Beiträge zur evangelischen Theologie
BFCT	Beiträge zur Förderung christlicher Theologie
BNTC	Black's New Testament Commentaries
BTN	Bibliotheca Theologica Norvegica
BZNTW	Beiheft zur Zeitschrift für die neutestamentliche Wissenschaft
CBC	Cambridge Bible Commentary
CNT	Commentaire du Nouveau Testament
ConNeot	Coniectanea Neotestamentica
EBC	Expositor's Bible Commentary
EkKNT	Evangelisch-katholischer Kommentar zum Neuen Testament
EPC	Epworth Preacher's Commentaries
EtBib	Etudes Bibliques
DJD	Discoveries in the Judean Desert
FRLANT	Forschungen zur Religion und Literatur des Alten und Neuen Testaments
Herm	Hermeneia
HNT	Handbuch zum Neuen Testament
HNTC	Harper's New Testament Commentary
HTKNT	Herders theologischer Kommentar zum Neuen Testament
IB	Interpreter's Bible
ICC	International Critical Commentary
JBC	Jerome Biblical Commentary
JSNT.SS	Journal for the Study of the New Testament. Supplement Series
JSOT.SS	Journal for the Study of the Old Testament. Supplement Series
KEKNT	Kritisch-exegetischer Kommentar über das Neue Testament
KNT	Kommentar zum Neuen Testament
LCL	Loeb Classical Library
LEC	Library of Early Christianity
MNTC	Moffatt New Testament Commentary
MNTS	McMaster New Testament Studies
MTS	Marburger Theologische Studien
NAC	New American Commentary
NCB	New Century Bible
NICNT	New International Commentary on the New Testament
NJBC	New Jerome Biblical Commentary
NovTSup	Novum Testamentum Supplement
NTAbh	Neutestamentliche Abhandlungen
NTC	New Testament Commentary
NTD	New Testament Deutsch
NTSR	New Testament for Spiritual Reading
NTTS	New Testament Tools and Studies

PNTC	Pelican New Testament Commentaries
RGRW	Religions in the Graeco-Roman World
RNT	Regensburger Neues Testament
SacPag	Sacra Pagina
SBJ	La Sainte Bible de Jérusalem
SBL.DS	Society of Biblical Literature — Dissertation Series
SBL.SBS	Society of Bible Literature — Sources for Biblical Study
SBLSemStud	Society of Biblical Literature — Semeia Studies
SBL.SP	Society of Biblical Literature — Seminar Papers
SBLTT.ECLS	Society of Biblical Literature — Texts and Translations: Early Christian Literature Series
SBL.WAW	Society of Biblical Literature — Writings from the Ancient World
SBS	Stuttgarter Bibelstudien
SBT	Studies in Biblical Theology
SD	Studies and Documents
SJLA	Studies in Judaism in Late Antiquity
SNT	Studien zum Neuen Testament
SNTS.MS	Studiorum Novi Testamenti Societas — Monograph Series
TBC	Torch Bible Commentaries
TBü	Theologische Bücherei
TH	Théologie Historique
THKNT	Theologischer Handkommentar zum Neuen Testament
TNTC	Tyndale New Testament Commentary
TU	Texte und Untersuchungen
VS	Verbum Salutis
WBC	Word Biblical Commentary
WUNT	Wissenschaftliche Untersuchungen zum Neuen Testament

Journals

ABR	*Australian Biblical Review*
AJP	*American Journal of Philology* (Baltimore)
ALUOS	*Annual of Leeds University Oriental Society*
ATR	*Anglican Theological Review* (Evanston)
AusBR	*Australian Biblical Review* (Melbourne)
AUSS	*Andrews University Seminary Studies* (Berrien Springs)
BA	*Biblical Archaeologist* (New Haven)
BBR	*Bulletin for Biblical Research* (Winona Lake)
BEvT	*Beiträge zur evangelischen Theologie*
Bib	*Biblica* (Rome)
Bijd	*Bijdragen* (Amsterdam/Heverlee)
BJRL	*Bulletin of the John Rylands University Library* (Manchester)
BSac	*Bibliotheca Sacra* (Dallas)

BTB	*Biblical Theology Bulletin* (St. Bonaventure)
BZ	*Biblische Zeitschrift* (Freiburg — Paderborn)
CBQ	*Catholic Biblical Quarterly* (Washington)
CJT	*Canadian Journal of Theology* (Toronto)
CP	*Classical Philology*
CQR	*Church Quarterly Review* (London)
EvQ	*Evangelical Quarterly* (Manchester — Aberdeen)
EvT	*Evangelische Theologie*
Exp	*Expositor*
ExpT	*Expository Times* (Banstead)
HeyJ	*Heythrop Journal* (London)
HibJ	*Hibbert Journal* (Liverpool)
HTR	*Harvard Theological Review* (Cambridge)
HUCA	*Hebrew Union College Annual* (Cincinnati)
Int	*Interpretation* (Richmond)
ITQ	*Irish Theological Quarterly* (Maynooth)
JAC	*Jahrbuch für Antike und Christentum* (Münster)
JAOS	*Journal of the American Oriental Society* (New Haven)
JBL	*Journal of Biblical Literature* (Philadelphia-Missoula-Chico-Decatur)
JETS	*Journal of the Evangelical Theological Society*
JJS	*Journal of Jewish Studies* (London — Oxford)
JP	*Journal of Philology*
JQR	*Jewish Quarterly Review* (Philadelphia)
JR	*Journal of Religion* (Chicago)
JRH	*Journal of Religious History*
JRS	*Journal of Roman Studies* (London)
JSJ	*Journal for the Study of Judaism* (Leiden)
JSNT	*Journal for the Study of the New Testament* (Sheffield)
JSOT	*Journal for the Study of the Old Testament* (Sheffield)
JTS	*Journal of Theological Studies* (Oxford)
JTSA	*Journal of Theology for Southern Africa*
Jud	*Judaica*
LexTQ	*Lexington Theological Quarterly* (Lexington)
MTZ	*Münchener theologische Zeitschrift* (Munich)
Neot	*Neotestamentica* (Pretoria)
NovT	*Novum Testamentum* (Leiden)
NTS	*New Testament Studies* (Cambridge)
OrT	*Oral Tradition*
PRS	Perspectives in Religious Studies
RB	*Revue biblique* (Paris — Jerusalem)
RBén	*Revue bénédictine* (Maredsous)
RBR	*Ricerche bibliche e religiose* (Milan)

ResQ	*Restoration Quarterly* (Abilene)
RevExp	*Review and Expositor* (Louisville)
RevistB	*Revista bíblica* (Buenos Aires)
RevQ	Revue de Qumran
RSPT	*Revue des sciences philosophiques et théologiques* (Paris)
RSR	*Recherches des sciences religieuses* (Strasbourg)
RTR	*Reformed Theological Review* (Melbourne)
SEA	*Svensk exegetisk arsbok* (Uppsala)
Semeia	*Semeia. An Experimental Journal for Biblical Criticism* (Missoula-Chico-Decatur)
SJT	*Scottish Journal of Theology* (Edinburgh)
ST	*Studia theologica* (Lund — Aarhus — Oslo)
TBlä	*Theologische Blätter*
TEvan	*Theologia Evangelica* (Pretoria)
ThStKr	Theologische Studien und Kritiken
TJT	*Toronto Journal of Theology* (Toronto)
TLZ	*Theologische Literaturzeitung* (Leipzig — Berlin)
TPAPA	*Transactions and Proceedings of the American Philological Association*
TS	Theological Studies
TSK	*Theologische Studien und Kritiken*
TTijd	Theologisch Tijdschrift
TV	*Theologia Viatorum*
TZ	*Theologische Zeitschrift* (Basel)
TZT	*Tübingen Zeitschrift für Theologie* (Tübingen)
VC	*Vigiliae christianae* (Amsterdam)
VD	*Verbum domini*
VT	Vetus Testamentum
WW	*Word and World* (St. Paul)
ZAW	Zeitschrift für die alttestamentliche Wissenschaft
ZKT	*Zeitschrift für katholische Theologie* (Innsbruck)
ZNW	*Zeitschrift für die neutestamentliche Wissenschaft* (Berlin)
ZTK	*Zeitschrift für Theologie und Kirche* (Tübingen)
ZWT	*Zeitschrift für wissenschaftliche Theologie*

Bibliography of Selected Commentaries

Note: References to the following commentaries will be by authors' names and abbreviated titles. Supplemental bibliographies of further sources, monographs, and articles will be provided at the end of each chapter.

I. THE PATRISTIC PERIOD

Major Greek Fathers (listed chronologically)

Origen (c. 185-254). *Commentarium in epistulam b. Pauli ad Romanos* (Rufinus's abridged Latin translation). *PG* 14.833-1291.

————. *Commentary on the Epistle to the Romans,* trans. T. P. Scheck. Washington, DC: Catholic University of America, 2001.

————. *The Writings of Origen,* trans. F. Crombie, in *Ante-Nicene Christian Library,* vols. 10 and 23, ed. A. Roberts and J. Donaldson. Edinburgh: T&T Clark, 1869.

Diodore of Tarsus (died c. 390). "Fragments of a Commentary on Romans," in *Die Pauluskommentare aus der griechischen Kirche,* ed. K. Staab. Münster: Aschendorff, 1933, 83-112.

John Chrysostom (c. 347-407). *Homilia XXXII in Epistolam ad Romanos. PG* 60.391-682.

————. "The Homilies of St. John Chrysostom on the Epistle of St. Paul the Apostle to the Romans," in *The Nicene and Post-Nicene Fathers of the Christian Church,* ed. P. Schaff, 14 vols. Buffalo: Christian Literature, 1886-90, 11.329-564; cf. also *PG* 64.1037-38; 51.155-208.

Theodore of Mopsuestia (c. 350-428). *In epistolam Pauli ad Romanos commentarii fragmenta. PG* 66.787-876.

————. Fragments of a Commentary on Romans, in *Die Pauluskommentare aus der griechischen Kirche,* ed. K. Staab. Münster: Aschendorff, 1933, 113-72.

Cyril of Alexandria (died c. 444). *Explanatio in Epistulam ad Romanos. PG* 74.773-856.

Theodoret of Cyrrhus (393-466). *Interpretatio Epistulae ad Romanos. PG* 82.43-226.

Major Latin Fathers (listed chronologically)

Tertullian (c. 145-220). *Adversus Marcionem. PL* 2.263-555.

————. *Adversus Valentinianos. PL* 2.558-662.

————. "The Five Books Against Marcion" and "Against the Valentinians," in *Ante-Nicene Christian Library,* ed. A. Roberts and J. Donaldson. Edinburgh: T&T Clark, 1868, 7.1-478, and 1870, 15.119-62; repr. in *The Ante-Nicene Fathers,* 10 vols. Grand Rapids: Eerdmans, 1986-1987, 3.269-475 and 503-20.

Ambrosiaster (wrote c. 366-384). *Commentarium in epistulam beati Pauli ad Romanos. PL* 17.47-197; *CSEL* 81.1.

Augustine (c. 354-430). *Expositio quarundam propositionum ex epistola ad Romanos. PL* 35.2063-88.

————. *Epistolae ad Romanos inchoata expositio. PL* 35.2087-2106.

————. *Augustine on Romans: Propositions from the Epistle to the Romans. Unfinished Commentary on the Epistle to the Romans,* ed. and trans. P. A. Landes. SBLTT.ECLS 23.6. Chico: Scholars, 1982.

Pelagius (c. 354-420). *In Epistolam ad Romanos. PL* 30.646-718.

————. *Pelagius's Commentary on St. Paul's Epistle to the Romans,* translated with introduction and notes by T. de Bruyn. Oxford: Clarendon, 1993.

II. The Reformation Period

Major Roman Catholic Scholars (listed chronologically)

Thomas Aquinas (1225-1274). "Expositio in omnes sancti Pauli epistolas: Epistola ad Romanos," in *Opera omnia,* 25 vols. Parma: Fiaccadori, 1852-1873; repr. New York: Musurgia, 1948-1950, 13.3-156.

Desiderius Erasmus (1469-1536). *The Collected Works of Erasmus,* vol. 42: *Paraphrases on Romans and Galatians,* trans. J. B. Payne, A. Rabil Jr., and W. S. Smith Jr., ed. R. D. Sider. Toronto: University of Toronto Press, 1984.

————. *Annotations on Romans,* ed. R. D. Sider, *et al.* Toronto: University of Toronto Press, 1994.

Major Protestant Scholars (listed chronologically)

Martin Luther (1483-1546). *Luthers Werke,* 61 vols. Weimar: Böhlaus, 1883-1983: vol. 56 (*Glossae & Scholia*), 1938; vol. 57 (*Nachschriften*), 1939.

————. *Luther's Works,* 55 vols., general editors J. Pelikan (vols. 1-30) and H. T.

Lehmann (vols. 31-55): vol. 25, "Lectures on Romans: Glosses and Scholia," trans. W. G. Tillmanns and J. A. O. Preus, ed. H. C. Oswald. St. Louis: Concordia, 1972.

―――. *Commentary on the Epistle to the Romans: A New Translation*, trans. and ed. J. T. Mueller. Grand Rapids: Zondervan, 1954.

―――. *Luther: Lectures on Romans, Newly Translated and Edited*, trans. and ed. W. Pauck. LCC 15. London: SCM; Philadelphia: Westminster, 1961.

Martin Bucer (1491-1551). "In epistolam ad Romanos," in *Metaphrases et enarrationes epistolarum d. Pauli apostoli*. Strasbourg: Rihel, 1536; repr. Basel: Pernan, 1562, 1-507.

Philip Melanchthon (1497-1560). *Melanchthons Werke in Auswahl*, 7 vols., ed. R. Stupperich. Gütersloh: Mohn, 1951-1975, 5.25-371.

―――. *Loci Communes Theologici*, trans. J. A. O. Preus. St. Louis: Concordia, 1992.

―――. *Commentary on Romans*, trans. F. Kramer. St. Louis: Concordia, 1992.

John Calvin (1509-1564). *Commentarii in omnes epistolas Pauli apostoli*. Strasbourg: Rihel, 1539.

―――. *Commentarius in epistolam Pauli ad Romanos*, ed. T. H. L. Parker. Leiden: Brill, 1981.

―――. *Commentary on the Epistle of Paul the Apostle to the Romans*, trans. J. Owen. Edinburgh: Calvin Translation Society, 1844; repr. Grand Rapids: Eerdmans, 1947.

―――. *The Epistles of Paul the Apostle to the Romans and to the Thessalonians*, trans. R. Mackenzie, in *Calvin's New Testament Commentaries*, 12 vols., ed. D. W. Torrance and T. F. Torrance. Edinburgh: Oliver & Boyd, 1960; Grand Rapids: Eerdmans, 1961, 8.5-328.

―――. *Calvin's New Testament Commentaries*, trans. and ed. T. H. L. Parker. London: SCM; Grand Rapids: Eerdmans, 1971.

Wesley, John (1703-1791). *Explanatory Notes upon the New Testament*. London: Epworth, 1950 (repr. of 1754 edition).

III. The Modern Critical Period (listed alphabetically)

Achtemeier, Paul J. *Romans. A Bible Commentary for Teaching and Preaching*. Interp. Atlanta: John Knox, 1985.

Barrett, C. Kingsley. *A Commentary on the Epistle to the Romans*. BNTC/HNTC. London: Black; New York: Harper & Row, 1957; 2nd ed. Peabody: Hendrickson, 1991.

Barth, Karl. *The Epistle to the Romans*, trans. E. C. Hoskyns. London, New York: Oxford University Press, 1933; original German publication: *Der Römerbrief*. Zollikon-Zurich: Evangelischer Verlag, 1919; ET from sixth edition. Munich: Kaiser, 1929; rev. ed. by H. Schmitt, Zurich: Theologischer Verlag, 1985.

―――. *A Shorter Commentary on Romans*. London: SCM; Richmond: John Knox,

1959; ET from *Kurze Erklärung des Römerbriefes*. Munich: Kaiser, 1956; repr. Munich-Hamburg: Siebenstern Taschenbuch, 1967.

Best, Ernest. *The Letter of Paul to the Romans*. CBC. Cambridge: Cambridge University Press, 1967.

Billerbeck, Paul. *Kommentar zum Neuen Testament aus Talmud und Midrasch*, 6 vols. Munich: Beck, 1926-1963, vol. 3 (4th ed. 1965), 1-320.

Black, Matthew. *Romans*. NCB. London: Oliphants; Grand Rapids: Eerdmans, 1973; 1989².

Bruce, Frederick F. *The Epistle of Paul to the Romans: An Introduction and Commentary*. TNTC. London: Tyndale; Grand Rapids: Eerdmans, 1963, 1969²; repr. Leicester: Inter-Varsity; Grand Rapids: Eerdmans, 1985.

Brunner, Emil. *The Letter to the Romans. A Commentary*, trans. H. A. Kennedy. London: Lutterworth; Philadelphia: Westminster, 1959; ET from *Der Römerbrief übersetzt und erklärt*. Stuttgart: Oncken, 1938; repr. 1956.

Byrne, Brendan. *Romans*. SacPag. Collegeville: Liturgical Press, 1996.

Cranfield, Charles E. B. *A Critical and Exegetical Commentary on the Epistle to the Romans*, 2 vols. ICC n.s. Edinburgh: T&T Clark, 1975, 1979.

Denney, James. *St. Paul's Epistle to the Romans*. EGT. London: Hodder & Stoughton, 1900, 2.555-725; repr. Grand Rapids: Eerdmans, 1970, 1983.

Dodd, Charles Harold. *The Epistle of Paul to the Romans*. MNTC. London: Hodder & Stoughton, 1932; London: Collins, 1959 rev. ed.

Dunn, James D. G. *Romans*, 2 vols. WBC. Dallas: Word, 1988-1989.

Fitzmyer, Joseph A. "The Letter to the Romans," in *JBC*, ed. R. E. Brown, J. A. Fitzmyer, and R. E. Murphy. Englewood Cliffs: Prentice-Hall, 1968, article 53, 2.291-331; revised one volume *NJBC*, article 51, 830-68.

⸻. *Romans: A New Translation with Introduction and Commentary*. AB. New York: Doubleday, 1993.

Gaugler, Ernst. *Der Brief an die Römer*, 2 vols. Zürich: Zwingli, 1945; repr. 1958.

Godet, Frédéric. *Commentary on St. Paul's Epistle to the Romans*, 2 vols., trans. A. Cusin. Edinburgh: T&T Clark, 1880-1881; New York: Funk & Wagnalls, 1883; repr. Grand Rapids: Kregel 1977; ET from *Commentaire sur l'épitre aux Romains*, 2 vols. Paris: Sandoz & Rischbacher; Geneva: Desrogis, 1879; repr. Geneva: Labor et Fides, 1879-1881.

Gore, Charles. *St. Paul's Epistle to the Romans: A Practical Exposition*, 2 vols. London: Murray; New York: Scribners, 1899-1900; repr. 1907.

Harrison, Everett F., and Donald A. Hagner. "Romans," in *The Expositor's Bible Commentary*, rev. ed., 13 vols., ed. T. Longman and D. E. Garland. Grand Rapids: Zondervan, 2008, 11.19-237.

Harrisville, Roy A. *Romans*. ACNT. Minneapolis: Augsburg, 1980.

Hendriksen, William. *Exposition of Paul's Epistle to the Romans*, 2 vols. NTC. Grand Rapids: Baker; Edinburgh: Banner of Truth, 1980-1981.

Hodge, Charles. *A Commentary on the Epistle to the Romans*. Philadelphia: Grigg &

Elliot, 1835; Philadelphia: Claxton, 1864[2]; repr. New York: Armstrong, 1896; repr. Grand Rapids: Eerdmans, 1980.

Huby, Joseph. *Saint Paul. Épître aux Romains: Traduction et commentaire.* VS. Paris: Beauchesne, 4th ed. 1940; new ed., rev. S. Lyonnet, 1957.

Hunter, Archibald M. *The Epistle to the Romans. Introduction and Commentary.* TBC. London: SCM, 1955; repr. with subtitle *The Law of Love,* 1968, 1977.

Jamieson, Robert, Andrew R. Fausset, and David Brown. *Commentary Practical and Explanatory on the Whole Bible,* rev. ed., ed. H. Lockyer. Grand Rapids: Zondervan, 1961, 1138-85.

Jewett, Robert. *Romans: A Commentary.* Hermeneia. Minneapolis: Fortress, 2007.

Johnson, Luke Timothy. *Reading Romans: A Literary and Theological Commentary.* Macon: Smyth & Helwys, 2001.

Käsemann, Ernst. *Commentary on Romans,* trans. G. W. Bromiley. London: SCM; Grand Rapids: Eerdmans, 1980; ET from *An die Römer.* HNT. Tübingen: Mohr-Siebeck, 1973, 1980[4].

Kertelge, Karl. *The Epistle to the Romans,* trans. F. McDonagh. NTSR. London: Sheed & Ward; New York: Herder & Herder, 1972; ET from *Der Brief an die Römer.* Düsseldorf: Patmos, 1971.

Knox, John, and Gerald R. Cragg. "The Epistle to the Romans: Introduction and Exegesis," in *The Interpreter's Bible,* 12 vols., ed. G. A. Buttrick *et al.* New York: Abingdon, 1954, 9.353-668.

Kuss, Otto. *Der Römerbrief übersetzt und erklärt,* 3 vols. (on chs. 1–11). Regensburg: Pustet, 1957, 1959, 1978.

Lagrange, Marie-Joseph. *Saint Paul. Épitre aux Romains.* EtBib. Paris: Gabalda, 1916; 4th ed. (with addenda) 1931; repr. 1950.

Leenhardt, Franz J. *The Epistle of Saint Paul to the Romans: A Commentary,* trans. H. Knight. London: Lutterworth; Cleveland: World, 1961; ET from *L'Épitre de saint Paul aux Romains.* CNT. Neuchatel-Paris: Delachaux et Niestlé, 1957; 2nd ed. Geneva: Labor et Fides, 1981.

Lenski, Richard C. H. *The Interpretation of St. Paul's Epistle to the Romans.* Columbus: Lutheran Book Concern, 1936; repr. Minneapolis: Augsburg, 1961.

Liddon, Henry P. *Explanatory Analysis of St. Paul's Epistle to the Romans.* London: Longmans, Green, 1893; repr. Grand Rapids: Zondervan, 1961.

Lietzmann, Hans. *Die Briefe des Apostels Paulus an die Römer.* HNT 8. Tübingen: Mohr-Siebeck, 1906, 1928[2], 1933[3], 1971[5].

Lightfoot, Joseph B. *Notes on Epistles of St. Paul from Unpublished Commentaries.* London: Macmillan, 1895, 237-305 (on chs. 1–7); repr. Grand Rapids: Zondervan, 1957.

Lohse, Eduard. *Der Brief an die Römer.* KEKNT. Göttingen: Vandenhoeck & Ruprecht, 2003.

Lyonnet, Stanislaus. *Les Épitres de Saint Paul aux Galates, aux Romains.* SBJ. Paris: Cerf, 1953; 2nd ed. 1959, 45-136.

Manson, Thomas W. "Romans," in *Peake's Commentary on the Bible,* 2nd ed., ed. M. Black and H. H. Rowley. London: Nelson, 1962, 940-53.

Metzger, Bruce M. *A Textual Commentary on the Greek New Testament.* New York: United Bible Societies, 1971; 1975 (corrected ed.); Stuttgart: Deutsche Bibelgesellschaft, 1994 (2nd rev. ed.).

Meyer, Heinrich A. W. *Critical and Exegetical Handbook to the Epistle to the Romans,* 2 vols. MCNT. New York: Funk & Wagnalls, 1884; rev. ed. by W. P. Dickson and T. Dwight, 1889; ET from *Der Brief an die Römer.* MKEKNT. Göttingen: Vandenhoeck & Ruprecht, 1836; 5th ed. 1872.

Michel, Otto. *Der Brief an die Römer.* MKEKNT. Göttingen: Vandenhoeck & Ruprecht, 1955; 1978[14].

Moo, Douglas J. *The Epistle to the Romans.* NICNT. Grand Rapids: Eerdmans, 1996.

Morris, Leon. *The Epistle to the Romans.* PC. Leicester: Inter-Varsity; Grand Rapids: Eerdmans, 1988.

Mounce, Robert H. *Romans.* NAC. Nashville: Broadman & Holman, 1995.

Murray, John. *The Epistle to the Romans: The English Text with Introduction, Exposition, and Notes,* 2 vols. NICNT. Grand Rapids: Eerdmans, 1959, 1965.

Nygren, Anders. *Commentary on Romans,* trans. C. C. Rasmussen. Philadelphia: Fortress, 1949, 1972; London: SCM, 1952; ET from *Der Römerbrief.* Göttingen: Vandenhoeck & Ruprecht, 1951; GT from *Pauli Brev till Romarna.* Stockholm: Svenska Kyrkans Diakonistyrelses Bokförlag, 1944.

O'Neill, John C. *Paul's Letter to the Romans.* PNTC. Harmondsworth, Baltimore: Penguin, 1975.

Pesch, Rudolf. *Römerbrief.* NEchB. Würzburg: Echter, 1983.

Robertson, Archibald T. "The Epistle to the Romans," in *Word Pictures in the New Testament,* 4 vols. New York: Smith, 1931, 4.320-430.

Robinson, John A. T. *Wrestling with Romans.* London: SCM; Philadelphia: Westminster, 1979.

Sanday, William, and Arthur C. Headlam. *A Critical and Exegetical Commentary on the Epistle to the Romans.* ICC o.s. Edinburgh: T&T Clark; New York: Scribner, 1895, 1896[2], 1902[5]; repr. 1922, 1958, 1962.

Schlatter, Adolf. *Romans: The Righteousness of God,* trans. S. S. Schatzmann. Peabody: Hendrickson, 1995; ET from *Gottes Gerechtigkeit. Ein Kommentar zum Römerbrief.* Stuttgart: Calwer, 1935, 1959[3], 1965[4]; 6th ed. (with preface by P. Stuhlmacher), 1991.

Schlier, Heinrich. *Der Römerbrief. Kommentar.* HTKNT. Freiburg, Basel, Vienna: Herder, 1977.

Schmidt, Hans W. *Der Brief des Paulus an die Römer.* THKNT. Berlin: Evangelische Verlagsanstalt, 1963, 1972[3].

Schmithals, Walter. *Der Römerbrief. Ein Kommentar.* Gütersloh: Mohn, 1988.

Schott, Theodor F. *Der Römerbrief.* Erlangen: A. Deichert, 1858.

Schreiner, Thomas R. *Romans.* Grand Rapids: Baker, 1998.

Stuhlmacher, Peter. *Paul's Letter to the Romans: A Commentary,* trans. S. J. Hafemann. Louisville: Westminster/John Knox, 1994; ET from *Der Brief an die Römer übersetzt und erklart.* NTD. Göttingen: Vandenhoeck & Ruprecht, 1989.

Talbert, Charles H. *Romans.* Macon: Smyth & Helwys, 2002.

Taylor, Vincent. *The Epistle to the Romans.* EPC. London: Epworth, 1955, 1962².

Weiss, Bernhard. *Der Brief an die Römer.* MK. Göttingen: Vandenhoeck & Ruprecht, 1881; 4th ed. 1891.

Wilckens, Ulrich. *Der Brief an die Römer,* 3 vols. EKKNT. Zürich: Benziger; Neukirchen-Vluyn: Neukirchener Verlag, 1978, 1980, 1982.

Witherington, Ben, III, with Darlene Hyatt. *Paul's Letter to the Romans: A Socio-Rhetorical Commentary.* Grand Rapids: Eerdmans, 2004.

Wright, N. Thomas. "The Messiah and the People of God: A Study in Pauline Theology with Particular Reference to the Argument of the Epistle to the Romans." D.Phil. Dissertation, University of Oxford, 1980.

Zahn, Theodor. *Der Brief des Paulus an die Römer ausgelegt.* KNT. Leipzig: Deichert, 1910, 1925².

Zeller, Dieter. *Der Brief an die Römer. Übersetzt und erklärt.* RNT. Regensburg: Pustet, 1985.

Ziesler, John A. *Paul's Letter to the Romans.* TPINTC. London: SCM; Philadelphia: Trinity Press International, 1989.

PART ONE

Important Matters Largely Uncontested Today

CHAPTER I

Author, Amanuensis, and Involvement of Others

The first thought in opening a letter is always: Who wrote this letter? Is it really from the one who claims to have written it? So when taking up Paul's letter to the Christians at Rome, it must be asked: Who wrote it? Was it really from the one who claims to have written it? Authorship, the use of an amanuensis or secretary, and the possible involvement of others in the letter's final composition are the necessary first considerations in the study of any NT letter.

1. Author

The most uncontroverted matter in the study of Romans is that the letter was written by Paul, the Christian apostle whose ministry is portrayed in the Acts of the Apostles. The author identifies himself as Paul in the first word of the salutation (1:1). He speaks of himself as both a Jew by birth (9:3) and "the apostle to the Gentiles" by vocation (11:13). And throughout the letter — whether in its personal references, theological presuppositions, christological affirmations, rhetorical modes of argument, epistolary conventions, or ethical appeals — there resounds the clear note of authenticity. Together with the letter to the Galatians, it must be said: If these two letters are not by Paul, no NT letters are by him, for none has any better claim to authenticity than Galatians and Romans.

Testimony as to Paul's authorship of Romans in "the sub-apostolic age" is, as William Sanday and Arthur C. Headlam have asserted, "full and ample."[1]

---

1. W. Sanday and A. C. Headlam, *Romans,* lxxix.

Likewise throughout church history — whether it be opinions expressed by the early Christian Gnostics, by such a second-century radical Christian deviant as Marcion, by Greek or Latin Church Fathers, by Roman Catholic or Eastern Orthodox scholars, or by Renaissance Humanists, Protestant Reformers, and modern critical scholars — Paul's authorship of Romans has been almost universally accepted. Every extant early list of NT writings includes Romans among Paul's canonical letters. There is, in fact, no recorded opposition to Paul's authorship of Romans until the late eighteenth century.

In his 1845 *Paulus, der Apostel Jesu Christi,* which summed up all of his previous NT studies, Ferdinand Christian Baur denied Paul's authorship of a number of letters in the Pauline corpus. But Baur accepted Romans as having been written by Paul (i.e., the first fourteen chapters; his views on the final two chapters of the letter will be discussed later in Chapter II, "Integrity"), and he built his case for early Christianity on "the four great Epistles of the Apostle which take precedence of the rest in every respect, namely, the Epistle to the Galatians, the two Epistles to the Corinthians, and the Epistle to the Romans" (i.e., the so-called *Hauptbriefe*). For, as Baur insisted, "there has never been the slightest suspicion of unauthenticity cast on these four epistles, and they bear so incontestably the character of Pauline originality that there is no conceivable ground for the assertion of critical doubts in their case."[2] In the first part of the twentieth century C. H. Dodd asserted: "The authenticity of the Epistle to the Romans is a closed question."[3] While in the latter part of the twentieth century C. E. B. Cranfield claimed: "The denial of Paul's authorship of Romans . . . is now rightly relegated to a place among the curiosities of NT scholarship. Today no responsible criticism disputes its Pauline origin."[4]

Shortly after the publication of F. C. Baur's *Paulus,* however, Bruno Bauer outdid his teacher F. C. Baur in the application of "Tendency Criticism" and denied that even Romans and the other three *Hauptbriefe* were written in the first century.[5] Bruno Bauer argued that the letter to the Romans is so full of obscurities, contradictions, improbabilities and *non sequiturs* that it could hardly have been written by Paul. And many on the European continent, following Bruno Bauer's lead, took a similar stance during the closing decades of the nineteenth century — as for example, the Dutch

---

2. F. C. Baur, *Paul,* 1.246.
3. C. H. Dodd, *Romans,* 9.
4. C. E. B. Cranfield, *Romans,* 1.2.
5. See B. Bauer, *Kritik der paulinischen Briefe,* 3.47-76.

critic A. D. Loman[6] and the Swiss theologian Rudolf Steck,[7] but most prominently the Dutch NT scholar W. C. van Manen.[8]

All of these nineteenth-century continental critics had been anticipated at the close of the eighteenth century by E. Evanson, who argued that (1) Paul could not have written to a church at Rome since the Acts of the Apostles makes it clear that no such church then existed, (2) Paul, having never visited Rome, could not have known so many people at Rome as the last chapter of the letter suggests, (3) Aquila and Priscilla could not have been at Rome at that time, (4) Paul's mother would hardly have wandered off to Rome (assuming, from a literal rendering of the possessive "my" of 16:13, that Rufus's mother, who is greeted at Rome, was also Paul's birth mother), and (5) such verses as 11:12, 15, 21 and 22 indicate that Romans was written after the fall of Jerusalem, and so after the death of Paul.[9] Echoes of many of these late-eighteenth- and nineteenth-century arguments continued, to some extent, in the writings of such early-twentieth-century scholars as W. B. Smith[10] and G. Schläger.[11] Scholars today, however, are united in recognizing Romans as having been written by Paul. And all earlier denials of his authorship are commonly viewed today as aberrations in the history of NT study, and rightly so.

2. Amanuensis

Every discussion of the authorship of Romans must also include reference to its probable amanuensis or secretary, for in 16:22 there is the statement: "I,

6. See A. D. Loman, "Quastiones Paulinae," *TTijd* 16 (1882) 141-63 and 20 (1886) 42-113; *idem*, "Paulus en de Kanon," *TTijd* 20 (1886) 387-406.

7. See R. Steck, *Der Galaterbrief, nach seiner Echtheit untersucht: Nebst kritischen Bemerkungen zu den paulinischen Hauptbriefen* (Berlin: Reimer, 1888).

8. See W. C. van Manen, *Paulus*, vol. 2, *De Brief aan de Romeinen* (Leiden: Brill, 1891); *idem*, "Romans (Epistle)," *Encyclopedia Biblica*, 4 vols., ed. T. K. Cheyne and J. S. Black (New York: Macmillan, 1899-1903), 4.4127-45 (esp. 4129-30 and 4141); *idem, Die Unechtheit des Römerbriefes* (Leipzig: Strübig, 1906).

9. See E. Evanson, *The Dissonance of the Four Generally Received Evangelists, and the Evidence of Their Respective Authenticity Examined: With That of Some Other Scriptures Deemed Canonical* (Ipswich: Jermyn, 1792), 257-61; (Gloucester, MA: Johnson, 1805), 305-12.

10. See W. B. Smith, "Address and Destination of Romans," *JBL* 20 (1901) 1-21; *idem*, "Unto Romans: XV and XVI," *JBL* 20 (1901) 129-51 and 21 (1902) 117-69; *idem*, "Did Paul Write Romans?" *HibJ* 1 (1903) 309-34.

11. See G. Schläger, "La Critique radicale de l'épître aux Romains," in *Congrès d'histoire du christianisme: Jubilé Alfred Loisy*, 3 vols., ed. P.-L. Couchoud (Paris: Rieder; Amsterdam: Van Holkema & Warendorf, 1928), 2.100-118.

Tertius, who wrote this letter, greet you in the Lord." Assuming that chapter 16 is an integral part of Paul's letter to the Christians at Rome (see Chapter II, "Integrity"), here is the clearest indication in all of Paul's letters that an amanuensis or secretary was involved in the composition of his correspondence — though there are also a number of other indicators in the other canonical letters of Paul and the other NT letters that secretaries were involved in most, if not all, of them as well.

The extant non-literary Greek papyri, the bulk of which (some 40,000 to 60,000 manuscripts) were found during the last decade of the nineteenth century in the Fayyum district of Egypt, indicate quite clearly that an amanuensis or secretary was frequently, if not commonly, used in the writing of letters in the years before, during, and after the first Christian century. And there are reasons to believe that the writers of the NT also followed this practice. Literary men of the day may have preferred, as did Quintilian (c. A.D. 35-95), not to use an amanuensis for their personal correspondence. Or they may have agreed with Cicero (106-43 B.C.) that dictation to a secretary was an expedient necessitated only by illness or the press of duties. But the non-literary papyrus materials show that the common practice for more ordinary people was to use an amanuensis to write out their letters, after which the sender would usually, though not always, add in his own handwriting a word of farewell, personal greetings, and often (at least about half the time, to judge by the letters studied so far) the date of writing.[12]

Writing skills among ancient amanuenses undoubtedly varied. A third-century A.D. Latin payment schedule reads: "To a scribe for best writing, 100 lines, 25 denarii; for second-quality writing, 100 lines, 20 denarii; to a notary for writing a petition or legal document, 100 lines, 10 denarii."[13] The Greek biographer Plutarch (c. A.D. 46-120) credited Cicero in the first century B.C. with the invention of a system of Latin shorthand, relating how Cicero placed scribes in various locations in the senate chamber to record the speeches and taught them in advance "signs having the force of many letters in little and short marks"[14] — though it may have been Tiro, the freedman of Cicero, who was actually the originator, for inventions of slaves were often credited to their masters. The reference by Seneca (c. 4 B.C.–A.D. 65) to slaves having invented among their other notable accomplishments "signs for words, with

---

12. Cf. R. N. Longenecker, "Ancient Amanuenses," 281-97; *idem*, "On the Form," 101-14.

13. *Edictum Diocletiani de Pretiis Rerum Venalium*, 7.39-41.

14. Plutarch, *Parallel Lives* 23, on Cato the Younger.

which a speech is taken down, however rapid, and the hand follows the speed of the tongue"[15] lends credence to Tiro, or someone like him, as the originator, and suggests that at least by A.D. 63-64, when Seneca's letters to Lucilius were written, a system of Latin shorthand was widely in use.

In the Greek-speaking world tachygraphy *(tachygraphos)*, or shorthand writing, may be assumed to have been fairly common in the first Christian century. Legend ascribes its invention among the Greeks to Xenophon of the fourth century B.C. In *POxy* 724, a letter dated March 1, A.D. 155 (i.e., "the fifth of Phamenouth in the eighteenth year of the emperor Titus Aiolios Hadrian Antonius Augustus Eusebius"), a former official of Oxyrhynchus by the name of Panechotes binds his slave Chaerammon to a stenographer named Apollonius for a term of two years in order to learn shorthand from him. Although Panechotes' letter is a second century A.D. writing, the developed system of shorthand that it assumes — which Chaerammon was to take two years to learn — presupposes an earlier workable system of Greek shorthand. And in the Wadi Murabba'at caves of southern Palestine, the site where Simeon ben Kosebah (who was called in Aramaic by his admirers "Bar Kokhbah," that is, "Son of the Star," but denounced by his detractors as "Bar Kozebah," that is, "Son of the Lie") made his headquarters in the early second century, there have been found, written on vellum, two pages of Greek shorthand writing, which are as yet undeciphered.[16]

The extent of the freedom that amanuenses had in drafting letters is impossible to determine from the evidence presently at hand. Undoubtedly it varied from case to case. Amanuenses may have written their clients' letters out in longhand, word for word or even syllable by syllable. They may have taken down their clients' messages in shorthand and then written them out in final form in longhand. They may have been given the sense of what their clients wanted to say and left to work out the wording themselves. Or they may have been asked to write on a particular subject in a sender's name without being given explicit directions as to how to develop the topic — especially if the sender felt his amanuensis already knew his mind on the matter. Scholarly opinion on this matter is divided. Otto Roller, for example, believed that ancient amanuenses had a great deal of freedom and that dictation of a word-for-word variety was rare,[17] whereas F. R. Montgomery

---

15. Seneca, *Ad Lucilium Epistulae Morales* 90.25.
16. Cf. P. Benoit, "Document en Tachygraphie Grecque," 275-79, Plates: CIII-CV.
17. O. Roller, *Das Formular der paulinischer Briefe,* 16-19.

Hitchcock drew exactly the opposite conclusion.[18] But whatever method or methods may have been used in the writing of any particular letter, and whatever freedom may have been given to the amanuensis involved, the sender usually added a personal subscription in his own hand, thereby not only concluding the letter with an intimate, personal touch but also attesting to all that was written. At times, there might even be included in the subscription a résumé of what had been said in the body of the letter, thereby acknowledging further the authenticity of the contents and highlighting some of its details.

We possess, of course, no autograph of any NT letter. It may be assumed, however, that their authors followed current conventions and so used amanuenses when writing — though for the authors of the NT writings their secretaries were probably more personal companions who possessed some literary ability than trained scribes. In 2 Thess 3:17 Paul says that it was his practice to add a personal subscription to his letters in his own handwriting ("I, Paul, write this greeting in my own hand, which is the attesting sign [σημεῖον] in all my letters"), thereby validating what was written and assuring his converts of the letter's authenticity. Such a statement is in line with the epistolary practice of the day and alerts us to the likely presence of other such subscriptions among his other letters, though it gives no guidance as to how to mark them off. Likewise, the words of 1 Cor 16:21 and Col 4:18 ("I, Paul, write this greeting in my own hand") suggest that the subscriptions were distinguishable in handwriting from the material that preceded — necessitating, of course, the involvement of an amanuensis in what preceded. Gal 6:11, while allowing some uncertainty as to the precise extent of the reference, recalls certain features in the subscriptions of Greco-Roman letters when it declares, "See what large letters I use as I write to you with my own hand!" Philemon 19 may also be the beginning of such a personal subscription: "I, Paul, am writing this with my own hand." And all of this suggests that the statement "I, Tertius, who wrote this letter in the Lord" of Rom 16:22 cannot be understood in any way other than that an amanuensis was involved in some way and to some extent in Paul's letter to the Christians at Rome.

Of the non-Pauline materials in the NT, 1 Peter and the Fourth Gospel are most plausibly also to be seen as having been written down by a close associate who served as the author's amanuensis or secretary. As George Milligan long ago observed:

18. F. R. M. Hitchcock, "The Use of *graphein*," 273-74.

In the case of the First Epistle of St. Peter, indeed, this seems to be distinctly stated, for the words *dia Silouanou,* "by Silvanus," in c. v. 12, are best understood as implying that Silvanus was not only the bearer, but the actual scribe of the Epistle. And in the same way an interesting tradition, which finds pictorial representation in many mediaeval manuscripts of the Fourth Gospel, says that St. John dictated his Gospel to a disciple of his named Prochorus.[19]

Just how closely Paul supervised his companions or associates in their writing down of his letters is impossible, based only on the data in his letters, to say. As suggested above, the responsibilities of an amanuensis could vary, ranging all the way from taking dictation verbatim to "fleshing out" a general line of thought. Paul's own practice probably varied with the circumstances encountered and the companions available. Assuming, as Otto Roller has proposed, that amanuenses were often identified in the salutations of letters (particularly if they were known to the addressees), more might be left to the discretion of Silas and Timothy (cf. 1 Thess 1:1; 2 Thess 1:1) or Timothy alone (cf. 2 Cor 1:1; Col. 1:1; Phil 1:1; Philem 1) than to Sosthenes (cf. 1 Cor 1:1) or Tertius (cf. Rom 16:22) — and perhaps much more to Luke, who is referred to as being the only one with Paul during his final imprisonment (cf. 2 Tim 4:11). And if in one case Paul closely scrutinized and revised a letter, at another time he may have only read it over and allowed it to go out practically unaltered.

Later, in Chapter VI, we will speak more extensively about the Greco-Roman epistolary conventions of Romans. It may be that some of these features should be credited more to Tertius than to Paul, particularly the epistolary conventions that appear at the beginning and end of the letter. Still, there are a number of reasons to suggest that what appears in the Greek text of Romans today is essentially what Paul dictated to Tertius — with all of it, however composed, standing under his approval and expressing what he wanted to say to the Christians at Rome. The similarities of style and language between Galatians, the Corinthian letters, and Romans suggest that in these earlier letters Paul was himself fully in charge of not only the arguments presented but also the diction used. Further, since his letter to Rome was undoubtedly viewed by him as one of his most important letters — one on which the success or failure of his proposed mission to the western regions of the Roman empire largely depended — it is not unreasonable to as-

19. G. Milligan, *New Testament Documents,* 22-23; cf. 160-61 and Plate V.

sume that Paul would have given a great deal of attention not only to the thoughts expressed but also to their precise wording.

Whether Tertius should be viewed as having written down Paul's dictation in longhand "syllable by syllable," as C. E. B. Cranfield postulates,[20] or as having taken Paul's dictation in shorthand and then written it out in longhand, as William Sanday and Arthur C. Headlam proposed,[21] Paul's letter to the Christians at Rome gives every indication of having been carefully composed by him in both its arguments and its diction — that is, in both its content and its wording. Paul may have used one of "the brothers" as his amanuensis when writing Galatians (Gal 1:2), Sosthenes when writing 1 Corinthians (1 Cor 1:1), his young colleague Timothy when writing 2 Corinthians (2 Cor 1:1), and Tertius when writing Romans (Rom 16:22). But in all of these four early letters, at least, he seems to have exercised a great deal of control over those who served as his secretaries, so that the letters produced may be seen to express not only his essential thoughts but also his precise wording.

3. Involvement of Others

In writing to the Christians at Rome, Paul undoubtedly drew on materials that he had earlier (1) used in various Jewish synagogues and (2) proclaimed in his outreach to Gentiles in the eastern part of the Roman empire. Such rather self-contained materials as found in 1:18-32 (on "God's wrath against humanity's godlessness and wickedness"), 7:1-6 (an illustration and comment regarding "the authority of the Mosaic law and Christian freedom"), and 9–11 (on "the Christian message vis-à-vis God's promises to Israel") may reflect Paul's earlier presentations in various Jewish contexts, while much of the theological material that he sets out in 5:1-11 (on "peace and reconciliation with God"), 5:12-21 (on "the one man [Adam] and the one man, Jesus Christ"), and chapter 8 (on "life 'in Christ' and life 'in the Spirit'") — together with the general ethical exhortations of 12:3-21 and 13:8-14 (on "a Christian love ethic") — may reflect materials that he proclaimed at various times in his outreach to Gentiles. Further, it may also be assumed that he

---

20. C. E. B. Cranfield, *Romans*, 1.3, citing Cicero's mention of *syllabatim* in *Ad Atticum* 13.25.3; cf. also *Ad Lucullum* 119.

21. W. Sanday and A. C. Headlam, *Romans*, lx, citing the manner in which Origen's lectures were taken down and subsequently written out, as described by Eusebius, *Eccl Hist* 6.23.2.

profited a great deal from discussions he had with both Jews and Gentiles with respect to the content of his message during those earlier presentations.

Likewise, it seems reasonable to suppose that Paul discussed various portions of his letter to Rome with some of his associates and with some of the Christian leaders in the city of Corinth and its environs. Such discussions would most likely have taken place between himself and Timothy his young colleague, who was then with him at Corinth and whose greetings Paul includes in his letter (cf. 16:21); probably also with Gaius, whose home became a meeting place for the Christians of Corinth and with whom Paul lived when in that city, and whose greetings are also included (cf. 16:23). Quite likely they would have taken place, as well, with the lady Phoebe, who was a "deacon" (διάκονον) of the church in the port city of Cenchrea, functioned in some manner as a "benefactor" or "patron" (προστάτις) to Paul and many other Christians of the area, was the one who seems to have actually carried the letter on Paul's behalf to Rome, and is warmly commended to the Christians at Rome by Paul (cf. 16:1-2). And certainly he would have discussed the contents of his letter with Tertius, who served as his secretary in writing down what he dictated, identified himself as a fellow believer in Jesus ("in the Lord"), and inserted his own greeting (cf. 16:22).

All of these people may very well have had some impact on the thought and wording of Paul's letter to the Christians at Rome, whether at some earlier time when he discussed its contents with them or as he was actually dictating its contents to Tertius. And others may have been involved as well — though, as must always be recognized, whatever input others may have had, the final composition was understood by all concerned as a letter by Paul himself.

Developing a "social scientific reconstruction" of the situation of Phoebe as Paul's benefactor or patron, the function of Tertius as Paul's amanuensis, and the circumstances of the Christians at Rome, Robert Jewett has gone further to "conjecture" (which is the word that Jewett himself uses to describe the nature of his proposal): (1) that Phoebe was an upper-class lady of considerable wealth who not only ministered as a deacon in one of the Christian congregations of the port city of Cenchrea, but also must be seen as the one who supported Paul financially during his writing of Romans, carried his letter to Rome at her own expense, lent her backing to the letter's reception by the Christians at Rome, was likely very much involved in explaining the letter's contents to the Roman Christians, and was financially as well as personally "directly involved with the missionary project promoted by the letter," and (2) that Tertius was in all likelihood "Phoebe's slave or employee," who not only served as Paul's secretary in writing the letter (at Phoebe's expense) but also traveled with Phoebe to Rome to deliver the letter (again, of course, at Phoebe's expense) — and, even more than that, was probably the one who actually both read and explained Paul's letter (as Phoebe's trusted slave or employee, and so on behalf of Phoebe) to the Jewish and Gentile believers in Jesus living at Rome and worshiping in their various Christian meeting places.[22] Thus Jewett proposes in a final sentence on this matter: "In conclusion, this commentary rests on the conjecture that Tertius and Phoebe were engaged in the creation, the delivery, the public reading, and the explanation of the letter."[23]

Such a proposal, at first glance, appears to have much in its favor, and so is quite likely. Further, it allows Robert Jewett, by reference to what he posits would have been the understanding of Phoebe and her trusted slave or employee Tertius regarding what Paul wrote to the Christians at Rome, to clarify a number of matters that may have been to its original addressees — as well as to scholars and general readers today — somewhat ambiguous (cf., e.g., Jewett's treatments of certain matters regarding both the structures and the wordings found in the body of the letter at 7:7, 25; 11:1; 12:3; and 15:24). Likewise, it permits Jewett to interpret a great deal of what is written in the letter in the light of his own understanding of the social situation of the day, as well as his understanding of the theological and social issues that were then present among the Roman Jewish and Gentile believers in Jesus in their various "house church" congregations.

Much more, of course, needs to be said about Phoebe and Tertius in any exegetical treatment of the verses where their names appear, that is, in 16:1-2 and 22 (which is what we intend to do in the future). Suffice it here to point out that (1) all that Paul explicitly says about Phoebe with respect to the writing and delivery of this letter is only that she "has been a benefactor (or, 'patron') of many and of myself as well," and (2) all that he requests of the Christians at Rome regarding her is only that she be welcomed "in the Lord in a way worthy of God's people" and given "any help she may need from you" (16:2). Further, it needs also to be noted that all that is said by Tertius in the letter regarding himself is only that he is the one "who wrote down this letter," that he includes his own greeting at the end of a long list of other greetings that he was instructed by Paul to send, and that he considered himself a believer "in the Lord" (16:22).

22. See R. Jewett, *Romans*, 22-23.
23. R. Jewett, *Romans*, 23.

There can hardly be any doubt that it was Tertius who served as Paul's secretary in the writing of Romans. Further, it has seemed highly plausible to almost all commentators that it was Phoebe, whom Paul identifies as a "deacon of the church at Cenchrea" and "a benefactor (or 'patron') of many people, including me," who was the one who actually carried the letter on Paul's behalf to Rome, probably at her own expense. But while it may be intriguing to speculate further about the persons, relations, and functions of Phoebe and Tertius — and while we will need to enter into such discussions later in a proposed commentary where their names are specifically included in the text — the rather general characterizations of these two people as given in 16:1-2 and 22 must suffice for now.

SUPPLEMENTAL BIBLIOGRAPHY

See also "Bibliography of Selected Commentaries." All references in the footnotes to works included in this list are by the authors' names and abbreviated titles.

Bahr, Gordon J. "Paul and Letter Writing in the First Century," *CBQ* 28 (1966) 465-77.
———. "The Subscriptions in the Pauline Letters," *JBL* 87 (1968) 27-41.
Bauer, Bruno. *Kritik der paulinischen Briefe,* 3 vols. Berlin: Hempel, 1850-1852, 3.47-76.
Baur, Ferdinand Christian. *Paul, the Apostle of Jesus Christ: His Life and Work, His Epistles and His Doctrine: A Contribution to a Critical History of Primitive Christianity,* 2 vols., trans. E. Zeller. Edinburgh: University of Edinburgh Press, 1846 (from the German 1845 first edition); London: Williams & Norgate, 1876, 1.245-49, 308-52.
Benoit, Pierre. "Document en Tachygraphie Grecque," in *Les Grottes de Murabba'at* [DJD 2], ed. P. Benoit *et al.* Oxford: Clarendon, 1961; Text: 275-79, Plates: CIII-CV.
Deissmann, Adolf. *Light from the Ancient East: The New Testament Illustrated by Recently Discovered Texts of the Graeco-Roman World,* trans. L. R. M. Strachan. London: Hodder & Stoughton, 1909.
Doty, William G. *Letters in Primitive Christianity.* Philadelphia: Fortress, 1973.
Epp, Eldon Jay. "New Testament Papyrus Manuscripts and Letter Carrying in Greco-Roman Times," in *The Future of Early Christianity: Essays in Honor of Helmut Koester,* ed. B. A. Pearson *et al.* Minneapolis: Fortress, 1991, 35-56.
Hitchcock, F. R. Montgomery. "The Use of *graphein*," *JTS* 31 (1930) 273-74.
Kim, Chan-Hie. "The Papyrus Invitation," *JBL* 94 (1975) 391-402.
Longenecker, Richard N. "Ancient Amanuenses and the Pauline Epistles," in *New Dimensions in New Testament Study,* ed. R. N. Longenecker and M. C. Tenney. Grand Rapids: Zondervan, 1974, 281-97.

————. "On the Form, Function, and Authority of the New Testament Letters," in *Scripture and Truth,* ed. D. A. Carson and J. D. Woodbridge. Grand Rapids: Zondervan, 1983, 101-14.

Milligan, George. *The New Testament Documents: Their Origin and Early History.* London: Macmillan, 1913, 21-30 and 241-47.

Milne, Herbert J. M. *Greek Shorthand Manuals. Syllabary and Commentary.* London: Oxford University Press, 1934.

Pack, Roger A. *The Greek and Latin Literary Texts from Greco-Roman Egypt.* Ann Arbor: University of Michigan Press, 1965[2].

Richards, E. Randolph. *The Secretary in the Letters of Paul.* WUNT 2.42. Tübingen: Mohr-Siebeck, 1991.

Roberts, Colin H. *Greek Literary Hands, 350 B.C.–A.D. 400.* Oxford: Clarendon, 1956.

Roller, Otto. *Das Formular der paulinischen Briefe: Ein Beitrag zur Lehre vom antiken Briefe.* Stuttgart: Kohlhammer, 1933, esp. 14-23, 191-99 and 295-300.

Sherk, Robert K. *Roman Documents from the Greek East:* Senatus Consulta *and* Epistulae *to the Age of Augustus.* Baltimore: Johns Hopkins University Press, 1969.

Turner, Eric G. *Greek Manuscripts of the Ancient World.* Princeton: Princeton University Press, 1971.

Wendland, Paul. *Die ürchristlichen Literaturformen.* HNT 1.3. Tübingen: Mohr, 1912, 339-45.

White, John L. *Light from Ancient Letters.* Philadelphia: Fortress, 1986.

CHAPTER II

Integrity

After author, amanuensis, and the involvement of others in the composition of Romans (as treated in the previous chapter), matters regarding the integrity of the text of Paul's letter must necessarily be addressed. For one can hardly deal with a letter's critical issues or discuss its contents in any meaningful manner without having some assurance about its undivided condition and some conviction that it has not been encumbered with materials inserted by others.

Matters regarding integrity may not be of any great concern when one reads a letter of no real importance or when one reads only casually. But issues having to do with integrity are always important when one has in hand a letter of great significance and attempts to read it seriously. In such a case, questions such as the following will inevitably arise: Are there any enclosures, glosses, or interpolations that have somehow been included with or incorporated into this letter? Is this a single letter written by one author? Or is this letter a compilation of two or more letters, whether composed by one author or by two or more authors?

Among the canonical letters of Paul, matters having to do with the integrity of 2 Corinthians and Philippians have been particularly perplexing. With regard to Paul's letter to the Christians at Rome, issues concerning integrity are also quite complex — though, of late, a convergence of scholarly opinion seems to have come about with respect to many of them. In what follows we will need to deal with (1) possible glosses and interpolations in the text, (2) the form of the original letter, whether "long" (chs. 1–16), "short" (chs. 1–14), or "intermediate" (chs. 1–15), and (3) the three most prominent text-critical issues today — setting out for each of these matters, in the main, the "state of the question" as it has taken shape among the great majority of contemporary NT scholars.

1. Glosses and Interpolations

Individual words, phrases or statements that appear in the margins or between the lines of MSS are referred to as glosses; foreign or extraneous materials incorporated into the texts themselves are called interpolations. At times, however, glosses were written into the texts by copyists, and so became interpolations. The terms *gloss* and *interpolation,* therefore, are often used somewhat interchangeably.

Based on the facts (1) that interpolation by later authors into earlier writings was a fairly common phenomenon in antiquity, (2) that editorial glosses are rather common in our extant biblical MSS, and (3) that a number of passages in Romans are not only difficult to interpret but also seem obscure or contradictory, some late-nineteenth-century scholars argued for a large number of glosses or interpolations in the text of Romans and claimed to be able to distinguish what Paul originally wrote from such later recensions. C. H. Weisse in 1867 was the earliest to so argue.[1] And he was followed "with greater indiscreetness" (to borrow Sanday and Headlam's characterization of their activities)[2] by A. Pierson and S. A. Naber (1886), J. H. A. Michelsen (1886-87), D. Voelter (1889-90), and W. C. van Manen (1887-1906).

The most vigorous and convincing of this group of scholars was W. C. van Manen, who attempted to reconstruct Marcion's text of Romans, which he held to be original, and then to identify everything else in the letter as a later interpolation.[3] Most ingenious, however, was Daniel Voelter, who argued on the basis of style and content:

> The original Epistle . . . contained the following portions of the Epistle: i.1a, 7; 5, 6; 8-17; v. and vi. (except v.13, 14, 20; vi.14, 15); xii, xiii; xv.14-32; xvi.21-23. This bears all the marks of originality; its Christology is primitive, free from any theory of pre-existence or of two natures. To the first interpolator we owe 1.18; iii.20 (except ii.14, 15); viii.1, 3-39; i.1b-4. Here

1. See C. H. Weisse, *Beiträge zur Kritik der Paulinischen Briefe* (1867).
2. Cf. W. Sanday and A. C. Headlam, *Romans,* lxxxvi.
3. See W. C. van Manen, *De Brief aan de Romeinen* (1891); idem, "Romans (Epistle)," *Encyclopaedia Biblica* (1899-1903), 4.4127-45; idem, *Die Unechtheit des Römerbriefes* (1906).

the Christology is different; Christ is the pre-existent Son of God. To the second interpolator we owe iii.21–iv.25; v.13, 14, 20; vi.14, 15; vii.1-6; ix, x; xiv.1–xv.6. This writer who worked about the year 70 was a determined Antinomian, who could not see anything but evil in the Law. A third interpolator is responsible for vii.7-25; viii.2; a fourth for xi; ii.14, 15; xv.7-13; a fifth for xvi.1-20; a sixth for xvi.24; a seventh for xvi.25-27.[4]

Theories about glosses and interpolations in Romans continue to abound today — as witness, for example, R. M. Hawkins's attempt to demonstrate glosses at 1:19-21, 32; 2:1, 16, 17; 3:10-18, 24-26; 4:1, 17, 18-19; 5:1, 6-7, 17; 7:6, 25; 8:1; 9:5; 10:9, 17; 11:6; 12:11; 13:1-7; 14:6; and 16:5, 24;[5] Charles Talbert's proposal that 3:24-26 is an interpolation;[6] Leander Keck's claim that 5:6-7 is by a post-Pauline author;[7] James Kallas's argument that 13:1-7 is a later non-Pauline addition;[8] and Robert Jewett's designation of 16:17-20 ("the warning against heretics") and 16:25-27 ("the concluding doxology") as interpolations.[9]

A more radical advocate of such views was Walter Schmithals, who argued that Romans is a conflation of two letters written by Paul at separate times and with different purposes to Gentile believers at Rome: "Letter A," which consisted of materials now found in 1–4; 5:12–11:36; 15:8-13; "Letter B," which contained materials now in chapter 12; 13:8-10; 14:1–15:4a; 15:5-6, 7, 14-32; 16:21-23; 15:33 — though with numerous non-Pauline glosses and interpolations present almost everywhere throughout these two letters, particularly where Jewish Christians are suggested as having been present in the Roman church and where Schmithals judged what is written to be "foreign" to Paul.[10] Equally extreme, though with quite a different analysis, are John O'Neill's insistence that "our present text groans under extensive overlay" and his identification of such large blocks of material as 1:18–2:29; 7:14-25, 9:14-23, 10:16–11:32 and 12:1–15:13 as later glosses — together with all of the

---

4. As summarized by W. Sanday and A. C. Headlam, *Romans,* lxxxvii.

5. R. M. Hawkins, "Romans: A Reinterpretation," 129-40; *idem, Recovery of the Historical Paul,* 14-20, 291-92.

6. C. H. Talbert, "Non-Pauline Fragment at Romans 3:24-26?" 287-96; though Talbert has considerably revised this position in his 2002 commentary *Romans,* 106-16.

7. L. E. Keck, "Post-Pauline Interpretation of Jesus' Death in Rom 5.6-7," 237-48.

8. J. G. Kallas, "Romans xiii.1-7: An Interpolation," 365-74.

9. R. Jewett, *Romans,* 30, 986-88, 998-1005, who sets out extended bibliographies in support of both interpolation and authenticity.

10. W. Schmithals, *Römerbrief als historisches Problem; idem, Römerbrief: Ein Kommentar.*

letter's references to Gentile Christians at Rome and numerous smaller texts that do not conform to his application of the criteria of logical compatibility, style and tone.[11] Somewhat more reserved, but still of the same variety, is Rudolf Bultmann's claim that there exist a number of short glosses at 2:16; 6:17b; 7:25b–8:1, and 10:17.[12]

Arguments against any large-scale incorporation of glosses or interpolations into the text of Romans, however, have proven far more convincing to most scholars than suppositions in their favor. For as Sanday and Headlam long ago pointed out: "The number, the variety, and the early character of the texts preserved for us in MSS., Versions, and Fathers, is a guarantee that a text formed on critical methods represents within very narrow limits the work as it left its author's hands."[13]

Writing at the end of the nineteenth century (their commentary being published in 1895, with only slight revisions thereafter until the fifth and final edition in 1902), William Sanday and Arthur C. Headlam did not have the opportunity to take into account the important contribution that the papyrus discoveries of Egypt would make with regard to this question of textual integrity. Today, however, the testimony of P[46] — that is, the Chester Beatty Papyrus II, which dates from about A.D. 200 and contains extensive portions of the text of Romans covering 5:17–6:14, 8:15–15:9 and 15:11–16:27 (folios 1-7 are missing, which evidently contained 1:1–5:16; also absent is the material from 6:15–8:14 and 15:10), with the doxology of 16:25-27 located between 15:33 and 16:1 (as will be treated later) — can be cited as external support for the basic authenticity of the Romans text, taking us back to at least the beginning of the third century. Similarly, though not as extensively, P[27] (containing 8:12-22, 24-27; 8:33–9:3; 9:5-9) and P[40] (containing 1:24-27; 1:31–2:3; 3:21–4:8; 6:4-5, 16; 9:16-17, 27), which both date from about the middle of the third century, augment P[46] and support our present critically-established text, as do also the much smaller fragments of P[10] (1:1-7), P[26] (1:1-16), and P[31] (12:3-8). While internally, the general flow of Paul's argument in the letter, together with the verbal connections that exist between its various parts, serves to weaken, if not actually put an end to, most (if not all) of the interpolation hypotheses.

It is always possible, of course, that minor glosses or extraneous interpolations have somehow become incorporated into a particular biblical text,

11. J. C. O'Neill, *Romans.*
12. R. Bultmann, "Glossen im Römerbrief," 197-202.
13. W. Sanday and A. C. Headlam, *Romans,* lxxxviii.

and every possible instance of such a phenomenon needs to be checked by the canons of textual criticism. Each postulated case needs to be looked at closely in its own context, for determinations will vary in particular contexts and circumstances. Yet it needs to be recognized that the positing of glosses and interpolations should always be considered a measure of last resort. Sadly, some commentators of the past, when faced with a difficulty of interpretation, have all-too-often dispensed with the problem simply by identifying the word, phrase, or passage in question as a gloss or interpolation, and so excised it from the text. Scholars today, however, are far more prepared to entertain the possibility of difficulties and obscurities — even of contradictions — in the interpretation of Romans than were scholars in previous generations, crediting such matters either to Paul's own somewhat convoluted logic or to the interpreter's misconceived perceptions of what Paul ought to be saying, or both, but not first of all to textual glosses or interpolations.

2. Form of the Original Letter

While accepting Paul's authorship of the first fourteen chapters of Romans, F. C. Baur concluded his discussion of chapters 15–16 with the following assertion:

> The criticism of the last chapters leads to but one result: they must be held to be the work of a Paulinist, writing in the spirit of the Acts of the Apostles, seeking to soothe the Judaists, and to promote the cause of unity, and therefore tempering the keen anti-Judaism of Paul with a milder and more conciliatory conclusion to his Epistle.[14]

Joseph B. Lightfoot, however, who in the latter half of the nineteenth century led the opposition against Baur and his Tübingen School of NT "tendency criticism," argued for all of the letter, including chapters 15–16, as having been written by Paul.[15] But though the views of Baur and his colleagues regarding the integrity of Romans 15–16 have been effectively countered by Lightfoot and others, there still remained serious questions about the textual history of these final two chapters.

All of our extant Greek MSS contain the long form of Romans, that is, 1:1–16:27, though they vary somewhat with regard to (1) the inclusion of the

---

14. F. C. Baur, *Paul*, 1.365; see his full treatment in 352-65.
15. J. B. Lightfoot, *Biblical Essays*, 315-20.

various grace benedictions at 16:20b, 16:24, and/or 16:28 (i.e., after the final doxology) and (2) the placement of the doxology at 16:25-27 (where it is found in most MSS) or after 15:33. Issues regarding the peace benediction of 15:33, the grace benediction of 16:20 (also, possibly, that of 16:24; far less likely a grace benediction that follows the doxology at 16:28), and the doxology of 16:25-27 are varied and complex, and will be considered on their own merits later. Here it is necessary to discuss the textual history of chapters 15 and 16, starting with the probable existence of an early "short" form, moving on to consider the possible existence of an "intermediate" form, and finally setting out arguments in favor of the originality of the "long" form.

The Probable Existence of an Early Short Form

Despite the unanimous testimony of the Greek MSS, there seems to have existed at an early time among many Christians (both orthodox and heretical), who were living in such areas as North Africa, Asia Minor, and France, a short form of Romans that did not have chapters 15–16 and that sometimes appended the doxology of 16:25-27 of the long form immediately after 14:23. Belief in the existence of such an early short form is based on a number of considerations:

1. Origen's statement in his commentary on Romans *apropos* 16:25-27 that Marcion not only "completely removed" *(penitus abstulit)* this doxology but also "cut away" *(dissecuit)* everything in the letter after the words "everything that does not come from faith is sin"[16] — that is, everything after 14:23. This statement is transmitted to us only in Rufinus's Latin translation of 405. But the accuracy of Rufinus's translation has been generally vindicated by comparison with the Tura Papyrus found in 1941, which contains twenty-eight pages of excerpts from Origen's Greek commentary on Rom 3:5–5:7.[17] And there seems no reason for Rufinus, for whom Marcionism was not a threat, to have invented it.

2. The fact that Irenaeus in his *Adversus Haereses*, Tertullian in his *Adversus Marcionem*, and Cyprian in his *Testimonia Adversus Judaeos* do not quote at all from the last two chapters of the long form of Romans. This is, of course, an argument from silence, and any argument from silence is notori-

---

16. See Origen, *Ad Romanos* (PG 14.1290).
17. Cf. H. Chadwick, "Rufinus and the Tura Papyrus of Origen's Commentary on Romans," *JTS* 10 (1959) 10-42.

ously insecure. But it is an argument that gains credence from the number of authors involved, the importance of the text in question, and the extent of the material not cited — especially so when such a passage as 16:17-19 ("Watch out for those who cause divisions and put obstacles in your way, contrary to the teaching you have learned. Keep away from them; etc.") would have been eminently suitable for the respective arguments of each of these three Church Fathers.

In addition, it needs to be noted that Tertullian speaks of Paul as threatening his readers in the conclusion *(in clausula)* of Romans with "the judgment seat of Christ"[18] — which, evidently, is an allusion to the apostle's statement Rom 14:10, "For we will all stand before the judgment seat of God." It cannot be absolutely determined as to whether Tertullian was here referring to the conclusion of Marcion's text of Romans or to the conclusion of his own text. Tertullian's usual practice was to refute Marcion on the basis of the heretic's text. Yet coupled with the facts (1) that Tertullian never rebukes Marcion for excising these chapters, though he does for other portions deleted, and (2) that Tertullian never quotes from Romans 15–16, it seems virtually certain that Tertullian himself also had in hand and used only a fourteen-chapter form of the letter. In all probability, therefore, the short form of Romans cannot be attributed simply to Marcion, but must have been accepted by Tertullian as well — and also, as may be argued from their lack of reference to anything in chapters 15 and 16, by Irenaeus and Cyprian.

3. The *capitula* or *breves,* that is, the précis or captions that appear in many MSS of the Vulgate, which function as something of a "table of contents" for what is being read, suggest the early existence of a text for Romans that consisted of 1–14 plus the doxology of 16:25-27, but without 15:1–16:23 (probably also 16:24). Codex Amiatinus (vg^A) of Romans, which dates from the eighth century, is particularly relevant, for it sets out fifty-one *capitula* that are meant to serve as summary captions for the various sections of the entire letter — with the fiftieth being pertinent to the material found in 14:15, 17, and the fifty-first pertinent to the doxology of 16:25-27, but without any précis or caption with reference to the material of 15:1–16:23/24.

The *capitula* that appear in Codex Fuldensis (vg^f) of the sixth century also presuppose a short form of Romans, though in this case without the final doxology. For though the *capitula* of this latter Latin MS are of two types, the first twenty-three captions or headings being pertinent to 1–14 and the second thirty-eight headings pertinent to 9–14 (thereby overlapping in their

18. Tertullian, *Adversus Marcionem* 5.14.

treatment of chapters 9–14), there are no *capitula* for anything in chapters 15–16. And this suggests a text made up of only chapters 1–14, without any appended doxology.

4. The fact that the so-called *Concordia Epistularum Pauli,* which is a sort of concordance to the Pauline corpus that appears in a number of Vulgate MSS, lists subject headings for all of the material in Romans from 1:1–14:23 and then for the doxology of 16:25-27, but has no subject headings for anything in 15:1–16:23/24. This seems to indicate that, at least in certain Latin quarters, Romans was read in only its short form plus the final doxology.

5. The fact that a few of the so-called "Marcionite" prologues of the Latin MSS speak of Romans as having been written "from Athens" *(ab Athenis)* also suggests the probable existence of an early short form of Romans. These Latin prologues, which have often (falsely) been attributed to Marcion's followers because of their supposed Marcionite tones and nuances, provide brief introductions to Paul's letters on such matters of provenance as (1) a particular letter's recipients and their location, (2) the occasion and purpose of the letter, and (3) the place of its composition. And while some of these prologues identify Corinth as the city from whence Paul wrote his letter to the Christians at Rome, a few of them read "from Athens" *(ab Athenis)* — which seems a strange inference if their authors had before them the materials from 15:25-27 or 16:1 as part of their text, for these verses appear to locate Paul at the time when he wrote Romans in the vicinity of Corinth.

The Possible Existence of an Intermediate Form

As well as a long form and a short form, it has frequently been argued that Romans originally existed in what is called an intermediate form, that is, 1–15 — with or without the doxology of 16:25-27, but not including 16:1-23. Such an intermediate form was first proposed in the eighteenth century by Johann S. Semler.[19] It was advocated in the early nineteenth century by Johann Gottfried Eichhorn[20] and David Schulz.[21] And it has since been championed by a number of other NT scholars.

19. J. S. Semler, *Paraphrasis Epistolae ad Romanos* (Halle, 1769), 277-311.

20. J. G. Eichhorn, *Einleitung in das Neue Testament,* 5 vols. (Leipzig, 1819-27), 3.243.

21. Cf. D. Schulz's reviews of Eichhorn's *Einleitung in das Neue Testament* and de Wette's *Lehrbuch der historisch-kritischen Einleitung in die kanonischen Bücher des Neuen Testaments,* in *TSK* 2 (1829) 563-636, esp. 609-12.

Arguments in support of a fifteen-chapter form of Romans have been primarily internal and mostly negative in nature. As usually stated, they are to the effect that 16:1-23 (or, at least, 16:3-23) cannot originally have been part of Romans 1–15 because of (1) the different character of 16:1-23 (or 16:3-23) from that of the rest of Romans; (2) the concluding peace benediction of 15:33, which reads like other Pauline benedictions that conclude their respective letters (cf. 1 Cor 16:23-24; 2 Cor 13:11; Phil 4:9); (3) the large number of persons, families, and house-church groups greeted in 16:3-16, often in a manner that reflects affectionate familiarity, whereas the material of chapters 1–15 seems hardly cognizant of any specific situation within the Roman church; (4) the Ephesian associations of a number of the people greeted, coupled with seeming difficulties in locating some of them at Rome; and (5) the sharp and authoritarian tone reflected in the admonitions against the schismatics in 16:17-20, whereas the material in chapters 1–15 is more irenic and solicitous. This identification of chapter 16 as being separate from the rest of the letter has been called "the Ephesian Hypothesis," for it usually posits that 16:1-23 (or, at least, 16:3-23) was originally addressed, in whole or in part, to believers at Ephesus rather than to believers at Rome — being only later attached in some manner to Paul's letter to Rome, and so sandwiched in between the peace benediction of 15:33 and the doxology of 16:25-27 in all of our extant Greek uncial MSS.[22]

With the discovery of P[46], the second of the Chester Beatty biblical papyri that contains the Pauline corpus of letters (including Hebrews), the view that 16:1-23 (or 16:3-23), either in whole or in part, was originally addressed to believers at Ephesus and that 1–15, with or without the doxology now located at 16:25-27, was originally addressed to believers at Rome gained greater cogency. For P[46] contains a papyrus version of Romans that dates from about A.D. 200, thereby antedating the major Greek uncial MSS by about a century and a half, and that arranges Paul's letter as follows (the first seven folios being missing): 5:17–6:14 + 8:15–15:9 + 15:11-33 + 16:1-23 + 16:25-27 + 16:1-23. The testimony of P[46] is, of course, somewhat confusing, for it includes the material of 16:1-23 not only after 15:33 but also after the doxology of 16:25-27. Yet in that it locates the final doxology after 15:33 and has 16:1-23 at the end, it has seemed to suggest to many (1) that the earliest form of Paul's letter to the Romans may have been either 1–15 alone or 1–15 plus the doxology of 16:25-27, and (2) that what now appears in 16:1-23 may have originally been a short letter of greetings and exhortations, whether pre-

22. Cf., e.g., K. Lake, *Earlier Epistles of St. Paul*, 325-70.

served in whole or in part, that was written by Paul to converts at Ephesus —
with that short letter then being appended, for some reason and at some
early time, to Paul's longer letter to Rome.[23]

Further support for the originality of a fifteen-chapter form of
Romans may be seen as arising from two other sources: (1) the discipline of
text criticism, and (2) comparative studies of the forms of ancient letters.
The first, as drawn from text criticism, highlights a comparison of the
tenth-century minuscule 1739 in Greek with Origen's commentary on
Romans as preserved in Rufinus's Latin translation — not only with respect
to the similarity of their underlying biblical texts, which has often been observed, but also as to how 1739 and Origen's comments on Romans are both
similarly divided into *scholia* (sections for comment) or *tomoi* (themes).
For not only is there a similarity between 1739 and the postulated Greek
text of Origen's commentary, which has suggested to most scholars that
1739 represents a later form of an earlier Greek uncial MS used by Origen,
but also the fifteen *scholia* written in the margins of 1739 correspond to the
fifteen *tomoi* of Origen's treatment of Romans, with the fifteenth theme in
both starting at Rom 14:10.[24] So it may be surmised — arguing (1) on the
basis of comparable lengths of the other *scholia* and *tomoi,* and (2) from the
fact that Origen does not comment on the personal details of 16:1-23 but
does comment on the doxology of 16:25-27 — that Origen used a fifteen-
chapter form of Romans that had the doxology of 16:25-27 immediately after the peace benediction of 15:33.

The second line of argumentation often used in support of an original
fifteen-chapter form of Romans compares chapter 16 with a type of hellenistic letter that seems to have been current in Paul's day. For 16:1-23 has many
of the structural features of a hellenistic "Letter of Recommendation," and so
it may be argued that such a letter could easily have originally existed separately.[25] But while certain features of 16:1-23 may be used in support of the
thesis that this material originally appeared as a separate letter of recommendation, they may also be seen as appropriate for an epistolary concluding section that includes a number of recommendations of individuals.

---

23. Cf., e.g., A. Deissmann, *Light from the Ancient East,* 234-36, who proposed that
because of their joint inclusion in a secretary's "copy-book" and their similar handwriting,
Paul's smaller letter of greetings and admonitions to Ephesus was later joined to his larger
letter of instructions and exhortations to Rome.

24. Cf., e.g., H. Gamble Jr., *Textual History,* 124-26.

25. Cf. A. Deissmann, *Light from the Ancient East,* 234-36; see also, with more detail,
C.-H. Kim, *Familiar Greek Letter of Recommendation,* 101, 113-15, 135-42.

Past Explanations

Various attempts have been made to explain the origin and history of the letter's final two chapters. Joseph B. Lightfoot, as noted above, argued (1) that Paul originally wrote 1:1–16:23, that is, the long form minus the second grace benediction of 16:24 and the doxology of 16:25-27, but (2) that it was Paul himself who, "during one of his sojourns in Rome" and as something of "an after-thought," deleted the designation "at Rome" in 1:7, 15 and all of the material of 15:1–16:23 in order to make 1–14 "a circular letter or general treatise" suitable for wider reading among Christians[26] — and (3) that to this "abridged recension" Paul then added the doxology, which now appears at 16:25-27, immediately after the last verse of his shorter, reconstructed treatise, that is, after 14:23.[27] A similar explanation was given by Hans Lietzmann.[28] But such a view is faced with a real problem: Why would Paul have cut his discussion of the weak and the strong, which runs throughout the whole of 14:1–15:13, into two parts and discard the latter?

Fenton J. A. Hort also accepted the originality of the long form of Romans, but felt the thrust of the criticism as to why Paul would have restructured his abridged recension to end at 14:23 without including 15:1-13.[29] So while he agreed, in the main, with his Cambridge colleague, Hort argued that it must certainly have been some ecclesiastical editor, at some time during the latter part of the first century or early second century, who abridged Romans for lectionary purposes.[30] A similar explanation was given by James Moffatt[31] and by C. H. Dodd.[32] But while such a solution preserved the intelligence of Paul, it hardly did credit to that of any editor who may have pared away materials in Romans in order to achieve its short form. For the problem still exists as to why *anyone* would want to break the continuity between chapter 14 and 15:1-13 and then dispose of the latter section. Other than "pure accident," which has often been proposed, the only other rationale able to be

---

26. J. B. Lightfoot, *Biblical Essays*, 315-20.

27. J. B. Lightfoot, *Biblical Essays*, 317-18.

28. Cf. H. Lietzmann, *An die Römer*, 27.

29. F. J. A. Hort, "On the End of the Epistle" (repr. in J. B. Lightfoot's *Biblical Essays*, 321-51).

30. F. J. A. Hort, "On the End of the Epistle," 337-44.

31. J. Moffatt, *An Introduction to the Literature of the New Testament* (Edinburgh: T&T Clark, 1911, 1918³), 140.

32. C. H. Dodd, *Romans* (1932), xvi.

offered by advocates of this view is that of "rash hands"[33] or "the illimitable stupidity of editors."[34]

The earliest and most common explanation for the short form of Romans is that of Origen: that it was Marcion who "completely removed" *(penitus abstulit)* the doxology of 16:25-27 and "cut away" *(dissecuit)* everything in the letter after the words "everything that does not come from faith is sin" of 14:23.[35] And the great majority of scholars and commentators have accepted this explanation — among whom, to name only a few of diverse proclivities and more recent vintage, have been Frederic Godet,[36] William Sanday and Arthur Headlam,[37] Rudolf Schumacher,[38] Franz Leenhardt,[39] Frederick Bruce,[40] Matthew Black,[41] Charles Cranfield,[42] and John Robinson.[43] The rationale usually given for Marcion having deleted chapters 15–16 is that there are features in these chapters that would have offended his theological sensibilities. The three most obvious of these features are (1) the OT quotations in 15:3, 9-12 and 21, (2) the commendation of the Jewish (OT) Scriptures as being valuable for Christian living in 15:4, and (3) the reference to Christ as "a minister of the circumcision" in 15:8. Perhaps Marcion also viewed the warning against false teachers in 16:17-20 as an indictment of himself — though just as likely, if he knew the passage at all, he would have understood it as referring to others.

All of the scholars cited above argued for the originality of the long form of Romans, differing only in their explanations as to how the short form came about — that is, whether by the action of (1) Paul himself, (2) a later ecclesiastical editor, or (3) Marcion. Others scholars, however, though not expressing a majority opinion, have argued for the originality of the short form. And in almost every case where the short form has been viewed as original, some thesis regarding Romans as an encyclical letter has been advanced.

---

33. So F. J. A. Hort, "On the End of the Epistle," 351.
34. So C. H. Dodd, *Romans,* xvi.
35. Origen, *Ad Romanos* (PG 14.1290).
36. F. Godet, *Romans* (1880), 1.109-12.
37. W. Sanday and A. C. Headlam, *Romans* (1895), xcvi-xcvii.
38. R. Schumacher, *Die beiden letzten Kapitel* (1929), 135.
39. F. J. Leenhardt, *Romans* (1961), 26.
40. F. F. Bruce, *Romans* (1963), 29.
41. M. Black, *Romans* (1973), 28-29.
42. C. E. B. Cranfield, *Romans* (1975), 1.8.
43. J. A. T. Robinson, *Wrestling with Romans* (1979), 3-5.

Kirsopp Lake, for example, argued:

> The short recension represents a letter written by St. Paul at the same
> time as Galatians, in connection with the question of Jewish and Gentile
> Christians, for the general instruction of mixed Churches [in Syria and
> Asia Minor] which he had not visited. It had originally nothing to do
> with Rome. Later on he sent a copy to Rome, with the addition of the
> other chapters to serve, as we should say, as a covering letter.[44]

Relations between this general "Anti-Judaistic Letter" (i.e., Romans 1–14),
the letter to converts in the province of Galatia (i.e., Galatians), the covering letter to Ephesus (i.e., Romans 16), and the final covering letter to
Rome (i.e., Romans 15) are to be seen, Lake proposed, as being "exactly the
same" as those between Ephesians, Colossians, and Philemon, where
"Ephesians is the general Epistle to the Christians in Asia, Colossians an
Epistle to a special Church in that province, and Philemon a private note
to an individual Christian either in Colossae or a neighbouring town."[45] So
Lake argued:

> Why should it not be, then, that "Romans" was originally a general Epis-
> tle written by St. Paul, at the same time as Galatians, to the mixed
> Churches which had sprung up round Antioch and further on in Asia
> Minor? In that case we should have another instance of St. Paul's custom
> of writing a general Epistle, and supporting it by a series of letters to the
> separate Churches, or groups of Churches, in the district for which it
> was intended.[46]

And as for the problem of the connection between chapter 14 and 15:1-13,
Lake explained matters in the following fashion:

> St. Paul was in Corinth, on the point of departure for Jerusalem, and, in-
> fluenced by the information of Aquila and Priscilla, sent a copy of his
> "Anti-Judaistic Letter" to the Roman Christians, adding at the end a few
> more paragraphs continuing the thoughts of his original writing, proba-
> bly because Aquila had told him that this was desireable. . . . I take it that
> what happened was that St. Paul told a copyist to make a copy of the
> "short recension," and then dictated the remainder. If the Romans

---

44. K. Lake, *Earlier Epistles,* 362; cf. *idem,* "Shorter Form," 504-25.
45. K. Lake, *Earlier Epistles,* 363.
46. K. Lake, *Earlier Epistles,* 363-64.

wished to know any more about the form of the document, they must ask the bearers.[47]

A similar understanding of the originality of the short form and secondary nature of the long form was proposed by John Knox, though without an appeal to any Ephesian-Colossian-Philemon complex of letters in support of Paul's practice. Knox, however, added to the argument the fact that Spain is not mentioned in chapter 1, which starts the general treatise, whereas it appears as an important feature in 15:14-33, the material appended for Roman consumption.[48] And this general approach to the matter has been approved by Robert Funk[49] and Jack Suggs.[50]

Contemporary Arguments for the Long Form

A highly significant investigation of the original form of Romans, as well as relations between the long and the short forms, is that published in 1977 by Harry Gamble Jr., which is titled *The Textual History of the Letter to the Romans*. Gamble's conclusions may be summarized in the following six propositions:[51]

1. The sixteen-chapter form was undoubtedly original, particularly because the closing portion of the sixteenth chapter (i.e., 16:1-23) reflects the style and structure of ancient hellenistic letters and exhibits the epistolary features and conventions of a typical Pauline letter. The short form completely lacks these epistolary closing conventions, and therefore must be considered a truncated version of the long form.
2. The short form cuts in two the clearly unified treatment of the strong and the weak in 14:1–15:13, which suggests that it is secondary and the long form is original.

47. K. Lake, *Earlier Epistles*, 365.

48. J. Knox, "Romans," in *IB*, 9.365-68; *idem*, "Note on the Text of Romans," 191-93.

49. R. W. Funk, *Language, Hermeneutic, and Word of God: The Problem of Language in the New Testament and Contemporary Theology* (New York: Harper & Row, 1966), 265, n. 66.

50. M. J. Suggs, "'The Word Is Near You': Romans 10:6-10 within the Purpose of the Letter," in *Christian History and Interpretation: Studies Presented to John Knox*, ed. W. R. Farmer, C. F. D. Moule, and R. R. Niebuhr (Cambridge: Cambridge University Press, 1967), 289-98.

51. H. Gamble Jr., *Textual History*, esp. 96-129; see also ch. 3, "The Problem of Integrity: The Pauline Epistolary Conclusions," 56-95.

3. Marcion is not to be blamed for shortening Paul's original letter and deleting "at Rome" in 1:7, 15; rather, he merely "took over a text of Romans which was already in circulation."[52]

4. The short form is the result of neither a later abridgment for liturgical purposes nor an accidental loss of some final pages in some early codex.

5. Probably the short form stems from a "conscious revision with a single intention, to convert the letter from a specific communication to a particular community into a document suitable for a wider and general audience, or, in a word, to 'catholicize' the letter,"[53] with this "catholic generalization" done sometime after Paul and before Marcion.

6. Though the short form was derived from the long form, the short form existed as a "catholicized" letter along with the long "particularized" form in many areas and within many circles of early Christendom. Both forms, at least in some localities, seem to have been available for use by Christians generally, whether "orthodox" or "heretical," though evidently not commonly by all.

With regard to a fifteen-chapter form of Romans, Gamble's conclusions, of course, depend heavily on what he has argued regarding the long form vis-à-vis the short form. Thus he says regarding the fifteen-chapter form vis-à-vis the sixteen-chapter form:

> Decisive arguments for the original unity of the sixteen-chapter text have emerged . . . through our examination of the style and structure of the Pauline epistolary conclusion. We have shown that all of the elements in ch. 16 are typically concluding elements, that without this chapter the fifteen-chapter text lacks an epistolary conclusion, and that the unusual aspects of some elements in ch. 16 find cogent explanation only on the assumption of its Roman address. Thus the unity of the sixteen-chapter text and its Roman address are established.[54]

As Gamble summarizes his position, he argues that "the emergence of both the fourteen- and the fifteen-chapter forms of the text must be sought at a later point in the tradition in the letter" when there was "an early effort to 'catholicize' the Roman letter."[55]

---

52. H. Gamble Jr., *Textual History*, 113.
53. H. Gamble Jr., *Textual History*, 115-16.
54. H. Gamble Jr., *Textual History*, 127.
55. H. Gamble Jr., *Textual History*, 128.

Later we will discuss the various epistolary conventions in Paul's letter to the Romans, and, in particular, deal with those of the closing section in chapter 16 (cf. Chapter VI, "Greco-Roman Oral, Rhetorical, and Epistolary Conventions"). Suffice it here to note, however, (1) that the most significant features in Gamble's study, which serve as the basis for his conclusions, are his appeals to both hellenistic epistolary practice and Paul's writing habits in his other letters, and (2) that Gamble uses such epistolary evidence to supplement the usual textual, literary, and canonical studies of the issues at hand. In so doing, he has been able to advance the discussion considerably.

Gamble's study is principally concerned with establishing the originality of the sixteen-chapter version of Romans (i.e., 16:1-23) and the derived, secondary nature of the two shorter versions. The issues involved are complex, but Gamble has done well in sorting them out, bringing together the pertinent evidence, and defending his main thesis. On some other matters, however, particularly those somewhat tangent to his central concern, it may be said that he has not spoken the last word. One may still wonder, for example, (1) why an ecclesiastical editor would so carelessly separate 15:1-13 from chapter 14 to achieve a short form of the letter, and (2) whether the "intermediate" form was motivated by a desire to correct the "short" form or simply to "catholicize" in another manner the "long" form. Further, one could argue with Gamble regarding (1) the extent of the autographic conclusion of Romans in 16:21-23 (i.e., the letter's "personal subscription"), (2) the authenticity of the second benediction in 16:24, and (3) the authorship and postulated history of the letter's final doxology in 16:25-27. Nonetheless, despite such lingering questions, Gamble's work on the textual history of the three basic versions of Romans must be judged as being the most thorough and judicious to date. And his arguments for the originality of the sixteen-chapter form and the secondary nature of the two shorter forms (assuming, of course, that a fifteen-chapter version of the letter ever existed), are, in the main, highly convincing. So Gamble's conclusions on these matters will be assumed where pertinent in the introductory and commentary portions to follow.

3. Major Text-Critical Issues Today

The major text-critical issues today with respect to the integrity of Romans have to do with (1) the phrase "at Rome" (ἐν ʽΡώμῃ) of 1:7 and 15, (2) the grace benedictions of 16:20b, 24, and/or 28 (after the final doxology), and

(3) the doxology of 16:25-27. Other text-critical issues that bear on particular interpretive matters will need to be treated in the textual notes and exegetical comments of a forthcoming exegetical commentary, and so must be reserved for that future commentary. But these three textual matters are so closely bound up with discussions of the integrity of the final two chapters that they must be considered here.

The Designation "at Rome" in 1:7 and 15

The designation "at Rome" (ἐν ʿΡώμῃ) in 1:7 and 15 is omitted in the ninth-century bilingual codex G (Boernerianus, Greek, and Latin) and the eleventh-century minuscules 1739 and 1908 (its omission being noted in the margins of these minuscules). It is also omitted in the ninth-century Old Latin recension "g" (Matthaei edition). More important, however, is the fact that "at Rome" is not referred to at all by some of the early commentary writers when dealing with these verses — not by Origen (*per* Rufinus's Latin translation), nor by Ambrosiaster or Pelagius. So it may be inferred that "at Rome" was not included in the texts used by these commentators.

If, however, Gamble's thesis is correct, that "Romans was subjected to conscious revision with a single intention, to convert the letter from a specific communication to a particular community into a document suitable for a wider and general audience, or, in a word, to 'catholicize' the letter"[56] — as we believe Gamble has sufficiently demonstrated — it follows, then, that an "explanation lies ready to hand at least for the omissions of the Romans address in 1:7 and 1:15, for which no other assumption is satisfactory."[57] And that explanation is that the designation "at Rome" was deleted when the last two chapters were excised, thereby forming a generalized version of fourteen chapters in length. Perhaps "at Rome" was also deleted in the fifteen-chapter version, but that is only speculation. For what is extant of P[46], which is our only MS support for the possibility of a fifteen-chapter version, begins only at 5:17 (the first seven folios being lost), and so provides no data for the question at hand.

Building on the work of Nils Dahl, his mentor, Harry Gamble has effectively shown that the excising of the localized phrase "at Rome" in 1:7 and 15 was not done because Romans stood at the head of the Pauline corpus in

56. H. Gamble Jr., *Textual History*, 115-16.
57. H. Gamble Jr., *Textual History*, 116.

those early listings that eventually became the canonical order, thereby effecting for the first letter a more generalized character, but was done in conjunction with the production of a fourteen-chapter version (perhaps also a fifteen-chapter version) in order to generalize further the content of the letter.[58] Perhaps the dropping of "at Rome" in 1:7 and 15 should be seen as somewhat parallel, at least in motivation, to the dropping of "at Ephesus" in Eph 1:1, which is omitted in P[46], א, B, and 1739 (as may also be inferred to have been the case in Origen's text because of his lack of reference to it, with Marcion and Tertullian evidently reading "at Laodicea" in their texts) — though it may also be argued that Ephesians was originally written as a generalized letter and only later became particularized when copies were sent to various Christian congregations (e.g., "at Ephesus," as canonized; or "at Laodicea," à la Marcion and Tertullian). Perhaps, as well, there is a parallel to be seen in the textual history of 1 Cor 1:2, where "which is at Corinth" (τῇ οὔσῃ ἐν Κορίνθῳ) follows rather than precedes "those sanctified in Christ Jesus" (ἡγιασμένοις ἐν Χριστῷ Ἰησοῦ) in P[46], B, D, F, G, etc., thereby suggesting some early uncertainty regarding both the inclusion and the placement of the phrase "at Corinth."

The Grace Benedictions of 16:20b, 24, and/or 28

The benediction of 16:20b, "The grace of our Lord Jesus [Christ] be with you," is strongly supported by the extant MS evidence (only uncials D and G, it[d*, e, f, g, x], and Sedulius-Scotus omit it), and so is hardly to be questioned. The central question among the major MSS is whether the name "Jesus" or "Jesus Christ" should be read. Also to be noted is that a few minuscules read "with us" instead of "with you." The greatest issue with regard to the grace benedictions of chapter 16, however, has to do with the inclusion and placement of the second benediction, "May the grace of our Lord Jesus Christ be with all of you. Amen," which appears in some texts at 16:24 and in a few other texts at 16:28. Issues regarding this second benediction and the doxology of Romans form something of an interlocking set of problems. Here, however, our focus will be on the second grace benediction, leaving treatment of the doxology for a following discussion.

It is most unlikely that Romans 16 would have originally concluded with both a second grace benediction (whether at v. 24 or v. 28) *and* a doxol-

58. Cf. H. Gamble Jr., *Textual History*, 115-21.

ogy. For as Harry Gamble has pointed out (also setting out a chart for visual comprehension):

> A solution to the problem posed by the variations of these benedictions in form and position becomes immediately obvious when it is recognized that the witnesses are grouped in a particular way in reading these benedictions, as the chart shows. It can be seen that witnesses which either lack the doxology altogether or place it only at the end of ch. 14 almost always offer the benediction at 16:24. Within this group of witnesses those reading the doxology after ch. 14 also read the benediction at 16:20b. On the other hand, texts which contain the doxology at the end of ch. 16 always offer the benediction at 16:20b, but almost never provide the benediction at 16:24, and only occasionally do they offer the benediction of 16:24 as 16:28, that is, after the doxology. Thus we can see that the benediction of 16:24 is lost (or displaced to 16:28) *only when the doxology is found at the end of ch. 16.*[59]

Gamble himself, of course, having argued for the doxology as composed by an early Christian editor to round off in proper ecclesiastical style the "catholicized" fourteen-chapter version of Romans, concludes (1) that it was only when the doxology was later moved from the end of chapter 14 to the end of chapter 16 that the grace benediction of 16:24 was dropped or displaced, (2) that before the doxology was moved to its present position at the end of chapter 16, the grace benediction of 16:24 served as the true conclusion of Paul's original letter, and (3) that Romans originally closed with two grace benedictions, the first at 16:20b and the second at 16:24.

Larry Hurtado, however, while applauding Gamble's explication of relationships between the long, the short, and the intermediate forms of Romans, has aptly pointed out that Gamble's understanding of the second grace benediction vis-à-vis the final doxology "seems to stand on its head a more likely interpretation of the data."[60] For, as Hurtado argues:

> The fact that a grace benediction appears at 16:24 in MSS that either omit the doxology or place it after 14:23 shows only that scribes desired some sort of "ceremonial" and "appropriate" ending of one kind or another for Romans. This variation does not in itself tell us which conclu-

---

59. H. Gamble, Jr., *Textual History,* 130 (emphasis his); see also page 131 for his chart that nicely tabulates the MS evidence.

60. L. W. Hurtado, "Doxology," 195.

sion, a grace benediction or the doxology (or neither!), may have been the original conclusion.[61]

Further, as Hurtado goes on to observe, two arguments drawn from the MS evidence may be mounted in support of deleting the second grace benediction at 16:24. The first is that "the doxology at 16:25-27 has for support what are judged generally as better quality witnesses [citing P[61], א, B, C, 81, 436, 630, 1739, and versions vg syr[p] cop[sa, bo]] than the witnesses supporting a benediction at 16:24 [citing L, Psy, 0209, 181, and most minuscules representing the Byzantine text]"[62] — which, when forced by the distribution of the data to pit one against the other, inclines one on the basis of external evidence to favor the inclusion of the doxology and the exclusion of the second grace benediction. The second is that "the witnesses that (for reasons that are not now clear) omit the benediction from 16:20 [i.e., D, G, it[d*, e, f g, x], and Sedulius-Scotus] have *instead* a benediction at 16:24"[63] — which suggests that Romans 16 did not originally have two grace benedictions, one at 16:20b and another at 16:24, but rather (1) that some early scribes moved the grace benediction from 16:20b to 16:24 (or to 16:28) in order to produce a suitable conclusion, and (2) that "at a later time, other scribes, aware of some MSS with the benediction at 16:20 and other MSS with the benediction at 16:24, produced the conflate text represented by the 'Byzantine' witnesses."[64] And it is this understanding of the benedictions of Romans 16 that, we believe, seems most supportable from the MS evidence: that 16:20b is the closing grace benediction of Paul's original letter (with vv. 21-23, perhaps also vv. 25-27, appended), and that a second grace benediction has entered into the textual tradition at either 16:24 or 28 via a combination of first scribal emendation and then scribal conflation.

The Doxology of 16:25-27

The textual history with respect to the doxology of Romans is, as noted above, not only varied but also quite contorted. Six positions as to its inclusion and placement can be taken, as seen in the Greek textual tradition, the ancient versions, and the commentaries of the early Church Fathers — though, of course, without all six being of equal significance:

61. L. W. Hurtado, "Doxology," 195.
62. L. W. Hurtado, "Doxology," 195.
63. L. W. Hurtado, "Doxology," 195 (emphasis his).
64. L. W. Hurtado, "Doxology," 196.

1. That the doxology is to be placed after 16:23/24, as it appears in P^{61}, ℵ, B, C, D, 81, 365, 436, 630, 1739, 1962, 2127, 2464; it$^{d, e, f}$, vg, syr^p, cop$^{sa, bo}$, eth; Origen^{lat} and Ambrosiaster.

2. That it should be placed after 14:23, as in L, Psy, 0209^{vid}, 181, 326, 330, 451, 460, 614, 1241, 1877, 1881, 1984, 1985, 2492, 2495, etc.; the Harclean Syriac; Cyril, Theodoret, and John of Damascus.

3. That it should be placed after 15:33, as in P^{46} (the Chester Beatty "Pauline" Papyrus).

4. That it should be placed after both 14:23 and 16:23/24, as in A, P, 5, 17, 33, 104, 109; Armenian.

5. That it should be placed after both 14:23 and 15:33 (16:1-23/24 being omitted), as in 1506.

6. That it should be entirely omitted, as in F, G, 629; it^g, goth; Marcion and Jerome.

The questions to be asked regarding the doxology of Romans are, therefore, the following: Was it written by Paul or someone else? Was it written to conclude the original sixteen-chapter form of the letter, or was it written to bring to an appropriate ecclesiastical conclusion a "catholicized" fourteen- or fifteen-chapter version of the letter? Should it be viewed as an entirely extraneous interpolation and so excised — or, less likely, should it be read either after both 14:23 and 16:23/24 or after both 14:23 and 15:33? And how does this doxology relate to what is said in the body of the Romans letter, that is, to the material of chapters 1–14 generally — but also to the material of chapter 15 in particular?

The integrity of the doxology and its placement at 16:25-27 have been defended by a number of late-nineteenth-century scholars.[65] Likewise, a number of contemporary scholars have argued for its Pauline authorship and its placement at the end of the sixteenth chapter.[66] The majority of NT

---

65. E.g., F. L. Godet, *Romans,* 2 vols. (1880-81); H. A. W. Meyer, *Romans,* 2 vols. (1884); F. J. A. Hort, "On the End of the Epistle to the Romans" (1893); H. P. Liddon, *Romans* (1893); W. Sanday and A. C. Headlam, *Romans* (1895); and B. W. Bacon, "The Doxology" (1899).

66. E.g., R. C. H. Lenski, *Romans* (1936); A. Nygren, *Romans* (ET: 1949); J. Huby, *Èpître aux Romains* (1957); J. Murray, *Romans,* 2 vols. (1959, 1965); H. W. Schmidt, *An die Römer* (1963); P. S. Minear, *The Obedience of Faith: The Purposes of Paul in the Epistle to the Romans* (London: SCM, 1971), 30-31; E. F. Harrison, "Romans" (1976; rev. ed. by D. A. Hagner, 2008); W. Hendrikson, *Romans,* 2 vols. (1980, 1981); P. Stuhlmacher, *Romans* (ET: 1994); D. J. Moo, *Romans* (1996); and I. H. Marshall, "Romans 16:25-27 — An Apt Conclusion" (1999).

scholars today, however, view the doxology as a post-Pauline creation that has been added to Romans for some reason by a later scribe — with many also postulating that it probably originated in the mid–second century during the time of Marcion, who, it is argued, excised chapters 15–16 (as based on Tertullian's statement in *Adv Marc* 5.13 that Marcion deleted "whole passages at his will") and whose followers then composed it as an appropriate conclusion to chapters 1–14.[67]

In support of such a "Marcionite" hypothesis, some have seen in the doxology certain features that reflect, to some degree, the teaching of Marcion, and so attribute its composition either to Marcion's followers[68] or to an ecclesiastical redaction of a doxology that was originally composed by his followers.[69] The most prominent Marcionite concepts usually found in the doxology are (1) that revelation was concealed before the appearance of Paul, and (2) that Paul himself was the bearer of that hidden revelation, assuming that the words "through the prophetic writings" refer not to the prophetic writings of the OT but to the Pauline letters. But as Harry Gamble has pointed out:

> These efforts to find in the doxology of Romans a distinctly Marcionite coloring are shown to be misguided by several more recent form-critical studies which effectively demonstrate that the conceptuality and terminology of Rom 16:25-27 are characteristic of a clearly defined pattern of early Christian proclamation.[70]

Gamble's own arguments against Paul's authorship of 16:25-27 are principally three: (1) that it is not Paul's usual epistolary style to conclude with a doxology, but, rather, to conclude with a grace benediction (which Gamble believes is in Romans a double grace benediction that appears at 16:20b and 16:24);

---

67. E.g., C. H. Dodd, *Romans* (1932); E. Gaugler, *An die Römer* (1945); C. K. Barrett, *Romans* (1957); F. F. Bruce, *Romans* (1963); T. W. Manson, "Romans" (1962); K. P. Donfried, "Short Note on Romans 16" (1970); H. Schlier, *Römerbrief* (1977); C. E. B. Cranfield, *Romans* (1975, 1979); U. Wilckens, *An die Römer,* 3 vols. (1978, 1980, 1982); E. Käsemann, *Romans* (ET: 1980); W.-H. Ollrog, "Abfassungsverhältnisse von Röm 16" (1980); J. K. Elliott, "Language and Style of the Concluding Doxology" (1981); J. D. G. Dunn, *Romans,* 2 vols. (1988); J. A. Fitzmyer, *Romans* (1993); and R. Jewett, *Romans* (2007).

68. So P. Corssen, "Zur Überlieferungsgeschichte des Römerbriefes" (1909) 32-34.

69. So A. Harnack, "Über I Kor. 14,32ff. und Röm. 16,25ff. nach der ältesten Überlieferung und der marcionitischen Bibel," in *Studien zur Geschichte des Neuen Testaments und der Alten Kirche,* vol. 1, *Zur neutestamentlichen Textkritik* (Berlin: Hinrichs, 1931), 180-90.

70. H. Gamble Jr., *Textual History,* 108, citing the studies of N. A. Dahl, D. Lührmann, and E. Kamlah.

(2) that the phrasing of the doxology is liturgical in character and more like the deutero-Pauline letters, particularly Ephesians and the Pastorals; and (3) that the textual history of Romans suggests that the doxology originated with the fourteen-chapter "catholicized" version of the letter, so appearing after 14:23, and only later moved to its canonical position after the second grace benediction of 16:24.[71] Gamble's arguments are cogent, but not altogether convincing.

Contrary to Gamble's arguments against Paul's authorship of 16:25-27, Larry Hurtado has drawn attention to certain matters that must also be taken into consideration. With regard to epistolary style, Hurtado has noted that while, indeed, the closing of Romans with a doxology is unusual, it is not entirely exceptional. 1 Cor 16:24, which is a concluding love wish that appears after the grace benediction of 16:23, is also an exception — an exception Gamble allows because he views it as an *ad hoc* addition that is best regarded as a postscript. But if we view Rom 16:20b as the closing grace benediction of Paul's original letter to believers at Rome, then all of 16:21-27 (minus v. 24) may also be seen as something of a postscript.[72] Further, with regard to the liturgical character of the passage: (1) "the apparent similarities between the doxology and the 'deutero-Paulines' (Eph. 3:4-7, 8-11; cf. 2 Tim. 1:9-11; Tit. 1:2-3) can be used against the authenticity of the doxology only if one can be certain that all these letters in no way come from Paul"; (2) on the basis of such portions as 1 Cor 16:22 and Rom 11:33-36, "it seems perilous . . . to presume because of its phrasing that Paul could not have written the doxology, for, just as his epistolary style shows variations, so does his language"; and (3) the close ideological connections between the doxology and the body of the Romans letter, which Gamble himself applauds and acknowledges not to exist for any other Pauline letter, suggest a dependence not on some other liturgical formulation but on what was said earlier in Romans itself.[73]

And with regard to the textual history of Romans as suggesting that the doxology came into existence only with the fourteen-chapter "catholicized" version of the letter — which Gamble considers "the decisive argument" for the passage's non-Pauline origin — Hurtado argues that "Gamble's interpretation of the text-critical data concerning the presence or absence of the doxology at the end of Romans 16 in connection with the positions of the grace benedictions in that chapter is unconvincing."[74] We have argued this

---

71. See H. Gamble Jr., *Textual History,* esp. 123-24.
72. Cf. L. W. Hurtado, "Doxology," 189-90.
73. H. Gamble Jr., *Textual History,* 191.
74. L. W. Hurtado, "Doxology," 194.

same point when dealing with the inclusion and placement of the benedictions, particularly debating Gamble's view of two grace benedictions at 16:20b and 16:24. So we find ourselves in essential agreement with Hurtado in his responses to Gamble's three principal arguments, and therefore cannot consider the non-Pauline origin of the doxology a closed question.

In addition to the above arguments, however, Hurtado makes the point that not only does the doxology echo the themes and vocabulary found in Romans 1–14, as many have observed — and which, of course, has been used to support the thesis that it was originally composed to round off a fourteen-chapter version of Romans — but also that it "seems to echo portions of Romans 15 and seems more understandable as to content as a conclusion to an edition of Romans with at least 15 chapters."[75] And after listing all of the possible echoes that can be found, Hurtado goes on to observe:

> If one reads 15:1-13 and then immediately reads 16:25-7, it becomes clear how perfectly the doxology, giving glory to God and referring to the message of Gentile salvation now disclosed through OT writings, gathers up the content of 15:1-13, where the glorification of God by and for converted Gentiles is spoken of, and where it is shown by examples that the OT points to their salvation.[76]

Hurtado's own conclusion is that "whoever composed the doxology seems to have done so, not only with 'special attention' to Romans, but, more specifically, with special attention to an edition of Romans with ch. 15." In so stating, Hurtado declares that he is not pressing the point in support of Pauline authorship, but only wants to leave that possibility open.[77]

Later, in a proposed exegetical commentary, we will deal with the echoes of themes and concerns in 16:25-27 that appeared in the earlier chapters of Romans, thereby attempting to make a positive case for its Pauline authorship and its canonical placement (in line with the data and arguments set out by Jeffrey A. D. Weima, *Neglected Endings* [1994], and I. Howard Marshall, "An Apt Conclusion" [1999]). Here, however, it is sufficient to declare our openness to Paul as the author of the doxology and its original placement at the end of chapter 16, reserving our more extended exegetical treatment for the commentary to follow.

75. L. W. Hurtado, "Doxology," 197
76. L. W. Hurtado, "Doxology," 198.
77. L. W. Hurtado, "Doxology," 198.

Supplemental Bibliography

See also "Bibliography of Selected Commentaries." All references in the footnotes to works included in this list are by the authors' names and abbreviated titles.

Aland, Kurt. "Glosse, Interpolation und Komposition in der Sicht der neutestamentlichen Textkritik," *Studien zur Überlieferung des Neuen Testaments und seines Textes.* ANTF 2. Berlin: de Gruyter, 1967, 35-57.

———. *Neutestamentliche Entwürfe.* TBü 63. Munich: Kaiser, 1979.

Aland, Kurt, and Barbara Aland. *The Text of the New Testament: An Introduction to the Critical Editions and to the Theory and Practice of Modern Textual Criticism,* trans. E. F. Rhodes. Grand Rapids: Eerdmans, 1987.

Bacon, Benjamin W. "The Doxology at the End of Romans," *JBL* 18 (1899) 167-76.

Baur, Ferdinand Christian. *Paul, the Apostle of Jesus Christ: His Life and Work, His Epistles and His Doctrine,* 2 vols., trans. E. Zeller. Edinburgh: University of Edinburgh Press, 1846 (from the German 1845 first edition); London: Williams & Norgate, 1876, 1.352-65.

Benoit, Pierre. "Le Codex paulinien Chester Beatty," *RB* 46 (1937) 58-82.

Brown, Raymond E. *An Introduction to the New Testament.* New York: Doubleday, 1997, 575-76.

Bultmann, Rudolf. "Glossen im Römerbrief," *TLZ* 72 (1947) 197-202; repr. in *Exegetica: Aufsätze zur Erforschung des Neuen Testaments,* ed. E. Dinkler. Tübingen: Mohr-Siebeck, 1967, 278-84.

Champion, L. G. *Benedictions and Doxologies in the Epistles of Paul.* Oxford: Kemp Hall, 1934.

Collins, Raymond F. "The Case of a Wandering Doxology: Rom 16,25-27," in *New Testament Textual Criticism and Exegesis. Festschrift J. Delobel,* ed. A. Denaux. Leuven: Leuven University Press/Peeters, 2002, 293-303.

Corssen, Peter. "Zur Überlieferungsgeschichte des Römerbriefes," *ZNW* 10 (1909) 1-45, 97-102.

Deissmann, Adolf. *Light from the Ancient East: The New Testament Illustrated by Recently Discovered Texts of the Graeco-Roman World,* trans. L. R. M. Strachan. London: Hodder & Stoughton, 1927, from the "fourth, completely revised" 1923 German edition.

Donfried, Karl P. "A Short Note on Romans 16," *JBL* 89 (1970) 441-49; repr. in *The Romans Debate,* revised and expanded edition (Peabody: Hendrickson, 1991), 44-52.

Dupont, Jacques. "Pour l'historie de la doxologie finale de l'épître aux Romains," *RBén* 58 (1948) 3-22.

Elliott, J. Keith. "The Language and Style of the Concluding Doxology to the Epistle to the Romans," *ZNW* 72 (1981) 124-30.

Emmet, Cyril W. "Romans XV and XVI: A New Theory," *ExpT* 8 (1916) 275-88.

Epp, Eldon Jay. "The Multivalence of the Term 'Original Text' in New Testament Textual Criticism," *HTR* 92 (1999) 245-81; repr. in E. J. Epp, *Perspectives on New Testament Textual Criticism: Collected Essays, 1962-2004.* NovTSup 116. Leiden: Brill, 2005, 551-93.

———. "Issues in New Testament Textual Criticism: Moving from the Nineteenth Century to the Twenty-First Century," in *Rethinking New Testament Textual Criticism,* ed. D. A. Black. Grand Rapids: Baker, 2002, 34-44.

Feine, Paul. *Die Abfassung des Philipperbriefes in Ephesus mit einer Anlage über Röm 16,3-20 als Epheserbrief.* BFCT 20.4. Gütersloh: Bertelsmann, 1916.

Feuillet, André. "Note complémentaire sur le dernier chapitre de l'épître aux Romains (xvi,1-24)," *RB* 57 (1950) 527-29.

Gamble, Harry, Jr. *The Textual History of the Letter to the Romans: A Study in Textual and Literary Criticism.* SD 42. Grand Rapids: Eerdmans, 1977.

Goodspeed, Edgar J. "Phoebe's Letter of Introduction," *HTR* 44 (1951) 55-57.

Hawkins, R. M. "Romans: A Reinterpretation," *JBL* 60 (1941) 129-40.

———. *The Recovery of the Historical Paul.* Nashville: Vanderbilt University, 1943, esp. 14-20, 291-92.

Hitchcock, F. R. Montgomery. "A Study of Romans XVI," *CQR* 121 (1935-36) 187-209.

Holtzmann, Heinrich J. "Der Stand der Verhandlungen über die beiden letzten Capitel des Römerbriefes," *ZWT* 17 (1874) 504-19.

Hort, Fenton J. A. "On the End of the Epistle to the Romans," *JP* 3 (1871) 51-80; repr. in J. B. Lightfoot, *Biblical Essays.* London: Macmillan, 1893; repr. Grand Rapids: Baker, 1979, 321-51.

Hoskier, Herman Charles. "A Study of the Chester-Beatty Codex of the Pauline Epistles," *JTS* 38 (1937) 148-63.

Hurtado, Larry W. "The Doxology at the End of Romans," in *New Testament Textual Criticism: Its Significance for Exegesis (Essays in Honour of Bruce M. Metzger),* ed. E. J. Epp and G. D. Fee. Oxford: Clarendon, 1981, 185-99.

Kallas, James G. "Romans xiii.1-7: An Interpolation," *NTS* 11 (1965) 365-74.

Keck, Leander E. "The Post-Pauline Interpretation of Jesus' Death in Rom 5.6-7," in *Theologia Crucis — Signum Crucis: Festschrift für Erich Dinkler zum 70. Geburtstag,* ed. C. Andresen and G. Klein. Tübingen: Mohr-Siebeck, 1979, 237-48.

Kenyon, Frederic G. *The Chester Beatty Biblical Papyri: Descriptions and Texts of Twelve Manuscripts on Papyrus of the Greek Bible.* III.1: *Pauline Epistles and Revelation.* London: Walker, 1934, 1-9; III.3 (Supplement): *Pauline Epistles, Text,* 1936; III.4: *Pauline Epistles, Plates* (f.8, verso–f.21, recto), 1937.

Kim, Chan-Hie. *The Form and Structure of the Familiar Greek Letter of Recommendation.* Missoula: University of Montana Press, 1972.

Kinoshita, J. "Romans — Two Writings Combined: A New Interpretation of the Body of Romans," *NovT* 7 (1965) 258-77.

Kling, Christian Friedrich. "Über den historischen Charakter der Apostelgeschichte und die Ächtheit der beiden letzten Kapitel des Römerbriefes, mit Beziehung auf Hrn. Dr. Baur," *ThStK* 10 (1837) 290-327.

Knox, John. "A Note on the Text of Romans," *NTS* 2 (1956) 191-93.

Kümmel, Werner Georg. *Introduction to the New Testament*, rev. ed., trans. H. C. Kee. Nashville: Abingdon, 1975, 314-20.

Lake, Kirsopp. *The Earlier Epistles of St. Paul. Their Motive and Origin.* London: Rivingtons, 1927², 325-70.

————. "The Shorter Form of St. Paul's Epistle to the Romans," *Exp* 7 (1910) 504-25.

Lampe, Peter. "Zur Textgeschichte des Römerbriefs," *NovT* 27 (1985) 273-77.

————. "The Roman Christians of Romans 16," in *The Romans Debate*, revised and expanded edition, ed. K. P. Donfried. Peabody: Hendrickson, 1991, 216-30.

Lightfoot, Joseph B. "M. Renan's Theory of the Epistle to the Romans," *JP* 2 (1869) 264-97; repr. as "The Structure and Destination of the Epistle to the Romans [Part A]," in J. B. Lightfoot, *Biblical Essays*. London: Macmillan, 1893, 287-320; repr. Grand Rapids: Baker, 1979, 287-320.

————. "The Epistle to the Romans," *JP* 3 (1871) 193-214; repr. as "The Structure and Destination of the Epistle to the Romans [Part C]," in J. B. Lightfoot, *Biblical Essays*. London: Macmillan, 1893, 352-74; repr. Grand Rapids: Baker, 1979, 352-74.

McDonald, James I. H. "Was Romans XVI a Separate Letter?" *NTS* 16 (1970) 369-72.

Manen, W. C. van. *Paulus*, vol. 2, *De Brief aan de Romeinen*. Leiden: Brill, 1891.

————. "Romans (Epistle)," *Encyclopaedia Biblica*, 4 vols., ed. T. K. Cheyne and J. S. Black. New York: Macmillan, 1899-1903, 4.4127-45 (esp. 4129-30 and 4141).

————. *Die Unechtheit des Römerbriefes*. Leipzig: Strübig, 1906.

Manson, T. W. "St. Paul's Letter to the Romans — and Others," *BJRL* 31 (1948) 224-40; repr. in *Studies in the Gospels and Epistles*, ed. M. Black. Manchester: Manchester University Press, 1962, 225-41; repr. in *The Romans Debate*, ed. K. P. Donfried. Minneapolis: Augsburg, 1977, 1-16; *The Romans Debate*, revised and expanded edition, Peabody: Hendrickson, 1991, 3-15.

Marshall, I. Howard. "Romans 16:25-27 — An Apt Conclusion," in *Romans and the People of God: Essays in Honor of Gordon D. Fee on the Occasion of His 65th Birthday.* Grand Rapids: Eerdmans, 1999, 170-84.

Michaelis, Wilhelm. "Die Teilungshypothesen bei Paulusbriefen: Briefkompositionen und ihr Sitz im Leben," *TZ* 14 (1958) 321-26.

Miller, James C. "Appendix ['Concluding Doxology: 16:25-27']," in *The Obedience of Faith, the Eschatological People of God, and the Purpose of Romans.* SBL.DS 177. Atlanta: SBL, 2000, 181-86.

Mowry, Lucetta. "The Early Circulation of Paul's Letters," *JBL* 63 (1944) 73-86.

Murray, John. "The Integrity of the Epistle," in *The Epistle to the Romans. The English Text with Introduction, Exposition, and Notes.* NICNT. 2 vols. Grand Rapids: Eerdmans, 1959, 1965, "Appendix F," 2.262-68.

Ollrog, Wolf-Hennig. "Die Abfassungsverhältnisse von Röm 16," in *Kirche: Festschrift für Günther Bornkamm zum 75. Geburtstag,* ed. D. Lührmann and G. Strecker. Tübingen: Mohr-Siebeck, 1980, 221-44.

Petersen, Norman R. "On the Ending(s) to Paul's Letter to Rome," in *The Future of Early Christianity: Essays in Honor of Helmut Koester,* ed. B. A. Pearson *et al.* Minneapolis: Fortress, 1991, 337-47.

Rengstorf, Karl Heinrich. "Paulus und die älteste römische Christenheit," *Studia Evangelica II,* ed. F. L. Cross. TU 87. Berlin: Akademie-Verlag, 1964, 447-64.

Schenke, Hans-Martin. "Aporien im Römerbrief," *TLZ* 92 (1967) 881-88.

Schmithals, Walter. *Der Römerbrief als historisches Problem.* SNT 9. Gütersloh: Mohn, 1975.

Schumacher, Rudolf. *Die beiden letzten Kapitel des Römerbriefes: Ein Beitrag zu ihrer Geschichte und Erklärung.* NTAbh 14.4. Münster: Aschendorff, 1929.

Seesemann, H. "Die Bedeutung des Chester-Beatty Papyrus für die Textkritik der Paulusbriefe," *TBlä* 16 (1937) 92-97.

Steinmetz, R. "Textkritische Untersuchung zum Röm 1,7," *ZNW* 9 (1908) 177-89.

Stuhlmacher, Peter. "Der Abfassungszweck des Römerbriefes," *ZNW* 77 (1986) 180-93; ET by R. and I. Fuller, "The Purpose of Romans," in *The Romans Debate,* revised and expanded edition, ed. K. P. Donfried. Peabody: Hendrickson, 1991, 231-42.

Talbert, Charles H. "A Non-Pauline Fragment at Romans 3:24-26?" *JBL* 85 (1966) 287-96.

Walker, William O., Jr. "The Burden of Proof in Identifying Interpolations in the Pauline Letters," *NTS* 33 (1987) 610-18.

———. "Text-Critical Evidence for Interpolations in the Letters of Paul," *CBQ* 50 (1988) 622-31.

Wedderburn, Alexander J. M. *The Reasons for Romans.* Edinburgh: T&T Clark, 1988; Minneapolis: Fortress, 1991, 25-29.

Weima, Jeffrey A. D. *Neglected Endings. The Significance of the Pauline Letter Closings.* JSNT.SS 101. Sheffield: Sheffield Academic Press, 1994, esp. 135-44, 229-30.

———. "Preaching the Gospel in Rome: A Study of the Epistolary Framework of Romans," in *Gospel in Paul: Studies on Corinthians, Galatians and Romans for Richard N. Longenecker,* ed. L. A. Jervis and P. Richardson. JSNT.SS 108. Sheffield: Sheffield Academic Press, 1994, 337-66, esp. 364-65.

Weisse, C. H. *Beiträge zur Kritik der Paulinischen Briefe an die Galater, Römer, Philipper und Kolosser.* Leipzig, 1867.

Wuellner, Wilhelm. "Paul's Rhetoric of Argumentation in Romans: An Alternative to the Donfried-Karris Debate over Romans," *CBQ* 38 (1976) 330-51; repr. in *The Romans Debate,* ed. K. P. Donfried. Minneapolis: Augsburg, 1977, 152-74; also in *The Romans Debate,* revised and expanded edition. Peabody: Hendrickson, 1991, 128-46.

Young, Frances M. "Romans xvi: A Suggestion," *ExpT* 47 (1935-36) 187-209.

CHAPTER III

Occasion and Date

Paul's letter to the Christians at Rome is a real letter, not a compendium of theology or a summation of religious truths. As a letter, it must be read with an eye to a number of rather obvious matters — principally, (1) the identity of its author, (2) the integrity of the letter, (3) the occasion and date of the letter, (4) the identity, character, circumstances, and perceived concerns of its addressees, and (5) the purpose or purposes of its author in writing. We have dealt with authorship, composition, and integrity of Romans in the previous two chapters. And we will deal with matters regarding the identity, circumstances, and concerns of its addressees and Paul's purpose or purposes in writing them in the following two chapters. Here in Chapter III we want to deal only with matters that pertain to the letter's occasion and date — with the hope that a determination of these rather elemental factors will provide a proper context for our later discussions of those much more complex issues regarding the identity, circumstances, and concerns of its addressees (Chapter IV) and Paul's purpose or purposes in writing them (Chapter V).

1. Occasion

Accepting the final two chapters of Romans as an integral part of the original letter (see Chapter II above) — that is, the integrity of the "apostolic parousia" of 15:14-32, the "peace benediction" of 15:33, the commendation of Phoebe in 16:1-2, the greetings of 16:3-16, the additional exhortations of 16:17-20a, the "grace benediction" of 16:20b, the further greetings of 16:21-23, and the "doxology" of 16:25-27 — a number of fairly clear inferences can be drawn regarding Paul's situation when writing Romans and the historical occasion for his writing. In fact, determination of the occasion and relative date for the letter, while not without interpretive problems, ranks a close second to a determination regarding the letter's author. For authorship, historical occasion, and relative date of Romans constitute the primary matters on which the majority of commentators today generally agree.

The Data in Romans

From his own plans as expressed in the letter itself, it is clear that Paul wrote Romans after having completed an extensive ministry to Gentiles throughout the eastern part of the Roman empire (15:17-22) — or, as he says rather expansively about his missionary activities up to that date, "from Jerusalem all the way around to Illyricum [on the northwest coast of Macedonia] I have fully proclaimed the gospel of Christ" (15:19). Further, having finished that eastern mission, he envisioned visiting the believers in Jesus at Rome, which he says he had wanted to do for a long time (15:23; cf. 1:13), and then traveling westward to inaugurate a further mission to Gentiles in Spain (15:22-24, 28-29). His desire to visit Rome, as he expresses it, was so as "to have you assist me on my journey there [to Spain], after I have enjoyed your company for a while . . . and together with you be refreshed" (15:24, 32). At present, however, he says he is committed to taking a monetary gift from his Gentile churches to the Jewish believers in Jesus at Jerusalem (15:25), which gift he viewed as a proper Christian response from his Gentile churches to the Jewish believers at Jerusalem — and which he says had been a matter of great concern to him for some time (15:26-27; cf. 1 Cor 16:1-4; 2 Cor 8–9). And he asks for the prayers of the Christians at Rome on his behalf (15:30-32). So, as expressed in the "apostolic parousia" or "travel plans" section of 15:14-32, the occasion and date for Paul's writing Romans must be located in that brief period of time between (1) the completion of his missionary activities in the eastern part of the empire and (2) his trip to Jerusalem in order to deliver the gift of money that he collected from his Gentile churches for the Jewish believers in Jesus of that city.

From his commendation, greetings, and exhortations in chapter 16, it is clear that Paul was writing from somewhere in the city of Corinth or its immediate environs (i.e., "greater Corinth") — probably from the home of Gaius in the city proper, though possibly from some lodging provided by Phoebe in the port city of Cenchreae, which was located about eight miles east of Corinth on the Saronic Gulf and served as the eastern port into the Aegean Sea for greater Corinth.[1] In 16:1-2 Paul commends to his Roman addressees the lady Phoebe, whom he identifies as a διάκονον ("deacon," "servant," or "minister") of the church at Cenchreae and a προστάτις ("patron" or "benefactor") to many people, including himself. And in 16:23a he concludes a long list of greetings with a greeting from Gaius, who was one of Paul's first converts at Corinth (cf. 1 Cor 1:14), whom he speaks of as having provided a place of meeting for believers in Jesus at Corinth and a place of residence in his home for Paul himself. Perhaps the greeting in 16:23b from Erastus, whom Paul identifies as ὁ οἰκονόμος τῆς πόλεως ("the city treasurer," NRSV; "the city's director of public works," NIV), reflects a Corinthian venue as well. For an inscription found at Corinth, which can be dated to the time of Nero, refers to a person named Erastus, who is called an *aedile* ("city commissioner") and is said to have "laid the pavement at his own expense" — which inscription may connect the Erastus of Paul's letter to Rome with a prominent official named Erastus of the city of Corinth, thereby rooting the writing of Romans more firmly to Corinth.[2] Suffice it here, however, to use this data from chapter 16 only by way of associating the writing of Romans with the city of Corinth and its eastern port Cenchreae (leaving all further treatments of the identities and functions of Phoebe and Gaius, as well as of all those greeted in the letter's final chapter, to our proposed commentary that will deal exegetically with the statements of 16:1-23).

Correlation with Indications in Luke's Acts

Correlating this data from Romans with indications in Acts, it seems rather clear that Paul wrote Romans toward the end of his third missionary journey in the eastern part of the Roman empire. For in Acts, after recounting an extensive ministry at Ephesus, Luke reports that Paul returned to Greece and spent three months at Corinth before setting out on a trip to Jerusalem, being accompanied by representatives from his Gentile churches, in order to present to Jewish believers in Jesus at Jerusalem the monetary gift he had

---

1. See Philo, *Flaccum* 155.3, who refers to Cenchreae as τὸ Κορίνθιον ἐπίνειον ("the Corinthian harbor").

2. See *Ancient Corinth: A Guide to the Excavations*, 6th ed. (Athens: American School of Classical Studies at Athens, 1954), 74; also J. H. Kent, *The Inscriptions 1926-1950*, in *Corinth* 8.3 (Princeton: American School of Classical Studies at Athens, 1966), 17-31, 99-100, pl. 21, n. 232; J. Murphy-O'Connor, *St. Paul's Corinth*, 37.

gathered for them from his Gentile churches (Acts 20:2-4). Evidently, it was during this three-month period — after having completed an extensive ministry throughout the eastern Roman empire and before his final trip to Jerusalem — that Paul turned his thoughts not only to Jerusalem but also to Rome and to Spain.

A few of the so-called Marcionite Prologues, which appear in some MSS of the Latin Vulgate, say that Paul wrote Romans when he was at Athens. Some scholars have proposed that Paul wrote Romans when he was at Ephesus;[3] others, when at Philippi;[4] and still others, when at Thessalonica.[5] A more supportable position, however, is that he wrote to the Christians at Rome when he was residing somewhere in "greater Corinth" during the three months *after* ministering at Ephesus and *before* he set out for Jerusalem, thereby preparing the way for his coming visit to Rome.

2. Date

The assignment of exact dates for Paul's missionary activities and letters is exceedingly difficult, if not impossible — as it is also for most of the other events portrayed in the NT. The only two dates in early apostolic history that we can be fairly certain about are both connected with Paul's first mission at Corinth, as reported by Luke in Acts — that is, (1) the Edict of Claudius in A.D. 49 (cf. our fuller discussion of the Edict of Claudius in Chapter IV, "Addressees"), which is referred to in Acts 18:2 ("There [at Corinth] he [Paul] met a Jew named Aquila, a native of Pontus, who had recently come from Italy with his wife Priscilla, because Claudius had ordered all the Jews to leave Rome"); and (2) Gallio's coming to Corinth to assume the post of Roman proconsul of the province of Achaia sometime shortly after July 1, A.D. 51,[6] which is referred to in Acts 18:12 ("When Gallio became proconsul of Achaia, the Jews made a united attack on Paul and brought him into the court"). On the basis of these two rather fixed dates, the beginning of Paul's

---

3. E.g., J. R. Richards, "Romans and I Corinthians"; W. Schmithals, *Römerbrief als historisches Problem.*

4. E.g., W. Michaelis, "Kenchreä"; T. M. Taylor, "Place of Origin."

5. E.g., F. Westberg, *Chronologie;* A. Suhl, *Paulus und seine Briefe.*

6. On the date of Gallio's coming to Corinth and the numerous laudatory statements about him by his brother Lucius Annaeus Seneca, by Pliny the Elder, and by Dio Cassius, see my *Acts,* EBC, 12 vols., ed. F. E. Gaebelein (Grand Rapids: Zondervan, 1981), 9.485; rev. ed., 13 vols., ed. T. Longman and D. E. Garland (2007), 10.994-95.

evangelistic ministry at Corinth can be dated to a time shortly after Aquila and his wife Priscilla left Rome and arrived at Corinth, that is, shortly after the Edict of Claudius in A.D. 49; while the conclusion of that first Corinthian mission can be dated to a time a few months after Gallio assumed office as proconsul of Achaia in mid-51 or early 52. But apart from these fairly well established dates, it is impossible to construct an absolute chronology for Paul's missionary activities or letter writing. All of the other dates for Paul's ministry must work from these two dates and can be proposed only in terms of a relative chronology, that is, by inferences based on the data of Paul's letters and Luke's Acts — with those inferences, necessarily, having always to be understood on the basis of some hypothesis as to how those various bits of data fit together.

By referring in 1 Cor 16:1-4 and 2 Cor 8–9 to his collection of money for the Jewish believers in Jesus at Jerusalem as being in progress, Paul clearly indicates that his letters to his converts at Corinth — whether regarded as two letters (i.e., 1 Corinthians followed by a unified 2 Corinthians), or one letter (i.e., 1 Corinthians) followed by a collection of two or more separate letters (i.e., what is canonically known as 2 Corinthians) — were written sometime not only *during* his final missionary journey in the eastern part of the Roman empire but also *shortly before* his final trip to Jerusalem. Likewise, Paul's letter to Rome can be assigned just as clearly to a time *shortly after* his writing of the final portion of 2 Corinthians, for Rom 15:25-32 alludes to that same collection for the Jerusalem believers in Jesus and indicates that the apostle had just received it. So it has usually been considered axiomatic in any relative chronology that Paul's letter to the Romans was written shortly after his Corinthian correspondence.

Kirsopp Lake has argued (1) that Romans originally consisted of only the first fourteen chapters, (2) that this "short form" of Romans was written about the same time as the letter to the Galatians, thereby explaining their many similarities of tone and temper, and (3) that "the short recension of Romans was originally sent to Churches in the neighbourhood of Syrian Antioch at the time, or before, the Council of Jerusalem."[7] But those are arguments that Harry Gamble has effectively silenced in his *Textual History of the Letter to the Romans.*[8] And though J. R. Richards has argued (based on a unique interpretation of Rom 15:23-28 and his compilation of somewhat

---

7. K. Lake, *Earlier Epistles of St. Paul,* 411-12.

8. Cf. our earlier treatments of K. Lake and H. Gamble on these matters in Chapter II, "Integrity," pp. 27-28 and 28-30.

misleading word statistics) that Paul wrote the Christians at Rome *shortly before* writing 1 Corinthians (as suggested by his interpretation of Acts 19:21-22), and so Romans should be dated at some time between 52 and 54,[9] the great majority of those in a position to know have rejected Richards's argument as being fallacious.

Scholars have usually dated 1 and 2 Corinthians (i.e., the material now found in those two canonical letters) as written sometime during 54-57 on Paul's third missionary journey and have dated Romans sometime during 55-58 before the apostle's final trip to Jerusalem. Werner Kümmel, for example, viewed 1 Corinthians as having been written "in the spring of 54 or 55," 2 Corinthians in the "late fall of the year 55 or 56," and Romans "about the spring of 55 or 56";[10] Raymond Brown, in general agreement with Kümmel though adjusting some details, considered 1 Corinthians to have been written in "late 56 or very early 57," 2 Corinthians in "late summer or very early autumn 57," and Romans "in the winter of 57/58."[11]

John Knox in his 1950 book *Chapters in a Life of Paul* proposed a chronology for Paul's missionary journeys that is based exclusively on data drawn from Paul's letters and largely disregards Acts.[12] In that book Knox argued for only two missionary journeys of Paul in the eastern empire and dated 1 and 2 Corinthians as "probably written in A.D. 51-53" and Romans "in A.D. 53-54."[13] And Knox's approach to Pauline chronology has been adopted, although with some variations, by Charles Buck and Greer Taylor,[14] John Hurd,[15] Robert Jewett,[16] and Gerd Lüdemann.[17]

Every date for the composition of Romans, whether worked out from a "traditional" or a "revisionist" perspective, must be based primarily on (1) Paul's travel plans as given in Rom 15:14-32, (2) his commendations and greetings of Rom 16:1-23, and (3) correlations between 1 Cor 16:1-4, 2 Cor 8–9, and Rom 15:25-32 with regard to Paul's collection of the monetary gift for

---

9. J. R. Richards, "Romans and I Corinthians," 14-30.

10. W. G. Kümmel, *Introduction to the New Testament,* 279, 293, 311.

11. R. E. Brown, *Introduction to the New Testament,* 512, 542, 560.

12. See J. Knox, *Chapters in a Life of Paul* (1950). Cf. my evaluation of Knox's chronology in R. N. Longenecker, *Galatians* (Dallas: Word, 1990), lxxv-lxxvii.

13. J. Knox, *Chapters,* 86.

14. C. Buck and G. Taylor, *Saint Paul* (1969).

15. J. C. Hurd, Jr., "Pauline Chronology and Theology" (1967); *idem,* "The Sequence of Paul's Letters" (1968).

16. R. Jewett, *Chronology of Paul's Life* (1979).

17. G. Lüdemann, *Paul, Apostle to the Gentiles* (1984).

believers in Jesus at Jerusalem. Further support in establishing a relative chronology, however, has also been gleaned (at least by more traditional scholars) from (1) the mention of the Edict of Claudius in Acts 18:2, (2) the reference to Gallio as proconsul of Achaia in Acts 18:12, and (3) the report about Paul's return to Corinth for three months at the end of his Ephesian ministry in Acts 20:1-4.

On a John Knox chronology, the date of Romans is usually viewed somewhat earlier than traditionally thought. Knox himself dated the letter about 53-54,[18] though those who take a similar stance regarding relations between Paul's letters and Luke's Acts have dated it anywhere from as early as 47 (as did Charles Buck and Greer Taylor)[19] to as late as 51/52 or 54/55 (as does Gerd Lüdemann[20]) — or dated it, as in a more revised "revisionist" chronology, to "the winter of 56-57" (as does Robert Jewett[21]).

Using a more traditional chronology, there are also various positions taken regarding the date of Romans, though all of them are within the range of 55 to 59. Thus the letter has been seen as having been written (1) "in the first three months of 55,"[22] (2) "in the winter of 55-56 or 56-57,"[23] (3) "during the early days of A.D. 57,"[24] (4) "at the beginning of either 57 or 58,"[25] or (5) "in the first quarter of A.D. 59, but a year or two earlier is possible."[26] A majority of NT scholars, however, have viewed Romans as written during the winter of 57-58.[27] In support of this date is the thesis of Johannes Friedrich, Wolfgang Pöhlmann, and Peter Stuhlmacher, who argued in 1976 (in a jointly authored article) that Paul's instructions about paying taxes in Rom 13:6-7 are best understood in the context of unrest at Rome concerning

18. J. Knox, *Chapters in a Life of Paul*, 86.

19. C. Buck and G. Taylor, *Saint Paul*, 29-30, 175.

20. G. Lüdemann, *Paul*, 262-63.

21. R. Jewett, *Chronology of Paul's Life, passim*; esp. note his attached "Graph of Dates and Time-Spans"; see also *idem, Romans*, 18-21.

22. E.g., C. K. Barrett, *Romans*, 5; A. Suhl, *Paulus und seine Briefe*, 249, 344.

23. E.g., M.-J. Lagrange, *Aux Romains*, xx; W. G. Kümmel, *Introduction*, 311; C. E. B. Cranfield, *Romans*, 16; R. Pesch, *Römerbrief*, 2; J. D. G. Dunn, *Romans*, 1.xliii; and C. B. Puskas, *Letters of Paul*, 72-73.

24. E.g., F. F. Bruce, *Romans*, 11-12; *idem, Paul*, 475; D. J. Moo, *Romans*, 3.

25. E.g., H. Schlier, *Römerbrief*, 2.

26. E.g., C. H. Dodd, *Romans*, xxvi.

27. E.g., J. B. Lightfoot, *The Epistle to the Galatians* (London: Macmillan, 1865, 1890[10]), 40, 43; W. Sanday and A. C. Headlam, *Romans*, xiii; O. Michel, *An die Römer*, 27; M. Black, *Romans*, 20; R. E. Brown, *Introduction to the New Testament*, 560; and J. A. Fitzmyer, *Romans*, 87.

the shady practices of the city's tax collectors, which led to the emperor Nero regulating their activities in A.D. 58.[28] It is this date of the winter of 57-58 that I believe best fits all of the data available from Paul's letter to Rome, Luke's Acts of the Apostles, and those external sources cited above. Thus the winter of 57-58 will be assumed in all that follows in this volume as being generally correct for the time of Paul's writing Romans.

SUPPLEMENTAL BIBLIOGRAPHY

See also "Bibliography of Selected Commentaries." All references in the footnotes to works included in this list are by the authors' names and abbreviated titles.

Brown, Raymond E. *An Introduction to the New Testament.* New York, London, Toronto: Doubleday, 1997, 559-60.
Bruce, Frederick F. *Paul: Apostle of the Heart Set Free.* Grand Rapids: Eerdmans, 1977 (British version: *Paul: Apostle of the Free Spirit.* Exeter: Paternoster, 1977), 379-89, 475.
Buck, Charles, and Greer Taylor, *Saint Paul: A Study of the Development of His Thought.* New York: Scribner's, 1969, 29-30, 163-75.
Campbell, T. H. "Paul's 'Missionary Journeys' as Reflected in His Letters," *JBL* 74 (1955) 80-87.
Fitzmyer, Joseph A. "The Pauline Letters and the Lucan Account of Paul's Missionary Journeys," *SBL Seminar Papers 1988.* Atlanta: Scholars, 1988, 82-89.
Friedrich, Johannes, Wolfgang Pöhlmann, and Peter Stuhlmacher. "Zur historischen Situation und Intention von Röm 13,1-7," *ZTK* 73 (1976) 131-66.
Gunther, John J. *Paul: Messenger and Exile. A Study in the Chronology of His Life and Letters.* Valley Forge: Judson, 1972, 13-14.
Hemer, Colin J. "Observations on Pauline Chronology," in *Pauline Studies* (Festschrift F. F. Bruce), ed. D. A. Hagner and M. J. Harris. Exeter: Paternoster, 1980, 3-18.
Hurd, John C., Jr. "Pauline Chronology and Theology," in *Christian History and Interpretation: Studies Presented to John Knox,* ed. W. R. Farmer, C. F. D. Moule, and R. R. Niebuhr. Cambridge: Cambridge University Press, 1967, 225-48.
———. "The Sequence of Paul's Letters," *CJT* 14 (1968) 189-200.
Jewett, Robert. *A Chronology of Paul's Life.* Philadelphia: Fortress, 1979, 51-52, 100-103.
Knox, John. *Chapters in a Life of Paul.* New York and Nashville: Abingdon-Cokesbury, 1950; London: Black, 1954, 86.

28. J. Friedrich, W. Pöhlmann, and P. Stuhlmacher, "Zur historischen Situation und Intention von Röm 13,1-7"), which time of unrest, shady practices, and official regulation is referred to by Tacitus (*Annales* 13.50-51) and Suetonius (*Vita Nero* 10).

Kümmel, Werner Georg. *Introduction to the New Testament,* rev. ed., trans. H. C. Kee. Nashville: Abingdon, 1975, 311-12.

Lake, Kirsopp. *The Earlier Epistles of St. Paul: Their Motive and Origin.* London: Rivingtons, 1927², 324-25, 369-70, 411-13.

Lüdemann, Gerd. *Paul, Apostle to the Gentiles: Studies in Chronology,* trans. F. S. Jones. Philadelphia: Fortress, 1984, 262-63.

Michaelis, Wilhelm. "Kenchreä (Zur Frage des Abfassungsortes des Rm)," *ZNW* 25 (1926) 144-54.

Murphy-O'Connor, Jerome. *St. Paul's Corinth: Texts and Archaeology.* Wilmington: Glazier, 1983.

Puskas, Charles B., Jr. *The Letters of Paul: An Introduction.* Collegeville: Liturgical Press, 1993, 72-73.

Ramsay, William M. *St. Paul the Traveller and the Roman Citizen.* London: Hodder & Stoughton, 1897; repr. Grand Rapids: Baker, 1962, 286-89.

Richards, J. R. "Romans and I Corinthians: Their Chronological Relationship and Comparative Dates," *NTS* 13 (1966) 14-30.

Roetzel, Calvin J. *The Letters of Paul: Conversations in Context.* Atlanta: John Knox, 1975; Louisville: Westminster/John Knox, 1991³, 104-13.

Schmithals, Walter. *Der Römerbrief als historisches Problem.* SNT 9. Gütersloh: Mohn, 1975.

Smiga, George. "Romans 12:1-2 and 15:30-32 and the Occasion of the Letter to the Romans," *CBQ* 53 (1991) 257-73.

Suhl, Alfred. *Paulus und seine Briefe. Ein Beitrag zur paulinischen Chronologie.* SNT 11. Gütersloh: Mohn, 1975, 264-82.

Taylor, T. M. "The Place of Origin of Romans," *JBL* 67 (1948) 281-95.

Wedderburn, Alexander J. M. "Keeping Up with Recent Studies: VIII. Some Recent Pauline Chronologies," *ExpT* 92 (1981) 103-8.

―――. *The Reasons for Romans.* Edinburgh: T&T Clark, 1988; Minneapolis: Fortress, 1991, 22-24.

Westberg, F. *Zur neutestamentliche Chronologie und Golgathas Ortslage.* Leipzig: Deichert, 1911, 72-73.

Wikenhauser, A., and J. Schmid. *Einleitung in das Neue Testament,* 6th ed. Freiburg: Herder, 1973, 449-62.

PART TWO

Two Pivotal Issues

CHAPTER IV

Addressees

The usual way of determining the identity, character, circumstances, and concerns of Paul's addressees at Rome has been first by "mirror reading" the letter and then by turning to historical sources and data outside the NT in order to supplement conclusions reached by such an internal process. But by using a mirror-reading methodology, interpreters appear to have arrived, at least in this case, at something of a dead end. It is better, therefore, we believe, to deal with questions about Paul's Roman addressees the other way around — that is, first by giving attention to the extant, historical data outside of the NT, and then by noting how a mirror reading of Romans might support (or refute) a hypothesis (or hypotheses) developed from historical sources and data outside of the NT. And this is what we intend to do in what follows — that is, to develop first a hypothesis regarding Paul's addressees on the basis of what is known from sources outside of the NT and then to ask how well a mirror reading of the letter either supports or refutes that hypothesis.

Wolfgang Wiefel has rightly argued that "the problem of the origin of the Christians referred to in Romans and the larger question of the origin of Christianity in Rome cannot be clarified without considering the entire phenomenon of Judaism in Rome."[1] In dealing with the matters regarding the addressees of Paul's letter to Rome, therefore, attention must be directed not only to (1) "Rome in Paul's day," thereby providing a broad panoramic background for the discussion, but also to the topics (2) "Jews and Judaism at Rome" and (3) "the rise of Christianity at Rome," thereby setting out the im-

1. W. Wiefel, "Jewish Community," in Donfried, ed., *Romans Debate* (1977), 101; (1991), 86.

mediate contexts of pertinence. Only then will we be able to make informed judgments about (4) "the identity, character, circumstances, and concerns of the letter's addressees."

1. Rome in Paul's Day

Legend has it that Rome was founded in 753 B.C. by Romulus and Remus, the twin sons of the Roman god Mars (i.e., the Greek god Ares, who was considered "the god of war") and a vestal virgin — with the infant boys abandoned to die, but found and raised by a she-wolf. To enhance their pedigree, the boys were also claimed to have been descendants of Aeneas, the hero of the Roman poet Virgil's great national epic the *Aeneid,* who escaped the sack of Troy and, after wandering seven years, settled in Italy. As the legend goes, Romulus killed Remus in a fit of jealous rage while laying out the first courses of the city's walls; and after building the city, he became Rome's first king. In actual fact, however, the origins of the city were much more mundane, though its rise to prominence and power could hardly have been more spectacular.

Rome's Beginning and Rise to Prominence and Power

Rome was originally only a loose cluster of farming villages and shepherd's coves on the left bank of the Tiber River. Early in their history the people of the area came under the control of the Etruscans, an ancient people whose kingdom of Etruria extended throughout west-central Italy (i.e., modern Tuscany and part of Umbria). But they were able to shake off the Etruscan yoke and became governed by their own kings for about two hundred years, with the Tiber separating the early Romans on the river's left bank from the Etruscans on its right bank.

In 510 B.C. Rome became a republic governed by two magistrates, who were called consuls and were elected each year to their posts. About 400 B.C. it began its wars of expansion, first taking the Etruscan city of Veii on the right bank of the Tiber and then conquering city after city throughout Italy. By 275 B.C. the Romans had gained complete control of all Italy.

In 264 B.C. Rome came into conflict with Carthage, the North African city-state that dominated the western Mediterranean. The conflict arose over the control of Sicily, which had been economically subservient to Carthage but which Rome wanted to annex. The result was the Punic Wars of 264-241 B.C. and 218-201 B.C., during which Rome gained control first of Sicily (241), then of Sardinia (238), and then of Spain (206). The second of the Punic Wars with Carthage almost resulted in disaster for Rome. But with the defeat of Hannibal, the Carthaginian general, at Zama in North Africa, Rome became the reigning power throughout the western Mediterranean.

Hardly had the exhausting struggle with Hannibal and his army come to an end when Rome found herself in conflict with the Greek kingdoms to the east, which had been formed when the empire of Alexander the Great was broken up: first in a war with the Macedonians; then, as an extension of those battles, in conflict with the Seleucids; and finally, using more subtle means, in various power struggles with the Ptolemaic rulers of Egypt. In 195 B.C. Rome swept through the Balkans, Greece, and Asia Minor, conquering the old city-states of Macedonia, granting them a measure of internal freedom, and bringing them under Rome's "protection." In 192 B.C., when the Seleucids tried to intervene, Roman legionaries invaded Cilicia and Syria, seriously crippling and impoverishing the Seleucid kingdom. And during 149-146 B.C., the so-called Third Punic War, Rome put an end not only to Carthage's domination of the western Mediterranean but also to the power of the old Aegean Confederacy of city-states in Greece and Asia Minor (including Crete), with Macedonia becoming a Roman province in 148 B.C. and Corinth being finally conquered in 146 B.C.

During the following century, all of the territories throughout Asia Minor, Cilicia, and Syria were transformed — one by one, in one way or another — either from "protectorates" to "provinces" or from "dependent kingdoms" to "client kingdoms" to "provinces." In 133 B.C. the last king of Pergamum, at his death, bequeathed his domains to the Roman senate and people, and so western Asia Minor became the Roman province of Asia. In 88 B.C. Mithridates VI, the king of Pontus, together with his confederates, revolted against Rome, and warfare between Rome and the northern territories of Asia Minor dragged on for about a quarter century. But with the defeat of Pontus in 64 B.C. by the Roman general Pompey, the whole political structure of Asia Minor was reorganized. Likewise, Syria was reconstituted a Roman province. And in 63 B.C. Pompey captured Jerusalem and occupied Judea, thereby bringing all of southern Palestine-Syria also under direct Roman rule.

Class struggles and slave wars racked Roman society during the last half of the second century B.C., especially during 135-132 and 103-101. Even more devastating were the civil wars and political upheavals at the end of that century and the beginning of the next. For in 107 B.C. a dictatorship was set up by Marius, the son of poor and obscure parents, who became a leading

Roman general and was in constant opposition to the aristocratic leaders of Rome. Marius, however, was later opposed by his own general Sulla, who returned from a number of successful foreign conquests to lead the Roman army under his command against Rome. And with his victory Sulla established himself as dictator from 88 to 79 B.C.

In 60 B.C. Rome became a Republic governed by a triumvirate of Sulla's generals — that is, by Pompey, Crassus, and Julius Caesar. Pompey had been the general who conquered the eastern areas of the Mediterranean, taking Jerusalem in 63 B.C. and making the Jewish nation part of the reorganized province of Syria. The triumvirate, however, soon broke up, and in 49 B.C. Julius Caesar, after defeating the forces of the Republic led at first by Pompey (until his death), took control of the empire. Then after further conflicts with the army of the Republic led by Pompey's followers — which included defeating Egypt, killing Ptolemy, subduing uprisings in the eastern part of the empire, and instituting numerous reforms and projects at Rome — Julius Caesar was murdered at Rome on March 15, 44 B.C.

After Julius Caesar's death, Octavian, his adopted son and political heir (and so later called Gaius Julius Caesar Octanianus), and Mark Antony vied for power. Mark Antony was defeated in the naval battle of Actium in September 31 B.C., along with Cleopatra, his consort, who was the last sovereign of Ptolemaic Egypt. Thus Octavian became the sole master of the Roman world, ruling officially as *Princeps* (the first citizen of the republic), but actually functioning as a constitutional monarch or benign dictator. In 27 B.C. the Roman Senate conferred on him the title *Augustus* ("the Venerable"; Greek: *Sebastos*) and he reigned another forty years until his death in A.D. 14. He was succeeded in the Julio-Claudian dynasty (i.e., those claiming relationship to Julius Caesar by birth or adoption) by Tiberius Caesar (14-37), Gaius Caligula (37-41), Claudius (41-54), and Nero (54-68).

Having disposed of his political opposition, Claudius Augustus put an end to civil strife and social unrest — at least at Rome, and as best he could in the provinces. Acting in the tyrannical manner of a benign dictator, he established *Pax Augusta* ("the Peace of Augustus") throughout the empire. At Rome he appointed a Prefect, a distinguished Roman senator, whose tasks were to keep peace and order, ensure the efficient collection of "tribute to Caesar," and govern wisely. Under him, Claudius Augustus set up local Aediles and Curators to handle the more mundane affairs in the city's fourteen regions. In towns near Rome, he established the Praetorian Guard, an elite corps of soldiers whose main task was to protect the emperor. He also reformed the army, making it the official protector of the people. And he created two paramilitary organizations: the *Vigiles* ("guards"), a sort of night watch and fire brigade combined, and the Urban Cohorts, a police force under the authority of the Prefect.

Among his many architectural triumphs, Augustus himself supervised the building of the Roman Forum, which was the city's civic center where much of its commercial, political, legal, and religious business was conducted, naming it the *Forum Augustae.* The Senate honored him with the construction of the strikingly beautiful *Ara Pacis Augustae* ("Altar of Peace") in the Campus Martius, an area outside the *pomerium* or sacred boundary of the city where a great deal of the political and social life of Rome also took place — with the sculptures on that "Altar of Peace" (which has recently been re-assembled and restored on a site not far from its original location) celebrating Augustus's victories in the West and representing members of his family.

In addition, with the enlistment of many wealthy individuals who served as patrons, like Marcus Vipsanius Agrippa and Gaius Maecenas, Augustus supported the arts and letters. He wanted to create a new *populus Romanus* ("People of Rome") of civilization and culture, both at Rome itself and throughout the empire. During his reign the Golden Age of Latin literature thrived, as represented by such writers as Virgil (79-19 B.C.), Horace (65-8 B.C.), Propertius (c. 47 B.C.–A.D. 2), and Livy (c. 64 B.C.–A.D. 12). And after Augustus's death, his interests and achievements were, in large part, carried on by his Julio-Claudian successors — particularly by Claudius throughout the whole fourteen years of his reign (41-54) and by Nero during the first part of his reign (i.e., from 54 through about 60).

Rome's Golden Age of Prosperity and Culture

Rome attained its apex architecturally, artistically, and culturally during the eight or nine decades from the early days of Augustus (after the battle of Actium in 31 B.C.) to about mid-point in Nero's reign (about A.D. 60). Augustus claimed to have "found Rome in brick and left it in marble," and his successors reveled in that claim. In fact, when Paul wrote his letter to believers at Rome, the city was basking in what Aurelius Victor, a fourth-century historian, called the *Neronis quinquennium,* "the five-year period of Nero,"[2] which was evidently viewed by most Romans as the most splendid period of the empire since the death of Augustus. And Nero during the first part of his

---

2. Aurelius Victor, *Caesares* 5, *Ep.* 12; cf. Lucan 1.33.

reign (i.e., 54–c. 60) carried on the traditions of his immediate predecessors, having not yet indulged in the tyrannical and murderous traits of his latter years (i.e., c. 60-68).

As the capital of the empire, Rome's impact on the Mediterranean world was profound. The aggressive policies of the Julio-Claudian dynasty made its presence felt in every province and district of the empire. But also, with political and commercial power centered at Rome, the city drew people like a magnet from all of the areas around the Mediterranean. Inscriptions on its funerary vaults and niches *(columbaria)* reveal quite clearly that many foreign people with foreign names lived and died at Rome during the imperial period. And with them came such eastern religions as Mithraism (from Persia), the worship of Isis and Osiris (from Egypt), Judaism (from Palestine and Jerusalem), and Christianity (from Judea and Jerusalem) — all vying for the people's allegiance, along with the worship of the ancient Italian fertility goddess Dea Dia, whose cult was reorganized by Augustus and whose religious ceremonies thereafter always included the presence of the emperor. The Roman satirist Juvenal (A.D. 60-140), decrying the decadence he saw at Rome and blaming it on the increasing dominance of such eastern cults, aimed one of his sharpest gibes at his own city when he said that "the Orontes had flowed into the Tiber."[3]

2. Jews and Judaism at Rome

Exactly when Jews first came to Rome is unknown. The evidence is not only scanty but also, at times, contradictory. Likewise, how the Jews organized themselves in the city, how they were viewed by the Roman authorities, and how they fared among the city's non-Jewish population are questions that have been extensively debated. Nonetheless, some generalizations can be made from the extant literary evidence and from recently discovered Jewish funerary inscriptions.

Literary Evidence about Jews at Rome

The earliest evidence of Jewish-Roman relations comes from 1 Maccabees, which was written about 110-100 B.C. 1 Macc 8:1-32 recounts how Judas

---

3. Juvenal, *Satires* 3.62.

Maccabeus, the leader of the Maccabean revolt during 166-160 B.C., sent envoys to Rome, probably about 161 B.C., with a letter asking for an alliance of peace and cooperation between "the nation of the Jews" and the Romans, and how the Roman Senate sent back a letter setting out a treaty of confederacy with the Jews. 1 Macc 12:1-18 relates how Jonathan (152-142 B.C.) also sent a delegation to Rome, probably about 150 B.C., asking for a renewal of that treaty. And 1 Macc 14:16-24, 40 speaks of the Romans, probably about 139 B.C., taking the initiative to renew that same treaty with Simeon (142-134 B.C.).

The earliest reference to Jews actually living in Rome comes from the Roman rhetorician and historian Valerius Maximus (flourished during the first part of the first century A.D.), who wrote that in 139 B.C. the Praetor ("judicial magistrate") of the city, Gnaeus Cornelius Hispalus, "forced the Jews to return to their own homes" — that is, to return to their homelands — because they "tried to contaminate Roman customs with the cult of Jupiter Sabazius."[4] Probably those who were expelled were Jewish merchants and Jewish "Freedmen," who did not enjoy the full rights of Roman citizenship. And probably the reason for their expulsion was that they tried to proselytize Romans to become Jewish adherents, either actual proselytes or "God-fearers," rather than that they were votaries of the cult of Sabazio.[5] For as Wolfgang Wiefel notes:

> One has to keep in mind that the general perception of the Jewish community in Rome was surrounded by misconceptions from the very beginning of its history. The Romans mistook them for followers of the hellenistic-oriental Sabazio cult for one of two good reasons: they misunderstood the Jewish word for God, Sabaoth, the Greek form of Zebaoth, and they might have made the same mistake with the word sabbath, the most conspicuous custom of Judaism.[6]

There appears to have existed at Rome during the first century B.C. an active Jewish community, which was augmented by a large number of Jewish slaves who had been brought to the city by Pompey from his conquests in the East. As reported in various Jewish sources, the Roman general Pompey, after his capture of Jerusalem in 63 B.C., "laid waste" Judea and "expelled" a great number of Jews "to the West" to suffer "harsh captivity" in Rome,[7] tak-

---

4. Valerius Maximus, *Factorum et Dictorum Memorabilium* 1.3.3.

5. Cf. E. N. Lane, "Sabazius and the Jews," 35-38.

6. W. Wiefel, "Jewish Community," in Donfried, ed., *Romans Debate* (1977), 102; (1991), 86.

7. *Pss Sol* 2:6-7; 17:11-14.

ing with them the then ruling Maccabean priest-king Aristobulus II (67-63 B.C., d. 49) "in chains, together with his family."[8] Josephus reports that Julius Caesar, who was the Roman emperor during 49-44 B.C., granted the right of free assembly and the practice of their "national customs and sacred rites" to the Jews "even in Rome," though other "religious societies" were forbidden to assemble in the city.[9] Philo of Alexandria tells of how during the reign of Augustus (44 B.C.–A.D. 14), and with his support, Jews resided in "the great section of Rome across the Tiber," with "most of them" being "emancipated Romans" or so-called Freedmen.[10] And Josephus recounts that when a delegation of fifty Judean Jews came to Rome in A.D. 6 to complain to Augustus about Archelaus's autocratic ways and to ask for autonomy, "more than eight thousand of the Jews in Rome" gathered to show their support.[11]

The fact of a large Jewish community at Rome during the first century B.C. is confirmed, as well, by Roman writers. Probably most illustrative of this fact are the actions and speech of the Roman orator, philosopher, and statesman Cicero (106-43 B.C.) in 59 B.C. in defense of Lucius Valerius Flaccus, who had been the Praetor ("judicial magistrate") of the province of Asia during 62-61 B.C. but was on trial for having misappropriated funds donated by the Jews of Asia for their temple at Jerusalem. For basing his defense on an old senatorial decree against the transfer of funds abroad, which decree had been renewed in 63 B.C., Cicero lowered his voice so as to be heard only by the judges before him — and not by the Jews who were present at the proceedings — and appealed to anti-Jewish Roman prejudice in referring to the Jews as follows: "You know how large a troop they are, how they stick together, how influential they are in political assemblies, . . . for there are plenty of people to stir them up against me and against every good citizen."[12] And he went on to charge the prosecution with cooperating with the Jews, considering their good will more important than the interests of the Roman state, and to identify the Jewish religion as a "barbarious superstition" that was not compatible with Roman customs. Likewise Horace (65-8 B.C.), one of the most celebrated Roman poets of the Augustan period, spoke of Jews at Rome in his day as a sect whose tenacious proselytizing of Gentiles was difficult to avoid.[13]

8. Josephus, *Antiq* 14.77; *War* 1.155.
9. Josephus, *Antiq* 14.213-15.
10. Philo, *Embassy to Gaius* 155-56.
11. Josephus, *War* 2.80; *Antiq* 17.300.
12. Cicero, *Oratio pro Flacco* 28.66-67.
13. Horace, *Satires* 1.4.142-43; cf. also 1.5.100; 1.9.67-72.

Attitudes toward the Jews at Rome varied considerably among the city's officials and populace, ranging from acceptance and toleration, on the one hand, to opposition and persecution, on the other. Many Romans viewed Jewish Sabbath observance and the practice of circumcision as "barbarous superstitions," and thought of their adherence to the Mosaic law and allegiance to the Jerusalem temple as subversive to Roman authority and unity. Caesar Augustus, however, in his desire for *Pax Augusta,* seems to have been not only tolerant, but also supportive of the Jews generally, both at Rome and throughout the empire. And at his death in A.D. 14, as Suetonius reports, there were among the foreigners who mourned at Caesar's pyre "above all the Jews, who even flocked to the place for several successive nights"[14] — which was an obvious response of respect and appreciation by the Jewish community for the tolerance and support shown them by Augustus.

The Roman Senate, however, made up of wealthy businessmen and politicians, seems usually to have been antagonistic to the Jews, whose interests must frequently have conflicted with theirs. Further, the emperors after Augustus often inaugurated legislation opposed to the Jews. One prominent example is the action taken in A.D. 19 by Tiberius Caesar, who ordered the expulsion of the entire Jewish community from Rome — perhaps excluding those who were Roman citizens — when it was reported that Fulvia, "a woman of high rank who had become a Jewish proselyte" who wanted to make a donation to the temple at Jerusalem, had been swindled out of a large sum of money by four Jews, whom Josephus calls "complete scoundrels."[15] Josephus's account of the emperor's action is as follows:

> Whereupon the latter [Tiberius] ordered the whole Jewish community to leave Rome. The consuls drafted four thousand of these Jews for military service and sent them to the island of Sardinia; but they penalized a good many of them, who refused to serve for fear of breaking the Jewish law. And so because of the wickedness of four men the Jews were banished from the city.[16]

The Jews of Rome certainly suffered by being expelled from the city in A.D. 19. Particularly was this so for the four thousand men sent to Sardinia,

---

14. Suetonius, *Iulii Vita* 84.5.

15. Cf. Josephus, *Antiq* 18.81-84; see also Tacitus, *Annals* 2.85.4; Suetonius, *Vita Tiberius* 36; Juvenal, *Satires* 3.10, 62-63; 6.542-47; 14.96-104; Dio Cassius, *Historia Romana* 57.18.5.

16. Josephus, *Antiq* 18.83b-84.

for their conscription into the Roman army, which was highly unusual for a Jew, was probably equivalent to a death sentence. Nonetheless, members of the Herodian family maintained close contacts with members of the imperial household during this period,[17] with benefits from that association spilling over to the Jewish populace generally. Yet despite such a major setback as the expulsion of A.D. 19 — and despite the frequent vacillation of policy toward the Jews under Tiberius[18] — Jews continued to live and prosper at Rome during the first sixty years or so of the first Christian century "without significant hindrance."[19]

Jewish Funerary Inscriptions at Rome

A great deal has been learned about the Jews of ancient Rome from the funerary inscriptions found in six Jewish catacombs at Rome. These were discovered in the areas of Monteverge (in 1602), the Via Appia (in 1859), and the Via Nomentana (in 1919) and have been extensively studied during the past century. "Thanks to the data from the catacombs," as Harry Leon has said in concluding his summary of the material, "we have more information about the Jews of ancient Rome than about any other community of the Diaspora in ancient times."[20] In particular, the funerary inscriptions indicate that there were as many as eleven, twelve, or even thirteen synagogues in Rome and its environs during the first century C.E., with members of the Jewish populace being associated with one or the other of them.[21]

The Greek word συναγωγή in these funerary inscriptions[22] seems not to denote a building, but an association of Jews who were gathered into an assembly or congregation, with each group apparently identified by the name of a particular ruler, a locality or city from which its members came, a district in which they lived or met, or some distinguishing characteristic. Yet

---

17. Cf. Josephus, *Antiq* 18.179-94.

18. Cf. Philo, *Embassy to Gaius* 24; also under Caligula (see Josephus, *Antiq* 18.261-304), and Claudius (cf. Josephus, *Antiq* 19.286-91).

19. So W. Wiefel, "Jewish Community," in Donfried, ed., *Romans Debate* (1977), 105; (1991), 89.

20. H. J. Leon, *Jews of Ancient Rome,* 259.

21. See *CIJ*, 1.lvi-ci and Plates 1-532; cf. J. B. Frey, "Le judaïsme à Rome," 129-56; H. J. Leon, *Jews of Ancient Rome,* 135-66; R. Penna, "Les Juifs à Rome," 328-30; P. Richardson, "Augustan-Era Synagogues in Rome," 17-29; L. M. White, "Synagogue and Society in Imperial Ostia," 30-68.

22. Note: All references in our text to Greek names, words, and phrases in the Jewish inscriptions of the Roman catacombs are in lower case, not in original capital or large letters.

while συναγωγή in these materials has primary reference to an assembly or association of people, the term seems also to have been used, as suggested by the archaeological evidence, with respect to particular buildings within which the Jewish congregations met.

Of those congregations called by the name of a ruler, there were at Rome: (1) the "Synagogue of the Augustesians,"[23] which probably was founded by Jews who had been set free (i.e., "Freedmen") by Caesar Augustus; (2) the "Synagogue of Agrippa,"[24] who was a minister of Augustus (also his son-in-law) and a friend of Herod the Great; (3) the "Synagogue of Volumnius,"[25] who was the procurator of the province of Syria at the time of Herod the Great; and (4) the "Synagogue of the Herodians,"[26] though this identification has been disputed by Harry Leon.[27] Of those called by the locality or city of origin of its members, there appear the following names: (1) "Valkarengian";[28] (2) "Eleas," which means "Olive Tree" but probably should be seen as a place name;[29] (3) "Tripolis";[30] (4) "Skina";[31] and (5) "Arca Libanon."[32] Of those incorporating the name of the district where its members lived or met, there appear the following names: (1) "Campesian,"[33] probably because the congregation met somewhere in the Campus Maritus on the left bank of the Tiber River; and (2) "Sibura,"[34] which was a heavily populated district between the Quirinal and Viminal hills. "More fascinating," as Wolfgang Wiefel observes, "are the designations Synagogue of the Hebrews[35] or of the Vernaculi,[36] since these go back to the time when the Greek-speaking Jews *(vernaculi),* who had settled in Rome a long time ago, lived together with the newer immigrants who still spoke Aramaic."[37]

23. *CIJ* 284, 301, 338, 368, 416, 496.
24. *CIJ* 365, 425, 503.
25. *CIJ* 343, 502, 517.
26. *CIJ* 173.
27. H. J. Leon, "Synagogue of the Herodians," 318-22.
28. *CIJ* 304, 316, 384, 433, 504.
29. *CIJ* 281, 509.
30. *CIJ* 390, 408.
31. *CIJ* 7.
32. *CIJ* 501.
33. *CIJ* 88, 319, 483(?), 523(?).
34. *CIJ* 18, 22, 37(?), 146(?).
35. *CIJ* 291, 317, 510, 535.
36. *CIJ* 318, 383, 398, 494.
37. W. Wiefel, "Jewish Community," in Donfried, ed., *Romans Debate* (1977), 106; (1991), 90.

It is clear from the funerary inscriptions that the various Jewish congregations of ancient Rome were fairly uniform in their organizational structures. Heading up each of the synagogues was a "council of elders" (γερουσία), with one of their number, "the chief elder" (γερούσιαρχ), serving as the principal leader. This executive body seems also to have been called "the rulers" (ἄρχοντες), with each "ruler" (ἄρχων) being elected to a term of one to three years. Also, there were a "head of the synagogue" (ἀρχισυνάγωγος) who had charge of the worship activities of the group, an "administrator" (φροντιστής) who supervised the community's material goods, a "scribe" (γραμματεύς) who served as secretary of the congregation, and those designated a "priest" (ἱερεύς), whose title was probably honorific for members of the priestly families in view of the fact that there was no temple at Rome.

However, also notable in the materials from the Roman catacombs is "the absence of a single, controlling organization supervising the individual synagogues."[38] And it is this lack of reference to any central Jewish governing body at Rome that has alerted scholars to a quite important factor in the understanding of (1) the character of Judaism in ancient Rome, and (2) the origin and early development of Christianity in the city.

By way of contrast, it needs to be observed that Josephus, when speaking about Alexandrian Jewry, reports that not only did the Jews of that city live together in certain sections, but also that they were socially and administratively cohesive: "an ethnarch of their own has been installed, who governs the people and adjudicates suits and supervises contracts and ordinances, just as if he were the head of a sovereign state."[39] Likewise at Cyrene, where Ptolemaic rulers also governed, a similar cohesiveness of Jews seems to have been allowed.[40] At Rome, however, there appears to have been considerably looser relations between the various Jewish groupings, with no central agency either controlling or coordinating the people's religious and social lives. Rather, the synagogues of ancient Rome seem to have maintained stronger links with Jerusalem Jewry than with one another — probably being discouraged by the Romans from being too intra-connected socially, and so forming an alien power bloc within the city, yet feeling the need on their own part to be inter-connected religiously with Jerusalem.

---

38. W. Wiefel, "Jewish Community," in Donfried, ed., *Romans Debate* (1977), 108; (1991), 91; see also H. J. Leon, *Jews of Ancient Rome*, 167-70.

39. Josephus, *Antiq* 14.117.

40. Josephus, *Antiq* 14.116.

Relations with Jewish Leaders at Jerusalem

The Mishnah speaks of four distinguished rabbis from ancient Palestine as having made visits to the Jewish communities at Rome, with all of them, evidently, coming during the reign of the Roman emperor Domitian (A.D. 81-96): Rabban Gamaliel, Rabbi Eleazar ben Azariah, Rabbi Joshua ben Hananiah, and Rabbi Akiba ben Joseph.[41] The traditions in the Mishnah, of course, were not codified until about 180-220 C.E. Yet in the few times they refer to Rome, they appear to reflect something of great significance regarding the circumstances of Roman Jewry in the first century C.E. — that is, that relations between the early groups or congregations of Jews living at Rome and the Jewish religious leadership at Jerusalem were stronger than they were between the various "synagogues" in the city of Rome itself.

Acts 28:21-22 lends some support to Roman Jewry's close links with the Jewish leaders at Jerusalem. For having been called together by Paul to hear his side of the story, the Jewish leaders at Rome, while acknowledging that they had received some general information from other sources about Paul's missionary activities and message, are portrayed as saying: "We have not received any letters from Judea concerning you, and none of those who have come from there has reported or said anything bad about you. But we want to hear what your views are, for we know that people everywhere are talking against this sect."

Relations with Roman Authorities and Rome's Non-Jewish Populace

Because of the establishment of *Pax Augusta* by Claudius Augustus, which was implemented (to various degrees) by succeeding emperors as *Pax Romana,* the Jews of ancient Rome were tolerated by the Roman authorities, allowed to practice their religion relatively undisturbed, and able to prosper economically and socially. There is no extant evidence for anything like a Roman "Magna Charta" for Jews. Rather, what guided Rome's policy toward the Jews of Rome, as well as toward everyone else in the empire, was a desire for law and order. Thus as long as they lived without disturbing *Pax Romana,* the Jews were left alone by the Roman authorities. Because of the

---

41. See, *Mish. Erubin* 4:1; *Mish. Abodah Zarah* 4:7; and *Mish. Shabbath* 16:8; also *JE* 5.560; cf. H. J. Leon, *Jews of Ancient Rome,* 35-36 — though in the Jerusalem Gemara, *Sanhedrin* 7:19 may be read as Eliezer ben Hyrcanus instead of Eleazar ben Azariah.

daily exigencies of living in a multi-cultural, non-Jewish city and a basically pagan environment, it was necessary for them to assimilate, at least to some extent, to the cultural and economic conditions at Rome. The Jewish catacomb inscriptions, for example, evidence that the Jews of Rome spoke mainly Greek and adopted some Latin names. They were, however, not required to renounce their religion; rather, they seem to have been permitted to develop their own Jewish heritage within their own Jewish circles.

Nonetheless, at times the Jews experienced opposition from the Roman authorities and turbulence in their relations with their non-Jewish neighbors — opposition because of occasional disturbances within their communities, which were viewed by the authorities as disturbing the *Pax Romana*, and turbulence because of some actions considered by non-Jews to be unlawful proselytizing. One such situation occurred in 139 B.C. when the magistrate of Rome, Gnaeus Cornelius Hispalus, expelled at least some of the Jews from Rome, evidently because they were disturbing the peace in their efforts to proselytize non-Jews.[42] Another occurred in A.D. 19 when the emperor Tiberius Caesar ordered the expulsion of "all the Jews" from the city — or, at least, all the Jews involved in "the Fulvia affair" who were not Roman citizens.[43]

Of particular importance for an understanding of both Judaism and Christianity at Rome in the days of Paul are (1) the mandate of the emperor Claudius in A.D. 41, which ordered the Jews of Rome, "while continuing their traditional mode of life, not to hold meetings,"[44] and (2) the Edict of Claudius in A.D. 49, which expelled Jews from Rome "since the Jews constantly made disturbances at the instigation of Chrestus."[45] Because both of these passages from the two Roman historians Dio Cassius and Suetonius deal with actions taken by Claudius against Jews living in Rome — and because both share vocabulary that can be associated with the language of expulsion — scholars have frequently equated the two events and used the separate accounts to shed light on each other.[46] A growing number of scholars

---

42. Cf. Valerius Maximus, *Factorum et Dictorum Memorabilium* 1.3.3 (as noted above).

43. Cf. Josephus, *Antiq* 18.81-84; Tacitus, *Annals* 2.85.4; Suetonius, *Vita Tiberius* 36; Juvenal, *Satires* 3.10, 62-63; 6.542-47; 14:96-104; Dio Cassius, *Historia Romana* 57.18.5 (as also noted above).

44. Dio Cassius, *Historia Romana* 60.6.6-7.

45. Suetonius, *Vita Claudius* 25.4.

46. So, e.g., E. Schürer, *History of the Jewish People,* 3.77; V. M. Scramuzza, *Emperor Claudius;* H. J. Leon, *Jews of Ancient Rome;* S. Benko, "Edict of Claudius of A.D. 49 and the

today, however, argue for the accounts of Dio Cassius and Suetonius to be referring to two separate events.[47] And it is this latter understanding that seems best supported, not only by a close reading of Dio Cassius and Suetonius, but also by parallel references in Josephus and the New Testament (see below).

The Edict of Claudius in A.D. 49 was undoubtedly traumatic for the Jews of Rome, whether it involved the expulsion of the entire Jewish populace — which has been estimated to have numbered anywhere from 15,000 to 60,000, with something closer to the larger number usually considered more probable — or only those Jews who were viewed by Rome as agitators in disturbing the *Pax Romana*. Likewise, repercussions from the invasion of Judea and the capture of Jerusalem by the Roman Tenth Legion during A.D. 66-70 must have had a tremendous impact on the ordinary lives of Jews living at Rome. For not only were Jerusalem and its temple destroyed, but a great number of Jews in the homeland were killed and many prisoners taken, with the bulk of those prisoners brought back to Rome as slaves. Josephus has it that "the total number of prisoners taken in the entire war amounted to ninety-seven thousand, and of those who perished during the siege, from first to last, to one million one hundred thousand"[48] — explaining that the casualty numbers for Jerusalem were exceptionally high because of the large number of pilgrims gathered in the city for the Feast of Unleavened Bread, who were trapped by the Roman siege.[49]

3. Christianity at Rome

As with questions regarding how and when Jews first came to Rome, so matters having to do with how and when Christianity first took root in the city are somewhat veiled in obscurity. Eusebius of Caesarea, writing about 303 (the date of the first editions of both his *Historia Ecclesiastica* and his

---

Instigator Chrestus," 407; also the earlier views of E. M. Smallwood, "Jews and Romans in the Early Empire," *History Today* 15 (1965) 236, and F. F. Bruce, *Commentary on the Book of Acts* (Grand Rapids: Eerdmans, 1954, 1966²).

47. So, e.g., A. Momigliano, *Claudius*, 31; J. P. V. D. Balsdon, *Romans and Aliens*, 106; W. Wiefel, "Jewish Community," in Donfried, ed., *Romans Debate* (1977), 105-8; (1991), 89-92; also the later positions of E. M. Smallwood, "Jews in Rome under the Julio-Claudians," 215, and F. F. Bruce, "Christianity under Claudius," 314.

48. Josephus, *War* 6.420.

49. Josephus, *War* 6.421.

Chronicon), attributed the gospel's entrance into Rome to Peter, "that power-ful and great apostle, who by his courage took the lead of all the rest" — and who, Eusebius claimed, arrived in the city in the second year of Claudius (i.e., in A.D. 42), hard on the heels of Simon Magus, and so, "like a noble commander of God, fortified with divine armor, bore the precious merchan-dise of the revealed light from the east to those in the west, announcing the light itself and the salutary doctrine of the soul, the proclamation of the kingdom of God."[50] Likewise, the *Catalogus Liberianus,* dating from A.D. 354, speaks of Peter as the founder of the Roman church, which he served as bishop for twenty-five years. And this tradition of Peter as the first Christian missionary to Rome and founder of the Roman church has been widely ac-cepted throughout history, especially by the Roman Catholic Church.

On the other hand, "Ambrosiaster" — that mysterious commentator on the Pauline letters, who lived in Rome during the fourth century and whose literal, rather straightforward commentary on Romans evidences a special interest in Jewish matters — wrote about A.D. 375 in the prologue to his commentary on Romans concerning Jews and Christians at Rome:

> It is evident that there were Jews living in Rome . . . in the time of the apostles. Some of these Jews, who had come to believe [in Christ], passed on to the Romans [the message] that they should acknowledge Christ and keep the law. . . . One ought not to be angry with the Romans, but praise their faith, because they came to embrace faith in Christ with-out seeing any sign of miracles and without any of the apostles, though according to the Jewish rite [*ritu licet Judaico*].[51]

Ambrosiaster's crediting of Christianity's entrance into Rome to Jewish be-lievers who already lived in the city — whether Jews by birth or Gentile proselytes; whether passing through as traveling merchants, living there as free or freed residents, or brought there as slaves — and who told others of the Christian message in the contexts of their synagogue meetings and secu-lar tasks, seems to be the proper understanding of the situation. For neither Paul in Romans nor Luke in Acts says anything about Peter, or any other apostle, as having founded the church at Rome, which would have been an almost intolerable omission on the part of either of them had Peter or an-other apostle been so involved. Further, Clement of Rome, writing about

---

50. Eusebius, *Eccl Hist* 2.14.6; cf. 2:17.1 and *Chron* 261F.
51. Ambrosiaster, *Epistulam ad Romanos* (*PL* 17.48; *CSEL* 81.1.5-6); the phrase *ritu licet Judaico,* however, appears only in codex K.

A.D. 95, though he identifies Peter and Paul as the "noble examples" of the faith and speaks of their "many labors,"[52] does not refer at all to Peter having been at Rome. And where Peter and Paul are spoken of together as "founders" of Roman Christianity by the early Church Fathers, it is not because they were the ones who first brought the gospel to Rome but because they both eventually ministered there, both suffered martyrdom there, and the mortal remains of both of them were preserved there.[53]

It may be that the "visitors from Rome, both Jews and proselytes" of Acts 2:10b-11a, whom Luke singles out for special mention in his list of Jewish pilgrims at Jerusalem on the Day of Pentecost, played an important part in bringing the Christian gospel to Rome — and it may be that this brief allusion was meant by Luke to suggest to discerning readers how that "good news" was first relayed to Rome. In Acts, of course, Luke is interested in showing how the Christian proclamation penetrated the empire, particularly through Paul's missions, and how Paul and his message finally came to Rome, the capital of the empire. So he may have wanted to set up something of an *inclusio* by referring to "visitors from Rome, both Jews and proselytes" in 2:10b-11a and then by portraying Paul's arrival and preaching at Rome in 28:16-31. Further, it may be that in sending greetings in Rom 16:7 to the Christian couple Andronicus and Junia (understanding the latter as the feminine name Junia) — whom he identifies as (1) Jewish Christian "compatriots" (τοὺς συγγενεῖς μου, "those who are akin to me" or "my fellow-countrymen"; i.e., "Jews"), (2) those who were "outstanding among the apostles" (with "apostle" here used in a broad sense), and (3) those who were "in Christ before I was," all of which suggests an earlier relationship with believers in Christ at Jerusalem — Paul is implying that they had some part not only in carrying on a Christian ministry at Rome but also in actually founding the church in the capital city of the Roman empire. But such suggestions are, at best, only inferential. And while they may be used in support of a particular theory, they cannot serve as a firm basis for any hypothesis as to how the Christian gospel entered Rome.

Taking all the data and possibilities into account, Ambrosiaster's explanation of the situation seems most credible: (1) that Christianity first entered Rome by way of Jewish believers in Christ who already lived in the city, whether as free or freed residents, slaves, or traveling merchants; (2) that Jewish believers formed the nucleus of the earliest Christian com-

---

52. *1 Clement* 5.
53. So Ignatius, *To the Romans* 4.3; Irenaeus, *Adv Haer* 3.1.1; 3.3.2.

munity; (3) that through the witness of those Jewish believers, a number of Gentiles also heard the message of the gospel and became believers in Christ; and (4) that the early Christian faith at Rome had a distinctly Jewish character, whether as practiced and proclaimed by Jewish believers themselves or as accepted by Gentiles, or both. The situation was probably analogous to that of Alexandria in Egypt, where Christianity seems to have entered the city and taken root apart from any missionary activity on the part of an apostle — though, of course, Eusebius, reflecting a tradition of his day, has it that "Mark . . . being the first sent to Egypt, proclaimed the gospel there which he had written, and first established churches at the city of Alexandria."[54]

Ambrosiaster's understanding of the origin and early development of Christianity at Rome also seems to fit remarkably well with recent studies regarding the organizational structure — or, perhaps better put, the lack of organizational structure — of the Jewish synagogues at Rome. For as Wolfgang Wiefel argues:

> The loose structure [of the Roman Jewish synagogues] provided an essential prerequisite for the early penetration of Christianity in Rome. The multitude of congregations, their democratic constitutions, and the absence of a central Jewish governing board made it easy for the missionaries of the new faith to talk in the synagogues and to win new supporters. Permission for missionaries to remain in the autonomous congregations could only be revoked if the governing body considered exclusion to be necessary and enforceable. However, since Rome had no supervising body which could forbid any form of Christian propaganda in the city, it was possible to missionize in various synagogues concurrently or to go successively from one to the other.[55]

It seems probable, therefore, that — both within and between the various Jewish synagogues of the empire's capital city — the gospel of Christ took root and grew rather indigenously during its earliest days at Rome, undoubtedly with a great variety of reactions to it among both Jews and Gentiles. In what must be classed as an understatement *par excellence*, Wiefel closed his paragraph above (as just quoted) with the words: "It is likely that the existence of newly converted Christians alongside the traditional members of

---

54. Eusebius, *Eccl Hist* 2.16.1.

55. W. Wiefel, "Jewish Community," in Donfried, ed., *Romans Debate* (1977), 108; (1991), 92.

the synagogue may have led to increased factions and even to tumultuous disputes."[56]

Such "increased factions" and "tumultuous disputes" were, it seems, what lay behind Claudius's Edict of A.D. 49 — which ties together the histories of the Jews and Christians at Rome and is part of the background to Paul's letter to the Romans. Writing about A.D. 120, Suetonius, who had been the private secretary of Hadrian and wrote biographies of the Roman emperors, reports that Claudius "expelled from Rome Jews who were making constant disturbances at the instigation of Chrestus [*Iudaeos assidue tumultuantes impulsore Chresto Roma expulit*]."[57] And Paulus Orosius, a Christian historian of the fifth century, dates this expulsion of the Jews in "the ninth year of Claudius' reign" (i.e., from January 25, A.D. 49, to January 24, A.D. 50).[58] It is a date that Orosius credited to Josephus, though there is no account of this incident in Josephus's writings. Nonetheless, most scholars today think the date A.D. 49 to be the most likely.[59]

On first reading, Suetonius's words may be taken to mean that some rabble-rousing Roman extremist (whether Gentile or Jew) named Chrestus had incited the Jews of Rome to a state of social and civil unrest, and so Claudius expelled the Jews from the city — for the Latin *Chrestus* and the Greek *Chrestos* were common Roman names for slaves and freedmen (meaning "useful" or "kindly"), though no instance of *Chrestus* or *Chrestos* has been found among the several hundred Jewish names inscribed in the Jewish catacombs of Rome. On such a reading, however, questions arise: How could a pagan Roman have caused such disturbances among the Jews as to bring about their expulsion? and, Why didn't Claudius just expel Chrestus the agitator, and not the Jews, thereby re-establishing *Pax Romana* among the Jewish populace? What appears more likely is that Suetonius, writing some seventy years after the event, had no clear understanding of who "Chrestus" really was, and so assumed him to have been a local Gentile troublemaker rather than the Jew from Nazareth who was revered by Christians as the Jewish Messiah. And if, indeed, Suetonius's reference is garbled and should be

---

56. W. Wiefel, "Jewish Community," in Donfried, ed., *Romans Debate* (1977), 108; (1991), 92.

57. Suetonius, *Vita Claudius* 25.4.

58. Orosius, *Historia Adversus Paganos* 7.6.

59. So, e.g., E. M. Smallwood, "Jews in Rome under the Julio-Claudians," 211-16; P. Lampe, *Die stadtrömischen Christen*, 4-8; W. Wiefel, "Jewish Community," in Donfried, ed., *Romans Debate* (1977), 110-11; (1991), 93-94; though *contra* G. Lüdemann, *Paul*, 6-7, 165-71, and others, who date it at A.D. 41.

read as actually meaning the *Christus* or *Christos* whom the Christians honored, as most scholars today believe was the case, then, as Wolfgang Wiefel has characterized the situation, "it is a dispute within the Roman synagogues about the messiahship of Jesus of Nazareth which led the emperor to act against the Jews," for "since there was no central Jewish authority to mediate the dispute, Claudius turned vigorously against all Jews."[60]

But even granting that Suetonius's reference may be garbled, one central question yet remains: How extensive in its application was Claudius's order of Jewish expulsion from Rome? Suetonius's statement may be read as either the expulsion of the entire Jewish population or the expulsion of only those Jews who were disruptive. Luke in Acts 18:2 says that Claudius expelled "all the Jews from Rome" (πάντας τοὺς Ἰουδαίους ἀπὸ τῆς Ῥώμης). Josephus, however, does not say anything about Jews being expelled by Claudius. Likewise, the Roman historian Dio Cassius, writing sometime in the early third century, does not refer to Jews having been expelled from Rome during the reign of Claudius, though he does report that during the second year of Claudius's reign (i.e., in A.D. 41, as noted above) they lost their right of free assembly in the city.[61]

It may be that Suetonius's statement should be understood as having in mind only those Jews whom Rome viewed as agitators, troublemakers, or disturbers of *Pax Romana* — whether those arguing for belief in Jesus of Nazareth as Israel's Messiah or those defending traditional Judaism, or both — and who were expelled by the Edict of Claudius in A.D. 49. This may still have constituted a sizable number, for Rome was not always too discriminating in its judgments. But it need not necessarily be understood as the entire Jewish population of the city. Further, it may be that Luke was somewhat hyperbolic in his statement in Acts 18:2. Or, perhaps, his words should be read as meaning "all the Jews who were believers in Christ," and so we should understand that only the Jewish Christian agitators were expelled.[62] Or it may be, indeed, that all of the Jews — with the exception, probably, of those who were Roman citizens — were expelled, thereby paralleling the expulsion of Jews from Rome by Tiberius Caesar in the year A.D. 19, and that Josephus refrained from recounting this event out of deference to his Roman audience.

We may never know exactly how extensive the intent and effects of Claudius's edict were. All that can be said is that (1) minimally viewed the

---

60. W. Wiefel, "Jewish Community," in Donfried, ed., *Romans Debate* (1977), 109; (1991), 93.

61. Dio Cassius, *Historia Romana* 60.6.6.

62. So, e.g., E. M. Smallwood, "Jews in Rome under the Julio-Claudians," 16.

Edict of Claudius served to expel the Jewish agitators, who in Rome's eyes may have numbered quite a few, and to continue to deny the remaining Jews free assembly in their synagogues, but (2) maximally understood it ordered the expulsion of the entire Jewish population from Rome, which, of course, would also effectively terminate any lingering right of free assembly for Jews in the city. Further, we do not know how long this edict of expulsion, with its resultant ban of free assembly, was in effect. Nor do we know what transpired between the time when it began to be less rigidly applied (*de facto*) and when it was legally repealed (*de jure*). For certainly Jews were living in Rome after Claudius's death in A.D. 54, and it may be presumed that many of them were living in the city even before the repeal of the Edict when he died.

But what is more important for our purpose than definitive answers to questions about the intent, extent, or duration of Claudius's Edict is the recognition that with first the emperor's order of A.D. 41, which restricted free assembly to the Roman Jews, and then his edict of A.D. 49, which expelled "all," or at least a great number of, Jews from the city, there came about the termination of free assembly for Jews at Rome. And this meant for the Christians of Rome after the order of A.D. 41 and the Edict of A.D. 49 that they could no longer function and be protected within the synagogues of Judaism — whether after the emperor's decree of A.D. 49 they were then all Gentiles (because all the Jews had been expelled) or part Jews and part Gentiles (because only the agitators had been expelled). Henceforth, those who pledged their allegiance to Jesus as the Messiah/Christ had to establish their own identity and to meet in their own meeting places, such as the "house churches" or "tenement congregations" mentioned in Rom 16:5 and 23 (probably also in vv. 10, 11, 14, and 15) and referred to in 1 Cor 16:19 and Philemon 2.

4. Identity, Character, Circumstances, and Concerns of Paul's Addressees

The crucial questions for an understanding of Paul's letter to the Christians at Rome, however, have to do with the identity, character, circumstances, and concerns of the apostle's addressees. Were they ethnically Jews or Gentiles, or were the Christian congregations at Rome comprised of both — and, if so, in what proportions? How did they think theologically? What were their civic and social circumstances in the city? And what concerns did they have about themselves as believers in Jesus and about their relationship to Paul "the apostle to the Gentiles" and his mission to Gentiles in the Roman empire?

Jewish Christians or Gentile Christians?

In the first half of the nineteenth century, Ferdinand Christian Baur, guided by his Hegelian views, read Romans as a letter of Paul that was directed against the Petrine party of early Christians. For him the true center of that letter is to be found in chapters 9–11, where Paul sets out his own vision of how the gospel proclamation relates to God's special choice of Israel — which is a discussion, he insisted, that would have been of pertinence only to Jewish believers in Jesus.[63] But Baur's dialectical understanding of the course of early church history, though once applauded by many, is today relegated to the intellectual dustbin of promising but lost causes.

Yet while many of Baur's arguments for identifying the addressees of Romans as early Jewish believers in Jesus have been generally discounted, a number of other features in the letter have since Baur's day been cited in support of such a view. Prominent among these more "Jewish" considerations are the following: (1) Paul's obvious interest in the spiritual welfare of his Jewish compatriots, as expressed particularly in 1:16b; 9:1-5; 10:1-3; and 11:13-36; (2) his conciliatory tone and tempered expressions when speaking about the Jews; (3) his appeal to Abraham in chapter 4 as the example of faith *par excellence,* even calling him "our father" in the first verse of that passage; (4) his express statement "I am speaking to those who know the law" in 7:1; (5) his repeated references to such essentially Jewish themes as the righteousness of God, the validity of the Mosaic law, the nature of redemption, and the election of Israel; (6) his distinctly Jewish manner of argumentation in developing his themes; (7) his extensive use of Scripture in support of his arguments, with over half of the biblical citations in the Pauline corpus being present in this letter; and (8) his invoking of certain Jewish rhetorical forms and patterns, paralleling in 1:18-32, for example, his use of the argument of *Wisdom of Solomon* 13–14 (though with a decidedly different thrust in 2:1-16 from that of *Wisdom of Solomon* 15:1-6) and his echoing of a remnant theology pattern of presentation in chapters 9–11 (though with decidedly different emphases). And such features, either separately or in concert, have convinced a number of scholars during the past century that the ad-

63. F. C. Baur, *Paul,* 1.313-52.

dressees of Romans must have been mainly, if not entirely, Jewish believers, for Paul would certainly not have written to Gentiles Christians in such a manner.[64]

On the other hand, a number of "Gentile" features in the letter have also been frequently highlighted, principally: (1) Paul's explicit identification of his addressees as being within the orbit of his Gentile ministry in 1:5-6, 13-15; 15:15-16); (2) his statement "I am speaking to you Gentiles" in 11:13, which clearly indicates that at least some, if not all, of those addressed were ethnically Gentiles; (3) his invoking of various Grecian rhetorical forms and patterns, as, for example, in chapter 2 (and perhaps elsewhere) where he uses a diatribe form of hellenistic argumentation; (4) his ethical appeals in 14:1–15:13 to "the strong," who seem to be Gentile Christians, asking them to express Christian love and tolerance toward "the weak," who seem to be Jewish Christians; and (5) his speaking of the Jews, "the people of Israel," as being "my brothers and sisters, those of my own race" in 9:3 and "my own people" in 11:14, thereby distinguishing his own Jewish ancestry from the Gentile ancestry of his addressees. These fairly overt statements, together with a number of more allusive indicators, have led the great majority of commentators today to hold that the addressees of Paul's letter to Rome were predominantly Gentile Christians, though with a minority of Jewish believers in Jesus also present in the various Christian congregations of the city.[65]

The Danish scholar Johannes Munck, in reaction to the claims of F. C. Baur, was certainly wrong to insist that the church at Rome was composed entirely of Gentile Christians, without any Jewish Christian component at all.[66] Even in nineteenth-century continental Europe, where Baur's opinions seemed to be taking over much of biblical scholarship, a more mediating and inclusive answer was being formed to the question "Which of these features found in Paul's letter to Rome, Jewish or Gentile, are we to think of as giving

---

64. So, e.g., E. Meyer, *Ursprung und Anfänge des Christentums* (1921), 1.431-32; J. H. Ropes, "The Epistle to the Romans and Jewish Christianity" (1928), 353-65; W. Manson, "Character of the Church at Rome" (1951), 172-84; *idem,* "Notes on the Argument of Romans" (1959), 150-64; T. Fahy, "St. Paul's Romans Were Jewish Converts" (1959), 182-91; and S. Mason, "The Gospel and the First Readers of Romans" (1994), 254-87.

65. So, e.g., W. Sanday and A. C. Headlam, *Romans* (1895[1]), xxxiii-xxxiv; (1902[5]), xxxi-xxxvi; J. Denney, *Romans* (1900), 2.561-67; M.-J. Lagrange, *Aux Romains* (1950), xxi-xxiv; W. Schmithals, *Römerbrief* (1988), 9-89; J. A. Fitzmyer, *Romans* (1993), 33-34, and D. J. Moo, *Romans* (1996), 9-13.

66. See J. Munck, *Paul and the Salvation of Mankind* (ET 1959), 196-209.

character to the church at Rome?"[67] And in Britain and North America it was the thesis of William Sanday and Arthur C. Headlam in their Romans commentary (ICC) of 1895, which in its fifth edition of 1905 was reprinted numerous times, that became definitive for most:

> The Church to which he [Paul] is writing is Gentile in its general com-
> plexion; but at the same time it contains so many born Jews that he
> passes easily and freely from the one body to the other. He does not feel
> bound to measure and weigh his words, because if he writes in the man-
> ner which comes most naturally to himself he knows that there will be in
> the Church many who will understand him.[68]

Sanday and Headlam believed that this thesis was "the natural construction to put upon the Apostle's language."[69] And that may, indeed, be true, as the majority of scholars today believe. Yet it needs to be recognized that such an identification and characterization stems almost entirely from a process of "mirror reading" — which is often quite a legitimate method when dealing with Paul's other letters, but must be recognized to be a somewhat tenuous enterprise with respect to his letter to the Christians at Rome.

On "Mirror Reading" Romans

Mirror reading an ancient letter in order to determine the identity, character, circumstances, and concerns of its addressees is always difficult. The main reason is that mirror reading works well only where there is a reasonable as-surance that one is dealing with either a polemic letter (an aggressive expli-cation that seeks to counter specific errors, whether doctrinal or ethical) or an apologetic letter (a defensive response to accusations) — that is, where one can be reasonably sure that the agenda of the letter is driven by some er-ror, some need, or some situation present among the addressees, and not just by a desire for contact or communication on the part of the author. The problem, however, is that it is not always easy to distinguish between (1) po-lemic, (2) apology, and (3) exposition, and mirror reading is only an appro-priate critical method when one is dealing with either (or both) polemic or

---

67. Cf., e.g., T. Schott, *Römerbrief* (1858); F. L. Godet, *Romans*, 2 vols. (ET 1880); and H. A. W. Meyer, *Romans*, 2 vols. (1884).

68. W. Sanday and A. C. Headlam, *Romans*, xxxiv.

69. W. Sanday and A. C. Headlam, *Romans*, xxxiv.

apology. And Paul's letter to the Christians at Rome, while forthright in its exposition, is notoriously vague when it comes to matters of polemic and apology.

We need not deny that circumstances among the Christians at Rome played a part in motivating Paul to write or that some knowledge of the situation of those who believed in Christ at Rome can be derived from Paul's letter. There is, of course, the direct reference in 16:17-19 to "those who cause divisions and put obstacles in your way," together with an explicit warning to "keep away from them" and an expressed desire for Christians to be "wise about what is good and innocent about what is evil." But that reference, warning, and desire play only a very minor role in the letter, located as they are almost parenthetically amidst its concluding greetings and closing benedictions. More important are the exhortations of 14:1–15:13 to "the strong" regarding their attitudes toward "the weak," which may profitably be "mirror read" for an understanding of the circumstances among believers at Rome at the time (see Chapter V, "Purpose"). Perhaps also the statements on paying taxes in 13:6-7 may be "mirror read" (see again Chapter V, "Purpose"). But in view of the lack of conviction among commentators — even, in fact, something of a "dead end," which seems to result when all of Romans is subjected to a close "mirror reading" in order to determine the identity, character, circumstances, and concerns of the letter's addressees (with data derived from external sources only later brought into consideration in order to supplement conclusions that have been reached by such an internal process) — it is probably better to start the other way around. And that is what we intend to do in what follows.

External Data regarding Jews at Rome

Beginning then with data drawn from materials external to the NT, three matters with respect to the Jews in first-century Rome seem to be particularly important for any treatment of the identity, character, circumstances, and concerns of Paul's addressees: (1) the decentralized situation, both socially and administratively, of the Jewish population at Rome; (2) their primary dependence on Palestinian Jewry religiously; and (3) their continued existence in Rome after Claudius's edict of expulsion ethnically. With regard to the first two of these matters, there can be little doubt that the decentralized situation of the Jews at Rome and their close ties with Palestinian Jewry had an impact on the character of the Christianity that first arose within the city's various synagogues. So it may be postulated that with the cradle of Roman Christianity being that of Roman Jewry, the first groups of believers in Jesus at Rome, though in fellowship with one another, probably also did not develop any central governing agency but rather looked primarily to the Jerusalem church for spiritual direction.

And with regard to the third of the above matters, that is, the continued existence of Jews at Rome after the Edict of A.D. 49, it probably also may be postulated that Claudius's order of expulsion was directed primarily against those Jews, Jewish believers in Jesus, and Gentile "God-fearers" — all of whom were seen by Roman authorities as associated with the Jewish synagogues, and so considered "Jews" — who were disturbing the *Pax Romana* in the city, whether by proclaiming Jesus of Nazareth as the Jewish Messiah (i.e., "the Christ") or by, conversely, defending traditional Judaism. The number of Jews expelled from Rome at that time may have been fairly substantial, for Rome was not overly discriminating in its evaluation of issues and persons involved in a civil disturbance. But judging by the silences of the Jewish historian Josephus and the Roman historian Dio Cassius regarding the expulsion of an entire Jewish populace — particularly when both Josephus and Dio Cassius had earlier reported how in A.D. 19 Tiberius had "ordered the whole Jewish community to leave Rome"[70] — it seems likely that many Jews continued to live in Rome even during the latter years of Claudius's reign.

Undoubtedly the life of Jews in Rome after Claudius's edict was severely restricted, particularly with the loss of their right to free assembly in their synagogue groupings. But we need not insist that a Jewish component was no longer part of the Christian presence at Rome. Likewise, it may be posited that Jewish believers in Jesus continued to live in the city and had some influence within the developing Roman church, whatever is postulated regarding their numbers compared to those of Gentile believers within the Roman Christian community.

External Data regarding Christians at Rome

Going further with regard to data drawn from materials external to the NT, the following matters need to be highlighted with regard to the origin and development of Christianity at Rome, with these matters being of impor-

---

70. Josephus, *Antiq* 18.82; Dio Cassius, *Historia Romana* 57.18.5a.

tance when attempting to determine the identity, character, circumstances, and concerns of the addressees of Paul's letter to Rome: (1) that the gospel entered the city in some manner by way of Jewish believers in Jesus as Israel's Messiah, (2) that the nucleus of the earliest Christian community was made up of Jewish believers in Jesus, (3) that through the witness of these Jewish believers, Gentiles also heard the message of the gospel and became Christians, (4) that Christianity at Rome had a distinctly Jewish character, whether as practiced and proclaimed by the Jewish believers themselves or as accepted by Gentiles, and (5) that connections between Roman Christianity and the Jerusalem church were particularly strong, not only among the earliest Jewish believers in Jesus but also among all of the Christians at Rome, whatever their ethnicity, even after the time of Claudius's death. As noted above, Ambrosiaster gives testimony to the first four of these features. And the Roman historian Tacitus, in writing in the second century about Nero's attempts to diffuse the suspicion that he had started the great fire of 64 at Rome, makes explicit the connection between Christianity at Rome and Christianity in Judea when he says:

> To suppress this rumor, Nero created scapegoats. He punished with every refinement of cruelty the notoriously depraved group who were popularly called Christians. The originator of the group, Christ, had been executed in the reign of Tiberius by the procurator, Pontius Pilate. But in spite of this temporary setback, this pernicious superstition had broken out again, not only in Judea (where the mischief had originated) but even in the capital city [i.e., Rome] where all degraded and shameful practices collect and become the vogue.[71]

To be noted in Tacitus's statement is the fact that the Christians at Rome were seen — after Claudius's Edict of A.D. 49, during Nero's emperorship of A.D. 54-68, and by Tacitus in the early second century — to be directly related to an event (i.e., the execution of Christ) and a movement (i.e., the activities of the Jerusalem church), both of which were located in Judea.

The Question of Theological Orientation

The question to be asked regarding the identity, character, circumstances, and concerns of those who believed in Jesus as Israel's Messiah/Christ in the

---

71. Tacitus, *Annals* 15.44.

city of Rome at the time when Paul wrote them is not, "Were they either Jewish or Gentiles ethnically, or dominantly one or the other?" — with the implications being that, if Jewish, they should be viewed as non-Pauline in their outlook, but if Gentile, then compatible with Paul's teaching. Raymond Brown conceded that probably the addressees of Romans constituted both Jewish and Gentile believers in Christ. Further, he argued that Gentile believers were undoubtedly in the majority, for Paul considered the church at Rome to be within the orbit of his Gentile ministry. But rather than trying to determine the addressees' character on the basis of ethnic origin, "the crucial issue," Brown argued, "is the theological outlook of this mixed Jewish/Gentile Christianity."[72] For if we take seriously the testimonies of the Christian writer Ambrosiaster and the pagan historian Tacitus, we should lay emphasis on the axis that runs from Roman Christianity back to the Jerusalem church in Judea as being of primary importance.

The stance often taken in working from ethnic origin to theological tendency has been well stated, for example, by Frédéric Godet over a century ago:

> The result of our study is, that the Roman church was mostly of Gentile origin and Pauline tendency, even before the apostle addressed our letter to it. The formation of the church was indirectly traceable to him, because its authors proceeded for the most part from the churches of the East, whose existence was due to his apostolic labours. Besides, the recruiting of the church having taken place chiefly in the midst of the Roman, that is to say, Gentile population, Paul was entitled to regard it as belonging to the domain of the apostle of the Gentile.[73]

But as Raymond Brown has pointed out:

> According to Acts, for the first two Christian decades, Jerusalem and Antioch served as the dissemination points of the Gospel. Because of his interest in Paul, the author keeps us well informed of missions to the West moving out from Antioch, but there is never a suggestion that a mission went from Antioch to Rome. (Indeed, in the first 15 chapters of Acts the only mention of Rome/Roman is 2:10 which notes the presence of Roman Jews at Jerusalem on the first Pentecost.) There are no arguments from Acts for a site other than Jerusalem as the source for Roman

72. R. E. Brown, *Antioch and Rome*, 109, note 227.
73. F. Godet, *Romans*, 1.74-75.

Christianity, and Acts 28:21 relates that Jews in Rome had channels of theological information coming from Jerusalem.[74]

So Brown concluded: (1) that for both Jews and Christians "the Jerusalem-Rome axis was strong," (2) "that Roman Christianity came from Jerusalem, and indeed represented the Jewish/Gentile Christianity associated with such Jerusalem figures as Peter and James," and (3) that both in the earliest days of the Roman church and at the time when Paul wrote them, believers at Rome could be characterized as "Christians who kept up some Jewish observances and remained faithful to part of the heritage of the Jewish Law and cult, without insisting on circumcision."[75] Or as Joseph Fitzmyer has described the character and concerns of Paul's addressees at Rome (citing Brown's article in *Antioch and Rome* in support): "Roman Christians seem to have been in continual contact with the Christians of Jerusalem";[76] further, their form of the Christian faith "seems to have been influenced especially by those associated with Peter and James of Jerusalem, in other words, by Christians who retained some Jewish observances and remained faithful to the Jewish legal and cultic heritage without insisting on circumcision for Gentile converts."[77]

It is this understanding of Paul's Roman addressees that will be explicated in what follows, arguing that (1) as for their ethnic identity, the Christians at Rome constituted both Gentile and Jewish believers in Jesus, but (2) as for their religious character and concerns, they considered themselves closely tied to the Jerusalem church and they thought and expressed themselves in ways congenial to Jewish Christianity. Gentile believers in Jesus were probably far more prominent than Jewish believers in the Christian congregations of Rome — with, perhaps, some of them having been former proselytes to Judaism or Jewish "God-fearers," though probably most of them had been converted to Christ directly from paganism. With respect to their theological thought and expression, however, it is likely that all of those at Rome who professed to be followers of Jesus — Gentile believers as well as Jewish believers in Jesus — generally (1) looked to the Jerusalem church as the Mother Church of Christendom, (2) thought and expressed their Christian convictions along the lines of Jewish Christianity, (3) had a high respect for the Mosaic law, and (4) followed certain Jewish Christian liturgical rites and ethical practices. They were not, however, "Judaizers" like those who in-

74. R. E. Brown, *Antioch and Rome,* 103-4.
75. R. E. Brown, *Antioch and Rome,* 104.
76. J. A. Fitzmyer, *Romans,* 33.
77. J. A. Fitzmyer, *Romans,* 33.

filtrated the churches of Galatia with what Paul called "a different gospel, which is no gospel at all" (Gal 1:6-7). Rather, they were considered by Paul to have been true Christians — though, as Charles Talbert has aptly characterized their position, they were followers of Jesus "who thought in Jewish categories."[78]

The Social Situation of Christians at Rome

At some time in their early experience, believers in Jesus at Rome — whether ethnically Jews or Gentiles — came to a time when they could no longer meet in the Jewish synagogues of the city, for Claudius's prohibition of free assembly had affected not only Jews but also everyone who in some manner was associated with the Jews. Further, the earliest Christians at Rome seem to have been without any overarching administrative agency, in common with the situation of the Jews generally at Rome. So they met in "house churches," that is, in the homes or tenement apartments of the more wealthy Christian believers in the city, with these various house church congregations being in fellowship with one another but not organizationally connected.

Studies of Roman cities and housing conditions within them — particularly of living conditions within the city of Rome in Paul's day — have highlighted the fact that while the wealthy lived very well in their own homes and villas, about 90 to 95 percent of Rome's free population lived in large apartment complexes of four or five stories in height *(insulae)*, which had shops on the ground floor, tenement apartments of varying sizes immediately above the shops, and as many small rooms as could be squeezed into the upper two or three floors — with most of these small upper-story cubicles having no windows, and therefore being without any natural light or ventilation.[79] Overcrowding and squalor were common, particularly in the small upper-floor living spaces that were rented out to the poor.

It is such a situation — that is, of a few prosperous believers in Jesus living in separate homes, but most living in tenement apartments *(cenaculae)* or dingy little upper-storied rooms — that we should keep in mind when attempting to reconstruct the lives of the early Christians at

78. C. H. Talbert, *Romans*, 16.

79. Cf. Z. Yavetz, "Living Conditions of the Urban Plebs in Republican Rome" (1969); J. E. Packer, *The Insulae of Imperial Ostia* (1971); A. G. McKay, *Houses, Villas and Palaces in the Roman World* (1975); B. W. Frier, *Landlords and Tenants in Imperial Rome* (1980); J. E. Stambaugh, *The Ancient Roman City* (1988); J. R. Clarke, *Houses of Roman Italy* (1991).

Rome. Further, it is in such circumstances that we should view the meetings of the Christians at Rome in Paul's day. For probably the Christians at Rome met together for corporate worship, teaching, and fellowship in rather small groups or congregations, whether in some Christian patron's home, some Christian family's tenement apartment, or some Christian person's small room or cubicle — particularly after Rome's prohibition of free assembly for Jews, as well as for all of those who were considered to have any past or present Jewish affiliation.

In an early and seminal study of Christian "house churches" in apostolic times, Floyd Filson enunciated the following five theses with respect to early Christian ecclesiology, generally, and the phenomenon of the house church, in particular:

1. while Christian worship was indebted to Jewish practices, the house church made possible "a distinctly Christian worship and fellowship from the very first days of the apostolic age";
2. the recognition of such house churches makes intelligible "the great attention paid to family life in the letters of Paul and in other Christian writings";
3. the "existence of several house churches in one city goes far to explain the tendency to party strife in the apostolic age";
4. "a study of the house church situation also throws light upon the social status of early Christians"; and,
5. "the development of church polity can never be understood without reference to the house Churches."[80]

And this understanding of early Christian communal meetings and association has been further explicated by many today.[81]

---

80. F. V. Filson, "Significance of the Early House Churches" (1939), 109-12.

81. See esp. H.-J. Klauck, *Hausgemeinde und Hauskirche im frühren Christentum* (1981); J. Gnilka, "Die neutestamentliche Hausgemeinde" (1983); A. J. Malherbe, "House Churches and Their Problems" (1983); R. Brändle and E. W. Stegemann, "Formation of the First 'Christian Congregation' in Rome" (1998); V. P. Branick, *House Church in the Writings of Paul* (1989); and on a more popular level J. M. Petersen, "House Churches in Rome" (1969) and R. Banks, *Paul's Idea of Community* (1994²). Cf. also many of the articles on early Christian "community formation" or "church order" in R. N. Longenecker, ed., *Community Formation in the Early Church and in the Church Today* (2002).

SUPPLEMENTAL BIBLIOGRAPHY

See also "Bibliography of Selected Commentaries." All references in the footnotes to works included in this list are by the authors' names and abbreviated titles.

Balsdon, J. P. V. D. *Romans and Aliens.* Chapel Hill: University of North Carolina, 1979.

Banks, Robert. *Paul's Idea of Community: The Early House Churches in Their Cultural Setting.* Peabody: Hendrickson, 1994².

Barnard, L. W. "The Early Roman Church, Judaism, and Jewish-Christianity," *ATR* 49 (1967) 371-84.

Baur, Ferdinand Christian. "Über Zweck und Veranlassung des Römerbriefs und der damit zusammenhangenden Verhältnisse der römischen Gemeinde," *TZT* (1836) 59-178.

————. *Paul, the Apostle of Jesus Christ: His Life and Work, His Epistles and His Doctrine,* 2 vols., trans. E. Zeller. Edinburgh: University of Edinburgh Press, 1846; London: Williams and Norgate, 1876, 1.105-45, 250-57.

Benko, Stephen. "The Edict of Claudius of A.D. 49 and the Instigator Chrestus," *TZ* 25 (1969) 407-18.

Brändle, Rudolf, and Ekkehard W. Stegemann. "The Formation of the First 'Christian Congregation' in Rome in the Context of the Jewish Congregations," in *Judaism and Christianity in First-Century Rome,* ed. K. P. Donfried and P. Richardson. Grand Rapids: Eerdmans, 1998, 117-27.

Branick, Vincent P. *The House Church in the Writings of Paul.* Wilmington: Michael Glazier, 1989.

Brown, Raymond E. "Not Jewish Christianity and Gentile Christianity, but Types of Jewish/Gentile Christianity," *CBQ* 45 (1983) 74-79.

————. "The Beginnings of Christianity at Rome" and "The Roman Church near the End of the First Christian Generation (A.D. 58 — Paul to the Romans)," in R. E. Brown and J. P. Meier, *Antioch and Rome: New Testament Cradles of Catholic Christianity.* New York: Paulist, 1983, 92-127.

————. "Further Reflections on the Origins of the Church of Rome," in *The Conversation Continues: Studies in Paul and John in Honor of J. L. Martyn,* ed. R. T. Fortna and B. R. Gaventa. Nashville: Abingdon, 1990, 98-115.

————. *An Introduction to the New Testament.* New York: Doubleday, 1997, 560-63.

Bruce, F. F. "Christianity under Claudius," *BJRL* 44 (1962) 309-26.

————. "St. Paul in Rome," *BJRL* 46 (1964) 326-45.

————. *New Testament History.* New York: Doubleday, 1972, 295-99, 393-97.

Caragounis, Chrys C. "From Obscurity to Prominence: The Development of the Roman Church between Romans and 1 *Clement,*" in *Judaism and Christianity in First-Century Rome,* ed. K. P. Donfried and P. Richardson. Grand Rapids: Eerdmans, 1998, 245-79.

Chadwick, Henry. "St. Peter and St. Paul in Rome: the Problem of the *Memoria Apostolorum ad Catacumbas*," *JTS* 8 (1957) 30-52.

Clarke, John R. *The Houses of Roman Italy, 100 B.C.–A.D. 250: Ritual, Space, and Decoration.* Berkeley: University of California Press, 1991.

Collins, John J. *Between Athens and Jerusalem: Jewish Identity in the Hellenistic Diaspora.* New York: Crossroad, 1983, 162-68.

Craffert, Pieter F. "The Pauline Household Communities: Their Nature as Social Entities," *Neot* 32 (1998) 309-41.

Donfried, Karl P., and Peter Richardson, eds. *Judaism and Christianity in First-Century Rome.* Grand Rapids: Eerdmans, 1998.

Fahy, Thomas. "St. Paul's Romans Were Jewish Converts," *ITQ* 26 (1959) 182-91.

Filson, Floyd V. "The Significance of the Early House Churches," *JBL* 58 (1939) 105-12.

Frey, J. B. "Les Communautés juives à Rome aux premiers temps de l'Église," *RSR* 20 (1930) 269-97.

———. "Le Judaïsme à Rome aux premiers temps de l'Église," *Bib* 12 (1931) 129-56.

———, ed. *Corpus Inscriptionum Judaicarum,* 2 vols. Rome: Pontificio Instituto de Archeologia Cristiana, 1936, 1952.

Frier, Bruce W. *Landlords and Tenants in Imperial Rome.* Princeton: Princeton University Press, 1980.

Gaston, Lloyd. "Reading the Text and Digging the Past: The First Audience of Romans," in *Text and Artifact in the Religions of Mediterranean Antiquity,* Essays in Honour of Peter Richardson, ed. S. G. Wilson and M. Desjardins. Waterloo: Wilfrid Laurier University Press, 2000, 35-44.

Gnilka, J. "Die neutestamentliche Hausgemeinde," in *Freude am Gottesdienst: Aspekte ursprünglicher Liturgie. Festschrift für Weihbischof Dr. J. Plöger,* ed. J. Schreiner. Stuttgart: Bibelwerk, 1983, 229-42.

Horst, P. W. van der. *Ancient Jewish Epitaphs: An Introductory Survey of a Millennium of Jewish Funerary Epigraphy* (300 BCE–700 CE). Kampen: Kok-Pharos, 1991, 85-101.

Howard, George E. "The Beginning of Christianity in Rome: A Note on Suetonius, *Life of Claudius* XXV,4," *ResQ* 24 (1981) 175-77.

Jeffers, James S. *Conflict at Rome: Social Order and Hierarchy in Early Christianity.* Minneapolis: Fortress, 1991.

———. "Jewish and Christian Families in First-Century Rome," in *Judaism and Christianity in First-Century Rome,* ed. K. P. Donfried and P. Richardson. Grand Rapids: Eerdmans, 1998, 128-50.

Johnson, Sherman E. "Jews and Christians in Rome," *LexTQ* 17 (1982) 51-58.

Judge, Edwin A., and G. S. R. Thomas. "The Origin of the Church at Rome: A New Solution?" *RTR* 25 (1966) 81-94.

Klauck, Hans-Josef. *Hausgemeinde und Hauskirche im frühen Christentum.* SBS 103. Stuttgart: Katholisches Bibelwerk, 1981.

————. *Gemeinde zwischen Haus und Stadt: Kirche bei Paulus.* Freiburg, Basel, Vienna: Herder, 1992.

Lake, Kirsopp. *The Earlier Epistles of St. Paul: Their Motive and Origin.* London: Rivingtons, 1927², 370-79, 411-13.

Lampe, Peter. *Die stadtrömischen Christen in den ersten beiden Jahrhunderten.* WUNT 2.18. Tübingen: Mohr-Siebeck, 1987, 1989².

————. "The Roman Christians of Romans 16," in *The Romans Debate,* revised and expanded edition, ed. K. P. Donfried. Peabody: Hendrickson, 1991, 216-30.

Lane, E. N. "Sabazius and the Jews in Valerius Maximus: A Re-examination," *JRS* 69 (1979) 35-38.

Lane, William L. "Social Perspectives on Roman Christianity during the Formative Years from Nero to Nerva: Romans, Hebrews, 1 Clement," in *Judaism and Christianity in First-Century Rome,* ed. K. P. Donfried and P. Richardson. Grand Rapids: Eerdmans, 1998, 196-244.

La Piana, George. "La primitiva communità cristiana di Roma e l'epistola ai Romani," *RBR* 1 (1925) 209-26 and 305-26.

————. "Foreign Groups in Rome During the First Centuries of the Empire," *HTR* 20 (1927) 183-403.

Leon, Harry J. "The Language of the Greek Inscriptions of the Jewish Catacombs of Rome," *TPAPA* 58 (1927) 210-33.

————. "The Names of the Jews of Ancient Rome," *TPAPA* 59 (1928) 205-24.

————. "The Synagogue of the Herodians," *JAOS* 49 (1929) 318-22.

————. *The Jews of Ancient Rome.* Philadelphia: Jewish Publication Society of America, 1960, 1980; Peabody: Hendrickson, 1995.

————. "The Jews of Rome in the First Century of Christianity," in *The Teacher's Yoke: In Memory of Henry Trantham.* Waco: Baylor University Press, 1964.

Levine, Lee I. *The Ancient Synagogue: The First Thousand Years.* New Haven: Yale University Press, 2000.

Lichtenberger, Hermann. "Jews and Christians in Rome in the Time of Nero: Josephus and Paul in Rome," in ANRW 2.26.3, ed. W. Haase and H. Temporini. New York: de Gruyter, 1996, 2142-76.

Longenecker, Richard N., ed. *Community Formation in the Early Church and in the Church Today.* Peabody: Hendrickson, 2002.

Lorenzen, Thorwald. "Das christliche Hauskirche," *TZ* 43 (1987) 33-52.

Lüdemann, Gerd. *Paul, Apostle to the Gentiles: Studies in Chronology,* trans. F. S. Jones. Philadelphia: Fortress, 1984, 6-7, 165-71.

Mackinnon, A. G. *The Rome of Saint Paul.* London: Religious Tract Society, 1930.

————. *The Rome of the Early Church.* London: Religious Tract Society, 1933.

Malherbe, Abraham J. "House Churches and Their Problems," in *Social Aspects of Early Christianity.* Philadelphia: Fortress, 1983, 60-91.

Manson, William. "Character of the Church at Rome: St. Paul's Epistle to the Romans," in *The Epistle to the Hebrews: An Historical and Theological Reconsideration.* The Baird Lecture, 1949. London: Hodder and Stoughton, 1951, 172-84.

―――. "Notes on the Argument of Romans (Chapters 1-8)," in *New Testament Essays: Studies in Memory of Thomas Walter Manson,* ed. A. J. B. Higgins. Manchester: Manchester University Press, 1959, 150-64.

Marcus, Joel. "The Circumcision and the Uncircumcision in Rome," *NTS* 35 (1989) 67-81.

Mason, Steve. "'For I Am Not Ashamed of the Gospel' (Rom. 1.16): The Gospel and the First Readers of Romans," in *Gospel in Paul: Studies on Corinthians, Galatians and Romans for Richard N. Longenecker,* ed. L. A. Jervis and P. Richardson. Sheffield: Sheffield Academic Press, 1994, 254-87.

McKay, A. G. *Houses, Villas and Palaces in the Roman World.* Ithaca: Cornell University Press, 1975.

Merrill, Elmer T. "The Expulsion of Jews from Rome under Tiberius," *CP* 14 (1919) 275-93.

Meyer, Eduard. *Ursprung und Anfänge des Christentums,* 3 vols. Stuttgart-Berlin: Cotta, 1921-23.

Miller, R. H. "Life Situations in the Roman Church as Reflected in Paul's Letters," *RevExp* 32 (1935) 170-80.

Moehring, H. "The Persecution of the Jews and the Adherents of the Isis Cult at Rome AD 19," *NovT* 3 (1959) 293-304.

Momigliano, Arnaldo. *Claudius: The Emperor and His Achievement,* trans. W. D. Hogarth. Oxford: Clarendon, 1934; repr. New York: Barnes & Noble, 1961.

Munck, Johannes. "The Manifesto of Faith: Comments on Romans," in *Paul and the Salvation of Mankind,* trans. F. Clarke. London: SCM; Richmond: John Knox, 1959, 196-209.

Orosius, Paulus. "*Historiarum adversum Paganos Libri VII*: Dating the Claudian Expulsions of the Jews," *JQR* 83 (1992) 127-44.

Packer, James E. *The Insulae of Imperial Ostia.* Rome: American Academy in Rome, 1971.

Penna, Romano. "Les Juifs à Rome au temps de l'Apôtre Paul," *NTS* 28 (1982) 321-47.

Petersen, Joan M. "House Churches in Rome," *VC* 23 (1969) 264-72.

Rajak, Tessa. "Was There a Roman Charter for the Jews?" *JRS* 74 (1984) 107-23.

―――. "Inscription and Context: Reading the Jewish Catacombs of Rome," in *Studies in Early Jewish Epigraphy,* ed. J. W. van Henten and P. W. van der Horst. Leiden: Brill, 1994, 226-41.

Rengstorf, Karl H. "Paulus und die älteste römische Christenheit," *Studia Evangelica* 2. TU 87. Berlin, 1964, 447-64.

Richardson, Peter. "Early Synagogues as Collegia in the Diaspora and Palestine," in *Voluntary Associations in the Ancient World,* ed. J. S. Kloppenborg and S. G. Wilson. London: Routledge, 1996, 90-109.

―――. "Augustan-Era Synagogues in Rome," in *Judaism and Christianity in First-*

Century Rome, ed. K. P. Donfried and P. Richardson. Grand Rapids: Eerdmans, 1998, 17-29.

Romanelli, Pietro. "The Jewish Quarters in Ancient Rome," *Quarterly Statement: Palestine Exploration Fund* (1914) 134-40.

Ropes, James H. "The Epistle to the Romans and Jewish Christianity," in *Studies in Early Christianity,* ed. S. J. Case. New York: Century, 1928, 353-65.

Roth, Cecil. *The History of the Jews of Italy.* Philadelphia: Jewish Publication Society of America, 1946.

Rutgers, Leonard V. *The Jews in Late Ancient Rome: Evidence of Cultural Interaction in the Roman Diaspora.* RGRW 126. Leiden: Brill, 1995.

————. "Roman Policy toward the Jews: Expulsions from the City of Rome during the First Century C.E.," in *Judaism and Christianity in First-Century Rome,* ed. K. P. Donfried and P. Richardson. Grand Rapids: Eerdmans, 1998, 93-116.

————. *The Hidden Heritage of Diaspora Judaism.* Leuven: Peeters, 1998.

Schelkle, Karl-Hermann. "Römische Kirche im Römerbrief. Zur Geschichte und Auslegungsgeschichte," *ZKT* 81 (1959) 393-404.

Schmidt, Karl. *Die Anfänge des Christentums in der Stadt Rom.* Heidelberg: Winter's Universität, 1879.

Schöllgen, G. "Probleme der frühchristlichen Sozialgeschichte: Einwände gegen Peter Lampes Buch über *Die stadtrömischen Christen in den ersten beiden Jahrhunderten,*" *JAC* 32 (1989) 23-40.

Schürer, Emil. *The History of the Jewish People in the Age of Jesus Christ (175 B.C.–A.D. 135),* 4 vols., rev. and ed. G. Vermes, F. Millar, and M. Goodman. Edinburgh: T&T Clark, 1973.

Scramuzza, V. M. *The Emperor Claudius.* Cambridge, MA: Harvard University Press, 1940.

Sherwin-White, Adrian N. *Racial Prejudice in Imperial Rome.* J. H. Gray Lectures, 1966. Cambridge: Cambridge University Press, 1967.

Simon, Marcel. "Les Juifs de Rome au debut de l'ère Chrétienne," *Bible et Terre Sante* 94 (1967) 9-15.

Slingerland, H. Dixon. "Chrestus: Christus?" in *New Perspectives on Ancient Judaism,* vol. 4: *The Literature of Early Rabbinic Judaism,* ed. A. J. Avery-Peck. Lanham: University Press of America, 1989, 133-44.

————. "Suetonius *Claudius* 25.4 and the Account in Cassius Dio," *JQR* 79 (1989) 305-22.

Smallwood, E. Mary. "The Jews in Rome under the Julio-Claudians," in *The Jews under Roman Rule: From Pompey to Diocletian.* SJLA 20. Leiden: Brill, 1976, 201-19.

Snyder, Graydon F. "The Interaction of Jews with Non-Jews in Rome," in *Judaism and Christianity in First-Century Rome,* ed. K. P. Donfried and P. Richardson. Grand Rapids: Eerdmans, 1998, 69-90.

Stambaugh, John E. *The Ancient Roman City.* Baltimore: Johns Hopkins University Press, 1988.

Styger, Paul. *Juden und Christen im alten Rom.* Berlin: Kunstwissenschaft, 1934.

Thomas, G. S. R. "The Origins of the Church at Rome: A New Solution?" *RTR* 25 (1966) 81-94.

Vogelstein, Hermann. "The Jews in Ancient Rome," in *Rome,* book 1, trans. M. Hadas. Philadelphia: Jewish Publication Society of America, 1941.

Vogler, W. "Die Bedeutung der urchristlichen Hausgemeinden für die Ausbreitung der Evangeliums," *TLZ* 107 (1982) 785-94.

Walters, James C. *Ethnic Issues in Paul's Letter to the Romans.* Valley Forge: Trinity Press International, 1993.

————. "Romans, Jews, and Christians: The Impact of the Romans on Jewish/Christian Relations in First-Century Rome," in *Judaism and Christianity in First-Century Rome,* ed. K. P. Donfried and P. Richardson. Grand Rapids: Eerdmans, 1998, 175-95.

Watson, Francis. "The Two Roman Congregations: Romans 14:1–15:13," in *The Romans Debate,* revised and expanded edition, ed. K. P. Donfried. Peabody: Hendrickson, 1991, 203-15.

Wedderburn, Alexander J. M. *The Reasons for Romans.* Edinburgh: T&T Clark, 1988; Minneapolis: Fortress, 1991, 44-65.

White, L. Michael. "Synagogue and Society in Imperial Ostia: Archaeological and Epigraphic Evidence," in *Judaism and Christianity in First-Century Rome,* ed. K. P. Donfried and P. Richardson. Grand Rapids: Eerdmans, 1998, 30-68.

Wiefel, Wolfgang. "The Jewish Community in Ancient Rome and the Origins of Roman Christianity," in *The Romans Debate,* ed. Karl P. Donfried. Minneapolis: Augsburg, 1977, 100-119; *The Romans Debate,* revised and expanded edition, Peabody: Hendrickson, 1991, 85-101 (trans. of "Die jüdische Gemeinschaft im antiken Rom und die Anfänge des römischen Christentums. Bemerkungen zu Anlass und Zweck des Römerbriefs," *Jud* 26 [1970] 65-88).

Williams, Margaret H. "The Expulsion of the Jews from Rome in A.D. 19," *Latomus* 48 (1989) 765-84.

————. *The Jews Among the Greeks and Romans: A Diasporan Sourcebook.* London: Duckworth, 1998.

Yavetz, Z. "Living Conditions of the Urban Plebs in Republican Rome," in *The Crises in the Roman Republic: Studies in Political and Social History.* London: Heffer, 1969, 500-517.

CHAPTER V

Purpose

The determination of Paul's purpose or purposes for writing Romans, that is, what his principal concerns were when writing and what he wanted to accomplish by writing, has been a perennial problem during the past two centuries. In his *Prolegomena to St. Paul's Epistles to the Romans and the Ephesians,* which was published posthumously in 1895, Fenton J. A. Hort observed: "That the problem is not very simple may be reasonably inferred from the extraordinary variety of opinion which has prevailed and still prevails about it."[1] In 1974 Karl Donfried pointed out: "Current research concerning the purpose of Romans is in a state of confusion. Almost every recent article or monograph on the subject proposes a different solution."[2] And that sentiment is echoed by many scholars today, as witness, for example, Alexander Wedderburn's opening remarks in his 1988 monograph on the subject: "Why Paul wrote Romans is still something of an enigma. There is as yet no consensus as to why Paul should write precisely this letter with these contents to this church at this moment in his, and its, history."[3]

Two opposing viewpoints have dominated all past discussions: (1) that Paul's purpose or purposes for writing must be seen as having originated principally from within his own consciousness and ministry — whether to introduce himself to an unknown audience, to seek support for a forthcoming mission to the western part of the Roman empire, to defend himself

---

1. F. J. A. Hort, *Prolegomena,* 5.
2. K. P. Donfried, "False Presuppositions," *CBQ* 36 (1974) 332; repr. in *Romans Debate* (1977), 120; (1991), 102.
3. A. J. M. Wedderburn, *Reasons for Romans,* 1.

against criticism and misrepresentation, to assert his apostolic authority over a church he considered within the orbit of his Gentile ministry, or to set out his own understanding of the Christian gospel as something of a summary of his message or a "last will and testament"; or, (2) that the letter was written primarily to counter some particular problem or set of problems, or some identifiable circumstance or set of circumstances, that existed among the Christians at Rome — whether doctrinal or ethical; whether arising from outside the church or from within. To frame these approaches somewhat differently, it may be asked: Was Paul's purpose in writing Romans *missionary* in nature, being motivated by his own consciousness as an apostle to the Gentiles, his own sense of mission, and/or his own desire to present to Christians at Rome a summation or testament of his message throughout the Greco-Roman world — perhaps incorporating into that tractate or letter some of the issues that had previously arisen in his ministry and that he wanted to present to believers at Rome for his own reasons? Or, was his purpose *pastoral,* being motivated by a desire to correct problems, whether doctrinal or ethical, that he knew existed — or, perhaps, potentially existed — among believers in Jesus at Rome?

These two approaches, while seemingly quite different, may not, however, express mutually exclusive options. Various interpretive possibilities exist both between and within them. Nevertheless, in asking whether Paul's purpose was motivated principally by factors arising from within his own ministry *or* primarily by conditions that existed (or potentially existed) within the church at Rome, scholars seem to have come to something of a watershed in sorting out the issues and proposing a solution to this most perplexing problem. And it is probably not too extreme to claim that from this watershed has flowed almost everything else that has been said regarding the character, form, and content of Paul's letter to the Christians at Rome.

In what follows, our treatment of the purpose of Romans will be set out along the lines of five discussions: (1) a survey of positions that view Romans as motivated principally by factors arising from within Paul's own consciousness and ministry; (2) a survey of positions that view the letter as motivated primarily by factors arising from conditions existing, or potentially existing, among the Christians at Rome; (3) a suggested methodology for determining Paul's purpose or purposes in Romans; (4) the impact of our proposed new understanding of the letter's addressees; and (5) our own thesis regarding Paul's primary and subsidiary purposes in writing Romans.

1. Positions Based on Paul's Own Consciousness and Ministry

The plethora of views regarding the purpose of Romans has often engendered bewilderment and frustration, even among experienced students of Paul. It is necessary, therefore, to survey the rather wide range of positions that have been proposed before going further by way of suggesting a proper method for determining such matters and proposing our own hypothesis. Treating the various positions that have been advanced in roughly historical order, we begin with those that understand Romans as having been motivated principally by factors arising from Paul's own consciousness and ministry.

A Theological Treatise or Tractate

Throughout the first eighteen centuries of the Christian church, Romans was most often understood as a theological treatise or tractate that sets out a relatively complete statement of Christian belief — or, at least, that clearly enunciates the basic features of Paul's teaching. The Muratorian Canon, which probably dates from the end of the second century (c. 180-200), seems to reflect this understanding when it says of Romans vis-à-vis the Corinthian correspondence and Galatians:

> The epistles of Paul themselves show to those who are willing to understand *what they are,* from what place they were written, or *for what reason.* First of all, he forbids the Corinthians to share in heretical schisms, and the Galatians to practice circumcision, but wrote at greater length to the Romans concerning the plan of the Scriptures [*ordine scripturarum*], showing that their foundation is Christ. (italics mine)

Tertullian in his *Adversus Marcionem* of 208 seems to have read Romans as a theological treatise; Melanchthon in his *Loci Communes Theologici* of 1521 called it a "compendium of Christian doctrine" *(compendium doctrinae Christianae).* Martin Luther in his *Preface to the Letters of St. Paul* of 1522, which reflects the introductory material of his 1515 lectures, said of Romans that "it appears that he [Paul] wanted in this one epistle to sum up briefly the whole Christian and evangelical doctrine." And John Calvin, in his introductory section, "The Theme of the Epistle of Paul to the Romans," in his Romans commentary of 1539, viewed Paul's "whole" *(tota)* purpose in Romans as being to expound "justification by faith" in a "methodical" *(methodica)* fashion.[4] In fact, Romans throughout the first eighteen centuries of Christian history was usually treated as the first systematic theology of the Christian church.

Even during the "modern critical period" of NT scholarship there have been many who, while acknowledging that Romans is in the form of a letter, have continued to speak of it as a theological treatise or tractate that summarizes Paul's essential teaching. For example, Joseph B. Lightfoot in 1865, comparing Galatians and Romans, gave voice to such a view when he wrote:

> The Epistle to the Galatians stands in relation to the Roman letter, as the rough model to the finished statue; or rather, if I may press the metaphor without misapprehension, it is the first study of a single figure, which is worked into a group in the latter writing. To the Galatians the Apostle flashes out in indignant remonstrance the first eager thoughts kindled by his zeal for the Gospel striking suddenly against a stubborn form of Judaism. To the Romans he writes at leisure, under no pressure of circumstances, in the face of no direct antagonism, explaining, completing, extending the teaching of the earlier letter, by giving it a double edge directed against Jew and Gentile alike. The matter, which in the one epistle is personal and fragmentary, elicited by the special needs of an individual church, is in the other generalised and arranged so as to form a comprehensive and systematic treatise.[5]

What needs to be noted here is that whereas Lightfoot understood Paul's purpose in writing Galatians as being historically and circumstantially rooted — with his commentary on that letter setting a new course for all future critical-historical-exegetical NT commentaries — his treatment of Romans was not only fragmentary but also quite traditional. Thus regarding Romans, Lightfoot could say (as quoted above): (1) Paul "writes at leisure, under no pressure of circumstances, in the face of no direct antagonism, explaining, completing, extending the teaching of the earlier letter [i.e., Galatians], by giving it a double edge directed against Jew and Gentile alike," and (2) the letter to the Romans is a "generalised" reworking of Galatians and "arranged so as to form a comprehensive and systematic treatise."

Likewise, Anders Nygren, to cite only one other prominent commentator on Romans, argued in 1944: (1) "to offer as the real explanation of the letter the accidental circumstances, of a more personal character, which sup-

---

4. J. Calvin, *Romans,* in *Calvin's New Testament Commentaries,* 12 vols. (ET 1960), 8.5.
5. J. B. Lightfoot, *Saint Paul's Epistle to the Galatians* (London: Macmillan, 1865), 49.

plied the occasion for its writing, does not contribute to the deeper understanding of its contents," (2) "the epistle . . . impresses one as a doctrinal writing, a theological treatise, which is only externally clad with the form of a letter," (3) "Romans does not deal, or deals only in slightest degree, with the conditions within the Roman congregation," and (4) "instead of the special problems of the congregation at Rome, we confront Paul's own life problem."[6] And this understanding of Romans as a theological treatise continues to appear — in greater or lesser degree, in theory or in practice — in the writings of a great many prominent scholars today.[7]

Indeed, as was early recognized within Christendom, Romans is in many ways unlike any of the other letters in the Pauline corpus, with the possible exception of Ephesians. The lengthy body middle of the letter (i.e., 1:16–15:13) has frequently been understood as a theological treatise set within an epistolary frame (i.e., 1:1-15 and 15:14–16:27). The letter is addressed to a church that was not founded by Paul, with most of its members unknown to him personally. Further, there seem to be few, if any, polemical responses to false teaching, very little recognition of local issues at Rome or of problems in the Christian congregations of the city, and no clear apologetic in defense of the apostle's person or ministry. Rather, the writing is strongly expositional in both tone and content, coming closer to being a reasoned and logical discourse than any of Paul's other letters. For such reasons, Romans has often been compared to the formal epistles of Seneca (c. 4 B.C.–A.D. 65), a prominent Spanish-Roman Stoic philosopher of the day, who communicated his teachings in the guise of ordinary letters — though comparisons between Paul and Seneca have proven to be more illusory than real.

Romans, however, is a real letter, not a contrived literary epistle. It contains personal allusions, definite travel plans, and rather specific instructions for a particular people. There are in it, as in Paul's other letters, digressions, parentheses, and unfinished sentences. More importantly, while the longest of the apostle's extant writings, Romans lacks a number of subjects that seem from his other letters to be absolutely essential to Paul's thought and proclamation — most obviously, (1) the omission of any discussion of the resurrection of believers, which was such an important topic in his earlier letters (cf. 1 Thessalonians 4-5, 2 Thessalonians 2, and 1 Corinthians 15),

6. A. Nygren, *Romans,* 6-8.

7. Cf., e.g., K. Barth, *Romans,* who often treated Romans as the original "Dogmatics in Outline"; F. F. Bruce, *Paul,* 325-26, who endorsed the position of J. B. Lightfoot (though with Lightfoot's stance somewhat moderated in Bruce's "Romans Debate — Continued"; L. E. Keck, *Paul and His Letters,* 15-16; and D. J. Moo, *Romans,* 21-22.

and (2) the lack of any reference to the Lord's Supper, which was a matter of great concern when writing to converts at Corinth (cf. 1 Cor 11:17-34). As a theological treatise, therefore, Romans is somewhat truncated and a bit disappointing in its coverage of important doctrinal themes.

A Summation of Earlier Teaching

In their important "International Critical Commentary" on Romans, which was first published in 1895, William Sanday and Arthur C. Headlam acknowledged that Romans was a real letter "full of direct human interest," containing "here and there side-glances at particular local circumstances," and including some emphatic warnings — and so they affirmed that various historical and circumstantial reasons could be given for the apostle having written it.[8] Yet while denying that Romans was "a compendium of *the whole of* Christian doctrine,"[9] they concluded their discussion of Paul's purpose in writing it with such statements as the following:

> The most powerful of all the influences which have shaped the contents of the Epistle is the experience of the writer.[10]

> It is natural that he [Paul] should cast back his glance over the years which had passed since he became a Christian and sum up the result as he felt it for himself. It is not exactly a conscious summing up, but it is a momentum of this past experience which guides his pen.[11]

> The Epistle is the ripened fruit of the thought and struggles of the eventful years by which it had been preceded.[12]

> The main theme of the letter is the gathering in of the harvest, at once of the Church's history since the departure of its Master, and of the individual history of a single soul, that one soul which under God had had the most active share in making the course of external events what it was.[13]

8. W. Sanday and A. C. Headlam, *Romans,* xxxix-xliv.
9. W. Sanday and A. C. Headlam, *Romans,* xli (italics mine, though emphasis theirs).
10. W. Sanday and A. C. Headlam, *Romans,* xlii.
11. W. Sanday and A. C. Headlam, *Romans,* xlii.
12. W. Sanday and A. C. Headlam, *Romans,* xliii.
13. W. Sanday and A. C. Headlam, *Romans,* xliv.

Such a treatment, while not explicitly calling Romans a theological treatise, nonetheless views its composition as motivated principally by factors arising from within Paul's own ministry and understands its content as being principally a summation of the apostle's earlier teaching. It was this thesis that C. H. Dodd picked up and worked out throughout his influential commentary, which was first published in 1932, and that he expressly stated in such comments as the following:

> Paul the restless traveller and pioneer missionary takes his leave of us in this great epistle, into which he has packed the ripe fruits of many years of thought and work, of preaching, controversy, and the cure of souls, of trial, suffering, and spiritual experience.[14]

> This epistle is far from being an occasional letter directed to this or that particular problem as it arose, like most of Paul's correspondence. It gathers up a great deal of his thinking of years past.[15]

And Ulrich Luz has carried on this approach in an article of 1969, insisting that Paul's letter to the Romans differs from all his other letters in that it is "a coherent exposition of the position which Paul had reached in his disputes with his churches. The subject-matter discussed in it is the key to understanding its structure, not the specific circumstances which occasioned it."[16]

Such an understanding of Romans is but a variation of the view that the letter should be seen as a theological treatise set within an epistolary frame. And it falls under the same judgments as that earlier proposal. For Romans presents itself as a real letter written for a genuine historical purpose — a letter in which Paul wanted to communicate intelligibly and effectively to the audience he was addressing and in which the Christian gospel is proclaimed and argued for a particular reason. The letter does not represent itself as only a truncated summary of the apostle's past teaching. Further, as has frequently been noted, Paul writes as a man in mid-career, with his ministry in the eastern part of the empire completed and his mission to the west yet to begin.

Romans, however, cannot be viewed as written entirely *de novo*. Undoubtedly Paul drew on what he had proclaimed and written earlier when he

---

14. C. H. Dodd, *Romans,* xxv-xxvi.
15. C. H. Dodd, *Romans,* xxix.
16. U. Luz, "Aufbau," 162-63; cf. also, e.g., D. E. Aune, *New Testament in Its Literary Environment,* 219; R. D. Anderson Jr., *Ancient Rhetorical Theory and Paul* (Kampen: Kok Pharos, 1996), 183-84.

wrote to the Christians at Rome. But to understand Romans only as a summary of Paul's earlier teaching, which was then set within an epistolary framework, is to fail to account for much that seems evident in the letter and to ignore what we believe to be a better explanation of the data (as will be set out below).

An Encyclical Letter for Paul's Churches

Another variant of Romans as a theological treatise is the view that the first fourteen chapters were not originally written with any particular church in mind, but, rather, meant as an encyclical letter for all of Paul's churches — or, at least, for his churches in certain provinces of the Roman empire. Advocates of this view argue that what was originally composed was what now appears in 1–14 (minus, of course, the designation "at Rome" in 1:7 and 15), to which was added the travel plans of 15:14-33 when sent to the Christians at Rome and the greetings of 16:1-24 when sent to the Christians at Ephesus.

Kirsopp Lake, for example, revived the thesis of Ernst Renan that Romans 1–14 was originally a circular letter, of which several copies with distinct and appropriate endings were sent to various churches — with the last editor of the letter that was sent to Christians at Rome combining all of the endings so that nothing might be lost.[17] Joseph Lightfoot had in 1869 decimated Renan's earlier version of this thesis.[18] But Lake reworked Renan's thesis in a manner that he believed to be simpler and more cogent, and so argued:

> The short recension represents a letter written by St. Paul at the same time as Galatians, in connection with the question of Jewish and Gentile Christians, for the general instruction of mixed Churches [in Syria and Asia Minor] which he had not visited. It had originally nothing to do with Rome. Later on he sent a copy to Rome, with the addition of the other chapters to serve, as we should say, as a covering letter.[19]

As Lake viewed matters, relations between this general "Anti-Judaistic Letter" (i.e., Romans 1–14), the letter to converts in the province of Galatia (i.e., Galatians), the covering letter to Ephesus (i.e., Romans 16), and the final

17. K. Lake, *Earlier Epistles of St. Paul*, 324-413; *idem*, "Shorter Form," 504-25.
18. Cf. J. B. Lightfoot, "Structure and Destination," in his *Biblical Essays* (London: Macmillan, 1893), 287-320.
19. K. Lake, *Earlier Epistles of St. Paul*, 362.

covering letter to Rome (i.e., Romans 15) are to be seen as "exactly the same" as those between Ephesians, Colossians, and Philemon, where "Ephesians is the general Epistle to the Christians in Asia, Colossians an Epistle to a special Church in that province, and Philemon a private note to an individual Christian either in Colossae or a neighbouring town."[20]

T. W. Manson proposed a similar view, though he suggested a different historical scenario. Manson argued that the material of 1–14 (without, of course, the designation "at Rome" in 1:7 and 15) was originally written at the close of Paul's Corinthian ministry as "the summing up of the positions reached by Paul and his friends at the end of the long controversy whose beginnings appear in 1 Corinthians" — that is, as a statement meant to incorporate the essential features of Paul's message — and that this statement was then sent out as an encyclical with covering letters to "others" in the areas where he had previously ministered.[21] And Manson concluded his analysis with the following scenario of what he believed probably occurred:

> Having got this statement worked out to his own satisfaction, Paul then decided to send a copy of it to his friends in Ephesus, which he did not intend to visit on his way to Jerusalem (Acts 20:16). This copy would be available for the information of all the churches in Asia. At the same time he conceived the idea of sending a copy to Rome with a statement of his future plans. It might be permissible to guess that a written record may have remained in Corinth, though that, I think, is not necessary on the assumption that the substance of what is now in Romans had been gone over in discussion with the members of the Corinthian community. The situation then is that the Corinthian church has had the Apostle's summing up by word of mouth; the church in Syria and Palestine may expect to hear it in the same way in the near future. The church in the province of Asia and the church in Rome will receive it in writing. Looked at in this way Romans ceases to be just a letter of self-introduction from Paul to the Roman church, and becomes a manifesto setting forth his deepest convictions on central issues, a manifesto calling for the widest publicity, which the Apostle did his best — not without success — to give."[22]

20. K. Lake, *Earlier Epistles of St. Paul,* 363.

21. T. W. Manson, "To the Romans — and Others," in Donfried, ed., *Romans Debate* (1977), 1-16; (1991), 3-15.

22. T. W. Manson, "To the Romans — and Others," in Donfried, ed., *Romans Debate* (1977), 16; (1991), 15.

The main problem with the reconstructions of both Kirsopp Lake and T. W. Manson is, of course, that they start with — and everything depends on — the acceptance of the short form of Romans (chs 1–14) as representing the original letter. But that is a thesis that has been disputed by many, and it seems to have been finally put to rest by Harry Gamble in his 1977 *Textual History of the Letter to the Romans*.[23] Ingenious as their scenarios are, the hypotheses of Lake and Manson can now be, we believe, safely set aside in favor of a more cogent understanding, as we will attempt to elucidate below in proposing a new understanding of Paul's primary and subsidiary purposes in writing to the Christians at Rome.

A Final Literary Testament ("Last Will and Testament")

A similar proposal with respect to Paul's purpose is that of Günther Bornkamm. For while recognizing Romans as a letter written by Paul from Corinth to believers in Jesus at Rome, but disclaiming that it was written to deal with any particular problem or issue then existing among his addressees, Bornkamm argued that Paul's purpose in writing was "to summarize and develop" his teaching for the benefit of the Roman Christians, thereby producing in the form of a letter his final literary achievement or testament.[24] Bornkamm also posited a further, though subsidiary, reason for the writing of such a literary testament: that Paul was anticipating a final trip to Jerusalem, and so had in mind "the impending important meeting with the mother church in Jerusalem and the rounding off of his work as an apostle."[25]

Admittedly, as Bornkamm himself acknowledged, "a testament is, strictly speaking, the declaratory act of a man in view of his death."[26] That is not, however, how Bornkamm wanted his use of the term "testament" to be understood with regard to Romans. Rather, he wanted it to be understood as characterizing Romans as "the historical testament of the Apostle" at a particularly significant time in his ministry — that is, after having completed an extensive evangelistic campaign throughout the eastern regions of the Roman empire, while reflecting on previous arguments with his churches in

23. See our earlier discussion of Gamble's work in Chapter II on "Integrity."
24. G. Bornkamm, "Paul's Last Will and Testament," in Donfried, ed., *Romans Debate* (1977), 17-31; (1991), 16-28.
25. G. Bornkamm, *Paul*, 96.
26. G. Bornkamm, "Paul's Last Will and Testament," in Donfried, ed., *Romans Debate* (1977), 30; (1991), 27.

Galatia and at Corinth, and before traveling to Jerusalem to defend himself and his gospel for the last time.[27]

Bornkamm's thesis is nicely summarized in the final statements of his article on the subject:

> Behind the letter to the Romans stands the history of the life, work, preaching, and struggles of Paul, and, here it has found its expression. This history is not only an external but more especially an inner history, a history particularly of his theological thinking. Nothing could be more incorrect than the opinion that Romans contains only a loose collection of thoughts which the Apostle had expressed at a much earlier time. No, the letter to the Romans shows how these thoughts have worked further in Paul and how he has further worked on them, until he could give them this great and significant formulation during his last stay in Corinth.[28]

> This great document, which summarizes and develops the most important themes and thoughts of the Pauline message and theology and which elevates his theology above the moment of definite situations and conflicts into the sphere of the eternally and universally valid, this letter to the Romans is the last will and testament of the Apostle Paul.[29]

But though Bornkamm's thesis views Romans as a real letter — enabling one to think of the letter as a creative writing and proposing a possible life setting for its composition — there remains, we believe, a better scenario for understanding why Paul wrote as he did to the Christians at Rome. And it is that scenario that we will attempt to develop at the close of this chapter.

A Brief Prepared Originally for Paul's Defense at Jerusalem

In his understanding of why Paul wrote Romans, Günther Bornkamm included (as noted above) a subsidiary reason: that during his last visit to Cor-

---

27. G. Bornkamm, "Paul's Last Will and Testament," in Donfried, ed., *Romans Debate* (1977), 30; (1991), 27.

28. G. Bornkamm, "Paul's Last Will and Testament," in Donfried, ed., *Romans Debate* (1977), 29; (1991), 26.

29. G. Bornkamm, "Paul's Last Will and Testament," in Donfried, ed., *Romans Debate* (1977), 31; (1991), 27-28.

inth Paul was also thinking about his forthcoming visit to Jerusalem, with the necessity to defend his message and the Gentile mission before the leaders of the Jerusalem church. Ernst Fuchs, however, saw that reason as being the primary reason for Paul writing Romans, and so argued that Jerusalem was, in fact, "the secret addressee" of the letter to the Romans.[30] Jack Suggs, building on Bornkamm's "subsidiary" reason and Fuchs's "primary" reason, proposed that the content of Romans was "a brief drawn up by Paul in anticipation of the renewed necessity of defending his gospel in Jerusalem."[31] And Ulrich Wilckens, restricting his focus to the first eleven chapters of Romans, argued that the central theological section of Romans (1:18–11:36) was first prepared for presentation at Jerusalem, with this material then supplemented by letter openings (1:1-17) and concluding exhortations, travel plans, greetings, and letter closings (chaps 12–16) when sent to the Christians at Rome for their approval and support.[32]

Jacob Jervell, however, has most clearly and fervently advocated this thesis, as can be seen by his renaming Romans with the title "The Letter to Jerusalem."[33] "The letter itself," as Jervell understands it, "states clearly that its raison d'être does not stem from the situation of the Roman congregation, but is to be found in Paul himself at the time of writing."[34] Thus Jervell states his thesis at the very beginning of his article, and then goes on to substantiate it, as follows:

> The essential and primary content of Romans (1:18–11:36) is a reflection upon its major content, the "collection speech," or more precisely, the defense which Paul plans to give before the church in Jerusalem. To put it another way: Paul sets forth and explains what he, as the bearer of the collection given by the Gentiles for the mother congregation in Jerusalem, intends to say so that he as well as the gift will not be rejected.[35]

As Jervell reads 15:30-32, he argues that in requesting prayer on his behalf "Paul is not asking support for his future missionary endeavors in

30. E. Fuchs, *Hermeneutik*, 191.

31. M. J. Suggs, "'The Word Is Near You,'" 295.

32. U. Wilckens, "Abfassungszweck," 167.

33. J. Jervell, "Der Brief nach Jerusalem," *ST* 25 (1971) 61-73; ET: "The Letter to Jerusalem," in Donfried, ed., *Romans Debate* (1977), 61-74; (1991), 53-64.

34. J. Jervell, "The Letter to Jerusalem," in Donfried, ed., *Romans Debate* (1977), 62; (1991), 54.

35. J. Jervell, "The Letter to Jerusalem," in Donfried, ed., *Romans Debate* (1977), 64; (1991), 56.

Spain"[36] — though Jervell admits that in 15:24 the apostle "is expressing hope for some aid, probably in terms of food and lodging, so that he will be able to continue his journey after his stay in Rome."[37] Further, as Jervell reads the epistolary portions that bracket the central body of Romans, he argues that Paul "is not specifically requesting such aid" for a mission to Spain. And as he reads the body of the letter, he concludes that Paul is neither (1) dealing with any problems or issues at Rome, nor (2) giving a summary of his preaching and teaching "designed to inform the congregation in Rome what he intends to say in Spain"; rather, "everything points to problems which are of particular concern to Jerusalem."[38]

Attempts by Bornkamm, Fuchs, Suggs, Wilckens, Jervell, and others to relate the central arguments of Romans — at least those theological presentations in 1:18–11:36 — to the concerns of the Jerusalem church are, in certain respects, quite laudatory, and need to be constantly kept in mind when formulating any thesis regarding Paul's purpose in writing. Many of their insights, however, can be better (as I believe) worked out in terms of another proposal, as will be presented later in this chapter. Nonetheless, their understanding of the central body of material in Romans as being addressed only to concerns that Paul believed would be of particular relevance to the leaders of the church at Jerusalem, and not to issues present among believers at Rome, can be faulted on a number of counts.

The major problem with any "Letter to Jerusalem" theory is that in 11:13-24, which material is accepted by everyone as part of the central body of Romans, Paul specifically addresses his readers as "Gentiles" and characterizes them as "wild olive branches" who have been grafted in among the "natural branches," and so supported and nourished by "the root" of the original olive tree. "Such an argument," however, as Alexander Wedderburn has aptly pointed out, "makes no sense addressed to the Jerusalem church, but makes excellent sense addressed to the Roman church and to what is . . . a predominantly gentile church."[39]

A second problem with the Jerusalem destination theory, however, has to do with the exhortations of 14:1–15:13. Admittedly, in some forms of the

36. J. Jervell, "The Letter to Jerusalem," in Donfried, ed., *Romans Debate* (1977), 66; (1991), 57.

37. J. Jervell, "The Letter to Jerusalem," in Donfried, ed., *Romans Debate* (1977), 66; (1991), 57.

38. J. Jervell, "The Letter to Jerusalem," in Donfried, ed., *Romans Debate* (1977), 66; (1991), 57-58.

39. A. J. M. Wedderburn, *Reasons for Romans*, 20.

theory this passage is not viewed as part of the apostle's intended presentation at Jerusalem. Yet the thrust of these exhortations in this context must still be dealt with, since, as it is proposed, prior to Paul's trip to Jerusalem these exhortations were associated with that original presentation and sent in a letter to believers at Rome. And so, on either form of the theory, a degree of incongruity is set up. For if viewed as part of the original body of Romans, these exhortations to "the strong," who evidently looked with disdain on certain Jewish dietary scruples (14:2-4, 6) and calendar issues (14:5), could hardly have been directed to Jewish believers at Jerusalem, who are identified in Acts 21:20 as being extremely "zealous for the law." But if these exhortations were not a part of that original material, yet associated with that central material before the apostle's trip to Jerusalem by inclusion in his letter to believers at Rome, no adequate rationale can be given for the joining of 14:1–15:13 to the earlier materials of Romans other than that in Paul's mind, at least in some manner, they cohered.

Further, Paul's identification of himself with "the strong" (15:1), together with his seeming identification of "the weak" as Jewish believers in Jesus (or believers "influenced" by Jewish scruples) throughout the passage, would hardly, if part of an original argument intended for presentation at Jerusalem, have endeared him to a Jerusalem audience. Nor would such identifications, if not a part of that original body of material but yet associated with that material prior to the apostle's trip to Jerusalem, be read without great difficulty by the Christians at Rome — unless, of course, Paul was addressing a particular issue that then existed at Rome among Gentile and Jewish believers in Jesus, which is a far better hypothesis than the above theory.

An Ambassadorial Letter of Self-Introduction That Solicits Support for Paul's Proposed Mission to Spain

Robert Jewett in 1982 characterized Romans as an "ambassadorial letter" of self-introduction that "seeks to elicit support for Paul's proposed mission to Spain" — with the classification of Romans as an "ambassadorial letter" being understood as a sub-type of epideictic rhetoric, which, in the case of Romans, includes a "unique fusion" of such epistolary types as a "parenetic letter" and a "hortatory letter" and incorporates "philosophical diatribe."[40]

---

40. R. Jewett, "Romans as an Ambassadorial Letter," 5-20.

And it is this thesis that Jewett has incorporated into his important Romans commentary of 2007, expanding it a bit further to read as follows:

> Romans is a unique fusion of the "ambassadorial letter" with several of the other subtypes in the genre: the parenetic letter, the hortatory letter, and the philosophical diatribe. Its purpose is to advocate in behalf of the "power of God" a cooperative mission to evangelize Spain so that the theological argumentation reiterates the gospel to be therein proclaimed and the ethical admonitions show how that gospel is to be lived out in a manner that would ensure the success of this mission.[41]

There is much in Jewett's thesis that is valid, intriguing, and ably argued. Certainly Jewett is right to understand Romans as a letter in which Paul (1) introduces himself to Christians at Rome, who, in the main, had only heard about him and did not know him personally, (2) sets out something of a précis of his Christian proclamation to Gentiles that he desires his Roman addressees to know, since he wants to continue preaching that same message to Gentiles in Spain, and (3) asks his addressees for their support for such a proposed Christian outreach — thereby, in effect, sending him out as their apostle to the Gentile world in the western region of the Roman empire, particularly to Spain, just as the church at Syrian Antioch had sent him out to evangelize Gentiles in the eastern region of the empire. There are, however, some features of Jewett's thesis that may be legitimately questioned, with respect both to what is argued and to what is not considered.

One feature of Jewett's thesis that may be questioned is his epistolary classification of Romans as an ambassadorial letter of self-introduction. This is not to deny that letters of introduction were often carried by officials, merchants, and people of rank in the ancient world when they traveled from one place to another — even by common people when they moved from one community to another — with such letters written by those who knew them introducing them to others at their proposed destination. In support of Romans as an ambassadorial letter, Jewett appeals to various examples of "ambassadorial speech" and "diplomatic correspondence" that can be found in a variety of forms and materials in Paul's day, both Greco-Roman and Jewish.[42] But these materials appear in a "great variety" of forms (as Jewett himself acknowledges), and it is therefore difficult to establish any discrete

---

41. R. Jewett, *Romans*, 44.
42. R. Jewett, *Romans*, 44.

epistolary category of Paul's day that would correspond to Jewett's proposal of Romans as an ambassadorial letter.

Letters of introduction are referred to in both the Jewish (OT) Scriptures and the Christian (NT) Scriptures.[43] Chan-Hie Kim has discussed the provenance and epistolary features of ancient letters of introduction (or "letters of recommendation" as Kim calls them) and has reproduced the Greek and Latin texts of eighty-three such letters — most of them, of course, being Greek nonliterary papyrus letters from Egypt.[44] And Stanley Stowers has dealt with a large number of Greco-Roman and Christian letters of introduction, which were written from the time of the Roman orator, philosopher, and statesman Cicero (106-43 B.C.) to the time of Aurelius Augustine (A.D. 354-430), the great fifth-century Church Father.[45] But ancient letters of introduction, as far as we know, (1) were always written by others on behalf of the person or persons being introduced or accredited, not by someone setting out his own credentials, and (2) usually included expressions of high praise for the person or people addressed, with those words of praise constituting an important part of the letter.

Further, Jewett's support of Romans as an ambassadorial letter by reference to Paul's consciousness of himself as "an apostle"[46] falls somewhat short of the mark. For while Paul certainly thought of himself as an apostle[47] and considered himself "Christ's ambassador,"[48] and while the tone and content of Romans can be spoken of as being broadly "ambassadorial," it may be questioned whether his letter to the Christians at Rome is any more ambassadorial than most, if not all, of his other NT letters.

Likewise, two major underlying suppositions of Jewett, which he uses in both defending and explicating his thesis, may also be questioned: (1) that an "indirect style of appealing to common values," which Jewett finds to be common in both Romans and his cited examples of "ambassadorial speech" and "diplomatic correspondence," is what really "places diplomatic rhetoric within the epideictic genre," and (2) that Paul in setting out his theological statements and ethical exhortations works extensively with the ancient rhetorical categories of "honor" and "shame" in an endeavor to get rid of the "prejudicial elements" that were "currently dividing the congregations in Rome" — which

43. Cf. 2 Kgs 5:5-6; Acts 9:1b-2; 18:27; 1 Cor 16:3; 2 Cor 3:1; see also 2 Macc 9:19-27.
44. C.-H. Kim, *Letter of Recommendation*, 150-238.
45. S. K. Stowers, *Letter Writing*, 153-65.
46. Cf. R. Jewett, *Romans*, 44-45.
47. E.g., Rom 1:1, *et passim*.
48. Cf. 2 Cor 5:20.

feelings of "honor" and "shame" were what, according to Jewett, evidently prejudiced the Christians at Rome against Paul and would have kept them from any united support of him in his proposed mission to Spain.

Even more to be questioned, however, at least from our perspective, is Jewett's inadequate understanding of the identity, character, and theological orientation of Paul's Christian addressees at Rome. For Jewett continues to view Paul's Roman addressees primarily in terms of their ethnicity (as almost all commentators of the past have viewed them) — that is, as Gentile Christians, who were in the majority and who espoused Paul's doctrinal and ethical teaching, vis-à-vis Jewish believers in Jesus, who were conditioned more by Jewish ways of thinking and a Jewish lifestyle. But if our thesis regarding Paul's addressees is anywhere close to the mark (see Chapter IV, "Addressees"), even some of the more congenial features of Robert Jewett's thesis will, we believe, need to be considerably adjusted.

An Attempt to Establish an Apostolic Church at Rome

Günter Klein has argued that while Paul viewed the Christian faith of his Roman addressees to be "beyond question," he also (1) did not view the Christian community at Rome "as having an apostolic foundation," (2) regarded that lack of apostolicity as "highly significant theologically," (3) considered the church's non-apostolic founding "a challenge to his apostolic mission," and (4) wanted to write to believers at Rome, and then visit them, in order to establish by his teaching and presence such an apostolic church.[49] Thus after reviewing and setting aside other proposed interpretations of Paul's purpose in writing Romans, Klein has insisted that there can be only one conclusion: "Paul can consider an apostolic effort in Rome because he does not regard the local Christian community there as having an apostolic foundation"[50] — and so, as the divinely accredited apostle to the Gentiles, he wanted to rectify that situation.

Klein concludes his article by asserting: "Romans, by the very nature of its existence, is striking evidence for a shockingly authoritarian understanding of the apostolic office, an understanding which, incidentally, established

49. G. Klein, "Paul's Purpose in Writing," in Donfried, ed., *Romans Debate* (1977), 32-49; (1991), 29-43.
50. G. Klein, "Paul's Purpose in Writing," in Donfried, ed., *Romans Debate* (1977), 45; (1991), 39.

norms for Christianity contemporary with Paul."[51] Such a stance, Klein notes, is "sufficiently annoying" to modern sensibilities. Nonetheless, as he proclaims in his final sentence: "Historical critical research in the field of theology was never meant to find in its texts the favorite dreams of the latest avant-garde scholarship; rather, it has always been committed to re-discovering that word which in contrast to all modernism remains a *verbum alienum* and precisely for that reason makes possible the discovery of faith."[52]

There is much in Klein's thesis that deserves comment — some commendatory, but most by way of opposition. Suffice it here to reproduce one short section from Karl Donfried's two-paragraph evaluation of Klein's thesis:

> Unfortunately, Klein's interesting suggestion has little exegetical support. Paul in no way indicates a weakness in the foundation. Quite the contrary, in 15:14 we hear, "I myself am satisfied about you, my brethren, that you yourselves are full of goodness, filled with all knowledge, and able to instruct one another." Then in the next verse he explicitly indicates that what he has just written is "by way of reminder" — hardly a situation which would indicate "that for Paul, Christianity in Rome still needed an apostolic foundation. . . ." Further, one would hardly expect Paul to do such a rebuilding job simply "in passing" (15:24) as he goes to Spain.[53]

Somewhat similar to Klein's proposal is that of Anton Fridrichsen, who argued that Paul's primary reason for writing Romans was to assert his apostolic authority in the Roman church.[54] But Donfried's response to Klein's proposal, as quoted above, speaks also to the essence of Fridrichsen's thesis, and with similar effect.

A Missions Document Soliciting Support

Among those who understand Romans as having been motivated principally by factors arising from within Paul's own ministry and consciousness, the most common position today is that which views the letter as a "missions

---

51. G. Klein, "Paul's Purpose in Writing," in Donfried, ed., *Romans Debate* (1977), 49; (1991), 43.

52. G. Klein, "Paul's Purpose in Writing," in Donfried, ed., *Romans Debate* (1977), 49; (1991), 43.

53. K. P. Donfried, "Short Note on Romans 16," in Donfried, ed., *Romans Debate* (1977), 51; (1991), 45.

54. A. Fridrichsen, "Apostle and His Message," 7.

document" that was written in order to solicit support from the Christians at Rome for the apostle's anticipated mission to Spain. It is a thesis that builds on Paul's express statements in 15:24 (as noted earlier in Chapter III, "Occasion and Date"): "I plan to do so [i.e., visit the Christians at Rome] when I go to Spain. I hope to visit you while passing through and to have you assist me on my journey there, after I have enjoyed your company for a while."

Gottlob Schrenk's 1933 article on Paul's letter to Rome as a missions document was important in establishing this thesis in the consciousness of contemporary NT scholarship.[55] Somewhat more inclusive, yet with the same basic thrust, is the depiction of Paul's purpose in writing Romans by Werner Kümmel:

> Since Paul is seeking ties with the Roman Christians in the interests of his ongoing missionary activity, it is quite appropriate that he presents himself to them and tells them what is the essence of Christianity and what is the content of the gospel that he preaches as apostle to the Gentiles. The desire to introduce himself to the Christians in Rome and to tell them who he is and what he preaches gives Paul the occasion to express himself at some length about the basic truths of Christianity as he sees and teaches it. Though it arose out of concrete necessity for his missionary work, Rom is the theological confession of Paul, which has been appropriately characterized as "the testament of Paul."[56]

And such a view of Romans as a missions document soliciting support appears widely in commentaries on Romans today, both scholarly and popular — perhaps set out in no more singular and explicit fashion than by Dieter Zeller in his 1985 commentary *Die Brief an die Römer*.

There is much to commend in this view of Romans as a missions document. Most obviously, it brings together issues regarding both the occasion and the purpose of the letter — which matters, while separable, must always be related. But the data of the letter itself seems to demand a more perceptive, incisive, and inclusive thesis regarding Paul's purpose or purposes in writing, particularly when Romans is read in light of what we have argued earlier regarding the identity, character, circumstances, and concerns of its addressees (cf. Chapter IV, "Addressees"). And that thesis is what we will attempt to spell out later in this chapter in proposing a new understanding of Paul's primary and subsidiary purposes.

55. G. Schrenk, "Der Römerbrief als Missionsdokument," 81-106.
56. W. Kümmel, *Introduction to the New Testament*, 312-13.

2. Positions Based on Conditions Existing
Among the Christians at Rome

There are also a number of positions that understand Paul's letter to Rome to have been motivated primarily by conditions that were then existing, or potentially existing, among the Christians at Rome. A survey of this latter set of views is here in order.

To Oppose Jewish Particularism and
Proclaim Christian Universalism

The earliest of the modern critical assessments of Paul's purpose for writing Romans based on what was thought to have existed among the Christians at Rome was that advanced by Ferdinand Christian Baur, who must be credited with having begun, in his own way, the "modern critical period" of NT study. F. C. Baur's thesis was that Paul was writing to a group of Gentile Christians at Rome who were being opposed by certain Jewish believers in Jesus in the city who, because of their inherited Jewish scruples, were antagonistic to his message, and so he wrote to remove "the last remnants of Jewish particularism" and to proclaim "the universalism of Christianity."[57] This was not an entirely new thesis, for Marcion in the second century had read Romans in a similar fashion — though, of course, without buttressing his views by a Hegelian analysis of history or by Baur's form of "tendency criticism" in determining the authenticity and date of a Christian writing.

All of the letters that Baur accepted as having been written by Paul, that is, the *Hauptbriefe* of Galatians, 1 and 2 Corinthians, and Romans, he believed were written in opposition to the deleterious effects of a lingering Judaism within early Christianity — with these hangovers from Jewish religion being propagated by Jewish Christians generally and Peter in particular. As Baur understood these four letters, Paul was in the process of developing his anti-judaistic theology along the following lines:

> In the Epistle to the Galatians he had emancipated Christianity from Judaism to the extent of casting off the outward symbol of bondage, the rite of circumcision, which the latter sought to impose upon the former as the necessary condition of salvation. In the two Epistles to

---

57. F. C. Baur, *Paul*, 1.309; see his full treatment in 1.308-65.

the Corinthians, he had asserted the principle that the call to, and the possession of, the Messianic salvation, were not conditioned by the authority of the Apostles, who had been called by Jesus himself: that he, the Gentile Apostle, was an Apostle quite as much, and to as good effect as they. In the Epistle to the Romans his task is to remove the last remnants of Jewish particularism, by showing that it is but a stage, a stepping-stone to the universalism of Christianity, in which all nations should be embraced.[58]

The dialectic that Baur saw inherent in Romans was (1) that Jewish Christianity "still maintained the absolute importance of Judaism," and could not accept that in the relationship between Jewish Christianity and Gentile Christianity "the latter was to assume an immense preponderance over the former," whereas (2) Paul could come "to no other conclusion than that the Jews were rejected and the Gentiles called."[59] And of this rejection of the Jews and call of the Gentiles, Baur declared: "This is the Apostle's position in the Epistle to the Romans; this is the theme which he works out in that Epistle."[60]

The Achilles' heel of Baur's understanding of Romans was, of course, that in order to make his thesis work he had to accept only the first fourteen chapters of the letter as authentic and reject its final two chapters. For in the first fourteen chapters, as Baur interpreted them, "the fundamental idea . . . is the absolute nullity of all the claims advanced by Jewish particularism,"[61] whereas chapters 15–16 — which speak of Paul's desire to go to Jerusalem in order to present "a contribution for the poor among the saints in Jerusalem," with the rationale being that since the "Gentiles have shared in the Jews' spiritual blessing . . . they owe it to the Jews to share with them their material blessings" (15:25-27) — "must be held to be the work of a Paulinist, writing in the spirit of the Acts of the Apostles, seeking to soothe the Judaists, and to promote the cause of unity, and therefore tempering the keen anti-Judaism of Paul with a milder and more conciliatory conclusion to his Epistle."[62] But such a discrediting of the textual evidence in favor of one's own thesis certainly raises a serious flag of caution regarding the validity of that thesis.

More serious for Baur's anti-judaistic theory regarding Paul's purpose

58. F. C. Baur, *Paul*, 1.309.
59. F. C. Baur, *Paul*, 1.309.
60. F. C. Baur, *Paul*, 1.309.
61. F. C. Baur, *Paul*, 1.341.
62. F. C. Baur, *Paul*, 1.365; see his full treatment in 1.352-65.

for writing Romans, however, is the widespread recognition today that a Hegelian understanding of early Christian history, as well as Baur's type of "tendency criticism" for determining authenticity and dates of the early Christian writings, provide inappropriate bases for understanding the biblical data and are largely contrived. Since the days of the Tübingen school's dominance in the nineteenth century, better understandings of the data and issues involved have been presented (as will be shown, as I would like to believe, in what follows in this chapter). For such reasons, even though he claimed that his views were based on a critical analysis of the history of ideas in early Christianity, Baur's view regarding Paul's purpose in writing Romans may be safely set aside as a fossil of an earlier age.

To Counter the Claims of the Judaizers, as Paul Did Earlier in Galatians

Of far greater significance throughout the course of Christian history, particularly during the past two centuries, has been the view that Paul's purpose in writing to the Christians at Rome was to counter the claims of the "Judaizers," just as he did earlier in his letter to his own converts in Galatia — only doing so in Romans in a more moderate and reflective manner. The fact that there appear in both letters the same topics of "law," "sin," "righteousness," "justification," and "faith," together with the same rejection of "works of the law," has led most interpreters to posit that something of the same "judaizing" agenda of Paul's opponents in the churches of Galatia also underlies the apostle's statements in his letter to the Christians at Rome. So most NT scholars have worked on the assumption that what Paul writes in Romans, like what he wrote earlier in Galatians, must be understood as basically apologetic and polemical responses (even though stated in somewhat more muted fashion) in opposition to a form of "Judaizing Christianity" that viewed the Christian religion as simply a part of Judaism, and so called on all believers in Jesus, whether ethnically Jews or Gentiles, to observe the Jewish law, either in whole or in part.

There are, of course, warnings about living "according to the Jewish law" in the writings of the Church Fathers,[63] thereby acknowledging that a "judaizing" problem continued to exist among early Christians even into the second century. But the major impetus for interpreting Romans along the

---

63. Cf., e.g., Ignatius, *To the Magnesians*, chs. 8–9.

lines of Galatians came from Martin Luther in the early sixteenth century. For in discovering Paul's teaching on "the righteousness of God" and "justification by faith" in Rom 1:17 — which became for him a catalyst for his own spiritual rebirth, an open door into "paradise" and "a gateway to heaven"[64] — Luther used these themes as something like "skeleton keys" to unlock the meaning of both Romans and Galatians. Thus for Luther, Romans and Galatians dealt with the same issues and proclaimed the same message, with the theme of that message found in Rom 1:17 but the details spelled out most clearly and graphically in Galatians.

Likewise, John Calvin in his 1540 commentary on Romans understood Paul to be speaking apologetically and polemically against a continuing "judaizing" threat among believers in Christ at Rome. In his introduction, "The Theme of the Epistle of Paul to the Romans," Calvin speaks of "the main subject of the whole Epistle" as being "that we are justified by faith," contrasting Paul's statements with what he perceived to be Jewish views on the topic.[65] And in his treatment of Rom 3:21-31 he understood Paul to be teaching justification "by faith" vis-à-vis Jewish views of justification by "works of the law."[66]

In arguing that Romans was written to remove "the last remnants of Jewish particularism" and to proclaim "the universalism of Christianity," Baur proposed his own theory about the "inner progress" of Paul's thought. In so doing, he used what he saw to be developments from the style and content of Galatians to the style and content of Romans: "the one [Galatians] being the first sketch of a bold and profound system as conceived in its characteristic and essential features; the other [Romans] the completed system, developed on all sides, and provided with all necessary argument and illustration."[67] And though Joseph B. Lightfoot differed radically with Baur in theological orientation and on many matters of interpretation, with respect to the relation of these two letters they were in basic agreement — as is clear from Lightfoot's statement of 1865, which has become for many the classic statement defining relations:

> The Epistle to the Galatians stands in relation to the Roman letter, as the rough model to the finished statue; or rather, if I may press the metaphor

64. See M. Luther, "Preface to Latin Writings," in *Luther's Works,* vol. 34, pp. 336-37; see also vol. 54, "Table Talk," pp. 193 and 309.

65. See J. Calvin, *Romans,* in *Calvin's New Testament Commentaries,* 8.5-11.

66. J. Calvin, *Romans,* 8.69-81.

67. F. C. Baur, *Paul,* 1.309.

without misapprehension, it is the first study of a single figure, which is worked into a group in the latter writing.[68]

So dominant, in fact, has been this understanding of the relation between the two letters that Kirsopp Lake, in defense of the theory of an original "short form" or "short recension" of Romans (i.e., chaps 1–14, minus the designation "at Rome" in 1:7 and 15), in 1927 could argue:

> The short recension represents a letter written by St. Paul at the same time as Galatians, in connection with the question of Jewish and Gentile Christians, for the general instruction of mixed Churches which he had not visited. It had originally nothing to do with Rome. Later on he sent a copy to Rome, with the addition of the other chapters to serve, as we should say, as a covering letter.[69]

Thus, as Lake reconstructed the situation, the letter that Paul eventually sent to Rome — which, he believed, consisted of what we now have as chapters 1–14, with the additions of "at Rome" in 1:7 and 15 and the further materials of chapter 15, but not the greetings of 16:1-23 — "belongs in the main to the same controversy as Galatians, that with Judaizing Christians."[70]

And the great majority of contemporary NT scholars, in fact, while not espousing Baur's understanding of Paul's message and not agreeing with Lake's views regarding the letter's integrity, have also interpreted Paul in Romans, as in Galatians, as arguing against "judaizing" opponents — whether "actual," "remembered," "potential," or simply "a rhetorical foil" for "an anti-Jewish agenda."[71] Likewise Alexander Wedderburn, in his highly acclaimed monograph given over entirely to the question of Paul's reasons for writing Romans, accepts as a major reason the presence of "Judaizing Christianity at Rome."[72]

Not everyone, of course, has interpreted Paul's statements in Romans regarding "law," "sin," "righteousness," "justification," and "faith" in an apolo-

---

68. J. B. Lightfoot, *Saint Paul's Epistle to the Galatians* (London: Macmillan, 1865), 49.

69. K. Lake, *Earlier Epistles of St. Paul*, 362.

70. K. Lake, *Earlier Epistles of St. Paul*, 369-70.

71. Cf., e.g., to cite only a diverse few, J. J. Gunther, *Paul's Opponents and Their Backgrounds: A Study of Apocalyptic and Jewish Sectarian Teachings* (Leiden: Brill, 1973), 314-17; C. E. B. Cranfield, *Romans*, 2.845-60; H. Räisänen, *Paul and the Law* (Philadelphia: Fortress, 1986), 162-98, *passim*; J. D. G. Dunn, *Romans*, xlii-xliii and lxiii-lxxii; and D. A. Campbell, "Determining the Gospel," 320-33.

72. A. J. M. Wedderburn, *Reasons for Romans*, 50-65.

getic or polemical fashion, and therefore understood him as speaking to a then existing "judaizing" theology among the Christians at Rome. William Sanday and Arthur C. Headlam, viewing Romans more in terms of a theological treatise, have argued:

> Both in the controversial portion [i.e., chapters 1–11] and in the admonitory portion [i.e., chapters 12–15], we find constant reminiscences of earlier situations, but always with the sting of controversy gone. St. Paul writes throughout with the remembrance of his own former experience, and not with a view to special difficulties in the Roman community. He writes on all these vexed questions, not because they have arisen there, but because they may arise. The Church of Rome consists, as he knows, of both Jewish and heathen Christians. These discordant elements may, he fears, unless wise counsels prevail, produce the same dissensions as have occurred in Galatia [as in "the controversial portion"] or Corinth [as in "the admonitory portion"].[73]

Ed Sanders, wanting to interpret the letter as "coming out of Paul's own situation" rather than as opposed to "covenantal" Judaism, also does not see any suggestion in Romans of a controversy with Christian Judaizers, even though such may be claimed for his writing of Galatians. So he draws the following distinction:

> Galatians is written in a polemical setting against the views of Christian missionaries who are undermining Paul's work. Romans . . . is written . . . not directly against Paul's opponents within the Christian movement.[74]

Yet it needs to be noted, as Wedderburn has acknowledged — even while advancing his arguments for the presence and problem of "Judaizing Christianity at Rome" — that:

> In the end, however, evidence for the nature of the Christian traditions at Rome remains tantalizingly scanty. That they were originally of a Judaizing character must remain a hypothesis, nothing more. But this will be a hypothesis that gains in plausibility the better it helps to explain the character of Paul's letter to the Christians of Rome.[75]

73. W. Sanday and A. C. Headlam, *Romans,* 401.
74. E. P. Sanders, *Paul, the Law, and the Jewish People* (Philadelphia: Fortress, 1983), 148.
75. A. J. M. Wedderburn, *Reasons for Romans,* 54.

It is this hypothesis, however, that not only needs to be tested by (1) its "plausibility" in providing a coherent picture of the life of the Christian community at Rome, (2) its "compatibility" with other data regarding the history of the earliest church, and (3) its "fit" with what Paul actually says in Romans — which are the three criteria proposed by Wedderburn[76] — but also must be judged against another hypothesis that will be proposed in what follows, which we believe fulfills these criteria better and with greater interpretive possibilities.

To Effect a Reconciliation between "the Strong" and "the Weak"

Commentators have, at times, noted a difference between the exhortations of chapters 12–13 and the exhortations of chapters 14–15. Sanday and Headlam, for example, introduced this hortatory section as follows:

> A definite division may be made between chaps. xii, xiii, in which the exhortations are general in character, and xiv–xv.12, in which they arise directly out of the controversies which are disturbing the Church.[77]

In their immediately following statement, however, they go on to say with respect to the exhortations of 14:1–15:12: "Yet even these are treated from a general point of view, and not in relation to any special circumstances"[78] — thereby defining the word "Church" in their previous sentence in a more universal manner, without any specific reference to the circumstances of the Christians at Rome.

During the second half of the twentieth century, the specificity of the exhortations of 14:1–15:12 has become increasingly emphasized, with the result that it became popular to view at least one of Paul's purposes for writing Romans as an attempt to effect a reconciliation between (1) Gentile Christians who espoused a broader view of Christian liberty, and who, it appears, called themselves "the strong," and (2) Jewish believers in Jesus who were more controlled by Jewish dietary scruples, and who, it seems, were called "the weak" by Gentile Christians. And this division, which was seen most explicitly in 14:1–15:12 (perhaps also in the doxological statement of 15:13), has been claimed to underlie much of what is presented elsewhere in the letter as well.

76. A. J. M. Wedderburn, *Reasons for Romans*, 64.
77. W. Sanday and A. C. Headlam, *Romans*, 351.
78. W. Sanday and A. C. Headlam, *Romans*, 351.

This thesis regarding Romans as having been written to effect a reconciliation between "the strong" and "the weak" at Rome was formulated in explicit form by Herbert Preisker in 1952-53,[79] Günther Harder in 1954,[80] Willi Marxsen in 1963,[81] and Hans-Werner Bartsch in 1967 and again in 1971.[82] As proposed by these German scholars, the conflict between the two groups arose when Jewish believers in Jesus, who had been expelled from Rome by the Emperor Claudius in A.D. 49, returned to Rome after Claudius's death in A.D. 54.

The thesis was further developed and popularized in North America by Paul Minear in his 1971 monograph *The Obedience of Faith: The Purposes of Paul in the Epistle to the Romans,* where he argued that not only did Paul write Romans in order (1) to set before Christians at Rome his plans for a future apostolic mission in the western regions of the Roman empire, asking for their aid, but also (2) to deal with a major dispute that had arisen among the Christians at Rome, which had been reported to him by some of those whom he lists in chapter 16. Minear proposed, in fact, that one could discern in 14:1–16:27 five groups of Christians at Rome who were arguing with one another: (1) the weak in faith who condemned the strong in faith; (2) the strong in faith who scorned and despised the weak in faith; (3) the doubters; (4) the weak in faith who did not condemn the strong in faith; and (5) the strong in faith who did not despise the weak in faith.[83]

Generally supportive of the Preisker-Harder-Marxsen-Bartsch understanding, but approaching issues from a Jewish perspective and adding greater specificity to the thesis, was Wolfgang Wiefel in his 1970 article "Die jüdische Gemeinschaft im antiken Rom und die Anfänge des römischen Christentums. Bemerkungen zu Anlass und Zweck des Römerbriefs" (ET = "The Jewish Community in Ancient Rome and the Origins of Roman Christianity").[84] Wiefel argued (1) that associated with the Edict of Claudius in A.D. 49 was a ban on formal Jewish synagogue meetings, (2) that this ban continued even after Claudius's edict was rescinded, (3) that Christians at Rome, both Jewish believers who remained in the city and Gentile believers

79. H. Preisker, "Das historische Problem des Römerbriefes."
80. G. Harder, "Der konkrete Anlass des Römerbriefes."
81. W. Marxsen, *Introduction to the New Testament,* 95-104.
82. H.-W. Bartsch, "Die antisemitischen Gegner des Paulus im Römerbrief"; *idem,* "Die Empfänger des Römerbriefes."
83. P. S. Minear, *Obedience of Faith,* 8ff.
84. W. Wiefel, "Jewish Community," in Donfried, ed., *Romans Debate* (1977), 100-19; (1991), 85-101.

who had been associated with the Jewish synagogues, were forced to meet for worship in smaller house congregations throughout the city, (4) that, with the return to Rome of the Jewish believers in Jesus who had been expelled, tensions arose between the then dominant group of Gentile Christians and the returning Jewish Christians in these various house churches, and (5) that Paul wrote Romans in order to effect a reconciliation between these respective factions (see Chapter IV, "Addressees," for a fuller discussion of Wiefel's thesis). In effect, what Wiefel did was to expand the discussion of Paul's purpose in writing Romans from strictly exegetical and theological concerns to include sociological analyses of not only Christianity at Rome but also the composition, organization, and circumstances of the Jewish community in the capital city of the Roman empire.

Combining a mirror reading of the passage and a sociological analysis of the addressees' situation, Francis Watson went further to argue (1) that 14:1–15:13, together with certain other indications in Romans, "presupposes two congregations, separated by mutual hostility and suspicion over the question of the law" — the one being a Gentile Christian congregation, which "like Paul himself had abandoned many of the ceremonial prescriptions of the law of Moses," and a Jewish Christian congregation, which "comprised the remnants of the original Roman congregation" and "for whom the whole law was still in force," and (2) that Paul's purpose in writing was to persuade the members of the Jewish Christian congregation to separate from the Jewish community and their legal commitments and to accept and unite with the Gentile Christian congregation.[85] But while Watson is certainly right in recognizing the specificity of the issues set out in 14:1–15:13 and in highlighting the need for a sociological analysis of the addressees' situation, his thesis may be faulted for being (1) overly simplistic in positing opposition between only two Christian congregations, particularly in view of the probability of a number of small house churches at Rome, (2) overly restrictive in assuming that the controversy was between Paulinist-type Gentile Christians and legalistic Jewish believers in Jesus, (3) wrong-headed in viewing Paul as calling on Jewish believers in Jesus to separate from everything Jewish, particularly when elsewhere in the letter he indicates that Christians are to recognize and maintain their bond with God's covenant people Israel, and (4) quite wrong in understanding Paul's words as being directed to "the weak," who were Jewish believers in Jesus, rather than to "the

---

85. F. Watson, "Two Roman Congregations," 94-105; repr. in Donfried, ed., *Romans Debate* (1991), 203-15.

strong," and therefore attempting "to persuade the Roman Jewish Christians to accept the Paulinists, in preparation for Paul's longer-term plans."[86] It seems far better to interpret the passage as Paul exhorting "the strong," with whom he identified, to respect "the weak" and welcome them into their fellowship — that is, to recognize the importance of mutual acceptance among believers in Jesus and to put into practice that Christian principle, whatever their respective scruples or lifestyles — and not as a call for "the weak" to divorce themselves from their Jewish past and convert to the views of "the strong."

We may dispute a particular scholar's interpretation of the exhortations of 14:1–15:13 — especially one that identifies the disputants too closely (as we believe Paul Minear has done) or one that redirects Paul's words to "the weak" rather than to "the strong," thereby reversing what seems to be the obvious intent of the apostle (as we believe Francis Watson has done). The specific details of Paul's statements in 14:1–15:13, however, are too numerous and involved to be spelled out here, and so must await our proposed exegetical treatment in a forthcoming commentary. Nonetheless, at least Paul Minear's general approach to the passage remains, in my opinion, entirely appropriate:

> It is true that Paul often incorporated into his letters didactic material which was typical of what he taught in all the churches. This catechetical material was often shaped by general practice rather than by particular situations. Chapters 12 and 13 contain material which is probably of this sort. . . . There is, however, a change in literary style between ch. 13 and 14. The apostle moves from general injunctions embodied in traditional oral forms of parenesis, to the consideration of a specific set of problems. The nearest analogy is I Corinthians (8.1-13; 9.19-23; 10.23–11.1). No one doubts that in Corinth he was wrestling directly with a specific situation. Why then should we doubt that this was also true in Rome?[87]

So in formulating our own understanding of Paul's primary and subsidiary purposes for writing Romans (as will be set out later in this chapter), this passage will again be brought to the fore and highlighted as having importance in that determination.

---

86. As Watson expresses the essence of his thesis in "Two Roman Congregations," 105; repr. in Donfried, ed., *Romans Debate* (1991), 215.

87. P. S. Minear, *Obedience of Faith*, 22.

To Counsel regarding the Relation of Christians to Civil Government

"In many respects," as Ernst Käsemann has pointed out, the discussion of the relation of Christians to civil government in 13:1-7 "is unique in Paul" and rather "surprising" in the context of the exhortations on love that surround it in 12:9-21 and 13:8-10.[88] It has appeared to many, in fact, that 13:1-7 is something of "an independent block" of material in the midst of the more general exhortations of chapters 12–13 — perhaps even "an alien body" — for these seven verses (1) are quite specific in scope and application, whereas the other exhortations are fairly general, (2) argue on the basis of what God has established by creation, whereas Christology, eschatology, and love (ἀγάπη) are the motivational factors that appear prominently throughout the rest of 12:1–15:13, and (3) seem to break the continuity of the exhortations given in 12:9-21 and 13:8-10.[89]

Much that needs to be said regarding this passage must be left for a later treatment in a forthcoming exegetical commentary. Suffice it here to say that (1) contrary to a number of scholars who have viewed 13:1-7 as a gloss or interpolation, there is no reason to deny the passage's authenticity on either external or internal grounds, and (2) the fact that Paul here discusses the relation of Christians to civil government, which is a theme not found in his other extant letters and is somewhat disruptive in the context of general exhortations regarding love, "must be connected," as Käsemann goes on to say, "with the fact that he is addressing the church in the capital city of the empire."[90] Or as Peter Stuhlmacher has argued, taking a somewhat different tack:

> In Rome they [the community of Christians] had the palace within view; everyone spoke of Caesar and his delegates. Therefore the question was always present: How is one to evaluate them [Caesar and his delegates] and associate with them in the light of God's will in the service of righteousness? It would be strange if the norm that orders the community's relationship to the state were missing in the message to the Romans.[91]

Further, it may well be, as Johannes Friedrich, Wolfgang Pöhlmann, and Peter Stuhlmacher argued in their co-authored article of 1976, that the

88. E. Käsemann, *Romans,* 350.
89. E. Käsemann, *Romans,* 350-52.
90. E. Käsemann, *Romans,* 350.
91. P. Stuhlmacher, *Romans,* 240.

exhortations of 13:6-7 regarding paying taxes and revenues to civil "authorities" — even offering them respect and honor — are to be understood against the background of unrest at Rome during the mid-50's regarding the rapacious practices of those who collected the city's revenues and tolls.[92] Tacitus (c. A.D. 55-117), the Roman historian and orator, who was during the year A.D. 88 a praetor (i.e., a magistrate with judicial functions) of the city of Rome, reports that in A.D. 58 there was such an outcry by the people of Rome against indirect taxation that the emperor Nero was forced to intervene, though he did not abolish those tolls and taxes but only ordered the collectors to be more strictly regulated.[93] Likewise, Suetonius (who flourished during the second century A.D.), the Roman biographer, historian, and teacher of rhetoric, who was also at one time private secretary to the emperor Hadrian, speaks of Nero as having mitigated the most grievous burdens of such tolls and taxes.[94]

As Friedrich, Pöhlmann, and Stuhlmacher have pointed out, instructions about paying taxes are not only absent in Paul's other letters, but also unusual in other Jewish and Greco-Roman writings of Paul's day. Therefore, the fact that Paul wrote Romans sometime during the winter of A.D. 57-58 (see our discussion in Chapter III, "Occasion and Date") — that is, at the very time when popular agitation against the collecting of various tolls and taxes was coming to a head at Rome (i.e., during the year A.D. 58) — suggests that 13:6-7 is best understood as Paul's counsel to Roman Christians as to how they should respond in their particular situation. And if that is so, then we must conclude as Alexander Wedderburn has aptly observed: (1) that 13:6-7 evidences "a surprisingly intimate knowledge by Paul, not only of the circumstances within the Roman church, but also of the situation in which its members had to live, and of the social, economic and political environment that surrounded them," and (2) that Paul's advice to his addressees "was written in the light of that knowledge, and is to be interpreted by us in the light of that situation."[95]

92. J. Friedrich, W. Pöhlmann, and P. Stuhlmacher, "Situation und Intention von Röm 13.1-7."

93. Tacitus, *Annals* 13.50-51.

94. Suetonius, *Lives of the Caesars: Nero* 10.1.

95. A. J. M. Wedderburn, *Reasons for Romans*, 63.

To Defend against Criticisms and Misrepresentations

There are a number of passing comments and veiled allusions in Romans — perhaps even some rhetorical questions and a pithy exhortation at the end of the letter — that have been seen by a few commentators as being apologetic and/or polemical in nature, and so, it is argued, to be understood as instances where Paul is defending himself against certain criticisms of his person and/or various misrepresentations of his message among the Christians at Rome. One such instance is in 1:16, where Paul begins what appears to be a clear introductory thesis statement with the words "I am not ashamed of the gospel." Kenneth Grayston, commenting in 1964 on these words of 1:16a, suggested that "the coherent structure of the epistle may be discerned if we begin by understanding that St. Paul was moved to write by an accusation that his gospel was a shameful thing, and that this charge was never far from his mind."[96] Walter Schmithals argued in 1975 that this rather personal comment is clearly to be understood as having reference to accusations against the apostle by certain Christians at Rome.[97] Peter Stuhlmacher proposed in 1986 (ET = 1991) that Paul was here, amidst criticisms of him by some Christians at Rome, "signaling to friend and foe alike among his recipients that he intends to stick to his embattled cause in Rome as elsewhere."[98] And Alexander Wedderburn developed in 1988 a rather full-blown case for the position that Paul's statement about being "not ashamed" — as well as all that he wrote from this statement in 1:16 on through to the end of his theological discussions in 11:36 — is best understood on the supposition that *"some in Rome had in fact claimed that he indeed ought to be ashamed of his gospel and his proclamation, for that gospel was in some way discredited and disgraceful."*[99]

Another instance where Paul appears to be defending himself against a criticism of his person and/or some misrepresentation of his message is in 3:8, which verse is situated within the dialogical argumentation of chapters 2–3 where he says that there are some who "slanderously report" and "claim" that his message boils down, in effect, to the libertine axiom "Let us do evil that good may result." It is a charge that Paul denounces in the strongest pos-

96. K. Grayston, "'Not Ashamed of the Gospel,'" 573.

97. W. Schmithals, *Römerbrief als historisches Problem,* 92.

98. P. Stuhlmacher, "Purpose of Romans," in Donfried, ed., *Romans Debate* (1991), 239.

99. A. J. M. Wedderburn, *Reasons for Romans,* 104 (italics his); see his full treatment of this position on pp. 104-42.

sible terms, saying: "Their condemnation is deserved" — with that response comparable to his denunciations in some of his other letters of those who opposed his message.[100] On the anathema expressed here in 3:8, Peter Stuhlmacher writes: "The Apostle is so infuriated by the slanderers who are saying this sort of thing behind his back that he declares them worthy of God's judgment."[101] Some scholars, in fact, have seen this charge as "just the tip of the iceberg" of an extensive body of criticism that had been mounted against Paul by at least some Christians at Rome — who were, as these scholars believe, "Jewish" Christians — and against which Paul was greatly concerned to defend himself throughout his entire letter to the Romans.[102]

Other scholars, however, argue that the so-called "diatribal texts" of Romans, which include the slanderous words of 3:8, are to be read as "the dramatic fiction of a dialogue with a Jewish interlocutor" and not as an attempt to counter real opponents at Rome. Stanley Stowers, for example, argued (1) that the dialogical style of Romans is "pedagogical and hortatory rather than polemical," being "motivated by concern rather than contempt," and so (2) that it is "a misunderstanding to read dialogical features (e.g. objections) as references to actual groups in the Roman church."[103] Likewise, David Aune says of Paul's "extended use of diatribe style throughout Romans 1–11":

> The diatribe was a classroom style featuring the Socratic method of indictment and persuasion to lead students out of ignorance and error to the truth. The imaginary opponents, hypothetical objections, and false conclusions that permeate diatribe rhetoric do not reflect the position of specific opponents whom the teacher attacks, but rather a range of possible objections. Paul's presentation of his gospel in Romans 1–11, therefore, is not occasioned by the *specific* epistolary situation, but rather introduces his *general* theological views and teaching style.[104]

---

100. Cf., e.g., Gal 1:9; 2 Cor 11:13-15; and Phil 3:18-19.

101. P. Stuhlmacher, "Purpose of Romans," in Donfried, ed., *Romans Debate* (1991), 239.

102. So, e.g., N. Elliott, *Rhetoric of Romans,* 97-98; D. A. Campbell, "Determining the Gospel," 325-27.

103. S. K. Stowers, "The Diatribe," in *Greco-Roman Literature and the New Testament,* ed. D. E. Aune, SBL.SBS 21 (Atlanta: Scholars, 1988), 81-82; *idem, The Diatribe and Paul's Letter to the Romans* (Chico: Scholars, 1981), esp. 55 and 203, n. 291, where 3:8 is listed among the "short responses, exhortations or thoughts for the day"; *idem,* "Paul's Dialogue with a Fellow Jew in Rom. 3.1-9," *CBQ* 46 (1984) 707-22.

104. D. E. Aune, *New Testament in Its Literary Environment,* 219-20 (italics his).

Rom 2:16, which appears as well within the dialogical argumentation of chapters 2–3, has also been viewed as a veiled allusion to some sort of misrepresentation of the apostle's message. For in the comment "as my gospel declares," Paul has been seen as defending his preaching of the gospel against any charge of "cheap grace,"[105] and so what he says about God judging people's secrets "through Jesus Christ" has been interpreted as "a pointed argument necessitated by the situation in Rome and by Paul's need to defend his proclamation."[106] Likewise, the final series of exhortations in the letter, that is, that in 16:17-20 — where Paul urges his addressees to "watch out for those who cause divisions and put obstacles in your way," to "keep away from them," to continue on in their Christian "obedience," and to rest in the confidence that "the God of peace will soon crush Satan under your feet" — has been seen as reflecting either some form of antagonism against Paul on the part of the Christians at Rome or some type of misunderstanding of his message, or both. Douglas Campbell, in fact, calls these final exhortations of the letter "the clearest direct textual indicator of the opponents in Romans."[107] And Stuhlmacher has rephrased Paul's words of 16:17-20 to read in condensed form: "The Romans should pay no attention to the insinuations of those in Rome who oppose the gospel planted there, for Paul is entirely in agreement with it."[108]

Further, the rhetorical questions that appear frequently in Romans have also been read as reflecting, at least to some extent, certain criticisms against Paul's person and various challenges to his message at Rome. Stuhlmacher, in particular, has argued:

> Nor are the rhetorical questions which punctuate the argument merely matters of style. They are more than that. Take for example Romans 3:31. Here the Apostle asks, "Do we overthrow the law by this faith?" Or 4:1, "What then shall we say about Abraham, our forefather according to the flesh?" Or 6:1, "Are we to continue in sin that grace may abound?" Or 6:15, "What then? Are we to sin because we are not under the law but under grace? By no means!" Or finally 7:7, 12, 14, "What shall we say then? That the law is sin? By no means! . . . the law is holy, and the commandment is holy and just and good." And a little later, "We know that the law is spiritual." In every case the Apostle is alluding to criticisms and chal-

---

105. So, e.g., P. Stuhlmacher, "Purpose of Romans," 239.
106. P. Stuhlmacher, "Purpose of Romans," 240.
107. D. A. Campbell, "Determining the Gospel," 328.
108. P. Stuhlmacher, "Purpose of Romans," 239.

lenges from his Jewish Christian opponents as they spread from Asia Minor and Greece to Rome. His intention is to refute and answer them. The dialogue we are witnessing in Romans is a real one in which Paul is wrestling for the hearts and minds of the Christians in Rome.[109]

Such an understanding of Romans as an apologetic letter written to counter certain criticisms of Paul and to correct various misrepresentations of his message that were then circulating among the Christians of Rome — especially, as many have proposed, among the *Jewish Christians* of the city; but also, as I have argued, among the greater body of *Gentile Christians* who had espoused the theology, liturgy, and practices of the Mother Church at Jerusalem — was, evidently, never suggested during the first eighteen centuries of Christian history. For during those first eighteen centuries of Christendom the passing comments and veiled allusions cited above seem not to have ever been noticed; while the rhetorical questions, when observed, were viewed as being directed against non-Christian Jews or the opposition of Judaism to Paul's message, but not in any way against Christians at Rome, whether ethnically Jewish or Gentile. During the twentieth century, however, the thesis that Romans should be understood as a letter of self-defense that was written in order to counter certain criticisms and to correct various misrepresentations by Christians at Rome has been argued, in various ways and to differing extents, not only by those interpreters of Paul cited above, but also by such scholars as Wilfred L. Knox,[110] Maurice Goguel,[111] John Knox,[112] Archibald M. Hunter,[113] Ernest Best,[114] John W. Drane,[115] and, extensively, Gerd Lüdemann.[116]

Separate Letters Written on Different Occasions for Different Purposes

A few scholars have maintained that Romans is a composite of two separate letters that were originally written on different occasions for different pur-

---

109. P. Stuhlmacher, "Purpose of Romans," 240.

110. W. L. Knox, *St. Paul and the Church of Jerusalem* (Cambridge: Cambridge University Press, 1925), 260, n. 26.

111. M. Goguel, *The Birth of Christianity*, trans. H. C. Snape (London: Allen & Unwin, 1953), 316-17.

112. J. Knox, "Romans: Introduction," *IB* 9.355-72.

113. A. M. Hunter, *Romans*, 14-15.

114. E. Best, *Romans*, 6.

115. J. W. Drane, "Why Did Paul Write Romans?" 223-24.

116. G. Lüdemann, esp. his *Opposition to Paul in Jewish Christianity*, 35-115.

poses, but which later became somehow united into a single composition. Walter Schmithals argued that "Letter A," which he posited is represented by 1–4; 5:12–11:36; and 15:8-13, was motivated by Paul's desire to bring Gentile Christians, who had decided leanings toward Judaism, into the apostle's understanding of the Christian gospel, whereas "Letter B," which he viewed as represented by chapters 12; 13:8-10; 14:1–15:4a; 15:7, 5-6, 14-32, 33; and 16:21-23, was written sometime later to those same Gentile Christian addressees who had by then accepted his gospel, urging them to be tolerant of other Gentile Christians who were not so enlightened — though with the insertion of numerous non-Pauline glosses and interpolations by some yet later editor almost everywhere throughout these two conflated letters, particularly where Jewish Christians are represented as having been present in the Roman church and where Schmithals judged the material "foreign" to Paul.[117] Somewhat along the same lines, Junji Kinoshita in his "new interpretation of the body of Romans" proposed that Romans consisted of two letters that had somehow been combined: (1) an original Pauline letter addressed to Gentile Christians, which he asserted is represented by 1:1-32; 2:6-16; 3:21-26; 5:1-11; 8; 12–13; and 15:14-33, to which were added (2) other materials from another Pauline letter addressed to Jewish believers.[118] But these theses of Schmithals and Kinoshita, though different in their understandings of the addressees and in their literary analyses, have generally been seen as "arguments of despair" motivated by the seeming complexity of the data and the inability of scholars to come up with a unified purpose or set of purposes for the writing of Romans.

More plausible is the proposal of Robin Scroggs, which is based on the rhetorical differences between chapters 1–4 and 9–11, on the one hand, and chapters 5–8, on the other. Highlighting these differences, Scroggs argued that chapters 1–11 should be seen as containing two Pauline sermons: one to a Jewish audience, which was originally made up of materials now in chapters 1–4 and 9–11, but whose parts have somehow become separated in our present canonical letter; the other to a Gentile audience, which is represented by chapters 5–8.[119]

But while Scroggs made a number of important points regarding the rhetoric of Paul in chapters 5–8 — as well as a number of apt observations re-

---

117. W. Schmithals, *Römerbrief als historisches Problem, passim; idem, Römerbrief, passim.*

118. J. Kinoshita, "Romans — Two Writings Combined."

119. R. Scroggs, "Paul as Rhetorician."

garding how the rhetoric of chapters 5–8 differs from that of chapters 1–4 and 9–11 — a better explanation, which we will attempt to explicate in this chapter below, can be given for the differences that exist between these two sets of material. And if that explanation is, indeed, credited as being better, then Scroggs's proposal must be judged, along with those of Schmithals and Kinoshita, as something of an "argument of despair."

3. Toward a Proper Method for Determining Paul's Purpose or Purposes

The determination of Paul's purpose or purposes in writing Romans is of great importance for an understanding of the letter. For unless Romans is read in a purely devotional, theological, homiletical, or "reader response" fashion, how one understands the author's purpose has a profound effect on how one understands the character and content of what is written. As Fenton J. A. Hort long ago observed, "so long as the purpose of the Epistle remains obscure, the main drift of its doctrinal teaching must remain obscure also."[120] Or as James Miller has more recently expressed it, "a decision regarding the letter's purpose inevitably shapes how one understands Paul's argument."[121]

Prior to such a determination, however, and especially because of the great variety of answers that have been proposed, consideration must be given to what may be called a "proper method" for defining the problem, sorting out the issues, assigning priorities, and arriving at a working hypothesis. In particular, a method needs to be established for resolving the tensions that have existed between (1) Romans as a letter directed to a particular group of Christians at Rome *and* Romans as a theological statement suitable for widespread distribution and use, (2) the epistolary nature of the frame of the letter *and* the expositional nature of its main body of material, and (3) the author's explicit and repeated references to his addressees as Gentile believers *and* his extensive use of what appears to be Jewish Christian argumentation.

The Epistolary Frame of the Letter

In the study of Paul's letters, as well as for every NT letter, the dictum enunciated by Robert Funk holds true: "The first order of business is to learn to

120. F. J. A. Hort, *Prolegomena*, 5.
121. J. C. Miller, *Obedience of Faith*, 1.

read the letter as a letter. This means above all to learn to read its structure."[122] Further, it is of very great importance when taking up any of Paul's letters to note what he says in the epistolary frame of that letter about (1) his personal concerns when writing and (2) his purpose or purposes for writing (or what might be called his "agenda"). For it is in the opening sections of Paul's letters (i.e., in the "salutations," "thanksgivings" [or θαυμάζω section of Gal 1:6-10], and "body openings" that begin a typical Pauline letter), together with the closing sections of his letters (i.e., the "body closings" [or so-called "apostolic parousia" sections], "final greetings," "admonitions," and "personal subscriptions" that conclude his letters), where Paul most explicitly expresses his concerns and his purpose or purposes in writing his letters.

It was Paul Schubert who in 1939 first undertook a formal analysis of the thanksgiving sections of Paul's letters and first argued: "Each thanksgiving not only announces clearly the subject matter of the letter, but also foreshadows unmistakably its stylistic qualities, the degree of intimacy and other important characteristics."[123] And Schubert's thesis has been spelled out, supported, clarified, and applied by others, most notably by Peter O'Brien[124] and Ann Jervis.[125]

As for the "closings" or "conclusions" of Paul's letters, Adolf Deissmann long ago argued: "More attention ought to be paid to the concluding words of the letters generally; they are of the highest importance if we are ever to understand the Apostle."[126] More recently Calvin Roetzel has bemoaned the fact that the Pauline letter closing has received scant attention among scholars, for there can be "discovered in it important clues to the viewpoint of the letter as a whole."[127]

It was not until the work of Ann Jervis in her 1991 *Purpose of Romans* and Jeffrey Weima in his 1994 *Neglected Endings,* however, that the closing sections of Paul's letters were formally treated as "carefully constructed units, shaped and adapted in such a way that they relate directly to — sometimes, in fact, even summarize — the major concerns and themes previously addressed in the body section of their respective letters."[128] And it was not

---

122. R. Funk, "The Form and Function of the Pauline Letter," *SBL Seminar Papers* (Missoula: Scholars, 1970), 8.

123. P. Schubert, *Form and Function of the Pauline Thanksgivings,* 77.

124. P. O'Brien, *Introductory Thanksgivings.*

125. L. A. Jervis, *Purpose of Romans,* 48-52, 86-109.

126. A. Deissmann, *Bible Studies,* trans. A. Grieve (Edinburgh: T&T Clark, 1901), 347.

127. C. Roetzel, *The Letters of Paul* (Atlanta: John Knox, 1975), 36.

128. Quoting J. A. D. Weima, "Pauline Letter Closings," 177-78 and 197.

until Jervis and Weima that the "salutation" (1:1-7) and the "thanksgiving" (1:8-12; or, perhaps, 1:8-15) at the beginning of Romans, together with the "apostolic parousia" (15:14-32) and the "closing" (15:33–16:27) at its end, were seen to be important for the determination of Paul's primary purpose or purposes and principal concerns in writing the letter — with a separate chapter devoted to each of these four sections by Jervis in her *Purpose of Romans* and a separate section to each of them by Weima in his "Preaching the Gospel in Rome."

When reading any Pauline letter, therefore, it is necessary to begin by noting what the apostle says about his concerns and his purpose or purposes in writing the letter. Otherwise, we might find ourselves engaged in some sort of "fishing expedition" — that is, in (1) cataloguing the features of a letter simply by the amount of material given to its various topics or by what appeals to us most, (2) setting out a letter's agenda in terms of our own theological agenda, or (3) identifying the apostle's purpose or purposes by reference to what they were in other letters (as in the case of Romans, what they were in Galatians and the Corinthian letters) or by what we think they ought to have been by some process of our own mirror reading of the letter. Paul's letters are letters, and, like any letter, we need to begin our reading of them by giving careful attention to what Paul says about his own concerns and about his purpose or purposes in the epistolary framework of his letters.

Mirror Reading the Letter

It is not sufficient, however, simply to organize all of Paul's statements in the opening and closing sections of his letters, compare those materials and statements with what has been found in other Greco-Roman and Jewish letters of the day, note similarities and differences in the various Pauline epistolary frames, and draw implications regarding the apostle's purpose or purposes for writing each of his extant letters. Mirror reading of what Paul says in his letters — particularly of what he argues in the bodies of those letters — is also important. For while the epistolary frames contain explicit statements regarding the particular occasion and respective purpose or purposes for each of his letters, and so provide guidance in identifying the apostle's principal concerns and primary purpose or purposes in writing, what Paul says in the bodies of those letters needs also to be carefully investigated with respect to (1) how that larger body of material correlates with what can be determined from the epistolary frames regarding his concerns and his purpose or purposes in writing, and (2) whatever else might be determined regarding his concerns and his purpose or purposes by means of a mirror reading of what is presented.

Karl Donfried's dictum, which he enunciated as "Methodological Principle I" when dealing with Rom 14:1–15:13, is certainly apropos — whether accepted as stated or nuanced in a more acceptable manner:

> Any study of Romans should proceed on the initial assumption that this letter was written by Paul to deal with a concrete situation in Rome. The support for such an assumption is the fact that every other authentic Pauline writing, *without exception,* is addressed to the specific situations of the churches or persons involved. To argue that Romans is an exception to this Pauline pattern is certainly possible, but the burden of proof rests with those exegetes who wish to demonstrate that it is impossible, or at least not likely, that Romans addresses a concrete set of problems in the life of Christians in Rome.[129]

Ever since Martin Luther, at least among most Protestant NT scholars, the common way to read Romans has been to turn its statements regarding "law," "sin," "righteousness," "justification," and "faith," together with its rejection of "works of the law," into polemical responses, and so to understand Paul's purpose in writing as being to counter the claims of legalistic Jewish Christians at Rome — just as Paul countered the teachings of the "Judaizers" in Galatians, only doing so in Romans in a more moderate and reflective manner. But evidence for that view of the "concrete situation" of Christians at Rome, as Alexander Wedderburn has rightly observed (even though he would like to believe otherwise), is "tantalizingly scanty."[130] In fact, as Mark Nanos has insisted, there is no evidence in Romans that Paul is polemicizing against either Judaism or Jewish Christianity in Romans.[131] The data used to support such a reading should be understood differently, as I will attempt to spell out below in discussing Paul's primary and subsidiary purposes for writing Romans.

During the last quarter of the twentieth century, other portions of Romans have also been viewed as able to be mirror read, and so used to identify other situations in the Roman house churches to which Paul might have been speaking and to determine something more of his purpose or purposes

---

129. K. P. Donfried, "False Presuppositions," in Donfried, ed., *Romans Debate* (1977), 122; (1991), 103-4 (italics his).

130. A. J. M. Wedderburn, *Reasons for Romans*, 54.

131. Cf. M. D. Nanos, *Mystery of Romans, passim.*

in writing as he did. Chief among these has been the series of exhortations regarding "the strong and the weak" in 14:1–15:13. Also to be classed among those materials that seem to reflect conditions among the Christians at Rome are (1) his counsel concerning the relation of Christians to civil government and the paying of taxes in 13:1-7, (2) a number of passing comments and veiled allusions in such passages as 1:16; 2:16; 3:8; and 16:17-20, as well as in certain rhetorical questions in 3:31; 4:1; 6:1; 6:15; 7:7; and 7:13, that can be understood as Paul defending himself against criticism and misunderstanding, and (3) the final exhortation of the letter to "watch out for those who cause divisions and put obstacles in your way," to "keep away from them," to continue on in Christian "obedience," and to rest in the confidence that "the God of peace will soon crush Satan under your feet" in 16:17-20.

All of this data drawn from a mirror reading of the letter — that is, (1) the data usually used in support of reading Romans as a polemical and/or apologetic response to legalistic Jews or Jewish Christians at Rome (which we would like to reinterpret) and (2) the data incorporated in certain of the apostle's exhortations, passing comments, veiled allusions, and rhetorical questions (which we would like to highlight) — is important in constructing a theory about Paul's purpose or purposes in writing Romans. And all this data we will attempt to take into account in setting out a new understanding of Paul's primary and subsidiary purposes below.

External Data

There are also valuable bits and pieces of information that can be gleaned from various external sources, both directly and indirectly, about Jews and Christians at Rome at the time of Paul's writing Romans, about the religious and societal circumstances of the Christians in the city, and about the nature of Paul's letter when compared to other writings of the day. Some of these matters we dealt with in Chapter III ("Occasion and Date"); others we highlighted in Chapter IV ("Addressees"); and still others we have referred to in passing, but must elaborate more fully in Chapter VI ("Greco-Roman Oral, Rhetorical, and Epistolary Conventions").

An important rule of hermeneutics for the understanding of any Pauline letter is that one must always start with the letter itself, interpreting it as a self-contained unit of material. But comparative studies of the letter's literary, historical, and ideological settings, as well as its particular teachings, are also important — not only with regard to how the letter relates in these matters to cognate letters in the Pauline corpus, to other writings of the NT, and to the whole of the Christian Bible, but also how it relates to information that can be gleaned from Greco-Roman and Jewish writings regarding historical events, religious attitudes, civic and social situations, and literary conventions and practices. For while one's interpretation of Scripture must not be determined simply by reference to what was taking place in the world of that day (or by what is taking place today), data drawn from the various historical, literary, and religious sources of that day (and from whatever such sources may be available today), when used perceptively, discriminatingly, and respectfully, can provide new insights, new methods, and new approaches in dealing with old problems and perennial conundrums.

4. The Impact of Our Proposed Understanding of the Letter's Addressees

The basic assumptions underlying our study of Romans are (1) that Paul wanted to communicate intelligibly and effectively to Christians at Rome in their particular circumstances, (2) that he viewed his addressees at Rome as being mainly Gentile believers in Jesus Christ, and so within the orbit of his Gentile ministry — even though he was not the one who had originally evangelized them and there were also many Jewish believers in Jesus among them, (3) that he had both primary purposes and subsidiary reasons for writing Romans, and (4) that he considered all of these purposes and reasons to be of real importance. We have, therefore, taken some time and space in Chapter IV to discuss matters regarding the identity, character, circumstances, and concerns of Paul's Christian addressees at Rome. Further, we have sketched out above various positions that have been advanced as to how Paul's purpose or purposes in writing those Roman believers in Jesus should be understood. It remains here to spell out how our proposed understanding of Paul's Roman addressees impacts the immediate question of his purpose or purposes in writing them and to suggest how that understanding moves forward the interpretation of this most important letter.

Our Understanding of the Addressees

Almost everything written about Romans in the past has been based on one or the other of the following views regarding the letter's addressees: (1) that they were Jewish Christians who were bound in some ways by their Jewish heritage, and so needed to be instructed about the law-free nature of the Christian gospel, (2) that they were Gentile Christians who were of a "Pauline tendency" but influenced by certain legalistic Jewish Christians, and so needed to be taught anew about the real nature of the gospel, or (3) that the church at Rome consisted of both Gentile Christians, who seem to have been in the majority but were somewhat uncertain about their faith theologically, and Jewish Christians, who were in the minority but felt strongly about certain legalistic matters that they carried over from their Jewish heritage, with Paul speaking at times to one of these groups and at other times to the other. Such understandings, however, have been challenged and considerably revised by both Raymond Brown on textual and theological grounds and Wolfgang Wiefel on historical and sociological bases.

Brown's point, as noted earlier (cf. Chapter IV, "Addressees"), is that the question to be asked regarding the identity and character of the letter's addressees is not "Were they either Jewish or Gentiles ethnically, or dominantly one or the other?" — with the implications being that if Jewish, they should be viewed as non-Pauline in their outlook, but if Gentile, then understood as being in accord with Paul's teaching. Brown believed that the addressees of Paul's letter constituted both Jewish and Gentile believers in Jesus, with the latter being in the majority since Paul considered the church at Rome to be within the orbit of his Gentile ministry. But rather than attempt to determine the addressees' identity, character, circumstances, and concerns on the basis of their particular ethnic origins, "the crucial issue," Brown argued, "is the theological outlook of this mixed Jewish/Gentile Christianity."[132] For as Brown insisted, if we take seriously the testimonies of the Christian commentator Ambrosiaster and the Roman historian Tacitus, we need to highlight the axis that runs from Roman Christianity back to the Jerusalem Church in Judea as being of major importance.

Further, as Brown has pointed out:

> According to Acts, for the first two Christian decades, Jerusalem and Antioch served as the dissemination points of the Gospel. Because of his interest in Paul, the author keeps us well informed of missions to the West moving out from Antioch, but there is never a suggestion that a mission went from Antioch to Rome. (Indeed, in the first 15 chapters of Acts the only mention of Rome/Roman is 2:10 which notes the presence

132. R. E. Brown, *Antioch and Rome*, 109, n. 227.

of Roman Jews at Jerusalem on the first Pentecost.) There are no arguments from Acts for a site other than Jerusalem as the source for Roman Christianity, and Acts 28:21 relates that Jews in Rome had channels of theological information coming from Jerusalem.[133]

So Brown concluded: (1) that for both Jews and Christians at Rome, "the Jerusalem-Rome axis was strong," (2) "that Roman Christianity came from Jerusalem, and indeed represented the Jewish/Gentile Christianity associated with such Jerusalem figures as Peter and James," and (3) that both in the earliest days of the Roman church and at the time when Paul wrote them, believers at Rome could be characterized as "Christians who kept up some Jewish observances and remained faithful to part of the heritage of the Jewish Law and cult, without insisting on circumcision."[134]

Wolfgang Wiefel's main points regarding Paul's addressees in Romans (as also set out earlier in Chapter IV, "Addressees") may be summarized as follows:[135]

1. that just as the Jewish populace in Rome was administratively disorganized, so the earliest believers in Jesus, who were Jews and proselyte Gentiles and who in those early days continued to meet and worship in the Jewish synagogues, lacked any formal organization;

2. that just as the Jerusalem-Rome axis was strong for Roman Jewry, with the ties between the various synagogues of Rome and Jerusalem Judaism being more important than relations between the city's separate synagogues, so the axis between the Jerusalem Church and Christians at Rome was strong, whether the believers in Jesus at Rome were ethnically Jewish, as at first, or dominantly Gentile, as later;

3. that just as the Jews of Rome were forbidden by the emperor Claudius in A.D. 41 the right of free assembly in their traditional synagogue associations, and therefore had to meet in smaller groups in their own homes, so Christians were compelled to meet for their worship of God through Jesus "the Christ" in household groupings or "house churches"; and,

4. that just as Christianity at Rome before the Edict of Claudius in A.D. 49 was Jewish in nature — being first espoused by Jews, composed of

133. R. E. Brown, *Antioch and Rome*, 103-4.
134. R. E. Brown, *Antioch and Rome*, 104.
135. Cf. W. Wiefel, "Jewish Community," in Donfried, ed., *Romans Debate* (1977), 100-119; (1991), 85-101.

Jews and Gentile proselytes within the Jewish synagogues, and heavily influenced from the start by the Jerusalem Church — so Christianity at Rome after the Edict of Claudius became essentially Gentile in its ethnological composition (or, as Wiefel himself believes, "entirely Gentile"), though with its theology, ecclesiology, and ethics still rooted in the Jewish Christianity of the Mother Church at Jerusalem.

It is the amalgam of these theses of Raymond Brown and Wolfgang Wiefel, coupled with renewed interests in the "house churches" of Paul's letters generally and the rhetoric of Romans in particular, that has impacted in new ways the old questions about the identity, character, circumstances, and concerns of Paul's addressees. And it is the insights gained from these theses and studies that provide, I propose, a new understanding of Paul's primary and subsidiary purposes in writing Romans.

Our thesis, therefore, may be spelled out as follows: (1) that ethnically Paul's addressees at Rome constituted both Jewish and Gentile believers in Jesus, though, since the Edict of Claudius in A.D. 49, the latter group had become increasingly dominant, (2) that theologically all the Christians at Rome, whether ethnically Gentile or Jewish, looked to the Jerusalem Church for inspiration and guidance, reverenced the Mosaic law, and followed some of the Jewish rites and practices, but were not "Judaizers" like those who troubled Gentile Christians in the Roman province of Galatia, and (3) that socially they were no longer meeting in the Jewish synagogues (Claudius's mandate of A.D. 41 and edict of A.D. 49 having put an end to such synagogue gatherings) and were without any overarching administrative structure (in common with the situation of the Jews in the city), but gathered for worship and fellowship in the homes and tenement accommodations of various Christians of the city — that is, in "house churches" and "tenement groups," which constituted a loose association of separate congregations. And if all this be true, as we believe it is, then it is necessary to read Romans in a different fashion than has usually been done.

Reading the Epistolary Frame of the Letter in a New Way

The study of any Pauline letter must begin, as we have argued, by giving attention to the letter's epistolary frame — that is, to its opening "salutation," "thanksgiving" (or, as with Gal 1:6-10, its θαυμάζω section), and "body opening" sections, together with its "body closing" (or "apostolic parousia") and its various concluding sections. This is especially important when reading Romans guided by our proposed new understanding of its addressees. It is necessary, therefore, to sketch out here how the epistolary frame of Romans should be read in light of this new understanding — giving attention first to what is not said (i.e., to certain negative observations) and then to what is said (i.e., to some important positive observations), and throughout asking how such a new understanding of the addressees affects an understanding of Paul's purpose or purposes when writing the letter.

1. Negative Observations

First of all, by way of negative observations, it needs to be noted that there is in the epistolary frame of Romans no disparagement by Paul of his addressees' Christian faith or theological commitments. Likewise, there is in this material very little reference to any difficulties among them. Contrary to the strident rebuke of his Gentile converts in the θαυμάζω section of Galatians, which begins with the words, "I am astonished that you are so quickly deserting the one who called you by the grace of Christ and are turning to a different gospel, which is not at all the same gospel" (Gal 1:6-7a), Paul begins the thanksgiving section of Romans by saying: "First, I thank my God through Jesus Christ for all of you, because your faith is being reported all over the world" (Rom 1:8). Admittedly, later, at the end of the letter, Paul warns his addressees about "those who cause divisions and put obstacles in your way, contrary to the teaching you have learned" (16:17). But such "divisions" and "obstacles" he credits not to any deficiency in their original teaching or lack in their present understanding, for, as he says, it is "contrary to the teaching you have learned." Rather, whatever divisions and obstacles existed among Christians at Rome he attributes to the "smooth talk and flattery" of others (16:18). And he goes on in the next verse to speak of his addressees' "obedience," which he says "everyone has heard about" and which has caused him great joy (16:19).

Further, it needs to be noted that there is no statement or suggestion anywhere in the epistolary frame of Romans that Paul viewed the Christians at Rome as being in any way deficient in their apostolic founding. Nor is there any hint in these materials that he thought of his writing to them as part of a process to correct such a deficiency — whether by asserting his own apostolic authority over them or by seeking to establish an apostolic foundation for the church by his presence. That thesis has been spawned by reading what Paul says about his apostleship in a polemical manner and with a monarchical view of church order. But there are, we believe, far better and more cogent explanations for such statements in Romans.

What Paul does say about the church at Rome in the opening sentence of the body closing section of Romans is: "I myself am convinced, my brothers, that you yourselves are full of goodness, complete in knowledge and competent to instruct one another" (15:14). Further, he goes on in the following verse to say that what he has written to them in the previous portions of his letter, even though "quite boldly on some points," has been written only in order "to remind you of them again" (15:15). These latter statements, as Karl Donfried has rightly pointed out, hardly reflect a situation in which Paul thought of Christians at Rome as still needing a proper apostolic foundation — or one that he thought, if in need of correction, could be supplied simply "while passing through" Rome on his way to Spain.[136]

The usual way of viewing the bombastic denunciations found in the epistolary frame of Galatians vis-à-vis the commendatory affirmations of the epistolary frame of Romans is to declare either (1) that Paul was somewhat overly brazen or extreme in writing to the Galatians or (2) that he was more muted, moderate, reflective, or diplomatic in Romans — often both, but at least certainly the latter. If, however, our new understanding of the addressees of Romans (as proposed above) is true, then the situations addressed in Galatians and Romans must be judged to have been not the same, despite the similarities of topics in the two letters, and Paul's purposes in writing Romans must be seen as having been different from his purposes in writing Galatians.

2. Positive Observations

Positively, however, it needs to be noted that in the epistolary frame of Romans Paul speaks almost entirely about his own person, his own desires, and his own concerns. This is quite different from what is found in the epistolary frames of most of the other Pauline letters, with the possible exception of Ephesians. For in most, if not all, of the epistolary frames of his other letters Paul speaks about the issues and concerns of his addressees — that is, usually about their theological lapses and their ethical failures, and so repeatedly uses the second person plural pronoun "you" — whereas in the epistolary frame of Romans it is his own desires and concerns that dominate, and so he uses the first person singular pronoun "I."

136. Cf. K. P. Donfried, "Short Note on Romans 16," in Donfried, ed., *Romans Debate* (1977), 51; (1991), 45.

This phenomenon is especially evident in Romans' thanksgiving section of 1:8-12, which, as Paul Schubert has observed is true with respect to all of Paul's letters, "not only announces clearly the subject matter of the letter, but also foreshadows unmistakably its stylistic qualities, the degree of intimacy and other important characteristics."[137] Or as Jeffrey Weima notes: "It is here [in the thanksgiving section of Romans] that we can expect Paul to tip his hand as to his primary purpose(s) in writing to the Roman believers."[138] Thus in the "thanksgiving" of 1:8-12 Paul speaks about *his* thankfulness for his addressees (1:8), *his* prayers for them (1:9-10), *his* desire to come to them (1:10-11, 13), and *his* wanting to give them some "spiritual gift" so that they might "be mutually encouraged by each other's faith" (1:11-12) — as well as, in what we will later identify as the "body opening" of 1:13-15, *his* obligation to preach to them, as he has to other Gentiles (1:14-15). And this highlighting of his desires and his concerns, as well as of his own person and qualities, also appears in the "salutation" of 1:1-7, when he speaks about himself as "a servant of Christ Jesus, called to be an apostle, and set apart for the gospel of God" (1:1) and about his own apostolic ministry to "all the Gentiles" (1:5).

Such an emphasis on Paul's own person, desires, and concerns appears, as well, in the concluding sections of the letter — which sections throughout the Pauline corpus, as Jeffrey Weima has ably argued, must be seen as "carefully constructed units, shaped and adapted in such a way that they relate directly to — sometimes, in fact, even summarize — the major concerns and themes previously addressed in the body section of their respective letters."[139] Thus in the letter's "body closing" (or "apostolic parousia") of 15:14-32, Paul discusses *his* ministry to the Gentiles and the inclusion of Christians at Rome within the orbit of *his* Gentile ministry (15:14-22), *his* travel plans, which include *his* presentation of a collection from his Gentile churches as "a contribution for the poor among the saints in Jerusalem," *his* visit to the Christians at Rome, *his* future ministry in Spain (15:23-29), and *his* request for his addressees' prayers as he is at Jerusalem and then as he journeys on to them (15:30-32). And in the concluding sections of 15:33–16:27 he greets his friends at Rome (16:1-16) and concludes with a reference to what he calls "my gospel" (16:25).

The "salutation" of 1:1-7 also highlights other matters of great concern

---

137. P. Schubert, *Form and Function of the Pauline Thanksgivings,* 77.
138. J. A. D. Weima, "Preaching the Gospel in Rome," 345.
139. J. A. D. Weima, "Pauline Letter Closings," 177-78 and 197.

to Paul when writing Romans, and these matters must be taken into account as well when asking about his primary purposes in writing to the Christians at Rome. Among these are (1) his concern for "the gospel of God" (1:1), (2) his consciousness of that gospel as being rooted in "the Holy Scriptures" (1:2), (3) his understanding of the Christian message as having its focus in "his [God's] Son," who is presented as "a descendant of David," "the Son of God," and "Jesus Christ our Lord" (1:3-4), (4) his consciousness of having been divinely appointed "to call people from among all the Gentiles to the obedience that comes from faith" (1:5), and (5) his recognition that the Christians of Rome were within the orbit of his divinely appointed Gentile ministry (1:6).

The "thanksgiving" of 1:8-12 continues many of the same features as found in the "salutation." But it also expresses Paul's desire (1) to visit his addressees at Rome (1:10; cf. also v. 13) and (2) to give them "some spiritual gift" (τι χάρισμα πνευματικόν), which would not only make them strong but also enable both them and him to mutually encourage one another (1:11-12). And in the "body opening" of 1:13-15 (see Chapter XI, "Structure and Argument") Paul goes on to speak of his obligation as God's appointed minister to the Gentiles as the basis for including the Christians at Rome within the orbit of his Gentile mission (1:14-15).

Further, while the "body closing" or "apostolic parousia" of 15:14-32 also highlights Paul's desire and plan to visit the Christians at Rome, it goes on (1) to suggest that their assistance in support of his proposed mission to Spain would be welcome (15:24, 32b), (2) to tell of the need to first take the money collected from his Gentile congregations to the Jerusalem Church in order to provide aid for the impoverished believers there (15:25-27), (3) to promise that after presenting that contribution at Jerusalem he will visit them at Rome (15:28-29, 32a), and (4) to ask for their prayers for a good reception at Jerusalem, both by the non-believing Jews of Judea and by the congregation of believers in Jerusalem (15:30-31).

And in the concluding sections of 15:33–16:27 there are (1) affectionate greetings sent to a large number of persons, families, and house-church groups at Rome, some thirty people in all being named (16:3-16), and (2) an acknowledgment that there existed within the Christian house churches at Rome certain people "who cause divisions and put obstacles in your way," giving a brief word of advice about not having relations with them (16:17-20a). Some scholars have argued, as we have noted earlier (cf. Chapter II, "Integrity"), that (1) since Paul could not have known so many people at Rome, (2) since the familiarity of these greetings hardly fits the non-personal tone of chapters 1–15, and (3) since the subject of "divisions" and "obstacles" was not raised in the body of the letter, chapter 16 must be viewed as having been added to the original material of Romans when that material was later sent to Christians at Ephesus — and so should be read as reflecting conditions at Ephesus rather than at Rome.[140] But accepting the integrity of at least 16:1-23, as has been cogently argued by Harry Gamble,[141] it must now be said, as Joel Marcus has appropriately observed: "If he [Paul] knew so many Roman Christians, it is credible that he was well enough informed about the situation of the Roman Christian community to address his letter to specific problems that had arisen there."[142] Further, accepting the probability of the integrity of the doxology of 16:25-27, it needs also to be noted that Paul's letter to the Romans concludes with an emphasis on the nature and substance of his proclamation of the gospel, which is characterized by the phrase "my gospel" (16:25-26).

All of this data in the opening and concluding sections of Romans, that is, in the epistolary frame of the letter, should be read as signaling Paul's major concerns and primary purposes in writing to the Christians at Rome. And when the letter is read in the light of our proposed new understanding of Paul's addressees, it must be read as addressing a different situation than was addressed in his letter to the Galatians. It cannot be doubted that Paul had, as well, some concerns about some of the particular circumstances of his addressees at Rome, as seem to be reflected in his rather general warning and advice of 16:17-20a. But his primary purposes for writing his letter to believers in Jesus at Rome, as seems evident from what he writes in the letter's epistolary frame, must be judged as having been mainly related to his own interests, his own desires, and his own concerns. And such interests, desires, and concerns should be given highest priority in any attempt to draw up a summary statement about Paul's purposes in writing Romans.

Reading the Body of the Letter in a New Way

Nonetheless, while recognizing the importance of the epistolary frame of the letter for understanding Paul's primary purposes in writing Romans, one must also read the entire body of his letter in the light of our suggested new

140. Cf., e.g., K. Lake, *Earlier Epistles of St. Paul,* 325-70; T. W. Manson, "St. Paul's Letter to the Romans — and Others."
141. Cf. H. Gamble Jr., *Textual History,* esp. 132-37.
142. J. Marcus, "The Circumcision and the Uncircumcision of Rome," 68.

understanding of the letter's addressees — and, in particular, "mirror read" at least certain portions of the body middle of the letter from such a perspective — in order to determine what other purposes he might have had for writing. For if the addressees are to be identified and characterized as we have done above, then the entire letter needs to be re-read in light of that new understanding and in terms of Paul's purposes as set out in the letter's epistolary frame. Further, if we accept the integrity of 16:17-20a, as we do, we may also believe that by a process of mirror reading at least some passages in the body of the letter can be viewed as reflecting conditions or circumstances at Rome that called for the apostle's warning and advice.

1. A Negative Observation

Negatively, it needs to be said at the very outset of any reading of the body of Romans that understanding Paul's statements about "law," "sin," "righteousness," "justification," and "faith" in the body of Romans, as well as his rejection of "works of the law," as polemical responses to the teachings of certain legalistic Jewish Christians at Rome rests on "tantalizingly scanty" evidence (to repeat Alexander Wedderburn's apt characterization of the basis for such an endeavor).[143] And if our new proposal regarding the letter's addresses is anywhere close to the mark, then it can no longer be said that the message of Romans was originally directed, as was that of Galatians, against the teachings of either Jewish or Gentile Christian "Judaizers" who were advocating the necessity of some form of legalism or nomism. Rather, the data often cited in support of an anti-judaistic polemic in Romans must now be understood in another manner, which is what we will attempt to do below in the final portion of this chapter.

2. Positive Observations

But while Romans is not to be read as an anti-judaistic polemic meant to counter a "judaizing" threat, whether real or anticipated, it needs to be recognized (1) that all of the material in the body middle of Romans (i.e., all of what is written in 1:16–15:13, which comprises the major theological sections of 1:16–11:36 and the major hortatory section of 12:1–15:13) is to be read as expressing Paul's concerns for his addressees at Rome, and (2) that there are certain individual statements and certain extended passages in these central

---

143. A. J. M. Wedderburn, *Reasons for Romans,* 54.

sections of the letter that can be mirror read as speaking to particular circumstances within the Christian house churches of Rome and/or to particular situations of believers in Jesus in the city, and therefore as reflecting something further about Paul's purposes in writing as he did. The individual statements appear throughout the central body middle of the letter, that is, throughout 1:16–15:13. The more extended passages, however, which seem able to be mirror read and so to reflect particular circumstances at Rome, appear in the hortatory section of the letter's body, that is, in 12:1–15:13. For pedagogical reasons, we will begin here with those more extended passages, attempting to determine by a process of mirror reading the circumstances that they reflect as existing among the Christians at Rome, and then we will move on to consider those individual statements that appear elsewhere throughout 1:16–11:36, attempting also to determine by mirror reading the situation at Rome of which they speak.

Chief among the passages frequently understood as addressing a then existing situation among the Christians at Rome is the series of exhortations about "the strong" and "the weak" in 14:1–15:13. It may be argued, as many have, that 14:1–15:13 should be viewed as "a theoretic development of the actual treatment of 1 Cor 8-10" — that is, as a "general Pauline paraenesis" or "general Pauline admonition" based on an earlier situation at Corinth.[144] Such an understanding of the statements in 14:1–15:13 as a reminiscence of an earlier situation, but "with the sting of controversy gone," is probably, as William Sanday and Arthur C. Headlam have called it, "the oldest explanation" of the passage.[145] And a large number of scholars today continue to interpret these exhortations in the hortatory section of Romans as, in the words of Victor Furnish, "a generalized adaptation of a position he [Paul] had earlier worked out respecting an actual, known situation in Corinth."[146]

Issues regarding relations between Rom 14:1–15:13 and 1 Cor 8:1–11:1 are too extensive and involved to be dealt with in any abbreviated fashion here, and so must be left for a more detailed treatment in a future commentary proper. Nonetheless, when judged on their own, the exhortations of 14:1–15:13 certainly seem to reflect a major concern of Paul about what was then taking place either within or between the various house churches of

144. So R. J. Karris, "Rom 14:1–15:13 and the Occasion of Romans," in Donfried, ed., *Romans Debate* (1977), 77, 83, 99; (1991), 66, 71, 84.

145. W. Sanday and A. C. Headlam, *Romans*, 400-401, citing Origen, Chrysostom, Augustine, and Neander; see their full treatment in 399-403.

146. V. P. Furnish, *The Love Command in the New Testament* (New York: Abingdon, 1972), 115.

Rome (not just some earlier situation he remembers as having occurred at Corinth and has earlier written about in 1 Cor 8:1–11:1). And we believe that when Paul's exhortations in this passage are judiciously mirror read, it may justifiably be postulated that a somewhat similar situation existed among the Christians at Rome as had earlier existed among the Christians at Corinth — though it needs also to be insisted that, while perhaps "somewhat similar," the circumstances were probably not the same.

Most important for our purposes here, however, is to insist that while almost every past treatment of 14:1–15:13 has taken it for granted that "the weak" represents Jewish Christians and "the strong" represents Gentile Christians, our thesis regarding the identity, character, circumstances, and concerns of the addressees of Paul's letter to Rome requires that we understand the Roman believers in Jesus at Rome differently than has usually been the case. Indeed, those designated "the strong" probably applied the term "strong" to themselves and the term "weak" to those they disagreed with, for hardly would those who thought of themselves as being scrupulous have called themselves "the weak" and their opponents "the strong." Further, those who identified themselves as "the strong" seem to have espoused views compatible with Paul's theology. Also to be noted is the fact that it is to this group that the apostle's exhortations regarding tolerance toward and the acceptance of others were directed. Likewise, it is beyond doubt that there are some features in Paul's rather sketchy depiction of "the weak" that could have been based — at least to an extent, though not entirely and probably not exclusively — on then current Jewish scruples.

Yet if our proposed new understanding of Paul's addressees be true, we cannot continue to align the two parties in the dispute simply on the basis of ethnicity — that is, as Gentile Christians with a "Pauline tendency," on the one side, and Jewish Christians with inherited Jewish scruples, on the other. For if all the Christians at Rome, whether ethnically Jews or Gentiles, looked to the Jerusalem Church for inspiration and guidance, reverenced the Mosaic law, and followed some of the Jewish rites and practices, then it may be postulated that the division spoken about in 14:1–15:13 was between certain individual Christians, whether ethnically Jews or Gentiles, who tended to group themselves along the lines of two opposing parties within some of the Christian house congregations of Rome. Or perhaps, as now seems probable from recent studies of house churches and community formation among the early Christians, the division should be seen as between certain entire household congregations composed of both Gentile and Jewish believers, which had become committed to one side of the issue, and other entire household congregations composed of both Gentile and Jewish believers, which held to the other side.

Also to be classed among the passages in Romans that should probably be mirror read as reflecting the situation of Christians at Rome, and so to suggest something further about the apostle's purposes in writing the letter, is Paul's counsel concerning the relation of Christians to civil government and the responsibility of believers in Jesus to pay their share of local taxes in 13:1-7. This is a passage that, as noted above, many have viewed as being a fairly unique and somewhat independent block of specific material, which appears in the midst of rather general exhortations on the subject of a Christian love ethic and seems to break the continuity of the exhortations in 12:9-21 and 13:8-10. Further, as Johannes Friedrich, Wolfgang Pöhlmann, and Peter Stuhlmacher have argued, Paul's exhortations about paying taxes and revenues to the civil authorities in 13:6-7 may very well be understood against the background of civil unrest at Rome during the mid-50's, which arose in opposition to the rapacious practices of those who collected the city's revenues and tolls.[147]

Much that needs to be said regarding this passage must be left for our proposed commentary later. Suffice it here to say (1) that contrary to a number of scholars who have viewed 13:1-7 as a gloss or interpolation, there is no reason to deny the passage's authenticity on either external or internal grounds, and (2) the fact that Paul here discusses the relation of Christians to civil government, which is a theme not found in his other extant letters and is somewhat disruptive in the context of general exhortations regarding love, "must be connected," as Ernst Käsemann has argued, "with the fact that he is addressing the church in the capital city of the empire."[148] And this is the approach to the passage that we take as well, agreeing with Alexander Wedderburn that 13:6-7 evidences "a surprisingly intimate knowledge by Paul, not only of the circumstances within the Roman church, but also of the situation in which its members had to live, and of the social, economic and political environment that surrounded them," and that Paul's advice to his addressees "was written in the light of that knowledge, and is to be interpreted by us in the light of that situation."[149]

Further, there are in the body of Romans a few passing comments and

147. Cf. again J. Friedrich, W. Pöhlmann, and P. Stuhlmacher, "Situation und Intention von Röm 13,1-7."

148. E. Käsemann, *Romans*, 350.

149. A. J. M. Wedderburn, *Reasons for Romans*, 63.

veiled allusions that can be mirror read as Paul defending himself against certain criticisms of his person and various misrepresentations of his message among the Christians at Rome. Such comments and allusions have been found in 1:16 ("For I am not ashamed of the gospel"), 2:16 ("as my gospel declares"), and 3:8 ("Why not say — as we are being slanderously reported and as some claim that we say — 'Let us do evil that good may result'?"). And an apologetic or polemical purpose can also be seen in the rhetorical questions of 3:31 ("Do we, then, nullify the law by this faith?"), 4:1 ("What then shall we say that Abraham, our forefather, discovered in this matter?"), 6:1 ("What shall we say, then? Shall we go on sinning so that grace may increase?"), 6:15 ("What then? Shall we sin because we are not under law but under grace?"), 7:7 ("What shall we say, then? Is the law sin?"), 7:13 ("Did that which is good, then, become death to me?"), and perhaps also in the implied rhetorical statement of 7:14 ("We know that the law is spiritual").

Such comments, allusions, and questions have usually been taken as part of Paul's anti-judaistic polemic against "judaizing" Jewish Christians at Rome. But if our proposed new understanding of Paul's addressees has merit — that they were dominantly Gentile Christians, with a minority of Jewish Christians among them, all of whom looked to the Jerusalem Church for inspiration and guidance, reverenced the Mosaic law, and followed some of the Jewish rites and practices, but were not "Judaizers" like those who troubled the Galatian congregations — it is not too difficult to mirror read these materials as what might be called "fervent knee-jerk responses" of the apostle to certain criticisms of his person and various misrepresentations of his message among the Gentile-Jewish believers in Jesus at Rome.

From reports that had probably come to them from various sources, the Gentile-Jewish believers in Jesus at Rome could very well have been a bit uneasy about Paul and his message, and so have expressed reservations about him. Conversely, having a number of friends at Rome, whom he greets in 16:3-16, Paul may have heard about their reservations. Assuming that such a scenario is reasonably accurate, his comments, allusions, and rhetorical questions cited above may, therefore, be justifiably mirror read in attempting to discern something further about his addressees' concerns and to learn something more about his purposes in writing them.

All of this data drawn from a mirror reading of the body middle of Romans — both that usually used in support of reading Romans as a polemical response to legalistic Jewish Christians at Rome (which view we have reinterpreted) and that found in some of the apostle's exhortations, comments, allusions, and rhetorical questions (which we have attempted to highlight)

— is important in constructing any theory about Paul's purposes in writing Romans. And all of this data we will attempt to take into consideration in setting out a new understanding of Paul's primary and subsidiary purposes.

5. Primary and Subsidiary Purposes for the Writing of Romans

Stanley Stowers has suggested that the "ambiguity" of scholars regarding the rhetoric and purpose of Romans would dissipate "if we suppose that Paul's literary audience represents something like those who have traditionally been called godfearers in modern scholarship."[150] That is a perceptive comment and an interesting suggestion. In some ways it brings us closer than many other proposals to understanding the addressees of Romans and solving the problem of Paul's purpose or purposes in writing to them. Nonetheless, we believe there is an even better way to view Paul's addressees, and so have argued: (1) that ethnically they constituted both Jewish and Gentile believers in Jesus, though with the latter becoming increasingly important after the Edict of Claudius and dominant at the time of Paul's writing, (2) that theologically they all, whether Jewish or Gentile believers, looked to the Jerusalem Church for inspiration and guidance, reverenced the Mosaic law, and followed some of the Jewish rites and practices, but were not "Judaizers" like those who troubled Paul's converts in the Roman province of Galatia, and (3) that socially they were no longer meeting in the Jewish synagogues, but gathered for worship and fellowship in the homes and tenement accommodations of various Christians of the city — that is, in "house churches" or "tenement groups," which made up a loose association of separate congregations. And it is this understanding of the addressees' identity, character, circumstances, and concerns that we believe not only to be true but also to provide the most likely basis for an understanding of Paul's purposes in writing Romans.

Occasion and Purposes in the Epistolary Frame of the Letter

A fairly clear distinction can usually be made in Paul's other letters between the occasion for his writing and his purpose or purposes in writing. In

---

150. S. K. Stowers, *Rereading of Romans,* 277, referring particularly to Romans 7, though viewed as true for much else in the letter as well; see also p. 279.

Romans, however, that distinction is not always clear. In fact, in the epistolary frame of Paul's letter to Rome the occasion for his writing and his purposes in writing are joined.

The occasion for writing Romans is identified in the epistolary frame
of the letter (i.e., in the "salutation," "thanksgiving," and "body opening" at
the beginning and the "body closing" and concluding sections at the end) as
being Paul's planned mission to Spain and his desire to visit the addressees
on the way (cf. esp. 1:10-15; 15:17-32). Within that occasion can be discerned
the apostle's two primary purposes for writing:

1. to give to the Christians at Rome what he calls "some spiritual gift" (τι
   χάρισμα πνευματικόν), which he thought of as something uniquely his
   (cf. his reference to "my gospel" in 16:25; also see 2:16), felt they needed
   if they were to "mutually encourage" one another (1:11-12), and evidently wanted them to know in order that they might understand accurately and more appreciatively what he was proclaiming in his mission to Gentiles; and,
2. to seek the assistance of the Christians at Rome for the extension of his
   Gentile mission to Spain (cf. 1:13; 15:24), which should probably be understood as including their financial support and their willingness to
   be used as a base for his outreach to the western regions of the Roman
   empire, just as the Christians at Antioch of Syria had served as the base
   for his outreach to the eastern regions of the empire.

Both of these purposes, it needs to be emphasized, arose from Paul's own
missionary consciousness and his plans for the future.

Also included within the epistolary frame of Romans, particularly
within the long salutation of 1:1-7, are statements about (1) the legitimacy of
Paul's apostleship (1:1; cf. 15:15b-16), (2) the supremacy of the gospel (1:1b-2a),
(3) the rootage of the gospel in God's promise given through the prophets in
the Holy Scriptures (1:2), (4) the focus of the gospel in the work and person
of God's Son, Jesus Christ our Lord (1:3-4, cf. 9a), (5) Paul's missionary mandate to the Gentile world (1:5; cf. 15:15-16), and (6) the inclusion of believers
at Rome within the orbit of his Gentile mandate (1:6; cf. 15:15-16). It may be
that some, if not all, of these statements should be mirror read as veiled responses of Paul to certain criticisms made against him and various misun-
derstandings of his proclamation — as, for example, in opposition to the
criticisms (1) that he was not an apostle like the Jerusalem apostles, (2) that
he was in some way confusing the pristine gospel of the Mother Church at

Jerusalem, (3) that the content of his preaching was far removed from the hope of Israel given through the prophets in Israel's Scriptures, (4) that in some manner he was obscuring the focus of the Christian gospel, (5) that by carrying on a direct mission to Gentiles he was actually subverting the Jewish Christian mission, of which they were a part, or (6) that believers at Rome should not be thought of as part of Paul's missionary enterprise, for they had their historical and theological roots in the Jewish Christianity of the Mother Church at Jerusalem. But a mirror reading of the statements in the salutation of the letter, while possibly signaling something of an apologetic or polemical purpose, cannot, of itself, support such a thesis, but may only be considered significant when combined with other indications from the body of the letter. And so we must hold our comments about this matter until a bit later, when the didactic material of the body of the letter is discussed below.

Likewise, there are a number of other statements in the epistolary frame of Romans that have a direct relevance to the occasion for writing the letter, with some of them also having a possible bearing on Paul's purposes for writing — such as (1) his thankfulness for the faith and maturity of the Roman Christians (1:8; 15:14), (2) his statement that he prays for them (1:9-10), (3) a summation of his past Gentile ministry in the eastern regions of the Roman empire (15:17-21, 23a), (4) his constant desire — in fact, his God-given obligation — to include Rome within his missionary endeavors (1:10, 13a, 14-15; 15:23b-24a), (5) an explanation of why he had not been able to come to Rome before (15:22), (6) his request that his addressees pray for him as he goes to Jerusalem (15:30-31), (7) his promise that he will, indeed, come to Rome after being at Jerusalem and before setting out for Spain (15:24, 32), and (8) his warning and general advice about "those who cause divisions and put obstacles in your way, contrary to the teaching you have learned" (16:17-20a). But, again, if these latter statements are to be understood as having any relevance in determining anything about Paul's purposes for writing, they need to be "unpacked" and seen in the context of what else the apostle says in the central body of Romans.

Purposes Explicated and Implied in the Didactic Materials of the Letter's Body

With their history, theology, and experience all rooted in the matrix of Jewish Christianity, it may be assumed that the Christians at Rome had some misgivings about Paul and his Gentile mission. Undoubtedly they had heard about him, his form of ministry, and his message, for news in the ancient world traveled relatively fast and Paul's outreach to pagan Gentiles would have been highly newsworthy among all believers in Jesus, whatever their ethnic background, circumstances, or location. And from what they heard, the Christians at Rome probably recognized that there were some differences between themselves and Paul. They may even have expressed their misgivings openly, with their criticisms being reported to Paul by some of the friends that he greets in 16:3-16.

But whatever scenario is constructed regarding his addressees' stance and views about Paul, it seems evident from the didactic materials of the letter's body, that is, from 1:16–11:36, that Paul wanted to allay their suspicions, to correct their misconceptions, to present what he was proclaiming elsewhere to Gentiles (which he calls "my gospel" in 2:16 and 16:25, but which they may have been pejoratively calling "Paul's gospel"), and to gain their support for a further advance of the Christian gospel to Gentiles in the western regions of the empire. And this is what he does in the three major theological sections of the letter's body middle, that is, in 1:16–4:25; 5–8; and 9–11 — which divisions and purpose we will attempt to justify and explicate further in discussing the structure and argument of the letter later in Chapter XI.

1. Explications of Paul's Primary Purposes

The pattern of argumentation that Paul exhibits in Galatians and 1 Corinthians — which, of course, are letters that the apostle wrote in roughly the same period of time when he wrote Romans — is as follows: (1) a statement or exposition of matters on which he and his addressees agree (i.e., points of agreement); (2) a statement or exposition of matters that are contested between them (i.e., points of disagreement), which he sets out in greater detail, which should be seen as the focus or major portion of his argument, and which he wants to convince his addressees about; and (3) a summation, which seems to include a refutation of a specific charge, a response to a particular criticism, or a correction of a certain misunderstanding. We have argued that such a pattern of argument is highlighted in the *propositio* of Gal 2:15-21 and explicated throughout the *probatio* of Gal 3:1–4:11.[151] And we would argue, as do many other commentators, that such a pattern can be

---

151. Cf. R. N. Longenecker, *Galatians,* WBC (Dallas: Word, 1990), 80-96 and 97-183.

seen as well in Paul's response to the questions posed by his converts in 1 Corinthians 7–14, where the apostle (1) begins his discussion of each of their questions with a statement or statements regarding where he agrees with them, then (2) presents an exposition on what he really wants them to know, which is the focus of his discussion in dealing with matters of disagreement between them and setting out his own position, and, finally, (3) gives a summation that deals with the particular issue or issues in question.

Based on this pattern of argumentation in Galatians and 1 Corinthians — as well as what may be surmised regarding what the apostle heard from his friends at Rome about criticisms of his person, ministry, and message — it may be postulated that, in seeking their support for his mission to Spain, Paul realized that the Christians of Rome needed to hear from him regarding (1) where they and he were in agreement in their understandings of the Christian gospel (i.e., their points of agreement), (2) what he proclaimed to Gentiles in the Greco-Roman world (i.e., their points of disagreement), which he wanted to present in detail for their understanding and to convince them about, and which, we believe, should be seen as the focus of his argument, and (3) how that message of God's direct acceptance of Gentiles through Christ, apart from any Jewish prolegomena or Jewish Christian contextualization, related to the hope of Israel, which they evidently saw as being fulfilled through the missionary outreach of Jewish Christians generally and in their midst at Rome in particular. And these three concerns are the three basic matters that Paul explicates in the three theological sections of 1:16–11:36, as we will attempt to spell out later in discussing the structure and argument of the letter (see Chapter XI, "Structure and Argument"): the first regarding where they were in agreement, as set out in 1:16–4:25; the second on what Paul proclaimed in his outreach to Gentiles, which he understood they were in disagreement about, as set out in 5–8; and the third on how God's acceptance of Gentiles relates to the hope of Israel, as set out in 9–11.[152]

Paul, it seems, had no problem with contextualizing the Christian gospel in Jewish ways of thinking and Jewish forms of expression. That was, indeed, his own background. Further, that was how he, at times in a Jewish context, proclaimed the "good news" of redemption in Christ Jesus;[153] and

---

152. Cf. R. N. Longenecker, "Prolegomena to Paul's Use of Scripture in Romans" (1997); idem, "The Focus of Romans: The Central Role of 5:1–8:39 in the Argument of the Letter" (1999).

153. Cf. 1 Cor 9:19-23; see also Luke's portrayal of Paul's preaching in a Jewish synagogue in Acts 13:16-41.

that was how he himself felt free, at times, to express his own Christian faith.[154] But Paul had been called by God to evangelize pagan Gentiles who had no contact with Judaism, no association with Jewish Christianity, and no appreciation of Jewish ways of thinking or forms of expression. So Paul's proclamation of the gospel, while in continuity with what was proclaimed by the apostles at Jerusalem and accepted by the Christians at Rome, was contextualized in a manner that resonated with the Gentile world, and so was somewhat different from what had been accepted as the Christian faith among believers at Rome.

Christianity at Rome had come to birth in a Jewish form and was nourished by the Mother Church at Jerusalem. After the Edict of Claudius, however, it became more and more dominated by Gentile believers in Jesus, who, nonetheless, continued on in the traditions they had inherited from their Jewish Christian predecessors. So as Gentile Christians — whether *exclusively* Gentile Christians (as some believe, including Wolfgang Wiefel) or *dominantly* Gentile Christians with also some Jewish Christians among them (as I think more likely, in agreement with Raymond E. Brown) — Paul viewed his addressees at Rome within the orbit of his God-given mandate. Further, the Christians of Rome were located very strategically in the capital city of the Roman empire, and so would provide an excellent base for an outreach to Gentiles in the western regions of the empire. Paul, therefore, desired their assistance for his proposed mission to Spain. But he also felt it necessary to spell out the nature and content of his proclamation to Gentiles vis-à-vis their traditional Jewish Christian understanding of the gospel, with the ultimate purpose being, as he says in 1:12, "that you and I may be mutually encouraged by each other's faith" — with that carefully constructed, but somewhat veiled, wording probably to be unpacked to mean: that they as Gentile Christians might be strengthened by the distinctive features of his message to the Gentile world, and so be prepared to join with him and support him in the extension of his Gentile mission to the western regions of the empire.

All of these matters must, of course, be dealt with further in an exegetical study of these three rather large didactic presentations in 1:16–11:36, which is what we plan to do later in a full-blown Romans commentary. Suffice it here to say, however, that in this expositional material of the body middle of his letter, Paul is explicating his two primary purposes for writing to the Christians at Rome: (1) to seek their assistance for the extension of his

---

154. Cf. R. N. Longenecker, "The Problem Practices of Acts," in *Paul, Apostle of Liberty* (New York: Harper & Row, 1964), 245-63.

Gentile mission to Spain, and (2) to give them "some spiritual gift" (τι χάρισμα πνευματικόν) in order to prepare them for his coming and to enable them to understand more accurately and appreciatively what he was proclaiming in his missionary outreach to Gentiles.

2. An Implied Purpose Embedded in Paul's Explications

Embedded in the didactic materials of 1:16–11:36 are also a few comments and veiled allusions that seem to carry something of an apologetic tone, and so probably should be understood as instances of Paul defending himself against certain criticisms of his person and various misrepresentations of his ministry by the Christians at Rome. These include, as noted earlier, such comments as "for I am not ashamed of the gospel" (1:16) and "as my gospel declares" (2:16), as well as an allusion to those who "slanderously report" and "claim" that Paul's message, in effect, boils down to the axiom "Let us do evil that good may result" (3:8).

Likewise, there are a number of rhetorical questions in the didactic body middle of Romans that probably should also be viewed as reflecting criticism of Paul and his message by at least some of the Christians at Rome. These include, as again noted above, the following: "Do we overthrow the law by this faith?" (3:31); "What then shall we say about Abraham, our forefather according to the flesh?" (4:1); "Are we to continue in sin that grace may abound?" (6:1); "What then? Are we to sin because we are not under the law but under grace?" (6:15); and "What shall we say then? That the law is sin?" (7:7, 13, 14). As Peter Stuhlmacher has said regarding the import of these rhetorical questions (though, of course, we differ with him regarding his understanding of "Jewish Christian opponents" at Rome), it seems probable that:

> In every case the Apostle is alluding to criticisms and challenges from his Jewish Christian opponents as they spread from Asia Minor and Greece to Rome. His intention is to refute and answer them. The dialogue we are witnessing in Romans is a real one in which Paul is wrestling for the hearts and minds of the Christians in Rome.[155]

Such an understanding of these comments, allusions, and rhetorical questions in the body middle of Romans lends credence to the case for understanding at least some of Paul's statements in the epistolary frame of his

---

155. P. Stuhlmacher, "Purpose of Romans," 240.

letter as also incorporating apologetic and polemical nuances, and so to be viewed as veiled responses to certain criticisms of his person and ministry that were being voiced by at least some of the Christians at Rome. Their criticisms, as also set out above, probably included the following: (1) that Paul was not an apostle like the Jerusalem apostles, (2) that he was confusing the pristine gospel of the Mother Church at Jerusalem, (3) that the content of his preaching was far removed from the hope of Israel given through the prophets in Israel's Scriptures, (4) that in some manner he was obscuring the focus of the Christian gospel, (5) that by carrying on a direct mission to Gentiles he was actually subverting the Jewish Christian mission, of which they were a part, and (6) that believers at Rome should not be thought of as part of Paul's missionary enterprise, for they had their historical and theological roots in the Jewish Christianity of the Mother Church at Jerusalem.

To mirror read all, or at least some, of the above comments, allusions, rhetorical questions, and statements as having an apologetic tone or polemical thrust is, of course, to suggest (as we do) that one of Paul's purposes in writing Romans was to defend himself against criticism and misrepresentation on the part of the Christians at Rome. But such an apologetic or polemical understanding of the data is not to be viewed as Paul's primary purpose for writing the letter. Rather, it more likely should be understood as one of Paul's subsidiary purposes, particularly because it is expressed more in tone and temper than in sustained exposition or didactic argumentation.

Additional Purposes in the Hortatory Materials of the Letter's Body

From the early 1950s through to today, the exhortations of 14:1–15:13 have often been viewed as reflecting a major purpose of Paul for writing Romans. Usually these exhortations have been understood as speaking to a breakdown of relations between Gentile Christians ("the strong") and Jewish Christians ("the weak"), and so taken as clear evidence for the existence of ethnic disputes among the Christians at Rome. In fact, some interpreters have built most, if not all, of their rationale for Paul's writing of Romans on the basis of these exhortations, with everything else in the letter understood as being anticipatory, supportive, or supplemental.[156]

---

156. See, e.g., the German scholars H. Preisker, "Das historische Problem des Römerbriefes" (1952-53); G. Harder, "Der konkrete Anlass des Römerbriefes" (1954); and H.-W. Bartsch, "Die antisemitischen Gegner des Paulus im Römerbrief" (1967) and "Die

But though the importance of 14:1–15:13 can be overstated, its exhortations over-analyzed, and the exegesis of the passage carried out in terms of questionable assumptions — particularly, the precise identification of "the strong" as being Gentile Christians and "the weak" as being Jewish Christians — it still remains most likely that Paul was speaking in 14:1–15:13 to a particular situation he had heard about, probably from some of his friends that he greets in 16:3-16, as existing among the house churches at Rome. William Sanday and Arthur C. Headlam, while not carrying out their introductory observations to a legitimate conclusion, were certainly right when they said regarding the exhortations of 12:1–15:13 (or, as they closed off the second part of the section, to 15:12):

> A definite division may be made between chaps. xii, xIii, in which the exhortations are general in character, and xiv–xv.12, in which they arise directly out of the controversies which are disturbing the Church.[157]

Likewise, while we do not agree with everything in his understanding of the situation at Rome or his exegesis of what Paul says, Paul Minear's general overview of the passage and his challenge to commentators are, we believe, still appropriate:

> The apostle moves from general injunctions embodied in traditional oral forms of parenesis, to the consideration of a specific set of problems. The nearest analogy is I Corinthians (8; 9.19 23; 10.23–11.1). No one doubts that in Corinth he was wrestling directly with a specific situation. Why then should we doubt that this was also true in Rome?[158]

So in formulating our own thesis regarding Paul's purposes in writing Romans, we believe it proper to include a consideration of 14:1–15:13 and consider it highly probable that the exhortations of the passage were written to speak to a situation that was then existing among the Christians of Rome.[159] Two caveats with respect to such a position, however, are in order:

Empfänger des Römerbriefes" (1971); see also such North American and British scholars as P. S. Minear, *Obedience of Faith* (1971); F. Watson, "Two Roman Congregations" (1986); J. C. Walters, *Ethnic Issues in Paul's Letter to the Romans* (1993); and J. C. Miller, *Obedience of Faith* (2000).

157. W. Sanday and A. C. Headlam, *Romans,* 351.

158. P. S. Minear, *Obedience of Faith,* 22.

159. Cf. also our treatment of the admonition of 16:17-20a in Chapter XI, "Structure and Argument."

(1) that we not import into our view of the situation an ethnic understanding of "the strong" as being Gentile Christians, who must have espoused views compatible with Paul's theology, and "the weak" as Jewish Christians, who held to some inherited Jewish scruples, and (2) that we not treat this passage as expressing a primary purpose of Paul for writing the letter. For, with respect to the first caveat, if all of the Christians at Rome, whatever their ethnicity, looked to the Jerusalem Church for inspiration and guidance, reverenced the Mosaic law, and followed some of the Jewish rites and practices, then it may be postulated that the division spoken about in 14:1–15:13 was either between certain individual Christians, whether ethnically Jews or Gentiles, who grouped themselves along the lines of opposing parties within the various Christian congregations at Rome, or between certain house churches that were composed of both Gentile and Jewish believers, which were committed to one side of the issue, and other house churches composed of both Gentile and Jewish believers, which held to the other side.

Further, with respect to the second caveat, the controversy reflected in 14:1–15:13, though important of itself (and probably recalled, at least in part, by Paul's "additional admonitions" of 16:17-20a), should, nonetheless, probably not be seen as one of Paul's primary reasons for writing Romans. Rather, it is more likely that the apostle's concern regarding this disturbance among the Roman Christians should be classed among his subsidiary purposes for writing, principally (1) because it is not included in the "thanksgiving" section (1:8-12) or "apostolic parousia" section (15:14-32) of the letter, where we would expect to find Paul's primary purposes and major concerns, and (2) because of the way in which Paul speaks about these "divisions" and "obstacles" and about his joy in their "obedience" and confidence in God's bringing about peace in the community.[160]

Based on a mirror reading of 13:1-7, where Paul gives rather specific teaching regarding the relation of Christians at Rome to the city's civil government and regarding their responsibility to pay legitimate taxes and revenues, an additional purpose for the writing of Romans has, of late, often also been found. As noted above, these seven verses are not only unique in the Pauline corpus with respect to their teaching, but they are also fairly distinctive in that they are specific statements that appear right in the middle of a series of general exhortations on the subject of Christian love — with those specific statements seeming to break the apparent continuity of the general

160. See our treatment of 16:17-20a in Chapter XI, "Structure and Arrangement."

exhortations in 12:9-21 and 13:8-10. Such a scanning of chapters 12–13 suggests that 13:1-7 should probably be seen as having been placed by Paul into an existing set of general exhortations regarding love, which set of exhortations he probably was accustomed to use widely in the course of his Gentile mission — with, then, the general exhortations and the specific statements that appear in their midst being both sent by the apostle in his letter to believers at Rome. And in support of such a thesis, which we believe to be credible, it has been argued that the statements about paying taxes, revenues, respect, and honor to civil authorities in 13:6-7, which are the last two verses of those seven verses of specific hortatory material, may very well be mirror read to reflect a background of civil unrest in Rome because of the unjust practices of Roman tax-collectors during the mid-50s,[161] which is a thesis we believe to be also credible.

So accepting the credibility of the above positions regarding the provenance, character, and purpose of 13:1-7, we conclude that an additional purpose for the writing of Romans was, in all probability, Paul's desire to counsel Christians at Rome regarding their relation to civil authorities and their responsibility to pay legitimate taxes and revenues. Here again, however, as with the exhortations of 14:1–15:13, at least one caveat needs to be voiced: that the purpose inferred by a mirror reading of 13:1-7 should probably not be considered one of Paul's primary purposes for writing Romans, principally because there is no statement or suggestion regarding such a purpose anywhere in the epistolary frame of the letter where we would expect to find such a purpose or concern. Rather, most likely the apostle's desire to counsel Christians at Rome regarding their relation to civil authorities and their responsibility to pay legitimate taxes and revenues should be understood as one of Paul's subsidiary purposes in writing Romans.

6. Summation and Broader Context

What, then, can be said about Paul's purpose or purposes in writing Romans? Undoubtedly it was more than simply to introduce himself. Based on reports they had heard during the decade prior to the winter of A.D. 57-58 (when Paul wrote them), Christians at Rome probably already knew a great deal about this prominent Christian evangelist to the Gentiles, about his

---

161. Cf. again J. Friedrich, W. Pöhlmann, and P. Stuhlmacher, "Situation und Intention von Röm 13,1-7."

ministry, and about his message — though what they knew seems to have been somewhat skewed and distorted. More than mere self-introduction, Paul's purposes appear to have been multiple and much more significant. And while some of his purposes in writing may be able to be identified as primary and others as subsidiary, it is necessary to appreciate all of them in order to have a more complete understanding of why Paul wrote as he did.

Of major importance are two primary purposes that are stated in the epistolary frame of the letter and then explicated throughout the letter's large body middle (i.e., throughout 1:16–15:13). These two purposes are related to the occasion for his writing and must be seen to have stemmed from his own missionary consciousness and future ministry plan. They are:

1. to give to the Christians at Rome what he calls in 1:11 a "spiritual gift" (χάρισμα πνευματικόν), which he thought of as something uniquely his (cf. his reference to "my gospel" in 16:25; also see 2:16), felt they needed if they were to "mutually encourage" one another (1:11-12), and evidently wanted them to know in order that they might understand accurately and more appreciatively what he was proclaiming in his mission to Gentiles;

2. to seek the assistance of the Christians at Rome for the extension of his Gentile mission to Spain (cf. 1:13; 15:24), which should probably be understood as including their financial support and their willingness to be used as a base for his outreach to the western regions of the Roman empire, just as the Christians at Antioch of Syria had assisted him and served as the base for his outreach to the eastern regions of the empire.

Also important is a purpose that can be discerned by a close mirror reading of various comments, veiled allusions, and rhetorical statements of Paul that appear in the explication of his message in the body middle of his letter, as well as a mirror reading of some of his statements in the epistolary frame surrounding that central letter body. But since this purpose is more muted and implied than directly stated, it seems best to call it not a primary purpose for writing Romans but a subsidiary purpose. This purpose may be identified as Paul's third purpose:

3. to defend himself against certain criticisms of his person and various misrepresentations of his message, with the intent that Christians at Rome would properly understand his person, ministry and message and thus happily assist him in his Gentile mission.

Two further purposes must also be included in any listing of Paul's reasons for writing Romans. Both seem to be discernible by a process of mirror reading, though, admittedly, they seem to carry somewhat different degrees of probability. The first is most probable and can be distilled by mirror reading the exhortations regarding "the strong" and "the weak" in 14:1–15:13, with that situation probably recalled in the additional admonitions of 16:17-20a. The second, while somewhat more inferential, can be ascertained by mirror reading the exhortations regarding the relation of Christians to civil authorities and their responsibilities in paying taxes and revenues in 13:1-7, which appear in the midst of the general exhortations on Christian love in chapters 12–13 and seem to break their continuity. These two purposes we list here as Paul's fourth and fifth reasons for the writing of Romans, listing them in the order of their greatest probability:

4. to counsel regarding a dispute that had arisen among Christians who called themselves "the strong" and other Christians who were designated "the weak," either within or between various house churches at Rome, as he does in 14:1–15:13 (and seems to recall in the further admonitions given in 16:17-20a);

5. to counsel regarding the relation of Christians at Rome to the city's governmental authorities and their responsibilities in paying legitimate taxes and revenues, as he does in 13:1-7.

These two additional purposes, however, should probably be seen as subsidiary purposes of Paul for writing the letter. For while reflecting the circumstances of Christians at Rome, they are not included in the epistolary "salutation" (1:1-7), "thanksgiving" (1:8-12), or "body opening" sections (1:13-15) at the letter's beginning or in the epistolary "body closing" or "apostolic parousia" section (15:14-32) at its end, where the primary purposes and major concerns of an ancient letter writer would be expected to be found.

Yet to speak of a specific occasion and certain primary and subsidiary purposes of Paul in writing Romans is not to conclude the discussion as to why the apostle wrote the Christians at Rome as he did. For underlying Paul's purposes were (1) a concern for the spiritual welfare of his addressees, (2) a desire that they might understand how he contextualized the Christian gospel in his ministry to the Gentile world and that as Gentile believers in Jesus they would both appreciate and appropriate that form of the gospel for themselves, and (3) a hope that they would assist him in his outreach to Gentiles in the western regions of the Roman empire.

In effect, what Paul wanted to accomplish by writing Romans was that Christians at Rome would (1) be transformed in their understanding of the gospel, (2) be renewed in their commitment to Jesus Christ, (3) come to appreciate the pattern of contextualization that his ministry and his form of the Christian message to the Gentile world represented, and (4) share in the conviction that this gospel must be proclaimed to all people in a form that is contextualized for the various cultures, societies, situations, and circumstances that it addresses and in a manner that transforms those who believe and the societies in which they live. And it is just such a transformation, commitment, contextualization, and missionary outreach that Paul's teaching in Romans has been used by God to bring about among Christians, their particular cultures and societies, and the Christian church today, whatever was the letter's original occasion and whatever were Paul's own purposes for writing it.

SUPPLEMENTAL BIBLIOGRAPHY

See also "Bibliography of Selected Commentaries." All references in the footnotes to works included in this list are by the authors' names and abbreviated titles.

Aune, David E. *The New Testament in Its Literary Environment*. Philadelphia: Westminster, 1987, 219-21.

Bartsch, Hans-Werner. "Die antisemitischen Gegner des Paulus im Römerbrief," in *Antijudaismus im Neuen Testament? Exegetische und systematische Beiträge*, ed. W. P. Eckert, N. P. Levinson, and M. Stöhr. Munich: Kaiser, 1967, 27-43.

———. "Die historische Situation des Römerbriefes," *Studia Evangelica* IV, ed. F. L. Cross. TU 102. Berlin: Akademie, 1968, 281-91; ET = "The Historical Situation of Romans," *Encounter* 33 (1972) 329-39.

———. "Die Empfänger des Römerbriefes," *ST* 25 (1971) 81-89.

Baur, Ferdinand Christian. "Über Zweck und Veranlassung des Römerbriefs und die damit zusammenhängenden Verhältnisse der römischen Gemeinde. Eine historisch-kritische Untersuchung," *TZT* 3 (1836) 59-178; repr. in *Ausgewählte Werke in Einzelausgaben*, 1: *Historisch-kritische Untersuchungen zum Neuen Testament*. Stuttgart: Frommann, 1963, 147-266.

———. *Paul, the Apostle of Jesus Christ: His Life and Work, His Epistles and His Doctrine*, 2 vols., trans. E. Zeller. Edinburgh: University of Edinburgh Press, 1846; London: Williams & Norgate, 1876, 1.309-65.

Beker, J. Christiaan. *Paul the Apostle: The Triumph of God in Life and Thought*. Philadelphia: Fortress, 1980, 59-63, 69-78, 89-93.

———. "The Faithfulness of God and the Priority of Israel in Paul's Letter to the

Romans," in *Christians Among Jews and Gentiles* (*Festschrift* Krister Stendahl), ed. G. W. E. Nickelsburg with G. W. MacRae. Philadelphia: Fortress, 1986, 10-16; repr. in Donfried, ed., *Romans Debate* (1991), 327-32.

Bornkamm, Günther. "The Letter to the Romans as Paul's Last Will and Testament," *AusBR* 11 (1963) 2-14; repr. in Donfried, ed., *Romans Debate* (1977), 17-31; (1991), 16-28.

————. *Paul.* New York: Harper & Row, 1971.

Brown, Raymond E. "Not Jewish Christianity and Gentile Christianity, but Types of Jewish/Gentile Christianity," *CBQ* 45 (1983) 74-79.

————. "The Beginnings of Christianity at Rome" and "The Roman Church near the End of the First Christian Generation (A.D. 58 — Paul to the Romans)," in R. E. Brown and J. P. Meier, *Antioch and Rome: New Testament Cradles of Catholic Christianity.* New York: Paulist, 1983, 92-127.

————. *An Introduction to the New Testament.* New York: Doubleday, 1997, 562-64.

Bruce, F. F. *Paul: Apostle of the Heart Set Free.* Grand Rapids: Eerdmans, 1977 (British title: *Paul: Apostle of the Free Spirit.* Exeter: Paternoster, 1977), 325-38.

————. "The Romans Debate — Continued," *BJRL* 64 (1982) 334-59; repr. in Donfried, ed., *Romans Debate* (1991), 175-94.

Campbell, Douglas A. "Determining the Gospel through Rhetorical Analysis in Paul's Letter to the Roman Christians," in *Gospel in Paul: Studies on Corinthians, Galatians and Romans for Richard N. Longenecker,* ed. L. A. Jervis and P. Richardson. Sheffield: Sheffield Academic Press, 1994, 315-36.

Campbell, William S. "Why Did Paul Write Romans?" *ExpT* 85 (1974) 264-69; repr. in his *Paul's Gospel in an Intercultural Context: Jew and Gentile in the Letter to the Romans.* New York: Peter Lang, 1991, 14-24.

————. "The Romans Debate," *JSNT* 10 (1981) 19-28.

————. "Romans III as a Key to the Structure and Thought of Romans," *NovT* 23 (1981) 22-40; repr. in Donfried, ed., *Romans Debate* (1991), 251-64.

Cancick, Hildegard. *Untersuchungen zu Senecas Epistulae Morales.* Spudasmata 18. Hildesheim: Olms, 1967.

Dahl, Nils A. "The Particularity of the Pauline Epistles as a Problem in the Ancient Church," in *Neotestamentica et Patristica: Eine Freundesgabe, Herrn Professor Dr. Oscar Cullmann zu seinen 60. Geburtstage überreicht.* NovTSup 6. Leiden: Brill, 1962, 261-71.

Dinkler, Erich. "Shalom — Eirene — Pax: Jüdische Sepulkralinschriften und ihr Verhältnis zum frühen Christentum," *Rivista Archeologia Christiana* 50 (1974) 121-44.

Donfried, Karl P. "A Short Note on Romans 16," *JBL* 89 (1970) 441-49; repr. in Donfried, ed., *Romans Debate* (1977), 50-60; (1991), 44-52.

————. "False Presuppositions in the Study of Romans," *CBQ* 36 (1974) 332-58; repr. in Donfried, ed., *Romans Debate* (1977), 120-48; (1991), 102-25.

————, ed. *The Romans Debate*. Minneapolis: Augsburg, 1977; *The Romans Debate*, revised and expanded edition, Peabody: Hendrickson, 1991.

————. "The Nature and Scope of the Romans Debate," in Donfried, ed., *Romans Debate* (1977), ix-xvii; (1991), xli-xlvii.

————. "The Romans Debate since 1977," in Donfried, ed., *Romans Debate* (1991), xlix-lxxii.

Drane, John W. "Why Did Paul Write Romans?" in *Pauline Studies: Essays Presented to F. F. Bruce on his 70th Birthday,* ed. D. A. Hagner and M. J. Harris. Exeter: Paternoster; Grand Rapids: Eerdmans, 1980, 208-27.

Drummond, James. "Occasion and Object of the Epistle to the Romans," *HibJ* 11 (1913) 787-804.

Dunn, James D. G. "The Formal and Theological Coherence of Romans," *Romans,* 1.lix-lxiii; repr. in Donfried, ed., *Romans Debate* (1991), 245-50.

————. "The New Perspective on Paul: Paul and the Law," *Romans* 1.lxiv-lxxii; repr. in Donfried, ed., *Romans Debate* (1991), 299-308.

Dupont, Jacques. "Appel aux faibles et aux forts dans la communauté romaine (Rom. 14,1–15,13)," in *Studiorum Paulinorum Congressus Internationalis Catholicus 1961.* Rome: Pontificio Instituto Biblico, 1963, 257-66.

Elliott, Neil. *The Rhetoric of Romans: Argumentative Constraint and Strategy and Paul's Dialogue with Judaism.* JSNT.SS 45. Sheffield: Sheffield Academic Press, 1990.

Fridrichsen, A. "The Apostle and His Message," *Uppsala Universitets Årsskrift* 3 (1947) 3-23.

Friedrich, Johannes, Wolfgang Pöhlmann, and Peter Stuhlmacher. "Zur historischen Situation und Intention von Röm 13,1-7," *ZTK* 73 (1976) 131-66.

Fuchs, Ernst. *Hermeneutik.* Bad Cannstatt: Müllerschön, 1954, 181-91.

Gamble, Harry, Jr. *The Textual History of the Letter to the Romans: A Study in Textual and Literary Criticism.* SD 42. Grand Rapids: Eerdmans, 1977, esp. 132-37.

Gaston, Lloyd. "Israel's Misstep in the Eyes of Paul," in *Paul and the Torah.* Vancouver: University of British Columbia Press, 1987, 135-50; repr. in Donfried, ed., *Romans Debate* (1991), 309-26.

————. "For *All* the Believers: The Inclusion of Gentiles as the Ultimate Goal of Torah in Romans," in *Paul and the Torah.* Vancouver: University of British Columbia Press, 1987, 116-34.

Grafe, Edward. *Über Veranlassung und Zweck des Römerbriefes.* Tübingen: Mohr-Siebeck, 1881.

Grayston, Kenneth. "'Not Ashamed of the Gospel': Romans 1:16a and the Structure of the Epistle," *Studia Evangelica* 2.1, ed. F. L. Cross. Berlin: Akademie Verlag, 1964, 569-73.

Haacker, Klaus. "Der Römerbrief als Friedensmemorandum," *NTS* 36 (1990) 25-41.

Harder, Günther. "Der konkrete Anlass des Römerbriefes," *TV* 6 (1954) 13-24.

Hort, Fenton J. A. *Prolegomena to St. Paul's Epistles to the Romans and the Ephesians.* London, New York: Macmillan, 1895.

Jervell, Jacob. "Der Brief nach Jerusalem: Über Veranlassung und Adresse des Römerbriefes," *ST* 25 (1971) 61-73; ET = "The Letter to Jerusalem," in Donfried, ed., *Romans Debate* (1977), 61-74; (1991), 53-64.

Jervis, L. Ann. *The Purpose of Romans: A Comparative Letter Structure Investigation.* JSNT.SS 55. Sheffield: Sheffield Academic Press, 1991.

Jewett, Robert L. "Romans as an Ambassadorial Letter," *Int* 36 (1982) 5-20.

———. "Following the Argument of Romans," *WW* 6 (1986) 382-89; adapted and expanded in Donfried, ed., *Romans Debate* (1991), 265-77.

Karris, Robert J. "Romans 14:1–15:13 and the Occasion of Romans," *CBQ* 25 (1973) 155-78; repr. in Donfried, ed., *Romans Debate* (1977), 75-99; (1991) 65-84.

———. "The Occasion of Romans: A Response to Prof. Donfried," *CBQ* 36 (1974) 356-58; repr. in Donfried, ed., *Romans Debate* (1977), 149-51; (1991), 125-27.

Kaye, B. N. "'To the Romans and Others' Revisited," *NovT* 18 (1976) 37-77.

Keck, Leander E. *Paul and His Letters.* Philadelphia: Fortress, 1979.

Kettunen, Marku. *Der Abfassungszweck des Römerbriefes.* ASF: Dissertationes Humanarum Litterarum 18. Helsinki: Suomalainen Tiedeakatemia, 1979.

Kim, Chan-Hie. *Form and Structure of the Familiar Greek Letter of Recommendation.* Missoula: Society of Biblical Literature, 1972.

Kinoshita, Junji. "Romans — Two Writings Combined: A New Interpretation of the Body of Romans," *NovT* 7 (1965) 258-77.

Klein, Günter. "Der Abfassungszweck des Römerbriefes," in *Rekonstruktion und Interpretation. Gesammelte Aufsätze zum Neuen Testament.* BEvT 50. Munich: Kaiser, 1969, 129-44; ET = "Paul's Purpose in Writing the Epistle to the Romans," in Donfried, ed., *Romans Debate* (1977), 32-49; (1991), 29-43.

Kümmel, Werner Georg. *Introduction to the New Testament,* rev. ed., trans. H. C. Kee. Nashville: Abingdon, 1975, 312-14.

Lake, Kirsopp. *The Earlier Epistles of St. Paul: Their Motive and Origin.* London: Rivingtons, 1927², 325-413.

———. "The Shorter Form of St. Paul's Epistle to the Romans," *Exp* 7 (1910) 504-25.

Lampe, Peter. "The Roman Christians of Romans 16," in Donfried, ed., *Romans Debate* (1991), 216-30; article is dependent on his book *Die stadtrömischen Christen in den ersten beiden Jahrhunderten.* WUNT 2.18. Tübingen: Mohr, 1987.

Longenecker, Richard N. "Prolegomena to Paul's Use of Scripture in Romans," *BBR* 7 (1997) 145-68.

———. "The Focus of Romans: The Central Role of 5:1–8:39 in the Argument of the Letter," in *Romans and the People of God: Essays in Honor of Gordon D. Fee on the Occasion of His 65th Birthday,* ed. S. K. Soderlund and N. T. Wright. Grand Rapids: Eerdmans, 1999, 49-69.

Lüdemann, Gerd. *Opposition to Paul in Jewish Christianity,* trans. M. E. Boring. Minneapolis: Fortress, 1989.

Lütgert, Wilhelm. *Der Römerbrief als historisches Problem.* BFCT 17.2. Gütersloh: Bertelsmann, 1913.

Luz, Ulrich. "Zum Aufbau von Röm. 1–8," *TZ* 25 (1969) 161-81.

MacRory, J. "The Occasion and Object of the Epistle to the Romans," *ITQ* 9 (1914) 21-32.

Manson, Thomas W. "St Paul's Letter to the Romans — and Others," *BJRL* 31 (1948) 224-40; repr. *Studies in the Gospels and Epistles,* ed. T. W. Manson. Manchester: University Press, 1962, 225-41; repr. in Donfried, ed., *Romans Debate* (1977), 1-16; (1991), 3-15.

Marcus, Joel. "The Circumcision and the Uncircumcision of Rome," *NTS* 35 (1989) 67-81.

Martyn, J. Louis. "Romans as One of the Earliest Interpretations of Galatians," in *Theological Issues in the Letters of Paul.* Nashville: Abingdon, 1997, 37-46.

Marxsen, Willi. *Introduction to the New Testament: An Approach to Its Problems.* Philadelphia: Fortress, 1968.

Meeks, Wayne A. "Judgment and the Brother: Romans 14:1–15:13," in *Tradition and Interpretation in the New Testament: Essays in Honor of E. Earle Ellis for His 60th Birthday,* ed. G. F. Hawthorne with O. Betz. Grand Rapids: Eerdmans, 1987, 290-300.

Miller, James C. *The Obedience of Faith, the Eschatological People of God, and the Purpose of Romans.* SBL.DS 177. Atlanta: SBL, 2000.

Minear, Paul S. *The Obedience of Faith: The Purposes of Paul in the Epistle to the Romans.* SBT 2.19. London: SCM, 1971.

Munck, Johannes. *Paul and the Salvation of Mankind,* trans. F. Clarke. London: SCM, 1959, 196-209.

Nanos, Mark D. *The Mystery of Romans.* Minneapolis: Fortress, 1996.

Nestingen, James A. "Major Shifts in the Interpretation of Romans," *WW* 6 (1986) 373-81.

Noack, Bent W. "Current and Backwater in the Epistle to the Romans," *ST* 19 (1965) 155-65.

O'Brien, Peter T. "Thanksgiving and the Gospel in Paul," *NTS* 21 (1974) 144-55.

———. *Introductory Thanksgivings in the Letters of Paul.* NovTSup 49. Leiden: Brill, 1977.

Preisker, Herbert. "Das historische Problem des Römerbriefes," *Wissenschaftliche Zeitschrift der Friedrich-Schiller-Universität Jena* 2 (1952-53) 25-32.

Roosen, A. "Le genre littéraire de l'Épître aux Romains," in *Studia Evangelica,* II.1: *The New Testament Scripture,* ed. F. L. Cross. TU 87. Berlin: Akademie, 1964, 465-71.

Russell, Walter B. "An Alternative Suggestion for the Purpose of Romans," *BSac* 145 (1988) 174-88.

Schmithals, Walter. *Der Römerbrief als historisches Problem.* SNT 9. Gütersloh: Mohn, 1975.

Schrenk, Gottlob. "Der Römerbrief als Missionsdokument," in *Aus Theologie und Geschichte der reformierten Kirche. Festgabe für E. F. Karl Müller-Erlangen.*

Neukirchen: Erziehungsverein, 1933; repr. in his *Studien zu Paulus*. ATANT 26. Zurich: Zwingli, 1954, 81-106.

Schubert, Paul. "Form and Function of the Pauline Letters," *JR* 19 (1939) 365-77.

————. *Form and Function of the Pauline Thanksgivings*. BZNTW 20. Berlin: Töpelmann, 1939.

Scroggs, Robin. "Paul as Rhetorician: Two Homilies in Romans 1–11," in *Jews, Greeks, and Christians* (*Festschrift* for W. D. Davies), ed. R. Hammerton-Kelly and R. Scroggs. Leiden: Brill, 1976, 271-98.

Smiga, George. "Romans 12:1-2 and 15:30-32 and the Occasion of the Letter to the Romans," *CBQ* 53 (1991) 257-73.

Smith, W. B. "Address and Destination of St. Paul's Epistle to the Romans," *JBL* 20 (1901) 1-21.

Snodgrass, Klyne R. "The Gospel in Romans: A Theology of Revelation," in *Gospel in Paul: Studies on Corinthians, Galatians and Romans for Richard N. Longenecker*, ed. L. A. Jervis and P. Richardson. JSNT.SS 108. Sheffield: Sheffield Academic Press, 1994, 288-314.

Stowers, Stanley K. *Letter Writing in Greco-Roman Antiquity*. Philadelphia: Westminster, 1986.

————. *A Rereading of Romans: Justice, Jews, and Gentiles*. New Haven: Yale University Press, 1994.

Stuhlmacher, Peter. "Der Abfassungszweck des Römerbriefes," *ZNW* 77 (1986) 180-93; ET: "The Purpose of Romans," in Donfried, ed., *Romans Debate* (1991), 231-42.

————. "The Theme of Romans," *AusBR* 36 (1988) 31-44; repr. in Donfried, ed., *Romans Debate* (1991), 333-45.

Suggs, M. Jack. "'The Word Is Near You': Romans 10:6-10 within the Purpose of the Letter," in *Christian History and Interpretation: Studies Presented to John Knox*, ed. W. R. Farmer, C. F. D. Moule, and R. R. Niebuhr. Cambridge: Cambridge University Press, 1967, 289-312.

Suhl, Alfred. "Der konkrete Anlass des Römerbriefes," *Kairos* 13 (1971) 119-30.

Trocmé, Étienne. "L'Épître aux Romains et la méthode missionaire de l'ápôtre Paul," *NTS* 7 (1961) 148-53.

Walters, James C. *Ethnic Issues in Paul's Letter to the Romans*. Valley Forge: Trinity Press International, 1993.

Watson, Francis. "The Two Roman Congregations: Romans 14:1–15:13," in *Paul, Judaism and the Gentiles: A Sociological Approach*. SNTS.MS 56. Cambridge: Cambridge University Press, 1986, 94-105; repr. in Donfried, ed., *Romans Debate* (1991), 203-15.

Wedderburn, Alexander J. M. "The Purpose and Occasion of Romans Again," *ExpT* 90 (1979) 137-41; repr. in *The Romans Debate* (1991) 195-202.

————. *The Reasons for Romans*. Edinburgh: T&T Clark, 1988; Minneapolis: Fortress, 1991.

Weima, Jeffrey A. D. *Neglected Endings: The Significance of the Pauline Letter Closings*. Sheffield: Sheffield Academic Press, 1994.

————. "Preaching the Gospel in Rome: A Study of the Epistolary Framework of Romans," in *Gospel in Paul: Studies on Corinthians, Galatians and Romans for Richard N. Longenecker*, ed. L. A. Jervis and P. Richardson. Sheffield: Sheffield Academic Press, 1994, 337-66.

————. "The Pauline Letter Closings: Analysis and Hermeneutical Significance," *BBR* 5 (1995) 177-97.

Wengst, Klaus. *Pax Romana and the Peace of Jesus Christ*. London: SCM, 1987, 79-84, 137-40.

Wiefel, Wolfgang. "The Jewish Community in Ancient Rome and the Origins of Roman Christianity," in Donfried, ed., *Romans Debate* (1977), 100-119; (1991) 85-101 (trans. of "Die jüdische Gemeinschaft im antiken Rom und die Anfänge des römischen Christentums. Bemerkungen zu Anlass und Zweck des Römerbriefs," *Jud* 26 [1970] 65-88).

Wilckens, Ulrich. "Über Abfassungzweck und Aufbau des Römerbriefes," in *Rechtfertigung als Freiheit: Paulusstudien*. Neukirchen-Vluyn: Neukirchener, 1974, 110-70.

Williams, Philip R. "Paul's Purpose in Writing Romans," *BSac* 128 (1971) 62-67.

Wood, John. "The Purpose of Romans," *EvQ* 40 (1968) 211-19.

Wuellner, Wilhelm. "Paul's Rhetoric of Argumentation in Romans: An Alternative to the Donfried-Karris Debate over Romans," *CBQ* 38 (1976) 330-51; repr. in Donfried, ed., *Romans Debate* (1977), 152-174; (1991), 128-46.

PART THREE

Conventions, Procedures, and Themes

CHAPTER VI

Greco-Roman Oral, Rhetorical, and Epistolary Conventions

Considerations of both content and form are essential in the scholarly study of any writing. When reading Paul's letters, therefore, it is important that we give attention not only to *what* he says but also to *how* he says it — that is, (1) to the forms of his day that he uses, whether consciously or unconsciously, to convey his message and (2) to the functions that these forms serve in expressing his message. So in any scholarly study of Romans, it is necessary to analyze Paul's letter in terms of (1) its Greco-Roman rhetorical and epistolary conventions, which, it may be assumed, had become commonplace among most educated people of antiquity, and (2) its Jewish and Jewish Christian procedures and themes, which were well known to him and evidently familiar to the Christians at Rome — always taking these analyses into account in the interpretation of the letter's content.

Yet prior to any rhetorical or epistolary analysis of the letter, it is necessary to recognize that there existed during the first Christian century, both in Greco-Roman society and within the world of Judaism, an extensive degree of "residual orality" — that is, "habits of thought and expression . . . deriving from the dominance of the oral as a medium in a given culture."[1] The speeches and addresses of antiquity were composed to be heard, and therefore were constructed with the oral features of discourse and the rhetorical conventions of argumentation that were common in that day so as to facilitate their being heard as their authors intended. Likewise the writers of letters in antiquity used those same patterns of oral speech and features of rhetorical argumentation, coupling them with then current epistolary practices,

---

1. W. J. Ong, *Rhetoric, Romance, and Technology,* 27-28.

in order to enable their communications to be understood by their address-ees as they intended.

The study of Greek and Roman rhetoric has had a long and venerable history. Further, analyses of epistolary conventions in the Greco-Roman world have been in vogue throughout the past century, coming to height-ened expression during the second half of the twentieth century and on into our present twenty-first century. And some work has been done on rhetori-cal modes and epistolary practices among the Jews during the period of Sec-ond Temple Judaism. Yet the study of oral conventions in the speeches and writings of antiquity — particularly of those oral features that have been in-corporated into the materials of the OT and the NT — seems to have largely "fallen between the cracks," with scholars only of late beginning to focus their attention on orality in the Jewish-Christian (OT) Scriptures and the distinctly Christian (NT) Scriptures. Nonetheless, attention to residual orality in the letters of the NT, as well as to the rhetorical, epistolary, the-matic, and procedural features that appear in them, is of great importance — particularly for the scholarly study of Romans.

Our own underlying conviction with regard to these matters is five-fold: (1) that Greek oral, rhetorical, and epistolary conventions were widely disseminated and extensively used in the Greco-Roman world, and so were common features of Paul's day; (2) that Jewish and Jewish Christian proce-dures and themes were not only well known to Paul but also familiar to his Christian addressees at Rome; (3) that studies of Greco-Roman oral, rhetori-cal, and epistolary conventions, together with studies of Jewish and Jewish Christian themes and procedures, cannot be undertaken in isolation from one another — certainly not, as has all too often occurred, in opposition to one another — but must always be understood as complementary endeav-ors, (4) that such studies are necessary for a more accurate appreciation not only of the forms but also of the contents of the NT letters, and (5) that all of this is particularly relevant with regard to Paul's letter to the Christians at Rome. In what follows, therefore, attention will be directed here in Chapter VI to Greco-Roman oral, rhetorical, and epistolary conventions that were widely prevalent in the ancient world and that appear in Romans; following that, we will deal in Chapter VII with Jewish and Jewish Christian proce-dures and themes that were common among Jews and Jewish Christians of Paul's day and that also appear in Romans. Our purpose in both of these chapters is to bring about a better understanding of what Paul has written in Romans by highlighting the oral, rhetorical, epistolary, thematic, and proce-dural conventions that he used (whether consciously or unconsciously) to convey his message to his Christian addressees at Rome — first in the present chapter, as drawn from the wider expanse of the Greco-Roman world in which he and his addressees lived; then in the following chapter, as drawn from the more particularly Jewish and Jewish Christian background not only of Paul but also of his Christian addressees at Rome (see Chapter IV, "Addressees").

1. Oral Conventions

Oral and written forms of expression existed side by side in the ancient world, and interaction between them was common. Today we assume the primacy of written texts over oral transmission. In antiquity, however, writing was usually used "as a help to memory rather than as an autonomous and independent mode of communication."[2] Thus as Paul Achtemeier has argued, "we need to keep in mind the essentially oral communication of the written texts of the NT and shape our examination of those texts, and their interpretation, accordingly."[3]

Orality in the Ancient World

The modern study of orality in antiquity began in the 1920s and 1930s with the writings of Milman Parry[4] and Marcel Jousse.[5] It became a recognizable discipline through the work of Albert B. Lord.[6] Beginning with analyses of Homer's *Iliad* and *Odyssey,* the study of orality blossomed to include oral traditions that were contained within written materials in Serbo-Croatian, Hispanic, medieval German, Byzantine, modern Greek, Irish, Arabic, Sumerian, Indian, Chinese, Norwegian, and Russian, as well as in Old English poetry, stories, and historical accounts.[7] Among recent scholars, the

---

2. Cf. P. J. Achtemeier, *Omne Verbum Sonat,* 5; quotation from W. J. Ong, *Orality and Literacy,* 40.

3. P. J. Achtemeier, *Omne Verbum Sonat,* 3.

4. Cf. M. Parry, *The Making of Homeric Verse: The Collected Papers of Milman Parry,* ed. A. Parry (New York: Oxford University Press, 1987).

5. Cf. M. Jousse, *Le Style oral rhythmique et mnémotechnique chez le Verbo-moteurs* (Paris: Beauchesne, 1925).

6. Cf. A. B. Lord, *The Singer of Tales* (1960; 2nd ed., 2004).

7. Cf. J. M. Foley, *Oral-Formulaic Theory and Research: An Introduction and Annotated Bibliography* (New York: Garland, 1985), who includes over 1,800 entries in his bibliog-

most significant has been Walter J. Ong, whose numerous studies of various cultural traditions have had a profound effect on understanding the writings of those societies.[8]

Techniques of oral communication were not formally taught in the curricula of antiquity, as one would learn literary composition in a school today. Rather, they were picked up and formed by association and usage. Yet though never organized into a formal curriculum, certain habits and characteristics of oral communication in the ancient world are able to be identified.[9]

One identifiable characteristic of oral communication is its *acoustical orientation.* As Albert Lord observed: "One word begins to suggest another by its very sound; one phrase suggests another not only by reason of idea or by a special ordering to ideas, but also by acoustic value."[10] Or as William Stanford has said in his study of Greek euphony (i.e., the harmonious succession of words having a pleasing sound): "Unlike a modern writer, who may write for the eye and the brain alone, the ancient Greek poet always had to choose *some* kind of sound-group for his composition, since the silent enjoyment of literature was out of the question in his time."[11]

With respect to the structuring of oral poetry and oral prose in antiquity, a number of features have been identified by scholars today. These include (1) the use of framing statements, sentences, phrases, or words to mark out blocks of material of varying lengths (i.e., *inclusio,* as later named by rhetoricians), (2) the repetition of words or expressions at the beginning of successive phrases, clauses, sentences, or verses (i.e., *anaphora,* as later named by rhetoricians), and (3) various types of "ring composition" in what is presented, where the speaker either returns to a previous point in order to frame a certain section of his discourse (i.e., a type of *inclusio*), resumes a discussion interrupted by another section of material (i.e., a type of *ana-*

---

raphy, with about 1,500 of them stemming either directly or indirectly from Parry's pioneering work; see also *idem, The Theory of Oral Composition: History and Methodology* (Bloomington: Indiana University Press, 1988).

8. Among the many books and articles by W. J. Ong, see esp. his *Presence of the Word* (1967); *Rhetoric, Romance, and Technology* (1971); *Interfaces of the Word* (1977); *Orality and Literacy* (1982); and "Writing Is a Technology That Restructures Thought" (1986).

9. For an extensive discussion of "oral patterning" in antiquity, see J. D. Harvey, *Listening to the Text,* 1-118.

10. A. B. Lord, "Characteristics of Orality," 54-62; see also W. J. Ong, *Orality and Literacy,* 37-41.

11. W. Stanford, *The Sound of Greek: Studies in the Greek Theory and Practice of Euphony* (Berkeley: University of California Press, 1967), 77 (italics his).

phora), or develops his argument symmetrically by inverting the order of corresponding elements (i.e., what modern scholars have called *chiasmus*).

Another characteristic of ancient oral communication, whether poetry or prose, is that it was heavily *formulaic in nature* — that is, that it incorporated and constructed its presentation around various formal statements or affirmations of the day, or that an orator expressed himself in ways that would resonate with statements and affirmations then current. Formulaic materials seem to have been included for a number of reasons, with some of the most prominent being (1) to anticipate efficient recognition of what will be said, (2) to highlight the importance of what was being said, (3) to enhance the understanding of what had been said, or (4) to gain acceptance and agreement by the hearers to what was said, and so create a greater persuasive impact.

Natural corollaries to the formulaic nature of oral communication include such features as *repetition, redundancy,* and *verbosity.* These habits of oral communication, whatever value judgments might be made regarding them, have been ingrained in the delivery of every orator or speaker throughout the ages, whether ancient or modern. For as Walter Ong has pointed out, "the orator's thoughts do not always come as fast as he would wish, and even the best orator is at times inclined to repeat what he has just said in order to 'mark time' while he is undertaking to find what move to make next."[12] But these habits have also been necessary for the understanding of every hearer, whether ancient or modern, simply because of the ephemeral nature of speech. For as Ong went on to note, citing two important reasons:

> First . . . spoken words fly away. A reader can pause over a point he wants to reflect on, or go back a few pages to return to it. The inscribed word is still there. The spoken word is gone. So the orator repeats himself, to help his hearers think it over. Second, spoken words do not infallibly carry equally well to everyone in an audience: synonyms, parallelisms, repetitions, neat oppositions, give the individual hearer a second chance if he did not hear well the first time. If he missed the "not only," he can probably reconstruct it from the "but also."[13]

Repetition seems to have been expressed in the oral poetry of antiquity principally by the *parallelism* of lines and the use of *synonyms* or *antonyms.* In

12. W. J. Ong, *Interfaces of the Word,* 114.
13. W. J. Ong, *Interfaces of the Word,* 114.

oral prose, however, it was expressed by a *parallelism* of ideas and the *same words* used to express those ideas.

But whatever the means, the goal of all ancient oral composition was to assist the hearer to understand and remember what the speaker said. This was accomplished by incorporating into both poetry and prose such mnemonic techniques and verbal patterns as would accomplish this purpose. Such techniques and patterns were not taught in any formal manner, but simply picked up and formed by association and usage. They became, almost unconsciously, the compositional habits of the ancient orators and speakers, who seem to have expected their hearers to recognize them rather easily.

Orality and the Scriptures

The study of oral features that appear in the Jewish and Christian Scriptures did not become an identifiable discipline in biblical scholarship until fairly recently.[14] Johann Gottfried Herder in 1880, Hermann Gunkel in 1910, and Henrik S. Nyberg in 1935 had argued for oral sources underlying the OT. But it was not until the 1950s that Eduard Nielsen proposed a number of formal criteria for the identification of such oral source materials as incorporated within the written texts of the OT: (1) monotonous style, (2) recurrent expressions, (3) paratactic style, (4) rhythm and euphony, (5) anacolutha, (6) repetition, (7) the use of twos and threes, (8) memory words, and (9) representative themes.[15] Since then there has arisen a growing interest in the impact of oral traditions on the composition of the OT, as witness the Society of Biblical Literature's 1976 publication "Oral Tradition and Old Testament Studies" in its *Semeia* series, volume 5 — which included not only Robert Culley's article ("Oral Tradition and the OT: Some Recent Discussion"), but also contributions by Burke O. Long ("Recent Field Studies in Oral Literature and the Question of *Sitz im Leben*"), Robert B. Coote ("The Application of Oral Theory to Biblical Hebrew Literature"), Albert B. Lord ("Formula and Non-Narrative Themes in South Slavic Oral Epic and the OT"), W. J. Urbrock ("Oral Antecedents to Job: A Survey of Formulas and Formu-

14. For surveys of the study of orality among biblical scholars prior to 1960, see R. C. Culley, "Oral Tradition and the OT: Some Recent Discussion" (1976); *idem*, "Oral Tradition and Biblical Studies" (1986); and J. D. Harvey, *Listening to the Text* (1998), 1-16.

15. See E. Nielsen, *Oral Tradition: A Modern Problem in Old Testament Introduction* (London: SCM; Naperville: Allenson, 1954).

laic Systems"), and John Van Seters ("Oral Patterns or Literary Conventions in Biblical Narrative"), and as can be found in a whole host of recent books and articles from various perspectives and with differing proposals on the subject.

Studies of orality and the NT have been less numerous, as well as somewhat more diverse, than studies of orality and the OT. In 1898 Eduard Norden identified various features pertaining to the oral composition of prose in his two-volume *Die antike Kunstprosa*.[16] More particularly, Norden went further in 1913 in his *Agnostos Theos: Untersuchungen zur Formengeschichte religiöser Rede* to highlight some of the oral characteristics of the religious language of the NT and to spell out a number of criteria for their identification. And from this beginning there developed during the twentieth century a fairly substantial number of studies dealing with early Christian confessional materials — which materials have been viewed as originally oral in nature and for which such terms as "formula of faith," "creed," "kerygma" ("proclamation"), "paradosis" ("tradition"), "hymn," "prayer," "confession," "liturgical formulation," "ecclesial tradition," "narrative portion," "story," and/or "saying" have been used.[17]

It is only of late, however, that scholars have begun to study in a more direct manner the oral patterning that underlies the writings of the NT and to spell out the impact of their studies on the interpretation of these materials. Werner Kelber has written more extensively than anyone on orality and the NT, especially with respect to the Gospels;[18] and Joanna Dewey has sought to understand Mark's narrative in terms of its oral background.[19] But as Arthur J. Dewey has pointed out, very little has been done to "bring the recent discussion of orality to the writings of Paul."[20] Indeed, interest in the subject of orality and the NT is just beginning to arise, with important programmatic studies of this fledgling discipline only recently being offered by

16. E. Norden, *Die antike Kunstprosa vom VI. Jahrhunderts vor Christus bis in die Zeit der Renaissance*.

17. For a survey of these studies, see R. N. Longenecker, *New Wine into Fresh Wineskins* (1999), 6-26.

18. See W. H. Kelber, "Mark and Oral Tradition," *Semeia* 6 (1979) 7-55; *idem, The Oral and Written Gospel: The Hermeneutics of Speaking and Writing in the Synoptic Tradition, Mark, Paul and Q* (Philadelphia: Fortress, 1983); *idem,* "The Authority of the Word in St. John's Gospel: Charismatic Speech, Narrative Text, Logocentrism, Metaphysics," *OrT* 2 (1987) 108-31.

19. See J. Dewey, "Oral Methods of Structuring Narrative in Mark," *Int* 43 (1989) 32-44.

20. A. J. Dewey, "A Re-Hearing of Romans 10:1-15," *SBLSP* (1990) 273.

Paul Achtemeier in his 1990 article *Omne Verbum Sonat* and John Harvey in his 1998 monograph *Listening to the Text*.

Oral Patterning in Romans

The recognition of residual orality in Paul's letter to the Romans is a study still very much in its infancy. Nonetheless, some of the more obvious instances of this phenomenon in Paul's letter to the Christians at Rome need to be highlighted here, with those features then taken into account in Chapter XI, "Structure and Argument" (and also discussed more fully, where appropriate, in a proposed forthcoming commentary).

1. Acoustical Orientation

The acoustical orientation of words and phrases is not an overly common phenomenon in Romans, for Paul was not rhapsodizing as a poet but writing prose. Yet there are a number of places in the letter where the repetition of words and sounds appears as a significant feature, with that repetition evidently meant as an aid to understanding and remembering what was said.

At least two instances appear in 1:18-32, a passage that denounces the idolatries, immoralities, and injustices of the non-Jewish world — and that may have been material having a previous oral history among Jews vis-à-vis the non-Jewish world, as drawn from *Wisdom of Solomon* 13-14, which Paul used for his own purposes. In verses 24, 26, and 28 there is the repetition of the refrain "God gave them over" (παρέδωκεν αὐτοὺς ὁ θεός), with each of these three uses of the statement serving to introduce a further feature in the downward spiral of the idolatrous Gentiles. Further, in verses 23, 25, and 26 the verb "they exchanged" (ἤλλαξαν . . . μετήλλαξαν . . . μετάλλαξαν) appears in describing that awful downward spiral, with the ominous sound of the final Greek syllable -ξαν undoubtedly meant to ring in the hearers' ears and resonate in their memory.

Commentators have frequently seen, as well, an instance of acoustical orientation in 5:12-21 — which likely incorporates material of major importance in Paul's preaching to Gentiles (on the centrality of 5:12-21 in the apostle's preaching, see Chapter XI, "Structure and Argument"), and so should probably be viewed as having been orally proclaimed by Paul at various times during the course of his Gentile mission. For in that passage the salvific work of Christ vis-à-vis the condition of humanity under sin, death, and judgment is presented in the form of a contrastive parallelism using a series of nouns that end with the Greek letters μα:

1. The sin of "the one man," who undoubtedly was viewed as being Adam (vv. 12-15), is spoken of as τὸ παράπτωμα ("the transgression") in verses 15, 16, 18, and 20, whereas what God has done through "the one man" Jesus Christ to counter sin, death, and judgment, which was brought into human experience through Adam's transgression, is spoken of as τὸ χάρισμα ("the grace") in verses 15 and 16.

2. The effect of Adam's transgression on humanity is spoken of as κρίμα (probably to be understood as "depravity") in verse 16, with its inevitable result being κατάκριμα ("divine judgment") in verses 16 and 18, whereas what God effected through Jesus Christ is spoken of as τὸ δώρημα ("the divine gift") in verse 16, which brings about the condition of δικαίωμα ("righteousness") in verses 16 and 18 and leads to "life eternal."

Such a pairing of nouns ending in μα, playing as it does on the sound of that final syllable of the words, would certainly have had significance both in Paul's oral proclamation and in his hearers' remembrance of what he said. They would have been accustomed to such a mnemomic technique, and he seems to have used it here to enhance their comprehension and retention. Thus in reporting to Christians at Rome regarding this matter of central importance in his proclamation of the Christian gospel to Gentile audiences throughout the eastern portion of the Roman empire, Paul should probably be viewed as having carried over, whether consciously or unconsciously, a characteristic feature of his oral preaching into his written letter.

Other instances of acoustical significance in Romans may be found in Paul's exhortations of chapters 12–13, particularly in what he wrote in chapters 12 and 13:8-14 — which exhortations on Christian love are, in all likelihood, also to be understood as incorporating materials that he had earlier proclaimed in his oral preaching to Gentiles. Particularly noteworthy in this regard are (1) the fourfold repetition in 12:3 of the infinitives "to think" or "think with sober judgment" (ὑπερφρονεῖν . . . φρονεῖν . . . φρονεῖν . . . σωφρονεῖν), which would undoubtedly have caught the attention of those who heard Paul preach, and (2) the almost liturgical cadence that is formed by the sevenfold (both explicit and implied) construction "if" (εἴτε) and "in" (ἐν) in 12:6-8, thereby reading: "If prophecy, in proportion to faith; if ministry, in ministering; if teaching, in teaching; if encouragement, in encouraging; if giving, in generosity; if leadership, in diligence; if showing mercy, in cheerfulness."

On a somewhat smaller scale, it should also be noted that in 5:6-8, which may very well be early Christian confessional material that Paul inserted parenthetically into his thesis paragraph of 5:1-11, each of the four clauses ends with a similar form of the verb "he [Christ] died" (ἀπέθανεν . . . ἀποθανεῖται . . . ἀποθανεῖν . . . ἀπέθανεν). And there may be other such acoustical features yet to be discovered in the letter (as we will attempt to note in a forthcoming exegetical commentary).

2. Chiastic Construction

Chiasmus is the name that modern rhetoricians have given to the phenomenon of paired words, statements, or texts that are arranged in a pattern of inverted symmetry around a focal word, statement, or text. The name is a transliteration of the post-classical Greek word χιασμός, which means "crossing." But the term is more directly derived from the Greek letter "χ," and so used for the structure's basic A-B-A' pattern of arrangement.

The identification and analysis of any particular *chiasmus* is often a matter of dispute — whether in the written materials of antiquity or in the oral delivery and written compositions of today. For the question always exists as to whether its presence is the result of deliberate intent or has been done inadvertently or somewhat unconsciously. Likewise, *chiasmus* in Paul's letter to Rome is also a fervently debated matter, both as to its identification and as to its significance. Extreme positions are those represented by (1) John W. Welch, who argues negatively that while the phenomenon of *chiasmus* appears elsewhere in the NT, Romans contains very few, if any, chiastic structures,[21] vis-à-vis (2) Peter Ellis, who, arguing positively, has analyzed the entire letter in terms of what he has perceived to be its major and minor A-B-A' and A-B-C-B'-A' formats.[22]

Most scholars have viewed 1 Corinthians as the "happy hunting ground" for the use of *chiasmus* in Paul's letters, as proposed by Nils Lund in 1942[23] and Joachim Jeremias in 1958.[24] Further, most have had no problem in seeing Paul as retaining the chiastic structures of the OT passages

21. J. W. Welch, "Chiasmus in the New Testament," in *Chiasmus in Antiquity: Structures, Analyses, Exegesis,* ed. J. W. Welch (Hildesheim: Gerstenberg, 1981), 211-49.

22. P. Ellis, *Seven Pauline Letters* (Collegeville: Liturgical Press, 1981).

23. Cf. N. Lund, *Chiasmus in the New Testament.*

24. Cf. J. Jeremias, "Chiasmus in den Paulusbriefen."

that he quotes in Romans, especially in 10:19 (quoting Deut 32:21), 11:3 (quoting 1 Kgs 19:10), and 11:10 (quoting Ps 69:23). But there remains a fairly high degree of uncertainty among contemporary commentators about where and how Paul used chiastic construction in the prose of his letter to the Romans.

Much of any discussion regarding *chiasmus* in Romans must be reserved for specific exegetical treatments of the various passages in question in a commentary proper, for it is only there that the schematics of particular verses can be adequately displayed (or discounted) and the implications appropriately spelled out (or set aside). Suffice it here to say that among the many passages in Romans often said to be chiastic in structure, the following have most frequently been viewed by NT scholars as including certain chiastic features: 2:14-27 (or, perhaps, 2:12-29); 3:4-8; 10:9-10; 11:30-31; and 11:33-35 — with some of these passages incorporating certain traditional materials that were, it may be assumed, originally formed in an oral environment.

3. Framing Statements, Sentences, Phrases, and Words

A further habit of oral prose is the framing of materials by the repetition of certain statements, sentences, phrases, and/or words. The materials of 5:1-11 at the beginning of chapters 5–8 and of 8:31-39 at the section's end express similar themes, and so have often been seen by commentators to represent what rhetoricians call an *inclusio.* More obviously, however, this characteristic feature of orality may be observed in the repeated refrain "through/by our Lord Jesus Christ" (διὰ τοῦ κυρίου ἡμῶν ᾽Ιησοῦ Χριστοῦ; or, as in 6:23 and 8:39, using the equivalent construction of ἐν followed by the dative) — not only at the beginning and the end of the section at 5:1 and 8:39, which represents again something of an *inclusio,* but also at the close of each individual unit within the section at 5:11; 5:21; 6:23; and 7:25. It has also been claimed that the phrase "both for the Jew first and for the Gentile" (᾽Ιουδαίῳ τε πρῶτον καὶ ῞Ελληνι) in 1:16 and 2:9-10 (twice) frames 1:16–2:10 as a single textual unit, but this proposal has been discounted by a number of recent scholars.[25]

25. For an evaluation of this thesis, see our discussions of 1:16-32 and 2:1-16 later in Chapter XI, "Structure and Argument."

2. Rhetorical Conventions

"Rhetoric," as George Kennedy has defined it, "is that quality in discourse by which a speaker or writer seeks to accomplish his purposes."[26] It is not just a matter of style. More importantly, rhetoric has to do with a speaker's or writer's choice and arrangement of words, use of evidence, type and form of argument, and control of emotions. Rhetorical criticism in the study of NT letters is somewhat similar to redaction criticism in the study of the Gospels, for rhetorical criticism, like redaction criticism, "takes the text as we have it, whether the work of a single author or the product of editing, and looks at it from the point of view of the author's or editor's intent, the unified results, and how it would be perceived by an audience of near contemporaries."[27]

Like grammarians — who analyze, describe, and catalogue the features and functions of a language, but do not invent the language itself — rhetoricians analyze, describe, and catalogue the features and functions of oral and written communication, but do not invent them. Yet also like grammarians — whose descriptive work not only provides an understanding of grammar (i.e., the forms of a language) and syntax (i.e., the function of those forms in communication), but also enhances a more effective and efficient use of language — the work of rhetoricians is meant not only to provide an understanding of acceptable conventions of speech and writing but also to enhance the more effective and efficient use of modes of persuasion and rhetorical techniques.

When applied to the biblical writings, rhetorical analysis serves as an additional tool in the hands of skilled interpreters for the purpose of gaining a better understanding of what was written. The emphasis of rhetorical analysis vis-à-vis the biblical materials is on (1) how a writing has been formulated in terms of the rhetorical conventions of its day, and (2) how that writing would have been perceived by its addressees at that time and in that culture. The classifications formulated by rhetoricians, whether ancient or modern, are but categories that have been invented to describe what best represents the types and modes of persuasion identifiable in the writings themselves. The invented categories, however, cannot be allowed to control what the biblical authors have written. They serve only as aids in helping modern readers understand what lies behind the written texts and

26. G. A. Kennedy, *New Testament Interpretation through Rhetorical Criticism*, 3.
27. G. A. Kennedy, *New Testament Interpretation through Rhetorical Criticism*, 4.

how the messages of those texts would have been understood in their day. In rhetorical analyses of Scripture, therefore, there must always be a balance on the part of interpreters between (1) allowing studies of rhetorical types, modes, and conventions, whether ancient or modern, to provide their particular contributions to a better understanding of what has been written, yet (2) not permitting the classifications or categories of the rhetoricians, whether ancient or modern, to dominate or excessively control one's reading.

Rhetoric in the Ancient World

Rhetoric is a universal phenomenon that is rooted in the basic workings of the human mind. Nonetheless, particular forms of rhetoric have been conditioned by the ideological perspectives and communal traditions of the various cultures in which they have come to birth. Classical rhetoric was not invented by the Greeks or the Romans. But the Greeks of antiquity, followed by many perceptive Romans, are to be credited with (1) studying the types, modes, and conventions of persuasive speech and effective writing of their day, (2) giving names to the rhetorical conventions and techniques they found in the oral and written materials of their culture and society, and (3) organizing those conventions and techniques into categories that could be taught and learned for the improvement of communication among people, and thereby for the betterment of people's lives generally.

1. The Classical Rhetoricians

The most important of the classical rhetoricians was the Greek philosopher Aristotle (384-322 B.C.), who, in addition to writing works on natural science, metaphysics, history, moral philosophy, and art, authored a handbook titled *The Art of Rhetoric,* which stemmed from his lectures at Athens during the mid-fourth century and was partly based on the principles set out by Plato (428-348 B.C.). Also important in the formulation of ancient rhetorical theory is the anonymous *Rhetoric ad Herennium,* which was written in Latin but based on Greek sources. It seems to have been composed about 84 B.C., probably by a rhetorician whose name was Cornificius. Cicero (106-43 B.C.), the renowned Roman orator, philosopher, and statesman, in his *De Inventione* (On Invention) and *De Partitione Oratoria* (On Partitions of Oratory), as well as in many of his other writings, is particularly helpful for providing insight into how rhetoric was understood and used in the first century before Christ. And Quintilian (c. A.D. 35-95), a Roman rhetorician of Spain and Rome, in his four-volume *Institutio Oratoria* (The Education of the Orator), which regularly summarizes the theories of a number of earlier rhetoricians, is important for understanding how rhetoric was used in speeches and written compositions during the time when the NT was written.

Two basic methods in the undertaking of rhetorical analysis can be discerned in the classical handbooks on rhetoric. The first is a historical, comparative method, which lays emphasis on the overall rhetorical form of an oration or writing and seeks to trace out lines of genetic relations with other speeches or writings of the time. It has been called "diachronic rhetorical analysis." The second is a strictly literary, compositional method, which examines the argument of an oration or writing on its own, identifying its modes of persuasion and classifying its argumentative conventions. It has been given the name "synchronic rhetorical analysis."[28] Each of these methods needs to be considered separately in what follows below.

2. Diachronic Rhetorical Analysis

Diachronic rhetorical analysis, the historical and comparative method, classifies speeches and written compositions in terms of their basic types or genres — that is, (1) "forensic," "judicial," or "legal" rhetoric (γένος δικανικόν), whose purpose was to establish right or wrong, and so functioned to defend or accuse; (2) "deliberative" or "advisory" rhetoric (γένος συμβουλευτικόν), which highlighted matters of advantage or disadvantage, and so functioned to exhort or commend the former and admonish against or dissuade the latter; and (3) "epideictic," "panegyric," or "eulogistic" rhetoric (γένος ἐπιδεικτικόν), which dealt with matters of honor or dishonor, praising the former and blaming the latter, and urged a proper response. It was Aristotle who seems to have first classified rhetorical theory in terms of this threefold classification.[29] And these three rhetorical types or genres were commonly recognized in antiquity as the basic categories of all oral and written composition[30] — though Quintilian speaks of

28. Cf. M. Kessler, "Methodological Setting for Rhetorical Criticism," 22-36; see also *idem*, "Introduction to Rhetorical Criticism of the Bible," 1-27.

29. Cf. Aristotle, *Rhetoric* 1.3.1-3.

30. Cf. Cicero, *De Oratore* 2.10; *De Inventione* 1.5.7; anon., *Rhetorica ad Herennium* 1.2; Quintilian, *Institutio Oratoria* 2.21.23; 3.3.14-15.

Anaximenes, a mid–fourth century B.C. author of a handbook on rhetoric, as categorizing speeches in terms of only two types, that is, either "forensic" or "deliberative."[31]

From the rhetorical handbooks and from the speeches and written materials extant from the ancient world, these three classical categories of rhetoric may be understood as follows:

A. Forensic (i.e., "judicial" or "legal") rhetoric, which sought to persuade a judge, a court, or an audience to make a judgment about something that occurred in the past. It consists of the following parts:
   1. *Exordium/Proem* (Introduction) — sets out the character of the speaker and defines the central issues being addressed;
   2. *Narratio* (Narration) — presents a statement of the facts that relate to the issues of the case;
   3. *Propositio* (Proposition) — states the points of agreement and disagreement, and then summarizes the central issues to be proved;
   4. *Probatio* (Confirmation/Argument/Proof) — develops the central arguments;
   5. *Refutatio* (Refutation) — gives a rebuttal to the opponents' arguments;
   6. *Peroratio/Epilogue* (Conclusion) — summarizes the case and evokes a sympathetic response.
B. Deliberative (i.e., "advisory") rhetoric, which sought to persuade a governing council or an audience to take some action in the future. It consists of the following parts:
   1. *Exordium/Proem* (Introduction) — sets out the character of the speaker and defines the central issues being addressed;
   2. *Propositio* (Proposition) — states the points of agreement and disagreement, and summarizes the central issues to be proved;
   3. *Narratio* (Narration) — presents a statement of the facts that relate to the issues of the case;
   4. *Probatio* (Confirmation/Argument/Proof) — develops the central arguments;
   5. *Exhortatio* (Exhortation/Appeal) — exhorts a desired action;
   6. *Peroratio/Epilogue* (Conclusion) — summarizes and evokes action.
C. Epideictic (i.e., "panegyric" or "eulogistic") rhetoric, which was used at various occasions such as victory celebrations, weddings and funer-

---

31. Quintilian, *Institutio Oratoria* 3.4.9.

als, and sought to persuade an audience to hold on to or reaffirm some point of view in the present, highlighting in the process what was to be viewed as honorable and what shameful, what was worthy of praise and what to be blamed. Generally it includes the following component parts:

1. *Exordium/Proem* (Introduction) — sets out the character of the speaker and defines the central issues being addressed;
2. *Probatio* (Body) — presents an orderly sequence of topics dealing with the life of the person being praised or the qualities of the concept under consideration, often adorned with vivid descriptions or comparisons of the subject to something else;
3. *Peroratio/Epilogue* (Conclusion) — summarizes and evokes action.

Since speeches and written materials were primarily fashioned by the Greeks and Romans for legal and political purposes, forensic rhetoric is what is most often discussed and analyzed in the ancient rhetorical handbooks. Forensic rhetoric, in fact, was usually understood as the rhetoric of the courtroom, and so it was natural for its structure and component parts to be dealt with at some length in the classical handbooks. Deliberative rhetoric was also extensively studied by the ancient rhetoricians. At times it was viewed as only a simplified version of forensic rhetoric. Usually, however, significant differences between forensic and deliberative rhetoric were recognized. The primary difference was that deliberative rhetoric was principally concerned with *exhortatio,* that is, with exhortation and appeal, with everything else in the speech or writing meant to prepare for this hortatory purpose (thus it has been called "the rhetoric of the assembly or council"), whereas forensic rhetoric was understood to include no hortatory element, since one does not exhort a judge or jury (thus it has been called "the rhetoric of the courtroom"). Also different was the development of their respective arguments, for in forensic rhetoric the *narratio* preceded the *propositio* whereas in deliberative rhetoric the *narratio* usually followed the *propositio.*

Analyses of epideictic rhetoric are often truncated in the classical handbooks. Epideictic rhetoric became something of a "catch-all" category for whatever did not fit either forensic or deliberative rhetoric. Its structure and component parts, therefore, are difficult to set out except in only very general terms. Further, epideictic rhetoric seems to have been seldom used by itself. Rather, it is usually found in connection with either forensic or deliberative rhetoric, with those two more prominent types including sections within them that contain certain epideictic features of either praise or blame, or both.

3. Synchronic Rhetorical Analysis

"Rhetorical study, in its strict sense," as was said by Aristotle, "is concerned with the modes of persuasion"[32] — that is, not primarily with historical types or genres of rhetoric (i.e., "diachronic rhetorical analysis"), but with rhetorical devices and techniques used in the formulation of an oral or written presentation (i.e., "synchronic rhetorical analysis"). For, as Aristotle continued, "it is not enough to know what we ought to say; we must also say it as we ought."[33] Further, Aristotle defined rhetoric as "the faculty of observing in any given case the available means of persuasion,"[34] thereby understanding rhetoric in its synchronic task as not confined to any particular art, science, or subject matter, but applicable to "almost any subject presented to us."[35]

Synchronic rhetoric was organized by Greco-Roman rhetoricians under three basic headings: (1) *ethos,* or proof derived from the character of the speaker himself; (2) *pathos,* or emotions induced in an audience with the purpose of eliciting a favorable response; and (3) *logos,* or the development of an argument as provided by the words of the speech itself. Or as Aristotle himself identified and defined these kinds of rhetoric in a synchronic analysis:

> Of the modes of persuasion furnished by the spoken word there are three kinds. The first kind depends on the personal character of the speaker [i.e., *ethos*]; the second on putting the audience into a certain frame of mind [i.e., *pathos*]; the third on the proof, or apparent proof, provided by the words of the speech itself [i.e., *logos*].[36]

Within these basic kinds of synchronic rhetoric — particularly within that of *logos,* which has to do with "the proof, or apparent proof, provided by the words of the speech itself" — there developed among the ancient rhetoricians a number of subcategories in their task of identifying and classifying the various modes of persuasion used in their day, and which they saw as being important for effective communication. And rhetoricians today have developed further rhetorical classifications and subcategories, largely by refining those of the classical rhetoricians but also by inventing new nomenclature to account for the data before them in the ancient written materials.

32. Aristotle, *Rhetoric* 1.1.
33. Aristotle, *Rhetoric* 1.1.
34. Aristotle, *Rhetoric* 1.2.
35. Aristotle, *Rhetoric* 1.2.
36. Aristotle, *Rhetoric* 1.2.

It is impossible to enumerate all of the conventions, practices, and techniques that have been identified and classified by classical and contemporary rhetoricians from Aristotle to today. Rhetoricians, whether past or present, have delighted in refining issues, subdividing matters, and constructing additional categories for the material studied, with the result that categories and classifications have been developed almost *ad infinitum,* often with conflicting understandings and nuances.[37] An inclusive or extensive listing of such categories and classifications is not necessary for our present purpose. However, some of the more prominent modes of persuasion that have been discussed and classified by the ancient rhetoricians may be listed here (arranged in alphabetic order for pedagogical purposes):

1. *Anaphora* (from the Greek word ἀναφορά or its synonym ἐπαναφορά, with the preposition ἐπί serving to intensify the noun; the verb ἀναφέρειν means "to carry back" or "bear again"): the repetition of a word or expression at the beginning of a series of successive phrases, clauses, sentences, or verses; or, as in an *extended anaphora,* the repetition of a word or expression at the resumption of a discussion that has been interrupted by another section of material.

2. *Apostrophe* (from the Greek word ἀποστροφή, which signified "a turning away"; the verb ἀποστρέφειν means "to turn away"): the interruption of a discourse in order to address a person or personified thing.

3. *Enthymeme* (from the Greek word ἐνθύμημα, which signified "thought," "consideration," or "argument"; with the verb ἐνθυμεῖσθαι meaning "to keep in mind," "reflect on," "consider"): an abbreviated or imperfect syllogism, whose premises may involve matters of character *(ethos),* emotion *(pathos),* or reason *(logos)* but whose conclusion must be supplied by the audience or addressees.

4. *Diatribe* (from the Greek word διατριβή, which may be translated "conversation," "discourse," "lecture," or even "school"; the verb διατρίβειν means "to spend time," "rub through," "wear away"): a lively dialogical style that made use of direct address to an imaginary interlocutor, hypothetical objections, and false conclusions. It involved rhetorical questions that called for an obvious answer. It was sometimes bitter and abusive in its invectives and pointed in its criticism. Yet it was always "motivated by concern rather than contempt" for the one

---

37. On ancient rhetorical terms, definitions, and nuancing, see H. Lausberg, *Handbuch der literarischen Rhetorik,* 2 vols.

(or those) to whom it was directed.[38] And it served to heighten the argument and to make the point of the argument in a fashion that would be remembered.

Diatribe was a type of discourse not employed by wandering Cynic or Stoic philosophers in their public teaching (as had been argued by R. Bultmann), but used principally by teachers of philosophy in a classroom setting in order to clarify what they taught, rebuke their students for their misconceptions, and refute any logical objections that might arise to their teaching (as argued by A. J. Malherbe and S. K. Stowers). By its use a teacher sought to lead a student from some erroneous or immature understanding to a proper or more mature comprehension of the issue at hand.

5. *Inclusio* (from the Latin word *inclusio* meaning "imprisonment" or "confinement"): similar phrases or clauses placed at the beginning and end of a relatively short unit of text that serve to frame the material presented.

6. *Metaphor* (from the Greek word μεταφορά, which signified "transference"; the verb μεταφέρειν means "to transfer," "carry away"): a word, group of words, or sentence that is used to stand for something different from the literal reference, but is linked to it by some perceived similarity and so suggests a likeness or analogy between them. Or as Aristotle defined it, a metaphor is "the application to a thing of a name that belongs to something else, the transference taking place from genus to species, from species to genus, from species to species, or proportionally."[39]

7. *Paradeigma* (from the Greek word παράδειγμα, which signified "pattern," "model," or "example"; the verb παραδειγματίζειν means "to expose," "make an example of"): a story that provides a pattern or example to be either imitated or avoided, or an argument based on the use of an example that is either positive or negative.

8. *Paronomasia* (from the Greek word παρονομασία, which signified "words that sound alike"; the verb παρονομάζειν means "to call with a slight change of name"): a play on two or more words in a relatively brief context that are similar in form, that sound alike, or that make use of different meanings of the same word.

9. *Prosopopoeia* (from the Greek word προσωποποιία, which signified "making a mask" and had to do with character delineation — the noun

---

38. Cf. S. K. Stowers, "Diatribe," 81-82.
39. Aristotle, *Poetica* 21.7; cf. *idem, Rhetoric* 3.10.7.

πρόσωπον, which means "face," with the verb ποίειν, which means "to do" or "make," connoting "to make a mask of someone's face"): the introduction of a specific character, whether person or thing, allowing that person or thing to speak for itself.

10. *Synkrisis* (from the Greek word σύγκρισις, "comparison"; the verb συγκρίνειν means "to bring together," "combine," "compare"): a comparison of comparable persons, objects, or things, with deficiencies and superiorities highlighted.

In addition to these classical classifications, modern scholars have identified a number of rhetorical conventions that appear in the writings of various ancient authors. Among these are what have been called:

1. *Alternation:* the interplay between two alternate choices or ideas, with the interplay involving the repetition of words, the use of synonyms, the discussion of results, or the listing of specific examples. Alternation serves to define the issues at stake, and so involves the hearer or reader in the decision-making process.

2. *Ring composition:* the correspondence in wording between sentences that frame a section, with similar wording being used both at the beginning and at the end. Ring composition often sets off a section of a discussion — though also, at times, it may resume a train of thought.

3. *Word chains:* the frequent repetition of a given word and its cognates within a clearly delimited context. The repetition emphasizes and gives color to the topic under discussion.

4. *Refrain:* the use of repeated wording or formulaic phrases to open or close the various sections of a discussion. Although this pattern is similar to "ring composition," it differs in that an opening statement may not be balanced by a closing statement, or vice versa. A refrain functions by way of beginning or ending successive sections, often, in effect, unifying extended portions of a writing.

5. *Concentric symmetry:* multiple correspondences that occur over an extended passage and have a single element at the center. The point of the correspondence should be verbal and grammatical, not just conceptual. Verbal parallels should involve central or dominant terminology not regularly found elsewhere in the structure. Concentric symmetry focuses attention on the central element of the structure, which usually is the significant point of the section.

6. *Chiasmus* (a transliteration of the post-classical Greek word χιασμός,

which means "crossing," but is more directly derived from the Greek letter "χ," pronounced "chi," which resembles the English letter "X" and so has come to suggest an inverted parallelism): the arrangement of paired words, statements, or texts in inverted symmetry around a focal word, statement, or text. *Chiasmus* is not a convention that was discussed in the Greco-Roman rhetorical handbooks; in fact, it seems not even to have been conceptualized by the classical theorists.[40] Nonetheless, as George Kennedy points out, "it is not uncommon in classical Greek literature, and very common in Latin."[41]

Rhetorical Analysis and the Scriptures

Rhetoric was highly prized in the Greco-Roman world. It was at the heart of the educational enterprise and the hallmark of a person of culture. As Henry Marrou has aptly noted:

> The thing that really showed whether a man was cultivated or not was not whether he had studied science or medicine . . . but whether he had received either of the two rival and allied forms of advanced education which were still the most widespread and characteristic . . . the philosophical and the rhetorical. Of these the dominant member was unquestionably the second, which left a profound impression on all manifestations of the Hellenistic spirit. For the very great majority of students, higher education meant taking lessons from the rhetor, learning the art of eloquence from him.[42]

Not surprisingly, many of the Church Fathers, having been trained in classical rhetoric, often used the rhetorical categories and modes of persuasion of their day in commenting on Scripture, thereby enabling them to speak and write intelligibly to the people of their day. Most notable in this regard were John Chrysostom[43] and Aurelius Augustine.[44] Likewise a num-

40. G. A. Kennedy, *New Testament Interpretation through Rhetorical Criticism*, 28-29.

41. G. A. Kennedy, *New Testament Interpretation through Rhetorical Criticism*, 28.

42. H. I. Marrou, *A History of Education in Antiquity*, trans. G. Lamb (New York: Sheed & Ward, 1956), 194.

43. See esp. Chrysostom's *Homily* 8 and *Homily* 31 on Romans, *Homily* 28 on 1 Corinthians, *Homily* 13 on 2 Corinthians, and *Homily* 7 on Colossians.

44. See esp. Augustine's *City of God* 11.18; also *idem, On Christian Doctrine* 4.7.11-15; 4.20.39-44.

ber of sixteenth-century Protestant Reformation leaders, having also been trained in classical rhetoric, used the conventions of the classical rhetoricians in their explications of Scripture. Most notable among these were Philip Melanchthon[45] and John Calvin.[46] And some post-Reformation writers, who had been exposed as well to Greco-Roman rhetoric in their secondary and university educations, continued to use the classical conventions, modes of persuasion, and nomenclature in their interpretations of Scripture. Most notable among these have been Hugo Grotius[47] and Johann Bengel.[48]

During the nineteenth and twentieth centuries, however, particularly from about 1825 to 1975 when "historical-critical-cultural" analyses and "comparative religionist" approaches dominated biblical studies, rhetorical analysis became almost a lost art in biblical scholarship. There were still a few scholars during that period who continued to argue, at least to some extent and in various ways, for the importance of rhetorical analysis for understanding the biblical writings. Among these, particularly dealing with the Pauline letters, were Johannes Weiss,[49] Friedrich Blass,[50] Rudolf Bultmann,[51] Ernest B. Allo,[52] Ernst von Dobschütz,[53] Nils W. Lund,[54] David Daube,[55] and Joachim Jeremias.[56] But despite these rather valiant, though somewhat diverse, attempts to reinstate rhetorical analysis as an important tool for the study of Scripture, interest in rhetoric, whether ancient or modern, was largely relegated to the backwaters of scholarly biblical study.

Much of the modern revival of interest in rhetoric vis-à-vis the biblical

45. Cf. R. Schäfer, "Melanchthons Hermeneutik im Römerbrief-Kommentar von 1532," *ZTK* 60 (1963) 216-35.

46. Cf. B. Girardin, *Rhétorique et Théologie. Calvin. Le Commentaire de l'Épître aux Romains,* TH (Paris: Beauchesne, 1979), who interacts, as well, with the rhetorical treatments of the Roman Catholic Religious Humanist Desiderius Erasmus and the lesser known Protestant Reformers Martin Bucer and Heinrich Bullinger.

47. See H. Grotius, *Annotationes in Novum Testamentum,* 3 vols. (Paris, 1641-50).

48. See J. A. Bengel, *Gnomon Novi Testamenti,* 2 vols. (1742); ET: *Gnomon of the New Testament,* 2 vols., trans. C. T. Lewis and M. R. Vincent (Philadelphia: Perkinpine & Higgins, 1860-1862; repr. as *New Testament Word Studies* (Grand Rapids: Kregel, 1978).

49. J. Weiss, "Beiträge zur paulinischen Rhetorik" (1897).

50. F. Blass, *Rhythmen der asianischen und römischen Kunstprosa* (1905).

51. R. Bultmann, *Stil der paulinischen Predigt und die kynisch-stoische Diatribe* (1910).

52. E. B. Allo, "Le défaut d'éloquence et le style oral de Saint Paul" (1934).

53. E. von Dobschütz, "Wortschatz und Stil des Römerbriefs" (1934).

54. N. W. Lund, *Chiasmus in the New Testament* (1942).

55. D. Daube, "Rabbinic Methods of Interpretation and Hellenistic Rhetoric" (1949).

56. J. Jeremias, "Chiasmus in den Paulusbriefen" (1959).

writings is rooted in the rhetorical studies of non-biblical scholars during the mid-1950s through the mid-1970s — with the attention of these scholars being directed either to classical rhetoric in its various forms or to the "New Rhetoric" that is concerned with contemporary modes of argumentation. Prominent in the renewed study of classical rhetoric have been Donald L. Clark,[57] Heinrich Lausberg,[58] R. F. Howes,[59] and George A. Kennedy.[60] The foundational study for the "New Rhetoric" was provided by Chaim Perelman and Lucie Olbrechts-Tyteca,[61] with the most prominent popularizers of this type of rhetorical analysis being Kenneth Burke,[62] Edward P. J. Corbett,[63] Edwin Black,[64] and William J. Brandt.[65]

In the field of OT studies, it was James Muilenburg who inaugurated and led a vigorous exploration of the impact of rhetorical analysis on the interpretation of the OT. In his presidential address of 1968 at the annual meeting of the Society of Biblical Literature, Muilenburg asked the question "After Form Criticism What?" (which was the title of his address), and he answered that question with the response: "rhetorical criticism, that's what."[66] That address, together with its publication, must be credited as having been epochal in the field of biblical studies generally and OT studies in particular. And through Muilenburg's teaching and leadership there has developed, as Wilhelm Wuellner (one of Muilenburg's early students) rightly declares, a "Muilenburg School" of scholars "whose publications have done much to make the reference to rhetoric acceptable, if not fashionable, again in biblical exegesis."[67]

In NT studies, Amos N. Wilder, because of his study of such literary forms as "dialogue," "story," and "parable" in the Gospels,[68] has often been

---

57. D. L. Clark, *Rhetoric in Greco-Roman Education* (1957).

58. H. Lausberg, *Handbuch der literarischen Rhetorik* (1960).

59. R. F. Howes, *Historical Studies of Rhetoric and Rhetoricians* (1961).

60. G. A. Kennedy, *Art of Persuasion in Greece* (1963); *idem, Art of Rhetoric in the Roman World* (1972).

61. C. Perelman and L. Olbrechts-Tyteca, *The New Rhetoric* (1958).

62. K. Burke, *Rhetoric of Motives* (1950); *idem, Grammar of Motives and a Rhetoric of Motives* (1962).

63. E. P. J. Corbett, *Classical Rhetoric for the Modern Student* (1965); *idem*, ed., *Rhetorical Analysis of Literary Works* (1969).

64. E. Black, *Rhetorical Criticism* (1965).

65. W. J. Brandt, *Rhetoric of Argumentation* (1970).

66. J. Muilenburg, "Form Criticism and Beyond" (1969), 1-18 (the title of his article being a reformulated form of the title of his 1968 address).

67. W. Wuellner, "Where Is Rhetorical Criticism Taking Us?" 454.

68. See A. N. Wilder, *Language of the Gospel* (1964).

called "the father of rhetorical analysis." But more significant for a rhetorical analysis of most of the writings of the NT — particularly for analyses of the canonical letters and apocalypse — have been Hans-Dieter Betz, George A. Kennedy, and Edwin A. Judge. For though their approaches, methods, and conclusions have often been quite different, these three scholars have shared a common insistence on the importance of rhetorical analysis for an understanding of the NT materials, and each of them has made important contributions toward such an understanding.

Hans-Dieter Betz, influenced by Heinrich Lausberg's analyses and classifications of classical rhetoric,[69] argued that Paul's letter to the Galatians, as well as some of his other letters, are best understood in terms of forensic or judicial rhetoric.[70] George Kennedy, building on his earlier studies of classical rhetoric,[71] set out various paradigmatic studies for the application of classical rhetorical conventions to the writings of the NT, proposing (*contra* H.-D. Betz) that most of the NT letters must be understood in terms of deliberative or advising rhetoric.[72] And Edwin Judge, focusing more on the ancient philosophers and their schools (who, of course, used the rhetoric of their day in their presentations), highlighted a number of rhetorical matters of significance for the interpretation of the early Christian movement generally and Paul in particular.[73]

Around each of these three seminal scholars has developed a "school" or cohort of scholars who have continued, with certain reservations and making some revisions, their respective teacher's approaches, methods, and conclusions. Yet the modern study of rhetoric vis-à-vis the interpretation of the NT is still very much in its infancy. There have been, of course, both advances and false starts in the discipline — and probably only in hindsight will later scholars be able to identify what was valid and what was invalid in those earlier studies. Nonetheless, despite the newness and difficulties of the

69. Cf. H. Lausberg, *Handbuch der literarischen Rhetorik* (1960).

70. See H.-D. Betz, esp. his *Apostel Paulus und die sokratische Tradition* (1972); *idem,* "Literary Composition and Function of Paul's Letter to the Galatians" (1975); *idem, Galatians,* Hermeneia (1979); *idem, Second Corinthians 8 and 9* (1985); and *idem,* "Problem of Rhetoric and Theology" (1986).

71. G. A. Kennedy, *Art of Persuasion in Greece* (1963); *idem, Art of Rhetoric in the Roman World* (1972); *idem, Classical Rhetoric and Its Christian and Secular Tradition* (1980).

72. G. A. Kennedy, esp. his *New Testament Interpretation through Rhetorical Criticism* (1984); see also *idem,* "Introduction to the Rhetoric of the Gospels" (1983).

73. E. A. Judge, see esp. his "Early Christians as a Scholastic Community" (1960); *idem, Social Pattern of Christian Groups* (1960); *idem,* "Paul's Boasting in Relation to Contemporary Professional Practice" (1968); and *idem,* "St. Paul and Classical Society" (1972).

modern use of rhetorical genres and conventions in biblical studies, there can be no doubt that rhetorical analysis must be appreciated and used as a significant tool in the study of the NT, and that it needs to be understood and developed more fully.

Rhetorical Analysis of Romans

Romans has frequently been the subject of rhetorical analysis — as witness, for example, (1) the theological affirmations drawn from Paul's letter by John Chrysostom and Aurelius Augustine (among the Church Fathers), (2) the commentaries on the letter by Philip Melanchthon and John Calvin (among the Protestant Reformers), (3) certain interpretations claimed to be derived from it by Hugo Grotius and Johann Albrecht Bengel (among post-Reformation writers), and (4) the great interest expressed today in its rhetorical genre and modes of persuasion. And interest in the rhetoric of Romans has been encouraged by the fact that Paul's letter to the Christians at Rome incorporates the longest and most sustained argument of any of the Pauline letters.

Paul and the Rhetoric of His Day

It is not necessary to view Paul as having been trained in rhetoric in order to appreciate the rhetorical features in his letters that correspond to the conventions of classical rhetoric. Rhetoric in the Greco-Roman world was "in the air" and intrinsic to the ethos of Paul's day. Burton Mack points out:

> By the first century B.C.E. the practice of rhetoric had been thoroughly enculturated, the system of techniques fully explored, the logic rationalized, and the pedagogy refined. Rhetoric permeated both the system of education and the manner of public discourse that marked the culture of Hellenism on the eve of the Roman age.[74]

Further, as Mack goes on to observe:

> All people, whether formally trained or not, were fully schooled in the wily ways of sophists, the eloquence required at civic festivals, the measured tones of the local teacher, and the heated debates where differences of opinion battled for the right to say what should be done. To be

74. B. L. Mack, *Rhetoric and the New Testament*, 28.

engulfed in the culture of Hellenism meant to have ears trained for the rhetoric of speech.[75]

But while rhetoric permeated the Greco-Roman world of Paul's day, it was never monolithic as to its generic types or constricted in the expression of its various features. Rather, it often took form in differing genres (analyzing the materials diachronically) and seems to have been frequently worked out using diverse modes of persuasion (analyzing the materials synchronically). The three classical genres of rhetoric were still recognized (i.e., forensic, deliberative, and epideictic) and the three basic modes of persuasion were still invoked (i.e., *ethos, pathos,* and *logos*). But there were also, as David Aune has rightly pointed out, (1) an eclectic use of these types and categories by the orators and authors of the day, and (2) a mixing of the rhetorical genres and modes of persuasion as seemed best to particular speakers or writers in carrying out their respective purposes when addressing their various audiences.[76]

For example, Dionysius of Halicarnassus (born at Halicarnassus in Caria and died at Rome in 8 B.C.) — a Greek rhetorician and historian who taught rhetoric in Rome sometime after 30 B.C., compiled a handbook on rhetorical style, wrote a number of critical works on the writings of various Greek philosophers (e.g., on Plato, Isocrates, Isaeus, and Polybius), and authored a history of Rome from its mythological beginnings to the Punic Wars (which was called *Archaeologia* or *Antiquitates Romanae*) — says of the writing of his history of Rome:

> As to the form I give this work, it does not resemble that which the authors who make wars alone their subject have given to their histories [e.g., Thucydides], nor that which others who treat of the several forms of government by themselves have adopted [e.g., Aristotle], nor is it like the annalistic accounts which the authors of the Attic histories have published. Rather, it is a combination (μικτός, "a mixture") of every kind — forensic, speculative and narrative — to the intent that it may afford satisfaction both to those who occupy themselves with political debates and to those who are devoted to philosophical speculations, as well as to any who may desire mere undisturbed entertainment in their reading of history.[77]

75. B. L. Mack, *Rhetoric and the New Testament,* 31.

76. Cf. D. E. Aune, "Mixtum Compositum" (i.e., "mixed genres") and "Rhetorical Genres," in his *Westminster Dictionary,* 307, 419-20.

77. Dionysius of Halicarnassus, *Antiq. Romanae* 1.8.3.

Likewise, the Greek rhetorician Publius Aelius Aristides (c. A.D. 120-180), in a handbook on the art of rhetoric, which was composed sometime in the mid-second century A.D., in analyzing a speech by Demosthenes (384-322 B.C.), the greatest of all the Greek orators, points out that in Demosthenes' speech all three classical genres of rhetoric are used (i.e., forensic, deliberative, and epideictic) — even taking pains to discuss where each type is present in the oration — yet he notes that because the speech was delivered before a court, the entire oration, despite its mixture of genres, was viewed as forensic or judicial in nature.[78]

Based on an analysis of the writings of Cicero (106–43 B.C.) and Quintilian (A.D. 35-95), both of whom were prominent Roman rhetoricians, Steven Kraftchick has argued that while "it is true that various rhetoricians suggested rules for the construction of a speech and that there were schools of thought," nonetheless "one is just as likely to find wide variation in these treatments of rhetoric as he or she is to find clear and universally shared rules or standards."[79] And it is this caveat that one must constantly keep in mind when reading any writing of antiquity, including the writings contained within the NT.

How, then, should we approach Paul's letter to Christians at Rome vis-à-vis the rhetorical genres, modes of persuasion, and conventions of his day? Duane Watson has not only captured the prevailing sentiment of contemporary biblical scholarship but also provided what is undoubtedly the most appropriate stance when undertaking a rhetorical analysis of any of Paul's letters:

> Paul's letters are not so occasional that they lack rhetorical sophistication, nor so carefully composed that they measure up to the finest Greek rhetorical standards. However, like anyone trying to persuade an audience, Paul's letters do have a rhetorical strategy. He works to persuade his congregations where he deems them faithful to the gospel and dissuade them where he finds them unfaithful — and he does so with all the means of persuasion available to him.[80]

It is necessary, therefore, to give attention to "all the means of persuasion available to him" when reading Paul's letter to the Romans — both those that

---

78. Publius Aelius Aristides, *Ars Rhetorica* 1.149-50.

79. S. J. Kraftchick, "Πάθη in Paul," 39.

80. D. F. Watson, "Paul's Appropriation of Apocalyptic Discourse: The Rhetorical Strategy of 1 Thessalonians," in *Vision and Persuasion: Rhetorical Dimensions of Apocalyptic Discourse*, ed. G. Carey and L. G. Bloomquist (St. Louis: Chalice, 1999), 61.

he assimilated almost unconsciously from his wide association with the Greco-Roman world and those that were ingrained within him from his Jewish background and traditions. It is also necessary in reading Paul, however, to give close consideration to how his Christian convictions and temperament impacted not only the content but also the form of what he wrote. For Paul, the apostle of Jesus Christ to the Gentiles, was not only in many ways "a product of his day"; he was, more importantly, "a man in Christ" (2 Cor 12:2).

Diachronic Rhetorical Analysis

Diachronic rhetorical analysis as a historical and comparative discipline seeks to understand the rhetorical genre of Romans within the context and categories of Greco-Roman rhetoric. Many of the subjects treated in Romans are, of course, comparable to those dealt with in Galatians. But the type of argument in Romans, that is, its rhetorical genre, can hardly be viewed the same as that in Galatians — whether entirely forensic (as per Betz's analysis of Galatians), entirely deliberative (as per Kennedy's analysis of Galatians), or part judicial and part deliberative, with features typical of Jewish rhetoric appearing as well (as I have analyzed Galatians). So there has been, of late, a great deal of effort attempting to categorize Romans in terms of its own form of argumentation, and thus in terms of its own rhetorical genre.

A number of scholars have argued that Romans is an example of epideictic rhetoric.[81] That seems to be because they understand epideictic rhetoric as something of a "catchall" or "overflow" category for materials that fit neither the category of forensic rhetoric (since Paul asks for no verdict) nor the category of deliberative rhetoric (since Paul expects no vote). It is probably also because they define epideictic rhetoric more generally, reflecting the broader definition of the term proposed by Chaim Perelman and Lucie Olbrechts-Tyteca as "including any discourse, oral or written, that does not aim at a specific action or decision but seeks to enhance knowledge, understanding, or belief, often through praise or blame, whether of persons, things, or values."[82] Others, however, propose that it should be understood

---

81. So, e.g., W. Wuellner, "Paul's Rhetoric of Argumentation in Romans" (1976); R. L. Jewett, "Romans as an Ambassadorial Letter" (1982); G. A. Kennedy, *New Testament Interpretation through Rhetorical Criticism* (1984), 152-56.
82. So G. A. Kennedy, "Genres of Rhetoric," 45.

as "a deliberative discourse which uses an epistolary framework, and in some ways comports with a protreptic letter."[83] And still others, while acknowledging that features from the various classical types of rhetoric can be discerned at places within the letter, have expressed a high degree of discomfort in describing the contents of Romans in terms of any of the usual genres of Greco-Roman rhetoric — certainly not forensic, but also neither epideictic nor deliberative.[84]

Several biblical scholars, building on earlier studies of protreptic ("exhortation") speeches and writings in antiquity, have proposed that Paul's letter to the Romans is best understood as a "word [i.e., 'speech' or 'message'] of exhortation" (λόγος προτρεπτικός), which was a type of address intended to win converts and attract people to a particular way of life. Those who argue for this understanding of the rhetorical genre of Romans include Klaus Berger,[85] Stanley Stowers,[86] David Aune,[87] Anthony Guerra,[88] and Christopher Bryan[89] (also, to an extent, R. Dean Anderson Jr.[90]). Their claim is that the rhetoric of Romans differs from all of the usual genres of ancient rhetoric — that, in fact, it cannot easily be made to fit within any of the usual three categories of "forensic," "deliverative," or "epideictic" rhetoric. It is not an apology in which Paul defends his apostleship or his message, nor a polemic that counters false teaching. Further, it lacks some of the important rhetorical sections that usually appear, in one order or another, in forensic, deliberative, and epideictic rhetoric — principally an *exordium,* but also a *narratio* and a *propositio.* Rather, as Stanley Stowers proposes: "In both form and function, Paul's letter to the Romans is a protreptic letter."[91] Or as Anthony Guerra enunciates the thesis: "Romans is a protreptic writing seeking to affirm Paul's ministry and the gospel which he preached."[92]

---

83. So, e.g., B. Witherington III, *Romans,* 20; see also 16-22 and *passim.*

84. So, e.g., N. Elliott, *Rhetoric of Romans* (1990), 64; C. J. Classen, "St. Paul's Epistles" (1992); R. D. Anderson Jr., *Ancient Rhetorical Theory and Paul* (1996, 1998), 98-109; S. J. Kraftchick, "Πάθη in Paul" (2001).

85. K. Berger, *Formgeschichte des Neuen Testament* (1984), see esp. 217.

86. S. K. Stowers, *Letter Writing* (1986), 112-14, 128.

87. D. E. Aune, "Romans as a *Logos Protrepikos*" (1991); *idem, Westminster Dictionary* (2003), 383-86, 430-31.

88. A. J. Guerra, *Romans and the Apologetic Tradition* (1995), 1-22.

89. C. Bryan, *Preface to Romans* (2000), 18-28.

90. R. D. Anderson Jr., in his treatment of "Ancient Letter-Speeches" in *Ancient Rhetorical Theory and Paul* (1996, 1998), 104-8.

91. S. K. Stowers, *Letter Writing,* 114.

92. A. J. Guerra, *Romans and the Apologetic Tradition,* Preface, ix.

The first explicit study of ancient λόγοι προτρεπτικοί ("speeches of exhortation") was done by Paul Hartlich in his Leipzig doctoral dissertation of 1889 entitled "*Exhortationum* (Προτρεπτικων) a Graecis Romanisque Scriptarum Historia et Indole.*" Theodore Burgess in 1902 also dealt briefly with this type of material in his cataloging of twenty-seven subtypes of epideictic speech.[93] But in classifying "speeches of exhortation" as a subtype of "epideictic" rhetoric, Burgess failed to recognize "protreptic" material as a distinguishable genre of ancient rhetoric — and he excused himself from any explicit treatment of a protreptic type of material since, as he reasoned, Hartlich had already provided one. In 1986, however, Mark Jordan explicated the nature of philosophic protreptic speech,[94] while in that same year Abraham Malherbe spelled out the inner logic of protreptic discourse.[95] The most readily accessible and up-to-date treatments of ancient protreptic speech and letters, building principally on the studies of Hartlich, Jordan, and Malherbe, are those by Stanley Stowers,[96] David Aune,[97] and Anthony Guerra.[98]

An apt summary of the purpose, setting, function, and structure of an ancient "speech of exhortation" is provided by David Aune in his article of 2003 entitled "Protreptic Literature." Regarding purpose and setting, Aune writes:

> The λόγος προτρεπτικός, or "speech of exhortation," is a speech intended to win converts and attract young people to a particular way of life. The primary setting for the *logos protreptikos* was the philosophical school, where it was the primary rhetorical tool used to attract adherents by exposing the errors of alternate ways of living and demonstrating the truth claims of a particular philosophical tradition over its competitors.[99]

As for the function of ancient speeches of exhortation:

---

93. T. C. Burgess, "Epideictic Literature," 112-13.

94. Cf. M. D. Jordan, "Ancient Philosophic Protreptic and the Problem of Persuasive Genres."

95. Cf. A. J. Malherbe, *Moral Exhortation* (1986).

96. S. K. Stowers, *Letter Writing* (1986), 112-14.

97. D. E. Aune, "Romans as a *Logos Protrepikos*" (1991); *idem,* "Protreptic Literature," *Westminster Dictionary* (2003), 383-86.

98. A. J. Guerra, *Romans and the Apologetic Tradition* (1995), 1-22.

99. D. E. Aune, *Westminster Dictionary,* 383.

The central function of λόγοι προτρεπτικοί ["speeches of exhortation"] was to encourage conversion, but it included a strong component of ἀποτρέπειν ("dissuasion") and ἐλέγχειν ("censure") as well, aimed at freeing the person from erroneous beliefs and practices.[100]

And regarding their basic structure:

They characteristically consist of three features: (1) a negative section centering on the critique of rival sources of knowledge, ways of living, or schools of thought that reject philosophy; (2) a positive section in which the truth claims of philosophical knowledge, schools of thought, and ways of living are presented, praised, and defended; (3) an optional section, consisting of a personal appeal to the hearer, inviting the immediate accepting of the exhortation.[101]

Aune highlights the prevalence of this genre of persuasion in the ancient world by a review of the protreptic writings of such philosophers as Plato (428/7-348/7 B.C.), Aristotle (384-322 B.C.), Philo of Larissa (c. 159/8-84/3 B.C.), Cicero (106-43 B.C.), Lucian of Samosata (c. 120-200 A.D.), and Iamblichus (c. A.D. 250-325). In the process, he shows how "speeches of exhortation" in antiquity (1) commonly combined features of forensic and epideictic rhetoric (though the combining of these features was not normally done in either forensic or epideictic speeches themselves), (2) frequently utilized the rhetorical strategy of *synkrisis* (σύγκρισις, "comparison"), and (3) often used a diatribe style of argumentation. Further, he notes that during the hellenistic period "Jewish intellectuals often conceptualized Judaism as a philosophy and attempted to present it in philosophical guise to outsiders."[102] Aune then goes on to analyze two Christian apologetic writings from the second century A.D., showing how Christians of that time also picked up this type of rhetoric for their own propaganda appeals. And throughout his presentation, his own proposal is evident: that Paul's letter to the Romans should also be seen as an example of a "word or message of exhortation" (λόγος προτρεπτικός) — a rhetorical genre that was common in the Greco-Roman world and among at least certain Jews during the hellenis-

100. D. E. Aune, *Westminster Dictionary,* 384.
101. D. E. Aune, *Westminster Dictionary,* 385.
102. D. E. Aune, *Westminster Dictionary,* 383; probably having in mind such writers as Philo of Alexandria (c. 30 B.C.–A.D. 45) and the pseudonymous author of the *Letter of Aristeas* (which was written sometime between 250 B.C. and A.D. 100).

tic period, which Paul "christianized" and used for his own purposes when writing the Christians at Rome.

The study of ancient protreptic literature is very much in its infancy, and, as would be expected with any new discipline, differing analyses of some of its details have been proposed. Nevertheless, viewing Romans as essentially a type of λόγος προτρεπτικός (i.e., a "word, speech, or message of exhortation") offers, we believe, a better diachronic rhetorical model for understanding Paul's argument in the extensive central section of the letter (i.e., 1:16–15:13) than does a forensic model (that assumes the genre of Romans to be comparable to that of Galatians), a deliberative model (that highlights the hortatory features of Romans), or an epideictic model (that highlights the persuasive features of the letter, with an accompanying emphasis on what is to be viewed as honorable and what as shameful). And this understanding will be spelled out more fully in Chapter XI ("Structure and Argument"), attempting to show (1) how Paul made use of the rhetoric of Greco-Roman protreptic discourse — whether deliberatively (i.e., in order to make the greatest impact on his addressees) or somewhat unconsciously (i.e., simply because it was a type of rhetorical communication that was common to him and his addressees), and (2) how he accommodated it to his own purposes and filled it with his own Christian theology.

Synchronic Rhetorical Analysis

Synchronic rhetorical analysis is a literary and compositional method that examines the argument of a speech or writing, identifies its modes of persuasion, and classifies its argumentative conventions. And Paul's letter to the Christians at Rome, as do all of his extant letters, reflects a number of such synchronic rhetorical devices that seem to have been current in his day. Among the more obvious of these rhetorical techniques in Romans, the following may be mentioned — thereby fleshing out the list given earlier in the section "Rhetoric in the Ancient World" by focusing on the identification of such claimed occurrences in Paul's letter:

1. *Anaphora* (i.e., the repetition of a word or expression at the beginning of a series of successive phrases, clauses, sentences, or verses; or, as in an *extended anaphora*, the repetition of a word or expression at the resumption of a discussion that has been interrupted by another section of material). The most obvious instance of *anaphora* in the NT is in Heb 11:3-31, where πίστει ("by faith") introduces eighteen examples of people who lived their lives trusting God. The nine occurrences of μακάριοι ("blessings") in

the "beatitudes" of Matt 5:3-12, as well as the four μακάριοι ("blessings") and four οὐαί ("woes") of Luke 6:20-26, are also instances of *anaphora*.[103]

Examples of *anaphora* in Paul's letters can be found in 1 Cor 6:12 and 10:23-24, where what was evidently a common adage of the day is enunciated, "'Everything is lawful' [or, 'permissible']" — but then is immediately conditioned by such statements as "but not everything is beneficial" (twice), "but I will not be dominated by anything," and "but not everything is constructive." In 1 Cor 12:4-6 Paul introduces three statements about spiritual gifts with the word διαιρέσεις ("diversities" or "different kinds of"), and in Phil 3:2 he begins each of three warnings about the Judaizers with the exhortation βλέπετε ("Watch out for!").

In Romans, which is our particular concern, the repetition of the ominous phrase παρέδωκεν αὐτοὺς ὁ θεός ("God gave them over") in 1:24, 26, and 28 is certainly a case of *anaphora*. Likewise, instances of extended rhetorical *anaphora* should probably be seen in (1) the thesis of 1:17 about "righteousness" and "faith" and its restatement and expansion in 3:21-23, and (2) the question of 11:1, "I ask then, Did God reject his people?," which is repeated in slightly different words in 11:11, "Again I ask, Did they stumble so as to fall beyond recovery?"

2. *Apostrophe* (i.e., the interruption of a discourse in order to address a person or personified thing). Two rather obvious examples occur in Romans 2: the first is in verses 1-16, "You, therefore, have no excuse, you who pass judgment on someone else," etc.; the second is in verses 17-19, "Now you, if you call yourself a Jew; if you rely on the law and brag about your relationship with God," etc.

3. *Enthymeme* (i.e., an abbreviated or imperfect syllogism, whose premises may involve matters of character [*ethos*], emotion [*pathos*], or reason [*logos*] but whose conclusion must be supplied by the audience or addressees). Being almost always expressed in the form of a single, interrogative sentence, it has often been seen in such questions as found in Gal 2:14 ("If you, though a Jew, live like a Gentile and not like a Jew, how can you compel Gentiles to live like Jews?"), Gal 3:3 ("After beginning with the Spirit, are you now trying to attain perfection by human fleshly effort?"), and 1 Cor 6:15 ("Shall I then take the members of Christ and unite them with a prostitute?").

In Romans, the rhetorical technique *enthymeme* has frequently been identified in the questions of 6:1 ("Shall we go on sinning so that grace may

---

103. Cf. also *Sirach* 14:20-27; *Gospel of Thomas*, 68-69, 79; *Acts of Paul* 5-6; *Acts of Thomas* 94; *Acts of Philip* 24.

increase?"), 6:2 ("How can we who died to sin still live in it?"), 6:15 ("Shall we sin because we are not under the law but under grace?"), and 7:7 ("Is the law sin?"). It is also, we believe, to be found in the statement or statements regarding Abraham's faith, God's promise, and the purpose of the Mosaic law in 4:14-15.

4. *Diatribe* (i.e., a lively dialogical style that makes use of direct address to an imaginary interlocutor, hypothetical objections, and false conclusions). The clearest and most sustained uses of this rhetorical convention in the NT are in Paul's letter to the Christians at Rome, particularly in 2:1-5 and 2:17-24, probably in 9:19-21 and 11:17-24, and perhaps in 14:4-11. A diatribal structure in Romans has also been seen in 3:1-8 (perhaps including verse 9) and 3:27-31 (perhaps including 4:1-2), though the classification of these latter passages as rhetorical diatribes has frequently been debated. Paul's use of a diatribal form of rhetoric in each of the passages cited above in Romans, however, varies somewhat, and each of them needs to be treated separately. Further, it needs to be noted that features resembling a Greek diatribe in Paul's other letters appear far less often than in Romans, with only 1 Cor 6:12-13; 15:35-38; and Gal 2:17; 3:21 sometimes so identified.

5. *Inclusio* (i.e., similar phrases or clauses placed at the beginning and the end of a relatively short unit of material, which function by way of framing a distinct portion of what is being said or written). Structurally, it is important to recognize that the repeated refrain "through our Lord Jesus Christ" (διὰ τοῦ κυρίου ἡμῶν Ἰησοῦ Χριστοῦ), which appears with only slight variation in Rom 5:1, 11, 21; 6:23; 7:25; and 8:39, not only frames the entire section of 5–8 but also nicely concludes each of the textual units within that section. It has also been claimed that the phrase "both for the Jew first and for the Gentile" (Ἰουδαίῳ τε πρῶτον καὶ Ἕλληνι) in 1:16 and 2:9-10 (twice) frames 1:16–2:10 as a single textual unit. But such a proposal has been discounted by a number of significant NT scholars today (for an evaluation of this thesis, see our later discussions of 1:16-32 and 2:1-16 in Chapter XI, "Structure and Argument"). And an *inclusio* construction has also been claimed to be present at a number of other places in Paul's letter to Christians at Rome, though with considerable less certainty.

6. *Metaphor* (i.e., a word, group of words, or sentence that is used to stand for something different from the literal reference, but is linked to it by some perceived similarity and so suggests a likeness or analogy between them). Paul's treatment of "the natural branches" and "engrafted wild branches" in Rom 11:17-24 is an obvious example of the use of metaphor.

7. *Paradeigma* (i.e., a story that provides a pattern or example to be ei-

ther imitated or avoided, or an argument that is based on the use of an example, whether positive or negative). The depiction of Abraham in Rom 4:1-24 is a clear example of a paradigmatic exhortation, as is also the list of faithful believers in Christ set out in the greetings of Rom 16:1-16. Likewise, the story of sin, frustration, and inability recounted in Rom 7:7-25, whether the "I" of the narrative is understood personally or gnomically, should probably be understood rhetorically in this light as well.

8. *Paronomasia* (i.e., the play on two or more words in a relatively brief context that are similar in form, that sound alike, or that make use of different meanings of the same word). The most famous NT example of this stylistic device, whether understood literally or with a shift of denotation, is, of course, Jesus' statement to Peter in Matt 16:18: "I tell you that you are Peter (Πέτρος), and on this rock (πέτρα) I will build my church." Probably *paronomasia* should also be seen, at least to some extent, in (1) the threefold repetition of the refrain παρέδωκεν αὐτοὺς ὁ θεός ("God gave them over") in Rom 1:24, 26, and 28, when recounting the downward spiral of idolatrous Gentiles, and (2) the series of nouns that end with the Greek letters μα in Rom 5:12-21, when setting out comparisons between Christ and Adam — that is, παράπτωμα ("transgression," cf. vv. 15, 16, 18, 20); χάρισμα ("grace," cf. vv. 15, 16); κρίμα ("depravity," cf. v. 16); κατάκριμα ("divine judgment," cf. vv. 16, 18); δώρημα ("divine gift," cf. v. 16); and δικαίωμα ("righteousness," cf. vv. 16, 18).

9. *Prosopopoeia* (i.e., the introduction of a specific character, whether person or thing, who or which is allowed to speak). Rom 7:7-25 has often been considered an instance of *prosopopoeia*, though more likely it should be viewed as a *paradeigma* or example. Rom 2:1-5, 17-29; 3:1-9; and 3:27–4:2 may also be understood as reflecting a *prosopopoeia* rhetorical style.

10. *Synkrisis* (i.e., the comparison of comparable persons, objects, or things, with deficiencies and superiorities highlighted). Hebrews is the most extended example of *synkrisis* in the NT, with its argument built almost entirely on comparisons and contrasts between "the Son" and all the past revelations of God — in particular, comparing and contrasting the Son with angels (chs. 1–2), Moses, Joshua, and "rest" in the land (chs. 3–4), the Levitical/Aaronic priesthood (ch. 5), Melchizedek (ch. 7), and the OT tabernacle, cult, and sacrificial system (chs. 8–10). Paul in his letters also uses this rhetorical technique in comparing himself with his converts in 2 Corinthians 10–13 (the so-called "severe letter"), especially in 11:21b-29. Most prominently, however, he uses *synkrisis* in Rom 5:12-21 when presenting what Christ effected through his obedience vis-à-vis what Adam brought about because of his sin.

Likewise, many of the rhetorical conventions that modern scholars have identified in the writings of antiquity have been claimed to exist also in Paul's letter to the Romans. Most prominent among these are (also following the order given earlier in the section "Rhetoric in the Ancient World"): *alternation* (i.e., the interplay between two alternate choices or ideas, with the interplay involving the repetition of words, the use of synonyms, the discussion of results, or the listing of specific examples); *ring composition* (i.e., the correspondence in wording between sentences that frame a section, with similar wording being used both at the beginning and at the end); *word chains* (i.e., the frequent repetition of a given word and its cognates within a clearly delimited context); *refrain* (i.e., the use of repeated wording or formulaic phrases to open or close the various sections of a discussion); *concentric symmetry* (i.e., multiple correspondences that occur over an extended passage and have a single element at the center); and *chiasmus* (i.e., the arrangement of paired words, statements, or texts in concentric symmetry around a focal word, statement, or text).

In many cases, such stylistic features as discovered by modern scholars in the writings of antiquity may represent only variations of what the ancient rhetoricians called *inclusio*. In other respects they may differ. Further, each of these rhetorical techniques as claimed to be found in Paul's letter to Rome — whether as discussed by the classical rhetoricians in their handbooks on rhetoric or as discovered by modern scholars in their study of the writings of antiquity — must be studied in its respective context. These stylistic features can, therefore, be appropriately treated only in an exegetical commentary that deals with the content and flow of argument of what Paul says in his letter to the Christians at Rome, and so any further discussion of them must await our proposed exposition in a proper Romans commentary.

3. Epistolary Conventions

Despite the fact that Romans has traditionally been considered, both exegetically and theologically, the most significant and comprehensive of Paul's writings — and despite current interests in its rhetorical practices and developing interests in its oral features — it needs always to be remembered that what Paul wrote to the Christians at Rome was a letter. And any reading of Romans must always take into account the fact that it is a letter.

Yet when reading Romans as a letter, it becomes immediately apparent that its epistolary conventions, while comparable in many ways, are also different in certain respects from most of the other ancient letters of Paul's day and all of the other NT letters. So it is necessary in dealing with Romans as a letter to explore such matters as (1) letter writing in the ancient world, giving attention to ancient epistolary types, forms, and practices, (2) epistolary analysis and the Scriptures, noting how the study of NT letters vis-à-vis ancient letters of the day has become a recognized discipline in NT scholarship and suggesting something of the importance of such studies, and (3) an epistolary analysis of Romans, highlighting the epistolary similarities and differences of Paul's letter to Rome vis-à-vis not only other letters of the day but especially the other letters of Paul that appear in the NT.

Letter Writing in the Ancient World

The writing of letters was common in the ancient world, for a letter was then (just as it is today) a means of communication that provided information, made requests, recommended, and promoted congenial relations between people who were spatially separated from each other. Letters functioned (and continue to function today) as a substitute for being personally present. So letters have always been important, with their contents as varied as the whole range of human activity.

Letter writing in antiquity was taught in the secondary schools "by the imitation of models rather than through theory and comprehensive rules."[104] It was not, however, included as a subject in the early handbooks on rhetoric, and so epistolary types and techniques were never developed as they were for rhetorical genres and conventions. Nonetheless, since content always influences form (as well as form having an impact on content), inevitably what was argued with respect to rhetoric came to be seen as having implications for epistolary styles and practices in the writing of letters. Thus in later Greco-Roman times there were set out in rather formal fashion a number of epistolary types and letter writing conventions — as, for example, in the first-century A.D. rhetorical handbook that was attributed to Demetrius of Phaleron, that is, Pseudo-Demetrius, *De Elocutione* (On Style), in which twenty-one different types of letters are enumerated along with examples of each, or in a still later fourth-century handbook that was usually attributed to Libanius of Antioch, that is, Pseudo-Libanius, *Epistolimaioi Charakteres* (Epistolary Styles), which lists forty-one styles of letters with definitions and examples.

104. S. K. Stowers, *Letter Writing*, 33.

There are many extant Greek "literary" letters of antiquity, both public and private, which are essentially literary tractates addressed to a writer's friend or friends (not just dedicated to them), exhibit many epistolary practices of the day, were transmitted through various literary channels, and have been collected and studied by classicists. Most important of these for our purposes are the hortatory writings of Isocrates (436-338 B.C.), an important speech writer and teacher of rhetoric, and of Aristotle (384-322 B.C.), one of the greatest of the philosophers and rhetoricians. There are also extant collections of the letters of Demosthenes (384-322 B.C.), the greatest of the Greek orators, and of Epicurus (341-270 B.C.), the founder of the Epicurean school of philosophy. Other collections of ancient Greek letters are probably to be judged as forgeries — such as those attributed to Phalarais of Sicily, the cruel "Tyrant of Acragas" (ruled c. 570-554 B.C.); Themistocles, the revered Athenian statesman and army commander (c. 528-462 B.C.); Socrates, who was one of the greatest of the philosophers (c. 470-399 B.C.); and Euripides, who was one of the triad of great tragic writers (c. 480-406 B.C.).

The most celebrated Roman writers of literary letters were the orator, philosopher, and statesman Cicero (106-43 B.C.), the poet Ovid (43 B.C.–A.D. 17/18), the Stoic philosopher Seneca (c. 4 B.C.–A.D. 65), the consul and governor Pliny "the Younger" (A.D. 61-112), and the rhetorician and orator Fronto (c. A.D. 100-166). Of these, there are extant a collection of 931 of Cicero's letters, which were written between 68 and 43 B.C. and published posthumously about A.D. 60, and a collection of 358 letters of Pliny the Younger, which he published in nine books in chronological order. Most prolific among the letter writers of late antiquity, however, was the fourth-century A.D. Greek rhetorician Libanius of Antioch, who wrote more than 1,600 such literary letters.

In the final decade of the nineteenth century, however, there occurred a major advance in our knowledge of ancient letters and the compositional conventions of ancient letter writing (and, correspondingly, a major advance in the scientific study of the letters of the NT) — that is, the discovery and initial publication of a large number of "nonliterary" or "common" (κοινή, *koine*) Greek papyrus letters, which dated principally from the Ptolemaic and Roman periods of Egyptian history. A few isolated collections of papyrus letters had earlier, almost by accident, come to light — such as those found at Herculaneum in 1752; in the Gizeh area of the Egyptian Fayyum in 1877; and at such other locations as Hermopolis, Heracleopolis, and Panopolis during the latter part of the nineteenth century. But these were either literary in nature, Byzantine in date, or very poorly preserved.

In the winter of 1889-90, however, W. M. Flinders Petrie inaugurated an entirely new epoch in the study of not only ancient letters generally but also the study of the letters of the NT in particular. For in his excavation at Gurob, in the Fayyum district of northern Egypt (south-southwest of Cairo), Petrie extracted from Ptolemaic mummy cases a large number of papyrus materials and sent them on to England to be deciphered and edited by John P. Mahaffy. During the decade that followed, the British carried on explorations at many places in the Fayyum district, most notably by Bernard P. Grenfell and Arthur S. Hunt at Oxyrhynchus during 1896-97 and the years following. Also, during the ten years from 1890 to 1900, the Germans excavated on the island of Elephantine in Upper Egypt, at Heracleopolis, and elsewhere; the French dug in the Fayyum, at Tanis in the Delta, and at Aproditopolis; the Italians and Americans dug at several locations in the Fayyum; and Egyptian archaeologists turned up a number of significant papyrus materials from a number of sites throughout Egypt, most importantly discovering the archives of Zenon that dated from the third century B.C. Following the lead of Flinders Petrie, archaeologists systematically investigated rubbish heaps outside former old towns and villages, ruins of old homes and other buildings, private graves, mummified crocodiles stuffed with or wrapped in old papyrus sheets, and mummy cases that had been formed by pressing discarded nonliterary papyrus letters and documents into a sort of thick cardboard. And great quantities of these papyri were sent off to the various museums, libraries, and institutions of the excavators who found them for storage, deciphering, editing, and further study.

The first publications of these newly found nonliterary papyrus letters followed closely on the heels of their discovery. In 1893 Frederic G. Kenyon published the first volume of his *Greek Papyri in the British Museum;* in 1895 was begun the famous German series *Ägyptische Urkunden aus den Königlichen* [now *Staatlichen*] *Museen zu Berlin: Griechische Urkunden;* and in 1898 Grenfell and Hunt released the first volume of *The Oxyrhynchus Papyri,* with Kenyon in that same year also publishing volume two of his *Greek Papyri in the British Museum.* Because of the condition of many of the papyrus materials (i.e., individual sheets stuck together and many fragments), and because of their wide dissemination among the various excavators' sponsoring institutions, it is almost impossible to speak of a total number of Greek papyri now available for study. It was estimated before World War II that there must be at least 40,000 to 60,000 papyrus texts of various types extant in the various collections, with the majority yet to be published. But what has been deciphered, edited, and published of these nonliterary letters and documents has thrown very welcome light on a number of matters of great importance for the scholarly study of the NT — at first on the language of the NT, as these materials opened up the whole subject of *koine* Greek philology and threw fresh light on the cognate use of *koine* Greek in the NT; then on the social conditions of the NT period; and latterly on the epistolary conventions and practices of the day that appear also in the letters of the NT. There are also extant a number of ancient letters in Aramaic and Hebrew, written on ostraca (pot shards and limestone flakes), papyri, and parchment. Most accessible for surveying these Aramaic and Hebrew letters are the recently published works of Edward Wente,[105] Bezalel Porten,[106] and James Lindenberger.[107]

Stanley Stowers has organized the nonliterary letters of the Greco-Roman and Jewish worlds according to the following six epistolary types: (1) "letters of friendship"; (2) "family letters"; (3) "letters of praise and blame"; (4) "letters of exhortation and advice"; (5) "letters of mediation"; and (6) "accusing, apologetic, and accounting letters."[108] Under the fourth heading, "letters of exhortation and advice," which type exhibits "much overlapping and ambiguous terminology" and most closely parallels the letters of the NT,[109] Stowers identifies seven subtypes: (a) "paraenetic letters"; (b) "letters of advice"; (c) "protreptic letters"; (d) "letters of admonition"; (e) "letters of rebuke"; (f) "letters of reproach"; and (g) "letters of consolation"[110] — with numerous examples given for each, primarily from antiquity generally but also from the NT.

There has been extensive study, particularly during the latter half of the twentieth century, of the form and epistolary features of ancient "nonliterary" or "common" letters. Differing features and various permutations can be identified in the data. Nonetheless, the epistolary conventions of the Greek papyrus letters of Egypt, as well as those reflected elsewhere in the Greco-Roman and Jewish worlds of the first Christian century, evidence a remarkable degree of similarity. And this convergence of epistolary forms

---

105. E. Wente, *Letters from Ancient Egypt* (1990).

106. B. Porten, "Egyptian Aramaic Texts" (1997), which includes an extensive bibliography of relevant writings by him and others.

107. J. M. Lindenberger, *Ancient Aramaic and Hebrew Letters* (1994); 2nd ed. (2003), with the addition of one letter in Edomite, one in Ammonite, and one in Phoenician; see also S. K. Stowers, *Letter Writing*, 41-42.

108. S. K. Stowers, *Letter Writing*, 49-173.

109. S. K. Stowers, *Letter Writing*, 91.

110. S. K. Stowers, *Letter Writing*, 91-152.

and features in ancient letters has been conveniently set out in summary fashion by David Aune in his article "Epistolography" in his *Westminster Dictionary of New Testament and Early Christian Literature and Rhetoric* of 2003,[111] wherein he highlights, with appropriate explanatory comments, the various parts of a hellenistic letter as being:

1. *Prescript* — superscription (sender), ascription (addressee), and salutation (greetings). "The basic pattern of Greek epistolary prescripts was subject to various forms of amplification and elaboration. The superscription and ascription could be expanded through the addition of epithets, titles, terms of relationship (e.g., 'X to his sister Y') and endearment (e.g., 'X to my dearest friend Y'), and geographical location. The salutation was also capable of expansion by using adjectives or adverbs emphasizing degree ('warmest greetings') or by adding a health wish ('greetings and health')."[112]

2. *Health wish* — often using the Greek verb ὑγιαίνειν, "to be in good health"; Latin: *formula valetudinis*. "Since there are several health formulas that exhibit some variation, the health wish might better be described as a *topos* or theme. The ἐρρῶσθαι wish (from the 3d cent. B.C.E. on) could occupy a separate position at the beginning of the main part of the letter separate from the prescript, or it could be joined syntactically to the salutation of the prescript: 'greetings and best wishes' (χαίρειν καὶ ἐρρῶσθαι)."[113]

3. *Prayer* — usually using the Greek noun προσκύνημα, which means "an act of worship" and often signifies a prayer with features of thanksgiving. "The *proskynema formula* . . . frequently either followed or was blended with the formula of health."[114]

4. *Body* — usually consisting of "three components: (1) the introductory section introducing the reasons for writing, (2) the middle section carrying the relevant details or disclosing new information, (3) the concluding section both reiterating the primary occasion for writing and laying the groundwork for future communication."[115]

5. *Closing formula* — most commonly using the Greek expressions ἔρρωσο or ἔρρωσθε ("farewell"), though also εὐτύχει or its intensified

---

111. D. E. Aune, *Westminster Dictionary*, 162-68.
112. D. E. Aune, *Westminster Dictionary*, 166.
113. D. E. Aune, *Westminster Dictionary*, 166.
114. D. E. Aune, *Westminster Dictionary*, 166.
115. D. E. Aune, *Westminster Dictionary*, 166.

form διευτύχει ("good luck" or "best wishes"). It could also have included a health wish, greetings, and a date when the letter was written. "The closing formula could also be omitted. Formulas at the conclusion of the main part included 'take care of yourself that you might be well' (from the 3d cent. B.C.E.). This was gradually replaced by the ἀσπάζεσθαι ('greeting') formula, from the 1st cent. B.C.E. on, in which the writer asked the recipient to greet acquaintances not directly addressed by the letter or conveyed the greetings of others. There was also the illiteracy formula: 'X writes on behalf of Y,' usually in business letters, such as sworn declarations and various official statements."[116]

Epistolary Analysis and the Scriptures

Twenty-one of the twenty-seven books of the NT are in the form of letters, with letters also appearing in Acts 15:23-29 and Rev 1:4–3:22. These twenty-one epistolary writings have traditionally been divided into two major groups: (1) thirteen Pauline letters, which were early recognized as a distinctive body of letters, and (2) eight sermons, tractates, or letters, from Hebrews through Jude in the canonical NT order, all of which are set out in epistolary form, which claim in seven cases to represent the teachings of various early Jewish Christian leaders — and which seem to have first circulated mainly within Jewish Christian circles, becoming generally known and accepted within the Gentile church of the Roman empire only in the third and fourth centuries. Whatever can be learned about the forms and features of ancient letters, therefore, as well as about the techniques of ancient letter writers, would seem, on the face of it, to have relevance for an understanding of a very large portion of the NT.

It was the nonliterary papyrus letters found in the Fayyum district of northern Egypt during the decade of 1890-1900 that entirely revolutionized NT philology. For in comparing the Greek of these papyrus letters with the Greek of the NT, the language of the NT was seen to be not some type of "debased" or "bastardized" classical Greek — nor, as some in the nineteenth century are said to have speculated, some type of "heavenly" language — but, rather, the "common" *(koine)* Greek that people used throughout the hellenized Roman empire. Adolf Deissmann had led the way in demonstrating the philological importance of the Egyptian papyrus materials for

116. D. E. Aune, *Westminster Dictionary,* 167.

an understanding of the language of the NT.[117] But Deissmann was also, in fact, the first to insist on the importance of these papyrus letters from the Fayyum district of northern Egypt for an understanding of the form of the NT letters, and thus the one who inaugurated the study of the NT letters as "not products of literary art but documents of life"[118] — that is, not *literary epistles,* comparable to the pedagogical treatises of various Greek, Roman, and Jewish teachers, but real *nonliterary letters,* which should be compared to the common *(koine)* papyrus letters found in Egypt and written as private communications.[119]

In many ways, as is widely acknowledged today, Deissmann overstated his case when he argued for the *entirely* personal, private, occasional, and nonliterary character of the NT letters. For the letters of the NT are hardly only "occasional and nonliterary" in form, and certainly were never meant to be only "private" in their proclamation. Nonetheless, it was Deissmann who not only spelled out many significant linguistic parallels between the Greek papyri and the NT, and so must be seen as a pioneer in NT philology, but also was the first to draw attention to the comparable epistolary features that appear in the Greek papyrus letters of Egypt vis-à-vis the letters of the NT, and so is rightly called the father of NT epistolary analysis.

During the second decade of the twentieth century, and building on Deissmann's earlier treatments, a number of scholars produced important seminal studies on the epistologial features of the canonical NT letters, particularly those of the Pauline corpus. Paul Wendland, for example, identified the basic components of the openings and closings of Paul's letters: a "salutation" section and a "thanksgiving" section in the openings; a "doxology," "greetings," and a "benediction" in the closings.[120] Francis Exler clarified the basic parts of a nonliterary hellenistic letter, both those papyrus letters from the Egyptian Fayyum and those in the NT, as being an opening, a body, and a closing, and he noted in the process a number of phraseological matters that tended to appear in each.[121] And Henry Meecham spelled out a number of relationships between the papyrus letters from Oxyrhynchus and the let-

---

117. Cf. A. Deissmann, *Light from the Ancient East,* 62-145.

118. A. Deissmann, *Light from the Ancient East,* 227.

119. Cf. A. Deissmann, *Light from the Ancient East,* 227-42; see also pp. 146-227, where Deissmann supports his thesis by the reproduction, with comments, of twenty-six papyrus letters that were then newly discovered.

120. See P. Wendland, *Urchristlichen Literaturformen* (1912).

121. See F. X. J. Exler, *Form of the Ancient Greek Letter* (1923).

ters of the NT, pointing out not only that many of the terms and expressions found in both sets of letters are similar but also that the use of formulas in Paul's letters is basically the same as found elsewhere in the Greco-Roman world.[122]

Closely following these seminal writings, there were produced during the second quarter of the twentieth century a number of further studies of importance that related the epistolary forms, formulas, and features of the nonliterary papyrus letter of Egypt to the letters of the NT. For example, Ernst Lohmeyer wrote on the Pauline greetings,[123] George Boobyer dealt with the "thanksgiving" sections of Paul's letters,[124] Johannes Sykutris developed a system for classifying ancient letters by type,[125] and Clinton Keyes analyzed Greek letters of introduction.[126] Probably most significant among these early epistolary analyses, however, was the publication of Paul Schubert's small book on the "thanksgiving" sections of the Pauline corpus, for in concentrating on a single type of material Schubert set the course for much that followed in establishing epistolary criticism as a recognized discipline of NT study.[127]

As a discipline of scholarly study, epistolary analysis of the letters of the NT came to bloom in the latter half of the twentieth century. A great deal of scholarly effort was expended during that time, and a great amount of significant literature produced, in analyzing the letters of the NT vis-à-vis the hellenistic letters of the Greco-Roman world generally and the nonliterary papyrus letters from Egypt in particular. Many of these studies have importance when dealing with various sections and specific verses of Paul's letter to Rome, and so must be interacted with in a future exegetical commentary on Romans. Suffice it here, however, to mention only a few of the most seminal studies of the last half of the twentieth century.

In 1956 Heikki Koskenniemi highlighted the purpose of nonliterary Greek letters as being that of turning "absence" into "presence" — that is, maintaining personal contacts between people spatially separated from one another and imparting information.[128] In 1962 James Sanders studied the

---

122. H. G. Meecham, *Light from Ancient Letters* (1923).

123. E. Lohmeyer, "Briefliche Grussüberschriften" (1927).

124. G. H. Boobyer, *"Thanksgiving" and the "Glory of God" in Paul* (1929).

125. J. Sykutris, "Epistolographie" (1931).

126. C. Keyes, "Greek Letter of Introduction" (1935).

127. P. Schubert, *Form and Function of the Pauline Thanksgivings* (1939).

128. H. Koskenniemi, *Studien zur Idee und Phraseologie des griechischen Briefes* (1956).

question of how Paul made the transition from the thanksgiving sections to the body sections in his letters.[129] From 1962 through 1980 Terence Mullins produced a series of articles that dealt with various literary forms and formulas within the NT letters.[130] In 1967 Robert Funk began the formal study of the body of a Pauline letter, dealing with its general epistolary structure ("formal opening," "connecting and transitional formulas," "eschatological climax," and "travelogue") and highlighting, in particular, its concluding travel section, which he renamed an "apostolic parousia."[131] In 1973, building on his 1966 doctoral dissertation and his 1969 article, William Doty argued that the basic structure of both hellenistic letters and Paul's letters was (1) an introductory section, which included sender, recipient, greetings, and a health wish or wishes, (2) the body, which was the largest portion and was introduced by stereotyped formulae, and (3) a concluding section, which included further greetings, wishes, and a prayer sentence.[132] In 1972 Chan-Hie Kim analyzed the form and structure of eighty-three Greek and Latin letters of recommendation, with most of them being Greek papyrus letters from Egypt.[133] In 1972-88 John White published a number of studies (1) on the body of Greek and NT letters, in which he argued for a similar structure in both groups of letters: a body opening, a body middle, and a body closing, and with similar introductory, transitional, and connecting formulas found in each, and (2) on various specific letter types.[134] And in 1986 Stanley Stowers classified the extant letters from the Greco-Roman world (including the NT letters) according to their various types, citing the most important texts and analyzing representative examples.[135]

Each of the above studies has spawned a number of other epistolary

129. J. T. Sanders, "Transition from Opening Epistolary Thanksgiving to Body" (1962).

130. T. Y. Mullins, "Petition as a Literary Form" (1962); "Disclosure: A Literary Form in the New Testament" (1964); "Greeting as a New Testament Form" (1968); "Formulas in New Testament Epistles" (1972); "Ascription as a Literary Form" (1973); "Visit Talk in the New Testament Letters" (1973); "Benediction as a New Testament Form" (1977); "Topos as a New Testament Form" (1980).

131. R. W. Funk, "The Apostolic 'Parousia'" (1967); also "The Letter: Form and Style," in his *Language, Hermeneutic, and Word of God* (1966).

132. W. G. Doty, *Letters in Primitive Christianity* (1973).

133. C.-H. Kim, *Letter of Recommendation* (1972).

134. See esp. J. L. White, *Body of the Greek Letter* (1972); *Official Petition* (1972); "Epistolary Formulas and Clichés" (1978); "Saint Paul and the Apostolic Letter Tradition" (1983); *Light from Ancient Letters* (1986); and "Ancient Greek Letters" (1988).

135. S. K. Stowers, *Letter Writing* (1986).

studies, with the ultimate purpose being to understand more accurately and adequately what was written in the letters of the NT. And it is to many of these critical studies of ancient epistolary practice — both as first set out in seminal fashion and then as worked out more fully — that every interpreter of Paul's letter to the Christians at Rome must look when attempting to understand more accurately the individual sections and specific passages of that important letter.

Epistolary Analysis of Romans

As with Paul's use of the rhetorical conventions of his day, so with his use of first-century epistolary practices: It is not necessary to view the apostle as having been formally trained in letter writing in order to appreciate the epistolary features in his letters that correspond to the epistolary conventions of his day. The conventions of how to write a letter, like those of how to frame an argument, were part of the ethos of the day (i.e., "in the air") and widely practiced. Paul's use of them, therefore, should probably be seen as more unconscious adaptations of standard practices than studied attempts to write in an acceptable fashion.

Yet Romans as a letter, while comparable in many ways to other letters in the Pauline corpus, differs in certain important respects from those other letters — not only in its content and rhetoric, but also with respect to its epistolary conventions. While it was often asked in earlier days "Why are the other letters of Paul so different from Romans?" the question more often asked today is "Why is Romans so different from Paul's other letters?" Modern questioners may not always realize the full extent of their query, nor be able to explicate what has given rise to their question. Ultimately, however, their unease with respect to the form of Romans as a letter boils down to asking about (1) its epistolary genre vis-à-vis those of Paul's other letters, and (2) its epistolary structure and formulas vis-à-vis those of Paul's other letters.

1. Epistolary Genre

Romans is far longer than a typical non-literary hellenistic letter — though Oxyrhynchus Papyri #237, which is a petition of Dionysia to a Roman Prefect that was written about A.D. 186, is not much shorter than Romans, but its length does not represent the norm of the day. Further, Romans is longer than all of the other letters of the NT, including all of the other letters of the Pauline corpus. More significantly, however, it differs from Paul's other letters with respect to its epistolary genre. For Romans is not, as is Galatians, a "rebuke and request" letter. Nor is it a strictly "paraenetic" or "exhortation" letter, as is 1 Thessalonians; nor a mixed letter of "response, exhortation, and advice," as is 1 Corinthians; nor a letter of "friendship and advice," as is Philippians; nor simply a letter of "recommendation," as is Philemon.

Frequently Romans has been classified as a *Lehrbrief* or "literary epistle" — that is, a letter written to instruct its readers.[136] But that is a designation far too general, for it could also be applied to a number of Paul's other letters (as well as to most, if not all, of the other NT epistolary writings). Some scholars have viewed it as some type of "letter of introduction" — perhaps even an "ambassadorial letter of self-introduction," as Robert Jewett does (see Chapter V, "Purpose"). Chan-Hie Kim has discussed the provenance and epistolary features of an ancient letter of introduction (or "letter of recommendation" as he calls it) and reproduced the Greek and Latin texts of eighty-three such letters — most of them, of course, being Greek nonliterary papyrus letters from Egypt.[137] Stanley Stowers has dealt with a large number of Greco-Roman and Christian letters of introduction, which were written from the time of the Roman orator, philosopher, and statesman Cicero (106-43 B.C.) — who, as Stowers points out, "wrote numerous letters of introduction and intercession of varying length and intensity"[138] — to the time of Aurelius Augustine (A.D. 354-430), the great fifth-century Church Father. And letters of introduction, as many have noted, are referred to in both the Jewish and the Christian Scriptures (cf. 2 Kgs 5:5-6; Acts 9:1b-2; 18:27; 1 Cor 16:3; 2 Cor 3:1; see also 2 *Macc* 9:19-27).

But ancient letters of introduction, as far as we know, always (1) were written by others on behalf of the person or persons being introduced or accredited, and not by someone setting out his own credentials, and (2) included expressions of high praise for the person or people addressed, with those words of praise constituting an important part of the letter. Further, repeating here what we have said earlier about Jewett's proposal (see Chapter V, "Purpose"), while Paul certainly thought of himself and of all believers in Christ as "ambassadors for Christ" (2 Cor 5:20), and while the tone and content of Romans could be classed as "ambassadorial," it may be questioned

---

136. Cf., e.g., O. Michel, *An die Römer*, 5; M. Black, *Romans*, 18.
137. C.-H. Kim, *Letter of Recommendation*, 150-238.
138. S. K. Stowers, *Letter Writing*, 159.

whether Romans is any more uniquely ambassadorial than many of Paul's other extant letters.

A more likely hypothesis is that suggested in 1977 by Martin Luther Stirewalt Jr., who argued that among the Greco-Roman letters of Paul's day there can be found evidence for a distinctive type of instructional letter — an epistolary genre for which the label "literary epistle" is misleading and "Lehrbrief" is too general, but for which the caption "letter essay" would be appropriate.[139] Stirewalt acknowledges that a "letter essay" cannot be shown to have been recognized as a separate or discrete epistolary genre by any author of the ancient world. Nonetheless, it is just this type of writing, he argues, that appears in letters of the Greek philosopher Epicurus (c. 342/334–271/270 B.C.), letters of the Greek rhetorician and historian Dionysius of Halicarnassus (died 8 B.C.), and certain writings of the Greek essayist and Pythian priest Plutarch (c. A.D. 46-120), as well as in the hellenistic Jewish composition known as 2 *Maccabees* (probably written sometime at the end of the second century B.C.) and the Christian *Martyrdom of Polycarp* (probably written sometime toward the end of the second century A.D.).

These writings Stirewalt characterizes as "written communications with epistolary characteristics, sent between identifiable parties, on particular subjects."[140] Or as Stirewalt defines further the ancient letter essays he has brought together for analysis — with, of course, his underlying thesis being that they offer close parallels to Paul's letter to the Romans:

> The pieces collected here were written out of a genuine letter-setting and they retain the formal and structural epistolary characteristics [of a genuine letter]. . . . On the other hand, they are losing some of the form, phraseology, and structure of the letter and are incorporating the more impersonal, objective style of the monograph. In fact, the writers themselves refer to them most often as *logoi* [i.e., literally "words," but here connoting "instruction"].[141]

Somewhat similar to Stirewalt's thesis is that of Klaus Berger, who in 1984 drew analogies between Paul's letter to the Romans and Greco-Roman

---

139. M. L. Stirewalt Jr., "Greek Letter-Essay," in Donfried, ed., *Romans Debate* (1977), 175-206; (1991), 147-71.

140. M. L. Stirewalt Jr., "Greek Letter-Essay," in Donfried, ed., *Romans Debate* (1977), 176; (1991), 147.

141. M. L. Stirewalt Jr., "Greek Letter-Essay," in Donfried, ed., *Romans Debate* (1977), 176; (1991), 148.

letters in which a teacher writes to his pupils, to a community of pupils, or even to certain cities and gives them instruction.[142] Yet Berger also recognized differences between Romans and ancient Greco-Roman didactic letters, principally in that (1) Paul does not write as a teacher who lords it over his pupils, since he was not the one who founded the church at Rome, and (2) the tone of Romans is more that of a general treatise, since Paul did not really know his addressees and so could not speak more personally.[143]

The proposal of Luther Stirewalt, as Karl Donfried characterized it when including his article as an appendix in the first edition of *The Romans Debate,* is "rich and creative," with "enormous relevance for the study of Romans."[144] And taken together, the theses of Stirewalt and Berger offer important contributions for an understanding of the epistolary genre of Romans. They do not, of course, provide an explanation as to why the Christians at Rome were singled out by Paul to be the recipients of such an instructional letter essay. One might have expected, in fact, that the apostle would have favored his own converts and his own churches with such a document, rather than writing to believers in Jesus who had not been brought to Christ through his ministry and who were largely unknown to him personally. Nor do the theses of Stirewalt and Berger, by themselves, offer any reason as to why Paul would have chosen the particular time he did to write such an instructional letter.

Nonetheless, when combined with our theses regarding the addressees of Romans, Paul's purposes in writing, and the protreptic nature of the letter's rhetoric (as argued above in Chapter V, "Purpose," and in the immediately preceding section of the present chapter, "Rhetorical Conventions"), understanding the epistolary genre of Romans as that of an ancient "letter essay" — that is, as instructional material set within an epistolary frame — seems to provide the most likely life setting and cultural context for a proper interpretation of the letter. And it is such an understanding that will underlie the treatment of structure and argument that follows in Chapter XI.

2. Epistolary Structures and Formulas of the Ancient World

In many ways, the extant nonliterary letters of the ancient world evidence a remarkable degree of similarity. This is true with respect to their general

---

142. K. Berger, "Hellenistische Gattungen," 1338-39.
143. K. Berger, "Hellenistische Gattungen," 1334-35.
144. K. P. Donfried, *Romans Debate* (1977), xv-xvi; (1991), xlvi.

structures: (1) an opening prescript (sender, addressee or addressees, and greetings), (2) a health wish (as set out separately or joined with the prescript), (3) a prayer, with features of thanksgiving frequently included (which establishes personal contact with the addressee), (4) the central body of the letter (which typically consists of a body opening, a body middle, and a body closing), and (5) a closing formula (which often includes a repetition of the health wish, further greetings, and the date when the letter was written — and, later, which may also incorporate a request to greet acquaintances who were not directly addressed in the letter and/or the greetings of others). But it is also true with respect to the particular epistolary formulas that appear in these nonliterary letters.

Analyses of the Greek papyrus letters have produced a fairly extensive list of common epistolary formulas, of which the following are probably the most significant when comparing these letters with the Pauline letters:[145]

> *Thanksgiving:* γινώσκειν σε θέλω, πάτερ, ὅτι εὐχαριστῶ πολλὰ Ἰσιδώρῳ τῷ ἐπιτρόπῳ ἐπεὶ συνέστηκέ μοι, "I wish you to know, father, that I am greatly thankful to Isidorus the guardian, since he has advised me" (BGU 816).
>
> *Prayer:* πρὸ μὲν πάντων εὔχομέ σαι ὑγιένειν καὶ προκόπτειν, ἅμα δὲ καὶ τὸ προσκύνημά σου ποιοῦμε ἡμερησίως παρὰ τοῖς πατρῴες θεοῖς, "before all things I pray for your health and success; at the time I also make daily obeisance for you before our ancestral gods" (PMich 209:3-6).
>
> *Expression of grief or distress:* ἀκούσας ὅτι νωθρεύῃ ἀγωνιοῦμεν, "I am anxious because I heard you were ill" (BGU 449:4).
>
> *Disclosure formula:* γινώσκειν σε θέλω ὅτι, "I want you to know that" (PGiess 11:4); or γνώριζε οὖν, "know therefore" (PMich 28:16); or ἀλλὰ οἶδα ὅτι, "but I know that" (POxy 1219:11).
>
> *Request formula:* παρακαλῶ σαι, μήτηρ, διαλάγητί μοι, "I beg you, mother, be reconciled to me" (BGU 846:10); or ἐρωτηθεὶς οὖν, ἀδελφέ, τάχιόν μοι γράφιν, "I therefore ask you, brother, to write me at once" (PMich 209:9-10); or δέομαι οὖν σου, βασιλεῦ, εἴ σοι δοκεῖ, "I entreat you therefore, king, if it pleases you" (PEnteux 82:6).

145. See esp. J. L. White, "Introductory Formulae" (1971); *idem, Body of the Greek Letter* (1972); and T. Y. Mullins, "Formulas in New Testament Epistles" (1972), with further documentation from the papyrus letters provided by White and Mullins; see also L. A. Jervis, *Purpose of Romans* (1991); J. A. D. Weima, *Neglected Endings* (1994); and J. D. Harvey, *Listening to the Text* (1998).

Expression of joy: λίαν ἐχάρην ἀκούσασα ὅτι, "I rejoiced exceedingly when I heard that" (PGiess 21:3).

Expression of astonishment: θαυμάζω πῶς, "I am surprised how" (POxy 113:20).

Reminder of past instruction: ὡς ἠρώτηκά σε, "as I have asked you" (PMich 202:3).

Formulaic use of the verb for hearing or learning: ἀκούσας δὲ τὰ κατὰ τὸν Πτολεμαῖον ἐλυπήθην σφόδρα, "I was deeply grieved to hear about the case of Ptolemaeus" (PTebt 760:20); ἐλοιπήθην ἐπιγνοῦσα παρά, "I was grieved to learn from" (POxy 930:4).

περί with the genitive: καὶ περὶ τῶν χωρίων, "and about the fields" (POxy 1220:23).

Notification of a coming visit: θεῶν οὖν βουλομένων, πρὸς τὴν ἑορτὴν . . . πειράσομαι πρὸς ὑμᾶς γενέσθαι, "If the gods will, therefore, I will try to come to you . . . for the feast" (POxy 1666:11).

Reference to writing: ἔγραψας ἡμῖν ὅτι, "you wrote us that" (PMich 36:1).

Verbs of saying and informing: ἐρῖ σοι δὲ Ἀπολινάρις πῶς, "Apolinarius will tell you how" (POxy 932:3); καὶ δηλωσόν μοι πόσαι ἐξέβησαν ἵνα εἰδῶ, "and inform me how many came out so that I may know" (PFay 122:14).

Expression of reassurance: τοῦτο μὴ νομίσης ὅτι, "do not think that" (PMich 206:11).

Responsibility statement: μὴ ἀμελήσης ἐν τῇ αὔριον ἀπαντῆσαι πρὸς ἡμᾶς, "do not neglect to come and meet us tomorrow" (PAmh 143:2).

Use of a vocative of direct address to indicate transition: φανερόν σοι ποιῶ, ἀδελφέ, "I make known to you, brother" (PMich 206:4-5).

With respect to the frequency and function of these epistolary formulas in the Greek papyrus letters, Terence Mullins has aptly pointed out that: (1) *"The use of one form tends to precipitate the use of others with it,"*[146] and (2) "They almost always punctuate a break in the writer's thought."[147] Thus, as Mullins goes on to elaborate:

The opening is a sort of warm-up for the main issue and provides a convenient clustering place for matters less important than the main issue

---

146. T. Y. Mullins, "Formulas in New Testament Epistles," 387 (italics his).
147. T. Y. Mullins, "Formulas in New Testament Epistles," 387.

(but not necessarily introductory to it). The closing constitutes the final communication and is a natural clustering place for matters of minor importance which the writer wants to add before breaking off. But in a letter of any considerable length there will be places where a writer will pause and break the flow of his thought for a moment. He may mark such places with epistolary forms whose relevance to the main subject matter will vary according to the way the writer thinks and expresses himself.[148]

So in the study of any Greek letter (including those by Paul), we need to be alert to the clustering of various epistolary formulas at certain strategic places *and* to the appearance of such formulas, whether used singly or in clusters, to signal significant breaks or turning points in the letter.

3. Epistolary Structures and Formulas of Romans

An analysis of Romans produces two major clusters of epistolary formulas that, by comparison with those found in the nonliterary papyrus letters of Egypt, should probably be judged as reflecting common epistolary conventions of the day. The first cluster of epistolary conventions appears in the opening sections of the letter, that is, in the "salutation" of 1:1-7, the "thanksgiving" of 1:8-12, and the epistolary "body opening" of 1:13-15:

1:1 — Sender: Παῦλος, "Paul."

1:7a — Addressees: πᾶσιν τοῖς οὖσιν ἐν ᾿Ρώμῃ, "to all those at Rome."

1:7b — Greeting: χάρις ὑμῖν καὶ εἰρήνη, "grace and peace to you."

1:8 — Thanksgiving: εὐχαριστῶ τῷ θεῷ μου διὰ ᾿Ιησοῦ Χριστοῦ περὶ πάντων ὑμῶν, "I thank my God through Jesus Christ for all of you."

1:9-10a — Attestation formula: μάρτυς μού ἐστιν ὁ θεός, "God is my witness."

1:10b — Prayer: δεόμενος εἴ πως ἤδη ποτὲ εὐοδωθήσομαι ἐν τῷ θελήματι τοῦ θεοῦ ἐλθεῖν πρὸς ὑμᾶς, "I pray that now at last by God's will the way may be opened for me to come to you."

1:11 — Visit wish: ἐπιποθῶ ἰδεῖν ὑμᾶς, "I long to see you."

1:13a — Disclosure formula, with vocative: οὐ θέλω ὑμᾶς ἀγνοεῖν, ἀδελφοί, "I do not want you to be unaware, brothers and sisters."

1:13b — Notification of a desired visit: πολλάκις προεθέμην ἐλθεῖν πρὸς ὑμᾶς, "I planned many times to come to you."

---

148. T. Y. Mullins, "Formulas in New Testament Epistles," 387.

1:14 — Responsibility statement: Ἕλλησίν τε καὶ βαρβάροις, σοφοῖς τε καὶ ἀνοήτοις ὀφειλέτης εἰμί, "I am obligated both to Greeks and non-Greeks, both to the wise and the foolish."

The second cluster of epistolary conventions appears in the closing sections of the letter, that is, in the "body closing" or "apostolic parousia" section of 15:14-32 and the concluding sections of 15:33–16:27:

15:14 — Confidence formula, with vocative of direct address: πέπεισμαι, ἀδελφοί, "I am convinced, brothers and sisters."

15:15 — Reminder statement: ἔγραψα ὑμῖν . . . ὡς ἐπαναμιμνῄσκων ὑμᾶς, "I have written you . . . so as to remind you."

15:22 — Visit wish: ἐνεκοπτόμην τὰ πολλὰ τοῦ ἐλθεῖν πρὸς ὑμᾶς, "I have often been hindered from coming to you."

15:23-24 — Notification of a coming visit: νυνὶ δέ . . . ἐλπίζω . . . θεάσασθαι ὑμᾶς, "but now . . . I hope . . . to visit you."

15:29 — Confidence formula: οἶδα δὲ ὅτι ἐρχόμενος πρὸς ὑμᾶς ἐν πλρώματι εὐλογίας Χριστοῦ ἐλεύσομαι, "I know that when I come to you, I will come in the full measure of the blessing of Christ."

15:30 — Request formula, with vocative of direct address: παρακαλῶ ὑμᾶς, ἀδελφοί, "I urge you, brothers and sisters."

16:1 — Commendation of the letter carrier: συνίστημι ὑμῖν Φοίβην τὴν ἀδελφὴν ἡμῶν, "I commend to you our sister Phoebe."

16:3-16 — Greetings sent to acquaintances: ἀσπάσασθε Πρίσκαν καὶ Ἀκύλαν, etc., "Greet Priscilla and Aquila, etc."

16:17 — Request formula, with vocative of direct address: παρακαλῶ ὑμᾶς, ἀδελφοί, "I urge you, brothers and sisters."

16:19 — Expression of joy: ἐφ᾽ ὑμῖν χαίρω, "I rejoice over you."

16:21 — Conveyance of greetings from others: ἀσπάζεται ὑμᾶς Τιμόθεος ὁ συνεργός μου καὶ Λούκιος καὶ Ἰάσων καὶ Σωσίπατρος οἱ συγγενεῖς μου, "Timothy, my co-worker, greets you, as do also Lucius, Jason, and Sosipater, my relatives."

16:22 — Greeting inserted: ἀσπάζομαι ὑμᾶς ἐγὼ Τέρτιος ὁ γράψας τὴν ἐπιστολήν, "I, Tertius, who wrote [down] this epistle greet you."

16:23 — Convenance of further greetings from others: ἀσπάζεται ὑμᾶς Γάϊος. ἀσπάζεται ὑμᾶς Ἔραστος . . . καὶ Κούαρτος, "Gaius greets you, Erastus greets you, . . . as does also Quartus."

A close examination of Romans also reveals within the letter's rather lengthy body middle a few other seemingly common epistolary phrases and expressions — chiefly, a few vocatives of direct address, some verbs of saying, and six or seven disclosure formulas, which may reflect, as well, certain epistolary conventions of Paul's day. A number of these phrases and expressions could be, of course, related more to certain rhetorical modes of expression that were then in vogue — as, for example, the words and phrases used to introduce a diatribial dialogue, rhetorical questioning, or the citation of a biblical passage. But however they are to be understood, whether as basically epistolary or basically rhetorical in nature, it needs always to be noted that these phrases and expressions appear frequently at breaks or turning points in the argument of the letter, and so serve to signal some type of transition of thought — either from one aspect of the argument to another aspect within the same discussion or from one topic to another topic.

The list of possible epistolary features within the body middle of Romans is not as long as what can be compiled from the letter's opening sections, its "body opening," its "body closing," and its concluding sections. Nonetheless, the following phenomena need also to be taken into account as possibly reflecting certain epistolary conventions of the day:

2:1 — Vocative of direct address: διὸ ἀναπολόγητος εἶ, ὦ ἄνθρωπε, "Therefore, O man, you are without excuse."

4:1 — Verb of saying: τί οὖν ἐροῦμεν; "What then shall we say?"

6:1 — Verb of saying: τί οὖν ἐροῦμεν; "What then shall we say?"

6:3 — Disclosure formula: ἀγνοεῖτε ὅτι, "Do you not know that . . . ?"

6:15 — Verb of saying (implied): τί οὖν; "What then [shall we say]?"

6:16 — Disclosure formula: οὐκ οἴδατε ὅτι; "Do you not know that . . . ?"

7:1a — Disclosure formula, with vocative of direct address: ἀγνοεῖτε, ἀδελφοί; "Do you not know, brothers and sisters?"

7:1b — Verb of saying/speaking: γινώσκουσιν γὰρ νόμον λαλῶ, "for I am speaking to those who know the law."

7:4 — Vocative of direct address: ὥστε, ἀδελφοι μου, "so, my brothers and sisters."

7:7 — Verb of saying: τί οὖν ἐροῦμεν; "What then shall we say?"

7:14 — Disclosure formula: οἴδαμεν γὰρ ὅτι; "For we know that. . . ."

8:12 — Vocative of direct address: ἄρα οὖν, ἀδελφοί, "so then, brothers and sisters."

8:22 — Disclosure formula: οἴδαμεν γὰρ ὅτι, "For we know that. . . ."

8:28 — Disclosure formula: οἴδαμεν δὲ ὅτι, "And we know that. . . ."

8:31 — Verb of saying: τί οὖν ερoῦμεν πρὸς ταῦτα; "What, then, shall we say in response to these things?"

8:38 — Confidence formula: πέπεισμαι γὰρ ὅτι, "For I am convinced that. . . ."

9:1 — Attestation statement: ἀλήθειαν λέγω ἐν Χριστῷ, οὐ ψεύδομαι, "I am speaking the truth in Christ, I am not lying."

9:14 — Verb of saying: τί οὖν ἐροῦμεν; "What then shall we say?"

9:30 — Verb of saying: τί οὖν ἐροῦμεν; "What then shall we say?"

10:1 — Vocative of direct address: ἀδελφοί, "brothers and sisters."

11:1 — Verb of saying: λέγω οὖν, "I say then. . . ."

11:11 — Verb of saying: λέγω οὖν, "I say then. . . ."

11:13 — Verb of saying/speaking: ὑμῖν δὲ λέγω τοῖς ἔθνεσιν, "Now, I am speaking to you Gentiles."

11:25 — Disclosure formula, with vocative of direct address: οὐ γάρ θέλω ὑμᾶς ἀγνοεῖν, ἀδελφοί, "I do not want you to be ignorant, brothers and sisters."

12:1 — Request formula, with vocative: παρακαλῶ οὖν ὑμᾶς, ἀδελφοί, "I urge you, brothers and sisters."

12:3 — Verb of saying: λέγω γὰρ . . . παντὶ τῷ ὄντι ἐν ὑμῖν, "for I say . . . to every one of you."

14:14 — Confidence formula: οἶδα καὶ πέπεισμαι ἐν κυρίῳ Ἰησοῦ ὅτι, "I know and am convinced in the Lord Jesus that. . . ."

It is immediately apparent from the data above that clusters of epistolary formulas appear most frequently in Romans in its beginning sections (i.e., the "salutation" of 1:1-7, the "thanksgiving" of 1:8-12, and the "body opening" of 1:13-15) and its closing sections (i.e., the "body closing" of 15:14-32, the "peace benediction," "commendation," and "greetings" of 15:33–16:16, and the "personal subscription" of 16:17-23, which contains additional "exhortations," the "grace benediction," and further "greetings"). A small cluster of epistolary phrases and expressions is also present in 12:1 (*request formula and vocative of direct address*) and 12:3 (*verb of saying*), when Paul moves from his theological discussions in 1:16–11:36 to his practical exhortations in 12:1–15:13 — which would seem to be a logical place for such a cluster when turning from exposition to exhortation. Elsewhere in the body of Romans, however, and particularly throughout the large body middle of the letter in 1:16–15:13, there appear relatively few epistolary formulas or phrases. Most of those that do appear in 1:16–15:13 are (1) the plural vocative of direct address ἀδελφοί ("brothers and sisters"), (2) various types of sayings formulas, and

(3) a few disclosure formulas, which function as transitional expressions at the head of a new section or sub-section. But apart from these rather few instances — all of which, of course, have some significance for an analysis of the letter's structure and argument, and so must be discussed further in Chapter XI ("Structure and Argument") — one looks hard to find the customary epistolary formulas and conventions of antiquity in the body middle of Romans, even though they are abundant in its beginning sections of 1:1-15 and closing sections of 15:14–16:27.

Many of Paul's other letters contain a relatively larger number of epistolary formulas in their body middle sections, with those formulas serving to introduce, connect, and close off the respective parts of those sections.[149] The apostle's letter to Christians at Rome, however, seems to be somewhat different in this regard.

It may be that in concentrating mostly on the opening and closing parts of ancient letters and of NT letters, which certainly are "epistolary" in style and function, scholars have given too little attention to the epistolary formulas contained in the bodies of those letters.[150] Or it may be that as a "protreptic" discourse (with respect to its rhetorical genre) or a "letter essay" (with respect to its epistolary type), the body middle of Romans, that is, 1:16–15:13, should be understood as instructional and hortatory materials set within an epistolary frame — with the implications being (1) that the four major sections of the body middle should be analyzed more in terms of their rhetorical features, and (2) that the opening and closing sections of the letter, including those portions of the letter's body that can be identified as a body opening and a body closing, are to be analyzed more in terms of their epistolary conventions.

Supplemental to this latter suggestion, it may be asked whether in writing to Christians at Rome Paul incorporated into the body middle of his letter (i.e., 1:16–15:13) certain materials that he had used earlier in his ministry, whether in oral fashion or written form. If that be so, or anything approximating such a scenario, it may then be conjectured (1) that at least some of the material within the body of Romans, particularly its central portion of 1:16–15:13, should be viewed as having had an earlier oral and rhetorical history before being cast into its present epistolary form, and, therefore, (2) that those materials should be evaluated more in terms of

149. Cf. R. N. Longenecker, *Galatians*, WBC (Dallas: Word, 1990), cvii-cviii, *passim*.
150. Note the complaint of J. L. White, "Introductory Formulae," 91; see also S. K. Stowers, *Letter Writing*, 22.

their oral and rhetorical conventions than in terms of any epistolary features they may reflect.

All three matters of oral, rhetorical, and epistolary conventions in the ancient world must be taken into account in any analysis of the structure and argument of Romans — with, in particular, all three being kept constantly in mind when studying each of the sections and sub-sections of the letter, whatever weight may be given to one factor vis-à-vis the other two in any particular passage. And these are matters that will be considered more closely in Chapter XI, which deals with the structure and argument of Paul's letter to the Christians at Rome.

SUPPLEMENTAL BIBLIOGRAPHY

See also "Bibliography of Selected Commentaries." All references in the footnotes to works included in this list are by the authors' names and abbreviated titles.

Achtemeier, Paul J. "*Omne Verbum Sonat:* The New Testament and the Oral Environment of Late Western Antiquity," *JBL* 109 (1990) 3-27.

Aletti, Jean-Noël. "La présence d'un modèle rhétorique en Romains: Son rôle et son importance," *Bib* 71 (1990) 1-24.

―――. "The Rhetoric of Romans 5–8," in *The Rhetorical Analysis of Scripture: Essays from the 1995 London Conference,* ed. S. E. Porter and T. H. Olbricht. JSNT.SS 146. Sheffield: Sheffield Academic Press, 1997, 294-308.

Allo, Ernest B. "'Le défaut d'éloquence' et le 'style oral' de Saint Paul," *RSPT* 23 (1934) 29-39.

Anderson, R. Dean, Jr. *Ancient Rhetorical Theory and Paul.* Kampen: Kok Pharos, 1996; rev. ed. Leuven: Peeters, 1998.

Aristotle. *The "Art" of Rhetoric,* trans. J. H. Freese. LCL. Cambridge, MA: Harvard University Press, 1932.

Audet, Jean-Paul. "Literary Forms and Contents of a Normal Εὐχαριστία in the First Century," *Studia Evangelica* 1, ed. F. L. Cross, K. Aland, *et al.* Berlin: Akademie, 1959, 632-43.

Aune, David E. *The New Testament in Its Literary Environment.* Philadelphia: Westminster, 1987, 158-225.

―――. ed. *Greco-Roman Literature and the New Testament: Selected Forms and Genres.* SBL.SBS 21. Atlanta: Scholars, 1988.

―――. "Romans as a *Logos Protreptikos* in the Context of Ancient Religious and Philosophical Propaganda," in *Paulus als Missionar und Theologe und das antike Judentum,* ed. M. Hengel and U. Heckel. WUNT 58. Tübingen: Mohr-Siebeck,

1991, 91-124; abbreviated version: "Romans as a *Logos Protrepikos*," in Donfried, ed., *Romans Debate* (1991), 278-96.

————. *The Westminster Dictionary of New Testament and Early Christian Literature and Rhetoric.* Louisville: Westminster/John Knox, 2003, 428-32, *passim.*

Bahr, Gordon J. "Paul and Letter Writing in the First Century," *CBQ* 28 (1966) 465-77.

————. "The Subscriptions in the Pauline Letters," *JBL* 87 (1968) 27-41.

Bailey, James L., and Lyle D. Vander Broek. *Literary Forms in the New Testament: A Handbook.* Louisville: Westminster/John Knox, 1992.

Berger, Klaus. *Formgeschichte des Neuen Testament.* Heidelberg: Quelle & Meyer, 1984.

————. "Hellenistische Gattungen im Neuen Testament," *ANRW,* II.25.2. Berlin: de Gruyter, 1984, 1031-1432, 1831-85.

Betz, Hans-Dieter. *Der Apostel Paulus und die sokratische Tradition.* Tübingen: Mohr, 1972.

————. "The Literary Composition and Function of Paul's Letter to the Galatians," *NTS* 21 (1975) 353-79.

————. *Galatians: A Commentary on Paul's Letter to the Churches in Galatia.* Herm. Philadelphia: Fortress, 1979.

————. *Second Corinthians 8 and 9: A Commentary on Two Administrative Letters of the Apostle Paul.* Herm. Philadelphia: Fortress, 1985.

————. "The Problem of Rhetoric and Theology according to the Apostle Paul," in *L'Apôtre Paul. Personalité, Style et Conception du Ministère,* ed. A. Vanhoye. Leuven: University Press, 1986, 16-48.

Bjerkelund, Carl J. *Parakalō: Form, Funktion und Sinn der parakalō-Sätze in den paulinischen Briefen.* BTN 1. Oslo: Universitetsforlaget, 1967.

Black, Clifton C. "Keeping Up with Recent Studies: XVI. Rhetorical Criticism and Biblical Interpretation," *ExpT* 100 (1989) 252-58.

————. "Rhetorical Questions: The New Testament, Classical Rhetoric, and Current Interpretation," *Dialog* 29 (1990) 62-70.

Black, Edwin. *Rhetorical Criticism: A Study in Method.* New York: Macmillan, 1965; Madison: University of Wisconsin, 1978.

Blass, Friedrich. *Die Rhythmen der asianischen und römischen Kunstprosa.* Leipzig: Deichert, 1905, esp. 42-78, 196-216.

Boobyer, George H. *"Thanksgiving" and the "Glory of God" in Paul.* Borna: Noske, 1929.

Botha, Pieter J. J. "The Verbal Art of the Pauline Letters: Rhetoric, Performance and Presence," in *Rhetoric and the New Testament: Essays from the 1992 Heidelberg Conference,* ed. S. E. Porter and T. H. Olbricht. JSNT.SS 90. Sheffield: Sheffield Academic Press, 1993, 409-28.

Boyarin, Daniel. "Rhetoric and Interpretation: The Case of the Nimshal," *Prooftexts* 5 (1985) 269-76.

Bradley, David G. "The *Topos* as a Form in the Pauline Paraenesis," *JBL* 72 (1953) 238-46.

Brandt, William J. *The Rhetoric of Argumentation.* New York: Bobbs-Merrill, 1970; rev. ed. New York: Irvington, 1984.

Brock, Bernard L., and Robert L. Scott, eds. *Methods of Rhetorical Criticism: A Twentieth-Century Perspective,* rev. ed. Detroit: Wayne State University, 1980.

Brunt, John C. "More on *'Topos'* as a New Testament Form," *JBL* 104 (1985) 495-500.

Bryan, Christopher. *A Preface to Romans: Notes on the Epistle in Its Literary and Cultural Setting.* Oxford: Oxford University Press, 2000.

Bultmann, Rudolf. *Der Stil der paulinischen Predigt und die kynisch-stoische Diatribe.* FRLANT 13. Göttingen: Vandenhoeck & Ruprecht, 1910, 1984.

Burgess, Theodore C. "Epideictic Literature," in *Studies in Classical Philology,* vol. 3. Chicago: University of Chicago Press, 1902, 89-261.

Burke, Kenneth. *A Rhetoric of Motives.* New York: Prentice-Hall, 1950.

―――. *A Grammar of Motives and a Rhetoric of Motives.* Cleveland: World, 1962.

Caird, George B. *The Language and Imagery of the Bible.* Philadelphia: Westminster, 1980.

Campbell, Douglas A. *The Rhetoric of Righteousness in Romans 3.21-26.* JSNT.SS 65. Sheffield: Sheffield Academic Press, 1992.

―――. "Determining the Gospel through Rhetorical Analysis in Paul's Letter to the Roman Christians," in *Gospel in Paul: Studies on Corinthians, Galatians and Romans for Richard N. Longenecker,* ed. L. A. Jervis and P. Richardson. JSNT.SS 108. Sheffield: Sheffield Academic Press, 1994, 315-36.

Capelle, Wilhelm, and Henri Marrou. "Diatribe," *Reallexikon für Antike und Christentum* 3 (1957) 990-1009.

Cicero. *De Inventione. De Optimo Genere Oratorum. De Topica,* trans. H. M. Hubbell. LCL. Cambridge, MA: Harvard University Press, 1949.

―――. *De Oratore. De Fato. Paradoxa Stoicorum. De Partitione Oratoria,* 2 vols., trans. E. W. Sutton and H. Rackham. LCL. Cambridge, MA: Harvard University Press, 1942.

―――. *Letters to Atticus,* 3 vols., trans. E. O. Winstedt. LCL. Cambridge, MA: Harvard University Press, 1912-1918.

―――. *Letters to His Friends,* 3 vols., trans. W. G. Williams. LCL. Cambridge, MA: Harvard University Press, 1958-1960.

Clark, Donald L. *Rhetoric in Greco-Roman Education.* New York: Columbia University Press, 1957.

Classen, Carl Joachim. "St. Paul's Epistles and Ancient Greek and Roman Rhetoric," *Rhetorica* 10 (1992) 325-32; repr. in *Rhetoric and the New Testament: Essays from the 1992 Heidelberg Conference,* ed. S. E. Porter and T. H. Olbricht. JSNT.SS 90. Sheffield: Sheffield Academic Press, 1993.

Clines, David J. A., David M. Gunn, and Alan J. Hauser, eds. *Art and Meaning: Rhetoric in Biblical Literature.* JSOT.SS 19. Sheffield: Sheffield Academic Press, 1982.

Corbett, Edward P. J. *Classical Rhetoric for the Modern Student.* New York: Oxford, 1965, 1971.

————, ed. *Rhetorical Analyses of Literary Works*. New York: Oxford, 1969.

Cosby, Michael R. "Paul's Persuasive Language in Romans 5," in *Persuasive Artistry: Studies in New Testament Rhetoric in Honor of George A. Kennedy*, ed. D. F. Watson. JSNT.SS 50. Sheffield: Sheffield Academic Press, 1991.

Culley, Robert C. "Oral Tradition and the OT: Some Recent Discussion," *Semeia* 5 (1976) 1-33.

————. "Oral Tradition and Biblical Studies," *OrT* 1 (1986) 30-41.

Daube, David. "Rabbinic Methods of Interpretation and Hellenistic Rhetoric," *HUCA* 22 (1949) 239-64.

Deichgräber, Reinhard. *Gotteshymnus und Christushymnus in der frühen Christenheit: Untersuchungen zur Form, Sprache, and Stil der frühchristlichen Hymnen.* Göttingen: Vandenhoeck & Ruprecht, 1967.

Deissmann, Adolf. *Light from the Ancient East: The New Testament Illustrated by Recently Discovered Texts of the Graeco-Roman World,* trans. L. R. M. Strachan; rev. ed. London: Hodder & Stoughton, 1927 (originally published in 1908), 146-251 (esp. 227-51 on NT nonliterary letters).

Dion, Paul E. "The Aramaic 'Family Letter' and Related Epistolary Forms in Other Oriental Languages and in Hellenistic Greek," *Semeia* 22 (1981) 59-76.

Dixon, Peter. *Rhetoric.* London: Methuen, 1971.

Dobschütz, Ernst von. "Zum Wortschatz und Stil des Römerbriefs," *ZNW* 33 (1934) 51-66.

Donfried, Karl P., ed. *The Romans Debate.* Minneapolis: Augsburg, 1977; *The Romans Debate,* revised and expanded edition. Peabody: Henrickson, 1991.

Doty, William G. "The Epistle in Late Hellenism and Early Christianity: Developments, Influences and Literary Form." Unpublished Ph.D. Dissertation, Drew University, Madison, NJ, 1966.

————. "The Classification of Epistolary Literature," *CBQ* 31 (1969) 185-89.

————. *Letters in Primitive Christianity.* Philadelphia: Fortress, 1973.

Dunn, James D. G. "How the New Testament Canon Began," in *From Biblical Criticism to Biblical Faith: Essays in Honor of Lee Martin McDonald,* ed. W. H. Brackney and C. A. Evans. Macon, GA: Mercer University Press, 2007, 122-37.

Elliott, Neil. *The Rhetoric of Romans: Argumentative Constraint and Strategy and Paul's Dialogue with Judaism.* JSNT.SS 45. Sheffield: Sheffield Academic Press, 1990.

Exler, Francis X. J. *The Form of the Ancient Greek Letter: A Study in Greek Epistolography.* Washington, D.C.: Catholic University of America, 1923.

Foley, J. M. *Immanent Art: From Structure to Meaning in Traditional Oral Epic.* Bloomington: Indiana University Press, 1991.

————. *The Singer of Tales in Performance.* Bloomington: Indiana University Press, 1995.

Fraikin, Daniel. "The Rhetorical Function of the Jews in Romans," in *Anti-Judaism in Early Christianity.* Vol. 1: *Paul and the Gospels,* ed. P. Richardson and D. Granskou. Waterloo: Wilfrid Laurier University, 1986, 91-106.

Funk, Robert W. "The Letter: Form and Style," in *Language, Hermeneutic, and Word of God: The Problem of Language in the New Testament and Contemporary Theology.* New York: Harper & Row, 1966, 150-74.

―――. "The Apostolic 'Parousia': Form and Significance," in *Christian History and Interpretation: Studies Presented to John Knox,* ed. W. R. Farmer, C. F. D. Moule, and R. R. Niebuhr. Cambridge: Cambridge University Press, 1967, 249-68.

Grobel, Kendrick. "A Chiastic Retribution-Formula in Romans 2," in *Zeit und Geschichte. Dankesgabe an R. Bultmann,* ed. E. Dinkler. Tübingen: Mohr-Siebeck, 1964, 255-61.

Guerra, Anthony J. *Romans and the Apologetic Tradition: The Purpose, Genre and Audience of Paul's Letter.* SNTS.MS 81. Cambridge: Cambridge University Press, 1995.

Harding, Mark. "The Classical Rhetoric of Praise in the New Testament," *RTR* 45 (1986) 73-82.

Hartlich, Paul. "*Exhortationum* (Προτρεπτικων) a Graecis Romanisque Scriptarum Historia et Indole" (Doctoral Dissertation). Leipziger Studien II (1889).

Harvey, John D. *Listening to the Text: Oral Patterning in Paul's Letters.* Grand Rapids: Baker, 1998.

Howes, R. F. *Historical Studies of Rhetoric and Rhetoricians.* Ithaca: Cornell University Press, 1961.

Jeremias, Joachim. "Chiasm in den Paulusbriefen," *ZNW* 49 (1958) 145-56.

―――. "Zur Gedankenführung in den paulinischen Briefen," in *Studia Paulina in honorem Johannis de Zwaan septuagenarii.* Haarlem: Bohn, 1953, 146-54.

Jervis, L. Ann. *The Purpose of Romans: A Comparative Letter Structure Investigation.* JSNT.SS 55. Sheffield: Sheffield Academic Press, 1991.

Jewett, Robert L. "The Form and Function of the Homiletic Benediction," *ATR* 51 (1969) 18-34.

―――. "Romans as an Ambassadorial Letter," *Int* 36 (1982) 5-20.

Jordan, Mark D. "Ancient Philosophic Protreptic and the Problem of Persuasive Genres," *Rhetorica* 4 (1986) 309-33.

Judge, Edwin A. "The Early Christians as a Scholastic Community," *JRH* 1 (1960) 4-15, 125-37.

―――. *The Social Pattern of Christian Groups in the First Century.* London: Tyndale, 1960.

―――. "Paul's Boasting in Relation to Contemporary Professional Practice," *ABR* 16 (1968) 37-50.

―――. "St. Paul and Classical Society," *JAC* 15 (1972) 21-36.

Kamlah, Ehrhard. *Die Form der katalogischen Paranese im Neuen Testament.* WUNT 7. Tübingen: Mohr-Siebeck, 1964.

Keck, Leander E. "*Pathos* in Romans? Mostly Preliminary Remarks," in *Paul and Pathos,* ed. T. H. Oldbricht and J. L. Sumney. Atlanta: Society of Biblical Literature, 2001, 71-96.

Kennedy, George A. *The Art of Persuasion in Greece*. Princeton: Princeton University Press, 1963.

―――. *The Art of Rhetoric in the Roman World: 300 B.C.–A.D. 300*. Princeton: Princeton University Press, 1972.

―――. *Classical Rhetoric and Its Christian and Secular Tradition from Ancient to Modern Times*. Chapel Hill: University of North Carolina Press, 1980.

―――. "An Introduction to the Rhetoric of the Gospels," *Rhetorica* 1 (1983) 17-31.

―――. *New Testament Interpretation through Rhetorical Criticism*. Chapel Hill: University of North Carolina Press, 1984.

―――. "The Genres of Rhetoric," in *Handbook of Classical Rhetoric in the Hellenistic Period, 330 B.C.–A.D. 400*, ed. S. E. Porter. Leiden: Brill, 1997, 43-50.

Kessler, Martin. "A Methodological Setting for Rhetorical Criticism," *Semitics* 4 (1974) 22-36.

―――. "An Introduction to Rhetorical Criticism of the Bible: Prolegomena," *Semitics* 7 (1980) 1-27.

Keyes, Clinton W. "The Greek Letter of Introduction," *AJP* 56 (1935) 28-44.

Kim, Chan-Hie. *Form and Structure of the Familiar Greek Letter of Recommendation*. SBL.DS 4. Missoula: University of Montana, 1972.

―――. "The Papyrus Invitation," *JBL* 94 (1975) 391-402.

Kornhardt, Hildegard. *Exemplum. Eine bedeutungsgeschichtliche Studie*. Göttingen: Noske, 1936.

Koskenniemi, Heikki. *Studien zur Idee und Phraseologie des griechischen Briefes bis 400 n. Chr.* Helsinki: Suomalaisen Tiedeakatemi, 1956.

Kraftchick, Steven J. "Πάθη in Paul: The Emotional Logic of 'Original Argument,'" in *Paul and Pathos*, ed. T. H. Oldbricht and J. L. Sumney. Atlanta: Society of Biblical Literature, 2001, 39-68.

Lambrecht, Jan. "Rhetorical Criticism and the New Testament," *Bijd* 50 (1989) 239-53.

Lausberg, Heinrich. *Handbuch der literarischen Rhetorik. Eine Grundlegung der Literaturwissenschaft*, 2 vols. Munich: Hueber, 1960, 1973² [ET = *Handbook of Literary Rhetoric: A Foundation for Literary Study*, ed. and trans. D. E. Orton and R. D. Anderson. Leiden: Brill, 1998].

―――. *Elemente der literarischen Rhetorik. Eine Einführung für Studierende der klassischen, romanischen, englischen und deutschen Philologie*. Munich: Hueber, 1963, 1976⁵.

Leeman, Anton D. *Orationis Ratio: The Stylistic Theories and Practice of the Roman Orators, Historians, and Philosophers*, 2 vols. Amsterdam: Hakkert, 1963.

Lindenberger, James M. *Ancient Aramaic and Hebrew Letters*. Atlanta: Scholars, 1994; 2nd ed., 2003.

Lohmeyer, Ernst. "Probleme paulinischer Theologie I: Briefliche Grussüberschriften," *ZNW* 26 (1927) 158-73.

Longenecker, Richard N. "Ancient Amanuenses and the Pauline Letters," in *New Di-*

mensions in New Testament Study, ed. R. N. Longenecker and M. C. Tenney. Grand Rapids: Zondervan, 1974, 281-97.

―――. "On the Form, Function, and Authority of the New Testament Letters," in *Scripture and Truth,* ed. D. A. Carson and J. D. Woodbridge. Grand Rapids: Zondervan, 1983, 101-14.

―――. *New Wine into Fresh Wineskins. Contextualizing the Early Christian Confessions.* Peabody: Hendrickson, 1999.

Lord, Albert B. *The Singer of Tales.* Cambridge, MA: Harvard University Press, 1960; 2nd ed., ed. S. Mitchell and G. Nagy. Cambridge, MA: Harvard University Press, 2004.

―――. "The Gospels as Oral Traditional Literature," in *The Relationships Among the Gospels: An Interdisciplinary Dialogue,* ed. W. O. Walker Jr. San Antonio: Trinity University Press, 1978, 33-91.

―――. "Characteristics of Orality," *OrT* 2 (1987) 54-62.

Louw, Johannes P. *A Semantic Discourse Analysis of Romans.* Pretoria: University of Pretoria, 1979.

Lund, Nils W. *Chiasmus in the New Testament: A Study in Formsgeschichte.* Chapel Hill: University of North Carolina Press, 1942.

Mack, Burton L. *Rhetoric and the New Testament.* Guides to Biblical Scholarship, New Testament Series. Minneapolis: Fortress, 1990.

Malherbe, Abraham J. "Ancient Epistolary Theorists," *Ohio Journal of Religious Studies* 5 (1977) 3-77; repr. *Ancient Epistolary Theorists.* SBL.SBS 19. Atlanta: Scholars, 1988.

―――. "ΜΗ ΓΕΝΟΙΤΟ in the Diatribe and Paul," *HTR* 73 (1980) 231-40; repr. in *Paul and the Popular Philosophers.* Minneapolis: Fortress, 1989, 25-33.

―――. *Social Aspects of Early Christianity,* 2nd ed. Philadelphia: Fortress, 1983.

―――. *Moral Exhortation: A Greco-Roman Sourcebook.* LEC 4. Philadelphia: Westminster, 1986.

Maurer, Christian. "Der Schluss 'a minore ad majus' als Element paulinischer Theologie," *TLZ* 85 (1960) 149-52.

Meecham, Henry G. *Light from Ancient Letters: Private Correspondence in the Non-Literary Papyri of Oxyrhynchus of the First Four Centuries and Its Bearing on New Testament Language and Thought.* London: Allen & Unwin, 1923.

Muilenburg, James. "Form Criticism and Beyond," *JBL* 88 (1969) 1-18.

Mullins, Terence Y. "Petition as a Literary Form," *NovT* 5 (1962) 46-54.

―――. "Disclosure: A Literary Form in the New Testament," *NovT* 7 (1964) 44-50.

―――. "Greeting as a New Testament Form," *JBL* 87 (1968) 418-26.

―――. "Formulas in New Testament Epistles," *JBL* 91 (1972) 380-90.

―――. "Ascription as a Literary Form," *NTS* 19 (1973) 194-205.

―――. "Visit Talk in the New Testament Letters," *CBQ* 35 (1973) 350-58.

―――. "Benediction as a New Testament Form," *AUSS* 15 (1977) 59-64.

―――. "Topos as a New Testament Form," *JBL* 99 (1980) 541-47.

Norden, Eduard. *Die antike Kunstprosa vom VI. Jahrhunderts vor Christus in die Zeit der Renaissance,* 2 vols. Leipzig: Teubner, 1898, 1909; repr. Stuttgart: Teubner, 1983.

————. *Agnostos Theos. Untersuchungen zur Formengeschichte religiöser Rede.* Leipzig: Teubner, 1913; repr. Stuttgart: Teubner, 1956, 348-53.

Oldbricht, Thomas H., and Jerry L. Sumney, eds. *Paul and Pathos.* Atlanta: Society of Biblical Literature, 2001.

Ong, Walter J. *The Presence of the Word.* New Haven: Yale University Press, 1967.

————. *Rhetoric, Romance, and Technology.* Ithaca: Cornell University Press, 1971.

————. *Interfaces of the Word: Studies in the Evolution of Consciousness and Culture.* Ithaca: Cornell University Press, 1977.

————. *Orality and Literacy.* London: Methuen, 1982.

————. "Writing Is a Technology That Restructures Thought," in *The Written Word: Literacy in Transition,* ed. G. Baumann. Oxford: Clarendon, 1986, 33-50.

Perelman, Chaim, and Lucie Olbrechts-Tyteca. *The New Rhetoric: A Treatise on Argumentation,* trans. J. Wilkinson and P. Weaver. Notre Dame: Notre Dame University Press, 1958, repr. 1969.

Plank, Karl A. *Paul and the Irony of Affliction.* SBL.SemStud 17. Atlanta: Scholars, 1987.

Plett, Heinrich F. *Einführung in die rhetorische Textanalyse,* 2nd ed. Hamburg: Buske, 1975.

————. *Textwissenschaft und Textanalyse. Semiotik, Linguistik, Rhetorik,* 2nd ed. Heidelberg: Quelle & Meyer, 1979.

Porten, Bezalel. "Egyptian Aramaic Texts," in *The Oxford Encyclopedia of Archaeology in the Near East,* 5 vols., ed. E. M. Meyers. New York, Oxford: Oxford University Press, 1997, 2.213-19.

Porter, Stanley E. "The Theoretical Justification for the Application of Rhetorical Categories to Pauline Epistolary Literature," in *Rhetoric and the New Testament: Essays from the 1992 Heidelberg Conference,* ed. S. E. Porter and T. H. Olbricht, JSNT.SS 90. Sheffield: Sheffield Academic Press, 1993, 110-16.

————, ed. *Handbook of Classical Rhetoric in the Hellenistic Period, 300 B.C.–A.D. 400.* Brill: Leiden, 1997.

Porter, Stanley E., and Thomas H. Olbricht, eds. *Rhetoric and the New Testament: Essays from the 1992 Heidelberg Conference.* JSNT.SS 90. Sheffield: Sheffield Academic Press, 1993.

————, eds. *Rhetoric, Scripture and Theology: Essays from the 1994 Pretoria Conference.* JSNT.SS 131. Sheffield: Sheffield Academic Press, 1996.

————, eds. *The Rhetorical Analysis of Scripture: Essays from the 1995 London Conference.* JSNT.SS 146. Sheffield: Sheffield Academic Press, 1997.

Porter, Stanley E., and Dennis L. Stamps, eds. *The Rhetorical Interpretation of Scripture. Essays from the 1996 Malibu Conference.* JSNT.SS 180. Sheffield: Sheffield Academic Press, 1999.

————, eds. *Rhetorical Criticism and the Bible: Essays from the 1998 Florence Conference.* JSNT.SS 195. Sheffield: Sheffield Academic Press, 2002.

Quintilian. *Institutio Oratoria* [The training of an orator], 12 bks., 4 vols., trans. H. E. Butler. LCL. Cambridge: Harvard University Press, 1920-1922.

Raymond, James C. "Enthymemes, Examples, and Rhetorical Method," in *Essays in Classical Rhetoric and Modern Discourse,* ed. R. J. Connors, *et al.* Carbondale: University of Southern Illinois Press, 1984, 140-51.

Reed, Jeffrey T. "Using Ancient Rhetorical Categories to Interpret Paul's Letters: A Question of Genre," in *Rhetoric and the New Testament: Essays from the 1992 Heidelberg Conference,* ed. S. E. Porter and T. H. Olbricht. JSNT.SS 90. Sheffield: Sheffield Academic Press, 1993, 292-324.

Roberts, J. H. "The Eschatological Transitions to the Pauline Letter Body," *Neot* 29 (1986) 29-35.

————. "Pauline Transitions in the Letter Body," in *L'Apôtre Paul. Personalité, Style et Conception du Ministère,* ed. A. Vanhoye. Leuven: Leuven University Press, 1986, 93-99.

Roller, Otto. *Das Formular der paulinischen Briefe. Ein Beitrag zur Lehre vom antiken Briefe.* Stuttgart: Kohlhammer, 1933.

Sanders, James T. "The Transition from Opening Epistolary Thanksgiving to Body in the Letters of the Pauline Corpus," *JBL* 81 (1962) 348-62.

Schmeller, Thomas. *Paulus und die 'Diatribe': Eine vergleichende Stilinterpretation.* NTAbh 19. Münster: Aschendorff, 1987.

Schnider, Franz, and Werner Stenger. *Studien zum Neutestamentlichen Briefformular.* NTTS 11. Leiden: Brill, 1987.

Schoedel, William R. "Apologetic Literature and Ambassadorial Activities," *HTR* 82 (1989) 55-78.

Schubert, Paul. *Form and Function of the Pauline Thanksgivings.* Berlin: Töpelmann, 1939.

Scroggs, Robin. "Paul as Rhetorician: Two Homilies in Romans 1–11," in *Jews, Greeks, and Christians (Festschrift* for W. D. Davies), ed. R. Hammerton-Kelly and R. Scroggs. Leiden: Brill, 1976, 271-98.

Smith, P. Christopher. *The Hermeneutics of Original Argument: Demonstration, Dialectic, Rhetoric.* Evanston: Northwestern University Press, 1998.

Standaert, Benoît. "La rhétorique ancienne dans saint Paul," in *L'Apôtre Paul. Personalité, Style et Conception du Ministère,* ed. A. Vanhoye. Leuven: University Press, 1986, 78-92.

Stirewalt, M. Luther, Jr. "Paul's Evaluation of Letter-Writing," in *Search the Scriptures,* ed. J. M. Myers, *et al.* Leiden: Brill, 1969, 179-96.

————. "The Form and Function of the Greek Letter-Essay," in Donfried, ed., *Romans Debate* (1977), 175-206; (1991), 147-71.

————. *Paul, the Letter Writer.* Grand Rapids: Eerdmans, 2003.

Stowers, Stanley K. *The Diatribe and Paul's Letter to the Romans.* SBL.DS 57. Chico: Scholars, 1981.

———. *Letter Writing in Greco-Roman Antiquity.* Philadelphia: Westminster, 1986.

———. "The Diatribe," in *Greco-Roman Literature and the New Testament,* ed. D. E. Aune. SBL.SBS 21. Atlanta: Scholars, 1988, 71-83.

———. "Diatribe," in *Anchor Bible Dictionary,* 6 vols., ed. D. N. Freedman. New York: Doubleday, 1992, 2.190-93.

———. *A Rereading of Romans: Justice, Jews, and Gentiles.* New Haven: Yale University Press, 1994.

Sykutris, Johannes. "Epistolographie," in *Realencyclopädie der classischen Altertums-wissenschaft,* ed. A. Pauly, G. Wissowa, *et al.* Suppl. 5. Stuttgart: Metzler, 1931, 186-220.

Thomson, Ian H. *Chiasmus in the Pauline Letters.* Sheffield: Sheffield Academic Press, 1995.

Thurén, Lauri. *Derhetorizing Paul.* WUNT 124. Tübingen: Mohr Siebeck, 2000.

Watson, Duane F. "Diatribe," in *Dictionary of Paul and His Letters,* ed. G. R. Hawthorne and R. P. Martin. Downers Grove: InterVarsity, 1993, 213-14.

———. "Rhetorical Criticism of the Pauline Epistles Since 1975," *Currents in Research: Biblical Studies* 3 (1995) 219-48.

———. "The Contributions and Limitations of Greco-Roman Rhetorical Theory for Constructing the Rhetorical and Historical Situations of a Pauline Epistle," in *The Rhetorical Interpretation of Scripture: Essays from the 1996 Malibu Confer-ence,* ed. S. E. Porter and D. L. Stamp. JSNT.SS 180. Sheffield: Sheffield Academic Press, 1999, 125-51.

———. "Rhetorical Criticism, New Testament," in *Dictionary of Biblical Interpretation,* 2 vols., ed. J. H. Hayes. Nashville: Abingdon, 1999, 399-402.

Watson, Duane F., ed. *Persuasive Artistry: Studies in New Testament Rhetoric in Honor of G. A. Kennedy.* JSNT.SS 50. Sheffield: Sheffield Academic Press, 1991.

Watson, Duane F., and A. J. Hauser. *Rhetorical Criticism of the Bible: A Comprehensive Bibliography, with Notes on History and Method.* Biblical Interpretation Series 4. Leiden: Brill, 1994.

Weima, Jeffrey A. D. *Neglected Endings: The Significance of the Pauline Letter Closings.* Sheffield: Sheffield Academic Press, 1994.

———. "Preaching the Gospel in Rome: A Study of the Epistolary Framework of Romans," in *Gospel in Paul: Studies on Corinthians, Galatians and Romans for Richard N. Longenecker,* ed. L. A. Jervis and P. Richardson. Sheffield: Sheffield Academic Press, 1994, 337-66.

Weiss, Johannes. "Beiträge zur paulinischen Rhetorik," in *Theologische Studien. Herrn Professor D. Bernhard Weiss zu seinem 70 Geburtstage dargebracht,* ed. C. R. Gregory *et al.* Göttingen: Vandenhoeck & Ruprecht, 1897, 165-247.

Wendland, Paul. *Die urchristlichen Literaturformen.* HNT 1.3. Tübingen: Mohr, 1912, 339-45.

Wente, Edward. *Letters from Ancient Egypt.* SBL.WAW 1. Atlanta: Scholars, 1990.

White, John L. "Introductory Formulae in the Body of the Pauline Letter," *JBL* 90 (1971) 91-97.

—————. *The Form and Function of the Body of the Greek Letter: A Study of the Letter-Body in the Non-Literary Papyri and in Paul the Apostle.* SBL.DS 5. Missoula: Scholars, 1972.

—————. *The Form and Structure of the Official Petition.* Missoula: University of Montana, 1972.

—————. "Epistolary Formulas and Clichés in Greek Papyrus Letters," *SBL Seminar Papers* 2 (1978) 289-319.

—————. "The Greek Documentary Letter Tradition, Third Century B.C.E. to Third Century C.E.," *Semeia* 22 (1981) 89-106.

—————. "Saint Paul and the Apostolic Letter Tradition," *CBQ* 45 (1983) 433-44.

—————. "New Testament Epistolary Literature in the Framework of Ancient Epistolography," *ANRW* II.25.2 (1984) 1730-56.

—————. *Light from Ancient Letters.* Philadelphia: Fortress, 1986.

—————. "Ancient Greek Letters," in *Greco-Roman Literature and the New Testament,* ed. D. E. Aune. SBL.SBS 21. Atlanta: Scholars, 1988, 85-106.

White, John L., and K. Kensinger. "Categories of Greek Papyrus Letters," in *SBL 1976 Seminar Papers,* ed. G. MacRae. Missoula: Scholars, 1976, 79-92.

Wilder, Amos N. *The Language of the Gospel: Early Christian Rhetoric.* New York: Harper & Row, 1964; repr. and retitled as *Early Christian Rhetoric: The Language of the Gospel.* Cambridge, MA: Harvard University Press, 1971.

Wuellner, Wilhelm. "Greek Rhetoric and Pauline Argumentation," in *Early Christian Literature and the Classical Intellectual Tradition: In honorem Robert M. Grant,* ed. W. R. Schoedel and R. L. Wilken. TH 53. Paris: Beauchesne, 1979, 177-88.

—————. "Paul's Rhetoric of Argumentation in Romans: An Alternative to the Donfried-Karris Debate over Romans," *CBQ* 38 (1976) 330-51; repr. in Donfried, ed., *Romans Debate* (1977), 152-74; (1991), 128-46.

—————. "Where Is Rhetorical Criticism Taking Us?" *CBQ* 49 (1987) 448-63.

CHAPTER VII

Jewish and Jewish Christian Procedures and Themes

Just as it is important in any scholarly study of Romans to give close attention to the Greco-Roman oral, rhetorical, and epistolary conventions that appear in the letter (as we have highlighted in the previous chapter), so it is necessary to take into account some of the more prominent Jewish and Jewish Christian procedures and themes that appear in the warp and woof of Paul's argument in his letter. Thus, having dealt in Chapter VI with certain oral, rhetorical, and epistolary conventions of antiquity that appear in Romans, here in Chapter VII we will give attention to some of the procedures and themes that were common among Jews and Jewish Christians of Paul's day and that also appear in his letter to the Christians at Rome.

1. Biblical Quotations and Allusions

The use of the OT by the writers of the NT has always been of interest to Christians. Sometimes the NT's use of the OT has been an embarrassment (as with Marcion and his followers); at times the OT has been treated in an allegorical fashion (as with Origen and the Alexandrian interpreters); frequently it has been understood in a historical fashion (as with Chrysostom and the Antiochean interpreters); and most often it has been used in a devotional manner (as by many Christians down through the centuries and today). Critical biblical scholarship of the nineteenth and twentieth centuries, however, was always interested in the use of the Jewish (OT) Scriptures by the NT authors.

The contemporary comparative study of Paul's use of the OT was inaugurated by Henry St. John Thackeray in his 1900 book *The Relation of St.* *Paul to Contemporary Jewish Thought*. And in that publication Thackeray began his discussion of Paul's use of Scripture with the following comment: "There is perhaps no aspect of Pauline theology in which the influence of the Apostle's Rabbinic training is so clearly marked as the use which is made of the Old Testament."[1] From this very important beginning, investigations (1) have expanded to deal with the use of the OT by all of the various NT writers, (2) have intensified by way of greater clarity and precision in the questions asked, (3) have developed by reference to comparable (whether the same, similar, or different) ways of using Scripture among the various groups of Jews and Jewish Christians in Paul's day, and (4) have moved forward, in what has often seemed a process of "trial and error," by means of the positing of a variety of hypotheses and methods that have sought to understand and explicate how Paul, as well as each of the other NT writers, used the OT Scriptures.[2]

Some Commonly Asked Questions about Paul's Use of Scripture in Romans

Prominent in this rather large body of research has been a focus on how Paul used Scripture in Romans, with a number of questions commonly being asked. One obvious question has been: Why did Paul quote and allude to so many biblical passages in writing the Christians at Rome, when elsewhere in his letters he is more reserved in his use of Scripture? For of the eighty-three or so places in the Pauline corpus where biblical quotations appear — which total approximately one hundred OT passages if one disengages the conflated texts and separates the possible dual sources — well over half of them are to be found in Romans: 45 of a total 83 in all of the thirteen canonical Pauline letters (or 55-60 biblical passages of about 100 passages total, if the conflated texts and dual sources are unpacked and counted separately). Likewise there can be identified in Romans a rather large number of OT allusions. Yet outside of Romans in the Pauline corpus there are far fewer quotations of Scripture and also fewer allusions: to count the explicit quotations

1. H. St.-J. Thackeray, *Relation of St. Paul to Contemporary Jewish Thought*, 180.
2. For a somewhat mechanical indicator of the burgeoning interest and rapidly increasing scholarly production in this field of study, see the bibliography of 530 books and articles (with about 186 having been published during the quarter century from 1975 to 1999) in R. N. Longenecker, *Biblical Exegesis in the Apostolic Period*, 2nd ed. (1999).

alone, only 15 in 1 Corinthians, 7 in 2 Corinthians, 10 in Galatians, 4 in Ephesians, 1 in 1 Timothy, and 1 in 2 Timothy, with none in 1 Thessalonians, 2 Thessalonians, Philippians, Colossians, Philemon, or Titus.

It might even, in fact, be asked: Why did Paul use biblical quotations and allusions at all in writing to the Christians at Rome, particularly when he identifies his addressees as those who were within the orbit of his Gentile ministry (1:5-6; 13-15; 15:15-16), explicitly calls them Gentiles (11:13), and distinguishes their ancestry from his Jewish ancestry (9:3; 11:14)? One could understand why he quoted Scripture and alluded to it so often when writing to the Galatians and the Corinthians, because (1) the problems at Galatia stemmed largely from a group of "Judaizers" who had infiltrated the Galatian Christian congregations and were themselves using the OT for their own purposes, and (2) the "Peter party" at Corinth had been proposing some form of Jewish Christian propaganda. The quotations of the OT in the letter to Ephesus and in the two letters to Timothy, though much less frequent, might even be justified on the bases of (1) the essential content of our canonical "Ephesians" as having been originally written as something of a circular letter to ethnically mixed congregations in western Asia Minor, and (2) the letters to Timothy as having been written to a young Christian convert who had been trained in the Jewish (OT) Scriptures by his grandmother and mother. But Romans cannot easily be "mirror read" so as to identify any Jewish or Jewish Christian problem among the Christian congregations at Rome, any Jewish opponents, or any distinctly Jewish Christian protagonists. And Paul's usual practice when writing Gentile Christians — especially when writing Gentile believers in Jesus who had not been influenced by Jewish or Jewish Christian thought, nor affected by a problem of Jewish Christian agitation — was not to quote or allude to OT passages at all in support of his arguments (though, of course, his language was always informed by biblical idioms and expressions), as witness his letters to his Gentile converts at Thessalonica, Philippi, and Colosse and to the two Gentile Christians named Philemon and Titus.

In addition, when dealing with the form of the biblical texts that Paul quotes, the question often arises: Why do the text forms of Paul's quotations of Scripture differ from those attributed to Jesus in the four Gospels and those credited to the earliest preachers in the Book of Acts? For in Paul's quotations, both in Romans and throughout his other letters, there appears a rather peculiar mix of textual readings. Over half of the Pauline text forms are either absolute or virtual reproductions of the LXX, with about half of these at variance with the MT. Yet almost another half vary from both the

LXX and the MT to a greater or lesser extent. And once in Romans (11:35, citing Job 41:11 in a traditional theocentric doxology), as well as three times elsewhere in the Pauline corpus (1 Cor 3:19, citing Job 5:13; 2 Cor 9:9, citing Ps 112:9; and 2 Tim 2:19, citing Num 16:5), the text of Paul's biblical quotation is in agreement with the MT against the LXX. By contrast, however, the texts used by Jesus, the earliest Christian preachers, and most of the NT writers seem to be almost exclusively septuagintal in form.

Likewise, in dealing with Paul's interpretation of OT texts, it has frequently been asked: How can the wide scope of his treatment be understood, ranging, as it does, from his quite literal "pearl-stringing" of biblical quotations in Rom 3:10-18 to his seeming disregard of the original text and context of the OT passage in Rom 10:6-8 (with Deut 30:12-14 being cited in an inexact and possibly proverbial manner to his own advantage; cf. also Eph 4:8, where Ps 68:18 is cited in a similar fashion)? Further, it needs to be asked: What does it mean to speak of Paul's "christocentric" exegesis, and how did such an orientation affect his interpretation of Scripture?

The Question about the Distribution of Biblical Quotations in Romans

What has not been asked as frequently, however, is the question: Why is the distribution of OT quotations in Romans, as well as the distribution of recognizable allusions to Scripture in the letter, so uneven? For to take the more observable and demonstrable cases of explicit biblical quotations: about 18 of them appear in eight or nine places in 1:16–4:25 and about 30 more appear in twenty-five or so places in 9–11 — with an additional 10 to be found in the ethical exhortations of 12:1–15:13 and 1 more in the body closing or "Apostolic Parousia" of 15:14-32 — whereas explicit biblical quotations occur only twice, and then somewhat tangentially, in what has seemed to many interpreters to be the apex of Paul's argument in 5–8 (i.e., once in 7:7, citing in illustrative fashion the tenth commandment "Do not covet" of Exod 20:17 and Deut 5:21, and once in 8:36, in what appears to be a traditional confessional portion that makes use of Ps 44:22).

What appears in 1:18–3:20 can be cited as one prominent example of the focused use of biblical quotations and allusions by Paul in his indictment of all humanity, Gentiles and Jews alike. For as Richard Hays has characterized the argument in this section of the apostle's letter: in 1:18–2:29 Paul "weaves together themes and language reminiscent of Old Testament wisdom and prophecy as well as of several intertestamental Jewish writings," with "the texture of Paul's language" in 2:1-16 being particularly "densely allusive"; then in 3:1-20 Paul's argument bursts forth "like a fireworks display toward a climactic explosion of scriptural condemnations in Rom 3:10-18," which is followed by two concluding verses on the purpose of the Mosaic law and the inability of anyone to gain righteousness through "works of the law."[3] And a similar concentration of biblical quotations, together at times with biblical allusions, appears in the positive affirmations of 3:21–4:25, in the exposition on the Christian gospel vis-à-vis God's promises to Israel of 9–11, and in the ethical exhortations of chapters 12 and 13:8-14 — though not in the second major section of the body middle of the letter, that is, in 5–8, which sets out the important themes of "peace," "reconciliation," and "life in Christ."[4]

This pattern of distribution in Romans is frequently ignored — or, when noted, is usually treated as being unimportant. There have been times, however, when this seemingly strange distribution of OT quotations and allusions in Paul's letters — and in Romans particularly — has been both observed and taken seriously, with various explanations given.

Adolf von Harnack, for example, long ago highlighted this phenomenon of OT usage and developed from it a circumstantial understanding of Paul's use of Scripture, arguing that the apostle quoted the Jewish (OT) Scriptures in his letters only when confronting Jewish opposition — which, of course, Harnack identified as opposition from "the Judaizers."[5] Robin Scroggs used this difference of distribution to argue that Romans 1–11 contains two Pauline sermons with two distinctly different types of rhetoric: one sermon that was originally preached to a Jewish audience in which Paul quoted Scripture, with this sermon now appearing in chapters 1–4 and 9–11 of Romans (whose parts have somehow become separated); the other sermon originally proclaimed to a Gentile audience in which Paul did not quote Scripture, which material now appears in chapters 5–8.[6] And Christiaan

---

3. R. B. Hays, *Echoes of Scripture in the Letters of Paul,* 41.

4. Allusions to Adam are often seen, as well, in the second major section of the body middle of the letter (i.e., in 5:1–8:39), particularly in 5:1-11 and 7:7-12 — though if that is the case (as seems probable) Paul draws such allusions into his argument in a manner that has a broad application even to Gentiles who would have known little or nothing about Adam himself (see Chapter XI, "Structure and Argument").

5. A. von Harnack, "Das alte Testament in den paulinischen Briefen und in den paulinischen Gemeinden," *Sitzungsberichte der Preussischen Akademie der Wissenschaften zu Berlin* (1928) 124-41.

6. R. Scroggs, "Paul as Rhetorician: Two Homilies in Romans 1–11," in *Jews, Greeks,*

Beker has spoken of "the peculiar appearance and disappearance of Scripture in Romans" as reflecting the factors of "coherence and contingency" in Paul's thought, and has proposed from this pattern of usage that "where the Jewish question is no longer an issue in the Gentile church, the hermeneutic of Old Testament Scripture is left behind."[7] (Further, by way of analogy, it may be observed that a similar pattern of distribution occurs in the Acts of the Apostles, where biblical quotations and clear allusions appear in the portrayals of the church's mission to the Jewish world in the first fifteen chapters and in the representations of Paul's words before Jewish audiences in chapter 13 [in a Jewish synagogue at Antioch], chapter 23 [before the Sanhedrin at Jerusalem], and chapter 28 [to Jewish leaders at Rome] — but not in the accounts of Paul's Gentile mission and his preaching to Gentiles.)

It is this pattern of the distribution of biblical quotations and allusions, in Paul's letters generally — as well as in his letter to the Christians at Rome in particular — that provides interpreters a significant interpretive key in the study of Paul.[8] For apart from a realization of this feature in the apostle's practice, the study of Paul's use of Scripture can easily become so generalized as to fail miserably in appreciating how he used biblical quotations and allusions circumstantially when addressing Jews, Jewish believers in Jesus, and Gentile Christians who have been influenced extensively by Jewish Christianity — in order (1) to build bridges of commonality with his hearers and addressees, and (2) to support and focus his arguments in ways that they would appreciate and understand.

The Question about Inner-Biblical Exegesis or Extra-Biblical Exegesis

One rather large question regarding the use of Scripture by Paul and the other NT writers, which lately has become something of a "burning issue" in certain quarters, has to do with methodology in the study of Paul's OT quotations. The question is this: Are we to understand the use of Scripture in the NT, and particularly by Paul, using what has been called an "inner-biblical" exegesis, which usually means among Christian scholars confining our in-

---

and Christians (Festschrift for W. D. Davies), ed. R. Hamerton-Kelly and R. Scroggs (Leiden: Brill, 1976), 271-98.

7. J. C. Beker, "Echoes and Intertextuality," 64-65.

8. Cf. my earlier treatments of the distribution of Paul's quotations in R. N. Longenecker, Biblical Exegesis in the Apostolic Period (1975[1], 1999[2]); idem, "Prolegomena to Paul's Use of Scripture in Romans," BBR 7 (1997) 145-68.

vestigations to the literary and theological parallels that exist between the two canonical testaments,[9] or also by means of an "extra-biblical" exegesis, which will be taken here to signify a comparative, historical analysis of the exegetical procedures of the NT authors vis-à-vis the conventions, practices, and themes that can be found in the Greco-Roman world generally and in the writings and traditions of Early Judaism in particular?[10] An inner-biblical method confines itself almost entirely to literary and theological parallels in the Jewish (OT) Scriptures and the Christian (NT) Scriptures, thereby working mainly with canonical "intertextuality," and is synchronic in nature. An extra-biblical method, however, while acknowledging the importance of an inner-biblical type of treatment, also (1) recognizes extra-canonical materials as being of aid in one's attempt to understand the hermeneutical mindsets and exegetical practices of the NT writers, (2) understands the term "intertextuality" in a broader sense to mean interpreted texts as they have been used and reused in a wider historical spectrum, and (3) is diachronic as well as synchronic in nature.

No one working in the field, of course, would deny — at least in theory — the presence of non-biblical influences on the writers of the NT. In practice, however, many NT interpreters have tended to bracket such historical investigations, preferring, as Richard Hays says of his own approach to the study of Paul's use of Scripture, to give "the place of honor to the privileged predecessor that Paul himself explicitly acknowledged [i.e., the OT]," and so to limit themselves "to an exploration of the intertextual echoes of Israel's Scripture in Paul."[11] This approach is reflected in the writings of a whole

9. Among Jewish scholars it means a focus on the Bible of Judaism — that is, on Scripture as read and interpreted by the rabbis of the early centuries of the Common Era.

10. I prefer to use the expressions "inner-biblical exegesis" and "extra-biblical exegesis" in comparing and contrasting these two exegetical approaches, rather than "intertextuality," "intratextuality," or "interpreted intertextuality." The term "intertextuality" is of recent coinage in both Jewish and Christian circles. It denotes not just relationships between texts, but also relationships between texts and their cultures. Understood in this broad manner, it is an expression I applaud. The designation is also used, however, more narrowly to connote "intra-textuality" — that is, a literary and theological comparison of texts that is confined to "authoritative revelation" (i.e., Scripture, or the Written Torah) and "authentic interpretation" (i.e., the Talmud, the Midrashim and cognate materials, or the codified Oral Torah), as among Jewish scholars, or to the two canonical testaments (i.e., the Old Testament and the New Testament), as among Christian scholars. Given this understanding, I prefer another term.

11. R. B. Hays, *Echoes of Scripture in the Letters of Paul*, 16. Cf. M. Fishbane: "The paramount concern of the present work is exegesis found within the Hebrew Bible" (*Biblical Interpretation*, 3, passim).

host of biblical scholars today, who, while differing widely among themselves on matters of interpretation and application, hold rather strictly to such an inner-biblical methodology.[12] And this approach is defended by proponents of what has been called "canonical criticism," however variously that expression has been defined.[13]

An inner-biblical or inner-canonical approach to NT exegesis was generally the rule prior to the 1950s, and scholars who espouse such an approach today often appeal to those earlier writers in support. The Dead Sea Scrolls, however, have brought about nothing less than a revolution in the scholarly study of the NT. They have done this directly by their contents. For as Joseph Fitzmyer points out, they provide "a remarkable parallel and background for the interpretation of the Old Testament by New Testament writers" — with Fitzmyer going on to say: "Herein lies the greatest contribution to the study of the New Testament which has come from the study of the Qumran scrolls."[14] But they have also done this indirectly by alerting biblical scholars to the importance of studying afresh the cognate writings and traditions of Early Judaism. Today, in fact, despite frequent protestations otherwise, it is impossible to give a fair hearing to the exegesis of the NT without also interacting with the various exegetical practices found in the writings of Early Judaism — whether it be those found in the Dead Sea texts themselves, in the other pseudepigraphical and apocalyptic writings of Second Temple Judaism, or in the later rabbinic codifications of earlier Pharisaic teaching.

It is possible, of course, to become overly enamored with historical, diachronic studies of the exegetical procedures of the NT vis-à-vis those of Early Judaism. "Parallelomania," as Samuel Sandmel once warned biblical scholars, is an ever-present danger.[15] Nonetheless, while attempting always to guard against that danger, I believe Geza Vermes's perspective is still valid and important:

> In inter-testamental Judaism there existed a fundamental unity of exegetical tradition. This tradition, the basis of religious faith and life,

---

12. For a list of representative scholars who take such a stance, see R. N. Longenecker, *Biblical Exegesis in the Apostolic Period,* 2nd ed. (1999), xx-xxi.

13. For a listing of such advocates and their proposals on this issue, see R. N. Longenecker, *Biblical Exegesis in the Apostolic Period,* 2nd ed. (1999), xxi.

14. J. A. Fitzmyer, "Dead Sea Scrolls and the New Testament after Thirty Years," 351-66. For examples, see idem, "Use of Explicit Old Testament Quotations in Qumran Literature and in the New Testament," 297-333.

15. S. Sandmel, "Parallelomania," 1-13.

was adopted and modified by its constituent groups, the Pharisees, the Qumran sectaries and the Judeo-Christians. We have, as a result, three cognate schools of exegesis of the one message recorded in the Bible, and it is the duty of the historian to emphasize that none of them can properly be understood independently of the others.[16]

It is such a stance, however derived, that is reflected in the work of a number of scholars today, both Jewish and Christian. And I join them in reaffirming my commitment to a historical and comparative study of the NT's use of the OT — not as "the be all and end all" of investigation, but as a highly significant aid in such a study.

A Brief Summation

In any serious study of Romans it is necessary, therefore, for interpreters to give attention to Paul's use of Scripture in building his arguments — particularly in his theological sections of 1:16–4:25 and 9–11, but also in his ethical exhortations of 12:1–15:13. And in all of these considerations of this critical issue, it is important to ask both "inner-biblical" and "extra-biblical" questions. That is, it is important to ask (1) How does Paul's use of Scripture in Romans compare to the use of the "earlier prophets" (including Moses in the Pentateuch) by the "later prophets" in the Jewish (OT) Scriptures? (2) How does it compare to the use of Scripture by the other NT writers? and (3) How does it compare to Paul's own use of Scripture in his other canonical letters, particularly in Galatians where there is an overlap of topics and similar expositions? But it is also important to ask (4) How does Paul's use of Scripture in Romans compare with that of the Jewish teachers of Second Temple Judaism and early Rabbinic Judaism, and what effect does an understanding of these exegetical practices have on our understanding of Paul's treatment of the OT? and (5) How does it compare to the exegetical practices of the Jewish sectarians of the Qumran community, as represented in the Dead Sea Scrolls, and to the practices of Philo of Alexandria, the Jewish philosopher-theologian and allegorical biblical interpreter, in his numerous writings?

16. G. Vermes, "The Qumran Interpretation of Scripture in Its Historical Setting," 85-97.

2. Confessional Affirmations and Other Traditional Materials

A further area of critical concern with regard to the study of Romans has to do with Paul's use of early confessional affirmations, religious aphorisms, and devotional or catechetical materials that presumably originated within the contexts of Jewish and/or Jewish Christian worship, instruction, and piety.[17] The identification and study of these traditional materials in the NT generally — and in Paul's letters in particular — began in the late nineteenth century and the early part of the twentieth century, and has been especially prominent during the last half of the twentieth century.[18] Form criticism is the necessary tool for identifying these pre-Pauline materials. And content analysis serves to highlight their central features and their use in early Christian thought and practice. Most important for a serious study of Romans, however, is the spelling out of how Paul used these materials to structure, support, and summarize the main points of his argument in his letter to the Christians at Rome.

There are a number of indications that there exists within Romans a "mother lode" of early Christian confessional material — as well as various aphoristic statements and certain devotional or catechetical formulations of Jewish and/or Jewish Christian origin — which have yet to be sufficiently mined out and whose nuggets of information can aid in understanding the nature of Paul's message and appreciating the methods that he used in its proclamation. Many of these confessional materials, aphoristic statements, and devotional or catechetical formulations will be highlighted in Chapter XI, "Structure and Argument" (and developed further in a forthcoming exegetical commentary). Suffice it here (1) to draw attention to these confes-

---

17. In Acts 17:28 Paul is portrayed as quoting two Gentile religious aphorisms ("In him we live and move and have our being"; "For we too are his offspring"); in 1 Cor 15:32-33 he quotes two Gentile ethical maxims ("Let us eat and drink, for tomorrow we die"; "Bad company ruins good morals"); and in Titus 1:12 he cites a statement of some unnamed Cretan prophet ("Cretans are always liars, vicious brutes, lazy gluttons") — using all of these materials from the Gentile world for his own purposes. In Romans, however, while he may in 7:14-24 be expressing some of the angst and phraseology of the tragic soliloquies of the Greek world (which is a matter that will be touched on in Chapter XI, "Structure and Argument," but must also be treated more extensively in a future exegetical commentary), Paul mainly confines himself to quoting confessional affirmations, religious aphorisms, and devotional or catechetical materials that seem to have originated within the contexts of Jewish and/or Jewish Christian worship, instruction, and piety.

18. For a brief history of such identifications and study, see R. N. Longenecker, *New Wine into Fresh Wineskins* (1999), 5-44.

sional and other traditional materials in Romans, and (2) to indicate how Paul uses them in his letter. What has been, to date, most commonly identified as early Christian confessional material within Paul's letter to the Christians at Rome are (1) the theocentric hymn of praise to God in 11:33-36, (2) the christological formulations that appear in 1:3-4; 3:24-26 (or, more narrowly, 3:25-26a); and 4:25, and (3) the single-statement affirmation of the Lordship of Christ in 10:9. Portions of the lyrical and almost defiant affirmation of 8:33-39 should probably also be seen as being confessional in nature. Perhaps there are also echoes of such material in 9:5b ("Who is God over all, forever praised! Amen") and 14:9 ("Christ died and returned to life so that he might be the Lord of both the dead and the living").

Each of these portions has a strategic place in the overall argument of Romans. The material of 1:3-4 appears in the salutation of the letter, with that salutation being used by Paul to highlight a number of the themes that he intends to develop later in the letter. Similarly, 3:24-26 (or, perhaps, 3:25-26a) is used to support what most commentators have viewed as a major thesis statement of the letter, that is, the paragraph thesis statement of 3:21-23 — whether that paragraph reiterates (or, as probably better stated, repeats and expands upon) the former thesis statement of 1:16-17. And 10:9 appears at the heart of Paul's discussion of the Christian gospel and the hope of Israel in chapters 9–11, while 14:9 appears at the heart of his exhortations regarding the weak and the strong.

Further, some of these confessional portions appear as the final items of their respective sections in the letter, and so serve to summarize and conclude what was said in those sections. Rom 4:25 ("Who was delivered over to death for our sins, and was raised to life for our justification") seems to function in this manner, summarizing, as it does, the central thesis statements of 1:16-17 and 3:21-31 and bringing to a climax the whole presentation of 1:16–4:25. Likewise, the forceful affirmations of 8:33-39, which probably include a number of early confessional statements, summarize and bring to a dramatic conclusion all that Paul has written in 5:1–8:32. And while it may be debated whether chapters 9–11 begin with a portion that includes a confessional doxology at 9:5b, certainly the majestic hymn of praise to God in 11:33-36 is confessional in nature and provides a fitting climax to those three chapters.

In addressing Christians at Rome, Paul seems to have used a number of early Christian confessional materials, whether in whole or in part, in at least two ways: (1) to support and focus his arguments, as he does with the materials of 1:3-4; 3:24-26; 10:9; and 14:9; and (2) to summarize and bring to a climax his presentations in the three main theological sections of his letter, as he does in 4:25; 8:33-39; and 11:33-36. Likewise, he appears to have incorporated certain traditional aphorisms and various then-existing Jewish and/ or Jewish Christian devotional and catechetical materials for much the same reasons, even though these latter materials may be less commonly recognized or discussed. The great body of exegetical detail that is necessary in order to identify properly and spell out adequately Paul's use of these confessional affirmations and other traditional materials must be left for a future Romans commentary. Suffice it here to say (1) that these pre-Pauline affirmations and materials were presumably known (whether in whole or in part) to Paul's Christian addressees at Rome (whether ethnically Jews or Gentiles), and (2) that Paul evidently used them to build bridges of commonality with his addressees, thereby instructing them in ways that they would understand and appreciate.

3. Remnant Theology and Rhetoric

Also of importance in any discussion of Jewish and Jewish Christian procedures and themes that have relevance for a serious study of Romans is "remnant theology and rhetoric." It is a type of thought and expression (1) that stems from a "remnant" (i.e., "chosen," "elect," and/or "survivor") understanding of God's people as expressed in the Jewish (OT) Scriptures, (2) that was used by the early Pharisees, the Dead Sea covenanters, and other Jewish sectarian groups to justify their existence, (3) that appears in a number of apocryphal and apocalyptic writings of Second Temple Judaism, (4) that was prominent in the ministry of John the Baptist in calling Jews to repentance and baptizing them,[19] (5) that was also present in the ministry of Jesus in inviting people to follow him,[20] referring to his followers as his "little flock,"[21] and calling them "my sheep";[22] and (6) that became, it seems, a major factor in the self-consciousness of the earliest Jewish believers in Jesus.[23] Further, it

19. Cf. Mark 1:2-6, par.; this theme is also implicit in John's warning to the Pharisees and Sadducees: "Do not think you can say to yourselves, 'We have Abraham as our father'" (Matt 3:9).

20. Cf. Mark 1:16-20, par.

21. Luke 12:32.

22. John 10:1-30.

23. For important treatments of "remnant theology" and "remnant rhetoric" with respect to the religion of Israel, Second Temple Judaism, John the Baptist, Jesus, and early Jewish Christianity, see F. Kattenbusch, "Der Spruch über Petrus und die Kirche bei Matthäus"

may be postulated that remnant theology and rhetoric would have been understood and appreciated by Paul's Christian addressees at Rome, rooted as they were (both Gentile and Jewish believers in Jesus) in the theology of the Mother Church at Jerusalem (see Chapter IV, "Addressees").

A highlighting of remnant theology, with its accompanying remnant rhetoric, may have been included in Paul's proclamation of the Christian message in various Jewish synagogues — not only prior to taking up his distinctive Gentile mission,[24] but also during his Gentile mission when he spoke in the various Jewish synagogues of the cities he visited.[25] And such a theology and rhetoric are highlighted in Romans 9–11 in the following ways:

1. by the quotation in 9:27 of Isa 10:22-23, which uses the articular and intensified form τό ὑπόλειμμα ("though the number of the Israelites should be like the sand by the sea, only 'the remnant' will be saved");
2. by the quotation in 9:29 of Isa 1:9, which uses the noun σπέρμα (literally: "seed," "posterity," or "descendant") in the figurative sense of "a few survivors" ("if the Lord of Hosts had not left us 'a few survivors,' we would have become like Sodom and been made like Gomorrah"), thereby paralleling the meaning of the terms λεῖμμα and ὑπόλειμμα;
3. by the use in 9:11 and 11:5, 7, 28 of ἐκλογή ("election," "selection," or "choosing"; passive: "that which is elected," "selected," or "chosen"); and,
4. by the use in 11:5 of λεῖμμα ("remnant"), even bringing λεῖμμα and ἐκλογή together in this verse in a manner not represented elsewhere in the NT ("so, too, at this present time there is a 'remnant' that is 'chosen' by grace").

There has been a considerable amount of discussion over the past century regarding the concept of "remnant" in (1) the OT (focusing on שְׁאָר, "rest," "residue," "survivor," "remnant," and its plural שְׁאֵרִית, "survivors" or

---

(1922); K. L. Schmidt, "Die Kirche des Urchristentums" (1927); G. Gloege, *Reich Gottes und Kirche im Neuen Testament* (1929), 212-19 and 241-49; A. Oepke, "Der Herrnspruch über die Kirche" (1948); J. Jeremias, "Der Gedanke des 'Heiligen Restes' im Spätjudentum und in der Verkündigung Jesu" (1949); W. G. Kümmel, "Jesus und die Anfänge der Kirche" (1953); B. F. Meyer, "Jesus and the Remnant of Israel" (1965); G. F. Hasel, *The Remnant* (1972); B. F. Meyer, *The Aims of Jesus* (1979), esp. 118-21, 197, 220-22, 225-29; and particularly, of late, the magisterial work of M. A. Elliott, *The Survivors of Israel* (2000), *passim*.

24. Cf., e.g., Acts 9:20, 28-30.
25. Cf., e.g., Acts 13:5, 14, 42-44; 14:1; 17:1-2, 10, 17; 18:4, 19; 19:8, 24:12.

"the remnant") and (2) the writings of Second Temple Judaism (focusing on λεῖμμα and its intensified form ὑπόλειμμα, "remnant," as well as on the passive form of ἐκλογή, "elected," "selected," or "chosen"). Amidst all of the debate, however, Gottlob Schrenk and Volkmar Herntrich have most aptly set out, in relative brevity, the characteristic features of a Jewish remnant theology and rhetoric in their TDNT article on λεῖμμα, ὑπόλειμμα, and cognates,[26] from which the following points are abstracted:

1. *The remnant is sovereignly established by God alone.* In Isa 8:16-18 the prophet Isaiah recognizes that the community of disciples (i.e., "the children") gathered about him was a gift of God. The prophet did not have the task of creating or gathering it, that is, "the remnant." Rather, God creates it. This is expressly stated in the prologue to Isaiah's prophecy in 1:9: "Unless the Lord Almighty had left us some survivors [i.e., 'a remnant'], we would have become like Sodom, we would have been like Gomorrah." As Herntrich has pointed out: "The remnant has its existence in Yahweh alone."[27] Further, the remnant has its origin not in the excellence or quality of those being saved, but in the saving action of God. Thus in Mic 4:7 God is represented as saying: "I will make the lame a remnant, those driven away a strong people." Likewise in Mic 2:12 God proclaims that he himself will gather the remnant of Israel. We are told nothing about the faith or holiness of the remnant. God establishes it. That is enough.[28]

2. *The remnant may be small, but envisioned also is its greatness.* In Mic 4:7 (as quoted above) the term "remnant" is paralleled by the expression "a strong people." In Mic 5:7-8 the remnant is pictured "like dew from the Lord, like showers on the grass" (v. 7), but also as becoming "like a lion among the beasts of the forest, like a young lion among flocks of sheep" (v. 8). In Jer 23:3 God is portrayed as promising that in the future day of his intervention the remnant will increase and be fruitful: "I myself will gather the remnant of my flock out of all the countries where I have driven them, and I will bring them back to their pasture, where they will be fruitful and multiply." And this idea of the present smallness but future greatness of the remnant is, as Herntrich points out, "often found in passages where the remnant concept is materially, if not linguistically, present."[29]

3. *The remnant is both a present and a future entity.* The uniqueness of

---

26. G. Schrenk and V. Herntrich, λεῖμμα, ὑπόλειμμα, καταλείπω, TDNT 4.194-214.
27. TDNT 4.203.
28. Cf. TDNT 4.203.
29. TDNT 4.205.

eschatological proclamation in the OT includes the fact that the remnant is referred to as both a present and a future entity. While various remnants are spoken about in what appear to be more quantitative terms in the earlier materials of the OT,[30] qualitative nuances having to do with election by God and faithfulness to God begin to appear in the writing prophets. In Isa 1:8-9, for example, though "the Daughter of Zion [i.e., Jerusalem]" is depicted as having been "left like a shelter in a vineyard, like a hut in a field of melons, like a city under siege," the "Lord Almighty" still protects the few "survivors" (i.e., the remnant) of the city; in Isa 8:16-18 the remnant that is constituted by God is the prophet Isaiah and his disciples; and in Isa 46:3-4 God promises to sustain and save "all the remnant of the house of Israel" (v. 3). Likewise in Amos 5:15 God promises to have mercy on "the remnant of Joseph."

It is particularly in the prophecy of Isaiah, however, that the interrelation of present historical events and future eschatological events is most clearly seen — especially in those messianic passages where the coming of the Messiah is represented as being both directly imminent (7:10-25) and in the process of enactment (9:5-7). The prophet also speaks of a sign given "to you" (7:14) and a son given "to us" (9:6), with both of those personal pronouns having reference to the remnant that is alluded to 8:16-18.[31]

4. *The remnant is commonly associated with Zion, the city of Jerusalem.* Throughout the writings of the OT prophets there is a common linking of the remnant with Zion, the city of Jerusalem. In the prophecy of Isaiah, Zion is itself represented as a remnant (cf. 1:8: "The Daughter of Zion [i.e., Jerusalem] is left like a shelter in a vineyard, like a hut in a field of melons, like a city under siege"). But also in the prophecy of Isaiah, Zion is the home of those who remain (4:2-6); the prophet and his followers are "signs and symbols in Israel from the Lord Almighty, who dwells on Mount Zion" (8:16-18); and God establishes the remnant in Zion (28:16-17). Further, in Isa 37:32 it is said that "out from Jerusalem will go a remnant, and out from Mount Zion a band of survivors" (cf. also 2 Kgs 19:31).

In Micah, as well, the remnant is closely associated with Zion, the city of Jerusalem (4:1-2), or with Bethlehem (5:1-4). In Zeph 3:11-13 the gathered remnant is brought into relation with the holy land (cf. also Isa 11:4; 14:32), and in Jer 31:6-7 the remnant is summoned to come to Zion. In Zechariah the new creation of the remnant by Yahweh will take place in Jerusalem (8:1-6) and a portion of the population of Jerusalem in the day of the Lord will

---

30. Cf. *TDNT* 4.205.
31. Cf. *TDNT* 4.205.

remain as the remnant (14:2). And in Ezra 9:8, 13, 15 and Neh 1:2-3 the delivered remnant and the city of Jerusalem are also closely connected.[32]

5. *While God establishes the remnant, the other side of that establishment is a response of faith and faithfulness on the part of the remnant.* The primary emphasis in remnant theology is on the deliverance by God of the remnant. A human response of trust or faith is not presented as a condition for belonging to the remnant, but simply assumed as the other side of its establishment. It is only after the establishment of the remnant that we read of the people's faith and faithfulness in response. Even in Zeph 3:12-13 ("But I will leave within you the meek and humble, who trust in the name of the Lord. The remnant of Israel will do no wrong; they will speak no lies, nor will deceit be found in their mouths"), qualities of trust, righteousness, and honesty are represented as being simply the other side of the establishment of the remnant by Yahweh.[33]

6. *Not only is there envisioned a remnant of Israel, but also a remnant from among the Gentiles.* Judgment on the nations is an established part of OT eschatological expectation. But the nations are not extirpated. A remnant of the Gentiles will remain. So in Isa 45:20-23 ("Gather together and come; assemble, you survivors of the nations! . . . . Turn to me and be saved, all you ends of the earth!" [vv. 20, 22]), those who remain of the Gentiles are called to gather together to find salvation and deliverance in Yahweh, their only Helper. And in Amos 9:11-12, which speaks of the promised restoration of "David's fallen tent," that promise seems to be extended at the conclusion of those verses to include "all the nations that bear my name."[34]

7. *Diverse opinions regarding the gathering of the Gentiles — whether on a proselyte basis or on a missionary basis — are expressed, with that having to do with a proselyte basis being most often expressed.* The mandate of the remnant in the closing verses of Isaiah's prophecy is not only to respond in faith and faithfulness to God, but also to bring "your brothers" from all the nations into relationship with Yahweh (cf. 66:18-21: "I am coming to gather all nations and tongues; and they will come and see my glory. . . . I will send some of those who survive to the nations. . . . They will proclaim my glory among the nations. And they will bring all your brothers, from all the nations, to my holy mountain in Jerusalem as an offering to the Lord. . . . And I will select some of them also to be priests and Levites, says the Lord"). Most

---

32. Cf. *TDNT* 4.205.
33. Cf. *TDNT* 4.206-7.
34. Cf. *TDNT* 4.208.

often this gathering of the Gentiles is portrayed on a "proselyte" basis or model (i.e., the bringing in of Gentiles to Jerusalem), though what might be called a "missionary" basis or model may also be involved (i.e., the reaching out to Gentiles from Jerusalem, as perhaps alluded to in Isa 66:19; cf. also Amos 9:12b). Ezek 36:3, 5 also refers to "the rest [or 'the remnant'] of the nations," and Ezek 36:36 speaks of "the nations that remain [i.e., 'the remnant of the nations']" as seeing God bringing back his people to Zion, which was once ruined and desolate.[35]

8. *The gathering of the remnant is not the final goal of God; rather, it is the re-adoption and salvation of all Israel.* The remnant will become the totality. It is, therefore, a productive number, not an unchangeable minority. Even the concept of the remnant in the Jewish apocalyptic writings and the Dead Sea Scrolls, which understands the survivors of Israel as being the elect of God in the last days, reflects such an expectation. In the Damascus Covenant (CD 2:9; 9:10b), for example, the Zadokite community is regarded as the elect remnant that is spared for the land — but also the chosen group who will become those of the whole land.[36]

With respect to the remnant concept in the writings of Second Temple Judaism, Gottlob Schrenk has added the following comment on the understanding of the remnant vis-à-vis the nation Israel:

> In apocal. as well as the OT the remnant is closely linked to Israel. It is what is left of the whole people. There are passages which are orientated to final cosmic catastrophes and which seem to leave Israel out of account, cf. Eth. En. 83:8 (date uncertain). Nevertheless, the definition in relation to Israel may be seen again in S.Bar. 40:2, where the Messiah protects the remnant of the people, which is located in the Holy Land. This ref. to the Holy Land along with the remnant is common in 4 Esr. 9:7f.; 13:48; 12:31-34: The Messiah destroys the Roman Empire, but will "graciously redeem the remnant of my people which have remained in my land." Messianic salvation appears in Palestine, for those who remain, and there is also ref. to the redemption of all creation, 13:26. In Eth. En. 90:30 (c. 135-105 B.C.) the remaining sheep, who with all other animals (the nations) do homage to the shepherd (the martyred leader), are the righteous remnant of Israel. The ref. to the remaining wise people of Israel in Sib. 5.384, however, seems to bear witness to the significance of Israel as a whole.[37]

35. Cf. *TDNT* 4.208.
36. Cf. *TDNT* 4.211-13.
37. *TDNT* 4.211-13.

There is much in the remnant theology of the Jewish (OT) Scriptures, of Second Temple Judaism, and of early Jewish Christianity that has yet to be more thoroughly investigated and more fully explicated.[38] Nonetheless, the recognition of remnant theology and rhetoric as being significant in the thought and expression of many Jews and Jewish believers in Jesus of Paul's day is of great importance for the study of Early Judaism and early Jewish Christianity. And it is particularly important for an appreciation of (1) what Paul is doing in the third major section of the body middle (i.e., in 9–11) of his letter to Rome, (2) how he builds his argument, and (3) how what he argues in this section relates to what has gone before and what follows in the letter.

4. Underlying Narrative Features

Scholarly study has recently also been enriched by (1) the explicit recognition that underlying the propositional statements of the NT letters are certain foundational "narratives" or "stories" — whether one central narrative or story, which was used somewhat differently on different occasions for differing purposes, or multiple narratives or stories, which possessed something of a common "sense of center" even though expressed at times somewhat differently, (2) the lively realization that these narratives or stories were generative for early Christian theologizing, proclamation, and counseling, and so they undergird all that the NT writers of letters wrote, and (3) the developed consciousness that the NT writers of letters were actually building on, arguing from, and using for their own purposes this substratum of narrative material. So in order to understand more fully what the NT writers are saying in their respective letters, one needs to have some appreciation for how their various statements function by way of "teasing out" (or, in some cases, "disentangling"), interpreting (or "re-interpreting"), and applying the principal features of that basic narrative or story material.

Such a narrative approach is not, of course, new to biblical study. It had often been used with respect to the historical materials of the OT, that is, (1) the patriarchal narratives of Genesis 12–50, (2) the accounts of the Exodus and the wilderness experience of Israel, (3) the histories of the fledgling nation of Israel from the conquest of Canaan through to the fall of Jerusalem in the books of Joshua through 2 Chronicles, and (4) the stories of the peo-

---

38. For a highly significant study of all these matters, see M. A. Elliott, *The Survivors of Israel* (2000).

ple's return from Babylonian captivity in the records of Ezra and Nehemiah
— with these narratives or stories underlying all of the prophetic and proverbial statements of the OT and providing the backdrop for the psalmists'
praise to God. Likewise, Christians have always viewed as foundational to
their faith (1) the portrayals of Jesus' ministry in the Gospels and (2) the accounts of the ministries of Peter and Paul in the Acts of the Apostles, with all
the rest of the NT writings being based, in some manner, on the events that
the canonical Gospels and Acts present. "For the most part, however," as
Bruce Longenecker has aptly pointed out, "the Pauline corpus has been relatively immune from narrative study for obvious reasons: Paul wrote letters,
not narratives."[39] It was not until the 1980s, however, that the letters of the
NT began to be studied as also encapsulating and reflecting an underlying
narrative or set of stories, which were known not only to the various authors
of these letters but also presumably, at least to some extent, by their respective addressees.

Much of the impetus for narrative analyses of the NT letters must be
credited to Richard Hays in his 1983 publication *The Faith of Jesus Christ*,
with its revealing subtitle *An Investigation of the Narrative Substructure of
Galatians 3:1–4:11*.[40] Hays argued that not only does a narrative "substructure" underlie the text of Gal 3:1–4:11, but it actually undergirds all of Paul's
statements, supports all of his arguments, animates his passion, gives coherence to the flow of his presentation, and constrains his discursive options.
Drawing on Northrop Frye's differentiation between *mythos* and *dianoia*,
Hays identified *mythos* as the "plot" or "linear sequence of events" in the
story or stories that provide the "narrative substructure" of the exposition of
a NT letter writer, and *dianoia* as the "theme" or "meaning of that sequence"
that he spells out in his "reflective discourse."[41] And this understanding of
relationships Hays summarized in the following three points:

1. There can be an organic relationship between stories and reflective
   discourse because stories have an inherent configurational dimension
   (dianoia) which not only permits but also demands restatement and
   interpretation in non-narrative language.
2. The reflective restatement does not simply repeat the plot *(mythos)* of
   the story; nonetheless, the story shapes and constrains the reflective

---

39. B. W. Longenecker, *Narrative Dynamics in Paul*, 3.
40. R. B. Hays, *The Faith of Jesus Christ* (1983; 2nd ed. 2001).
41. R. B. Hays, *The Faith of Jesus Christ*, 21-22; 2nd ed. 22-24.

process because the *dianoia* can never be entirely abstracted from the story in which it is manifested and apprehended.

3. Hence, when we encounter this type of reflective discourse, it is legitimate and possible to inquire about the story in which it is rooted.[42]

Thus with respect to the narrative substructure that underlies a NT letter writer's exposition, Hays proposed a twofold procedure: "we may first identify within the discourse allusions to the story and seek to discern its general outlines; then, in a second phase of inquiry, we may ask how this story shapes the logic of argumentation in the discourse."[43]

A narrative approach to Paul's letters has been picked up by a number of scholars during the past few decades, developed in various ways, and is today the subject of rather intense scrutiny and critical assessment.[44] Debates are frequent with regard to (1) whether a narrative underlying a particular Pauline presentation is to be viewed as one "Grand Story" or multiple "stories" having something of a "sense of center," and (2) whether that narrative is to be found within the text, behind the text, or in front of the text. But however evaluated with regard to these particular matters, the importance of a narrative approach for the study of Paul's letters has become increasingly evident. For though all of his letters are concerned with various problems and issues to which he speaks, all of what he writes in all of his letters is based on the story (or stories) about what God has done redemptively on behalf of humanity and the world through the work of Jesus Christ — which redemptive narrative also includes the story (or stories) about (1) God's purpose for his creation, (2) God's dealing with his people Israel, (3) humanity's response (or lack of response) to divine grace, and (4) the divine mandate to Paul personally and to all believers in Christ corporately.

Such a narrative substructure is especially evident in Romans in Paul's use of Abraham as the preeminent example of a person of faith in 4:1-24, his contrast between what Adam brought into human experience and what Christ effected on behalf of humanity in 5:12-21, and his analysis of relations between Israel and the church and his sketching out of "salvation history" in chapters 9–11. It can also be seen elsewhere in the letter, particularly in the early Christian confessional materials that Paul quotes and his use of those

---

42. R. B. Hays, *The Faith of Jesus Christ,* 28 (in both 1st and 2nd eds.).

43. R. B. Hays, *The Faith of Jesus Christ* 28; 2nd ed., 29.

44. Cf., e.g., the collection of articles and responses in B. W. Longenecker, ed., *Narrative Dynamics in Paul* (2002).

materials (see above in this chapter on the early Christian confessional materials that are incorporated into his letter).

The recognition that a narrative substructure underlies all that is written in the NT is not new. Christians have always believed that the "good news" that the earliest believers in Jesus proclaimed was about what God had decreed in his eternal counsels and then brought about historically on behalf of humanity — primarily, about what he brought about at a particular time in the course of human history through the person and work of Jesus Christ. Only recently, however, have scholars come to realize that not only were the principal features of that redemptive story generative for early Christian proclamation and theology, but also such a foundational redemptive story (or such a cluster of redemptive episodes in history) was instructional in the writing of the NT letters as well as in the composition of the NT Gospels. And it is this approach that needs to be taken into account at every point when interpreting Romans — both as an exegetical tool and as an interpretive control in analyzing what Paul presents in this particular letter.

Thus we need to read Paul's letter to the Christians at Rome with an eye to such underlying narratives, recognizing that they had a profound effect on (1) the theologizing of the earliest believers in Jesus, which took the form of "early Christian confessions" in spontaneous hymns, formal statements, and condensed sayings (as discussed above), (2) the eventual composition of the four canonical Gospels, which brought these narratives into a more formalized form, and (3) the writing of letters, particularly those of Paul, which not only incorporate many of those early Christian confessional materials but also reflect the narrative substructure on which they were founded.

Supplemental Bibliography

See also "Bibliography of Selected Commentaries." All references in the footnotes to works included in this list are by the authors' names and abbreviated titles.

Allen, Leslie C. "The Old Testament in Romans I–VIII, *Vox Evangelica,* vol. 3, ed. R. P. Martin. London: Epworth, 1964, 6-41.

Barrett, C. Kingsley. "The Interpretation of the Old Testament in the New," in *The Cambridge History of the Bible,* ed. P. R. Ackroyd and C. F. Evans. Cambridge: Cambridge University Press, 1970, 1.377-411.

Batemann, Herbert W. *Early Jewish Hermeneutics and Hebrews 1:5-13: The Impact of Early Jewish Exegesis on the Interpretation of a Significant New Testament Passage.* New York: Lang, 1997 (esp. Part One, "Early Jewish Hermeneutics," 9-116).

Beker, J. Christiaan. "Echoes and Intertextuality: On the Role of Scripture in Paul's Theology," in *Paul and the Scriptures of Israel*, ed. C. A. Evans and J. A. Sanders. Sheffield: JSOT, 1993, 64-65.

Black, Matthew. "The Christological Use of the Old Testament in the New Testament," *NTS* 18 (1971) 1-14.

———. "The Theological Appropriation of the Old Testament by the New Testament," *SJT* 39 (1986) 1-17.

Bloch, Renée. "Midrash," trans. M. H. Callaway, in *Approaches to Ancient Judaism: Theory and Practice*, ed. W. S. Green. Missoula: Scholars, 1978, 29-50.

———. "Methodological Note for the Study of Rabbinic Literature," trans. W. S. Green, in *Approaches to Ancient Judaism: Theory and Practice*, ed. W. S. Green. Missoula: Scholars, 1978, 51-75.

Bonsirven, Joseph. *Exégèse allégorque et exégèse paulinienne.* Paris: Beauchesne, 1939.

Bornkamm, Günther. "Der Lobpreis Gottes: Röm 11,33-36," *Aufbau und Besinnung* 5 (1951) 70-75.

———. "Lobpreis, Bekenntnis, und Opfer," in *Apophoreta: Festschrift für Ernst Haenchen*, ed. W. Eltester. Berlin: Töpelmann, 1964.

Bowker, John. *The Targums and Rabbinic Literature: An Introduction to Jewish Interpretations of Scripture.* Cambridge: Cambridge University Press, 1969; repr. 1979.

Boyarin, Daniel. *Intertextuality and the Reading of Midrash.* Bloomington, Indianapolis: Indiana University Press, 1990.

Brown, Raymond E. *The 'Sensus Plenior' of Sacred Scripture.* Baltimore: St. Mary's University, 1955.

———. "The Sensus Plenior in the Last Ten Years," *CBQ* 25 (1963) 262-85.

———. "Hermeneutics," in *The Jerome Biblical Commentary*, ed. R. E. Brown, J. A. Fitzmyer, and R. E. Murphy. Englewood Cliffs: Prentice-Hall, 1968, 605-23.

Brownlee, William H. "Biblical Interpretation among the Sectaries of the Dead Sea Scrolls," *BA* 14 (1951) 54-76.

———. *The Text of Habakkuk in the Ancient Commentary from Qumran.* Philadelphia: Society of Biblical Literature, 1959.

Bruce, Frederick F. *Biblical Exegesis in the Qumran Texts.* London: Tyndale; Grand Rapids: Eerdmans, 1960.

———. *This Is That: The New Testament Development of Some Old Testament Themes.* Exeter: Paternoster, 1968.

Carson, Donald A., and Hugh M. G. Williamson, eds. *"It Is Written": Scripture Citing Scripture: Essays in Honour of Barnabas Lindars.* Cambridge: Cambridge University Press, 1988.

Cerfaux, Lucien. "Hymnes au Christ des letters de Saint Paul," *Revue diocésaine de Tournai* 2 (1947) 3-11.

Charlesworth, James H. "A Prolegomenon to a New Study of the Jewish Background of the Hymns and Prayers in the New Testament," *JJS* 33 (1982) 265-85.

———. "Jewish Hymns, Odes, and Prayers (ca. 167 B.C.E.–35 C.E.)," in *Early Judaism and Its Modern Interpreters,* ed. R. A. Kraft and G. W. E. Nickelsburg. Philadelphia: Fortress, 1986, 411-36.

Cullmann, Oscar, *The Earliest Christian Confessions,* trans. J. K. S. Reid. London: Lutterworth, 1949.

————. *The Christology of the New Testament,* trans. S. C. Guthrie and C. A. M. Hall. London: SCM, 1959.

Daube, David. "Rabbinic Methods of Interpretation and Hellenistic Rhetoric," *HUCA* 22 (1949) 239-64.

————. "Alexandrian Methods of Interpretation and the Rabbis," in *Festschrift Hans Lewald.* Basel: Helbing & Lichtenbahn, 1953, 27-44.

Deichgräber, Reinhard. *Gotteshymnus und Christushymnus in der frühen Christenheit: Untersuchungen zu Form, Sprache, and Stil der frühchristlichen Hymnen.* Göttingen: Vandenhoeck & Ruprecht, 1967.

Dodd, Charles H. *According to the Scriptures: The Sub-Structure of New Testament Theology.* London: Nisbet, 1952.

————. *The Old Testament in the New.* London: Athlone, 1952; Philadelphia: Fortress, 1963.

Elliott, Mark A. "Romans 9–11 and Jewish Remnant Theology." Th.M. Dissertation, Wycliffe College — Toronto School of Theology, University of Toronto, 1986.

————. *The Survivors of Israel: A Reconsideration of the Theology of Pre-Christian Judaism.* Grand Rapids: Eerdmans, 2000.

Ellis, E. Earle. *Paul's Use of the Old Testament.* Edinburgh: Oliver & Boyd; Grand Rapids: Eerdmans, 1957; repr. Grand Rapids: Baker, 1981.

————. "Midrash, Targum and New Testament Quotations," in *Neotestamentica et Semitica,* ed. E. E. Ellis and M. Wilcox. Edinburgh: T&T Clark, 1969, 61-69.

————. "How the New Testament Uses the Old," in *New Testament Interpretation: Essays on Principles and Methods,* ed. I. H. Marshall. Grand Rapids: Eerdmans, 1977, 199-219.

————. "Biblical Interpretation in the New Testament Church," in *Mikra: Text, Translation, Reading and Interpretation of the Hebrew Bible in Ancient Judaism and Early Christianity,* ed. M. J. Mulder. Philadelphia: Fortress, 1988, 691-725.

Eslinger, L. "Inter-Biblical Exegesis and Inner-Biblical Allusion: The Question of Category," *VT* 42 (1992) 47-58.

Evans, Craig A. "Paul and the Hermeneutics of 'True Prophecy': A Study of Romans 9–11," *Bib* 65 (1984) 560-70.

Evans, Craig A., and James A. Sanders, eds. *Paul and the Scriptures of Israel.* Sheffield: JSOT, 1993.

Finkelstein, Louis. "The Transmission of Early Rabbinic Tradition," *HUCA* 16 (1941) 115-35.

Fishbane, Michael. "Revelation and Tradition: Aspects of Inner-Biblical Exegesis," *JBL* 99 (1980) 343-61.

————. *Biblical Interpretation in Ancient Israel.* Oxford: Clarendon, 1985.

Fitzmyer, Joseph A. "'4QTestimonia' and the New Testament," *TS* 18 (1957) 513-37; repr. in his *Essays on the Semitic Background of the New Testament.* Missoula: Scholars, 1971, 59-89.

————. "The Dead Sea Scrolls and the New Testament after Thirty Years," *Theology Digest* 29 (1981) 351-66.

————. "The Use of Explicit Old Testament Quotations in Qumran Literature and in the New Testament," *NTS* 7 (1961) 297-333.

Fowl, Stephen E. *The Story of Christ in the Ethics of Paul: An Analysis of the Function of the Hymnic Material in the Pauline Corpus.* Sheffield: JSOT, 1990.

Fox, Michael V. "The Identification of Quotations in Biblical Literature," *ZAW* 93 (1981) 416-31.

Gloege, Gerhard. *Reich Gottes und Kirche im Neuen Testament.* Gütersloh, 1929.

Gloer, William H. "Homologies and Hymns in the New Testament: Form, Content, and Criteria for Identification," *PRS* 11 (1984) 115-32.

Goltz, Eduard van der. *Das Gebet in der ältesten Christenheit.* Leipzig: Hinrichs, 1901.

Goppelt, Leonhard. *Typos: The Typological Interpretation of the Old Testament in the New,* trans. D. V. Madvig. Grand Rapids: Eerdmans, 1982 (from 1939 German edition).

Gordis, Robert. "Quotation as a Literary Usage in Biblical, Oriental and Rabbinic Literature," *HUCA* 22 (1949) 157-219.

Hagner, Donald A. "The Old Testament in the New Testament," in *Interpreting the Word of God: Festschrift in Honor of Steven Barabas,* ed. S. J. Schultz and M. A. Inch. Chicago: Moody, 1976, 78-104 (with notes on 275-76).

Hahn, Ferdinand. *The Titles of Jesus in Christology: Their History in Early Christianity,* trans. H. Knight and G. Ogg. London: Lutterworth, 1969.

Harnack, Adolf von. "Das alte Testament in den paulinischen Briefen und in den paulinischen Gemeinden," *Sitzungsberichte der Preussischen Akademie der Wissenschaften zu Berlin* (1928) 124-41.

Hasel, Gerhard F. *The Remnant: The History and Theology of the Remnant Idea.* Berrien Springs, MI: Andrews University Press, 1972.

Hays, Richard B. *The Faith of Jesus Christ: An Investigation of the Narrative Substructure of Galatians 3:1–4:11.* SBL.DS 56. Chico: Scholars, 1983[1], 2001[2].

————. *Echoes of Scripture in the Letters of Paul.* New Haven: Yale University Press, 1989.

————. "Echoes of Scripture in the Letters of Paul: Abstract," with critiques by C. A. Evans, J. A. Sanders, W. S. Green, and J. C. Beker, and a response by Hays, in *Paul and the Scriptures of Israel,* ed. C. A. Evans and J. A. Sanders. Sheffield: JSOT, 1993, 42-96.

Hengel, Martin. "Hymns and Christology," in *Papers on Paul and Other New Testament Authors,* vol. 3 of *Studia Biblica 1978,* ed. E. A. Livingstone. Sheffield: JSOT, 1983, 173-97; repr. in *idem, Between Jesus and Paul: Studies in the Earliest History of Christianity.* Philadelphia: Fortress, 1983, 78-96 and 188-90.

Hunter, Archibald M. *Paul and His Predecessors.* London: Nicholson & Watson, 1940; rev. ed. London: SCM, 1961.

Jeremias, Joachim. "Der Gedanke des 'Heiligen Restes' im Spätjudentum und in der Verkündigung Jesu," *ZNW* 42 (1949) 184-94.

Johnson, S. Lewis. *The Old Testament in the New.* Grand Rapids: Zondervan, 1980.

Juel, Donald H. *Messianic Exegesis: Christological Interpretation of the Old Testament in Early Christianity.* Philadelphia: Fortress, 1988.

Kaiser, Walter C. *The Uses of the Old Testament in the New.* Chicago: Moody, 1985.

Karris, Robert J. *A Symphony of New Testament Hymns: Commentary on Philippians 2:5-11, Colossians 1:15-20, Ephesians 2:14-16, 1 Timothy 3:16, Titus 3:4-7, 1 Peter 3:18-22, and 2 Timothy 2:11-13.* Collegeville: Liturgical Press, 1966.

Kattenbusch, Ferdinand. "Der Spruch über Petrus und die Kirche bei Matthäus," *TSK* 94 (1922) 96-121.

Kramer, Werner. *Christ, Lord, Son of God,* trans. B. Hardy. London: SCM, 1966.

Kroll, Josef. "Die Hymnendichtung des frühren Christentums," *Antike* 2 (1926) 258-81.

Kümmel, Werner Georg. "Jesus und die Anfänge der Kirche," *ST* 7 (1953) 1-27.

Lindars, Barnabas. *New Testament Apologetic: The Significance of the Old Testament Quotations.* London: SCM, 1961.

Lindars, Barnabas, and Peter Borgen. "The Place of the Old Testament in the Formation of New Testament Theology: Prolegomena and Response," *NTS* 23 (1976) 59-66 (Lindars's prolegomena) and 67-75 (Borgen's response).

Longenecker, Bruce W. *Narrative Dynamics in Paul: A Critical Assessment.* Louisville: Westminster/John Knox, 2002.

Longenecker, Richard N. *The Christology of Early Jewish Christianity.* London: SCM, 1970 (repr. Grand Rapids: Baker, 1981).

———. *Biblical Exegesis in the Apostolic Period.* Grand Rapids: Eerdmans, 1975[1]; 1999[2].

———. "Prolegomena to Paul's Use of Scripture in Romans," *BBR* 7 (1997) 145-68.

———. *New Wine into Fresh Wineskins: Contextualizing the Early Christian Confessions.* Peabody: Hendrickson, 1999.

———. "Early Church Interpretation," in *Dictionary of Biblical Criticism and Interpretation,* ed. S. E. Porter. London, New York: Routledge, 2007, 78-89.

Martin, Ralph P. "Some Reflections on New Testament Hymns," in *Christ the Lord: Studies in Christology Presented to Donald Guthrie,* ed. H. H. Rowden. Leicester: Inter-Varsity, 1982, 37-49.

McNamara, Martin. *The New Testament and the Palestinian Targum to the Pentateuch.* Rome: Pontifical Biblical Institute, 1966.

———. *Targum and Testament: Aramaic Paraphrases of the Hebrew Bible. A Light on the New Testament.* Shannon: Irish University Press; Grand Rapids: Eerdmans, 1972; rev. ed. Grand Rapids: Eerdmans, 2010.

Metzger, Bruce M. "The Formulas Introducing Quotations of Scripture in the New Testament and the Midrash," *JBL* 70 (1951) 297-307.

Meyer, Ben F. "Jesus and the Remnant of Israel," *JBL* 84 (1965) 123-30.

260

————. *The Aims of Jesus.* London: SCM, 1979, esp. 118-21, 197, 220-22 and 225-29.

————. "The Pre-Pauline Formula in Rom 3.25-26a," *NTS* 29 (1983) 198-208.

Michel, Otto. *Paulus und seine Bibel.* Gütersloh: Bertelsmann, 1929, 1972².

Moo, Douglas J. "The Problem of Sensus Plenior," in *Hermeneutics, Authority and Canon,* ed. D. A. Carson and J. D. Woodbridge. Leicester: Inter-Varsity; Grand Rapids: Zondervan, 1986, 179-211.

Moule, Charles F. D., "The Church Explains Itself: The Use of the Jewish Scriptures," in his *The Birth of the New Testament.* London: Black; New York: Harper & Row, 1962, 1966², 53-85.

————. "'Through Jesus Christ Our Lord': Some Questions about the Use of Scripture," *Theology* 80 (1977) 30-36.

Neufeld, Vernon H. *The Earliest Christian Confessions.* Grand Rapids: Eerdmans, 1963.

Norden, Eduard. *Die antike Kunstprosa vom VI. Jahrhundert vor Christus bis in die Zeit der Renaissance,* 2 vols. Leipzig: Teubner, 1898; repr. Stuttgart: Teubner, 1983.

————. *Agnostos Theos: Untersuchungen zur Formengeschichte religiöser Rede.* Leipzig: Teubner, 1913; repr. Leipzig: Teubner, 1956.

Oepke, Albrecht. "Der Herrnspruch über die Kirche, Mt 16,17-19 in der neuesten Forschung," *ST* 2 (1948) 110-65.

Patte, Daniel. *Early Jewish Hermeneutics in Palestine.* Missoula: Scholars, 1975.

Robinson, James M. "Die Hodayot-Formel in Gebet und Hymnus des Frühchristentums," in *Apophoreta: Festschrift für Ernst Haenchen,* ed. W. Eltester. Berlin: 1964, 194-235.

Sanders, Jack T. *The New Testament Christological Hymns: Their Historical Religious Background.* Cambridge: Cambridge University Press, 1971.

Sandmel, Samuel. "Parallelomania," *JBL* 81 (1962) 1-13.

Schattenmann, J. *Studies zum neutestamentlichen Prosahymnus.* Munich: Beck, 1965.

Schille, Gottfried. *Frühchristliche Hymnen.* Berlin: Evangelische, 1962.

Schmidt, Karl L. "Die Kirche des Urchristentums," in *Festgabe für Adolf Deissmann zum 60. Geburtstag.* Tübingen: Mohr (Siebeck), 1927, 258-319 (esp. 290-92).

Schrenk, Gottlob, and Volkmar Herntrich. "λεῖμμα, ὑπόλειμμα, κτλ," *TDNT* 4.194-214.

Schüssler Fiorenza, Elisabeth. "Wisdom Mythology and the Christological Hymns of the New Testament," in *Aspects of Wisdom in Judaism and Early Christianity,* ed. R. L. Wilken. Notre Dame: University of Notre Dame Press, 1975, 17-41.

Scroggs, Robin. "Paul as Rhetorician: Two Homilies in Romans 1-11," in *Jews, Greeks, and Christians (Festschrift for W. D. Davies),* ed. R. Hammerton-Kelly and R. Scroggs. Leiden: Brill, 1976, 271-98.

Seeberg, Alfred. *Der Katechismus der Urchristenheit.* Leipzig: Deichertschen, 1903; repr. Munich: Kaiser, 1966.

Segert, Stanislav. "Semitic Poetic Structures in the New Testament," in ANRW, II.25.2, ed. H. Temporini and W. Hasse. Berlin: de Gruyter, 1984, 1432-62.

Silva, Moises. "The New Testament Use of the Old Testament: Text Form and Authority," in *Scripture and Truth,* ed. D. A. Carson and J. D. Woodbridge. Grand Rapids: Zondervan, 1983, 147-65 (with notes on 381-86).

————. "Old Testament in Paul," in *Dictionary of Paul and His Letters,* ed. G. F. Hawthorne, R. P. Martin, and D. G. Reid. Downers Grove: InterVarsity, 1993, 630-42.

Silberman, Louis H. "Unriddling the Riddle: A Study in the Structure and Language of the Habakkuk Pesher (1QpHab)," *RevQ* 3 (1962) 323-64.

Smith, D. Moody, Jr. "The Use of the Old Testament in the New," in *The Use of the Old Testament in the New and Other Essays: Studies in Honor of William Franklin Stinespring,* ed. J. M. Efird. Durham: Duke University Press, 1972, 3-65.

Stanley, Christopher D. *Paul and the Language of Scripture: Citation Technique in the Pauline Epistles and Contemporary Literature.* Cambridge: Cambridge University Press, 1993.

Stauffer, Ethelbert. "Twelve Criteria of Creedal Formulae in the New Testament," in his *New Testament Theology,* trans. J. Marsh. London: SCM, 1955, Appendix III.

Thackeray, Henry St.-J. *The Relation of St. Paul to Contemporary Jewish Thought.* London: Macmillan, 1900.

Vermes, Geza. *Scripture and Tradition in Judaism.* Leiden: Brill, 1961, 1973².

————. "The Qumran Interpretation of Scripture in Its Historical Setting," *ALUOS* 6 (1966-1968) 85-97.

————. "Bible and Midrash: Early Old Testament Exegesis," in *The Cambridge History of the Bible,* 3 vols., ed. P. R. Ackroyd and C. F. Evans. Cambridge: Cambridge University Press, 1970, 1.199-231.

————. "The Impact of the Dead Sea Scrolls on Jewish Studies during the Last Twenty-Five Years," in *Approaches to Ancient Judaism: Theory and Practice,* ed. W. S. Green. Missoula: Scholars, 1978, 201-14.

————. "Jewish Studies and New Testament Interpretation," *JJS* 31 (1980) 1-17.

————. "Jewish Literature and New Testament Exegesis: Reflections on Methodology," *JJS* 33 (1982) 362-76.

Vielhauer, Philipp. "Paulus und das Alte Testament," in *Studien zur Geschichte und Theologie der Reformation,* ed. L. Abramowski. Neukirchen-Vluyn: Neukirchener Verlag, 1969, 33-62.

Weiss, Johannes. "Beiträge zum paulinischer Rhetorik," in *Theologische Studien (Festschrift B. Weiss),* ed. C. R. Gregory, *et al.* Göttingen: Vandenhoeck & Ruprecht, 1897, 165-247.

Wengst, Klaus. *Christologische Formeln und Lieder des Urchristentums.* Gütersloh: Mohn, 1972.

Wright, A. G. *The Literary Genre Midrash.* Staten Island: Alba House, 1967.

Zeitlin, Solomon. "Hillel and the Hermeneutical Rules," *JQR* 54 (1963) 161-73.

PART FOUR

Textual and Interpretive Matters

CHAPTER VIII

Establishing the Text

Of critical importance in the study of Romans (as well as, of course, in the study of any portion of Scripture) is "establishing" the text of the letter — that is, reconstructing the letter's present text as closely as possible to its original text. This involves (1) giving attention to the extensive textual tradition of the writing, (2) developing procedures for evaluating the textual data, and (3) making valid judgments regarding the most likely reading in those many places where variant readings have appeared.

1. An Overview of the New Testament's Textual Tradition

It is impossible in only a few paragraphs to spell out in any detail what has transpired in the scholarly study of the NT's textual tradition. That has been done most adequately by Kurt and Barbara Aland in their book *The Text of the New Testament.*[1] Yet certain phenomena, events, scholars, and advances need to be here identified in order to provide some consciousness of what has taken place in the past, where we are today, and what challenges lie before us for the future — particularly, as is our purpose in this chapter, with respect to establishing the Greek text of Paul's letter to the Christians at Rome. At risk of oversimplification, it may be said that three periods stand

---

1. K. Aland and B. Aland, *The Text of the New Testament: An Introduction to the Critical Editions and to the Theory and Practice of Modern Textual Criticism,* trans. E. F. Rhodes (Leiden: Brill; Grand Rapids: Eerdmans, 1987; 2nd ed. 1989; translated from the German 1983 first edition and 1988 revised edition, respectively).

out as being especially important in the history of the NT text generally and the text of Romans in particular: (1) the patristic period, (2) the Reformation period, and (3) the modern critical period.

The Patristic Period

The patristic period, which may be dated from Clement of Rome in the late first century to Jerome and Augustine in the mid-fifth century, is of primary importance in any study of the NT text. It is necessary, however, not to treat the patristic textual tradition of the NT generally — or of Romans in particular — in a monolithic fashion. Two phases of this period need to be distinguished: (1) a time when certain Christian communities possessed their own favored "apostolic" writings and when various textual traditions were developing with some degree of freedom, which is a span of time that can be dated from the late first or early second century through to the middle of the third century, and (2) a time when Christians were officially persecuted by Rome — as instituted in 250-260 by Decius (who reigned 249-251), Valerius (who reigned 253-260), and the tetrarchy that ruled during the two years between them, and then re-instituted in 303 by Diocletian (who reigned 284-305) — with those imperial policies of state persecution dramatically reversed by Constantine (who reigned 306-337) after his conversion to Christianity in 313. It was during this latter phase that Christians, both when suffering official persecution and then when enjoying a time of acceptance and peace inaugurated by Constantine, came to realize that they needed to standardize their NT writings — thus a period of time that can be dated from the last quarter of the third century through to the end of the fifth century.

That a diversity of text forms existed during the earlier phase, that is, during the first two centuries of the Christian era, is attested (1) by variant readings in the Old Latin, the Old Syriac, and certain Coptic versions that may be presumed to have incorporated some earlier readings, (2) by variations in the biblical texts quoted by such early Greek church fathers as Irenaeus and Origen (even though their writings were preserved by the Western church only in Latin translations), and (3) by differences in the text forms of the NT papyri, which were found among other papyrus materials in the Fayyum district of Egypt over a century ago. More allusively, early textual diversity is also suggested by what can be known about Marcion's text of Luke's Gospel and ten of the Pauline letters (Marcion's so-called *Apostolikon* or "Apostolic Writings"), as reported mainly by Tertullian and Origen, which readings seem not to have been unique to Marcion but were evidently accepted widely by certain other groups of early Christians.

Some of the more obvious examples of diverse textual traditions during these first two Christian centuries have to do with: (1) the inclusion or omission of the negative οὐδέ in Gal 2:5 ("we did *not* give in to them for a moment, so that the truth of the gospel might remain with you"), with Irenaeus and Tertullian quoting this passage as though the negative was omitted in their circles; (2) the inclusion or omission of chapters 15–16 in Paul's letter to the Romans; (3) the inclusion and placement of the doxology of Rom 16:25-27, whether after 14:23, after 15:33, after 16:23/24, after both 14:23 and 15:33, after both 14:23 and 16:23/24, or omitted entirely; (4) the inclusion or omission of ἐν ῾Ρώμη ("at Rome") in Rom 1:7 and 15; (5) the inclusion or omission of ἐν ᾿Εφέσῳ ("at Ephesus") in Eph 1:1; (6) the plural αἱ διαθῆκαι ("the covenants") or the singular ἡ διαθήκη ("the covenant") in Rom 9:4; (7) the accusative plural αὐτούς ("them") or the dative plural αὐτοῖς ("to them") in Heb 8:8; and (8) the reading of the Greek substantival passive participle at the beginning of Rom 1:4 — that is, whether it appeared in Greek as τοῦ ὁρισθέντος ("the one appointed" or "designated") or as τοῦ προορισθέντος ("the one predestined"), as suggested by the Latin *praedestinatus* that is to be found in the Old Latin, Jerome's Vulgate, and many Latin writers (though Origen, as preserved in Rufinus's abridged Latin version of his Romans commentary, insisted that the true reading is *destinatus*, "designated," and not *praedestinatus*, "predestined"). Each of these cases (and more, of course, could be cited) reflects a particular theological dispute that occurred during the first two centuries of the Christian era — with each of them also giving evidence of a text that was somewhat fluid before the "families" of texts (or, at least, before the Byzantine family of texts) became standardized. And a number of these textual variants continue to influence and support some of those same theologies today.

It was, however, during the latter part of the third century and throughout the fourth century — in response to both persecution by antagonistic emperors and then acceptance and the restoration of peace by Constantine — that the major text types or "families" came into existence. For under Roman persecution there was not only a systematic destruction of Christian churches and Christian centers but also public burnings of Christian writings and texts, with a resultant widespread scarcity of NT manuscripts; whereas during the Age of Constantine there was a rapid growth of Christianity, with the resultant need for a large number of NT texts.

The Reformation Period

The end of the fifteenth century and the entire sixteenth century constituted a time of intense interest in the Bible, with Christians being challenged by the Renaissance (which began in the fourteenth century in Italy) and motivated by the Protestant Reformation (which took definitive form in the early sixteenth century in Germany) to return to their biblical roots. With respect to the text of the NT, the most important scholar of the day was Desiderius Erasmus of Rotterdam (1469-1536), the religious humanist, who was trained as a Roman Catholic theologian but worked principally as a Latin and Greek linguist. He was a highly significant figure throughout Europe, becoming even Professor of Divinity at Cambridge University in England from 1509 to 1514.

Erasmus is best known today for having produced, based on only four or five twelfth- to thirteenth-century Byzantine manuscripts, a critical Greek text of the NT (or, in Latin, the *Novum Instrumentum*), which was comparable in many ways to what in the seventeenth century came to be known as the "received text" *(Textus Receptus),* with accompanying textual notes and Latin translation. In his day, however, Erasmus was more applauded — though also often criticized — as a paraphraser of the NT, appropriating a method used by the Greek rhetorician Quintilian (late first century A.D.) and the Latin rhetorician Themistius (fourth century A.D.) on writings of classical authors and applying it to the contents of the NT. For to paraphrase a text was (so it was thought) to improve its clarity, and therefore to facilitate its translation from one language to another.

Erasmus's Greek text quickly became the basis for some of the most important NT commentaries of the sixteenth century — not only those by Protestant Reformers, but also some of those written by Roman Catholics. Martin Luther in his lectures on Romans, for example, while working basically from the Basel edition of the Vulgate of 1509 and Faber Stapulensis's Latin edition of the Epistles of St. Paul of 1512 and 1515 (especially for the first eight chapters of Romans), often corrected the Vulgate (particularly in chapters 9–16) by reference to the first edition of Erasmus's *Greek New Testament,* which was published and became available to him early in 1516. And Thomas de Vio (surnamed "Cajetan"), the Roman Catholic bishop of Gaeta — who was a scholastic theologian of great stature and influence, and who in 1518 had presided as the Papal Legate in the examination of Luther at Augsburg — devoted himself during the latter years of his life (i.e., 1525-1534) entirely to the writing of biblical commentaries: first on the Psalms; then on the Gospels, Acts, and the letters of the NT; and finally on the Pentateuch, Joshua,

Proverbs, Ecclesiastes, and Isaiah 1–3. But he got into trouble with his ecclesiastical superiors when writing his NT commentaries because (1) he departed from the Latin text of the Vulgate, using instead the critical editions of the Greek prepared by Erasmus and Faber, and (2) he sounded, at times, too much like Luther, at least to those who claimed to be his judges.

Erasmus's Greek text also became the basis for Luther's German translation of the NT (his so-called *Septembertestament,* because it was published in September of 1522), which, in turn, was incorporated into his complete German Bible of 1546. And Erasmus's Greek text was the text for William Tyndale's very important English translation of the NT that he began to publish in 1525 while in exile, which was, in turn, the prototype for such lesser English translations as the Great Bible of 1539, the Geneva Bible of the 1550s, and the Bishops' Bible of 1568 — with Tyndale's translation, together with many of these lesser English versions, culminating in the King James Version of 1611.

The Modern Critical Period

The modern period of NT textual criticism may be somewhat difficult to characterize, simply because we are all a part of it and much too close to developments to be objective in our evaluations. Nonetheless, at least three phases of this period, which dates from about the mid–nineteenth century to today (and will undoubtedly continue), can be identified: (1) a time when a number of important early Greek uncial manuscripts of the Bible became known to the scholarly world, when judgments regarding the text of the NT were based primarily on external manuscript evidence alone, and when relations between the Greek texts and their "families" were becoming fairly well "established"; (2) a time when internal data also became important in textual criticism; and (3) a time when papyrus texts of the NT were discovered and then later seen to be of great importance in the identification of early traits and features in the textual traditions of the second and third centuries, before efforts were made to standardize the NT text and the main "families" of texts were formed in the third and fourth centuries.

1. Phase One

The primary impetus for the first phase of modern NT textual criticism was (1) the coming to light of the contents of Codex Vaticanus (B, 03), which had been housed in the Vatican Library since at least the end of the fifteenth century and whose text the Vatican authorities finally allowed to become known in the mid–nineteenth century, and (2) the recovery of Codex Sinaiticus (ℵ, 01), which Konstantin von Tischendorf (1815-1877) of Leipzig discovered in 1844 amidst piles of waste paper in the monastery of St. Catherine on Mount Sinai and arranged in 1859 to be moved to St. Petersburg (with the Russian government later selling it to the British Museum, where it resides today). Earlier, in 1830 the Berlin philologist Karl Lachmann (1793-1851), who was the first scholar to make a decisive break with the *Textus Receptus,* had called for NT scholarship to go "back to the text of the early-fourth-century church." But now with the Greek NT texts of Codex Vaticanus and Codex Sinaiticus, von Tischendorf — who had been sponsored by Czar Nicholas I to search for ancient biblical materials, and who had also found in his extensive travels some twenty-one other uncial manuscripts — was able, supported by the writings of Samuel P. Tregelles (1813-1875), to provide evidence for earlier and more reliable readings than those provided by the *Textus Receptus.*

Inspired by the "discoveries" (or, more properly, the "recoveries") of Codex Vaticanus and Codex Sinaiticus — and building on the challenge of Karl Lachmann (first in 1831 and then throughout 1842-1850) and on the studies of von Tischendorf (during 1841-1872) and Samuel Tregelles (during 1857-1879) — Brooke F. Westcott (1825-1901) and Fenton J. A. Hort (1828-1892) set out in 1863 to establish the Greek text of the NT on a more critically assured basis. Hort seems to have been the one who was principally responsible for the original conception and early development of the theory of "family" relations between the ancient Greek texts, whereas Westcott took the lead in applying that theory in practice. On all points, however, the two worked in close collaboration with one another. And in 1881-1882 they published the results of their labors in *The New Testament in the Original Greek,* with those results having a profound effect on all NT study thereafter.[2]

As a result of the work of Westcott and Hort, most scholars today recognize three basic types or "families" of texts (or, perhaps, four types, if we accept a distinct "Caesarean" family) in the textual tradition of the Greek NT, with various subtypes and combinations of these families identified as well. These will be discussed in greater detail below. Here we will simply list

---

2. B. F. Westcott and F. J. A. Hort, *Introduction to the New Testament in the Original Greek,* vol. 1: *Text,* 1881; vol. 2: *Introduction* and *Appendix,* 1882 (2nd ed. of vol. 1 in 1898 and 2nd ed. of vol. 2 in 1896; repr. in one volume, Peabody: Hendrickson, 1988).

the three basic types: (1) the "Alexandrian" text (what Westcott and Hort called the "Neutral" text); (2) the "Western" text; and (3) the "Byzantine," "Syrian," or "Antiochene" text (also called the "Koine" ["common"] text, the "Majority" text, or the "Received Text").

2. Phase Two

The inauguration of phase two of the modern critical period of NT textual criticism must be credited to Martin Dibelius (1883-1947), Rudolf Bultmann (1884-1976), and Karl Ludwig Schmidt (1891-1956). None of these scholars was a text critic in the strict sense of that term — though, of course, all three worked extensively with the NT text and made numerous pronouncements about it. More important for NT textual criticism, however, is the fact that in their advocacy and development of *Formgeschichte* and the *formgeschichtliche Methode* (which expressions and method they undoubtedly picked up from Eduard Norden's monograph entitled *Agnostos Theos: Untersuchungen zur Formgeschichte religiöser Rede* of 1913), Dibelius, Bultmann, and Schmidt, who worked independently but along very similar lines, highlighted in their writings (beginning in 1919 and continuing on throughout the mid–twentieth century) the redactional activities of the NT evangelists in their composition of the Gospels (also, as with Dibelius, in the composition of Acts).

What we as English-speaking scholars today call "Form Criticism" and "Redaction Criticism" has been used in a wide diversity of ways, both destructively and constructively. This has been true not only with respect to the traditions that underlie the NT generally but also with reference to the actual composition of our canonical Gospels and Acts. And much has transpired in the development of these scholarly NT disciplines since their inauguration. Yet it must be stated that what Dibelius, Bultmann, and Schmidt did for text-critical studies — as well as what many others after them have done in these areas, whatever their various motivations and however they have proceeded — has been to lay emphasis on the necessity of always taking into consideration the internal features of a NT author's purpose, compositional habits, expressional patterns, and theology, as well as the external factors having to do with the extant textual manuscripts and the "families" of texts, when making text-critical judgments. And it is this understanding that has become more and more important in modern text-critical studies — whether it be called "form" or "redaction" criticism with respect to the canonical Gospels and Acts, "epistolary" or "rhetorical" analysis when dealing with the NT letters, or "narrative theology" as underlying everything written.

3. Phase Three

Discoveries during the 1890s of NT *koine* Greek papyrus manuscripts and fragments among the many non-literary papyri found in the Fayyum region of Egypt, as well as continuing identifications of further NT papyrus texts, have been a boon in all sorts of ways for NT study. With respect to matters regarding text criticism, these papyrus materials of whole and partial texts (which today number a total of 116 relatively whole manuscripts and very brief portions of NT Greek texts) have always been brought into the text-critical data bank of NT scholarship as they have become known and studied — but usually only in a subsidiary fashion and often only in a supporting role.

Of late, however, a thorough re-evaluation of the textual history of the NT has been inaugurated by Kurt and Barbara Aland and their associates at the Institute for New Testament Textual Research, Münster, Germany. It is a re-evaluation that builds on the work of Westcott and Hort with respect to the family relations of uncial and minuscule manuscripts, and so seeks to spell out with greater clarity the NT textual traditions of the fourth through the fifteenth centuries. More importantly, it attempts to clarify the textual situation of the second and third centuries — principally by reference to data drawn from the NT *koine* Greek papyri that can be dated in those centuries and from later biblical papyrus texts that continue some of those particular traits and features. So the Alands' re-evaluation of the NT's textual history — which in many ways is not just a re-evaluation but more like a revolution — lays primary emphasis on the earlier papyrus NT materials and only then seeks to show how what is found in those earlier texts was continued, developed, adjusted, or omitted in the later families of texts.

2. The Contemporary Re-evaluation of the Textual Tradition

The re-evaluation of the textual history of the NT by Kurt and Barbara Aland and their associates has presented to NT scholarship a promising challenge — in fact, something of a revolution in "the theory and practice of modern textual criticism" (as the subtitle of their book expresses their major concerns). For it begins with the extant papyrus NT texts that stem from the second and third centuries (or, at least, that reflect texts of that time), attempting always to interpret them in their historical and sociological contexts, and then seeking to understand how those textual traditions were used in the families of texts that came about during the third and fourth centuries and continued on through to the fifteenth century — rather than the other way around of first studying the relations and features of the later textual families and then inferring from them what must have been the situation before. So in the Alands' arrangement of a critical apparatus, the NT *koine* Greek papyri are cited first, then the uncial MSS, then the minuscule MSS, followed by evidence drawn from the other language versions and the Church Fathers — as can be seen in the twenty-seventh edition of the Nestle-Aland critical Greek text (NA[27]) and the fourth edition of the United Bible Societies' *Greek New Testament* (GNT[4]), both of which were published in 1993 and both of which have been thoroughly revised to reflect the Alands' re-evaluation of the NT's early textual history. Further, this approach is also "promising," "challenging," and "revolutionary" in that it often highlights different significances in the data than had previously been seen, brings about different arrangements of the evidence, and results in somewhat different conclusions with respect to particular variant readings — as witness their treatments of the numerous textual variants in both NA[27] and GNT[4].

The genius of Brooke F. Westcott and Fenton J. A. Hort in the area of NT text criticism was expressed in their new understanding of "family" relations between the numerous Greek manuscripts of the NT — both those previously known and those that were then being discovered. Based on Westcott and Hort's thesis of family relationships, most scholars today recognize three basic types or "families" of Greek texts in the textual tradition of the NT, with a variety of combinations of these families often also identified as subtypes. The earliest and probably the primary family of texts is the "Alexandrian" text, or what Westcott and Hort called the "Neutral" text because it seems relatively uncontaminated by later scribal alterations. It was prominent in the region of Alexandria, hence its name. But it was also used in various churches throughout the eastern part of the Roman empire. A second type is a bilingual Greek-Latin text often called the "Western" text, which may have had its roots among some Christians as early as the mid-second century and was used dominantly in western portions of the empire. A third is the "Byzantine" text, which is also called the "Syria" or "Antiochene" text because it is thought to have originated in Antioch of Syria during the late-third century. This third family of texts has also been called the "Koine" ("common") text — or often today the "Majority Text," simply because, being represented by a few later uncial manuscripts and the great bulk of minuscule manuscripts from the ninth through the fifteenth centuries, it is numerically the most prevalent. It is frequently also called the "Received Text" since it is generally comparable to the text proposed in the early sixteenth century by the Dutch religious humanist Desiderius Erasmus, with that text then developed in the seventeenth century and called the *Textus Receptus*.

The *Alexandrian* or *Neutral* text is represented most directly by two fourth-century uncial manuscripts: Codex Vaticanus (B, 03) and Codex Sinaiticus (‎‎א, 01), which are usually in agreement — though on the few occasions where they differ, Codex Vaticanus, as Westcott and Hort argued, is most often to be preferred. It also appears in the fifth-century uncial manuscript Codex Alexandrinus (‎‎א, 02), whose text is Byzantine in the Gospels but Alexandrian in the Acts and the letters of Paul, and in the fifth-century uncial manuscript Codex Ephraemi Rescriptus (C, 04) — which, as its name suggests, is a palimpsest that was erased in the twelfth century and reused by Ephraem for a Greek translation of thirty-eight tractates — whose text is generally Alexandrian but contains other mixed readings.

Of even greater importance is the fact that the Alexandrian or Neutral type of text is dominant in the biblical papyrus manuscripts of the third and fourth centuries. It appears most extensively in P^{46} ("Chester Beatty II"), which contains eight of Paul's letters and the Epistle to the Hebrews (though with numerous lacunae because of many broken edges in the folios of this papyrus codex and the omission of 2 Thessalonians, Philemon, and the Pastorals) and which dates from about A.D. 200 (with some leeway on either side). It is also to be found, to a large extent, in P^{45} ("Chester Beatty I"), which contains the Gospels and Acts (beginning at Matt 20:24 and ending at Acts 17:17) and dates from the mid–third century. Further, it is dominant as well in those other manuscripts, whether papyrus, uncial, or minuscule, that are included by Kurt and Barbara Aland in their Category I (see below) — and, though with "alien influences" usually derived from the Byzantine text, in those manuscripts that the Alands have included in their Category II (see below).

The so-called *Western* text appears in the bilingual manuscripts Codex Bezae Cantabrigiensis (D, 05) of the fifth century, which contains the Gospels and Acts, and Codex Claromontanus (D, 06) of the sixth century, which contains the Pauline letters — with both of these manuscripts often identified simply as Codex Beza, since they were at one time both possessed by Theodore Beza (1519-1605), who was an important text critic and Latin translator of his day (as well as John Calvin's successor at Geneva). This type of text, however, seems to have had roots in a much earlier period, for certain rather distinctive expressions, phrases, deletions, and additions in the two manuscripts of Codex D also appear earlier at various places in the Greek texts of the biblical papyri and the Latin biblical quotations of such Church Fathers as Tertullian (c. 145-220), Cyprian (died c. 258), and Augustine (354-430).

The *Byzantine* text is found in some of the uncial Greek manuscripts, principally in codices H, L, and P — that is, (1) in Codex H (013), which contains the Gospels and dates from the ninth century, and Codex H (015), which contains the Pauline letters and dates from the sixth century, (2) in Codex L (019), which contains the Gospels and dates from the eighth century, and Codex L (020), which contains Acts, the Catholic or General Epistles, and the Pauline letters and dates from the ninth century; and (3) in Codex P (024), which contains the Gospels and dates from the sixth century, and Codex P (025), which contains Acts, the Catholic or General Epistles, the Pauline letters, and Revelation and dates from the ninth century. But it appears far more commonly in the very large number of minuscule manuscripts that date from the ninth to the fifteenth centuries.

All of this understanding of family relationships among the various textual traditions remains, at least to date, basically true. But Kurt and Barbara Aland's new approach to "the theology and practice of textual criticism," which bases itself extensively on the evidence of the early papyrus NT texts, gives promise of opening up new vistas for our understanding of the textual history of the second and third centuries of Christendom — thereby taking scholars back to an earlier time before attempts were made to standardize the NT text and before the families of texts were formed.

3. The Impact of This New Approach on New Testament Textual Determinations

As a result of the work of Kurt and Barbara Aland and their colleagues, the textual variants of every disputed passage in both *GNT*[4] and NA[27] have undergone a complete review, with different significances often seen in the data from what had been previously accepted, different arrangements made of the available evidence, and different conclusions drawn with respect to particular variants. So, for example, the Introduction to *GNT*[4] states:

> The selection of passages for the apparatus has undergone considerable revision since the Third Edition (corrected). . . . Accordingly the Com-

mittee selected 284 new passages for inclusion in the apparatus. Meanwhile 273 passages previously included were removed, because the variants were of less significance for translators and other readers.[3]

Likewise, each of the previously assigned letter evaluations of "A" ("certain"), "B" ("almost certain"), "C" ("difficulty in deciding which variant to place in the text"), and "D" ("great difficulty in arriving at a decision") in *GNT*[4] — which represent the degree of certainty among the five editors of the Fourth Revised Edition (i.e., Barbara Aland, Kurt Aland, Johannes Karavidopoulos, Carlo M. Martini, and Bruce M. Metzger) with respect to the readings chosen — have been reconsidered and, where felt necessary, have been revised.[4] Further, the "Preface to the Fourth Edition" of *GNT*[4] declares that "very careful consideration was given to the selection of representatives for each group of witnesses in order to reflect faithfully the character of the textual tradition and exclude elements of uncertainty."[5] Thus the text-critical analysis of every disputed NT passage must now take into account this most recent re-evaluation of the NT's textual history.

Of greatest importance for any "establishing" of the various disputed texts of the NT is, of course, the evidence that can be drawn from the Greek textual tradition — that is, from the extant papyrus, uncial (or majuscule), and minuscule manuscripts. These materials have been grouped by Kurt and Barbara Aland and their associates into five categories, with that fivefold classification based on the quality of the respective Greek texts and their importance for establishing the original readings of the NT writings.[6] And it is this categorization that has been used in both *GNT*[4] and NA[27] as the basis for including or excluding a manuscript in the textual apparatus with respect to a variant reading.[7]

These five categories of NT manuscripts, as abstracted from the Alands' *The Text of the New Testament*,[8] may be characterized as follows:

Category I: Manuscripts of a "very special quality," corresponding to the Alexandrian or so-called Neutral text. These manuscripts must

---

3. *The Greek New Testament,* 4th rev. ed. (Stuttgart: Deutsche Bibelgesellschaft/ United Bible Societies, 1993), 2.

4. Cf. *GNT*[4], 3.

5. *GNT*[4], v.

6. See K. and B. Aland, *Text of the New Testament,* 2nd ed. (1989), 106, 159, 332-37.

7. See the Introduction to *GNT*[4], 4.

8. Cf. K. and B. Aland, *Text of the New Testament,* 2nd ed. (1989), 335-36.

always be given primary consideration in attempting to establish the text. To this category belong all of the papyri and uncial manuscripts of the third and fourth centuries, and so these manuscripts represent what Kurt and Barbara Aland have called the "early text."

Category II: Manuscripts of a "special quality." These are manuscripts that, while similar to those of Category I, must be distinguished from the manuscripts of Category I because of the presence of "alien influences," which have usually been derived from the Byzantine text. To this category belongs the "Egyptian" text, which was evidently developed from the Alexandrian tradition.

Category III: Manuscripts of a "distinctive character" with an "independent text." These are manuscripts that often exhibit a strong Byzantine influence, and so they are not to be used as primary evidence for establishing the text. Yet they are important for understanding the history of the textual tradition.

Category IV: Manuscripts of the so-called "Western" text (a designation that is no longer favored by Kurt and Barbara Aland, but has continued to be used by Bruce Metzger) — that is, principally and perhaps exclusively, D (Codex Beza) in both of its two volumes (i.e., 05, which contains the Gospels and Acts, and 06, which contains the Pauline letters).

Category V: Manuscripts that exhibit a purely or dominantly Byzantine text.

As the Introduction to GNT^4 puts it, "the Committee made use of these categories in selecting manuscripts because they provide the only tool presently available for classifying the whole manuscript tradition of the New Testament on an objective statistical basis."[9] So GNT^4 in its text-critical apparatus includes (1) all of the *papyri*, most of which are from categories I and II, though a few from categories III and IV, (2) all of the *uncial manuscripts* from categories I, II, III, and V, and (3) a relatively small group of *minuscule manuscripts* from categories I and II, plus some ten manuscripts from category III that have been selected as representative for the various parts of the NT (i.e., Gospels, Acts, Paul, Catholic or General Epistles, and Revelation).

There are no minuscules in category IV that represent the text type of the so-called "Western" text of Codex D, whether 05 (the Gospels and Acts) or 06 (the Pauline letters). Category V includes the major minuscule manu-

---

9. GNT^4, 4*.

scripts that the Alands have identified as being the most important of the Byzantine family of texts — that is, those manuscripts that bear "constant witness" to this family of texts. There are, of course, many hundreds of other minuscule manuscripts that belong to the more developed Byzantine text. But all of the Byzantine manuscripts included within Category V, as well as all of the hundreds more of the Byzantine family of texts, are inferior to those of Categories I, II, and III, and so are never used by Kurt and Barbara Aland and their associates in their attempts to establish the NT text[10] (and will never be cited in the "Textual Notes" or "Exegetical Comments" of our forthcoming Romans commentary).

4. The Challenge of Establishing the Text of Romans Today

What, then, can be said regarding the challenge of "establishing" the text of Romans today? The past course of debate during the patristic period and the past course of investigation during the Reformation period have not always been the most helpful, largely because (1) the most important codices and texts were not in hand, and even much of what was then at hand was not used, (2) methods for the interpretation of the available textual data had not been developed, and (3) tools for handling the vast amount of material were not available. As Christians who respect tradition, we honor our fathers — but we are not required always to agree with them.

In the last two centuries, however, we have been blessed with new discoveries of immense relevance for the establishment of the NT text — principally, (1) the recoveries of Codex Vaticanus (from the restraints of Vatican officialdom) and Codex Sinaiticus (from St. Catherine's Monastery on Mount Sinai), together with the coming to light of a number of other uncial Greek biblical manuscripts, and (2) the unearthing of 116 (to date) Greek NT papyri from the Fayyum district of Egypt, some relatively intact and others fragmentary. Further, we have gained immensely from the work of a number of scholars who have proposed various methods of interpretation in using these materials in order to understand more adequately the textual history of the NT — with some of these proposals only demonstrating the "dead end" quality of some of these methods and approaches, but others setting out a basis for and pointing the way toward real advances. Obviously, being so close temporally to the major textual discoveries of the past two centuries

---

10. See K. and B. Aland, *Text of the New Testament,* 138-42.

— and, of course, having sympathies with certain of the major text-critical endeavors of particular scholars in their understanding and interpretation of these more recent materials — it is difficult to be entirely objective. Nonetheless, I believe that B. F. Westcott and F. J. A. Hort in the latter part of the nineteenth century and Kurt and Barbara Aland and their associates more recently in our own day must be considered the primary scholars who have provided a basis for and pointed the way toward real advances in NT textual criticism. In addition, during the past few decades we have been provided with computer tools to enable us to handle more adequately and rapidly the vast amount of textual data now at our disposal.

The Greek Manuscripts

Of the approximately 3,200 manuscripts that make up the Greek textual tradition of the NT, the most important for establishing the text of Romans are the following:

1. Papyrus Manuscripts

There are eight papyrus manuscripts or leaves of manuscripts that are of primary importance for establishing the text of Paul's letter to the Christians at Rome. None of them contains the full text of the letter. Most of them, however, either date from or reflect a time earlier than the uncial manuscripts that preserve the text in its entirety, and so must be considered of great significance in any evaluation of the text of Romans.

The most important of these eight papyri, both because of its early date and because of the uncontaminated nature of its readings, is P[46] in the Chester Beatty collection ("Chester Beatty II"), which can be dated about A.D. 200 and contains eight of Paul's letters and the Epistle to the Hebrews (though with numerous lacunae because of damaged leaves and the omission of 2 Thessalonians, Philemon, and the Pastorals). It exhibits what Kurt and Barbara Aland have called a "free" text — that is, a text that does not clearly or consistently correlate with any of the families of texts that developed at a later period.[11] Unfortunately, the first seven folios of P[46], which evidently contained Rom 1:1–5:16, are missing. Further, a number of the remaining folios of Romans in P[46] — particularly those containing 5:17–6:14;

---

11. Cf. K. and B. Aland, *Text of the New Testament,* 2nd ed., esp. 95.

8:15–15:9; and 15:11–16:27 — are somewhat defective because of their damaged edges. Nonetheless, as Werner Kümmel has rightly insisted, because of its date and the uncontaminated or "free" nature of its text, P[46] is "a valuable witness to the unrevised Pauline text of the second century and hence to the early component parts of all later textual forms."[12]

The other biblical papyri that reflect Category I texts of Romans are P[10] (1:1-7), P[26] (1:1-16), P[27] (8:12-22, 24-27; 8:33–9:3, 5-9), P[31] (12:3-8), and P[40] (1:24-27; 1:31–2:3; 3:21–4:8; 6:4-5, 16; 9:16-17, 27). Category II papyrus texts of Romans are P[61] (16:23-27) and P[94] (6:10-13, 19-22), but these contain even smaller portions of the letter. All of these eight collections of biblical papyri, it needs to be noted, have pages that have writing on both sides of the page, that is, on both the "recto" and the "verso" sides — and so seem to stem from codices (i.e., from a book form that contained folios with pages or leaves) and not from scrolls — as do also most of the other biblical papyri that contain other writings of the NT. And this suggests that the early Christians must have used the codex or book form for their sacred writings from the very beginning.

2. Uncial Manuscripts

The Greek uncial (or "majuscule") manuscripts of the fourth to the ninth centuries have played a dominant role in NT textual criticism well into the twentieth century, being superseded only in the latter part of the twentieth century by the witness of the earlier third- and fourth-century biblical papyri. For Konstantin von Tischendorf, who published his two-volume *Novum Testamentum Graece* in 1869-1872, it was Codex Sinaiticus (‭א‬ 01) that was the critical standard for establishment of the text of the NT. On the other hand, Brooke F. Westcott and Fenton J. A. Hort, who published their two-volume *The New Testament in Original Greek* in 1881-1882, proposed that the touchstone for all NT text criticism was Codex Vaticanus (B 03) — especially when it was in agreement with Codex Sinaiticus (‭א‬ 01), but also in those relatively few cases where B and ‭א‬ differed. And this B-‭א‬ textual approach (i.e., basing primary textual dependence on the two fourth-century uncial manuscripts B and ‭א‬, but favoring B over ‭א‬ where they differed) gained almost universal acceptance among NT scholars through its incorporation by Eberhard Nestle in his *Novum Testamentum Graece*, which was published by the Württemberg Bible Society of Stuttgart in 1898.

12. W. G. Kümmel, "History of the Text," in his *Introduction to the NT,* 363.

However, Kurt and Barbara Aland, together with their associates, have argued that in comparing the texts of Codex Vaticanus and Codex Sinaiticus the conclusion must be that "the textual quality of Codex Vaticanus is inferior in the Pauline corpus: in the Gospels and elsewhere it is far superior to Codex Sinaiticus (and the other uncials), but not in the letters of Paul."[13] Thus even when dealing with these two primary fourth-century uncial witnesses, which together support an Alexandrian or Neutral family of texts, a "reasoned eclecticism" must be invoked — that is, an establishing of the text that takes into consideration for each particular passage not only the external data of the respective manuscripts but also the internal data of the author's argument and usage (which is, in effect, much the same methodology as that used in establishing the text of the canonical Gospels by the use of both source criticism and redaction criticism).

3. Minuscule Manuscripts

The minuscule manuscripts have long played an important role in NT textual studies — even a dominant role up through the mid–nineteenth century. For while Desiderius Erasmus knew of Codex Basilensis, the eighth-century Byzantine uncial manuscript that was brought to the Council of Basel in 1431 and is now designated E (07), he depended almost entirely on later Byzantine minuscule texts and seems to have made no use of that then well-known Basel uncial in constructing his "received text." And while Theodore Beza published critical editions of the NT text, he never referred to what is now called Codex Beza, whose two volumes are now designated D (05) on the Gospels and Acts and D (06) on the Pauline letters — even though both of these bilingual volumes were in his possession and are today called by his name. But with new discoveries of many NT manuscripts, new finds of papyri containing biblical Greek materials, and new studies of relationships between the various families of Greek texts — all of which began in the mid–nineteenth century and have continued unabated since — that dominance of the minuscule tradition has been dramatically reduced.

Of the over 2,800 minuscule manuscripts that have been identified, numbered, and studied to date, all of which stem from the ninth through the fifteenth or sixteenth centuries, more than 80 percent represent the Byzantine or so-called "majority" text almost exclusively. Only a few of the minuscule manuscripts on Romans, as Kurt and Barbara Aland have

---

13. K. and B. Aland, *Text of the New Testament,* 14.

pointed out, "offer a valuable early text which can compete with . . . the best of the uncials."[14] Chief among these is the ninth-century minuscule manuscript 33, which has often been called the "Queen of the Minuscules"; also valuable are portions of the tenth-century minuscule manuscript 1739 and the eleventh-century minuscule manuscript 1175.

Kurt and Barbara Aland also include in Category I (i.e., manuscripts of a "very special quality") and Category II (i.e., manuscripts of a "special quality") a few minuscule manuscripts that reflect, to some extent, the Alexandrian or Neutral family of texts — with most of these evidencing, as well, various "alien influences," which usually means that they represent Byzantine readings. In Category III (i.e., manuscripts of a "distinctive character" with an "independent text") the Alands itemize a number of textual materials that, while evidencing a distinctive character and an independent text, also often exhibit a strong Byzantine influence, and so the Alands conclude that though these texts may be of some importance for understanding the history of the textual tradition of Romans they cannot be used as primary evidence for establishing the letter's text. There are no Category IV or "Western" text minuscule manuscripts for Romans. And the minuscule manuscripts of Category V (i.e., manuscripts that exhibit a purely or predominantly Byzantine text) are inferior to those of Categories I, II, and III, and so should not be used in establishing the text of Romans (and will not be taken into account in either the "Textual Notes" or the "Exegetical Comments" of our proposed Romans commentary).

Nonetheless, even though there is only a small group of minuscule manuscripts that are able to be included in Categories I and II, some attention must also, at times, be paid to the Byzantine family of texts when exegeting Romans. Thus with respect to certain passages in Romans, a "reasoned eclecticism" must also take into consideration certain Byzantine variants — not by way of establishing the text, but by way of understanding how it was interpreted in certain quarters and thereby adding another dimension to a contemporary exegesis of the passage.

Other Textual Witnesses

In addition to the Greek papyrus, uncial, and minuscule manuscripts, which reflect, in whole or in part, a continuous text for Romans, there are also

14. K. and B. Aland, *Text of the New Testament,* 128.

other textual materials that have a bearing on one's attempts to establish the original biblical text. These include early versions of the NT, patristic citations, and church lectionaries.

1. Early Versions

The earliest versions of the NT — that is, the Old Latin (the Itala or *it*), the Old Syriac (the Vetus Syra, and surviving materials derived from Tatian's Diatessaron), and a presumed Coptic prototype of the many extant Coptic translations — can be dated sometime toward the end of the second Christian century (probably about A.D. 180-190). The Latin versions are usually referred to as the Old Latin *(it)*, a translation that was produced at the end of the second century or first part of the third century, and the Vulgate *(vg)* of the fourth and fifth centuries — with both of these versions represented by a large number of manuscripts that present a great variety of textual variants. The Syriac versions are (1) the early Old Syriac, which is represented by the Sinaitic (syr^s) and/or the Curetonian (syr^c), as well as by the fifth-century Peshitta (syr^p); (2) the Philoxeniana (syr^{ph}), which was commissioned by bishop Philoxenus of Mabbug and translated by Polycarp in the year 507-508 (but is now as a manuscript extinct); (3) the Harklensis (syr^h), which was translated in 616 by the monk Thomas of Harkel, who was also at some time bishop of Mabbug; and (4) the Palestinian (syr^{1pa}) of the sixth century, which is a partially preserved translation written in an Aramaic dialect with an Syriac script, and so can only rather indirectly be called a Syriac version. The Coptic versions of the NT are very numerous, with the most commonly cited being the Sahidic (cop^{sa}), the Bohairic (cop^{bo}), and the fragmentary Fayyumic (cop^{1fay}), all three of which stem from some time in the third century or beginning of the fourth century.

All of these versions either were translated directly from a Greek text or give evidence that they have been thoroughly revised from a Greek base if originally dependent on another version. And all of these translations, as the Introduction of GNT^4 expresses matters, "are important witnesses for the Greek text of the New Testament because they derive from a relatively early stage of the tradition. They witness to the early form of the text as it was used at the time and place of their origin and development."[15]

A number of other ancient versions, however, were either only partially dependent on the Greek text or give evidence of having been influ-

---

15. GNT^4, 22.

enced by the Greek text only at various later stages in the revision of their texts. These derived versions include the Armenian version and the Georgian version, both of which appear to be based on an Old Syriac type of text. Likewise, the Ethiopic version is probably to be viewed as something of a derived translation. For while the Ethiopic translations of Acts, the General Epistles, and the Apocalypse of John seem to be based on a Greek text, though with subsequent influences from various Coptic and Arabic translations, the character of the readings and their textual sources in many of the other portions of the Ethiopic version are highly controversial. So like the United Bible Societies' fourth edition of *The Greek New Testament* (*GNT*[4]) and Nestle-Aland's twenty-seventh edition of *Novum Testamentum Graece* (NA[27]) — which both limit the citation of versions in their apparatuses to instances where there is a clear witness to the original Greek text — the policy to be followed by all interpreters of Paul is undoubtedly this: that these other ancient versions should be taken into account "only in instances where their underlying Greek text may be determined with certainty or with a high degree of probability."[16]

2. Patristic Citations

Using quotations of the NT by the Church Fathers generally, as well as their quotations of Paul's letter to the Christians at Rome in particular, to establish the biblical text poses numerous problems. And this is true even when a Church Father writes a commentary on a NT book, where, obviously, the greatest number of patristic citations are to be found. For there was always the temptation, both for the patristic authors themselves and for later copyists of their writings, to rephrase the quoted biblical materials in terms of familiar forms of the text, rather than to give attention to how that text was actually worded in the passage under consideration. Further, there are always problems as to whether a particular Church Father was (1) paraphrastically alluding to a text or actually quoting a NT passage, (2) quoting from memory or copying from a biblical manuscript, or (3) intentionally rephrasing a NT text for his own purposes. And, of course, when Latin- or Syriac-speaking Fathers wrote in their own language, there is always the additional problem of determining how the text of the translation they quoted relates to the original Greek text.

Nonetheless, as Kurt and Barbara Aland have rightly pointed out, "es-

---

16. *GNT*[4], 22.

tablishing the New Testament text of the Church Fathers has a strategic importance for textual history and criticism. It shows us how the text appeared at particular times and in particular places: this is information we can find nowhere else."[17] So while a great deal still remains to be done by way of evaluating the use of Scripture by the Church Fathers and identifying the text forms that they used, it is always important in any scholarly study of Romans to give attention to how various early Church Fathers read Romans in our attempts to establish the Greek text of the letter and then to interpret that text.

3. Church Lectionaries

Church lectionaries, of which there are about 2,300 whole or partial manuscripts in existence, are collections of biblical texts that were divided into separate pericopes and arranged according to their sequence as lessons appointed for the church year. These ecclesiastical lectionaries, however, are not principally to be related to the history of the NT text, but are to be understood more with respect to the history of church liturgy. For they are the products of particular liturgical needs, with the result that their form and wording are to be seen as having been heavily influenced by certain liturgical necessities.

Nonetheless, while only a few may be of any help in establishing the text of a NT passage, the ancient church lectionaries are important for the study of the later history of particular biblical texts. For since scribes copying a biblical text would have been familiar with the constant repetition of that text in their worship services — and so, either consciously or inadvertently, may have incorporated portions of their worship expressions into that text — the lectionaries may be presumed to have exercised some influence on the biblical texts themselves, and therefore on the textual traditions that are represented in the later manuscripts. Yet as Kurt and Barbara Aland have rightly insisted: "We can only conclude that for New Testament textual criticism, so far as the original text and its early history is concerned, nearly all of the approximately 2,300 lectionary manuscripts can be of significance only in exceptional cases."[18]

17. K. and B. Aland, *Text of the New Testament*, 172.
18. K. and B. Aland, *Text of the New Testament*, 169.

SUPPLEMENTAL BIBLIOGRAPHY

See also "Bibliography of Selected Commentaries." All references in the footnotes to works included in this list are by the authors' names and abbreviated titles.

Aland, Kurt. *Kurzgefasste Liste der griechischen Handschriften des Neuen Testaments,* vol. 1: *Gesamtübersicht.* ANTF 1. Berlin, New York: de Gruyter, 1963.

―――. "Der Schluss und die ursprüngliche Gestalt des Römerbriefes," *Neutestamentliche Entwürfe.* TBü 63. Munich: Kaiser, 1979, 284-301.

―――. "Die Entstehung des Corpus Paulinum," in *Neutestamentliche Entwürfe.* TBü 63. Munich: Kaiser, 1979, 302-50.

Aland, Kurt, *et al.,* eds. *Text und Textwert der griechischen Handschriften des Neuen Testaments,* vol. 2: *Die paulinischen Briefe.* Berlin, New York: de Gruyter, 1991.

Aland, Kurt, and Barbara Aland. *The Text of the New Testament: An Introduction to the Critical Editions and to the Theory and Practice of Modern Textual Criticism,* trans. E. F. Rhodes. Leiden: Brill; Grand Rapids: Eerdmans, 1987; 1989 2nd rev. ed.

Bardy, G. "Le texte de l'Épître aux Romains dans le commentaire d'Origène-Rufin," *RB* 17 (1920) 229-41.

Bauernfeind, Otto. *Der Römerbrieftext des Origenes, nach den Codex von der Geltz (Cod. 184 B 64 des AtheMsklosters Laura) untersucht und herausgegeben.* TU 44. Leipzig: Hinriche, 1923.

Colwell, Ernest C. *Studies in Methodology in Textual Criticism of the New Testament.* NTTS 9. Leiden: Brill, 1969.

Corssen, P. "Zur Überlieferungsgeschichte des Römerbriefes," *ZNW* 10 (1909) 1-45, 97-102.

Ehrman, Bart D. "The Use of Group Profiles for the Classification of New Testament Documentary Evidence," *JBL* 106 (1987) 465-86.

Ehrman, Bart D., and Michael W. Holmes, eds. *The Text of the New Testament in Contemporary Research: Essays on the* Status Quaestionis. Grand Rapids: Eerdmans, 1995.

Elliott, J. Keith. *Essays and Studies in New Testament Textual Criticism.* Cordoba: Ediciones El Almendro, 1992.

―――. "Thoroughgoing Eclecticism in New Testament Textual Criticism," in *The Text of the New Testament in Contemporary Research: Essays on the* Status Quaestionis, ed. B. D. Ehrman and M. W. Holmes. Grand Rapids: Eerdmans, 1995, 321-35.

Epp, Eldon J. "The Twentieth Century Interlude in New Testament Textual Criticism," *JBL* 93 (1974) 386-414.

―――. "New Testament Textual Criticism Past, Present, and Future: Reflections on the Alands' Text of the New Testament," *HTR* 82 (1989) 213-29.

Epp, Eldon J., and Gordon D. Fee, eds. *New Testament Textual Criticism: Its Significance for Exegesis (Essays in Honour of Bruce M. Metzger).* Oxford: Clarendon, 1981.

Epp, Eldon J., and Gordon D. Fee, eds. *Studies in the Theory and Method of New Testament Textual Criticism.* Grand Rapids: Eerdmans, 1993.

Fee, Gordon D. "P[75], P[66], and Origen: The Myth of Early Textual Recension in Alexandria," in *New Dimensions in New Testament Study,* ed. R. N. Longenecker and M. C. Tenney. Grand Rapids: Zondervan, 1974, 19-45.

———. "Rigorous or Reasoned Eclecticism: Which?" in *Studies in New Testament Language and Text: Essays in Honour of George D. Kilpatrick on the Occasion of His Sixty-fifth Birthday,* ed. J. K. Elliott. Leiden: Brill, 1976, 1974-97; repr. in *Studies in the Theory and Method of New Testament Textual Criticism,* ed. E. J. Epp and G. D. Fee. Grand Rapids: Eerdmans, 1993, 124-40.

———. "The Textual Criticism of the New Testament," in *Biblical Criticism: Historical, Literary, and Textual,* ed. R. K. Harrison, *et al.* Contemporary Evangelical Perspectives. Grand Rapids: Zondervan, 1978, 127-55; repr. in *The Expositor's Bible Commentary,* 12 vols., ed. F. E. Gaebelein. Grand Rapids: Zondervan, 1979, 1.419-33.

———. "Modern Textual Criticism and the Revival of the *Textus Receptus*," *JETS* 21 (1978) 19-34 (see also 157-60, "A Rejoinder").

———. "The Majority Text and the Original Text of the New Testament," *The Bible Translator* 31 (1980) 107-18; repr. in E. J. Epp and G. D. Fee, *Studies in the Theory and Method of New Testament Textual Criticism.* SD 45. Grand Rapids: Eerdmans, 1993, 183-208.

———. "Origen's Text of the New Testament and the Text of Egypt," *NTS* 28 (1982) 348-64.

———. *New Testament Exegesis: A Handbook for Students and Pastors.* Philadelphia: Westminster, 1983; rev. ed. Louisville: Westminster/John Knox, 1993, 81-91.

———. "Textual Criticism," in *Dictionary of Jesus and the Gospels,* ed. J. B. Green, S. McKnight, and I. H. Marshall. Downers Grove: InterVarsity, 1992, 827-31.

———. "The Use of the Greek Fathers for New Testament Textual Criticism," in *The Text of the New Testament in Contemporary Research: Essays on the Status Quaestionis,* ed. B. D. Ehrman and M. W. Holmes. Grand Rapids: Eerdmans, 1995, 191-207.

Finegan, Jack. *Encountering New Testament Manuscripts: A Working Introduction to Textual Criticism.* Grand Rapids: Eerdmans, 1974.

Gregory, Caspar R. *Canon and Text of the New Testament.* Edinburgh: T&T Clark; New York: Scribner's Sons, 1907, 297-528.

Hammond, C. P. "Notes on the Manuscripts and Editions of Origen's Commentary on the Epistle to the Romans in the Latin Translation by Rufinus," *JTS* 16 (1965) 338-57.

Hatch, William H. P. "A Recently Discovered Fragment of the Epistle to the Romans," *HTR* (1952) 81-85.

Holmes, Michael W. "Textual Criticism," in *Dictionary of Paul and His Letters,* ed. G. F. Hawthorne, R. P. Martin, and D. G. Reid. Downers Grove: InterVarsity, 1993, 927-32.

———. "Reasoned Eclecticism in New Testament Textual Criticism," in *The Text of the New Testament in Contemporary Research: Essays on the* Status Quaestionis, ed. B. D. Ehrman and M. W. Holmes. Grand Rapids: Eerdmans, 1995, 336-60.

———. "Reasoned Eclecticism and the Text of Romans," in *Romans and the People of God: Essays in Honor of Gordon D. Fee on the Occasion of His 65th Birthday.* Grand Rapids: Eerdmans, 1999, 187-202.

Kenyon, Frederic G. *Handbook to the Textual Criticism of the New Testament* (1926).

———. *Recent Developments in the Textual Criticism of the Greek Bible* (1933).

———. *The Chester Beatty Biblical Papyri: Descriptions and Texts of Twelve Manuscripts on Papyrus of the Greek Bible.* III.1: *Pauline Epistles and Revelation.* London: Walker, 1934, 1-9; III.3 (Supplement): *Pauline Epistles, Text,* 1936; III.4: *Pauline Epistles, Plates* (f.8, verso–f.21, recto), 1937.

———. *The Text of the Greek Bible.* London: Duckworth, 1937; revised and enlarged by A. W. Adams, 1958.

Kümmel, Werner G. "The History of the Text of the New Testament," in *Introduction to the New Testament,* trans. A. J. Mattill Jr. London: SCM, 1966, 359-86.

Lagrange, Marie-Joseph. "La Vulgate latine de l'Epître aux Romains et le texte grec," *RB* (1916) 225-39.

———. *Critique textuelle,* vol. 2: *La critique rationnelle.* Paris: Gabalda, 1935.

Lampe, Peter. "Zur Textgeschichte des Römerbriefes," *NovT* 27 (1985) 273-77.

Lietzmann, Hans. *An die Römer.* HNT. Tübingen: Mohr-Siebeck, 1906; 5th ed. 1971.

———. *Einführung in die Textgeschichte der Paulusbriefe.* HNT. Tübingen: Mohr-Siebeck, 1926, 1933.

Longenecker, Richard N. "*Quo vadis?* From Whence to Where in New Testament Text Criticism and Translation," in *Translating the New Testament: Text, Translation, Theology,* ed. S. E. Porter and M. J. Boda. MNTS. Grand Rapids: Eerdmans, 2009, 327-46.

Metzger, Bruce M. *Chapters in the History of New Testament Textual Criticism.* Leiden: Brill, 1963.

———. *The Text of the New Testament: Its Transmission, Corruption, and Restoration.* New York: Oxford University Press, 1964; 2nd ed. 1968; 3rd enlarged ed., 1992, 207-46.

———. *A Textual Commentary on the Greek New Testament.* London, New York: United Bible Societies, 1971, 1975 (corrected edition); 4th ed. revised Stuttgart: Deutsche Bibelgesellschaft/United Bible Societies, 1994.

———. *The Early Versions of the New Testament: Their Origin, Transmission, and Limitations.* New York: Oxford University Press, 1977.

———. *New Testament Studies: Philological, Versional, and Patristic.* Leiden: Brill, 1980.

Milligan, George. *The New Testament and Its Transmission*. London: Hodder and Stoughton, 1932.

Moulton, James Hope. *A Grammar of New Testament Greek*, vol. 1: *Prolegomena*, 3rd ed. Edinburgh: T&T Clark, 1908.

Nestle, Eberhard. *Introduction to the Textual Criticism of the Greek New Testament*, trans. W. Edie, ed. (with preface) by A. Menzies. London, New York: Williams and Norgate, 1901.

Souter, Alexander. *The Text and Canon of the New Testament*, rev. by C. S. C. Williams. London: Duckworth, 1913; 2nd ed. 1954.

Sturz, H. A. *The Byzantine Text-Type and New Testament Textual Criticism*. Nashville: Nelson, 1984.

Suggs, M. Jack. "The Use of Patristic Evidence in the Search for a Primitive New Testament Text," *NTS* 4 (1958) 139-47.

Tasker, R. V. G. "The Text of the 'Corpus Paulinum,'" *NTS* 1 (1955) 180-91.

Tischendorf, Konstantin von. *Novum Testamentum Graece* [editio octava critica maior], 2 vols. Leipzig: Hinrichs, 1869-1872; vol. 3, *Prolegomena*, ed. C. R. Gregory. Leipzig: Hinrichs, 1894.

Vaganay, Leon. *An Introduction to New Testament Textual Criticism*, trans. J. Heimerdinger; 2nd ed. updated and expanded by C.-B. Amphoux and J. Heimerdinger. Cambridge: Cambridge University Press, 1991, 129-45.

Wallace, Daniel B. "The Majority Text Theory: History, Methods, and Critique," in *The Text of the New Testament in Contemporary Research: Essays on the Status Quaestionis*, ed. B. D. Ehrman and M. W. Holmes. Grand Rapids: Eerdmans, 1995, 297-320.

Westcott, Brooke F., and Fenton J. A. Hort. *Introduction to the New Testament in the Original Greek*. Peabody: Hendrickson, 1988; repr. of *The New Testament in the Original Greek*, vol. 1: *Text;* vol. 2: *Introduction* and *Appendix*, 1881-1882; 2nd ed. of vol. 1 in 1898 and 2nd ed. of vol. 2 in 1896.

Zimmermann, Heinrich. *Neutestamentliche Methodenlehre: Darstellung der historisch-kritischen Methode*, 6th ed. Stuttgart: Katholisches Bibelwerk, 1978; 7th ed. rev. by K. Kliesch, 1982.

Zuntz, Günther. *The Text of the Epistles: A Disquisition upon the Corpus Paulinum*. British Academy Schweich Lectures, 1946. London: British Academy, 1953.

―――. "Réflexions sur l'Histoire du Texte Paulinen," *RB* 59 (1952) 5-22.

CHAPTER IX

Major Interpretive Approaches Prominent Today

A rather large number of interpretive approaches, with their respective methodologies, have been proposed during the past nineteen or twenty centuries for an understanding of Paul and his letters — particularly for an understanding of Paul's letter to the Christians at Rome. And many of these approaches have continued on, in one form or another, among both scholars and lay people today. There have also been a number of "dead ends," as well as some rather impossible (even aberrant) hypotheses.

The approaches highlighted in this chapter have been of major importance and especially prominent during the modern critical period of NT study, that is, from about 1850 through to today. And while the issues raised by these more contemporary approaches can be properly treated only in an exegetical commentary, the most significant of them are able also to be explicated (at least to an extent) in a thematic manner. So the following major interpretive approaches that seem particularly prominent today will be briefly set out in thematic fashion as critical issues that need to be taken into account in a scholarly study of Romans.

1. "The Righteousness of God" and "Righteousness"

The expression "the righteousness of God" (δικαιοσύνη θεοῦ) and the abstract noun "righteousness" (δικαιοσύνη) have always been to the fore in the interpretation of Romans, though often treated in somewhat diverse ways. During the past one and one-half centuries, however, discussions regarding what Paul meant when he spoke of "the righteousness of God" and of "righteousness" have been particularly extensive, with whole volumes dedicated to such expositions. In order, therefore, to appreciate what Paul is saying in his letter to Rome regarding this expression and this noun, the following matters need to be set out.

Patterns of Usage in Paul's Letters and the Rest of the New Testament

The expression "the righteousness of God" (δικαιοσύνη θεοῦ) appears in Paul's letters mainly in the first section (1:16–4:25) of the body middle of Romans, that is:

1. in 1:17a, "the righteousness of God is revealed (δικαιοσύνη θεοῦ ἀποκαλύπεται)," where it appears in the thesis statement of 1:16-17;
2. in the rhetorical question of 3:5, "But if our unrighteousness (εἰ δὲ ἡ ἀδικία ἡμῶν) establishes/demonstrates/brings out more clearly God's righteousness (θεοῦ δικαιοσύνην συνίστησιν), what shall we say?";
3. in 3:21a and 3:22a, reading first "the righteousness of God has been revealed" (δικαιοσύνη θεοῦ πεφανέρωται) and then repeating the phrase "the righteousness of God" (δικαιοσύνη θεοῦ), with that double use of the expression appearing in the context of the second thesis statement of 3:21-23, which repeats and expands on the first thesis statement of 1:16-17; and,
4. in 3:25 and 3:26, "He did this in order to show/demonstrate/prove (εἰς ἔνδειξιν and πρὸς τὴν ἔνδειξιν) his righteousness/justice (τῆς δικαιοσύνης αὐτοῦ)," where it appears in what seems to be early Christian confessional material that is quoted by Paul in support of his repeated and expanded thesis statement of 3:21-23.

It is also found twice in 10:3, which verse is in the third major section (9–11) of the body middle (1:16–15:13) of Romans: "For being ignorant of the righteousness that comes from God (τὴν τοῦ θεοῦ δικαιοσύνην), they sought to establish their own; they did not submit to God's righteousness (τῇ δικαιοσύνῃ τοῦ θεοῦ)" — with the twofold use of the article in these two instances evidently meant to refer back to the use of the expression earlier in 1:17; 3:21-22; and 3:25-26 (perhaps also 3:5) in the first part of the first major section of the body middle of the letter.

As for the noun δικαιοσύνη ("righteousness," "uprightness," "justice"), it is frequently found in a religious sense in the LXX, the writings of Early Judaism, and throughout the NT — as are also the adjective δίκαιος ("righteous," "upright," "just"), the verb δικαιόω ("justify," "vindicate," "acquit"), and the adverb δικαίως ("uprightly," "justly," "in a just manner"). In Romans the singular noun "righteousness" (δικαιοσύνη) appears in 5:17, "the gift of righteousness" (τῆς δωρεᾶς τῆς δικαιοσύνης); in 5:21, "so that grace might reign through righteousness (οὕτως καὶ ἡ χάρις βασιλεύσῃ διὰ δικαιοσύνης) to bring eternal life through Jesus Christ our Lord"; and in 9:30, "What then shall we say? That the Gentiles, who did not pursue righteousness (δικαιοσύνην), have obtained righteousness (δικαιοσύνην), a righteousness (δικαιοσύνην) that is by faith?" — while in 2 Corinthians the articular noun "the righteousness" is to be found in 3:9, "the ministry of [or, 'that brings'] the righteousness (τῆς δικαιοσύνης)." All four of these verses use the noun in an objective or communicative fashion to speak of a righteousness that God gives as a gift to those who have faith in him.

What is to be noted here regarding Paul's pattern in using the expression "the righteousness of God," however, is that, apart from its multiple occurrences in Romans, it is found in his other letters only twice — that is, in 2 Cor 5:21, "so that in him [Christ] we might become the righteousness of God (δικαιοσύνην θεοῦ)," and Phil 3:9, "the righteousness of God (τὴν ἐκ θεοῦ δικαιοσύνην) that is based on faith." And in both of these passages the expression quite clearly refers to a righteousness that is bestowed by God — that is, it is used in an objective or communicative sense (with the genitive τοῦ θεοῦ being read as an objective genitive, which signifies that God is the source or originating agent of the righteousness that is communicated), and so to be understood as "the gift of righteousness" (cf. Rom 5:17) that is given by God to those who respond "by faith."

Further, "the righteousness of God" as an expression appears elsewhere in the NT only three times. First in Matt 6:33, that is, in Jesus' "Sermon on the Mount" — where, evidently, the evangelist has redacted a "Q" saying by the incorporation of the words "his [God's] righteousness" (τὴν δικαιοσύνην αὐτοῦ; note the phrase's omission in Luke 12:31): "Seek first the kingdom of God and his righteousness (τὴν δικαιοσύνην αὐτοῦ), and all these things will be given to you as well." Then it appears in the warning of Jas 1:20: "A person's anger (ὀργή) does not bring about the righteousness of God (δικαιοσύνην θεοῦ)" — which is somewhat reminiscent of Sir 1:22, "Unrighteous wrath [reading ὀργή with A*] cannot be justified, for the wrath of his anger will prove to be a person's ruin." It also occurs in a slightly varied form (i.e., with the article τοῦ and possessive pronoun ἡμῶν) in the salutation of 2 Pet 1:1: "To those who through/in the righteousness of our God (ἐν δικαιοσύνῃ τοῦ θεοῦ ἡμῶν) and Savior Jesus Christ have received a faith as precious as ours." In all of these three non-Pauline NT occurrences, however, the expression connotes a strong subjective or attributive nuance.

Thus with regard to the expression "the righteousness of God" (δικαιοσύνη θεοῦ), it is to be noted that its occurrences are extremely limited in the NT — appearing only a relatively few times in Paul's letters, being primarily grouped together in the first major section (i.e., 1:16–4:25) of the body middle of Romans, and found less often elsewhere in the NT. Further, it needs to be observed that whereas in its three NT occurrences outside of the Pauline corpus (as well as in its appearance in Rom 3:5) the expression is used in a distinctly subjective or attributive sense — which, it may be postulated, reflects or echoes the vocabulary and usage of Early Judaism and early Jewish Christianity — Paul speaks of "the righteousness of God" in a more objective or communicative sense, which is a usage that calls for particular attention.

The Use of Δικαι-Terminology in Classical Greek and Early Patristic Writings

What, then, did Paul mean in Romans by "the righteousness of God" (δικαιοσύνη θεοῦ) — particularly when he used the expression in 1:17 and then again in 3:21-22 (twice) in his two thesis statements of 1:16-17 and 3:21-23? And extending that question somewhat further, How did Paul understand the cognate expression "his [God's] righteousness" (ἡ δικαιοσύνη αὐτοῦ) in 3:25-26, which appears twice in what seems to be a portion of early Christian confessional material that he quoted in support of his expanded thesis statement of 3:21-23? The matter has been extensively debated throughout the course of Christian history, and it remains a vital question today.

It is not enough, however, to deal only with the explicit expression δικαιοσύνη θεοῦ. Paul's use of the abstract noun δικαιοσύνη (i.e., without the possessive noun θεοῦ or pronoun αὐτοῦ), as well as his uses of the adjective δίκαιος, the verb δικαιόω, and the adverb δικαίως, must also be taken into account. Further, it must always be asked how this complex of δικαι-terminology (i.e., the noun, the adjective, the verb, and the adverb) was used by authors before Paul and by other writers of his day — not only as can be determined from a study of its use in the LXX, the writings of Early Judaism, and other NT authors, but also by classical Greek writers and the early Church Fathers.

In the Greek classical period the noun δικαιοσύνη had to do with the observance of law and the fulfillment of duty,[1] and so was used in legal contexts for the punishment that a person justly deserved according to the law.[2] And in the Greco-Roman world of earliest Christianity, the term continued to be closely associated with judicial justice and most often connoted the idea of retributive punishment. So the common Latin translation of δικαιοσύνη θεοῦ came to be *iustitia Dei* ("the justice of God"), both in the Old Latin translation, which was produced at the end of the second or first part of the third century, and in Jerome's Vulgate, which was translated during the latter part of the fourth and first part of the fifth centuries. Thus most Latin theologians came to understand "the righteousness of God" in primarily an attributive sense — that is, as an attribute of God, with an emphasis on his character as being absolutely just and his actions as always expressed justly and in terms of justice.

This sense of δικαιοσύνη θεοῦ as referring primarily to God's just nature and his acts of justice was buttressed by the writings of Tertullian of Carthage (c. 145-220), who was trained as a lawyer and philosopher before his conversion to Christ but excelled as a Christian apologist and theologian after his conversion. Tertullian was extremely prolific, writing literally scores of apologetic and theological tractates (both orthodox and sectarian) — many of which were kept and cherished, though others have been lost and forgotten. It was Tertullian who took away the reproach of theological and literary barrenness that was commonly leveled in his day against Latin Christianity. For he developed a system of juridical and forensic Christian doctrine that instructed such contemporary Roman Christian thinkers and writers as Cyprian, Minucius Felix, Arnobius, and Lactantius — and that continued to inspire many later Christian worthies, such as Jerome and Augustine.

Such a subjective or attributive understanding of "the righteousness of God" was expressed in the fourth century by a Latin commentator, whose commentary on the Pauline letters was thought to have been written by Ambrose but who was later dubbed "Ambrosiaster" by Erasmus. In Ambrosiaster's treatment of the phrase *iustitia Dei* in Rom 1:17, he writes:

> It is the justice of God, because he has given what he has promised; hence the one who believes that he has acquired that which God had promised through his prophets shows that God is just and becomes a witness to his justice.[3]

1. Cf. Plato, *Republic* 4.433a.
2. Cf. Aristotle, *Rhetoric* 1.9.
3. Ambrosiaster, *Ad Romanos* on 1:17 (*CSEL* 81.1.36-37).

Further, connecting "justice," "mercy," and "promise," Ambrosiaster says of the phrase as it appears in Rom 3:21:

> That is said to be God's justice which seems to be his mercy, because it is rooted in his promise. . . . And when he welcomes those who take refuge in him, it is said to be justice, because not to welcome those who seek refuge is iniquity.[4]

Augustine, however, writing during the final decade of the fourth century and the first three decades of the fifth (i.e., from 391 until his death in 430), came more and more to interpret the expression *iustitia Dei* in his Latin Bible not only in a subjective or attributive sense but also in an objective or communicative sense — that is, not only as an attribute of God and his actions, but also with reference to God's justification of repentant sinners, his bestowal on them a status of righteousness, and his endowment of them with his own quality of righteousness.[5] For after returning to North Africa in 391 (some four years after his conversion to Christ in Milan), and shortly following his ordination as a presbyter in the diocese of Hippo, Augustine, in response to questions asked him at a conference in Carthage, wrote a series of expository comments on selected passages from chapters 5–9 of Romans (which he grouped into eighty-four sections and published in 394 as *Expositio quarundam propositionum ex epistula ad Romanos*) that highlighted the important feature of God's unmerited grace in Paul's letter to the Christians at Rome. It was probably during this period that Augustine first began to think seriously about the nature of God's grace — though his understanding of God's grace developed considerably over the next few years, as seems evident from the letters that he wrote later to his friend Simplicianus on the subject during 396-398 in *De diversis Quaestionibus ad Simplicianum*. And it was this topic of God's grace that dominated all of Augustine's thought throughout the last thirty years of his life (i.e., from the beginning of the fifth century until his death in 430) and redirected much of Christian theology thereafter. Further, it may be assumed that it was this deep-seated conviction regarding the nature of God's unmerited grace that caused Augustine to understand the phrase *iustitia Dei* not only as an attribute of God (i.e., in the subjective or attributive sense) but also as the righ-

---

4. Ambrosiaster, *Ad Romanos* on 3:21 (*CSEL* 81.1.116-17).

5. Augustine, *De Trinitate* 14.12.15 (*CCLat* 50A.443); *De Spiritu et Littera* 1.9.15 (*CSEL* 60.167); 1.11.18 (*CSEL* 60.171); *Ep* 140.72 (*CSEL* 44.220); *In Johannis Evangelium* 26:1 (*CCLat* 36.260).

teousness that God gives to repentant sinners in redeeming them by his grace (i.e., the objective or communicative sense).

Interpretations During the Middle Ages

In the Middle Ages, that is, from the fifth through the fifteenth centuries of European history, two interpretations of "the righteousness of God" (δικαιοσύνη θεοῦ in Greek; *iustitia Dei* in Latin) vied for acceptance. The first, which has been called "the classical view" because of its dominance among the Latin Fathers, understood the phrase as having reference to the righteous and just nature of God, his fidelity to his promises, and the justice of his actions in dealing with humanity (i.e., the subjective or attributive sense). The other, influenced by Augustine and by Paul's use of the expression in 2 Cor 5:21 and Phil 3:9, viewed δικαιοσύνη θεοῦ (in Greek) and *iustitia Dei* (in Latin) more in the context of God's salvific activity in human history (i.e., the objective or communicative sense), though also understood it as referring to God's righteous and just nature. In speaking about "God's justice/righteousness," therefore, theologians during the fifth through the fifteenth centuries frequently combined, in various ways, both (1) what is true about God's character and actions and (2) what God gives to those who believe the gospel and commit themselves to him.

This collation of interpretations was expressed by some of the better Roman Catholic commentators during the Middle Ages. Thomas Aquinas (1224-1274), for example, spoke of "the justice of God" in Rom 1:17 as that "by which God is just and by which he justifies human beings *(iustitia qua Deus iustus est et qua Deus homines justificat),*" thereby joining Augustine's understanding of God's grace in justifying people with Anselm's understanding of God's mercy as being the fullness of his justice.[6] This union of views appears also in the commentary writings of Thomas de Vio, surnamed Cajetan (1469-1534), a scholastic theologian of immense stature and great influence who had in 1518 presided as the Papal Legate in the examination of Luther at Augsburg — and who during the final decade of his life (i.e., from 1525 to 1534) devoted himself entirely to the writing of biblical commentaries, first on the Psalms, then on the Gospels, the Acts, and the letters of the NT (including Romans), and finally on the Pentateuch, Joshua, Proverbs, Ecclesiastes, and Isaiah 1–3. But though Thomas de Vio was considered the most eminent Roman Catho-

---

6. Cf. Thomas Aquinas, "Ad Romanos," in *Opera Omnia,* 13.3-156, on 1:17.

lic theologian of his day, he got into trouble with his ecclesiastical superiors when his NT commentaries were published — not only because he had departed from the Vulgate text, using instead the critical editions of the Greek text prepared by Erasmus and Faber, but also, and much more seriously in the eyes of his detractors, because he often sounded too much like Luther in his interpretation of "God's justice/righteousness" and "faith." Further, while Augustine of the fifth century was widely revered during the Middle Ages as one of the church's greatest theologians, he was also frequently rather diversely understood — with the result that his broader understanding of "the righteousness of God" was often combined with the more strictly attributive views of such writers as Anselm and "Ambrosiaster."

Luther's Understanding of "The Righteousness of God" and "Righteousness"

It was Martin Luther, however, who most effectively highlighted the communicative sense of "the righteousness of God" and the vital importance of "faith" in Paul's letters, and so brought about a new appreciation in western Christendom of Augustine's emphasis on God's unmerited grace. In his earlier experience as a monk Luther had pondered deeply, with considerable consternation and great sorrow, the meaning of the phrase *iustitia Dei* ("the justice of God") in his Latin Bible. In 1515, however, Luther came to what was for him an entirely new discovery regarding Paul's teaching on "the justice/righteousness of God" and "justification by faith" in Rom 1:17 and 3:21-24 (also 5:1), which new discovery became the catalyst for his own spiritual rebirth, "an open door into paradise" and "a gateway to heaven" — and so the start of a thoroughgoing religious revolution in his life, which, of course, eventuated in the Protestant Reformation. Later, in 1545, recalling the resolution of his spiritual struggles when he came to what he believed was a proper understanding of this phrase, Luther wrote (with the translation of the Latin *iustitia Dei*, "the justice of God," in the text, and that of the Greek δικαιοσύνη θεοῦ, "the righteousness of God," in brackets):

> I greatly longed to understand Paul's Epistle to the Romans, and nothing stood in the way but that one expression, "the justice ['righteousness'] of God," because I took it to mean that justice ['righteousness'] whereby God is just ['righteous'] and deals justly ['righteously'] in punishing the unjust ['unrighteous']. My situation was that, although an impeccable

monk, I stood before God as a sinner troubled in conscience, and I had no confidence that my merit would assuage him. Therefore I did not love a just ['righteous'] and angry God, but rather hated and murmured against him. Yet I clung to the dear Paul and had a great yearning to know what he meant.

Night and day I pondered until I saw the connection between the justice ['righteousness'] of God and the statement that "the just ['righteous'] will live by his faith." Then I grasped the truth that the justice ['righteousness'] of God is that justice ['righteousness'] whereby, through grace and sheer mercy, he justifies us by faith. Thereupon I felt myself to be reborn and to have gone through open doors into paradise. The whole of Scripture took on a new meaning, and whereas before "the justice ['righteousness'] of God" had filled me with hate, now it became to me inexpressibly sweet in greater love. This passage of Paul became to me a gateway to heaven.[7]

Luther's discovery was in line with Augustine's emphasis on the unmerited nature of God's grace. Like Augustine, Luther was not opposed to understanding "just" and "justice" (in Latin), or "righteous" and "righteousness" (in Greek), as attributes of God and his actions (i.e., in the subjective or attributive sense). His emphasis, however, was on "God's righteousness as a divine gift" (i.e., in the objective or communicative sense) that puts the person who receives that gift "by faith" in an entirely new relationship with the one true, righteous Divine Being (i.e., in a state of "forensic justness or rightness") and causes that person to live in an entirely new way both personally and in society (i.e., in an experience of "ethical justice or righteousness").

A New Focus on the Old Testament and the Writings of Early Judaism

An important new focus in biblical scholarship with regard to the understanding of the expression "the righteousness of God" and the noun "righteousness" was begun by Augustus Hermann Cremer in his *Die Paulinische Rechtfertigungslehre* of 1900. For Cremer argued that NT interpreters should not treat these expressions in terms of the use of the noun δικαιοσύνη in Greek classical writings, nor deal with them just theologically, but, rather, must first understand them with reference to their rootage in the OT. So he

---

7. Martin Luther, "Preface to Latin Writings," in *Luther's Works*, 34.336-37; see also *idem*, "Table Talk," in *Luther's Works*, 54.193, 309, 442.

argued that Paul's use of δικαιοσύνη and δικαιοσύνη θεοῦ must be viewed primarily vis-à-vis the OT Hebrew masculine noun צדק and its feminine counterpart צדקה, which in both genders denoted broadly a whole range of concepts having to do with "justness," "justice," "rightness," and "righteousness," and thus were used in the religion of Israel to connote both (1) an attribute of God and the quality of his actions (cf., e.g., Ps 36:7 [6]: "Your 'righteousness' is like the mighty mountains, your justice like the great deep"; Ps 71:19: "Your 'righteousness' reaches to the skies, O God") and (2) what God accomplishes redemptively on behalf of his people, often in conjunction with the concept of "salvation" (cf., e.g., Isa 46:13: "I am bringing my 'righteousness' near, it is not far away; and my salvation will not be delayed. I will grant salvation to Zion, my splendor to Israel"; Isa 56:1: "Maintain 'justice' and do what is right, for my salvation is close at hand and my 'righteousness' will soon be revealed").

This understanding of "righteousness" and "the righteousness of God" as rooted in the OT Scriptures, with both attributive and communicative nuances being present, is supported by a number of other OT passages that (1) speak of the character and actions of God in terms of "rightness" and "righteousness" (cf. Deut 33:21; Judg 5:11; Pss 89:16[17]; 96:13; 98:9; 111:3; 143:1, 11; Mic 6:5) and (2) refer to God's deliverance and salvation of his people as "his acts of righteousness" (cf. 1 Sam 12:7; Isa 45:8, 24-25; 51:4-8; Dan 9:16). Further, such a joining of nuances is supported by various passages in the LXX and the Dead Sea Scrolls where God's righteous nature and just actions are depicted as including both his granting of a new status to people as a result of his removal of their sins (cf., e.g., LXX Ps 50 [51]:1-14; 1QS 11.3; 1QH 12.37) and the transformation of his people by means of his enablement (cf., e.g., LXX Ps 71 [72]:1-2; 1QS 11.14; 1QH 13.37).

In addition to these passages, "the best perception of God's righteousness" in writings that may be claimed to represent the better Jewish spiritual milieu of Paul's day is probably, as Peter Stuhlmacher has suggested, the "Jewish prayers of repentance" that appear in the later writings of the OT and in the Dead Sea Scrolls — particularly those of Dan 9:4-19; 4 Ezra 8:20-36; and 1QS cols. 10-11.[8] For the prayer of repentance of Dan 9:4-19 incorporates toward its close the following words:

> O Lord, in keeping with all your righteous acts, turn away your anger and your wrath from Jerusalem, your city, your holy hill. . . . We do not

---

8. P. Stuhlmacher, *Romans*, 30.

make requests of you because we are righteous, but because of your great mercy.[9]

Ezra's prayer of repentance in 4 Ezra 8:20-36 concludes with the following statement:

For in this, O Lord, your righteousness and goodness will be declared, when you are merciful to those who have no store of good works.[10]

And the Qumran covenanters' hymn of repentance in 1QS cols. 10-11 includes the following words of confidence, which reflect not only an attributive but also a communicative understanding of God's righteousness:

If I should waver, God's mercies will be my salvation; if I stumble in the waywardness of flesh, I shall be set aright through God's righteousness ever-enduring. . . . In His righteousness he will cleanse me from all the pollution of man and from the sin of humanity, that I may acknowledge to God His righteousness, and to the Most High His majestic splendor.[11]

When Paul's use of "the righteousness of God (δικαιοσύνη θεοῦ)" is understood in terms of its rootage in the Jewish (OT) Scriptures and the writings of Early Judaism, its range of meaning and comprehensive nature can be more fully appreciated. No longer can such past alternatives be proposed as (1) whether the possessive "of God" (τοῦ θεοῦ), or its cognate "of him" (αὐτοῦ), is to be interpreted as a subjective or an objective genitive, (2) whether the expression should be understood in an attributive or a communicative sense, (3) whether it is best viewed soteriologically or eschatologically, or (4) whether its thrust has to do primarily with theology or with anthropology. In light of Paul's Jewish background, all of these dichotomies, as H. Graf Reventlow has observed, "quickly show themselves to be much too narrow."[12] It is not whether one or the other of these alternative views is correct for an understanding of Paul's use of the expression δικαιοσύνη θεοῦ (or, δικαιοσύνη αὐτοῦ) in Rom 1:17; 3:5; 3:21-22 (twice); 3:25-26 (twice); 10:3; 2 Cor 5:21; and Phil 3:9. Rather, the more comprehensive range of meaning found in the OT and in the literature of Early Judaism must be credited, as well, to Paul's use of the expression — particularly in his thesis statements of

9. Dan 9:16, 18.
10. *4 Ezra* 8:36.
11. 1QS 11.12, 14-15.
12. H. G. Reventlow, *Rechtfertigung im Horizon des Alten Testaments,* 113 (my trans.).

1:16-17 (at v. 17a) and 3:21-23 (at vv. 21a and 22a). For "the righteousness of God" that Paul speaks of in these passages is a righteousness that is both (1) an attribute of God and a quality that characterizes all of his actions (the attributive sense) and (2) a gift that God gives to people who come to him "by faith" (the communicative sense). It is a type of righteousness that enables God to be both δίκαιον ("just") and δικαιοῦντα ("justifier" or "the One who justifies"), as the confessional material of 3:24-26 affirms at its close in verse 26b.

Righteousness as a Forensic Status or an Ethical Quality

But even when a communicative sense of "the righteousness of God" and "righteousness" is included within the range of meaning of these expressions, the question remains as to whether in speaking of the gift of "God's righteousness" and "righteousness" Paul is referring (1) to a status of righteousness that God confers (i.e., a forensic, declaratory understanding) or (2) to an ethical quality of life that God empowers (i.e., an effective, ethical understanding). Roman Catholics have laid stress on the noun δικαιοσύνη ("righteousness," "uprightness," "justice") and the adjective δίκαιος ("righteous," "upright," "just"), interpreting the verb δικαιόω ("to justify," "vindicate," "acquit," "make free") in terms of its noun and adjective — and so have concluded that δικαιοσύνη means primarily an acquittal from past sins and a "making righteous" in an ethical sense, but that a final declaration of righteousness awaits the last judgment. Protestants, on the other hand, have emphasized that the verb δικαιόω must be viewed in the sense of "to account as righteous" or "declare righteous," and so have interpreted the entire cluster of δικαι-words in terms of a "right relationship" established by God (i.e., forensic, declaratory, or sometimes called "imputed" righteousness) rather than as first of all "ethical uprightness" (i.e., effective, ethical, or sometimes called "real" righteousness). Or to put the question in a more modern form: Is Paul's use of δικαι-words to be viewed as "transfer terminology"[13] or as applicable to "the day-to-day conduct of those who had already believed"?[14]

John Ziesler, based on his study of "about 481 cases" of the use of the Hebrew term צדק as a noun, a verb, and an adjective in the Jewish (OT)

---

13. So E. P. Sanders, *Paul and Palestinian Judaism*, 470-72; idem, *Paul, the Law, and the Jewish People*, passim.

14. So J. D. G. Dunn, "New Perspective on Paul," 121.

Scriptures, has largely, we believe, resolved this dilemma in demonstrating how Paul, in continuity with OT usage, employed (1) the verb δικαιόω in a forensic or declaratory fashion to mean "to justify," "vindicate," or "acquit," but also used (2) the noun δικαιοσύνη in a more comprehensive manner to signify both a status or standing before God (the objective or communicative sense) and an ethical "uprightness," "righteousness," or "justice" (the subjective or attributive sense), with (3) the adjective δίκαιος being used to connote an ethical "uprightness," "righteousness," or "justice" in primarily an attributive sense.[15] In so doing, Ziesler has shown how Paul was able to join both the forensic and the ethical nuances in his understanding of righteousness, with the one always involving the other.

Proposed Rationale for the Varied Nuances in Paul and in Other New Testament Occurrences

There yet remains, however, a further rather nagging difficulty for many interpreters of Paul. This has to do with a rationale for the varied nuances of the expression "the righteousness of God" (δικαιοσύνη θεοῦ) in Paul's letters and in its three other NT appearances. As Peter Stuhlmacher has stated the difficulty:

> It has long been a matter of debate in Pauline exegesis whether one should understand the righteousness of God in Paul's thought above all, on the basis of Phil. 3:9, as the gift of God, the righteousness of faith, or "the righteousness which is valid before God" (Luther); or whether the accent is to be placed, with Schlatter among others, on God's own juridical and salvific activity (in and through Christ).[16]

Stuhlmacher himself seeks to settle this debate with the following comment, which, as far as it goes, is quite appropriate:

> One should not establish a false alternative between the two [understandings]. The expression incorporates both, and it must be determined from passage to passage where Paul places the accent.[17]

---

15. Cf. J. A. Ziesler, *Meaning of Righteousness in Paul* (1972).
16. P. Stuhlmacher, *Romans*, 31.
17. P. Stuhlmacher, *Romans*, 32.

Likewise, Joseph Fitzmyer — while acknowledging the probable presence of both an attributive and a communication sense in Paul's understanding of the expression (and speaking in a Roman Catholic fashion) — recognizes this dilemma faced by all Pauline interpreters regarding the apostle's use of "the righteousness/justice of God" in Romans when he says: "What is debatable, however, is whether the gift idea of *dikaiosynē theou* is suitable anywhere in Romans."[18] For while Fitzmyer seems to have little doubt about the communicative sense of the expression being present in 2 Cor 5:21 and Phil 3:9, he has difficulty in seeing anything but the attributive sense in its more numerous appearances in Paul's letter to Rome.

Such a dilemma, however, may be somewhat mitigated if we understand, as I have argued above (see Chapter IV, "Addressees"): (1) that Romans was written to believers in Jesus who had been extensively influenced by Jewish Christian theology and vocabulary, whatever their particular ethnic backgrounds, and (2) that in writing to the Christians at Rome Paul often used certain theological expressions and religious vocabulary that he believed they would have understood and appreciated, particularly in the first section (1:16–4:25) and third section (9–11) of the body middle of his letter. On such a thesis, the following fourfold scenario may be proposed as being present in Romans:

1. that in 1:17 and 3:21 Paul uses "the righteousness of God" in a comprehensive fashion, including in its range of meaning both a subjective or attributive sense and an objective or communicative sense;

2. that in 3:22 (where he expands on his usage in 1:17 and 3:21) and in 3:25-26 (where he supports his expanded usage by the quotation of a portion of early Christian confessional material) Paul not only has in mind "God's righteousness" in an attributive sense but also wants to highlight "God's righteousness" in a communicative sense — thereby in 3:22 defining "God's righteousness" in terms of "the faithfulness of Jesus Christ," which is applicable to "all of those who believe," and then in 3:25-26 including not only an attributive understanding of "divine righteousness/justice" but also a communicative understanding of God as being "the One who justifies";

3. that in 3:5 the attributive sense is certainly to the fore: "If our injustice/unrighteousness serves to confirm the justice/righteousness of God, what shall we say?"; and,

18. J. A. Fitzmyer, *Romans*, 262.

4. that in 10:3 the expression is clearly used in the first part of the verse in a communicative sense — though with, perhaps, both attributive and communicative nuances present in the last part of the verse: "They did not know the righteousness that comes from God. . . . They did not submit to God's righteousness."

An attributive sense, however, is dominant in all three of the NT uses of the expression "the righteousness of God" outside of the Pauline corpus, that is, in Matt 6:33; Jas 1:20; and 2 Pet 1:1 — probably because all three represent, in some fashion, the theological language of early Jewish Christianity. That may have been how the Christians at Rome understood the expression as well, rooted as they were in the theology, language, and ethics of Jerusalem Christendom (see Chapter IV, "Addressees"). But Paul's emphasis in his Gentile mission was on God's righteousness as a gift given by God to those whom he reconciles to himself through the work of Christ, the ministry of his Holy Spirit, and their response of faith. Therefore, while always acknowledging the "justness," "justice," and "righteousness" of God in an attributive sense, Paul's emphasis in proclaiming the Christian gospel to Gentiles was on "the righteousness of God" in a communicative sense — as can be seen most clearly in 2 Cor 5:21, "God made him who had no sin to be sin for us, so that in him we might become 'the righteousness of God,'" and Phil 3:9, that I may gain Christ "and be found in him, not having a righteousness of my own that comes from the law, but that which is through faith in Christ, that is, 'the righteousness that comes from God and is by faith'" (cf. also his use of "righteousness" as a "gift" from God based solely on God's "grace" in Rom 5:15-17 and 10:3).

A Suggested Hypothesis

It may have been that some Christians at Rome objected to what they perceived to be an imbalance in Paul's proclamation of the Christian message in his Gentile mission — that is, that he preached well "the righteousness of God" in a communicative sense, but was less vocal about God's righteousness in an attributive sense. In writing them, therefore, Paul begins by affirming the broad range of meaning that the expression "the righteousness of God" incorporates. In effect, he agrees with his addressees in their attributive understanding — which, however, may have been conceptualized by them in a somewhat static manner with respect to the character and actions of God. But he also wants them to think in revelatory, historical, and redemptive terms — and so, it may be presumed, in a more dynamic fashion. Thus he emphasizes the fact that God's righteousness "is now being revealed" by God himself (using the present indicative passive verb ἀποκαλύπτεται) in the Christian gospel — which is a truth that he believed both they and he confessed, and so held in common. And in the course of his argument in 1:16–4:25 he develops his thesis, which is first presented in 1:16-17 and then repeated and expanded in 3:21-23 (with all of what he has declared being supported by an early Christian confessional portion that he quotes in 3:24-26, explicates further in 3:27-31, and finally illustrates by the example of Abraham in ch. 4), by laying more and more emphasis on the communicative nuances of a traditionally Jewish and Jewish Christian understanding of "the righteousness of God" while still keeping in balance the important attributive nuances.

All of these matters regarding "the righteousness of God" and "righteousness" are issues of critical concern in the study of Romans, and they call for careful consideration on the part of every interpreter. They are matters that must be dealt with exegetically and more rigorously in a forthcoming commentary proper. Suffice it here to present them in thematic fashion as introductory issues of great significance for any study, whether popular or scholarly, in the study of Paul's letter to the Christians at Rome.

2. "Justification" and "Faith"

Martin Luther came (as noted above) to understand Paul's use of the expression "the righteousness of God" and the term "righteousness" in a new way. The Roman Catholic Church of Luther's day proclaimed (and continues to proclaim) that a person receives an initial "righteousness" or "justification" at his or her baptism, with then a final "righteousness" or "justification" being attainable only after a lifetime of "good works" that strives (always, of course, in cooperation with God) to do God's will. Luther, however, came to the realization from his reading of Rom 1:16-17 and 3:21-24 that "righteousness" (i.e., "justification") is a sovereign act of God in which, because of his great love and apart from any human merit, God declares a person to be righteous at any time in that person's life when he or she responds positively to God's provision of relationship with him through the work of Jesus Christ and God's call through the ministry of his Holy Spirit. Salvation, therefore, is a gift given by God to repentant sinners, which is based historically on the redemptive work of Jesus Christ and is to be received only by faith.

In his *On the Bondage of the Will* (Latin: *De Servo Arbitrio*) of 1525, which was one of his earliest writings and was written in response to Desiderius Erasmus's 1524 attack against him entitled *On Free Will* (Latin: *De Libero Arbitrio*), Luther set out the essence of the Protestant Reformation. The issue between Luther and Erasmus had to do with whether human beings are, after the Fall, free to choose good or evil — and, in particular, whether people could cooperate with God by their own merits, as aided by God, in the attainment of their own justification and a righteous standing before God. Among the many biblical passages that Luther cited in refutation of Erasmus's defense of a doctrine of meritorious cooperation with God in the achievement of one's own justification, Luther highlighted the expression "justified freely by his grace" in Rom 3:24, commenting as follows:

> Paul here gives you an answer: That there is no such thing as merit at all; but that all who are justified are justified "freely" — that this is ascribed to no one but to the grace of God. And when this righteousness is given, the kingdom and eternal life are given with it![19]

It was this thesis, which has been concisely expressed by the phrase "justification by faith," that characterized all of Luther's preaching and epitomized all of the theology of the succeeding Protestant Reformation — and which has provided the primary interpretive approach for almost all Protestant Christians in their reading of Romans.

Included within an adherence to the principle of "justification by faith" for Luther — as well as for most "reformation" or "reformed" Protestant theologians — were the accompanying doctrinal emphases on (1) God's righteousness, sovereignty, and grace; (2) bestowed or imputed righteousness as a free gift from God to repentant sinners; (3) the impossibility of any human merit as being efficacious before God; (4) the work of Jesus Christ as the only sufficient basis for the salvation of anyone; and (5) the work of the Holy Spirit in condemning sin, effecting faith, and enabling a believer in Jesus to think and live in a righteous manner. Thus there have been a great many studies by numerous "reformation" or "reformed" biblical interpreters on all of these particular doctrinal matters.

Nonetheless, "justification by faith" was understood by Martin Luther, as well as by almost all Protestant interpreters who have followed him, as expressing the central theme of Paul's Christian proclamation. And it is this

---

19. M. Luther, *The Bondage of the Will*, Discussion, Third Part, Section 148.

theme that Luther saw highlighted throughout the first major section of the body middle of Romans, that is, in 1:16–4:25 — particularly in Paul's statements in 1:16-17 and 3:21-24 — and as echoed at many places elsewhere in the letter.

3. "In Christ" and "Christ by His Spirit in Us"

Another important interpretive approach to Paul and his letters, including what Paul has written in Romans, is that proposed by Adolf Deissmann in his *Die neutestamentliche Formel "in Christo Jesu"* of 1892. Based on his survey of the expression "in Christ Jesus" in Paul's letters, together with its cognates "in Christ," "in the Lord," and "in him," Deissmann argued that at the heart of all that Paul proclaimed and did was a consuming consciousness of an intensely personal relationship that existed between the exalted Christ and himself — with that consciousness being present, as well, in all those who are truly committed to and followers of Jesus Christ (i.e., "Christians"). It is a consciousness of a relationship between Christ and believers in Christ that is, in fact, so close, lively, and personal that it can properly be called "Christian mysticism."[20]

Building on Deissmann's thesis (though without any acknowledgment to him), Albert Schweitzer asserted in his *The Mysticism of Paul the Apostle* of 1910 that central to the "developed" thought of Paul, and therefore the main theme in his letter to the Romans, was not "justification by faith" — which Schweitzer called "a subsidiary crater" in the Pauline landscape "formed from the rim of the main crater" — but "the mystical doctrine of redemption through being-in-Christ."[21] And ever since Deissmann's original thesis, as well as its somewhat aberrant employment by Schweitzer, NT interpreters have frequently spoken of Paul's theology as being "personal," "relational," "participationistic," and even "mystical" — thus (1) at times setting out his "personal," "relational," and/or "participationistic" language in contrast to his "forensic" soteriological statements; (2) at other times viewing his "in Christ," "in the Lord," or "in him" expressions as simply extensions or elaborations of his forensic statements; though (3) usually just allowing the "personal," "relational," "participationistic," or "mystical" features to reside

---

20. Cf. A. Deissmann, *Die neutestamentliche Formel "in Christo Jesu"* (1892).

21. Cf. A. Schweitzer, *Mysticism of Paul the Apostle* (ET: 1931; first German edition 1910), quoting 225.

side by side with the "forensic" features of his message, without any attempted resolution.

Various Interpretations of Paul's "in Christ" Motif

During the past century there has been a considerable amount of discussion regarding Paul's "in Christ" motif, with various interpretations proposed. One prominent understanding frequently expressed during the first half of the twentieth century was that Paul's "in Christ" expression was a carry-over from the Greek mystery religions. Wilhelm Bousset and Richard Reitzenstein argued that the phrase was one of many items that Paul borrowed, both in form and in content, from the Greek mystery religions;[22] Alfred Loisy and Kirsopp Lake went further to claim that "Christianity has not borrowed from the Mystery Religions, because [under the influence of Paul] it was always, at least in Europe, a Mystery Religion itself";[23] and Erwin Goodenough, agreeing with the hellenistic nature of the expression, insisted that there was no need for Paul to borrow from a pagan source since the synagogues of Diaspora Judaism had themselves become homes for the mysteries — as witness Philo.[24] Thus it was argued that Paul's "in Christ" carries with it connotations found in the Greek mystery religions — that is, sacramental initiation, absorption into divinity, mystic identity, ecstatic experience, and all. But such a view has failed to carry conviction for both methodological and comparative reasons.

Methodologically, the question of Greek influence on Paul at this point can never be as decisively settled in the affirmative as this view claims, for the information concerning the ancient mystery religions is both meager and late of date. The dangers are (1) to be more precise than the evidence allows[25] and (2) to assume uncritically that the influence between the mys-

22. W. Bousset, *Kyrios Christos* (1934), 104-20; R. Reitzenstein, *Hellenistischen Mysterienreligionen* (1927, 3rd ed.), 333-93.

23. Quoting K. Lake, *Earlier Epistles of St. Paul* (1934), 215; see also A. Loisy, "The Christian Mystery" (1911), 50-64.

24. E. R. Goodenough, *By Light, Light: The Mystic Gospel of Hellenistic Judaism* (1935).

25. As E. Bevan caustically commented in 1950: "Of course, if one writes an imaginary description of the Orphic mysteries, as Loisy, for instance, does, filling in the large gaps in the picture left by our data from the Christian eucharist, one produces something very impressive. On this plan, you first put in the Christian elements, and then are staggered to find them there" ("Mystery Religions and Christianity," 43).

teries and Christianity always moved in one direction.[26] Most scholars today recognize that the question is not only how much Christianity was influenced by Greek thought and culture, but also how much the Greek mystery religions were a perversion of early Christianity.

Comparatively, the differences between Paul's "in Christ" and the concept of union with divinity in the mystery religions are most convincing against the view that Paul incorporated the religious speculations and forms of the latter into Christianity. For in addition to the fact that he does not proclaim a sacramental initiation, Paul does not advance the fundamental salvific tenet of the Greek mystery religions, that is, the ultimate absorption of the personhood of an adherent into whatever is viewed as the divine. Similarly, while the mystery religions present a salvation that is solely individualistic, Paul's "in Christ" is both personal and corporate. Likewise, while salvation in the mystery religions is freedom from fate, Paul accepts creatureliness and announces a salvation from sin and its associations; while faith is intellectual acceptance in the mystery religions, it is personal and ethical commitment with the apostle; and while ecstatic rapture is the goal of the mysteries, the ecstatic is only reluctantly spoken of by Paul and is not considered characteristic of the Christian life.

Even the form of the expression "in Christ," while similar to that of the Greek mystery religions, cannot with certainty be attributed to that milieu for its occurrence in Paul. For the question must always be asked whether the phraseology is a true "genealogical" parallel that has resulted from direct borrowing, or merely an "analogical" parallel to be regarded as arising from a more or less similar religious experience and temper. The facts that Paul's Jewish background included the concept of identification, that his Christian experience was one of close personal fellowship with the exalted Christ, and that he likely knew at least something about Jesus' teaching regarding an intimate relationship existing between himself and his own as later recorded in John's Gospel[27] all make it probable that the latter situation is the true one. It

---

26. For an excellent discussion of such methodological considerations, see B. M. Metzger, "Considerations of Methodology in the Study of the Mystery Religions and Early Christianity," 1-20.

27. Note particularly the "abide in me and I in you" motif that appears repeatedly as a feature of Jesus' teaching in John's Gospel — most prominently in (1) John 6:48-58, the discourse on the bread of life, which draws to a close in the words "he who eats my flesh and drinks my blood abides in me and I in him"; (2) John 14:20, where Jesus is reported as telling his disciples "In that day you shall know that I am in my Father and you in me and I in you"; (3) John 15:1-11, the analogy of the vine and the branches, whose imagery focuses a number

will always remain a question regarding just how hellenistically orientated so-called hellenistic Judaism really was. But the argument that Paul's "in Christ" theme reflects the thought and language of the Greek mystery religions seems to have fallen into disrepute today, and rightly so.

Adolf Deissmann himself argued that the phrase should be interpreted as a literal local dative of personal existence in the pneumatic Christ. He asserted that Paul viewed the Spirit as a semiphysical, ethereal entity, and so by equating the resurrected Christ with the ethereal Spirit could quite easily think of the Christian life as being "in Christ" and Christ "by his Spirit living in us." Deissmann's favorite analogy was that of air, of which it can truly be said that we are in it and it is in us. But while many considered Deissmann's treatment of Paul's "in Christ" theme a significant advance in NT studies, he actually left the discussion open to two unwarranted allegations: (1) that since Paul could so closely equate Christ and the Spirit, what is true of the Spirit as semiphysical and nonpersonal existence must to some extent also be true of Christ; and (2) that in advocating the incorporation of a person into the ethereal and semiphysical substance of the pneumatic Christ, Paul has shown himself to be a very primitive metaphysical thinker.

Thus Johannes Weiss, while agreeing with Deissmann in the main, argued that Deissmann did not go far enough, for while what is true of Christ is true of the Spirit, what is true of the Spirit is also true of Christ.[28] This association of Christ with the Spirit, insisted Weiss, is one place where "it cannot be denied that Paul's Christology is inclined, upon one side, to abandon the firm lines laid down by concrete ideas of a definite personality"[29] — for here Paul enters into "abstract speculation" and effects "the sublimation and dissolution of personality."[30] Going further, and in opposition to Deissmann's literal local thesis, Friedrich Büchsel asserted that to view Paul's "in Christ" as a local dative is to degrade both the Pauline presentation of Christ, representing him as "ein halb sachliches Fluidum,"[31] and the person

---

of times on the exhortation "abide in me as I abide in you"; (4) John 17:21, where Jesus' prayer to God his Father includes the request for his own: "that they also may be one in us"; (5) John 17:23 and 26, which include the expression "I in them"; and (6) John 16:33, where Jesus uses locative language in saying "In me you may have peace; in the world you have tribulation" (cf. also the language of close relationship in Jesus' statements of Matt 18:20 and 25:40-45).

28. Cf. J. Weiss, *Primitive Christianity,* 2.464.

29. J. Weiss, *Paul and Jesus,* 22.

30. J. Weiss, *Paul and Jesus,* 24; cf. *idem, Primitive Christianity,* 2.464-71.

31. F. Büchsel, "'In Christus' bei Paulus," 146.

of Paul himself, portraying him as a "primitiver Denker."[32] And, indeed, it is at these points that Deissmann's interpretation fails to do justice to Paul's understanding of Jesus.

Therefore, many scholars have proposed, in reaction to Deissmann's local interpretation, that Paul's "in Christ" expression must be viewed as simply a dative of instrumentality, causality, and/or source. In a methodical piece of research, Büchsel concluded that "es ist instrumental, kausal, modal und im übertragenen Sinne lokal gebraucht"[33] — that is, that while a figurative sense may at times be found, the primary meaning is more adequately expressed by applying the instrumental idea "by Christ" to Paul's phrase "in Christ"[34] and the dynamic idea "through the empowerment of Christ" to his formulation "Christ in us."[35]

Such an understanding, of course, often yields a perfectly intelligible and theologically sound meaning. No one would disagree that, whatever Paul meant by the expression, he did not exclude the ideas of Christ as the source, cause, and power of the Christian's life. But the question that stands over all of Büchsel's work — and which he neglects to raise — is this: Why, then, didn't Paul just continue to use the Greek constructions διὰ Χριστοῦ and ἐκ Χριστοῦ, and not also use the expression ἐν Χριστῷ, if he desired to express only the ideas of instrumentality, causality, and/or source? And further, Why did he use all three expressions within a single presentation when, according to Büchsel, his thought was roughly singular?

Similarly in opposition to Deissmann's local interpretation is the view that understands the phrase as simply a metaphor of personal communion with Christ. It is not that this position desires to minimize the personal element of intimate relation between Christ and the Christian contained in the expression, but it considers it "hazardous to press the 'local' significance of the formula."[36] It accepts the more general, but still profound, truth that Paul proclaims regarding a close and personal communion with Christ, but it shies away from trying to be more explicit in the exposition of that relationship by an emphasis on the form of the term. In its insistence that the metaphor stands for the believer's "supremely intimate relation of union with

32. F. Büchsel, "'In Christus' bei Paulus," 152. Somewhat similarly, H. Lietzmann referred to Paul's "in Christ" motif as representing "a plastically conceived mysticism" in his *Beginnings of the Christian Church*, 183.

33. F. Büchsel, "'In Christus' bei Paulus," 156.

34. F. Büchsel, "'In Christus' bei Paulus," 146.

35. F. Büchsel, "'In Christus' bei Paulus," 152.

36. So H. A. A. Kennedy, *Theology of the Epistles*, 121.

Christ,"[37] it has certainly caught the main theme of the apostle's teaching. Nonetheless, as William Barclay has aptly observed, "the cumulative effect of all Paul's uses of the phrase 'in Christ' demands something even more than this."[38]

During the twentieth century there also arose to prominence a different type of objection to Deissmann's interpretation. This position agrees with the local emphasis, but interprets it not as denoting an individual and personal relationship with Christ but as being a locution for corporate communion in the Church. The Roman Catholic Church, of course, has always taken this position, asserting that to be in the living Christ was to be in "the Church with its centre in Rome."[39] But in a reaction to philosophic individualism and the rediscovery of "corporate personality" in the Scriptures, many non-Romanists have also viewed the phrase as speaking primarily of corporate life in the Body of Christ — that is, in the organic Church. Albert Schweitzer, for example, argued that "'being-in-Christ' is the prime enigma of the Pauline teaching"[40] if we view it as "an individual and subjective experience" rather than "a collective and objective event."[41] Thus he insisted that "the expression 'being-in-Christ' is merely a brachyology for being partakers in the Mystical Body of Christ."[42] And while "in Christ" language may be common in Paul's letters, it is, Schweitzer asserted, not the most appropriate expression for union with Christ. It becomes the most usual, not only because of its shortness but because of the facility which it offers for forming antitheses with the analogous expressions "in the body," "in the flesh," "in sin," and "in the spirit," and thus providing the mystical theory with a series of neat equations.[43]

Likewise, Rudolf Bultmann argued that "'in Christ', far from being a formula for mystic union, is primarily an ecclesiological formula," and so "to belong to the Christian Church is to be 'in Christ' or 'in the Lord.'"[44] And in Britain this position was strongly advanced by John A. T. Robinson and L. S. Thornton as a corollary to their insistence that "the Church as literally now

37. H. A. A. Kennedy, *Theology of the Epistles,* 124.

38. W. Barclay, *Mind of St. Paul,* 128.

39. So the Roman Catholic biblical scholar C. Cary-Elwes, *Law, Liberty and Love* (London: Hodder & Stoughton, 1949), 247.

40. A. Schweitzer, *Mysticism of Paul,* 3.

41. A. Schweitzer, *Mysticism of Paul,* 123.

42. A. Schweitzer, *Mysticism of Paul,* 122-23.

43. A. Schweitzer, *Mysticism of Paul,* 123.

44. R. Bultmann, *Theology of the New Testament,* 1.311.

the resurrection 'body' of Christ" was the dominant motif in the proclamation of Paul.[45]

The Significance of Being "in Christ"

Endless debate will probably continue to gather around Paul's expression "in Christ," for it signifies a central feature of the Christian life that is better experienced than explained. Further, the more confident we are that we have reduced the expression to the cold prose of the psychologist's laboratory, the more assured we can be that we have lost its central significance. The inexplicable must always remain in a truly personal relationship. Yet that relationship can be intellectually understood and expressed up to a point — and it is to that point, and I trust only to that point, that I would seek to go in understanding Paul's thought here.

It is true that there are many places in Paul's letters where the expression could be viewed as being merely synonymous with the noun and adjective "Christian." For example, in his greeting to his addressees in his letters by such phraseology as "to all the saints 'in Christ Jesus,'" Paul could mean simply "to all the Christians";[46] in his reference to "the dead 'in Christ,'" he need mean no more than "the Christian dead";[47] and in his mention of certain individuals who were "in the Lord" or "in Christ," his use of the phrase could be only in order to identify them as Christians.[48] Similarly there are a host of passages where διὰ Χριστοῦ or ἐκ Χριστοῦ could be read just as well as ἐν Χριστῷ, and a perfectly intelligible meaning would emerge. The most prominent examples are:

> *2 Cor 3:14,* where Paul speaks of the veil that "is done away ἐν Χριστῷ" (RSV: "through Christ"; AV, NIV, NRSV: "in Christ");
> *Rom 5:10,* which speaks of being "saved ἐν τῇ ζωῇ αὐτοῦ" (AV, ASV, RSV, NRSV: "by his life"; NIV: "through his life");
> *Rom 14:14,* where Paul says, "I know and am persuaded ἐν κυρίῳ Ἰησοῦ" (AV: "by the Lord Jesus"; RSV, NIV, NRSV: "in the Lord Jesus"); and,

45. J. A. T. Robinson, *The Body,* 51; cf. L. S. Thornton, *Common Life in the Body of Christ* (London: Dacre, 1950), *passim.*
46. So Phil 1:1; cf. Eph 1:1 and Col 1:2.
47. So 1 Thess 4:16; cf. 1 Cor 15:18.
48. E.g., Rom 16:7, 11.

Phil 4:13, where Paul asserts that he "can do all things ἐν τῷ
ἐνδυναμοῦντί με" (AV: "through Christ which strengtheneth me";
RSV: "in him who strengthens me"; NRSV: "through him who
strengthens me"; NIV: "through him who gives me strength").

Nonetheless, the fact that in the following passages Paul distinguishes
ἐν from διά and ἐκ with respect to Christ suggests that he used these prepositions somewhat more exactly than has at times been thought in the past:

2 Cor 1:20: "All the promises of God have their 'Yes' ἐν αὐτῷ. Where-
fore also we utter the 'Amen' δι' αὐτοῦ to the glory of God";
2 Cor 2:17: "As ἐκ θεοῦ in the presence of God we speak ἐν Χριστῷ";
Col 1:16: "ἐν αὐτῷ were all things created. . . . All things were created δι'
αὐτοῦ and εἰς αὐτόν"; and,
Col 1:19-20: "ἐν αὐτῷ it was considered proper for all the fullness of
God to dwell, and δι' αὐτοῦ to reconcile all things to himself."

Moreover, in most of the passages where it is possible that Paul used
the term only as a synonym for the noun or the adjective "Christian," or
where it is asserted that the instrumental, causal, source, or dynamic idea
was uppermost in his thought, the local designation, if it were not for the re-
vulsion of the interpreter to the seeming crudity of the idea, can just as easily
be seen. The following instances certainly savor strongly of a local flavor:

Rom 8:1: "There is therefore now no condemnation for those who are
ἐν Χριστῷ Ἰησοῦ";
2 Cor 5:17: "If anyone is ἐν Χριστῷ, that person is a new creation";
2 Cor 5:19: "God was ἐν Χριστῷ reconciling the world to himself";
Eph 1:20: God's work was accomplished ἐν τῷ Χριστῷ when he raised
him from the dead"; and,
Phil 3:9: "That I might gain Christ and be found ἐν αὐτῷ."

Thus, while not assenting to all of Deissmann's positions, nor insisting
that there be a unitary exegesis of the expression, it seems that one must recognize that Paul's "in Christ" motif often carries a quite definite local flavor.[49] It is not just a bit of "verbal ingenuity";[50] nor is it one of many meta-

49. As argued by E. Best, *One Body in Christ, passim.*
50. As asserted by A. Schweitzer, *Mysticism of Paul,* 117.

phors subservient to the controlling concept of "the Body of Christ."[51] Rather, it is the dominant expression of Paul for the intimate and personal relationship that exists between the exalted Christ and those who have committed themselves to him. While the expression certainly has corporate overtones and social implications, it is used so often[52] and in such individualistic settings[53] that it must be viewed as much more than just an extension of meaning from a more fundamental concept of corporeity. Of two books written on the subject during the heyday of its heightened scholarly interest, Ernest Best's title and treatment in his 1955 *One Body in Christ* is much more representative of Paul's thought than is John Robinson's 1957 *The Body,* for Best recognizes the personal emphasis contained in the expression "in Christ" while also stressing the corporate nature of the Christian life as contained in the metaphor "the body of Christ," whereas Robinson subdues everything under the corporate concept of "the body."

A Concluding Statement

Paul uses the expression "in Christ Jesus" — as well as its cognates "in Christ," "in Christ Jesus our Lord," "in the Lord Jesus," and "in the Lord" — a number of times in writing to the Christians at Rome (cf. 6:11, 23; 8:1, 39; 9:1; 14:14; 15:17; 16:2, 11-13). In 8:1-12 he focuses particular attention on this theme in speaking of the Christian as being "in Christ Jesus" and of Christ by his Spirit being "in the Christian." The question arises, however, regarding how Paul in his use of such local terminology understood the intermingling of personalities — that is, of believers being "in Christ" and of Christ by his Spirit living "in believers."

Adolf Deissmann wrestled with this question and proposed that Paul must have thought along the lines of the joining of an ethereal Spirit and a pneumatic Christ, into which union the Christian lives as in a sort of rarified air — and which could also, as can air, indwell the believer. But such an analogy is not really Pauline. Rather, Paul seems to have thought of the exalted Christ as a cosmic, redemptive, and eschatological "Universal Personality,"[54]

---

51. As claimed by J. A. T. Robinson, *The Body,* esp. 58-67.

52. A total of 164 times in ten of the Pauline letters (i.e., minus the Pastorals) according to A. Deissmann, *Die neutestamentliche Formel "in Christo Jesu,"* 1-2, 118-23.

53. Cf. esp. 2 Cor 5:17; Phil 3:9.

54. A. Oepke, "ἐν," *TDNT* 2.542 (translating Oepke's cosmic and eschatological term "Universalpersönlichkeit" in *TWNT,* 2.538).

as his statements regarding Jesus Christ, "the Son/the One whom he [God] loves," in Col 1:15-20 and Eph 1:3-14 reveal.[55]

As the OT can say "And he [Abraham] trusted in Jahweh" (וְהֶאֱמִן בַּיהוָה)[56] (and, likewise, can often use that same Hebrew preposition בְּ ["in"] rather than the more usual relational Hebrew preposition לְ ["to," "for," "in regard to"] when speaking about people either trusting or not trusting God)[57] — and as Jesus is reported to have spoken of his relationship to the Father as being that of "the Father in me" (ἐν ἐμοὶ ὁ πατήρ) and "I in the Father" (κἀγὼ ἐν τῷ πατρί) without diminishing in any way the personality either of God or of Jesus[58] — so Paul with his high Christology could speak of being "in Christ" without suggesting any softening or dissolving of the personality either of Christ or of the Christian. To have been forced to give a psychological analysis of this relationship would probably have left Paul speechless. Yet he was convinced that he had experienced just such an intimacy with the exalted Christ.

Of course, in positing a local and personal flavor for the expression "in Christ," one is admitting to a form of mysticism. But this need not be abhorred if we mean by the term *mysticism* "that contact between the human and the Divine which forms the core of the deepest religious experience, but which can only be felt as an immediate intuition of the highest reality and cannot be described in the language of psychology."[59] It is not the pagan mysticism of absorption, for the human "I" and the divine "Thou" of the relationship retain their identities. Rather, it is fellowship between the human

55. Note especially the following christological statements in these passages: "In him all things were created in heaven and on earth, things visible and invisible" (Col 1:16); "In him all things consist" (Col 1:17); "In him it was considered proper for all the fullness of God to dwell" (Col 1:19); God "has blessed us in the heavenly realms with every spiritual blessing in Christ" (Eph 1:3); "In him we have redemption through his blood, the forgiveness of sins" (Eph 1:7); God "made known to us the mystery of his will according to his good pleasure, which he purposed in Christ" (Eph 1:9); and "In him" God's plan for the fullness of time will be brought to completion in "bringing to summation all things in the Christ, things in heaven and on earth" (Eph 1:10).

56. Gen 15:6.

57. See 2 Kgs 18:5-6 (of Hezekiah who "trusted in the Lord"); Ps 78:22 (of Israel's lack of "belief/trust in God"); Prov 28:25 (of one who "trusts in the Lord"); Isa 50:10 (on the prophet's call for Israel to "trust in the name of the Lord"); Jer 17:5-7 (on the blessedness of the one who "trusts in the Lord"); Nah 1:7 (on God's care for the one who "trusts in him"); Zeph 3:2 (woe to the one who "does not trust in the Lord"); and Zeph 3:12 (on the meek and humble who "trust in the name of the Lord").

58. Cf. John 10:38; 14:10, 11, 20; 17:21.

59. H. A. A. Kennedy, *Theology of the Epistles,* 122.

"I" and the divine "Thou" at its highest, which for Paul epitomizes the essence of personal relations between the exalted Christ and those who believe in and are committed to him.

4. The πίστις Ἰησοῦ Χριστοῦ Theme

A further critical issue in the study of Romans has to do with what Paul meant by πίστις Ἰησοῦ Χριστοῦ. This has been a matter vigorously debated during the past century, and it is an issue that must be faced by every interpreter today.

The phrase πίστις Ἰησοῦ Χριστοῦ (or the more compact phraseology πίστις Χριστοῦ, πίστις Ἰησοῦ, or πίστις αὐτοῦ) appears in Paul's letters only seven or eight times — that is, in Rom 3:22 and 3:26, in Gal 2:16 (twice) and 3:22 (perhaps also 3:26, which in P⁴⁶ concludes with the phrase διὰ πίστεως Χριστοῦ), in Eph 3:12, and in Phil 3:9. The prepositions διά ("through," "by means of") and ἐκ ("from," "based on," "by reason of"), which variously precede and condition the genitive form πίστεως in these seven or eight instances, are probably used interchangeably, as is particularly evident in their synonymous use in Gal 2:16 — though elsewhere in other contexts they may very well signal some distinctions in meaning.

The generally accepted view has been that Ἰησοῦ Χριστοῦ is syntactically an objective genitive, and therefore διὰ/ἐκ πίστεως Ἰησοῦ Χριστοῦ in these passages should be read as "through [or 'based on'] faith in Jesus Christ." The vast majority of commentators on Romans have understood the expression in this manner — as, for example, William Sanday and Arthur Headlam,[60] Anders Nygren,[61] Franz Leenhardt,[62] Kingsley Barrett,[63] F. F. Bruce,[64] Charles Cranfield,[65] Heinrich Schlier,[66] Ernst Käsemann,[67] James Dunn,[68] Douglas Moo,[69] and Robert Jewett.[70] Likewise, almost all contem-

---

60. W. Sanday and A. C. Headlam, *Romans* (1895), esp. 83-84.
61. A. Nygren, *Romans* (1949), esp. 150-61.
62. F. J. Leenhardt, *Romans* (1957), esp. 99-101.
63. C. K. Barrett, *Romans* (1957), esp. 74.
64. F. F. Bruce, *Romans* (1963), esp. 102.
65. C. E. B. Cranfield, *Romans,* 2 vols. (1975, 1979), esp. 1.203.
66. H. Schlier, *Römerbrief* (1977), esp. 105, 115.
67. E. Käsemann, *Romans* (ET 1980), esp. 94, 101.
68. J. D. G. Dunn, *Romans,* 2 vols. (1988, 1989), esp. 1.166-67.
69. D. J. Moo, *Romans* (1996), esp. 224-26.
70. R. Jewett, *Romans* (2007), esp. 277-78.

porary English versions of the Bible have translated διὰ/ἐκ πίστεως Ἰησοῦ Χριστοῦ in Romans in this way — and a number of articles by highly accredited scholars have recently been written in defense of such an objective genitive translation.[71] From the late nineteenth century to the present, however, there has been a rising tide of scholarly opinion that understands Ἰησοῦ Χριστοῦ as a subjective genitive, and so argues that πίστις Ἰησοῦ Χριστοῦ should be read as "the faith/faithfulness of Jesus Christ." This reading was first proposed by Johannes Haussleiter at the close of the nineteenth century.[72] It was then argued by Gerhard Kittel at the beginning of the twentieth century.[73] Karl Barth was the first commentary writer on Romans to espouse such an understanding in his *Römerbrief* of 1919, not only translating Paul's words ἐκ πίστεως εἰς πίστιν in 1:17 in this fashion (i.e., *auf Treue dem Glauben*, "from faithfulness unto faith") but also explicating all of the other references to πίστις in 3:21-31 in this manner.[74]

It was largely through Karl Barth's influence that this position was popularized in the English-speaking world in the mid-1950s by Gabriel Hebert[75] and Thomas Torrance.[76] It was then advocated by T. W. Manson in his Romans commentary of 1962,[77] and has since begun to be accepted by a few commentators on Romans — particularly by Charles Talbert in his commentary of 2002.[78] As something of an indication of the growing acceptance among scholars of such a subjective genitive understanding, it should be noted that the NRSV includes a footnote at 3:22 that suggests the possibility of such an alternative view, reading "through the faith of Jesus Christ," with TNIV doing somewhat the same, reading "through the faithfulness of Jesus Christ" — though neither of these subjective genitive readings were included as translation footnotes earlier in either the RSV or the NIV (nor are they included in the text of either the NRSV or TNIV). Of contemporary English translations, only NET (New English Translation)

71. See esp. A. J. Hultgren, "The πίστις Χριστοῦ Formulation in Paul" (1980), 248-63; J. D. G. Dunn, "Once More *Pistis Christou*" (1991), 730-44; and C. E. B. Cranfield, "On the Πίστις Χριστοῦ Question" (1998), 81-97.

72. J. Haussleiter, *Der Glaube Jesu Christi und der christliche Glaube* (1891); *idem*, "Eine theologische Disputation über den Glauben Jesu" (1892), 507-20; *idem*, "Was versteht Paulus über christlichen Glauben" (1895), 159-81.

73. G. Kittel, "Pistis Iesou Christou bei Paulus" (1906), 419-36.

74. K. Barth, *Römerbrief* (1919; rev. ed. 1929; first ET 1933), *ad loci*.

75. A. G. Hebert, "'Faithfulness' and 'Faith'" (1955), 373-79.

76. T. F. Torrance, "One Aspect of the Biblical Conception of Faith" (1956), 111-14.

77. T. W. Manson, "Romans," in *Peake's Commentary on the Bible*, 2nd ed., 942.

78. C. H. Talbert, *Romans*, 41-47 (on 1:17) and 107-10 (on 3:22 and 26).

has the subjective genitive reading "through the faithfulness of Jesus Christ" in its text.

Prominent among the list of scholars who have argued for a subjective genitive treatment of πίστις Ἰησοῦ Χριστοῦ — whether understood as "the faith of Jesus Christ," "the faithfulness of Jesus Christ," or "the fidelity [of God] in Jesus Christ") — have been the following: Ernst Fuchs,[79] Pierre Vallotton,[80] Karl Kertelge,[81] Markus Barth,[82] George Howard,[83] D. W. B. Robinson,[84] Sam Williams,[85] Richard Hays,[86] Luke Timothy Johnson,[87] Morna Hooker,[88] and Bruce Longenecker.[89] I also argued for this understanding in my *Paul, Apostle of Liberty* of 1964, my Galatians commentary of 1990, and my article "The Foundational Conviction of New Testament Christology: The Obedience/Faithfulness/Sonship of Christ" of 2004.[90]

Linguistically, πίστις Ἰησοῦ Χριστοῦ has always been difficult to interpret, and so to translate. But when πίστις is understood in terms of the Hebrew noun אמונה, which includes the nuances of both "faith" and "faithfulness," it is not too difficult to view Paul as using πίστεως Ἰησοῦ Χριστοῦ in Rom 3:22 in much the same way as he used (1) τὴν πίστιν τοῦ θεοῦ ("the faithfulness of God") earlier in 3:3, (2) τῆς πίστεως τοῦ πατρὸς ἡμῶν Ἀβραάμ ("the faith of our father Abraham") later in 4:12, and (3) πίστεως Ἀβραάμ ("the faith of Abraham") in that same later context in 4:16.

As has often been observed, Jerome in the Vulgate translated πίστις

---

79. E. Fuchs, "Jesus und der Glaube" (1958), 170-85.

80. P. Vallotton, *Le Christ et la Foi* (1960).

81. K. Kertelge, "Rechtfertigung bei Paulus" (1967), 162-66.

82. M. Barth, "The Faith of the Messiah" (1969), 363-70; idem, *Ephesians*, 2 vols. (New York: Doubleday, 1974), esp. 1.224, 347.

83. G. E. Howard, "On the 'Faith of Christ'" (1967), 459-65; idem, "The 'Faith of Christ'" (1974), 212-15, and idem, *Paul, Crisis in Galatia* (1990), 57-65.

84. D. W. B. Robinson, "'Faith of Jesus Christ' — a New Testament Debate" (1970), 71-81.

85. S. Williams, "The 'Righteousness of God' in Romans" (1980), 241-90; idem, "Again Πίστις Χριστοῦ" (1987), 431-47.

86. R. B. Hays, *The Faith of Jesus Christ* (1983), esp. 170-74; idem, "ΠΙΣΤΙΣ and the Pauline Christology: What Is at Stake?" (1997), 35-60.

87. L. T. Johnson, "Rom 3:21-26 and the Faith of Jesus" (1982), 77-90.

88. M. D. Hooker, "ΠΙΣΤΙΣ ΧΡΙΣΤΟΥ" (1989), 321-42.

89. B. W. Longenecker, "Πίστις in Romans 3.25" (1993), 478-80; idem, *The Triumph of Abraham's God* (1998), 98-103.

90. R. N. Longenecker, *Paul, Apostle of Liberty* (1964), 149-52; idem, *Galatians*, WBC (1990), 87-88; idem, "The Foundational Conviction of New Testament Christology" (2004), esp. 132-37.

Ἰησοῦ Χριστοῦ quite literally as *fides Iesu Christi,* as did also Erasmus — though, unfortunately, this Latin phrase may be understood almost as ambiguously as the Greek expression itself. Also often noted is the fact that the translators of the KJV, apparently influenced by Paul's reference to "the faith of Abraham" in 4:12 and 16 (though evidently not by "the faithfulness of God" in 3:3), translated διὰ πίστεως Ἰησοῦ Χριστοῦ here in 3:22 as "by the faith of Jesus Christ," thus understanding Ἰησοῦ Χριστοῦ syntactically as a subjective genitive. Further, it needs to be noted that five of the other occurrences of this expression that are worded in almost exactly the same manner are also translated in the KJV in a subjective genitive fashion: twice in Gal 2:16 ("by the faith of Jesus Christ" and "by the faith of Christ"), once in Gal 3:22 ("by faith of Jesus Christ"), once in Eph 3:12 ("by the faith of him"), and once in Phil 3:9 ("through the faith of Christ") — though the single name Ἰησοῦ in the roughly synonymous phrase τὸν ἐκ πίστεως Ἰησοῦ of Rom 3:26 was apparently viewed by those early-seventeenth-century English scholars as an objective genitive, and therefore translated as "him which believeth in Jesus" (or, as reworded by the RSV: "him who has faith in Jesus").

Inspired by Karl Barth's treatment of πίστις Ἰησοῦ Χριστοῦ in his *Römerbrief,* which was based on the earlier studies of that expression by Johannes Haussleiter and Gerhard Kittel, Gabriel Hebert argued that just as אמונה meant both "faithfulness" and "faith" in Jewish writings, so Paul used "the one word *pistis* for the two things, Divine faithfulness and human faith."[91] And Hebert went on to point out (1) that the Hebrew idea of faithfulness often emerges in the LXX's use of πίστις (citing Ps 36:5-7; Isa 28:16; Hab 2:4), and (2) that there is no disagreement as to the fact that Paul and the other NT authors often used πίστις (πιστός) elsewhere in their writings in this Hebrew sense (citing Rom 3:3: "The *pistis* of God"; 1 Cor 1:9; 10:13: "God is *pistos*"; 1 Thess 5:24: "*Pistos* is the one who calls you"; 2 Thess 3:3: "But the Lord is *pistos*"; also Heb 2:17; 3:2; 1 Jn 1:9; Rev 1:5; 3:14; 19:11). Further, Hebert noted that in three of the passages where πίστις Ἰησοῦ Χριστοῦ appears in Paul's letters (i.e., in Rom 3:22; Gal 3:22; and Phil 3:9) the phrase εἰς πάντας τοὺς πιστεύοντας ("to all who believe"), which appears immediately afterward, is, at least to some extent, redundant if an objective genitive reading "through faith in Jesus Christ" is accepted — and so he argued that πίστις Ἰησοῦ Χριστοῦ, rather than setting up a redundancy with what follows, is best translated "the faithfulness of

91. A. G. Hebert, "'Faithfulness' and 'Faith'" (1955), 376.

Jesus Christ," with that translation understood by him to mean "God's faithfulness revealed to him."[92]

In those early days of the *Pistis Christou* debate, the expression πίστις Ἰησοῦ Χριστοῦ was often understood as referring in some manner to "divine faithfulness." Karl Barth, for example, translated πίστις Ἰησοῦ Χριστοῦ as "his [God's] faithfulness in Jesus Christ," giving the following explanation: "The faithfulness of God and of Jesus the Christ confirm one another. The faithfulness of God is established when we meet the Christ in Jesus."[93] Gabriel Hebert, however, translated the expression as "the faithfulness of Jesus Christ," but understood it to mean "God's faithfulness revealed to him (i.e., 'to Jesus')," while Thomas Torrance translated it simply as "the faithfulness of Jesus Christ." And considering (1) Paul's hebraic background in the dual use of the Hebrew term אמונה, (2) his other uses of πίστις in Romans 3 in this sense (cf. also 3:25, 26; and possibly 3:30), and (3) the redundant nature of the immediately following expression εἰς πάντας τοὺς πιστεύοντας in Rom 3:22, as well as the equivalent dual expressions that appear in Gal 3:22 and Phil 3:9, the emphasis on divine faithfulness (whether of God or of Jesus Christ) and the translation "through the faithfulness of Jesus Christ" seem most linguistically convincing.

Yet the interpretation of any statement or expression in Scripture, whether OT or NT, is not just a linguistic matter. Biblical exegesis is also vitally interested in (1) the context of every statement or expression in question, that is, both its immediate context and its broader context, and (2) the overall theology of the particular author involved. Proponents of both positions in the present *Pistis Christou* debate readily acknowledge the importance of bringing together all of the relevant linguistic, contextual, and theological issues that pertain to this particular exegetical enterprise — as does, for example, Arlan Hultgren in arguing for an objective genitive view,[94] and as does Luke Timothy Johnson in arguing for a subjective genitive understanding.[95] So it is necessary also to speak here regarding the contextual and theological issues involved, as well as to deal with those features of linguistic relevance cited above.

Contextually, first it needs to be noted that throughout the material just prior to his use of the phrase διὰ πίστεως Ἰησοῦ Χριστοῦ in 3:22, that is,

---

92. A. G. Hebert, "'Faithfulness' and 'Faith'" (1955), 373.
93. K. Barth, *Romans* (ET 1933), 96.
94. Cf. A. J. Hultgren, "The πίστις Χριστοῦ Formulation in Paul," 263ff.
95. Cf. L. T. Johnson, "Romans 3:21-26 and the Faith of Jesus," 78ff.

throughout 2:17–3:20, Paul has been speaking about the "unfaithfulness" of Jews vis-à-vis the "faithfulness of God," with that discussion coming to explicit expression in his two rhetorical questions of 3:3: "What if some of them were unfaithful (τί εἰ ἠπίστησάν τινες)? Will their unfaithfulness (ἡ ἀπιστία αὐτῶν) nullify the faithfulness of God (τὴν πίστιν τοῦ θεοῦ)?" — with those questions then being immediately followed by his vociferous, even vehement, response of 3:4a: "Certainly not (μὴ γένοιτο)!" Further, it needs to be noted (1) that the central affirmation of the early Christian confession quoted by Paul in Phil 2:6-11, which affirmation appears in 2:8, has to do with the "obedience" (ὑπακοή) of Jesus: "he became obedient (γενόμενος ὑπήκοος) to the extent (μέχρι) of death (θανάτου)" — which, it appears, Paul wanted to emphasize, and therefore added the awesome statement "even death on a cross (θανάτου δὲ σταυρου)," and (2) that later, at the beginning of "Section Two" of the body middle of Romans, that is, in 5:19b, Paul picks up on this theme of Christ's "obedience" (διὰ τῆς ὑπακοῆς τοῦ ἑνός) as effecting "righteousness" (δίκαιοι) for "the many" (οἱ πολλοί), and so may be seen as using the noun "obedience" (ὑπακοή) as a synonym for the noun "faithfulness" (πίστις) in connection with the work of Christ.

Admittedly, apart from its appearance in Phil 2:8, which occurs at the focal point in the confessional material that Paul quotes in Phil 2:6-11, only once elsewhere in his letters, that is, in Rom 5:19, does Paul use ὑπακοή ("obedience") when speaking about the work of Christ. But theology is more than mathematics; and while the literary-historical criterion of "multiple attestation" is always important, one does not appeal only to frequency counts in support of significance. The context of a concept or expression is much more important. And with respect to context, it needs to be observed that Paul's use of διὰ πίστεως Ἰησοῦ Χριστοῦ in 3:22 (as well as his use of ἐκ πίστεως Ἰησοῦ only four verses later in 3:26) appears (1) almost immediately after his treatment of "the unfaithfulness" of Jews vis-à-vis "the faithfulness" of God in 2:17–3:20 (particularly as expressed in 3:3), and (2) shortly before his contrast between "the disobedience of the one man [Adam]" and "the obedience of the one [Christ]" in 5:19 (cf. also 5:18 on his contrast between Adam's "one trespass" and Christ's "one righteous act").

Theologically, it needs also to be taken into account that Paul's "high" Christology allows him to make an easy association of (1) the titles "Son" and "Son of God" as rightfully applied to Jesus, Israel's Messiah and humanity's Lord, (2) his and the early church's references to Christ's "obedience," and (3) his references to Christ's "faithfulness" — all of which speak in a functional manner of Jesus' fulfillment of the will of God in effecting human redemption through his earthly ministry, sacrificial death, and physical resurrection.[96] In effect, what seems most likely is that Paul used πίστις Ἰησοῦ Χριστοῦ (and its cognate forms) to signal the extremely important historical basis for the Christian gospel — that is, to highlight the fact that the objective basis for the Christian proclamation of "good news" in this time of the eschatological "now" is the perfect response of obedience and faithfulness that Jesus, the Son, offered to God, the Father, both actively in his life and passively in his death.

Perhaps Paul came to such a subjective genitive understanding of πίστις Ἰησοῦ Χριστοῦ ("the faithfulness of Jesus Christ") — or, at least, he developed his understanding of the salvific work of Jesus along these lines — on the basis of his meditation on some early Christian confessional material that was circulating among Jewish believers in Jesus, was known to the Christians at Rome, and was cherished by Paul. It was, it seems, a portion of such traditional material that Paul quotes in 3:24-26 (or 3:25-26) in support of his thesis statement of 3:21-23. It may even have been that that early Christian confessional material quoted in 3:24-26 (or 3:25-26) had become highly significant to Paul personally — and that he believed it would be of great importance to his Christian addressees at Rome — because of the way in which it used the expressions διὰ τῆς πίστεως in 3:25a (which may be translated "through his [i.e., Christ's] faithfulness") and ἐκ πίστεως Ἰησοῦ in 3:26a (which may be translated "on the basis of the faithfulness of Jesus"). Such "possible" theses require a great deal more exegetical treatment than can be given here in order to speak about their "probable" nature, and so must await further examination and explication in our proposed exegetical commentary. Nonetheless, however all of that might be, Paul certainly seems in 3:21-22 to be repeating, expanding on, and developing the earlier rather cryptic expression ἐκ πίστεως εἰς πίστιν (which literally translated reads "out of faith unto faith") that he used at the close of his original thesis statement in 1:16-17.

Thus we feel compelled to believe that the expression πίστις Ἰησοῦ Χριστοῦ — which appears six, seven, or eight times in Romans, Galatians, Ephesians, and Philippians, and whose content is alluded to in other ways throughout the Pauline corpus of letters — has reference to the "obedience" and/or "faithfulness" of Jesus in his earthly ministry and death. And so we have highlighted here this πίστις Ἰησοῦ Χριστοῦ theme as a matter of criti-

96. Cf. R. N. Longenecker, "The Foundational Conviction of New Testament Christology: The Obedience/Faithfulness/Sonship of Christ" (2004), 122-44.

cal concern in the study of Romans, which every interpreter of Paul must examine, evaluate, and (if convinced of its truth) explicate as he or she is able.

5. The "New Perspective" on Palestinian Judaism and Paul

An interpretive approach of great significance in the study of Romans that has come to the fore during the latter decades of the twentieth century is what has been called "The New Perspective," which has to do with (1) how one understands what Paul wrote regarding the Jews and Judaism in Rom 2:17–3:20 and 9:6–11:36 (as well as earlier in his Galatian letter) and (2) how one understands what he wrote regarding the Christian message in Rom 3:21–4:25 and 5–8 (as well as throughout Galatians). This recently proposed approach offers (1) a corrective to the imbalance in biblical scholarship during the past centuries regarding the mainline Judaism of Paul's day (as well as later rabbinic Judaism, as represented by the tannaitic rabbis whose teachings are codified in the Talmud), and so a "new perspective" on what Paul wrote regarding the Jews and the Jewish religion in Rom 2:17–3:20 and 9:6–11:36 (as well as in Galatians), and (2) a somewhat different understanding, in light of that "corrected" treatment of Palestinian Judaism, regarding what Paul wrote with respect to the Christian gospel vis-à-vis the Jews and the Jewish religion, and so a "new perspective" on what he wrote regarding the Christian proclamation in Rom 3:21–4:25 and 5–8 (as well as in Galatians).

The "New Perspective" on Palestinian Judaism

The new perspective on Palestinian Judaism is rightly credited, in large part, to Ed Sanders, as he set it out in "Part One" of his *Paul and Palestinian Judaism: A Comparison of Patterns of Religion* of 1977 and then developed further in his *Paul, the Law, and the Jewish People* of 1983 (though see also my 1964 chapter, "The Piety of Hebraic Judaism," in *Paul, Apostle of Liberty,* 65-85). What Sanders argued is that (1) Palestianian Judaism was not a legalistic religion, that is, it did not require Jews to observe the Mosaic law in order to "get in" or be accepted by God into his covenant, and so become God's people — for Jews always believed themselves to be, by God's grace and mercy, already in God's covenant, and so in a right relationship with God; yet (2) Palestinian Judaism also taught that, having been received into God's covenant by

God's grace and mercy, the Jewish relationship with God within his covenant was to be maintained and expressed by obedience to the Mosaic law, that is, that Jews must obey the precepts of the Mosaic law in order to "stay in" or remain within that covenantal relationship with God, and so be, in truth, God's people.

Sanders called this type of religious orientation "covenantal nomism,"[97] distinguishing it from "a 'works-righteousness' concern, as commonly conceived."[98] And he delineated the "pattern" or "structure" of this Jewish covenantal nomism, as depicted by the earliest portions of the Talmud and other early rabbinic writings, as follows:

> The "pattern" or "structure" of covenantal nomism is this: (1) God has chosen Israel and (2) given the law. The law implies both (3) God's promise to maintain the election and (4) the requirement to obey. (5) God rewards obedience and punishes transgression. (6) The law provides for means of atonement, and atonement results in (7) maintenance or re-establishment of the covenantal relationship. (8) All those who are maintained in the covenant by obedience, atonement and God's mercy belong to the group which will be saved. An important interpretation of the first and last points is that election and ultimately salvation are considered to be by God's mercy rather than human achievement.[99]

Such an understanding of mainline Palestinian Judaism, of course, raises a number of questions about Paul's statements regarding the Jews and Judaism in his letters, and particularly about his pejorative use of the phrase "works of the law" and the noun "works" in Galatians and Romans. So in "Part Two" of his *Paul and Palestinian Judaism,* Sanders explicated further what he understood was the pattern or structure of Paul's theology, focusing particularly on Paul's differences with the mainline Judaism of his day. And in his portrayal of Paul's theology, Sanders argued that Paul's Christian proclamation was not rooted in first-century Jewish "patterns" or "theological constructs," but was based on his conviction that Jesus of Nazareth was the Jewish Messiah and the Savior of the world. Thus, according to Sanders, "Paul's type of religion is basically different from anything known from Palestinian Judaism," for whereas "there was a generally prevailing religious type in Palestinian Judaism," that of "covenantal nomism," "Paul's pattern of

---

97. E. P. Sanders, *Paul and Palestinian Judaism,* 75, 236, 422-23.
98. E. P. Sanders, *Paul and Palestinian Judaism,* 74-75.
99. E. P. Sanders, *Paul and Palestinian Judaism,* 422.

religious thought" was that of "participationist eschatology."[100] Sanders proposed, therefore, that Paul must not be seen as faulting Judaism as a "legalistic, self-righteousing, self-aggrandizing" religion of works; rather, Paul faults Judaism simply because, as Sanders put it, *"it is not Christianity."*[101] Traditional interpreters, Sanders insisted, have misunderstood Paul. And because of their failure to understand Paul, they have failed also to understand Palestinian Judaism. Thus with respect to Paul's use of the expression "works of the law" in Gal 2:16 (also 3:2, 5) and in Rom 3:20 (also 3:27; 4:2, 6), interpreters today need to understand that Paul was "not against a supposed Jewish position that enough good works earn righteousness" but was simply expressing his own view, which had been drawn from his own convictions about Jesus and his own type of participationistic-eschatological soteriology, that "one need not be Jewish to be 'righteous.'"[102]

A great deal of Ed Sanders's appreciation of early rabbinic theology and quite a bit of his understanding of Paul's relation to the mainline Judaism of his day came about from his study under W. D. Davies, whose treatments of these matters had been set out in his 1955 *Paul and Rabbinic Judaism*.[103] In large measure, Davies turned the tide in NT study from viewing Paul's thought as rooted in hellenistic Jewish religious speculation to understanding his basic modes of thought and expression as having deep rootage in hebraic Jewish theology and ways of thinking — and while Sanders did not always follow Davies in his understandings of either Paul or early rabbinic Judaism, he highly appreciated his professor's attempts to spell out relations that existed between their respective theologies and exegetical methods. Further, some of the ethos for Sanders's argument was provided by Krister Stendahl in his 1963 article "The Apostle Paul and the Introspective Conscience of the West."[104] For in that article Stendahl argued that Christians of the western world have misread Paul as being anti-Jewish and anti-Judaism — and so as speaking pejoratively about Jewish "works of the law"

---

100. E. P. Sanders, *Paul and Palestinian Judaism*, 552.

101. E. P. Sanders, *Paul and Palestinian Judaism*, 552 (italics his); *idem, Paul, the Law, and the Jewish People*, 45-48 and 154-62.

102. E. P. Sanders, *Paul, the Law, and the Jewish People*, 46.

103. See W. D. Davies, *Paul and Rabbinic Judaism: Some Rabbinic Elements in Pauline Theology* (London: SPCK, 1955). Note Davies's response to Sander's *Paul and Palestinian Judaism* in the "Preface to the Fourth Edition" of his *Paul and Rabbinic Judaism* (Philadelphia: Fortress, 1980), xxix-xxxviii.

104. K. Stendahl, "The Apostle Paul and the Introspective Conscience of the West," *HTR* 56 (1963) 199-215.

and "works" in obedience to the Mosaic law — largely because they have been overly influenced by Martin Luther's anxieties about his guilty conscience, his struggles to gain personal justification, and his polemic against the "Papists" of his day, whom Luther viewed as essentially the same as the "Judaizers" of Paul's day, and *vice versa.*

The "New Perspective" on Paul

Much of Ed Sanders's depiction of mainline Palestinian Judaism was accepted by James Dunn, who then attempted to describe Paul's teaching in a manner that both affirmed the apostle's basic Christian convictions and was compatible with Sanders's understanding of the Judaism of Paul's day. Dunn first argued his understanding of Paul's proclamation of the Christian gospel vis-à-vis Sanders's views of Palestinian Judaism in his "Manson Memorial Lecture" of 1982, in which he coined the expression "The New Perspective on Paul."[105] Since then James Dunn has lectured and written extensively in support of this "new perspective,"[106] and in the process has influenced a large number of students and scholars.[107]

Building on Sanders's understanding of Palestinian Judaism (and, to an extent, in agreement with Sanders's understanding of Paul's message), Dunn argues not only that Paul had no quarrel with the Mosaic Law, but also that he did not have any fundamental problem with what the Jewish teachers within mainline Palestinian Judaism understood with respect to that God-given law. What Paul opposed, according to Dunn, was the perverse habit among the Jews of his day of turning the traditional Jewish regulations regarding circumcision, Sabbath observance, and dietary matters for God's people into "identity markers" and "boundary markers," which they then used to exclude all others who did not follow these regulations — that is, the Gentiles — from the salvific benefits of God's grace. In effect, the message of "grace" that dominated the "religion of Israel" (as per the OT) and early "formative Judaism" of Paul's day (as per the tannaitic materials later codified in the Talmud and the other rabbinic writings) was perverted into a prideful

---

105. See J. D. G. Dunn, "The New Perspective on Paul," *BJRL* 65.2 (1982-1983) 95-122.

106. For a collection of Dunn's articles on the subject, together with a further article in response to his critics, see J. D. G. Dunn, *The New Perspective on Paul: Collected Essays.* WUNT 185. Tübingen: Mohr-Siebeck, 2005.

107. Perhaps most obviously N. T. Wright, as evidenced in his *Paul: In Fresh Perspective* (Minneapolis: Fortress, 2005).

focus on "race" — which, of course, was diametrically opposed to Paul's message, which focused on the God of mercy and grace, through the work of Jesus Christ and the ministry of the Holy Spirit, as (1) having effected salvation for all people, irrespective of their ethnicity, and (2) now offering that salvation to all people, whatever their racial or ethnic backgrounds, in response to their trust in him and their acceptance by faith of his provision.

Thus Paul's pejorative references to "works of the law" and "works" in Galatians and Romans, Dunn argues, do not have in mind any legalistic observances by which Jews might have thought they could gain righteousness — for mainline Palestinian Judaism, as Sanders has demonstrated, did not think in this way. Rather, Paul's disparaging remarks about "works of the law" and "works" were, as Dunn views matters, directed against certain aberrant understandings that were entertained by some of the Jews of his day with respect to circumcision, Sabbath observance, and dietary matters — that is, against using these particular traditions of the Mosaic law as (1) "identity markers" that function to identify only Jews as the true people of God, (2) "boundary markers" that separate Jews from all other people and nations, and (3) God-given criteria that serve to exclude all Gentiles from God's mercy and grace — unless, of course, they became "proselyte Jews" by their acceptance of these identity and boundary markers.

An Evaluation and Response

By way of evaluation and response, I want first of all to say that a number of features in Sanders's analysis of Palestinian Judaism are both noteworthy and important. In my *Paul, Apostle of Liberty* of 1964[108] I also argued that the theology of mainline Judaism in Paul's day was not — at least as taught by the better Jewish rabbis — an "acting legalism" (i.e., that one must observe the Mosaic law *in order to* gain acceptance by God and be accounted righteous in his sight), but, rather, that Judaism's teaching on the necessity of Jews to observe the law must be understood in terms of a "responding" or "reacting nomism" (i.e., that, *because of* having been brought into God's covenant by his mercy and grace, one must respond to God in a life of faithful obedience to his will, as expressed in the Mosaic law).

Where my 1964 analysis of first-century mainline Judaism differed with

---

108. Cf. R. N. Longenecker, "The Piety of Hebraic Judaism," in *Paul, Apostle of Liberty*, 65-85.

Sanders's portrayals in his *Paul and Palestinian Judaism* of 1977 — and where I continue to differ with him — was (and is) principally with respect to his confidence that "covenantal nomism" dominated the totality of Palestinian Jewish thought and practice in Paul's day. For the same rabbinic writings that Sanders uses for an understanding of Palestinian Judaism also contain some Jewish teachings, refer to some Jewish teachers, and report some Jewish situations that reflect an outlook that can only be called "legalistic" and not "nomistic" — and which, at times, some of the leading rabbis of the period denounced. Further, it needs always to be recognized that even lofty principles can be viewed and practiced in legalistic ways — which is, sadly, true with respect to every religious philosophy, including both Judaism and Christianity.

Sanders's treatment of Palestinian Judaism has been a highly important corrective to much that has been assumed and written about Judaism by uninformed and over-zealous Christians. It may be, however, that scholarship has swung too far, in pendulum-like fashion, from one extreme position to another extreme position, exchanging blind condemnation for an almost equally blind approbation — which, at times, goes even beyond the evaluations of the better Jewish teachers as represented in the Talmud and the other rabbinic writings that claim to represent an earlier period. Nonetheless, one matter seems to be fairly well established among most NT interpreters today (a matter which, as we have said above, must be credited in large part to Sanders): No longer can the Jewish religion of Paul's day be simply written off as a legalistic religion of "works righteousness." Further, it needs to be noted that students of Paul today have been alerted to the facts (1) that there is much in the apostle's writings that he took over from Judaism, though with all of his earlier Jewish training and piety "rebaptized" into his Christian experience, and (2) that the basic structures of Jewish thought and the underlying ethos of Jewish piety continued to play a large part in Paul's life as a follower of the exalted Jesus of Nazareth, whom he accepted as Israel's Messiah and humanity's Lord.

There are, as well, many other matters in the analyses of Sanders and Dunn that may rightly be acclaimed as laudatory. It would, however, be extraneous to enumerate all of these positive matters here. Suffice it here to say, by way of criticism, that I believe both Sanders and Dunn have twisted the evidence in support of an alien thesis in arguing (1) that Paul's disparaging remarks about "works of the law" and "works" probably came about because he was under some type of foreign influence (i.e., "hellenistic" influence) when he wrote those words (as does Sanders), or (2) that Paul was using "works of the law" and "works" with reference only to Jewish legislation on circumcision, Sabbath laws, and certain dietary matters, which some Jews of that day were using in a nationalistic fashion as their "identity markers" and "boundary markers," and not to any form of Jewish "legalism" as usually understood (as does Dunn).

Ed Sanders and James Dunn, each in his own way, seem to be attempting to exonerate Paul from the charge of being anti-Jewish, anti-Judaism, or anti-Semitic — and that is, at least to a certain extent, highly laudatory. More importantly, however, both Sanders and Dunn have wanted to highlight the emphases in the teachings of mainline Judaism in Paul's day on (1) God's election of Israel, (2) divine grace and mercy, (3) human faith in response to God, and (4) a doctrine of forgiveness — which are features of great importance that need to be highlighted, particularly in response to the bleak picture of Jewish theology that was painted by many Christian interpreters during the nineteenth and early twentieth centuries. But as important as their motivations and these emphases may be, it still must be said that the treatments of both Sanders and Dunn on Paul's pejorative statements regarding "works of the law" and "works" in Galatians and Romans — and particularly his disparaging words about Jews and the Mosaic law in Rom 2:17–3:19 (as well as elsewhere in his letters) — misconstrue Paul's teaching, and so fall short of a true understanding of what he said about the Jews and what his attitude was toward the mainline Judaism of his day.

It will be necessary to deal with all of these matters more fully in a forthcoming exegetical commentary, giving attention particularly to some of the Jewish writings from the period of Second Temple Judaism that throw light on them (including, especially, the six recently reconstructed Qumran texts identified as 4QMMT and published as 4Q394-399). Suffice it here to say that one's understanding of "the New Perspective" with respect to both Palestinian Judaism and Paul's teaching — whether one is in support of or opposed to such a stance, or views matters in a more nuanced fashion — is a critical issue in the study of Paul's letter to the Christians at Rome.

6. "Honor" and "Shame"

During the 1960s there arose among philosophers and cultural anthropologists an understanding of Mediterranean society, both ancient and modern, as founded on the values of "honor" (i.e., "respect/recognition from one's peers," "dignity," "status," "prestige") and "shame" (i.e., "dishonor in the eyes of one's peers," "disgrace," "disdain," "rebuke") — which factors, whether inherited or acquired, functioned as a foundational set of social values for all of life, whether personal or corporate. And since Christianity came to birth and was nurtured in the cradle of Mediterranean culture, a number of biblical interpreters since the 1980s have seen the motifs of "honor" and "shame" as being present throughout the NT, not only in the narratives of the Gospels and Acts but also in many of the statements and exhortations that appear in the canonical letters and the Johannine Apocalypse. Christian interpreters and preachers today, therefore, have been urged to take these cultural motifs into account in their reading of the NT, both for a more accurate understanding of its contents and for a more relevant application of its message.

Philosophical and Anthropological Foundations

The great Greek philosopher Aristotle (384-322 B.C.) spoke of "honor" and "pleasure" as the two primary positive motivations that people have for the choosing of one course of action over another[109] — though the caveat of his teacher, the Athenian orator Isocrates (436-338 B.C.), always tempered Aristotle's judgment with respect to these matters: that while honor with pleasure was a great good, pleasure without honor was the worst of evils; for to put pleasure ahead of honor was to be ruled by passion and desire, and so to be more animal-like than human.[110] Further, on the importance of "shame" as a negative means of controlling conduct, Aristotle commented as follows: "There are many things that they [the people] either do or do not do owing to the feeling of shame, which these men [i.e., those who form the public consensus, whose opinion matters to the doers] inspire."[111] Isocrates, Aristotle's teacher, even insisted that one's honor was more important than one's safety[112] — which ordering of "honor" above "pleasure" and "safety" was what evidently compelled Isocrates at the ripe old age of 98 to starve himself to death after the Battle of Chaeronea (338 B.C.), because he was convinced that all honor and all freedom had come to an end with the defeat of the Athenians by Philip of Macedon. Among the Roman intelligentsia, Seneca "the Younger" (i.e., Lucius Annaeus Seneca, born c. 4 B.C. and died A.D. 65), the Stoic philosopher, statesman, and writer of a number of prose works and

109. Aristotle, *Nicomachean Ethics*, 3.1.11 (1110b. 11-12).
110. Isocrates, *Ad Demonicum* 17.
111. Aristotle, *Rhetoric* 2.6.26.
112. Isocrates, *Ad Demonicus* 43.

tragedies, said of "honor": "The one firm conviction from which we move to the proof of other points is this: that which is honorable is held dear for no other reason than that it is honorable."[113]

Picking up on such Greco-Roman statements, Arthur Adkins published his *Merit and Responsibility: A Study in Greek Values* in 1960,[114] and Julian Pitt-Rivers produced his *The People of the Sierra* in 1961[115] — both, in their own ways, seeking to demonstrate the thesis that the social values of "honor" and "shame" possessed fundamental importance in the culture of the Mediterranean world, both of antiquity and today. And much of this early philosophical and anthropological understanding of Mediterranean culture was brought together in a 1966 symposium volume edited by John Peristiany entitled *Honour and Shame: The Values of Mediterranean Society*,[116] within which the article by Julian Pitt-Rivers entitled "Honour and Social Status" is probably the most significant in its defining of the issues and setting the course for all further discussion of the subject.[117]

The Identification of "Honor and Shame" Motifs in the New Testament Generally

While it can be shown that themes of "honor" and "shame" were prominent in the writings of several ancient Greek, Latin, and Jewish authors,[118] the most significant occurrences of these themes for our purposes are in the NT. The pioneer in the identification of these motifs in the NT is Bruce Malina, who in 1981 published his book *The New Testament World: Insights from Cultural Anthropology*.[119] Later, in 1991, Malina and Jerome Neyrey produced a

---

113. Seneca, *De Beneficiis* 4.16.2.

114. A. W. H. Adkins, *Merit and Responsibility: A Study in Greek Values* (Oxford: Clarendon Press, 1960).

115. J. Pitt-Rivers, *The People of the Sierra* (Chicago: University of Chicago Press, 1961).

116. J. G. Peristiany, *Honour and Shame: The Values of Mediterranean Society* (London: Weidenfeld & Nicholson, 1966).

117. J. Pitt-Rivers, "Honour and Social Status," in *Honour and Shame*, ed. J. G. Peristiany (London: Weidenfeld & Nicholson, 1966), 19-77.

118. For an apt summary of such materials in several major Greek, Latin, and Jewish writings, see D. A. deSilva, *Despising Shame: Honor Discourse and Community Maintenance in the Epistle "to the Hebrews"* (1995; 2nd ed. 2008), chs. 2 and 3.

119. B. J. Malina, *The New Testament World: Insights from Cultural Anthropology* (Atlanta: John Knox, 1981).

highly significant article entitled "Honor and Shame in Luke-Acts," which they subtitled "Pivotal Values of the Mediterranean World."[120] Further, in 1992 Malina and Richard Rohrbaugh published their *Social-Science Commentary on the Synoptic Gospels*,[121] and in 1998 Jerome Neyrey edited a volume of articles entitled *Honor and Shame in the Gospel of Matthew*.[122]

Of importance, as well, is Halvor Moxnes's programmatic "Readers Guide" article of 1993, "Honor and Shame,"[123] and John Elliott's study of 1994 on the use of these themes in 1 Peter, which he subtitled *The Gospel According to 1 Peter in the Key of Honor and Shame*.[124] Of particular importance, however, not only because of the author's expertise but also because of his sensitivity and balance in the presentation of his material, are the publications on the subject by David A. deSilva — that is, (1) his well known 1995 publication of his earlier doctoral thesis in the SBL Dissertation Series entitled *Despising Shame: Honor Discourse and Community Maintenance in the Epistle to the Hebrews*,[125] (2) his 1996 article "Honor Discourse and Social Engineering in 1 Thessalonians,"[126] (3) his 1999 monograph *The Hope of Glory: Honor Discourse and New Testament Interpretation*, which discusses the whole subject of NT occurrences of the theme more broadly,[127] and (4) his 2000 commentary on Hebrews, which is titled *Perseverance in Gratitude: A Socio-Rhetorical Commentary on the Epistle to the Hebrews*.[128]

120. B. J. Malina and J. H. Neyrey, "Honor and Shame in Luke-Acts: Pivotal Values of the Mediterranean World," in *The Social World of Luke-Acts*, ed. J. H. Neyrey (Peabody: Hendrickson, 1991), 25-65.

121. B. J. Malina and R. L. Rohrbaugh, *Social-Science Commentary on the Synoptic Gospels* (Minneapolis: Fortress, 1992).

122. J. H. Neyrey, ed., *Honor and Shame in the Gospel of Matthew* (Louisville: Westminster/John Knox, 1998).

123. H. Moxnes, "Honor and Shame" (BTB Readers Guide), *BTB* 23 (1993) 167-76.

124. J. H. Elliott, "Disgraced yet Graced: The Gospel According to 1 Peter in the Key of Honor and Shame," *BTB* 24 (1994) 166-78.

125. D. A. deSilva, *Despising Shame: Honor Discourse and Community Maintenance in the Epistle to the Hebrews*, SBL.DS 152 (Atlanta: Scholars Press, 1995; rev. ed. 2008).

126. D. A. deSilva, "Worthy of His Kingdom: Honor Discourse and Social Engineering in 1 Thessalonians," *JSNT* 64 (1996) 49-79.

127. D. A. deSilva, *The Hope of Glory: Honor Discourse and New Testament Interpretation* (Collegeville: Liturgical Press, 1999).

128. D. A. deSilva, *Perseverance in Gratitude: A Socio-Rhetorical Commentary on the Epistle to the Hebrews* (Grand Rapids: Eerdmans, 2000).

The Identification of "Honor" and "Shame" Motifs in Romans

Much of what has been done to date in the use of the motifs of "honor" and "shame" as interpretive approaches for an understanding of the NT has pertained (1) to the narratives of the Synoptic Gospels and Acts, and (2) to the hortatory materials in the Corinthian letters, Hebrews, 1 Peter, and the Johannine Apocalypse. Sociological studies of the motifs of "honor" and "shame" in the writings of the NT are yet in their infancy, and a great deal of work has yet to be done by way of investigation and explication of this rather new interpretive approach — particularly with regard to Paul and his letters.

Paul's letter to the Christians at Rome has, in fact, just begun to receive serious treatment along these lines. Halvor Moxnes led the way in his 1988 article "Honor, Shame, and the Outside World in Paul's Letter to the Romans"[129] and in his 1994 article "The Quest for Honor and the Unity of the Community in Romans 12 and in the Orations of Dio Chrysostom."[130] It is, however, Robert Jewett who has given the fullest expression to this interpretive approach with regard to the study of Romans — first in his 1997 article "Honor and Shame in the Argument of Romans"[131] and then most extensively in his 2007 Romans commentary in the Hermeneia series.[132]

In the first two sentences of his "Introduction" to his Romans commentary, under the heading "The Approach of the Commentary," Jewett states his basic critical concerns (as I have called them) that underlie all that he seeks to accomplish in his commentary on Paul's letter to Rome — which include his intent to engage extensively in "cultural analysis of the honor, shame, and imperial systems in the Greco-Roman world":

> This commentary employs all of the standard methods of historical-critical exegesis. This includes historical analysis; text criticism, form criticism, and redaction criticism; rhetorical analysis; social scientific

129. H. Moxnes, "Honor, Shame, and the Outside World in Paul's Letter to the Romans," in *The Social World of Formative Christianity and Judaism: Essays in Tribute to Howard Clark Kee,* ed. J. Neusner, P. Borgen, E. S. Frerichs, and R. Horsley (Philadelphia: Fortress, 1988), 207-18.

130. H. Moxnes, "The Quest for Honor and the Unity of the Community in Romans 12 and in the Orations of Dio Chrysostom," in *Paul and Hellenism,* ed. T. Enberg-Pedersen (Minneapolis: Fortress, 1994).

131. R. Jewett, "Honor and Shame in the Argument of Romans," in *Putting Body and Soul Together: Essays in Honor of Robin Scroggs,* ed. A. Brown, G. F. Snyder, and V. Wiles (Valley Forge: Trinity Press International, 1997), 257-72.

132. R. Jewett, *Romans* (2007).

reconstruction of the audience situation; an historical reconstruction of the situations in Rome and Spain; *historical and cultural analysis of the honor, shame, and imperial systems in the Greco-Roman world;* and a theological interpretation that takes these details into account rather than following traditional paths formed by church traditions.[133]

Jewett readily acknowledges, of course, that "there is room to disagree" with what he calls "the historical, social, and rhetorical premises on which this commentary rests"[134] — that is, with what he later identifies as (1) "the pyramid of honor" that controlled the mentality and all of the affairs of the imperial government of Rome ("the historical premise"), (2) the culture of "honor and shame" that dominated all of Greco-Roman society ("the social premise"), and (3) the "epideictic type of rhetoric" that Paul uses throughout his letter to the Christians at Rome, which praises matters of honor, denounces matters of shame, and calls for a proper response (i.e., "the rhetorical premise").[135] Nonetheless, engaging in a bit of introspective autobiography and some pastoral concern, Jewett goes on to state how these particular premises have radically changed his own understanding of Paul's message in Romans and to offer an opportunity for his readers to change their understanding of Paul's letter to Rome as well — stating these more personal matters in the following words:

> These premises have led to an interpretation of the letter that differs from the one I was taught by my church and by the theological professors at Chicago and Tübingen. It is also different from the interpretation of Romans that I myself advocated through most of my teaching career. But difference is no proof of final adequacy, and the assessment of the results is left up to others.[136]

An Evaluation and Challenge

The thesis that controls most of Jewett's commentary on Romans is that Paul in his letter to Rome "employs honor categories from beginning to end."[137] It is a thesis that makes use of passages where the motifs of "honor and shame"

---

133. R. Jewett, *Romans*, 1 (italics mine).
134. R. Jewett, *Romans*, 4.
135. See particularly R. Jewett, *Romans*, 46-53; but also *passim*.
136. R. Jewett, *Romans*, 4.
137. R. Jewett, *Romans*, 49, *et passim*.

seem most obviously present — such as in 1:16, where Paul says that he is "not ashamed of the gospel" (possibly reflecting an accusation against him of some of the Christians at Rome); in 13:1-7, where he urges "respect," "honor," and "submission" to those in governmental authority (probably in opposition to the stances taken by some of his addressees); and in 14:1–15:13, where he speaks against dishonoring and shaming a weaker believer in Jesus and urges the supposedly "stronger" members in some of the various Roman congregations to accept them, encourage them, and seek to please them. Much of Jewett's case for the dominance of "honor categories" elsewhere in Romans, however, is based on his twofold insistence (1) that Paul uses a form of epideictic (i.e., "panegyric" or "eulogistic") rhetoric throughout his letter to the Christians at Rome, which type of rhetoric sought to persuade an audience to hold on to or reaffirm some point of view by highlighting what was to be viewed as honorable and what shameful — that is, what was worthy of honor and praise and what was shameful and to be blamed, and (2) that a large part of Paul's polemic in Romans is focused on "the pyramid of honor" that characterized the mentality and actions of the imperial government of Rome, which, in turn, had filtered down into all of the Greco-Roman culture of Paul's day.

Our proposal with regard to Paul's rhetoric in Romans, however, is that the extensive central portion of the letter (i.e., the "body middle" of 1:16–15:13) cannot easily be made to fit any of the usual three classical models of "forensic," "deliberative," or "epideictic" rhetoric, but, rather, that the form of rhetoric lately identified as "protreptic" rhetoric — that is, "a word, speech, or message of exhortation" (λόγος προτρεπτικός) — offers a better diachronic rhetorical model for the development of Paul's argument in 1:16–15:13, which form of presentation the apostle accommodated, whether consciously or unconsciously, to his own purposes and filled with his own Christian theology (cf. Chapter VI, "Greco-Roman Oral, Rhetorical, and Epistolary Conventions"). And if that is so, then it cannot be assumed (1) that since Paul used an epideictic form of rhetoric in Romans (which we dispute), and (2) that since epideictic rhetoric includes an emphasis on what is to be viewed as honorable and what is to be seen as shameful (which we acknowledge), it follows (3) that one must interpret Paul's statements in the central section of his letter to Rome, that is, in 1:16–15:13, as being directed mainly against the "honor and shame conventions" present in the Mediterranean culture of his day.

Admittedly, the fact that Romans has most often been interpreted only in a theological manner, without attention also to the cultural conventions of

Paul's day or to Paul's response to certain criticisms, can be faulted. But that does not mean that one must correct that error by focusing principally on the cultural conventions of that earlier day or on certain criticisms of Paul. As Halvor Moxnes rightly says with respect to one modern commentator's treatment of Paul's statement in Rom 1:16, "I am not ashamed of the gospel": it is possible to make "an unfortunate distinction between a 'social' and a 'Christian' condition and between 'Paul's relation to his environment' and the 'nature of the Gospel'" — to which statement Moxnes then appends the following appropriate note:

> Although the ground for Paul's confidence is found in the gospel, the fact that he is not ashamed expresses his relations to his environment. Even in their most theological use, "shame" and "not to be ashamed" do not relinquish their everyday meaning, in which a person stands within a relationship not only to God but [also] to other people within a community.[138]

In Paul's own understanding, God "called" him to be "an apostle" to the Gentiles, and therefore he considered that he had been "set apart for the gospel of God" (Rom 1:1) — not appointed a reformer of society (whether as one of the great societal reformers of history or as a "Don Quixote" simply tilting at windmills). Nonetheless, while it was the message of the Christian gospel, its content as focused in "Jesus Christ our Lord" — and its outreach to Gentiles through his God-ordained ministry — that motivated Paul and were his central concerns, he was not unaware of the cultural features within the Greco-Roman world of his day and he used them to the advantage of his mission and message.

Such a combination of emphases, arranged in their proper order of emphasis in the appropriate portions of Paul's letter to Rome, need to be elaborated more fully in our proposed exegetical commentary. Yet they need also to be highlighted here as part of our listed critical issues in the study of Romans, with the reader alerted to their presence and the need for their proper interpretation.

7. "Reconciliation" and "Peace"

"Reconciliation" and "peace" are important features in Paul's proclamation of the Christian gospel, rooted as they are in (1) God's love and purpose,

---

138. H. Moxnes, *The Social World of Formative Christianity and Judaism,* 207.

(2) Christ's earthly ministry and sacrificial death, and (3) the earliest Christian confessions. James Denney in his 1917 book *The Christian Doctrine of Reconciliation* was in many ways ahead of his time in highlighting the theme of reconciliation as a primary Christian teaching.[139] T. W. Manson in 1963 referred to "reconciliation" as "the keyword of Paul's Gospel."[140] Joseph Fitzmyer in 1967 highlighted the importance of "reconciliation" in Paul's theology, relating it also to the apostle's emphases on "peace" and "union with the Father" in saying: "The main effect of Christ's passion, death, and resurrection is the reconciliation of man [i.e., 'of responsive people'] to a state of peace and union with the Father."[141] Ralph Martin in 1981 and Seyoon Kim in 1982, each in his own way, have set out in detail the arguments for "reconciliation" as being central in Paul's understanding of the Christian gospel and basic to all that he proclaimed.[142] And Willard Swartley in 2006 has highlighted the importance of the theme of "peace" throughout the NT as well as in Paul's letters.[143]

The Language of Reconciliation and Peace

The Greek verbs καταλλάσσω and διαλάσσομαι ("reconcile"), as well as the Greek noun καταλλαγή ("reconciliation"), are compound forms of the verb ἀλλάσσω ("alter" or "change") and the noun ἄλλος ("other"), and so they basically mean "to make otherwise" and connote "a change of relationship or situation." They appear frequently in Greek writings to signify a change of circumstances or relationships in the political, social, familial, and moral spheres of life. Yet they did not play any part in the cultic expiatory rites of the Greco-Roman world and are almost entirely absent in Greek religious writings, for pagan religions did not think of relations between divinity and humanity in terms of personal nearness. Only Sophocles, who was one of the three great tragic poets of the fifth century B.C., in depicting the humiliation

---

139. J. Denney, *The Christian Doctrine of Reconciliation* (London: Hodder & Stoughton, 1917).

140. T. W. Manson, *On Paul and John* (London: SCM, 1963), 50.

141. J. A. Fitzmyer, *Pauline Theology: A Brief Sketch* (New York: Prentice-Hall, 1967), 43-44.

142. R. P. Martin, *Reconciliation: A Study of Paul's Theology* (Atlanta: John Knox, 1981; rev. ed. Grand Rapids; Zondervan, 1990); S. Kim, *The Origin of Paul's Gospel* (Tübingen: Mohr-Siebeck, 1981; Grand Rapids: Eerdmans, 1982; rev. ed. Tübingen: Mohr-Siebeck, 1984).

143. W. M. Swartley, *Covenant of Peace* (Grand Rapids: Eerdmans, 2006).

and suicide of the warrior Ajax, speaks about a person as reconciling himself to the gods[144] — but he does not say anything about how that reconciliation was accomplished.

There are no equivalents to the language of reconciliation in Hebrew or Aramaic. The closest terms in the Jewish (OT) Scriptures, as well as in the later rabbinic codifications, are the terms רצה and פנים, which mean "to please," "appease," "satisfy," or "placate." When used in the context of a wrongdoer placating a person who had been wronged by some act of restitution, these terms may be seen as connoting certain features that correspond, at least to some degree, to the idea of "reconciliation" — though without any change of personal relationships or one's emotions being necessarily involved.

The somewhat parallel Greek verb ἐπιστρέφω ("turn," "turn around," "turn back," "return") is used in a purely secular fashion in Judg 19:3 (LXX) with reference to a Levite "returning his concubine to himself." The noun διαλλαγή ("reconciliation") appears in Sir 22:22 and 27:21 with respect to friends being reconciled (cf. also the use of the second person aorist, imperative, passive διαλλάγηθι in Matt 5:24 with respect to a person being reconciled to a brother or a sister). In Mishnah Yoma ("Day of Atonement") 8:9 it is said: "For transgressions that are between man and God, the Day of Atonement effects atonement; but for wrongs that are between a man and his fellow, the Day of Atonement effects atonement only if he [i.e., the wrongdoer] has appeased his fellow" — that is, only if a form of reconciliation has taken place between the two parties, as inaugurated by the wrongdoer.

The Greek noun εἰρήνη ("peace," "harmony") translates the Hebrew שלום ("completeness," "soundness," "welfare," "peace"), which was a central motif in the Jewish (OT) Scriptures and Early Judaism in speaking of the health and welfare of persons individually and of people corporately. In the NT it is spoken of repeatedly in statements, greetings, and benedictions as one of the greatest benefits that God through Jesus Christ bestows on his people (cf., e.g., John 14:27; 16:33; 20:19, 21, 26; Acts 10:36; Rom 1:7; 15:33; 1 Cor 1:3; 2 Cor 1:2; 13:11; Gal 1:3; 6:16; Eph 1:2; 6:23; Phil 1:2; 4:7, 9; Col 1:2; 3:15; 1 Thess 1:1; 5:23; 2 Thess 1:2; 3:16; Titus 1:4; Phlm 3; Heb 13:20; 1 Pet 1:2; 5:14; 2 John 3; 3 John 14; Jude 2; Rev 1:4). And since according to the OT prophets "peace" will be an essential characteristic of the messianic kingdom, what comes to God's own through their reception of the Christian gospel is spoken of as uniquely God's peace — especially by Paul in his letter to the believers in Jesus at Rome (see esp. Rom 5:1; 8:6; 14:17, 19; 15:13; 16:20).

144. Sophocles, *Ajax* 744.

"Reconciliation" as a Religious Term among the Jews

A religious use of the term "reconciliation" among Jews first appears in 2 Maccabees, where the writer prays: "May he [God] be reconciled to you [i.e., the writer's Jewish addressees], and not forsake you in the time of trouble" (2 Macc 1:5). Later in that same writing the writer expresses the common Jewish belief that after God has chastened his people because of their sins — and so when he becomes, in effect, reconciled to his people — the Jerusalem temple will be restored to its former glory (2 Macc 5:20; 7:33). Further, after the early successes of Judas Maccabeus against the Seleucids, the author of 2 Maccabees tells his readers that the Israelite warriors "united in supplication and besought the Lord of mercy to be reconciled to his servants for ever" (2 Macc 8:29). Josephus twice uses the terminology of reconciliation (both as a noun and as a verb) in a religious manner — first, in telling his Roman readers that he had earlier declared at the close of his address to the Jewish insurgents of his day that "The Deity is reconciled to those who confess and repent" (*War* 5.415); and second, in speaking of Samuel, at a time of King Saul's "contempt and disobedience," as pleading with God "to be reconciled to Saul and not angry with him" (*Antiq* 6.143).

Paul's Concept and Language of Reconciliation

It was Paul, however, who focused on the concept and language of reconciliation in his evangelistic preaching to pagan Gentiles and in his letters to Gentile believers in Jesus. The term appears in highly significant portions of his letters and is used in these letters almost entirely in a theological sense: the noun καταλλαγή being used four times in Rom 5:11; 11:15; and 2 Cor. 5:18, 19; the verb καταλλάσσω five times in Rom 5:10 (twice) and 2 Cor 5:18, 19, 20); and the verb ἀποκαταλλάσσω (an emphatic form, as prefaced by an additional preposition) three times in Eph 2:16 and Col 1:20, 22 — with only one secular use to be found in his letters, that is, in 1 Cor 7:11, where he exhorts a wife who may have thoughts about separating from her husband: "If she does separate, let her remain unmarried or else be reconciled (καταλλαγήτω, 'let her be reconciled') to her husband."

Somewhat surprising, however, is the fact that reconciliation language does not appear in any of the other writings of the NT. Nor can it be found in any of the extant Christian writings of the second century. It may, therefore, be viewed as having been distinctive to Paul among the earliest Christian writers. Nonetheless, because of the form and context in which this reconcil-iation language is used in 2 Cor 5:19 ("In Christ God was reconciling the world to himself, not counting their trespasses against them, and entrusting the message of reconciliation to us"), it may be postulated that Paul was ac-tually quoting in this verse a portion of some early Christian confession. For his statement of 2 Cor 5:19 suggests his use of such early Christian confes-sional material for the following reasons: (1) it evidences a certain balance of structure, (2) it is introduced by the particle ὅτι (i.e., a *hoti recitativum*), which was often used by Paul and other NT writers to introduce a quotation from some traditional material, (3) it incorporates in a formal manner the essence of early Christian proclamation, and (4) it serves as the linchpin or central feature of all that is said by way of exposition in 5:18 and 20.

It is probably best, therefore, to surmise that Paul came to know of this reconciliation language because of its inclusion in some early Christian con-fessional material — and, further, that he came to appreciate it as being most expressive of what he had personally experienced in his relationship with God through the work of Christ and the ministry of God's Spirit. It may also be postulated that he made this relational and personal soteriological lan-guage central in his preaching to pagan Gentiles in the Greco-Roman world simply because he believed it to be (1) more culturally meaningful, (2) more theologically significant, and (3) more ethically compelling than many of the traditional soteriological expressions of a forensic nature (such as the terms "justification," "redemption," and "propitiation" or "expiation") that were be-ing used by both Jews and Jewish Christians.

Paul's Theology of Reconciliation

Two important theological points are always made by Paul when he speaks of reconciliation. The first is that he always refers to God as the subject of the verb καταλλάσσω and never its object — which is a feature contrary to a Jewish understanding of reconciliation, where God is spoken of as being rec-onciled to his people or situations (cf. the references cited above from the LXX, Josephus, and rabbinic literature). In Paul's proclamation, it is God who reconciles "people" and "the world," and never the reverse (cf. 2 Cor 5:18: "God reconciled us to himself"; 2 Cor 5:19: "in Christ God was reconcil-ing the world"; Rom 5:10: "we were reconciled to God"; Rom 5:11: "through whom [i.e., 'our Lord Jesus Christ'] we have now received reconciliation"; Rom 11:15: "the reconciliation of the world"). The second point to be observed is that Paul always proclaims that God's reconciliation of people and the world is based on the salvific work of Jesus Christ — that is, on his faithfulness/obedience to God the Father in his earthly life (his "active obedience") and his faithfulness/obedience to the purposes of God in his death on a cross (his "passive obedience") — and never on what people might do in their endeavors to please God by their own merits (cf. 2 Cor 5:15: "He [Christ] died for all, so that those who live might live no longer for themselves, but for him who died and was raised for them"; 2 Cor 5:21: "He [God] made him [Christ] to be sin who knew no sin, so that in him we might become the righteousness of God"; Rom 5:10: "We were reconciled to God through the death of his Son"; Rom 5:11: "through whom ['our Lord Jesus Christ'] we have now received reconciliation").

Further, it needs to be observed that in Romans 5 Paul explicitly relates this theme of reconciliation to such important theological matters as "peace with God" (5:1), "access into this grace in which we stand" (5:2), and "no longer being God's enemies" (5:10) — while later, in Romans 14–15, he inferentially relates this teaching to such important practical concerns as "accepting a person whose faith is weak, without passing judgment on disputable matters" (ch. 14), "bearing with the failings of the weak, without trying to please only ourselves" (15:1-7), and "accepting one another, just as Christ accepted you" (15:7-8).

Also to be noted regarding the apostle's language of reconciliation is the fact that it is inclusive in its applications, for it refers not only to the reconciliation of "people" (2 Cor 5:18; Rom 5:10-11) but also to the reconciliation of "the world" (2 Cor 5:19; Rom 11:15). Further, Paul's proclamation of reconciliation has reference not only to what God has already accomplished (cf. 2 Cor 5:19; Rom 5:10), but also to what he is presently doing in the lives of believers (cf. 2 Cor 5:17) and to what he will yet bring about both for those who have responded positively to him and for his entire creation (cf. Rom 5:10-11; 8:19-25).

Yet inherent in Paul's understanding of reconciliation — which has been accomplished already by God through the work of Christ Jesus, is a present reality for those who turn to him in faith, and will be fully brought about in the future for all of his people and all of his creation — is what has been characterized as "the twofold absurdity" of the Christian gospel. This double absurdity has to do with the facts that (1) reconciliation with God comes about by means of death — that is both objectively by means of the physical death of Jesus of Nazareth, God's Messiah, and subjectively because of a person's "death" to self-reliance before God, and so his or her turning to God in complete trust in God's provision through Jesus Christ alone; and

(2) "the ministry of reconciliation," in both its proclamation and its practice, has been delegated by God to finite and failing human beings who have themselves, by God's grace and apart from their own merits, been reconciled to God (cf. 2 Cor 5:18b, 19b).

The Ministry Component and Ethical Compulsion of Reconciliation

Involved in Paul's teaching regarding reconciliation, therefore, is a ministry component. For God has not only reconciled people to himself, he has also "entrusted the message of reconciliation to us" (2 Cor 5:18). Thus believers in Christ, who have been reconciled to God and are presently experiencing that reconciliation in an initial measure, are those who have been commissioned by God as "ambassadors for Christ," and so called by God to "entreat" all people "on behalf of Christ" to be "reconciled to God" (2 Cor 5:20). It is a component that stems directly from the compulsion of the message and the experience of the "good news" of God's reconciliation, with none of the three essential features in Paul's proclamation of reconciliation — the message, the experience, and the compulsion — ever able to be separated off from the others, but all meant to be part and parcel of the same reality.

Likewise, there is a vitally important ethical factor in Paul's proclamation of reconciliation. For just as being loved by God we are motivated to love — and just as being forgiven by God we are motivated to forgive — so being reconciled by God to himself we are motivated "on behalf of Christ" to be agents of reconciliation to people individually and to the world inclusively. God's love for us is expressed in our love for others; God's forgiveness of us takes bodily form in our forgiveness of others. So also God's reconciliation of us to himself and his bestowing on us his peace compels our involvement in working for the reconciliation and peace of others, whatever their needs and as God directs us. For to divorce the ethic of reconciliation from the doctrine of reconciliation is, sadly, to deny them both.

8. A Concluding Remark regarding Patterns of Distribution and Paul's Use of These Themes and Features in Romans

Each of the above interpretive approaches to Paul and his letters — and particularly those having to do with the interpretation of his letter to the Christians at Rome — has, of late, been seen as important for an understanding of

Paul's thought, ministry, and letter writing. Yet what has often been ignored are (1) the patterns of distribution in Paul's letters with respect to the themes and features that underlie these various interpretive approaches and (2) how Paul uses these themes and features in his letters — particularly his patterns of distribution and his usage in Romans. What follows in the final two chapters of this book, therefore, will highlight the various patterns of distribution of certain major themes and features in Romans and how Paul develops these themes and features in his Letter. For it is essential in a scholarly study of Romans not only to note the major themes and features of the letter but also to observe where, how, and for what purpose he uses them. Thus we will deal with "the focus or central thrust" of Paul's letter to Rome in Chapter X and with "the structure and argument" of that letter in Chapter XI, believing that only when matters regarding the distribution, purpose, and development of the major themes and features of Romans are highlighted and then explicated will readers of Paul's most famous letter be truly aided in their understanding of the message of this important letter today.

Supplemental Bibliography

See also "Bibliography of Selected Commentaries." All references in the footnotes to works included in this list are by the authors' names and abbreviated titles.

Adkins, Arthur W. H. *Merit and Responsibility: A Study in Greek Values.* Oxford: Clarendon Press, 1960.

Barclay, William. *The Mind of St. Paul.* London: Collins, 1958.

Barth, Markus. "The Faith of the Messiah," *HeyJ* 10 (1969) 363-70.

―――. *Justification: Pauline Texts Interpreted in the Light of the Old and New Testaments,* trans. A. M. Woodruff. Grand Rapids: Eerdmans, 1971.

Bayer, Oswald. *Living by Faith: Justification and Sanctification,* trans. G. W. Bromiley. Grand Rapids: Eerdmans, 2003.

Best, Ernest. *One Body in Christ.* London: SPCK, 1955.

Bevan, Edwin. "Mystery Religions and Christianity," in *Contemporary Thinking about Paul: An Anthology,* ed. T. S. Kepler. New York: Abingdon-Cokesbury, 1950.

Bousset, Wilhelm. *Kyrios Christos.* Göttingen: Vandenhoeck & Ruprecht, 1934.

Braaten, Carl E. *Justification: The Article by Which the Church Stands or Falls.* Minneapolis: Fortress, 1990.

Brauch, Manfred T. "Perspectives on 'God's Righteousness' in Recent German Discussion," in E. P. Sanders, *Paul and Palestinian Judaism: A Comparison of Patterns of Religion.* Philadelphia: Fortress, 1977, "Appendix," 523-42.

Breytenbach, Cilliers. *Versöhnung. Eine Studie zur paulinischen Soteriologie.* Neukirchen-Vluyn: Neukirchener Verlag, 1989.

Büchsel, Friedrich. "'In Christus' bei Paulus," *ZNW* 42 (1949) 141-58.

Bultmann, Rudolf. *Theology of the New Testament,* 2 vols., trans. K. Grobel. London: SCM, 1951.

————. "ΔΙΚΑΙΟΣΥΝΗ ΘΕΟΥ," *JBL* 83 (1964) 12-16.

Campbell, Douglas A. "Rom. 1:17 — A Crux Interpretum for the ΠΙΣΤΙΣ ΧΡΙΣΤΟΥ Debate," *JBL* 113 (1994) 265-85.

Conzelmann, Hans. "Die Rechtfertigungslehre des Paulus: Theologie oder Anthropologie?" *EvT* 28 (1968) 389-404.

Corrigan, Gregory M. "Paul's Shame for the Gospel," *BTB* 16 (1986) 23-27.

Cranfield, C. E. B. "On the Πίστις χριστοῦ Question," in *On Romans and Other New Testament Essays.* Edinburgh: T. & T. Clark, 1998, 81-97.

Cremer, Augustus Hermann. *Die Paulinische Rechtfertigungslehre im Zusammenhang ihrer geschichtlichen Voraussetzungen.* Gütersloh: Bertelsmann, 1900.

Deissmann, Adolf. *Die neutestamentliche Formel "in Christo Jesu."* Marburg: Elwert, 1892.

Denney, James. *The Christian Doctrine of Reconciliation.* London: Hodder & Stoughton, 1917.

deSilva, David A. *Despising Shame: Honor Discourse and Community Maintenance in the Epistle to the Hebrews.* SBL.DS 152. Atlanta: Scholars, 1995; rev. ed. 2008.

————. "Worthy of His Kingdom: Honor Discourse and Social Engineering in 1 Thessalonians," *JSNT* 64 (1996) 49-79.

————. *The Hope of Glory: Honor Discourse and New Testament Interpretation.* Collegeville: Liturgical Press, 1999.

————. *Perseverance in Gratitude: A Socio-Rhetorical Commentary on the Epistle "to the Hebrews."* Grand Rapids: Eerdmans, 2000.

Dunn, James D. G. "The New Perspective on Paul," *BJRL* 65 (1983) 95-122.

————. "Once More *Pistis Christou*," in *Society of Biblical Literature 1991 Seminar Papers,* ed. E. H. Lovering Jr. Atlanta: Scholars Press, 1991, 730-44.

————. "The Justice of God: A Renewed Perspective on Justification," *JTS* 43 (1992) 1-22.

Elliott, John H. "Disgraced yet Graced: The Gospel According to 1 Peter in the Key of Honor and Shame," *BTB* 24 (1994) 166-78.

Fitzmyer, Joseph A. "Reconciliation in Pauline Theology," in *No Famine in the Land: Studies in Honor of John L. MacKenzie,* ed. J. W. Flanagan and A. W. Robinson. Missoula: Scholars, 1975, 155-77.

Forde, Gerhard O. *The Captivation of the Will: Luther vs. Erasmus on Freedom and Bondage.* Grand Rapids: Eerdmans, 2005.

Fridrichsen, Anton. "Aus Glauben zum Glauben, Röm 1,17," in *Walter Bauer Gottingensi Novi Testamenti philologia optime merito sacrum.* ConNeot 12. Lund: Gleerup, 1948, 54.

Fuchs, Ernst. "Jesu und der Glaube," *ZTK* 55 (1958) 170-85.

Gilmore, David G. *Honor and Shame and the Unity of the Mediterranean.* Washington, DC: American Anthropological Association, 1987.

Goodenough, Erwin R. *By Light, Light: The Mystic Gospel of Hellenistic Judaism.* New Haven: Yale University Press, 1935.

Goppelt, Leonhard. "Versöhnung durch Christus," in *Christologie und Ethik. Aufsätze zum Neuen Testament.* Göttingen: Vandenhoeck & Ruprecht, 1968, 147-64.

Hagner, Donald A. "Paul and Judaism: Testing the New Perspective," in *Revisiting Paul's Doctrine of Justification: A Challenge to the New Perspective,* ed. P. Stuhlmacher. Downers Grove: InterVarsity, 2001, 75-105.

Hanson, Anthony T. *Studies in Paul's Technique and Theology.* London: SPCK, 1974.

Haussleiter, Johannes. *Der Glaube Jesu Christi und der christliche Glaube: Ein Beitrag zu Erklärung des Römerbrief.* Leipzig: Dörffling & Franke, 1891.

————. "Eine theologische Disputation über den Glauben Jesu," *Neue kirchliche Zeitschrift* (1892) 507-20.

————. "Was versteht Paulus unter christlichen Glauben," in *Theologische Abhandlungen Hermann Cremer dargebracht.* Gütersloh: Bertelsmann, 1895, 159-81.

Hays, Richard B. *The Faith of Jesus Christ: An Investigation of the Narrative Substructure of Galatians 3:1–4:11.* SBL.DS 56. Chico: Scholars, 1983, esp. 170-74.

————. "ΠΙΣΤΙΣ and the Pauline Christology: What Is at Stake?" in *Pauline Theology,* vol. 4: *Looking Back, Pressing On,* ed. E. E. Johnson and D. Hay. Atlanta: Scholars, 1997, 35-60.

Hebert, A. Gabriel. "'Faithfulness' and 'Faith,'" *Theology* 58 (1955) 373-79.

Hooker, Morna D. "ΠΙΣΤΙΣ ΧΡΙΣΤΟΥ," *NTS* 35 (1989) 321-42.

Howard, George E. "Notes and Observations on the 'Faith of Christ,'" *HTR* 60 (1967) 459-65.

————. "The 'Faith of Christ,'" *ExpT* 85 (1974) 212-15.

————. *Paul, Crisis in Galatia: A Study in Early Christian Theology.* Cambridge: Cambridge University Press, 1990, esp. 57-65.

Hultgren, Arland J. "The *Pistis Christou* Formulation in Paul," *NovT* 22 (1980) 248-63.

Jewett, Robert. "Honor and Shame in the Argument of Romans," in *Putting Body and Soul Together: Essays in Honor of Robin Scroggs,* ed. A. Brown, G. F. Snyder, and V. Wiles. Valley Forge: Trinity Press International, 1997, 257-72.

Johnson, Luke Timothy. "Romans 3:21-26 and the Faith of Jesus," *CBQ* 44 (1982) 77-90.

Jüngel, Eberhard. *Justification: The Heart of the Christian Faith.* Edinburgh: T&T Clark, 2001 (ET of German publication by J. C. B. Mohr, 1999).

Käsemann, Ernst. "'The Righteousness of God' in Paul," in *New Testament Questions of Today,* trans. W. J. Montague. London: SCM; Philadelphia: Fortress, 1969, 168-82 (from his "Gottesgerechtigkeit bei Paulus," *ZTK* 58 [1961] 367-78).

————. "Justification and Salvation History in the Epistle to the Romans," in *Perspectives on Paul,* trans. M. Kohl. London: SCM; Philadelphia: Fortress, 1971, 60-78.

————. "Some Thoughts on the Theme 'The Doctrine of Reconciliation in the New Testament,'" in *The Future of Our Religious Past*, ed. J. M. Robinson. London: SCM, 1971, 49-64.

Kennedy, Harry A. A., *The Theology of the Epistles*. London: Duckworth, 1919.

Kertelge, Karl. *"Rechtfertigung" bei Paulus. Studien zur Struktur und zum Bedeutungs-gehalt des paulinischen Rechtfertigungsbegriffs*. Münster: Aschendorff, 1967.

Kim, Seyoon. *The Origin of Paul's Gospel*. Tübingen: Mohr-Siebeck, 1981; Grand Rapids: Eerdmans, 1982; rev. ed. Tübingen: Mohr-Siebeck, 1984.

Kittel, G. "Pistis Iesou Christou bei Paulus," *ThStKr* (1906) 419-36.

Klein, Günter. "Gottes Gerechtigkeit als Thema der neuesten Paulus-Forschung," in *Rekonstruktion und Interpretation*. Munich: Kaiser, 1969, 225-36.

Lake, Kirsopp. *The Earlier Epistles of St. Paul*. London: Christophers, 1934.

Lambrecht, Jan. "Righteousness in the Bible and Justice in the World," *TEvan* 27 (1988) 6-13.

Lietzmann, Hans. *The Beginnings of the Christian Church*, trans. B. L. Woolf. London: Nicholson & Watson, 1937.

Loisy, Alfred. "The Christian Mystery," *HibJ* 10 (1911) 50-64.

Longenecker, Bruce W. *Eschatology and the Covenant: A Comparison of 4 Ezra and Romans 1–11*. JSNT.SS 57. Sheffield: JSOT Press, 1991, esp. 203-15.

————. "Πίστις in Romans 3.25: Neglected Evidence for the 'Faithfulness of Christ'?" *NTS* 39 (1993) 478-80.

————. *The Triumph of Abraham's God: The Transformation of Identity in Galatians*. Edinburgh: T&T Clark, 1998, esp. 98-103.

Longenecker, Richard N. *Paul, Apostle of Liberty*. New York: Harper & Row, 1964, esp. 149-55, 160-80.

————. *Galatians*. WBC. Dallas: Word, 1990, esp. 87-88.

————. *Biblical Exegesis in the Apostolic Period*, 2nd ed. Grand Rapids: Eerdmans, 1999, esp. 88-116.

————. "The Foundational Conviction of New Testament Christology: The Obedi-ence/Faithfulness/Sonship of Christ," in *Studies in Hermeneutics, Christology, and Discipleship*. Sheffield: Phoenix Press, 2004, 122-44.

Luther, Martin. *The Bondage of the Will*, trans. J. I. Packer and O. R. Johnston. Grand Rapids: Baker, 1957.

Lyonnet, Stanislas. "De 'iustitia Dei' in Epistola ad Romanos 1,17 et 3,21-22," *VD* 25 (1947) 23-34.

Malina, Bruce J. *The New Testament World: Insights from Cultural Anthropology*. Atlanta: John Knox, 1981.

Malina, Bruce J., and Jerome H. Neyrey. "Honor and Shame in Luke-Acts: Pivotal Values of the Mediterranean World," in *The Social World of Luke-Acts*, ed. J. H. Neyrey. Peabody: Hendrickson, 1991, 25-65.

Malina, Bruce J., and Richard L. Rohrbaugh. *Social-Science Commentary on the Synop-tic Gospels*. Minneapolis: Fortress, 1992.

McGrath, Alister E. "The Righteousness of God from Augustine to Luther," *ST* 36 (1982) 63-78.

―――――. *Iustitia Dei: A History of the Christian Doctrine of Justification,* 2 vols. Cambridge: Cambridge University Press, 1986.

Mannermaa, Tuomo. *Christ Present in Faith: Luther's View of Justification.* Minneapolis: Augsburg-Fortress, 2005.

Marshall, I. Howard. "The Meaning of 'Reconciliation,'" in *Unity and Diversity in New Testament Theology: Essays in Honor of G. E. Ladd,* ed. R. Guelich. Grand Rapids: Eerdmans, 1978, 117-32.

Martin, Ralph P. *Reconciliation: A Study of Paul's Theology.* Atlanta: John Knox, 1981; rev. ed. Grand Rapids: Zondervan, 1990.

Mattill, Andrew J., Jr. "Translation of Words with the Stem Δικ- in Romans," *AUSS* 9 (1971) 89-98.

Metzger, Bruce M. "Considerations of Methodology in the Study of the Mystery Religions and Early Christianity," *HTR* 48 (1955) 1-20.

Moxnes, Halvor. "Honor, Shame, and the Outside World in Paul's Letter to the Romans," in *The Social World of Formative Christianity and Judaism: Essays in Tribute to Howard Clark Kee,* ed. J. Neusner, P. Borgen, E. S. Frerichs, and R. Horsley. Philadelphia: Fortress, 1988, 207-18.

―――――. "Honor and Shame" (BTB Readers Guide), *BTB* 23 (1993) 167-76.

―――――. "The Quest for Honor and the Unity of the Community in Romans 12 and in the Orations of Dio Chrysostom," in *Paul and Hellenism,* ed. T. Enberg-Pedersen. Minneapolis: Fortress, 1994.

Neyrey, Jerome H., ed. *The Social World of Luke-Acts: Models for Interpretation.* Peabody: Hendrickson, 1991.

Neyrey, Jerome H., ed. *Honor and Shame in the Gospel of Matthew.* Louisville: Westminster/John Knox, 1998.

Oden, Thomas C. *The Justification Reader.* Grand Rapids: Eerdmans, 2002.

Oepke, Albrecht. "Δικαιοσύνη θεοῦ bei Paulus in neuer Beleuchtung," *TLZ* 78 (1953) cols. 257-63.

―――――. "ἐν," *TDNT* 2.537-43.

Peristiany, John G., ed. *Honour and Shame: The Values of Mediterranean Society.* London: Weidenfeld & Nicholson, 1965.

Piper, John. *The Future of Justification: A Response to N. T. Wright.* Wheaton: Crossway, 2007.

Pitt-Rivers, Julian. *The People of the Sierra.* Chicago: University of Chicago Press, 1961.

―――――. "Honour and Social Status," in *Honour and Shame: The Values of Mediterranean Society,* ed. J. G. Peristiany. London: Weidenfeld & Nicholson, 1965, 1977.

Reitzenstein, Richard. *Die hellenistischen Mysterienreligionen.* Leipzig: Teubner, 1927, 3rd ed.

Reventlow, H. Graf. *Rechtfertigung im Horizont des Alten Testaments.* Munich: Kaiser, 1971.

Robinson, D. W. B. "'Faith of Jesus Christ' — a New Testament Debate," *RTR* 29 (1970) 71-81.

Robinson, John A. T. *The Body: A Study in Pauline Theology.* London: SCM, 1957.

Sanders, E. P. *Paul and Palestinian Judaism: A Comparison of Patterns of Religion.* Philadelphia: Fortress, 1977.

————. *Paul, the Law, and the Jewish People.* Philadelphia: Fortress, 1983, 29-64.

Schenk, Wolfgang. "Die Gerechtigkeit Gottes und der Glaube Christi: Versuch einer Verhältnisbestimmung paulinischer Strukturen," *TLZ* 97 (1972) 161-74.

Schmithals, Walter. *Der Römerbrief als historisches Problem.* SNT 9. Gütersloh: Mohn, 1975.

Schrenk, Gottlob. "δίκη, δίκαιος, δικαιοσύνη, δικαιόω," *TDNT* 2.174-225.

Schweitzer, Albert. *The Mysticism of Paul the Apostle,* trans. W. Montgomery. London: Black, 1931.

Seifried, Mark A. *Christ, Our Righteousness: Paul's Theology of Justification.* Downers Grove: InterVarsity, 2001.

Stendahl, Krister. "The Apostle Paul and the Introspective Conscience of the West," *HTR* 56 (1963) 199-215.

Stuhlmacher, Peter. *Gerechtigkeit Gottes bei Paulus.* FRLANT 87. Göttingen: Vandenhoeck & Ruprecht, 1965.

————. "The Apostle Paul's View of Righteousness," in *Reconciliation, Law, and Righteousness: Essays in Biblical Theology,* trans. E. R. Kalin. Philadelphia: Fortress, 1986, 68-93.

Swartley, Willard M. *Covenant of Peace: The Missing Piece in New Testament Theology and Ethics.* Grand Rapids: Eerdmans, 2006.

Taylor, Vincent. *Forgiveness and Reconciliation: A Study in New Testament Theology.* London: Macmillan, 1941.

Torrance, Thomas F. "One Aspect of the Biblical Conception of Faith," *ExpT* 68 (1956-1957) 111-14 and 221-22.

Vallotton, Pierre. *Le Christ et la Foi: Étude de théologie biblique.* Geneva: Labor et Fides, 1960.

Waters, Guy Prentiss. *Justification and the New Perspective on Paul: A Review and Response.* Phillipsburg, NJ: Presbyterian and Reformed Publishing Co., 2004.

Weiss, Johannes. *Paul and Jesus,* trans. H. J. Chaytor. New York: Harper & Brothers, 1909.

————. *The History of Primitive Christianity,* 2 vols., trans. by "four friends," ed. F. C. Grant. London: Macmillan, 1937.

Williams, Bernard. *Shame and Necessity.* Berkeley: University of California Press, 1993.

Williams, Sam K. "The 'Righteousness of God' in Romans," *JBL* 99 (1980) 241-90.

————. "Again Πίστις Χριστοῦ," *CBQ* 49 (1987) 431-47.

Wright, N. T. *Justification: God's Plan and Paul's Vision.* Downers Grove: InterVarsity, 2009.

Ziesler, John A. *The Meaning of Righteousness in Paul: A Linguistic and Theological Enquiry.* SNTS.MS 20. Cambridge: Cambridge University Press, 1972.

PART FIVE

Focus, Structure, and Argument of Romans

CHAPTER X

Focus or Central Thrust of the Letter

In his highly significant *magnum opus* on "the Holy Spirit in the letters of Paul,"[1] Gordon Fee, in dealing with Rom 1:11, correctly observes (1) that a letter in antiquity (as also today) was meant to serve as "a second-best substitute for a personal visit," (2) that the opening thanksgiving sections of Paul's letters reveal the apostle's central concerns and purposes in writing, and (3) that in the thanksgiving section of Romans, which begins at 1:8, Paul states his reasons for writing believers at Rome and wanting to be with them — somewhat generally in verse 13b ("in order that I might have fruit also among you") and verse 15 ("so that I might preach the gospel also to you who are in Rome"), but expressly in verse 11: "In order that I might share with you *some spiritual gift* (τι χάρισμα πνευματικόν) so that you might be strengthened." In fact, as Fee rightly asserts, it is the expression "spiritual gift" (χάρισμα πνευματικόν) that Paul uses to characterize what he writes in the letter.

But the question arises: How, then, should Romans be understood in the light of that expression? More specifically, was Paul referring by that expression to his whole letter generally, or did he have in mind a particular focus or central thrust? Fee points out that the combination of the noun χάρισμα ("gift") and the adjective πνευματικόν ("spiritual") is a "unique collocation" of terms in Paul's letters, which requires both linguistic and contextual explication.[2] Investigating the expression linguistically, he concludes

---

1. G. D. Fee, *God's Empowering Presence: The Holy Spirit in the Letters of Paul* (Peabody: Hendrickson, 1994).

2. G. D. Fee, *God's Empowering Presence*, 486-89.

that Paul is not here talking about some "gifting" by the Spirit, as in 1 Cor 12:8-10 and Rom 12:6-8, but about the present letter as a "Spirit gift" sent to believers at Rome in lieu of a personal visit in order to strengthen them (Rom 1:11) — and so, as more generally stated, to bring about "some fruit" (τινὰ καρπόν) among them as among other Gentiles (v. 13) and to fulfill his obligation to proclaim the gospel to them at Rome as he did among other Gentiles throughout the eastern part of the Roman empire (vv. 14-15). With approval Fee cites James Denney: "No doubt, in substance, Paul imparts his spiritual gift through this epistle."[3]

Then, referring to the immediate and extended contexts of the expression, Fee goes on to suggest:

> In its present context, and especially in light of the letter as a whole, the "Spirit gift" that he most likely wishes to share with them is his understanding of the gospel that in Christ Jesus God has created from among Jews and Gentiles one people for himself, apart from Torah. This is the way they are to be "strengthened" by Paul's coming, and this surely is the "fruit" he wants to have among them when he comes (v. 13). If so, then in effect our present letter functions as his "Spirit gifting" for them. This is what he would impart if he were there in person: this is what he now "shares" since he cannot presently come to Rome.[4]

I am in complete agreement with Fee's general introductory observations and his linguistic analysis of the expression "spiritual gift" in 1:11, and so will not reconsider here the points he has already made. In particular, I am sure Fee is right in understanding χάρισμα πνευματικόν as having reference to the letter itself, either in its entirety or with particular reference to its central thrust. Likewise, I agree that what Paul "most likely wishes to share with them [his addressees] is his understanding of the gospel." I would, however, argue that the focus or central thrust of Romans is not to be found in 1:16–4:25, which can be epitomized by the statement "in Christ Jesus God has created from among Jews and Gentiles one people for himself, apart from Torah," as Fee suggests in the quotation cited above and as has been traditionally understood. Rather, I propose that the focus of the letter — which Paul refers to as "my gospel" in 16:25 of the doxology (see also 2:16) — is to be found in 5–8, which highlights the themes of "peace" and "reconcilia-

---

3. G. D. Fee, *God's Empowering Presence*, 488, n. 48, quoting James Denney, *St. Paul's Epistle to the Romans*, EGT, 2.588.

4. G. D. Fee, *God's Empowering Presence*, 488-89.

tion" with God, the antithesis of "death" and "life," and the relationships of being "in Christ" and "in the Spirit."

In support of such a thesis it is necessary to scan Romans contextually. In particular, it is necessary to deal critically with certain features regarding the structures and arguments of the letter. For any complete treatment, of course, since these features appear throughout the whole of the letter, the entire letter ought to be taken into account. Here, however, because of space and time limitations, only the structures and arguments of the first eight chapters will be considered and only preliminary comments made regarding these matters. More detailed explication of these chapters, as well as further analyses of the last eight chapters of the letter, will be reserved for a forthcoming commentary.

1. The Materials of Rom 1:18–3:20

A number of perplexing issues arise in any critical reading of Romans. Many of these reflect what has been called the "dual character" of the letter. And most of them come to the fore when comparing the materials set out in 1:18–4:25 with the materials of 5–8. It seems best, therefore, especially in a preliminary survey and with limited space available, to deal only with the development of Paul's arguments in the first half of his letter. We will begin by highlighting first those materials that appear in 1:18–3:20, with special attention to chapter 2.

Some Important Issues

The interpretation of 1:18–3:20 has been notoriously difficult for almost every commentator. Problems begin to take form when one attempts to identify exactly who is being talked about or addressed in the passage. Is it Gentiles in 1:18-32, Jews in 2:1-5, Gentiles in 2:6-16, then Jews again in 2:17–3:19, with a conclusion in 3:20? Or is it Gentiles in 1:18-32 and Jews in 2:1–3:19, with a conclusion pertaining to both in 3:20? Or is it humanity generally in 1:18–2:16 and Jews (or a particular type of Jew) in 2:17–3:19, with a conclusion in 3:20? Earlier interpreters such as Origen, Jerome, Augustine, and Erasmus wrestled with this issue, and it continues to plague commentators today.

Likewise, problems arise when one tries to evaluate the presentations within 1:18–3:20. In the first part of that section, in 1:18-32, there appears a denunciation of the idolatry and immorality of the Gentile world that parallels quite closely the denunciation of Gentile idolatry and immorality in *Wisd of Sol* 13–14, with scholars generally agreed that Paul must have drawn on this work for his portrayal in 1:18-32 (perhaps also in 2:1-15) or that he and the writer of *Wisdom* drew from similar traditions. Further, the second part of the section, 2:1–3:8, abounds with characteristic features and stylistic traits that correspond to what was practiced in the Greek diatribal dialogues. And 3:10-18, which is the longest catena of biblical passages in the Pauline corpus, has been seen by many to be a collection of passages that was originally brought together within Judaism and/or Jewish Christianity and then used by Paul in support of his thesis (and theirs?) that "Jews and Gentiles alike are all under sin" (3:9; cf. 3:19, 23).

More importantly, however, problems of interpretation multiply when one asks: How does what Paul says about Gentiles and Jews in chapter 2 correspond to what he says about humanity generally and Jews in particular in the rest of his letter? For while his conclusions regarding God's impartiality (2:11), Jews and Gentiles being alike under sin (3:9-19, 23), and no one being able to be declared righteous by observing the law (3:20) are clear, there are four texts in Romans 2 that seem to espouse a theology of salvation by works or by obedience to the Mosaic law. And only once in this chapter, in verse 16, does explicit Christian language come to the fore.

The first problem of interpretation appears in 2:7, 10, where it is said that God will give "eternal life" — or, "glory, honor and peace" — to those who persist in doing good works, which seems to conflict with what is said about being justified solely by faith in 3:21-30; ch. 4; and throughout 9–11. The second problem text is 2:13, where it is said that "those who obey the law [are the ones] who will be declared righteous," which seems to be in conflict with (1) Paul's statement that no one is declared righteous by observing the law in 3:20, (2) his references to humans being unable to obey the law in 7:14-25, and (3) his denunciation of Israel for attempting to gain righteousness by means of the Mosaic law in 9:30–11:12. The third is 2:14-15, where there is the parenthetical statement that some Gentiles do by nature "the things of the law" and "show the work of the law written in their hearts," with the inference being that in so doing they are justified before God. But assuming that Paul is using "law" throughout this passage in much the same way, such an inference seems to contradict his earlier picture of the Gentiles in 1:18-32 and his conclusion about the impossibility of righteousness before God being obtained by observing the law in 3:20. And the fourth problem text is 2:25-27, which appears to be built on the assumption that righteousness is associated with the practice of the Mosaic law. But, again, this seems to fly in the face of (1) Paul's express conclusion to this section in 3:19-20, (2) his thesis statement regarding the "righteousness of God" being "apart from the law" in 3:21-23, (3) his use of Abraham as the exemplar of faith in chapter 4, and (4) his entire depiction of the relation of the gospel to the hope of Israel in 9–11 — as well as, of course, his arguments in Gal 2:15-16; 3:6-14; and exhortations in Gal 4:12–5:12, as repeated here and there in his other letters.

Some Preliminary Observations

What has been made of these seemingly non-Pauline statements in Romans 2? One popular way of reconciling them with Paul's thought elsewhere in Romans and in his other letters is to propose that the apostle is here speaking of *Christian* Gentiles, not pagan Gentiles — that is, of Gentiles who obey the Jewish law through faith in Christ and life in the Spirit.[5] Another way is to posit that Romans 2 is speaking primarily about *pre-Christian* Gentiles who had faith in God or about godly Jews *before* the coming of the gospel — or perhaps, in some blended manner, about pre-Christian Gentiles who possessed a God-given faith, faithful Jews who before the coming of Christ expressed their trust in God through the forms of the Mosaic law, *and* Christian believers.[6]

Still other ways of viewing these statements have been proposed, mostly by means of some combination of the above two approaches.[7] Ernst

---

5. Cf., e.g., K. Barth, *Shorter Commentary on Romans*, 36-39; M. Black, *Romans*, 55-56; and C. E. B. Cranfield, *Romans*, 1.152-62, 173-76; see also R. Bultmann, *Theology of the New Testament*, trans. K. Grobel (New York: Scribner's, 1951), 261; A. König, "Gentiles or Gentile Christians? On the Meaning of Romans 2:12-16" (1976), 53-60; A. Ito, "Romans 2: A Deuteronomist Reading" (1995), 33-34.

6. Cf., e.g., A. Schlatter, *Gottes Gerechtigkeit. Ein Kommentar zum Römerbrief*, 74-112; and C. K. Barrett, *Romans*, BNTC/HNTC (London: Black; New York: Harper & Row, 1957), 42-51; see also J.-M. Cambier, "Le jugement de tous les hommes par Dieu seul, selon la vérité, dans Rom 2:1–3:20," *ZNW* 67 (1976) 187-213, esp. 210; K. R. Snodgrass, "Justification by Grace — To the Doers: An Analysis of the Place of Romans 2 in the Theology of Paul," *NTS* 32 (1986) 72-93; and G. N. Davies, *Faith and Obedience in Romans* (Sheffield: JSOT, 1990), 53-71, esp. 55-56 (both OT and NT believers). Snodgrass epitomizes this position in saying: "Those people who have seen Romans 2 as a description of circumstances prior to the coming of the gospel are correct" ("Justification by Grace — To the Doers," 81).

7. C. E. B. Cranfield cites and evaluates eight such ways (*Romans*, 1.151-53).

Käsemann, for example, interprets Romans 2 in terms of "three distinct moments in the chapter":[8] pagan Gentiles in 2:12-16; a "purely fictional" Gentile soteriology in 2:24-27; and the "true Jew" as a Gentile Christian in 2:28-29.[9] Joseph Fitzmyer argues that in 2:7, 10 Paul is referring to Christians "whose conduct (good deeds) is to be understood as the fruit of their faith,"[10] but that in 2:14-15 and 2:26 he is referring to pagan Gentiles and not Christian Gentiles.[11] And James Dunn believes that in 2:7, 10 and 2:26-29 Paul is thinking of Christian Gentiles, whereas in 2:14-15 he is referring to pagan Gentiles.[12]

Quite another approach has been to understand Romans 2 as referring to the *hypothetical* possibility of being justified by good works or obedience to the law, but then to deny that possibility in order to highlight the reality of righteousness before God as being only by faith — that is, arguing that *if people could* obey the law they would be justified, *but no one can.* This is basically an Augustinian approach, which was reiterated by Martin Luther in his insistence that "All the Scriptures of God are divided into two parts: commands and promises" — the former being "God's strange work" to bring us down; the latter "God's proper work" to raise us up.[13] Such a view was established in modern critical scholarship by Hans Lietzmann, who argued that Paul is here viewing matters "from a pre-gospel standpoint" and setting out what would have been the case "if (1) there were no gospel, and (2) it were possible to fulfill the Law."[14] Essentially the same position has been espoused by many scholars both before and after Lietzmann.[15] I also adopted this ap-

8. To use E. P. Sanders's expression in characterizing Käsemann's understanding, which Sanders calls an example of "tortured exegesis" (*Paul, the Law, and the Jewish People,* 127).

9. E. Käsemann, *Romans,* 59, 65, 73.

10. J. A. Fitzmyer, *Romans,* 297, cf. 302.

11. J. A. Fitzmyer, *Romans,* 310, 322.

12. J. D. G. Dunn, *Romans,* 1.86, 98, 100, 106-7, 122-25. Cf. also T. R. Schreiner, "Did Paul Believe in Justification by Works? Another Look at Romans 2" (1993), 131-55. Somewhat similarly, H. Schlier held that pagan Gentiles are designated in 2:14-15, while in 2:27 Paul passes unconsciously into describing Christian Gentiles, *Der Römerbrief,* 77-79, 88.

13. M. Luther, "A Treatise on Christian Liberty," in *Works of Martin Luther,* vol. 2, trans. W. A. Lambert (Philadelphia: Holman, 1916), 317.

14. H. Lietzmann, *An die Römer,* 39-40 (my translation). Cf. also 44.

15. Cf., e.g., J. Knox, *Romans,* 409, 418-19; O. Kuss, *Der Römerbrief,* 1.64-68, 70-71, 90-92; U. Wilckens, *An die Römer,* 1.132-33, 145; F. F. Bruce, *Romans* (1985²), 90; R. A. Harrisville, *Romans,* 43-50; and D. J. Moo, *Romans,* 155-57, 171-72; see also M. Kähler, "Auslegung von Kap. 2,14-16 in Römerbrief" (1974), 274, 277; A. Friedrichsen, "Der wahre Jude und sein Lob: Röm. 2.28f." (1922), 43-44; G. Bornkamm, "Gesetz und Natur (Röm. 2,14-15)" (1959), 110.

proach in 1964, arguing in my *Paul, Apostle of Liberty*: "The contrast we see between Romans 2:6ff. and 3:21ff. is the same as that between Law and Gospel. In Romans 2:6ff. the Apostle cites the Law, which promises life and would bring life *if* the factors of human sin and inability were not present."[16]

On the other hand, there are a number of scholars today who assert that some or all of the above-listed problem passages of Romans 2 are flatly contradictory to Paul's thought elsewhere in Romans, though they offer diverse explanations for the texts in question. John O'Neill, as might be expected from his treatment of Galatians, sees all of Rom 1:18–2:29 as contradictory to Paul's teaching and irrelevant to his purpose, and so declares this section to be an interpolation by a later glossator who drew on material from a hellenistic Jewish missionary tractate.[17] Heikki Räisänen, rejecting an interpolation theory, argues that 2:14-15 and 26-27 are flatly contradictory to Paul's main thesis in 1:18–3:20 that all are under sin, and so evidence quite clearly that "Paul's mind is divided" with respect to humanity's ability to keep the Mosaic law.[18] And Ed Sanders believes that in 1:18–2:29 "Paul takes over to an unusual degree homiletical material from Diaspora Judaism, that he alters it in only insubstantial ways, and that consequently the treatment of the law in chapter 2 cannot be harmonized with any of the diverse things which Paul says about the law elsewhere."[19]

Douglas Campbell has proposed a more rhetorically based argument that, while decidedly different from the theses of John O'Neill, Heikki Räisänen, and Ed Sanders, comes to similar conclusions about the non-Pauline nature of the materials of 1:18–3:20. For based on a plausible view that in exercising his rhetorical skills "Paul at times displays great argumentative sophistication" and "seems to be something of a master at taking the terminology and/or basic position of some rival and turning it inside-out and using it to his own advantage"[20] — which is a thesis that I have also often proposed (though with applications that differ from those that Campbell develops) — Douglas Campbell has argued that in 1:18–3:20 Paul uses "an *ad hominem* strategy" that he employs in ironic fashion "as a critique of 'another Gospel.'"[21] That *ad hominem* strategy, as Campbell understands it,

16. R. N. Longenecker, *Paul, Apostle of Liberty*, 121-22.
17. J. C. O'Neill, *Romans*, 41-42, 49, 53-54, 264-65.
18. H. Räisänen, *Paul and the Law*, 100-107. For a critique of Räisänen, see C. E. B. Cranfield, "Giving a Dog a Bad Name," 77-85.
19. E. P. Sanders, *Paul, the Law, and the Jewish People*, 123.
20. D. C. Campbell, *The Quest for Paul's Gospel*, 259.
21. D. C. Campbell, *The Quest for Paul's Gospel*, 246.

"begins by mimicking its opponent" — that is, "by recapitulating the proba-ble *elenchic* [i.e., syllogistic refutations] or condemnatory opening of the po-sition that it intends ultimately to undermine" — and then "flushes out" the presuppositions of its opponents by means of "a series of devastating reduc-tions" to demonstrate their impossible conclusions, with "the result of these moves" being "the discrediting of the entire programme, in its own terms."[22] Thus as Campbell understands Paul's purpose in the rhetorical movements of his argument in 1:18–3:20: "The end result of this process of exposure and extrapolation is consequently a thorough discrediting of the entire position. It is a useless and contradictory 'gospel', on several counts."[23]

By way of introducing his understanding of Paul's rhetorical strategy in 1:18–3:20, Campbell characterizes his position as follows: "My alternative reading shifts Paul's own commitments within the argument as it unfolds. Essentially, it places him on the other side of the argumentative tensions as they are developed from 1.18 through to 3.20, so the initial voice of the text is not, in my view, Paul's."[24] And in concluding his treatment of Paul's rhetori-cal strategy, Campbell says with regard to all of the statements in 1:18–3:20 (with, of course, the exception of what Paul writes in 2:16, though even what is said there must be read in the context of irony): "They would belong to the gospel of Paul's opponents, the Teachers, hence the attribution of those pre-mises to Paul himself through much of Romans' interpretive history is an unintended irony that, as we have said, he would greatly resent."[25]

Most attempts to understand Romans 2 — other than those of O'Neill, Räisänen, Sanders, and Campbell (as cited above) — are based on the as-sumption, whether stated or implied, that everything in the chapter repre-sents Paul's teaching, however derived, and therefore try to reconcile what is stated in 2:12-16 with what Paul says elsewhere in Romans and in his other letters. For most of those who begin on such a conciliatory assumption, it has always seemed incredible that Paul would speak about justification with-out also having the idea of faith in mind. So scholars have usually found it necessary in commenting on what is said in 2:12-16 either (1) to clarify the nature of the referents beyond what the apostle himself has done or (2) to understand what is said as a hypothetical presentation, which functions rhe-torically to prepare for a later discussion.

22. D. C. Campbell, *The Quest for Paul's Gospel*, 246.
23. D. C. Campbell, *The Quest for Paul's Gospel*, 246.
24. D. C. Campbell, *The Quest for Paul's Gospel*, 233.
25. D. C. Campbell, *The Quest for Paul's Gospel*, 261.

How, then, should the seemingly non-Pauline statements of Roman 2 — and particularly those in verses 12-16, which constitute our present concern — be understood? That certainly is a question of critical concern to every commentator. To some extent that question will be dealt with in our discussion of some of the proposals that follow. Yet for pedagogical reasons, it seems best to reserve a more extended treatment of this matter for our discussion of 1:18–3:30 (and particularly of 2:12-16) in Chapter XI, "Structure and Argument" (as well as to hold our specific exegetical treatments of these matters for a future Romans commentary).

Some Proposals

How, then, can the issues that arise in 1:18–3:20 be understood? Personally, while I am prepared to relinquish the designation "hypothetical," I still believe that 1:18–3:20 was written in order to prepare for the discussion of 3:21–4:25 — with 1:16-17 being the thesis for the entire section, 3:21-23 the repetition and expansion of that thesis, and 9–11 the climatic resumption of the issues raised in 2:17–3:20 regarding a Jewish response (or lack of response) to the gospel. But 1:18–3:20 is not properly understood when seen only as containing declarations about God's impartiality (2:11),[26] Jews and Gentiles being alike under sin (3:9-19, 23), and no one being able to be declared righteous by observing the law (3:20). What also needs to be recognized is (1) that 2:1–3:8 is structured along the lines of two diatribal dialogues,[27] and (2) that 2:17–3:8 is entirely, both in the objections raised and the answers given, set out in terms of an intramural Jewish debate.[28]

The first of the diatribal dialogues is introduced at 2:1 by the sudden address to an imaginary interlocutor in the second person singular, "O man!" It follows on the heels of the depiction of humanity's idolatry and immorality presented in 1:18-32 — which, as noted above, has often been seen to parallel the depiction of the Gentile world given in *Wisd of Sol* 13–14. It begins in 2:1 with an indicting statement addressed to a censorious person; it

26. While J. M. Bassler's structural analysis of 1:18–3:20 can be questioned, she is certainly correct in arguing that "divine impartiality" is a central axiom of the passage (*Divine Impartiality*, esp. 121-23, 137).

27. Cf. S. K. Stowers, *The Diatribe and Paul's Letter to the Romans*, esp. 93-98, 110-13; *idem*, "Paul's Dialogue with a Fellow Jew," 707-22; *idem*, *Rereading of Romans*, 83-193.

28. In addition to S. K. Stowers cited above, see G. P. Carras, "Romans 2,1-29: A Dialogue," 183-207.

continues with a series of questions addressed to that imaginary interlocutor in 2:2-5; and it concludes in 2:6-11 with a quotation from Ps 62:12 (MT 62:13) and an explication of the significance of that passage — with such quotations from ancient sources being not uncommon in Greek diatribal dialogues. Its theme is God's impartiality in dealing with humanity. And its referent is humanity in general, both Gentiles and Jews. For while 1:18-32 seems to have Gentiles primarily in mind, the diatribe of 2:1-11 and the further comments of 2:12-16 broaden out to include both Gentiles and Jews.

A second diatribal dialogue is introduced at 2:17, not by a vocative but by the second person singular pronominal phrase, "You a Jew!" — which is a form of address that was also common in ancient diatribes. It, too, begins with a number of questions addressed to an imaginary interlocutor in 2:17-23, with an appended quotation from Isa 52:5 in 2:24. As it continues, it poses another set of questions in 3:1-8. And it ends with a conclusion in 3:9-19, which contains what was probably a traditional catena of biblical passages (vv. 10-18) stitched together by a sixfold repetition of the phrase "there is no one" (οὐκ ἔστιν) and an enumeration of various parts of the body ("throats," "tongues," "lips," "mouths," "feet," and "eyes") to make the point that all human beings in their totality are sinful. The referent throughout this whole latter section of 2:17–3:19 is certainly Jewish — probably, however, not Jews generally or Judaism *per se*, but rather some type of proud and inconsistent Jew who viewed himself as a moral teacher of Gentiles, but who caused the name of God to be dishonored among the Gentiles because he failed to live up to the standards of the Mosaic law.

More important to note with regard to 1:18-3:20, however, is the fact that in both its structures and its arguments the passage is exceedingly Jewish. In fact, as George Carras has observed (particularly with regard to chapter 2), the entire passage reflects an "inner Jewish debate" and "is best understood as a diatribe whereby two Jewish attitudes on the nature of Jewish religion are being debated."[29] The thesis statement of 1:16, "first for the Jew, then for the Gentile," alerts readers to expect that what follows will deal with relationships between Jews and Gentiles before God. And that is what is spelled out throughout all of 1:18–4:25 — first in 1:18–3:20 in depicting God's impartiality in judging all people, both Gentiles and Jews; then in 3:21–4:25 in proclaiming God's impartiality in bestowing his righteousness on all people, whether Jews or Gentiles.

So I propose that here in 1:18–3:20 we see Paul beginning his argument

29. G. P. Carras, "Romans 2,1-29: A Dialogue on Jewish Ideals," 185 and 206.

in Romans by agreeing with both Judaism generally and Jewish believers in Jesus in particular about (1) the impartiality of divine judgment (2:11), (2) Jews and Gentiles being alike under sin (3:9-19, 23), and (3) no one able to be declared righteous by observing the law (3:20). Further, I propose that in arguing these points Paul used what he considered to have been rather standard Jewish and Jewish Christian sources and arguments, believing that such materials were used in similar ways in those same circles. And if all this be true, then it cannot be said that the focus of Paul's teaching in Romans — and therefore what he specifically had in mind in speaking about imparting "some spiritual gift" to his addressees in 1:11 — is to be found in 1:18–3:20.[30] Rather, it seems that what he sets out in 1:18–3:20 is something that he believed he held in common with his addressees and that he used in preparation for what appears later in his letter.

2. The Materials of Rom 3:21–4:25

Coupled with 1:18–3:20 is 3:21–4:25, which presents a counterbalance to what has just been depicted. And though this second part of the first major section of the body middle of Romans is similar in tone and language to the first, a critical reading of this latter part highlights certain distinctive issues that need to be observed and evaluated as well.

Some Important Issues

The passage begins in 3:21-23 with what appears to be a thesis paragraph that repeats and expands on the opening thesis statement of 1:16-17. Immediately readers are faced with an issue of some significance for interpretation. For while the emphatic "but now" (νυνὶ δέ) marks a shift to a new level in Paul's argument, commentators vary as to whether the expression is to be understood as having a purely logical function (i.e., signaling a further aspect of the subject, without necessarily contrasting the two parts of the section) or as having a temporal force (i.e., contrasting the two parts). Likewise, interpreters have varied widely with respect to the meaning of "the righteousness of God," principally as to whether it signifies an attribute of God that determines his actions on behalf of humanity or a quality of existence that he be-

30. As, e.g., H. P. Liddon, *Romans*, 43; C. Gore, *Romans*, 1.106.

stows on those who respond to him — and, if the latter, whether it should be viewed in a forensic or an ethical manner. Further, interpreters vary widely in their treatment of the two sets of statements that are used ascriptively with regard to "the righteousness of God," which has been manifested in the gospel: (1) "apart from the law," yet "witnessed to by the Law and the Prophets" (v. 21); and (2) "through faith in [or 'by the faithfulness of'] Jesus Christ" and "to all who believe" (v. 22).

A shift in style certainly occurs in 3:21-26, set as it is between the question-and-answer styles of 3:1-8 and 3:27-31. And repeating, as it does, the declarative tone and content of 1:16-17, the passage not only ties together the two parts of the first section of Romans, but also seems to be kerygmatic in nature. For by its emphatic repetition of the phrase "the righteousness of God" in verses 22-23, its ascriptive statements regarding that righteousness in those same verses, its emphasis on divine impartiality in verse 23, and its weighty soteriological affirmations in verses 24-26, the passage highlights the central thrust of what Paul writes at least throughout 1:16–4:25.

The question, however, must be asked: Is 3:21-26 (in conjunction with 1:16-17) the structural center and argumentative focus of all of Romans, which provides "the key to the structure and thought of the letter"[31] — as has traditionally been argued, at least since the Protestant Reformation? Does it, in fact, embody the heart of the Christian gospel in miniature?[32] Or, stated more prosaically, the issue is this: Does 3:21-26 (in conjunction with 1:16-17) set out the controlling thesis of the whole of Romans? Or, alternatively, should 3:21-26, together with 1:16-17, be understood as the thesis of the first eight chapters of the letter — or perhaps, more narrowly, the thesis of only the first four chapters?

Also at issue in any discussion of 3:21–4:25 are questions regarding (1) the provenance of what appears to be early Christian confessional material in 3:24-26 (or, perhaps, 3:25-26a), (2) the nature of the argument about the oneness of God and God's impartial treatment of all people in 3:27-31, (3) the use of Abraham as the exemplar of faith in 4:1-24, and (4) the inclusion of an early Christian confessional portion at the end of this section in 4:25. For 3:24-31 has been seen, particularly of late, to incorporate many fundamentally Jewish ideas about "justification," "justice," "redemption," "re-

---

31. Quoting W. S. Campbell, "Romans 3 as the Key to the Structure and Thought of the Letter," *NovT* 23 (1981) esp. 24, 32-35.

32. So A. Hultgren, *Gospel and Mission: The Outlook from His Letter to the Romans* (Philadelphia: Trinity Press International, 1985), 47, who expresses the view of many.

pentance," and "atonement" — with 4:1-24 highlighting the major Jewish exemplar of relationship with God and 4:25 epitomizing the essence of the earliest Christian proclamation. Further, the two key terms of the thesis statements of 1:16-17 and 3:21-23, that is, δικαιοσύνη and πίστις, which appeared also throughout 1:18–3:20, come to dominant expression in 3:24–4:25 as well. And so this "word chain" appears to tie together these two parts of the first section of Romans.

Some Preliminary Observations

How has this important section of Romans been treated by commentators? The subject is too vast for any brief, comprehensive answer. Suffice it here to say that, since at least the Protestant Reformation, the materials of 3:21–4:25 have been seen by most interpreters to be at the heart of Paul's teaching in his letter to the Christians at Rome. Reading Romans as a compendium of Christian theology, ignoring Paul's own religious background and possible literary sources, and caricaturing the Judaism of the apostle's day as a religion of "works-righteousness," Christians have felt fairly secure in understanding 3:21–4:25 as the focus of what Paul writes in this letter. So the central thrust of Romans has been seen as (1) a polemic against any form of acceptance before God by human endeavor, and (2) a proclamation of righteousness through faith alone — with these two emphases taken to be the central features of the Christian religion vis-à-vis Judaism and all other religions.

But quite a revolution has taken place among Christian scholars during the past few decades in understanding the Judaism of Paul's day and that of the early (tannaitic) rabbis whose teachings are codified in the Talmud.[33] No longer can the mainline Judaism of Paul's day be simply written off as a legalistic religion of human works-righteousness. And interpreters of Paul have today been alerted to the fact that there is much in the apostle's writings that he took over from Judaism. Though all of his earlier thought and piety

---

33. Rightly credited, in large part, to E. P. Sanders, *Paul and Palestinian Judaism: A Comparison of Patterns of Religion* (Philadelphia: Fortress, 1977). But just for the record, I quote T. L. Donaldson's comment in his *Paul and the Gentiles: Remapping the Apostle's Convictional World* (Minneapolis: Fortress, 1997), 311: "Aspects of Sanders's analysis, including the use of 'nomism' itself, were anticipated in significant ways by Richard N. Longenecker, *Paul, Apostle of Liberty* (New York: Harper & Row, 1964)." See esp. chapter 3, "The Piety of Hebraic Judaism," in R. N. Longenecker, *Paul, Apostle of Liberty*, 65-85.

were "rebaptized" into Christ, the basic structures of Paul's Jewish thought and the basic ethos of his Jewish piety continued to play a large part in his life as a Christian.

Scholars, of late, have demonstrated that much of what Paul says in 3:21–4:25 about "the righteousness of God," "justification," "redemption," "expiation-propitiation," "divine impartiality," and "faith" rests solidly on Jewish foundations, and have argued that much of what he affirms with respect to these matters was voiced by Jewish and Jewish Christian teachers of the day as well.[34] Likewise, scholars have shown that a portion of early Christian confessional material has been used by Paul in 3:24-26 in support of his thesis paragraph in 3:21-23 — material that Rudolf Bultmann, Ernst Käsemann, and others have seen as contained in verses 24-26a, starting with the participle δικαιούμενοι ("being justified"), but that Eduard Lohse and others view as contained in verses 25-26, starting with the relative personal pronoun ὅν ("who").[35] Yet however we evaluate the specific details of the materials in 3:24-26 — or, for that matter, the presence and use of traditional structures and language elsewhere in Paul's letters — the suggestion seems irresistible that what Paul writes in 3:21–4:25 was part and parcel of the shared faith of his Christian addressees at Rome. And further, it may be claimed that what he writes them was based immediately on the confessions of the earliest Jewish believers in Jesus and ultimately on the fundamental structures and thought of Early Judaism.

A Proposal

What needs to be noted here from our contextual scanning above is that 3:21–4:25 is extensively Jewish and/or Jewish Christian in both its structures and its expressions, as we found also to be true for 1:18–3:20. On the basis of

34. Note particularly J. D. G. Dunn, "Paul and Justification by Faith," 85-101. Among Dunn's many other writings on the subject, see also his "New Perspective on Paul," 95-122; *idem, Romans*, 1.161-241; *idem, The Partings of the Ways between Christianity and Judaism* (London: SCM; Philadelphia: Trinity Press International, 1991), 117-39; *idem*, "How New Was Paul's Gospel? The Problem of Continuity and Discontinuity," in *Gospel in Paul: Studies on Corinthians, Galatians and Romans for Richard N. Longenecker*, ed. L. A. Jervis and P. Richardson (Sheffield: Sheffield Academic Press, 1994), 367-88.

35. For a history of the interpretation of 3:24-26 as a pre-Pauline tradition, see the published dissertation of H. Koch, *Römer 3,21-31 in der Paulusinterpretation der letzten 150 Jahre* (Göttingen: Andreas Funke, 1971), 107-34.

such observations, therefore, I propose that Paul begins his letter to the believers in Jesus at Rome in 1:16–4:25 in quite a traditional manner — not only praising them for their faith in Christ Jesus, but also using materials and arguments that they and he held in common. He believes, as he said in the first part of the *Propositio* of Gal 2:15-21, that all true believers in Jesus — particularly Jewish believers, but also, by extension, Gentile believers who have been influenced by Jewish thought in some way — know that a person is not justified "by the works of the law" (ἐξ ἔργων νόμου), but by what Christ has effected (διά/ἐκ πίστεως Ἰησοῦ Χριστοῦ, which I understand to be a subjective genitive and so to mean "by the faith/faithfulness of Jesus Christ") and because of one's faith in him (ἐπιστεύσαμεν εἰς Χριστὸν Ἰησοῦν, vv. 15-16). So he writes with confidence to the Christians at Rome, setting out in the two parts of 1:16–4:25 what he believes both they and he held in common, before then going on in 5–8 to speak of matters that pertain to the distinctive nature of his preaching (i.e., "my gospel") within the Gentile mission.

If our proposal be true, then, of course, it cannot be said that the focus of Paul's teaching in Romans — and therefore what he had in mind in speaking about imparting "some spiritual gift" to his addressees in 1:11 — is to be found in 3:21–4:25, as has been traditionally held. Rather, it may be argued that what he sets out in his thesis paragraph of 3:21-23, in the portion of early Christian confessional material that he quotes in 3:24-26, in the highlighting of God's oneness and impartiality in 3:27-31, in the illustration of Abraham as the exemplar of faith in 4:1-24, and in the traditional portion incorporated in 4:25 are matters that he believed he held in common with his addressees and that he used in preparation for what he would write later in his letter, particularly in 5–8.

3. The Materials of Rom 5–8

The relation of 5–8 to 1:16–4:25 has been a perennial problem for interpreters. One common way has been to understand 1:16–4:25 as being about sin in the first part and justification in the second, whereas 5–8 deals with sanctification. Another way is to view these two sections as setting forth somewhat parallel lines of thought: first by the use of judicial and forensic language in 1:16–4:25; then in language more personal, relational, participatory, and even mystical in 5–8. The issues are complex, but they call for some evaluation here.

Some Important Issues

When moving from 1:16–4:25 to 5–8, the reader is immediately confronted with the problem of how the two forms of "therefore" in 5:1 and 5:12 function to set up the materials of 5–8. For 5:1 begins with the statement, "Therefore being justified by faith," with the postpositive transitional conjunction οὖν ("therefore") connecting "being justified by faith" with what was argued in 1:16–4:25; while in 5:12 there appears the prepositional phrase διὰ τοῦτο ("therefore"), which seems not to be a transition forward from 5:1-11 but to signal some type of logical break and (perhaps) to reach back to 1:16–4:25. Likewise, one must determine whether 5:1a should be read as "let us have (ἔχωμεν, a hortatory subjunctive) peace with God," which is the better-supported reading in the manuscript tradition, or "we have (ἔχομεν, an indicative) peace with God," which most scholars prefer for internal reasons. In effect, what one concludes regarding these seemingly minor linguistic points has a profound effect on how one relates 5:1-11 (also, perhaps, 5:12-21) to the flow of the argument from chapters 1–4 to chapters 5–8 — that is, whether it is the conclusion to what precedes in 1:16–4:25, whether it serves as transitional material between 1:16–4:25 and 5:12–8:39, or whether it functions as an introduction to what follows in 5:12–8:39.

There are, of course, a number of similarities between these first and second major sections of the body middle of Romans, however the sections are precisely delineated — with the similarities often continuing on throughout the rest of the letter as well. For example, the theme of righteousness, which was prominent in 1:16–4:25, appears also in 5–8 (i.e., in 5:17, 21; 6:13, 16, 18, 19, 20; 8:10) and throughout 9:30–10:21. Likewise, issues concerning the Mosaic law, which were raised in 3:20, 21, 31 and 4:13-15, receive further treatment in 5:13-14, 20; 7:1-6, 7-25; and 8:1-4 — with the conclusions reached in these passages underlying the whole presentation of 9–11. And convictions about Jesus Christ that were implicit in the thesis statement of 1:16-17, interjected almost parenthetically into the discussion at 2:16, and further expressed in the thesis paragraph of 3:21-26 are elaborated in 5–8 — with these convictions then presupposed throughout 9–11 and the exhortations of 12:1–15:13.

On the other hand, there are a number of striking differences between these two sections. Most obvious is their difference in the use of Scripture.[36]

---

36. Cf. R. N. Longenecker, "Prolegomena to Paul's Use of Scripture in Romans," esp. 146-47, 158-67; see also *idem*, "Paul and the Old Testament," in *Biblical Exegesis in the Apostolic Period*, 2nd ed. (1999), 88-116.

For while there are about eighteen quotations of Scripture in eight or nine places in 1:16–4:25 — with about thirty quotations in twenty-five or twenty-six places in 9–11, an additional ten in the exhortations of 12:1–15:13, and one more in the so-called "Apostolic Parousia" of 15:14-32 — only two biblical quotations appear in 5–8, and then somewhat tangentially: once in 7:7, citing in illustrative fashion the tenth commandment, "Do not covet," of Exod 20:17 and Deut 5:21; and once in 8:36, in what appears to be an early Christian confessional portion that makes use of Ps 44:22. Likewise, the word chain shifts from δικαιοσύνη and πίστις/πιστεύω in 1:16–4:25 to the dominance of ζωή/ζάω vis-à-vis ἁμαρτία and θάνατος in 5–8 (though also, of course, with the appearance of δικαιοσύνη in eight verses of this section, as noted above).

Further, the form of address varies in these two sections. For whereas imaginary interlocutors are addressed in 2:1 ("O man!") and 2:17 ("You a Jew!"), with a rhetorical "we" appearing in 4:1 ("What then shall we say?"), Paul — for the first time since the salutation of 1:1-7 and the thanksgiving of 1:8-12 — speaks directly to his addressees in 5–8. He sets up his direct address in this latter section by the pronoun "us" in 4:24, which concludes his illustration of Abraham in chapter 4, and the pronoun "our" in the incorporated traditional portion of 4:25, which closes off the first section. In 5–8, however, he speaks directly and consistently to his readers by the use of the pronouns and verbal suffixes "we," "you," "yourselves," and "us" — addressing them also as "brothers and sisters" (ἀδελφοί) in 7:1, 4. He uses, as well, a type of rhetorical προσωποποιία or "speech-in-character" in 7:7-25 as he expresses in the first person singular "I" the tragic soliloquy of humanity in its attempts to live by its own insights and strength. In addition, the style in these two sections shifts from being argumentative, particularly in the diatribes of 2:2-11 and 2:17–3:8 and the rhetorically structured presentation of God's oneness and impartiality in 3:27-31, to being more "confessional," cast as it is in 5–8 in the first person plural.

Also significant are the differences in content between these two sections of Romans. Two matters, in particular, call for mention here. The first has to do with the differing diagnoses of the "human predicament." For in depicting humanity's situation apart from God, the narrative of 1:18-32 unfolds in terms of humanity's *decline* into idolatry and immorality *during the course of history* — without any reference to Adam's sin; whereas in 5:12-21 (probably also in 7:7-13) the focus is on the disobedience of the "one man" and how his transgression has affected all human beings. The diagnosis of 1:18-32, of course, may be built on *Wisd of Sol* 13–14 and/or similar Jewish traditions (as postulated above), and so conditioned by the materials used.

Nonetheless, while the story of Adam's sin in Genesis 2–3 was certainly retained within the Jewish Scriptures, it seems not to have been widely used as an explanation for humanity's predicament during the time of Early Judaism (except in *4 Ezra* 3:7-8, 21-22; 7:116-26 and *2 Bar* 23:4; 48:42-43; 54:15; 56:5-6). Certainly it was not used by the tannaitic rabbis whose teachings were codified in the Talmud.

Likewise, 7:7-25 poses numerous problems with respect to both its content and its possible parallels. Commentators have traditionally been concerned with the identity of the speaker and the type of experience described. Questions, however, have also been raised regarding the rhetoric of the passage, with parallels pointed out between 7:14-24 and the tragic soliloquies of the Greek world.[37] In particular, Paul's use of the first person singular and his laments throughout verses 14-24 have been compared to Euripides' Medea, who, driven by rage and thoughts of revenge, determined to murder her own children, and who, in reflecting on such a heinous act, cries out: "I am being overcome by evils. I know that what I am about to do is evil, but passion is stronger than my reasoned reflection; and this is the cause of the worst evils for humans."[38] This "famous Medean saying," as Stanley Stowers has pointed out, was widely known in Paul's day, occurring "not only in drama and philosophers' debates, but also in such contexts as letters and public orations."[39]

Some Preliminary Observations

What can be said with respect to such issues? Though many have taken Paul's discussion in 1:16–4:25 to continue on through 5:11,[40] or on through 5:21,[41] most scholars today view 5–8 as a distinguishable unit of material.[42] That is not only because the example of Abraham as a "proof from Scripture" is a fit-

---

37. Cf. H. Hommel, "Das 7 Kapitel des Römerbriefs im Licht antiker Überlieferung," *Theologia viatorum* 8 (1961) 90-116; G. Theissen, *Psychological Aspects of Pauline Theology* (Philadelphia: Fortress, 1987), 211-19; S. K. Stowers, *Rereading of Romans*, 260-64.

38. Euripides, *Medea*, 1077-80. Among the many parallel Greek texts that could be cited, note also Ovid, *Metamorphoses* vii.19-20: "Desire persuades me one way, reason another. I see the better and approve it, but I follow the worse."

39. S. K. Stowers, *Rereading of Romans*, 263.

40. E.g., M. Luther (with 5:12-21 considered an excursus), P. Melanchthon, T. Zahn, F. Leenhardt, M. Black, and J. A. T. Robinson.

41. E.g., J. Calvin, U. Wilckens, O. Kuss, F. F. Bruce, and J. D. G. Dunn.

42. E.g., H. Schlier, A. Nygren, O. Michel, C. H. Dodd, N. Dahl, C. E. B. Cranfield, E. Käsemann, J. A. Fitzmyer, and D. J. Moo.

ting conclusion to what precedes, but also because 5:1-11 appears to function as thesis material for what follows — with most of the themes and some of the terms of 5:1-11 reappearing in 8:18-39, thereby setting up an *inclusio* or type of "ring composition." Further, as noted above, (1) 5:1 seems to be something of a literary hinge, first summarizing the argument of 1:16–4:25 — particularly that of 3:21–4:25 ("since, therefore, we have been justified through faith") — and then preparing for what follows in 5:2–8:39 ("we have peace [or, 'let us have peace'] with God through our Lord Jesus Christ"); (2) the word chain shifts from δικαιοσύνη and πίστις/πιστεύω in 1:16–4:25 to the dominance of ζωή/ζάω vis-à-vis ἁμαρτία and θάνατος in 5–8; (3) the tone shifts from being argumentative in 1:16–4:25 to more confessional in 5–8; and (4) there appears throughout the section the repeated refrain διὰ/ἐν τοῦ κυρίου ἡμῶν Ἰησοῦ Χριστοῦ, not only as an *inclusio* at 5:1 and 8:39 but also at the end of each separate unit at 5:11; 5:21; 6:23; and 7:25.

Interpreters have usually not been too concerned about the differences identified above between these two sections of material in 1:16–4:25 and 5–8 — that is, about differences in their use of Scripture, their respective word chains, their forms of address, or their tones or styles. Usually these matters are viewed as being only circumstantial in nature, without any inferences drawn as to their significance. On the other hand, where such differences are recognized, they have often been seen as evidencing either later interpolations by some undiscerning Paulinist or outright contradictions in Paul's own thought. One scholar has even proposed that Romans 1–11 should be viewed as two distinctly different Pauline sermons: one to a Jewish audience, which is now found in chapters 1–4 and 9–11, but whose parts have somehow become separated; the other to a Gentile audience, which is preserved in chapters 5–8.[43]

Likewise, though analyses of humanity's condition are set out differently in 1:18-32 and 5:12-21, most interpreters have been content to read 1:18-32 as "the obviously deliberate echo of the Adam narratives,"[44] and so have denied or minimized any difference between them. And though scholars have frequently noted parallels between 7:14-24 and the tragic soliloquies of the Greek world, most have dismissed them as being somewhat trivial in comparison to the seemingly more significant parallels between 7:7-13 (also,

43. So R. Scroggs, "Paul as Rhetorician," 271-98.

44. J. D. G. Dunn, *Romans*, 1.53; cf. M. D. Hooker, "Adam in Romans 1," *NTS* 6 (1960) 297-306; *idem*, "A Further Note on Romans 1," *NTS* 13 (1966) 181-83; A. J. M. Wedderburn, "Adam in Paul's Letter to the Romans," in *Studia Biblica* 3, ed. E. A. Livingstone (Sheffield: JSOT, 1980), 413-30; and many others.

of course, 3:21–4:25) and the Jewish world.[45] But it may be doubted whether the differences between 1:16–4:25 and 5–8 or the parallels between 7:14-24 and the tragic soliloquies of the Greeks can be treated so summarily.

A Proposal

I have not dealt here directly with matters pertaining to the identity and circumstances of Paul's Roman addressees. That is not because I consider such questions unimportant. On the contrary, I consider them highly significant. But I have discussed Paul's Roman addressees and Roman Christianity early in Chapter IV ("Addressees") and in a recent article,[46] and I have space here only to refer to what I have argued earlier and to repeat those conclusions.

My argument, in agreement with Raymond Brown,[47] is that the important question to ask regarding the Christians at Rome is not the ethnic question, "Were they Jews or Gentiles, or, if ethnically mixed, dominantly one or the other?" — with the implications being that if Jewish believers, then they should be viewed as non-Pauline in outlook, but if Gentile believers, then adherents to Paul's teaching. Probably the addressees constituted both Jewish and Gentile believers in Jesus. And most likely the Gentile believers were in the majority, for Paul considered the Roman church to be within the orbit of his Gentile ministry.

Rather than trying to determine the addressees' character on the basis of their ethnicity, "the crucial issue," as Brown has pointed out, "is the theological outlook of this mixed Jewish/Gentile Christianity."[48] In analyzing the factors to be considered for any judgment regarding the theological outlook of the Roman Christians, Brown concludes (1) that for both Jews and Christians "the Jerusalem-Rome axis was strong," (2) "that Roman Christianity came from Jerusalem, and indeed represented the Jewish/Gentile Christianity associated with such Jerusalem figures as Peter and James," and (3) that

---

45. Cf. E. Käsemann, *Romans,* 198-211, and many others.

46. See my "Prolegomena to Paul's Use of Scripture in Romans," 148-52.

47. Cf. R. E. Brown, "The Beginnings of Christianity at Rome" and "The Roman Church near the End of the First Christian Generation (A.D. 58 — Paul to the Romans)," in *Antioch and Rome: New Testament Cradles of Catholic Christianity,* ed. R. E. Brown and J. P. Meier (New York: Paulist, 1983), 92-127; *idem,* "Further Reflections on the Origins of the Church of Rome," in *The Conversation Continues: Studies in Paul and John in Honor of J. L. Martyn,* ed. R. T. Fortna and B. R. Gaventa (Nashville: Abingdon, 1990), 98-115.

48. R. E. Brown, "Beginnings of Christianity at Rome," 109, n. 227.

both in the earliest days of the Roman church and at the time when Paul wrote them, believers at Rome could be characterized as "Christians who kept up some Jewish observances and remained faithful to part of the heritage of the Jewish Law and cult, without insisting on circumcision."[49] And it is this understanding that I bring to the discussion here, believing it to be the position best supported by all the available data — and believing that it casts Paul's argument in Romans in an entirely new light.

My proposal, then, is that the materials of 5–8 should be viewed as expressing the focus of what Paul writes in Romans, and particularly the section that contains the "spiritual gift" that he says he wants to give the Christians at Rome in 1:11 and that he speaks about as being "my gospel" in 2:16 and 16:25. This is not to discredit what he writes in 1:16–4:25, for that is what he held in common with his addressees. Indeed, it was probably on the basis of their acceptance of the message of 1:16–4:25 that both they and he originally became believers in Jesus.

It may be surmised that Paul often proclaimed the materials contained in 1:16–4:25 when addressing Jews or when addressing those who had been influenced by Jewish thought for the better (as had the believers in Jesus at Rome, whatever their ethnic backgrounds) — or when addressing those who had been influenced by Jewish thought for the worse (as had Paul's own Gentile converts to Christ in Galatia). But what he also wanted the Christians at Rome to know was the gospel that he had been preaching to pagan Gentile audiences. For believers at Rome, too, were predominantly Gentiles, and he wanted to include them within the orbit of his Gentile proclamation and so to strengthen them. Further, he wanted them to become partners in his Gentile mission as the sending church to the western regions of the Roman empire, just as the church at Antioch of Syria had functioned as the sending church to the eastern regions of the Roman world.

So Paul addresses the recipients of his letter as Gentiles within his Gentile mission (cf. 1:5-6, 13-15; 11:13; 15:15-18), distinguishing between them and his "own people" (e.g., 11:14). He also, however, speaks of Abraham as "our forefather" (4:1), refers to his addressees as "those who know the law" (7:1), presupposes that they have lived under the law (7:4-6; 8:3-4), and lays

---

49. R. E. Brown, "Beginnings of Christianity at Rome," 104. For a different attempt to deal with the same data, arguing that the addressees were "a group of Judean Christians" at Rome, see S. Mason, "'For I Am Not Ashamed of the Gospel' (Rom. 1.16): The Gospel and the First Readers of Romans," in *Gospel in Paul: Studies on Corinthians, Galatians and Romans for Richard N. Longenecker*, ed. L. A. Jervis and P. Richardson (Sheffield: Sheffield Academic Press, 1994), 254-87.

stress on the messianic tradition in this letter more than anywhere else in his extant writings (cf. 1:3-4; 9:5; 15:12, quoting Isa 11:10). More particularly, in 1:16–4:25 he argues in a thoroughly Jewish and Jewish Christian manner. And he continues that type of argumentation in relating the gospel to the hope of Israel in 9–11 (perhaps also, to an extent, in his exhortations of 12:1–15:13).

In 5–8, however, Paul sets out the essence of what he proclaims in his Gentile mission — that is, to pagan Gentiles who had not been prepared for the gospel by Jewish or Jewish Christian teaching, and so did not think in Jewish categories. That message, he acknowledges in 5:1a, is based on being "justified by faith." Its thrust, however, consists of (1) a proclamation of "peace" and "reconciliation" with God "through our Lord Jesus Christ," which is unfolded in the theme or thesis section of 5:1-11; (2) the telling of the universal, foundational story of sin, death, and condemnation having entered the world by "one man," but grace, life, and righteousness brought about "through Jesus Christ our Lord" in 5:12-21; (3) the spelling out of the relations of sin, death, and the law, on the one hand, and grace, life, and righteousness, on the other, through the use of three rhetorical questions at 6:1; 6:15; and 7:7 — with a particularly tragic soliloquy, which had many parallels in the Greek world, coming to voice in 7:14-24; (4) the highlighting of relationships "in Christ" and "in the Spirit" in 8:1-30; and (5) a triumphal declaration, which verges on being a defiant assertion, of God's love and care for his own "in Christ Jesus our Lord" in 8:31-39, with that final portion probably incorporating a number of early Christian confessional statements.

It is in this section that the three basic features of classical rhetoric — that is, *logos* (content or argument), *ethos* (the personal character of the speaker or writer), and *pathos* (the power to stir the emotions) — come most fully to expression in Paul's letter to the Romans. It is in this section that themes most distinctly Pauline are clustered: "peace" and "reconciliation" with God,[50] and the believer being "in Christ" and "in the Spirit." And it is in Romans 8, using John A. T. Robinson's analogy of "a journey by canal across an isthmus" with its "series of locks" rising to and then falling away from "a central ridge," that "the heights of the epistle are reached" and there occurs "a sustained climax which takes the argument across the watershed."[51]

50. This is, in particular, the insight of S. Kim, "God Reconciled His Enemy to Himself," 102-24; *idem,* "2 Cor. 5:11-21 and the Origin of Paul's Concept of 'Reconciliation,'" 360-84.

51. J. A. T. Robinson, *Wrestling with Romans* (London: SCM, 1979), 9.

4. Conclusion

While different in many respects in its tone and content from the letter that he wrote to Gentile Christians living in the Roman province of Galatia, the approach that Paul takes in Romans has some parallels to the approach he took earlier in Galatians — for in both letters he begins with matters of agreement and then moves on to those matters having to do with either disagreement or his own distinctive proclamation of the gospel. The *Propositio* or proposition statement of Gal 2:15-21, as Hans Dieter Betz has argued (and I have agreed), sets out Paul's argument in terms of three movements: first acknowledging matters of agreement with his addressees (vv. 15-16), then setting out matters of disagreement (vv. 17-20), and finally drawing a conclusion (v. 21)[52] — with, then, in the *Probatio* or argument section of Galatians the matters of agreement spelled out in 3:1-18, the matters of disagreement explicated in 3:19–4:7, and expressions of concern for the believers appended in 4:8-11.[53] Most commentators have taken the central thrust of Galatians to be Paul's argument against "legalism" in 3:1-18. I have argued, however, on the basis of his *Propositio* ("proposition") in 2:15-21 and his *Probatio* ("arguments") in 3:1–4:11, that (1) Paul's principal arguments in Galatians are against "nomism," which are to be found in 3:19–4:11, and (2) his experiential and biblical arguments in 3:1-18, while valid and meaningful, are primarily given to prepare for his major arguments in 3:19–4:11.[54]

Likewise in his pastoral counsel set out in 1 Corinthians, Paul often begins with statements that he and his addressees agreed on — though, in this case, they seem to have interpreted the statements in one way and he in another. The most obvious of these statements are "Everything is permissible" (6:12; 10:23), "It is good for a man not to have sexual relations with a woman" (7:1), "We all possess knowledge" (8:1), "An idol is nothing at all in the world" (8:4), and "There is no God but one" (8:4). In all of these instances Paul begins by seeking common ground and then moves on to explicate his own understanding.

Something similar, I suggest, is taking place in Paul's letter to believers at Rome, though with the parallels closer to the pattern in Galatians than to that in 1 Corinthians. Thus, while the presentations of God's impartiality, Jews and Gentiles being alike under sin, no one being able to be declared

---

52. Cf. R. N. Longenecker, *Galatians,* WBC (Dallas: Word, 1990), 80-96.
53. Cf. R. N. Longenecker, *Galatians,* 97-183.
54. R. N. Longenecker, *Galatians,* 97-178.

righteous by observing the law, and justification by faith in 1:16–4:25 are vitally important, these seem to have been matters of agreement between Paul and his addressees. What Paul wanted to give his readers as a "spiritual gift," which he refers to in 2:16 and 16:25 as "my gospel," is to be found preeminently, I suggest, in 5–8: a gospel that focuses on "peace" and "reconciliation" with God, that deals with humanity's essential tension of "death" and "life," and that highlights the personal relationships of being "in Christ" and "in the Spirit."

Understanding Romans in this fashion, of course, has rather revolutionary implications for NT criticism and for Christian theology. Most of all, however, it has great significance for our living as Christians, our proclamation of the gospel, and our contextualization of the essential Christian message in our own day and culture.

Supplemental Bibliography

See also "Bibliography of Selected Commentaries." All references in the footnotes to works included in this list are by the authors' names and abbreviated titles.

Bassler, Jouette M. *Divine Impartiality: Paul and a Theological Axiom.* Chico: Scholars, 1982.

Bornkamm, Günther. "Gesetz und Natur (Röm. 2,14-15)," in *Studien zu Antike und Urchristentum* II. Munich: Kaiser, 1959.

Cambier, J.-M. "Le jugement de tous les hommes par Dieu seul, selon la vérité, dans Rom 2:1–3:20," *ZNW* 67 (1976) 187-213.

Campbell, Douglas A. "A Rhetorical Suggestion concerning Romans 2," in *Society of Biblical Literature Seminar Papers,* ed. E. Lovering. Atlanta: Scholars, 140-64.

———. *The Quest for Paul's Gospel: A Suggested Strategy.* London, New York: T&T Clark International, 2005.

———. *The Deliverance of God: An Apocalyptic Rereading of Justification in Paul.* Grand Rapids: Eerdmans, 2009.

Carras, George P. "Romans 2,1-29: A Dialogue on Jewish Ideals," *Bib* 73 (1992) 183-207.

Cranfield, Charles E. B. "Giving a Dog a Bad Name: A Note on H. Räisänen's *Paul and the Law,*" *JSNT* 38 (1990) 77-85.

Davies, Glenn N. *Faith and Obedience in Romans.* Sheffield: JSOT, 1990.

Dunn, James D. G. "The New Perspective on Paul," *BJRL* 65 (1983) 95-122; repr. in *Jesus, Paul and the Law: Studies in Mark and Galatians.* London: SPCK; Louisville: Westminster, 1990, 183-214.

———. "Paul and Justification by Faith," in *The Road from Damascus: The Impact of*

Paul's Conversion on His Life, Thought, and Ministry, ed. R. N. Longenecker. MNTS. Grand Rapids: Eerdmans, 1997, 85-101.

Fee, Gordon D. *God's Empowering Presence: The Holy Spirit in the Letters of Paul*. Peabody: Hendrickson, 1994.

Friedrichsen, Anton. "Der wahre Jude und sein Lob: Röm. 2.28f.," in *Symbolae Arctoae* I (1922) 43-44.

Ito, A. "Romans 2: A Deuteronomist Reading," *JSNT* 59 (1995) 33-34.

Kähler, Martin. "Auslegung von Kap. 2,14-16 in Römerbrief," *TSK* 47 (1974) 274, 277.

Kim, Seyoon. "God Reconciled His Enemy to Himself: The Origin of Paul's Concept of Reconciliation," in *The Road from Damascus: The Impact of Paul's Conversion on His Life, Thought, and Ministry*, ed. R. N. Longenecker. MNTS. Grand Rapids: Eerdmans, 1997, 102-24.

—————. "2 Cor. 5:11-21 and the Origin of Paul's Concept of 'Reconciliation,'" *NovT* 39 (1997) 360-84.

König, A. "Gentiles or Gentile Christians? On the Meaning of Romans 2:12-16," *JTSA* 15 (1976) 53-60.

Longenecker, Richard N. *Paul, Apostle of Liberty*. New York: Harper & Row, 1964; repr. Grand Rapids: Baker, 1976; repr. Vancouver: Regent College Publishing, 1993 and 2003.

—————. "Paul and the Old Testament," in *Biblical Exegesis in the Apostolic Period*. Grand Rapids: Eerdmans, 1975; 2nd ed. 1999, 88-116.

—————. "Prolegomena to Paul's Use of Scripture in Romans," *BBR* 7 (1997) 145-68, esp. 146-47, 158-67.

Räisänen, Heikki. *Paul and the Law*. Tübingen: Mohr, 1983, 1987^2.

Sanders, E. P. "Appendix: Romans 2," in *Paul, the Law, and the Jewish People*. Philadelphia: Fortress, 1983, 123-35.

Schreiner, Thomas R. "Did Paul Believe in Justification by Works? Another Look at Romans 2," *BBR* 3 (1993) 131-55.

Scroggs, Robin. "Paul as Rhetorician: Two Homilies in Romans 1–11," in *Jews, Greeks, and Christians* (*Festschrift* W. D. Davies), ed. R. Hamerton-Kelly and R. Scroggs. Leiden: Brill, 1976, 271-98.

Snodgrass, Klyne R. "Justification by Grace — To the Doers: An Analysis of the Place of Romans 2 in the Theology of Paul," *NTS* 32 (1986) 72-93.

Stowers, Stanley K. *The Diatribe and Paul's Letter to the Romans*. Chico: Scholars, 1981, esp. 93-98, 110-13.

—————. "Paul's Dialogue with a Fellow Jew in Romans 3:1-9," *CBQ* 46 (1984) 707-22.

—————. *A Rereading of Romans*. New Haven: Yale University Press, 1994, 83-193.

Thielman, Frank. *From Plight to Solution: A Jewish Framework for Understanding Paul's View of the Law in Galatians and Romans*. Leiden: Brill, 1989.

CHAPTER XI

Structure and Argument of the Letter

Issues regarding the structure and argument of Romans have been of critical concern, not only to NT scholars but also among many Christian ministers, theological students, and earnest laypeople. There has been, in fact, a vast host of proposals advanced regarding how the structure of the letter is to be viewed and how the flow or development of its argument should be understood. Indeed, the often repeated pseudo-scholarly adage (though expressed somewhat flamboyantly) is true with respect to the letter's structure and argument: "The ocean of opinion has lashed the shores of human conviction with repeated tides of varying intensity, and there are many undercurrents."

The most important questions with respect to the structure and argument of Romans have to do with (1) the delineation of the various sections and subsections of the letter, (2) the identification of the letter's central theme or themes, and (3) how what is identified as the central theme or themes is worked out throughout the letter. And with respect to the delineation of the letter's sections and subsections, the question must be asked: Are such matters to be determined by subject matter, or by the epistolary and rhetorical conventions reflected in the materials, or by some combination of these two approaches?

With respect to the identification of the letter's central theme or themes, the following questions immediately come to the fore: (1) Is the major thrust of the letter to be found in chapters 1–4, which denounce all attempts to obtain righteousness or justification before God based on human "works," declare God's impartiality in dealing with all people, and set forth a proper understanding of "righteousness" and "justification by faith"? Or (2) is the primary focus of the letter to be found in chapters 5–8, which begin with "peace" and "reconciliation" with God, go on to highlight the scenario of "sin and death" through Adam but "grace and life" through Christ, and culminate with the believer being "in Christ" and "in the Spirit"? Or (3) should the letter's primary focus be seen in chapters 9–11, which set out relations between the Christian gospel and Israel's hope or expectations, with that section often understood to include teaching on "predestination" and "election," an exposition on the course of "salvation history," and a "theodicy" in vindication of God's salvific actions? Or (4) is the theme, thrust, or focus of Romans to be found in its hortatory materials of 12:1–15:13, with those admonitions anticipated by the apostle's reference to "the obedience of faith" in 1:5? And if any of these four major sections of the letter's body middle is understood to incorporate the focus or central theme of the letter, and so to represent its major argument and concerns, it must then be asked: How do the other sections of Romans relate to and complement the argument of that section?

Building on what has been argued earlier in this book — particularly in our treatments of the identity, character, circumstances, and concerns of the addressees (Chapter IV); Paul's purpose or purposes for writing (Chapter V); and the oral, rhetorical, and epistolary conventions reflected in the letter (Chapter VI) — it is necessary here, in preparation for a more intensive exegetical study of the contents of the letter in a forthcoming commentary proper, to scan Romans, giving particular attention to its basic structure and the flow or development of its argument. It might be possible to treat "structure" and "argument" separately. But since these matters are so integrally intertwined, it seems better to deal with them together — organizing our discussion not by topics but, rather, in terms of the letter's major epistolary divisions: its opening sections (i.e., "salutation" and "thanksgiving"); its body sections (i.e., "body opening," four "body middle" sections, and "body closing"); and its concluding sections (i.e., "peace" and "grace" benedictions, commendation of Phoebe, two sets of greetings, additional admonitions, and "doxology").

In our earlier discussion of ancient oral, rhetorical, and epistolary conventions in Chapter VI we dealt with orality first, then with rhetorical types and modes of persuasion, and finally with epistolary practices — that is, in terms of the various uses of these features and the development of their nomenclature. Here, however, in discussing the structure and argument of Paul's letter to the Christians at Rome, we will treat these matters in reverse order. For since Romans is a letter, what Paul wrote must first of all be analyzed in terms of its epistolary features; yet since the central content of the letter corresponds to a particular type of rhetoric of the day and reflects various ancient modes of rhetorical and oral argumentation, it must then also be analyzed in terms of its rhetorical and oral features.

1. The Opening Sections

Paul begins his letter to Rome with a "salutation" section and a "thanksgiving" section. Each of these can be fairly well delineated — though it may be questioned where exactly the thanksgiving ends and the body of the letter (i.e., the "body opening") begins. More importantly, each of these sections, in its own way, expresses something of Paul's major concerns, anticipates features of his primary purposes in writing, and highlights what he wants to develop more fully in the rest of the letter.

Salutation (1:1-7)

As is true for most of the extant letters of antiquity, as well as for all of Paul's other NT letters, the salutation of Romans has a threefold structural framework: (1) an "identification of sender" unit; (2) a "designation of recipient" unit; and (3) a "greetings" unit. This basic structure, together with the fact that an εὐχαριστῶ formula ("I give thanks") appears at the beginning of verse 8 and so signals the start of the "thanksgiving" section at that point, indicates quite clearly that the salutation of Romans is to be identified as 1:1-7.

The salutation of Romans, however, is longer than the salutation of any of Paul's other letters. The most obvious reason for this is that Paul has added further material to each of the usual salutatory units in this letter. Thus to his own name "Paul" as the sender he adds "a servant of Christ Jesus, called [by God] an apostle, and set apart for the gospel of God" (v. 1); to the designation of his addressees as being "all those at Rome" he adds "who are loved by God and called his holy people" (v. 7a); and to the twofold greeting "grace and peace" he adds "from God our Father and the Lord Jesus Christ" (v. 7b).

Each of these additions highlights in telescopic fashion certain important matters that will be taken up later in his letter: (1) that Paul is truly a prophetic "servant of Christ Jesus," a divinely called "apostle," and has been "set apart for the gospel of God," which are qualifications that may have been questioned by some of the Christians at Rome; (2) that his addressees at

Rome were considered by him to be true Christian believers, for they are "loved by God" and called his "holy people"; and (3) that "grace and peace" have as their ultimate source "God our Father" and "the Lord Jesus Christ." While "grace" and "peace" may, at first glance, appear to be only traditional greetings expressed in two languages — the first, a typical Greek greeting; the second, the usual Jewish greeting — Paul seems to be using these terms here, as he does elsewhere in Romans (as well as in all of his other letters), to epitomize in compressed fashion something of the fullness of the Christian proclamation: that through the "grace" of God our Father, as expressed in the work of Christ (e.g., Rom 5:15-21), there has been brought about "peace" with God, as effected through the work of Christ (e.g., Rom 5:1-11).

It is also important to note, however, that the salutation of Romans highlights as well a number of themes that Paul will be explicating in what follows throughout his letter. The first is "the gospel of God," which he affirms was "promised beforehand through his [God's] prophets in the Holy Scriptures" (vv. 1b-2). In referring first to "the gospel" among these themes and in speaking of that gospel the way he does, Paul signals that he wants to emphasize at least three things: (1) that his primary concern in writing to the Christians at Rome has something to do with the nature of the Christian gospel; (2) that his way of proclaiming that gospel to pagan Gentiles in the Greco-Roman world is "of God"; and (3) that the Christian message is integrally related to the prophetic message of the OT Scriptures.

A second theme highlighted in the letter's salutation is that the focus of Christian proclamation is on the work and person of Jesus Christ, God's Son (v. 3a). In support of this affirmation — and perhaps by way of anticipating some extraneous thoughts among his Roman addressees about the co-equal importance of Jewish thought forms, rituals, and/or lifestyles for believers in Jesus — Paul cites in verses 3-4 what many scholars have come to believe is an early Christian confession, which was in all likelihood known and accepted by the Christians at Rome. It is a confession that proclaimed (1) Jesus' Jewishness and kingly status humanly in the words "descended from David according to the flesh" and (2) Jesus' accreditation by God spiritually in the proclamation "declared to be the Son of God with power, according to the Spirit of holiness, by [his] resurrection from the dead" (vv. 3-4).

A third theme that is highlighted in this salutation has to do with Paul's own apostleship and mandate to carry on a Christian mission to Gentiles, which he (1) says was "to call people from among all the Gentiles to the obedience that comes from faith"; he then (2) states quite explicitly that such a mandate came "through him [Jesus Christ] and for his name's sake," and (3) implies that his addressees were to consider themselves as part of that God-given mission (vv. 5-6).

All of these themes, which are enunciated rather cryptically in the salutation, Paul will unpack and develop more fully in the body of Romans. It needs also, however, to be recognized that these three matters — that is, (1) the centrality of the gospel, (2) the focus of the gospel as being on Jesus Christ, and (3) the legitimacy of Paul's Gentile mission — represent, in condensed fashion, the major concerns of the apostle at the time when he wrote his letter to the Christians at Rome. And these statements in the salutation of Romans, which Paul has added to the usual threefold structure of an ancient epistolary salutation, become particularly significant when they are understood in light of what may be postulated about the identity, character, concerns, and circumstances of his addressees at Rome, as we have proposed earlier (cf. Chapter IV, "Addressees"): (1) that the various congregations of Christians at Rome probably included both Jewish and Gentile believers in Jesus, though with the Gentile contingent being more prominent at the time when Paul wrote them, and (2) that all of the Christians at Rome, both Jews and Gentiles ethnically, looked to the "Mother Church" at Jerusalem for their doctrinal and ethical instruction, followed at least some of the Jewish Christian rites, and reverenced the Mosaic law — though they were not "Judaizers" like those who infiltrated the churches of Galatia with what Paul called "a different gospel, which is no gospel at all" (Gal 1:6-7).

Thanksgiving (1:8-12)

There can be no doubt about where the thanksgiving section of Romans begins. The salutation is a discrete unit of material, which extends from verse 1 through verse 7. And the εὐχαριστῶ formula ("I give thanks") — which begins almost all of the thanksgiving sections in Paul's other uncontested letters (except, of course, Galatians, where θαυμάζω, "I am amazed," functions in much the same manner; also note the similar use of the adjective εὐλογητός, "Blessed" or "Praised," which functions equivalently in 2 Cor 1:3; cf. also Eph 1:3 and 1 Pet 1:3) — appears at the beginning of verse 8. Questions, however, may legitimately be raised regarding where the thanksgiving section ends.

Commentators have usually viewed 1:8-15 as also a single unit of material that introduces the entire letter of Romans, for it follows the salutation of 1:1-7 and appears before the thesis statement of 1:16-17. Theodor Zahn, for example, captioned 1:8-15 "Der Briefeingang" ("The Letter's Introduction"), understanding it as a discrete unit of eight verses that introduces the whole letter.[1] But if Romans is to be understood as a letter, then its epistolary features must be seriously taken into account. And that means, in particular, that the disclosure formula οὐ θέλω δὲ ὑμᾶς ἀγνοεῖν ("I do not want you to be unaware") at the beginning of 1:13, which is coupled with the vocative ἀδελφοί ("brothers and sisters"), needs to be seen as signaling the start of a new section, which would be the "body opening" of the letter — as do similar expressions in many letters of antiquity and in 2 Cor 1:8 and Phil 1:12 (perhaps also Gal 1:11).[2]

Of even greater importance when studying the thanksgiving of Romans, however, is to observe how Paul sets out in this section something of an agenda for what he will deal with later in the body of his letter and how he highlights some of his major concerns when writing. Paul Schubert, as noted earlier, was the first to observe this phenomenon in the Pauline thanksgiving sections,[3] and his seminal observations have been spelled out more fully by many others since.[4] So when reading the "thanksgiving" of Romans — together, of course, with the preceding "salutation," the immediately following "body opening," the later "body closing" (or "apostolic parousia"), and the concluding sections of the letter — we need to read it in terms of Paul's own agenda and major concerns, and thus as an important introduction to what will appear later in the body of the letter.

The three themes highlighted in the salutation also appear in the thanksgiving section of the letter: the first when Paul speaks of serving God with his whole heart "in preaching *the gospel*" (1:9a); the second when he defines that gospel as being "the gospel of *his* [God's] *Son*" (1:9a); the third when he alludes to his *Gentile mission* and his desire to include his addressees within that mission (1:12). Likewise included within this thanksgiving of Romans are (1) a recognition by the apostle of the Christian faith of his addressees (1:8), (2) an assurance of the apostle's prayers for his addressees (1:9-10a), and (3) a reference to the apostle's prayer and desire to visit the Christians at Rome (1:10b; cf. also v. 13).

But the most significant of the features in this thanksgiving section for an understanding of Paul's agenda and his concerns when writing Romans

---

1. T. Zahn, *An die Römer*, 27.

2. Cf. J. L. White, *Body of the Greek Letter*, 66, 76, 84-85.

3. P. Schubert, *Form and Function of the Pauline Thanksgivings* (1939).

4. See esp. P. T. O'Brien, *Introductory Thanksgivings* (1977); L. A. Jervis, *Purpose of Romans* (1991), 48-52, 86-109.

are the two suggested in verses 11-12 — that is, (1) the statement "I am longing to see you in order that (ἵνα) I may share with you (μεταδῶ ὑμῖν) some spiritual gift (τι χάρισμα πνευματικόν) to make you strong," and (2) the explication "so that (τοῦτο δέ ἐστιν) we may be mutually encouraged (συμπαρακληθῆναι) by each other's faith, both yours and mine (ὑμῶν τε καὶ ἐμοῦ)." The first is introduced by the conjunction ἵνα (here understood as signifying purpose, and so "in order that") and expressed in the phrase "some spiritual gift" (τι χάρισμα πνευματικόν), which Paul wants to share with his addressees to make them strong (1:11).

What was this "spiritual gift" that Paul wanted to share with his addressees? In the previous chapter (Chapter X, "Focus or Central Thrust") I argued that the focus of Paul's letter to Rome is not to be found in 1:16–4:25 (or more expressly in 3:21–4:25), but, rather, in the theological exposition of 5–8, which highlights the themes of "peace" and "reconciliation" with God, the antitheses of "death" and "life," and the relationships of being "in Christ" and "in the Spirit" — with that central theological thrust then applied, as we will propose later in this chapter, in the ethical exhortations of chapters 12 and 13:8-14, which set out a Christian love ethic that is integrally related to the didactic message of the Christian gospel.

The second of these highly significant features to note in the thanksgiving of Romans is expressed in 1:12, which explicates what was said in 1:11: "that is (τοῦτο δέ ἐστιν), to be mutually encouraged (συμπαρακληθῆναι) by each other's faith, both yours and mine (ὑμῶν τε καὶ ἐμοῦ)." But what did Paul have in mind when he spoke of being "mutually encouraged by each other's faith" and then emphasized the reciprocal nature of that encouragement by the addition of the phrase "both yours and mine"? The language of verse 12, while suggestive, is considerably compressed. Later, in the "apostolic parousia" of 15:14-32, it will be unpacked to mean (1) Paul's sharing the gospel message that he proclaims in his Gentile mission with his Christian addressees at Rome (15:14-22), which he believed they needed to understand and accept as a group of predominantly Gentile believers in Jesus, and (2) their assisting him in his proposed journey to Spain and its environs in the western outreach of his Gentile mission (15:23-24, 32b), which would include both their prayers and their financial support — much as the church at Antioch of Syria had prayed for and assisted him throughout his ministry in the eastern part of the Roman empire.

These two matters — that is, (1) his exposition to believers at Rome of what he was preaching as the Christian gospel in his Gentile mission and (2) their support of him in his planned outreach to Gentiles in the western portion of the Roman empire — were, as noted earlier (cf. Chapter V, "Purpose"), Paul's two primary purposes for the writing of Romans. So here in the thanksgiving section of the letter, combined with data derived from the salutation, we have in compressed form the apostle's major concerns and purposes when writing. These are the matters that Paul (1) will develop throughout the four sections of his letter's body middle in 1:16–15:13, and then (2) finally unpack in rather specific fashion in the "apostolic parousia" of 15:14-32 and the closing sections of 15:33–16:27. In effect, these concerns and purposes provide the reader with something of an agenda for what will follow. So we need to begin our reading of Romans by giving careful attention to what Paul says about his own concerns and purposes at the time when he wrote.

2. The Body Sections

The body of ancient letters, whether Greco-Roman letters generally or Paul's letters in particular, "has proved," as David Aune has pointed out, "most resistant to formal analysis."[5] Or as John White has said: "Regarding the body portion of Paul's letters, common [epistolary] features are less evident than in the opening and closing."[6] Nonetheless, it is generally recognized (1) that the body of a Pauline letter usually consists of three distinct parts: a body opening, a body middle, and a body closing,[7] and (2) that every Pauline letter, except Philemon, evidences at least two body middle sections: the first, a well-organized theological section; the second, a hortatory section, where in a less structured manner the message that was set out and developed in the theological section is made personal by means of exhortations.[8]

All of this is generally true of Paul's letters. Yet it also needs to be recognized, as David Aune has noted, that "there is an important sense in which the attenuated literary styles and forms that percolated down the social strata of antiquity tended toward eclecticism."[9] And with particular reference to the writings of Luke and Paul, Aune in that same article has appropriately gone on to say:

---

5. D. E. Aune, *New Testament in Its Literary Environment*, 188.
6. J. L. White, "Ancient Greek Letters," 99.
7. Cf. J. L. White, *Body of the Greek Letter*, 62-66, 73-74.
8. Cf. J. L. White, *Body of the Greek Letter*, 87-88.
9. D. E. Aune, "*Mixtum compositum*," in *Westminster Dictionary*, 307, col. 1.

Luke-Acts and the letters of Paul, when compared with the stylistic and structural prescriptions of the literary theory and practice of the educated, are eclectic. Yet unlike Dionysius of Halicarnassus [who, as Aune has observed, evidences in his *Antiquitates Romanae* that he was "very conscious of the eclectic character of his history"], if they were aware of their eclecticism, they betray no hesitation, nor do they feel the need to defend what they are doing.[10]

Among all of the Pauline letters, Romans is the most eclectic of the lot. For not only is it longer than most extant ancient letters and all of Paul's other letters, it is also (1) more composed of elements drawn from various sources and (2) more reflective of various rhetorical modes of argumentation than most, if not all, of the letters of antiquity and Paul's other letters — and so has proved itself to be more resistant to formal analysis than them all.

The body of Romans consists of three main parts: (1) a brief body opening (1:13-15); (2) an extensive body middle (1:16–15:13), which may be subdivided into four quite lengthy major sections (i.e., 1:16–4:25; 5–8; 9–11; and 12:1–15:13); and (3) a body closing (15:14-32), which has, of late, been called an "apostolic parousia." The body opening of 1:13-15 and body closing of 15:14-32 reflect a number of the usual epistolary conventions of the ancient world. The extensive body middle of 1:16–15:13, however, except for the use of a few vocatives of direct address, a few verbs of saying, and some disclosure formulas that can be found at strategic places in the presentation, evidences very few of the customary epistolary conventions of the day. Rather, it is more amenable to rhetorical analyses, both diachronic and synchronic. Its four large subsections, as we have proposed earlier, most likely should be understood along the lines of a "protreptic word/speech/message (λόγος προτρεπτικός) of instruction and exhortation" that is set within an epistolary frame — that is, a presentation intended to win someone over to a particular enterprise or way of life by exposing the errors of an alternate view and demonstrating the truth claims of its author's position, with that presentation being set within the structure of a letter (see Chapter VI, "Greco-Roman Oral, Rhetorical, and Epistolary Conventions").

---

10. D. E. Aune, *"Mixtum compositum,"* in *Westminster Dictionary,* 307, col. 2.

A. BODY OPENING

A Brief Introduction to Paul's Protreptic Message (1:13-15)

The beginning of the body opening of Romans is signaled by a disclosure formula that appears at the start of verse 13, οὐ θέλω ὑμᾶς ἀγνοεῖν ("I do not want you to be unaware"), which is coupled with the vocative ἀδελφοί ("brothers and sisters"). A body opening in a typical Greek letter states the reason or reasons for writing and introduces what the writer wants to say in the body middle section that follows. And Paul's body opening in Romans does this by including (1) a notification of a desired visit in verse 13, πολλάκις προεθέμην ἐλθεῖν πρὸς ὑμᾶς ("I planned many times to come to you"), and (2) a responsibility statement in verse 14, Ἕλλησίν τε καὶ βαρβάροις, σοφοῖς τε καὶ ἀνοήτοις ὀφειλέτης εἰμί ("I am obligated both to Greeks and non-Greeks, both to the wise and the foolish").

More importantly, in these few verses Paul (1) speaks of his purpose for wanting to be in contact with his addressees as being "in order that I might have a harvest among you, just as I have had among the other Gentiles" (v. 13b), (2) includes his addressees within his Gentile mission in saying "that is why I am so eager to preach the gospel also to you who are at Rome" (v. 15), and (3) suggests that what follows in the four subsections of the letter's body middle is what he wants to proclaim to them, whether in person or by letter. These three verses, therefore, pick up from the apostle's desires as expressed at the end of his thanksgiving of 1:8-12: "that now at last by God's will the way may be opened for me to come to you" (v. 10) and "that I may impart to you some spiritual gift to make you strong — that is, that you and I may be mutually encouraged by each other's faith" (vv. 11-12). And they function to introduce what Paul wants to say to his addressees in his letter by way of presenting to them his "spiritual gift" in the body middle of that letter.

Were it not for this brief body opening, one would have some difficulty in moving from Paul's general desires and purposes, as expressed in 1:8-12, to what he wants to do in particular in his protreptic type of message of instruction and exhortation, as set out in 1:16–15:13. As it is, however, his desire to be with his addressees in person, which was stated earlier in 1:10 (and will be repeated later in the body closing of 15:14-32) — together with the major purposes motivating that desire, which were expressed in rather compressed fashion in 1:11-12 — are now elaborated more fully in 1:13-15. So Paul's statement "in order that (ἵνα) I might have a harvest among you, just as I have had among the other Gentiles" (v. 13b), coupled with his clarification of that statement to mean "to preach the gospel [i.e., the Christian message as he had been proclaiming it throughout his Gentile mission] also to you who are at Rome" (v. 15), serves as a compressed and more particular introduction to what he wants to present in the four major sections of the letter's body middle in 1:16–15:13.

B. BODY MIDDLE

Ancient "words [i.e., 'speeches' or 'messages'] of instruction and exhortation" (λόγοι προτρεπτικοί) were characteristically structured in terms of three sections: (1) a negative section, which dissuaded and censured an opposing view, (2) a positive section, which set forth and defended the author's position, and (3) a hortatory section, which appealed to the hearers or addressees by way of inviting them to accept what was presented in the two previous sections.[11] To each of these customary sections of protreptic discourse, however, Paul adds in his letter to the Christians at Rome his own distinctive emphases and gives his own spin to the data he presents — often, as well, speaking to his addressees on their own grounds and interjecting material of particular relevance to them. Notable in this regard are the facts that (1) Paul restructures the first section of his protreptic discourse (i.e., 1:16–4:25) to include not only negative statements about what he opposes but also positive affirmations of what he holds in common with his addressees, and (2) he adds a fourth section (i.e., 9–11) between the first two theological sections and the final hortatory section, which material would have been of particular interest to the believers at Rome who understood and expressed their commitment to Jesus in ways that had been largely transmitted to them by Jewish Christians from the Mother Church at Jerusalem.

Section I: Righteousness, Faithfulness, and Faith (1:16–4:25)

In the first section of the body middle of Romans, that is, in 1:16–4:25, Paul sounds very much like a righteous Jew or an authentic Jewish Christian in (1) rebutting the false concept of religious legalism and (2) arguing for faith as the only proper response to what God has done redemptively for people.

---

11. Cf. D. E. Aune, "*Mixtum compositum*," in *Westminster Dictionary*, 383-85.

His purpose, as in the first part of any ancient protreptic "word of instruction and exhortation" (λόγος προτρεπτικός), is to dissuade and censure — that is, to dissuade any believer in Jesus, whether ethnically Jewish or Gentile, who might be enticed by some form of judaistic legalism, and to censure any such legalistic view of acceptance by or relationship with God. But Paul goes beyond dissuasion and censure in this section to enunciate, as well, the teachings of the Jewish (OT) Scriptures with regard to "righteousness" and "justification by faith" — which principles were foundational (1) for the religion of Israel (as represented by the OT), (2) among the better teachers of Early Judaism (as represented by many of the early "tannaitic" rabbis of the Talmud), and (3) in early Jewish Christianity (as founded on the OT and the apostolic testimony regarding the person, teaching, and work of Jesus). So Paul makes the point throughout this first section of the letter's body middle that, with respect to the nature of righteousness and the importance of justification by faith, he and his addressees are in basic agreement — and he does so believing that such a recognition of their essential agreement is an important first step by way of preparation for what he wants to set out for his addressees about his own proclamation of the Christian gospel in the following section of his letter.

1. The Structure of the Section

Typical epistolary conventions have been seen at two places in this first section of the letter's body middle: (1) at the beginning of 2:1 with the vocative "O man" (ὦ ἄνθρωπε), and (2) at the start of chapter 4 with verbs of "saying" in the question of verse 1, "What then shall we say?" (τί οὖν ἐροῦμεν), and the question of verse 3, "What does the Scripture say?" (τί γὰρ ἡ γραφὴ λέγει). These instances, however, as we have noted above, may also be related to certain rhetorical modes of expression that were then in vogue: the vocative "O man," which begins the diatribe of 2:1-5, and the verbs of saying in the questions "What then shall we say?" and "What does the Scripture say?," which begin the paradigmatic illustration of Abraham in 4:1-24. Nonetheless, these two textual indicators — whether strictly epistolary in nature or incorporating a combination of epistolary and rhetorical features — provide the reader with some understanding of how Paul's presentation should be delineated.

More important, however, are the rhetorical conventions in this section of the letter, which serve to mark off various movements in the apostle's argument. Among the more obvious examples of rhetorical phenomena in the section, as noted earlier (cf. the section entitled "Rhetorical Analysis of Romans" in Chapter VI, pp. 193-204), are the following:

1. *Anaphora* (i.e., the repetition of a word or expression at the beginning of a series of successive statements; or, as in an *extended anaphora*, the repetition of a word or expression at the resumption of a discussion that has been interrupted by another section of material). The thesis enunciated about "righteousness" and "faith" in 1:16-17, coupled with its restatement and expansion in 3:21-23, should probably be viewed as an extended form of rhetorical *anaphora*. The repetition of the ominous phrase "God gave them over" (παρέδωκεν αὐτοὺς ὁ θεός) in 1:24, 26, and 28 should be classified, as well, as a case of *anaphora* — though, possibly, that repetition could also be understood as *paronomasia* (i.e., the play on two or more words in a relatively brief context that are similar in form, that sound alike, or that make use of different meanings of the same word).

2. *Apostrophe* (i.e., the interruption of a discourse in order to address a person or personified thing). Two rather obvious examples occur in Romans 2: the first in verses 1-16, "You, therefore, O man, whoever you are who passes judgment on someone else," etc.; the second in verses 17-29, "Now you, if you call yourself a Jew; if you rely on the law and brag about your relationship with God," etc.

3. *Diatribe* (i.e., a lively dialogical style that makes use of direct address to an imaginary interlocutor, hypothetical objections, and false conclusions). It is in Romans that the techniques of the Greek diatribe are most conspicuous in the NT. And it is in 2:1-5 and 2:17-24 that they appear most prominently in the letter — probably also in 9:19-21 and 11:17-24; possibly in 3:1-8 (or 3:1-9); and perhaps in 3:27-31 (or 3:27–4:2) and 14:4-11. All of these passages could also be seen as reflecting a rhetorical style that was called *prosopopoeia* (i.e., the insertion of a specific character, whether person or thing, who or which is allowed to speak).

4. *Paradeigma* (i.e., a story that provides a pattern or example to be either imitated or avoided, or an argument that is based on the use of an example, whether positive or negative). The example of Abraham in 4:1-24 is a clear instance of a paradigmatic exhortation, whether its "verb of saying" in verse 1 is judged to be purely epistolary or the opening element of a rhetorical *paradeigma*.

Among the less obvious, though often proposed, examples of rhetorical phenomena in this first section of the body middle of Roman, that is, in 1:16–4:25, are the following:

1. *Chiasmus* (i.e., an inverted relationship between syntactical elements

of parallel phrases). Because of the question of intentionality — that is, "Just because a *chiasmus* is discernible to the reader of a text, should it be viewed as having been intentionally created by its author?" or, "Should it be seen as having come about somewhat unintentionally, with its discovery to be credited more to the reader than to the author, as so often happens in both oral and written compositions?" — the significance of chiastic structures in the NT, especially in Paul's letters, has often been debated. Of those portions in Romans that have been claimed to be chiastic in nature, 2:7-10 (or, perhaps, 2:6-11) and 3:4-8 in this first section have frequently been so identified — with 2:12-29 sometimes also said to reflect certain chiastic features.

2. *Inclusio* (i.e., similar verbal phenomena, which would include similar sentences, statements, phrases, clauses, or words, placed at the beginning and the end of a relatively short unit of text that serve to frame the material presented). The framing of material by the repetition of certain fixed statements, sentences, phrases, and/or words was in antiquity, and still continues today, a common convention of oral speech. It was called *inclusio* by the ancient rhetoricians.

The expression "through our Lord Jesus Christ" (διὰ τοῦ κυρίου ἡμῶν Ἰησοῦ Χριστοῦ), which in the following section of 5–8 is repeated six times (with only slight variation), that is, in 5:1, 11, 21; 6:23; 7:25; and 8:39, is assuredly a case of such a rhetorical convention, for it not only frames the entire section but also concludes each of the textual units within that section. More questionable, however, is the identification of an *inclusio* in Paul's use of the phrase "both for the Jew first and for the Gentile" (Ἰουδαίῳ τε πρῶτον καὶ Ἕλληνι), which appears first in 1:16 and then twice more in 2:9-10. On the basis of this two- or threefold use of the expression, together with the repetition of several words and phrases that appear first in 1:18-20 and then again in 2:1-9, Jouette Bassler has argued for the structural unity of 1:16–2:10 — even proposing that 1:16–2:10 should be viewed in terms of a "ring-structure," which she sees as coming close to being worked out in terms of a *chiasmus*.[12]

But Bassler's thesis, together with her working out of that thesis, has failed to convince most scholars today. Its major problems are (1) that it does not sufficiently take into account the shift from the third person plural in 1:18-32 to the second person singular that begins at 2:1, which change of pro-

---

12. J. M. Bassler, *Divine Impartiality* (1982), esp. 121-70 and "Appendix D," p. 199, building on the work of M. Pohlenz, "Paulus und die Stoa" (1949), and J. A. Fisher, "Pauline Literary Forms and Thought Patterns" (1977).

noun suggests that a new focus begins or a new group of people comes into view at 2:1, and so a new section (or subsection) of Paul's overall argumentation must be seen as beginning at 2:1, (2) that it does not take seriously enough the vocative expression "O man" (ὦ ἄνθρωπε), which heads up all of what follows in 2:1-16 and seems to provide the reader with an epistolary clue for the identification of a new section (or subsection) in the apostle's argument, and (3) that it fails to account for the dramatic shift of style between 1:18-32 and 2:1-10, with a diatribe form of argumentation, which was not evident in 1:18-32, being prominent in 2:1-5 and continuing on in the sections (or subsections) of Paul's argument that follow (cf. 2:17-29 and 3:1-9). Thus, though Bassler has argued that 1:16–2:10 must be understood in terms of its "ring-structure," which structure, she argues, comes close to being a *chiasmus,* most scholars believe that she has not worked out her thesis with sufficient perception or stringency. For a common theme, similar phrases, parallel expressions, and the repetition of words, while significant in the development of an overall argument, need not imply some form of rhetorical or structural ring composition — and certainly not the presence of a *chiasmus.*

Significant, as well, are some of the conventions of ancient orality that appear in this section of the letter's body middle. Among the more obvious examples of oral patterning in 1:16–4:25, as noted earlier (cf. the section entitled "Oral Patterning in Romans" in Chapter VI), are the following:

1. *Acoustical orientation* (i.e., the repetition of words and phrases that sound alike, which was used as an aid to understanding and remembering what was said). Acoustical orientation is not, as noted earlier, an overly common phenomenon in Romans, for Paul was not rhapsodizing as a poet but writing prose. Nonetheless, two instances appear in 1:18-32, which is a passage that denounces the idolatries, immoralities, and injustices of humanity — and which may have been material that had a previous oral history among Jews vis-à-vis pagan Gentiles, having been drawn from *Wisdom of Solomon* 13–14 (and certain tangent verses of the third section of this apocryphal book), and which Paul used for his own purposes.

The first instance of acoustical orientation appears in 1:24, 26, and 28, where there is the repetition of the refrain "God gave them over" (παρέδωκεν αὐτοὺς ὁ θεός). It may be that each of these phrases serves to introduce a further stage in the downward moral spiral of idolatrous humanity. More likely, however, these three appearances of the phrase function to hold together the structure of verses 24-31 and to drive home to the minds and hearts of Paul's addressees the impact of what is being said in this subsection of the passage. The second instance of acoustical orientation appears in 1:23, 25, and 26, where the verb "they exchanged" is used three times, first as a simple aorist (ἤλλαξαν) and then twice more as a compound aorist (μετήλλαξαν) — with the compound form of the verb evidently meant to intensify the significance of the verb's action and the ominous sound of the final Greek syllable of the word (-ξαν) serving to ring in the ears and resonate in the memory of the hearers.

Both of these instances, however, as classified by the rhetoricians of antiquity (see above), may be called either *anaphora* or *paronomasia*, or both. Rhetorical categories were (and are today) only invented by rhetoricians to describe what occurs in oral speech and/or in written composition, and so any particular linguistic phenomenon may be described in terms of both its oral and its rhetorical nomenclatures.

2. *Framing statements, sentences, phrases, and/or words* (i.e., similar verbal phenomena placed at the beginning and end of a relatively short unit of text that serve to frame the material presented). As noted above under the rhetorical rubric *inclusio*, this is a feature that appears in the sixfold repetition (with only slight variation) of the expression "through our Lord Jesus Christ" (διὰ τοῦ κυρίου ἡμῶν Ἰησοῦ Χριστοῦ) in 5:1, 11, 21; 6:23; 7:25; and 8:39, with that expression not only framing the entire section of 5–8 but also nicely concluding each of the textual units within it. It may also be found, though probably much less likely, in the repetition of the phrase "both for the Jew first and for the Gentile" (Ἰουδαίῳ τε πρῶτον καὶ Ἕλληνι) that appears first in 1:16 and then two times more in 2:9-10 (see discussion above).

3. *Formulaic confessional materials* (i.e., early Christian confessional portions that were, presumably, originally oral, and that seem to have been incorporated, either whole or in part, by the authors of the NT at strategic places into their writings). As was seen with respect to the christological formulation of 1:3-4 in the salutation of the letter, so in this first section of the letter's body middle Paul seems to have quoted material drawn from certain early Christian confessions in 3:24-26 (or, perhaps, 3:25-26) and at 4:25. Each of these passages must be treated more fully in a forthcoming commentary proper. Suffice it here to note that both of these confessional portions are strategically placed in the argument of this first section: (1) that of 3:24-26 being used in support of the thesis statement of 3:21-23, which most commentators take to be a repetition and expansion of the thesis statement of 1:16-17 (rhetorically, as noted above, an extended form of *anaphora*); (2) that of 4:25 serving as a fitting climax to what is proclaimed in 3:21-31 and the Abrahamic illustration of 4:1-24 — but also, it may be ar-

gued, to highlight Paul's christological thought that underlies his whole presentation in 1:16–4:25.

From such data drawn from the world of ancient epistolary, rhetorical, and oral conventions, what then can be said about the structure of this first section of the letter's body middle? Well, first of all, analyzing the section in terms of its macro-structure, it needs to be noted (1) that the extended *anaphora* of a thesis statement in 1:16-17 and its repetition and expansion in 3:21-23 implies that this first large portion of material in the letter's body middle is to be understood as one rather self-contained section that is set out in two parts: the first in 1:16–3:20, which is introduced by 1:16-17; the second in 3:21–4:25, which is introduced by 3:21-22; and (2) that the sixfold repetition (with only slight variation) of the expression "through our Lord Jesus Christ" (διὰ τοῦ κυρίου ἡμῶν Ἰησοῦ Χριστοῦ) in 5:1, 11, 21; 6:23; 7:25; and 8:39, which not only frames the entire section of 5–8 but also nicely concludes each of the textual units within it, suggests that the material of 5–8 should be viewed as a second rather self-contained section of the body middle of the letter that follows this first section of 1:16–4:25. And on the basis of these two rather elementary observations, it may be proposed (1) that while 1:16-17 contains an important thesis statement, it probably does not constitute the thesis or caption for all that Paul wrote in his letter to the Christians at Rome (as is usually assumed), but, rather, should likely be viewed as the thesis statement for the first section of the body middle of Romans, which is then repeated and expanded in anaphoric rhetorical fashion in 3:21-23, and (2) that 5:1-11 is not to be understood as the conclusion of what precedes it (thereby forming a textual unit comprised of 1:16–5:11, as some have proposed), but as the opening unit of what follows it (thereby forming a unit of material comprised of chs. 5–8).

Also important for an analysis of 1:16–4:25 are the following factors: (1) that *Wisdom of Solomon,* which pre-dates Paul's letter by at least a half-century and was (presumably) known by Jews and Jewish Christians of that day, lies in some fashion behind what Paul wrote in 1:18–2:15, with the substance of chapters 13–14 of *Wisdom of Solomon* most likely used by him in 1:18-32 and the self-congratulatory emphasis of *Wisd of Sol* 15:1-6 probably alluded to and reacted against in 2:1-15; (2) that much of what appears in 2:1–3:9 echoes in rather allusive fashion a large number of passages drawn from the Jewish (OT) Scriptures; (3) that the materials of chapter 2 suggest Paul's use of various Jewish and/or Jewish Christian aphorisms, doctrinal affirmations, and ethical teachings, all of which he redacted for his own purpose; (4) that a diatribe form of argumentation appears in 2:1-5 and 2:17-29 (possibly also, though less likely, in 3:1-8); (5) that the longest catena of biblical passages in the Pauline corpus is to be found in 3:10-18, which may be understood as a collection of OT texts that was originally brought together within Judaism and/or Jewish Christianity and used here by Paul in support of his thesis that "Jews and Gentiles alike are all under sin" (3:9; cf. 3:19, 23); and (6) that Abraham "our forefather" (τὸν προπάτορα ἡμῶν), who was extolled not only by Jews and Jewish Christians but also by Gentile Christians who looked to the Jerusalem church for guidance in their doctrine and practice, is used by Paul in 4:1-24 as the illustration of the type of response desired from his addressees. Further, what needs also to be taken into account are (1) that the two key terms of the thesis statements of 1:17 and 3:21-23, that is, "righteousness" (δικαιοσύνη) and "faith" (πίστις; πιστεύειν), dominate the discussion throughout this section; (2) that Paul's statements in 1:16–4:25 are replete with explicit OT quotations, with about eighteen of them appearing in eight or nine places throughout this section; (3) that Paul seems to draw into his argument in 2:1–3:20 a number of Jewish religious aphorisms and some Jewish Christian catechetical materials; and (4) that what appears in 3:24-26 and 4:25 may very well be drawn from certain early Christian confessional portions, the first (in 3:24-26) in support of the thesis statement of 3:21-23 and the second (in 4:25) as an appropriate christological conclusion to all that Paul has written in 1:16–4:25.

Analyzing this first section of the body middle of Romans in terms of its micro-structure, a number of other points can be made as well. It is evident, whether on an epistolary or a rhetorical basis, that the vocative "O man" of 2:1 signals the start of some new section (or subsection) in the argument and that the verb of saying "What then shall we say?" of 4:1 begins another. And on a strictly rhetorical basis it can be postulated: (1) that the *apostrophe* of 2:1 ("You, therefore, have no excuse, you who pass judgment on someone else," etc.) and the *apostrophe* of 2:17-29 ("Now you, if you call yourself a Jew; if you rely on the law and brag about your relationship with God," etc.) function to mark off the beginning of some further phases or subsections in the presentation; (2) that the *diatribe* pattern of dialogue in 2:1-5 and 2:17-29 (possibly also 3:1-8/9 and 3:27–4:2), which may also reflect a type of rhetoric labeled *prosopopoeia*, suggests that all of the material in 2:1–3:20 should be somehow drawn together; and (3) that 3:4-8 may, to some extent, reflect certain chiastic features (in all likelihood, less so 2:14-27).

With respect to structure, therefore, this first section of the body middle of Romans in its main movements should probably be understood as follows:

Part I (1:16–3:20)

1. A thesis statement on righteousness and faith (1:16-17)
2. God's wrath against humanity's godlessness and wickedness (1:18-32)
3. God's judgment expressed impartially against all who sin (2:1-16)
4. Denunciations of Jewish failures to keep the Mosaic law (2:17-29)
5. The situation of the Jews before God (3:1-20)

Part II (3:21–4:25)

6. The thesis statement repeated, expanded, supported, and elucidated (3:21-31)
7. The example of Abraham regarding righteousness and faith (4:1-24)
8. A concluding early Christian confessional statement (4:25).

2. The Argument of the First Part of the Section

Tracing out Paul's argument in the first part of this first section of the letter's body middle, that is, in 1:16–3:20, has been notoriously difficult for every commentator. A number of perplexing issues arise in any critical reading of 1:16–3:20. These have to do chiefly with (1) the identification of those who are being talked about or addressed, particularly in 2:1–3:20; (2) the evaluation of various literary and rhetorical structures that seem to be incorporated by Paul throughout this portion of material; and (3) the interpretation of what Paul says about Gentiles and Jews in chapter 2 vis-à-vis what he says about humanity generally and Jews in particular in the rest of Romans and his other letters.[13]

All of these matters must be dealt with exegetically and more extensively later in a forthcoming commentary proper. Suffice it here to say that the material of 1:16–3:20 appears to be exceedingly Jewish — not only with regard to its subject matter and structures, but also with respect to how and what is being argued. In fact, as George Carras has observed with regard to chapter 2, the entire passage reflects an "inner Jewish debate" and "is best understood as a diatribe whereby two Jewish attitudes on the nature of Jewish religion are being debated."[14] The thesis statement of 1:16, "both for the Jew first and for the Gentile," alerts readers to expect that what will follow will deal with relationships between Jews and Gentiles before God. And the type of argumentation that appears throughout all of this first section of the

13. See "Some Important Issues" above, pp. 355-57.
14. G. P. Carras, "Romans 2,1-29: A Dialogue on Jewish Ideals," 185 and 206.

body middle of the letter — first in 1:16–3:20 in depicting God's impartiality in his judgment of all people, both Gentiles and Jews; then in 3:21–4:25 in proclaiming God's impartiality in bestowing his righteousness on all people, whether Jews or Gentiles — suggests that Paul is writing to his Christian addressees at Rome, whether Jews or Gentiles ethnically, in terms they would understand, attempting to build on the theological foundations that they had received from the Mother Church at Jerusalem.

So here in 1:16–3:20, I propose, Paul begins his argument in Romans by agreeing with both Judaism generally and Jewish believers in Jesus in particular about (1) the impartiality of divine judgment (2:11-12), (2) Jews and Gentiles being alike under sin (3:9-19, 23), and (3) no one being able to be declared righteous by observing the law (3:20). Further, I suggest that in arguing these points Paul used what he considered to have been rather standard Jewish and Jewish Christian sources and arguments, believing that such materials were used in similar ways among his addressees. What is set out in 1:16–3:20, therefore, should be understood as material that Paul believed he held in common with his addressees and that he used in preparation for what he will present later in his letter.

3. The Argument of the Second Part of the Section

Since at least the time of the Protestant Reformation, the second part of this first section of the letter's body middle, that is, 3:21–4:25, has been seen by most interpreters to contain the central thrust or focus of Paul's teaching in Romans. Reading Romans as a compendium of Christian theology, ignoring Paul's own religious background, discounting his use of literary sources, and caricaturing the Judaism of the apostle's day as "a religion of works righteousness," Christians have felt fairly secure in understanding 3:21–4:25 as containing the central thrust or focus of what Paul writes in Romans. So the major themes of the letter have often been seen as (1) a polemic against humanity's godlessness and wickedness (i.e., in 1:18–2:16, or perhaps only 1:18-32), (2) a polemic against Jewish failures to keep the Mosaic law and against Jewish legalism (i.e., in 2:17–3:20, or perhaps 2:1–3:20), and (3) the proclamation of righteousness by faith alone (i.e., in 3:21–4:25, or perhaps 3:21–5:11).

Quite a revolution, however, has taken place among Christian scholars during the past few decades with regard to an understanding of mainline Judaism in Paul's day and that of the early tannaitic rabbis whose teachings are codified in the Talmud (see Chapter IX, section 5, "'The New Perspective' on Palestinian Judaism and Paul"). No longer can the Judaism of Paul's day be simply written off as a legalistic religion of "works righteousness." Interpreters of Paul have today been alerted to the facts (1) that there is much in the apostle's writings that he took over from Judaism, though with all of his earlier thought and piety "rebaptized" into his Christian experience, and (2) that the basic structures of his Jewish thought and the basic ethos of his Jewish piety continued to play a large part in his life as a follower of Jesus, the Christ, who is Israel's Messiah and humanity's Lord. Further, much of what he writes in 3:21–4:25 about "righteousness," "justification," "redemption," "propitiation/expiation/sacrifice of atonement," and "faith" rests solidly on OT foundations — and much of what he affirms with respect to these matters was also voiced by Jewish and Jewish Christian teachers of his day. Likewise, many scholars have shown that at least a portion of some early Christian confessional material is quoted by Paul in 3:24-26, with such early Christian confessional material also used by him in 4:25.

But however we evaluate the specific details regarding Paul's use of Jewish theological themes and early Christian confessions — or, for that matter, his use of Jewish aphorisms and/or Christian confessions elsewhere in his letters — the suggestion seems irresistible that what Paul writes in both parts of 1:16–4:25, that is, in the more negative portion of 1:18–3:20 and the distinctly positive portion of 3:21–4:25, was part and parcel of the Christian faith that he shared with his addressees at Rome. Further, it may be claimed that what he writes to them regarding "righteousness" and "faith" was not only based on the basic convictions of the earliest Jewish and Gentile believers in Jesus, as expressed in their confessional materials, but also on the foundational thought of the OT, which formed the basis for what is today called "Early Judaism" or "Formative Judaism" during Paul's day. Thus I propose that Paul begins his letter to the Christians at Rome in quite a traditional manner, not only praising them for their faith in Christ (as in 1:8 of the "thanksgiving") but also using materials and arguments that both they and he held in common (as in 1:3-4 of the "salutation" and throughout this first section of his letter's body middle).

A parallel can be drawn between Paul's argument in Galatians and what he does here in Romans. For in the first part of the *propositio* of Gal 2:15-21, Paul argues, on the basis of what he believes to be common ground with his addressees, that all true believers in Jesus — that is, particularly Jewish believers, but also, by extension, Gentile believers who have been influenced by Jewish thought in some way — know that a person is not justified by "works of the law" (ἐξ ἔργων νόμου), but rather, (1) on the basis of what Christ has effected (διὰ/ἐκ πίστεως Ἰησοῦ Χριστοῦ, which I have argued, along with others, should be taken as a subjective genitive grammatical construction and so be understood as "by the faithfulness [or 'faith'] of Jesus Christ"), and (2) because of one's response of faith (or trust) in him and what he has done (ἐπιστεύσαμεν εἰς Χριστὸν Ἰησοῦν).[15] So it may be postulated that Paul does something similar here in writing to believers in Jesus at Rome: first setting out in the two parts of 1:16–4:25 what he believed he held in common with his addressees, before then going on in 5–8 to speak of matters that pertain to the distinctive nature of the gospel message that he proclaims in his evangelistic outreach to Gentiles in the Greco-Roman world (cf. his references to "my gospel" in 2:16 and 16:25).

4. Conclusions

In this first section of his protreptic type of message of instruction and exhortation, therefore, Paul begins by enunciating in 1:16-17 the basic tenets of the Christian gospel, which he believed that both he and his addressees — though they might have had their differences with respect to other matters and their respective emphases — basically agreed on: (1) that the gospel "is the power of God for the salvation of everyone who believes"; (2) that this gospel message is "both for the Jew first and for the Gentile"; (3) that "in the gospel a righteousness of [or 'from'] God (δικαιοσύνη θεοῦ) is revealed (ἀποκαλύπτεται)"; (4) that this righteousness is ἐκ πίστεως εἰς πίστιν (lit.: "out of faith unto faith"), that is, is "based on divine faithfulness unto a human response of faith"; and (5) that this message of faith is in line with the express teaching of the OT. All of these rather compact statements must be unpacked and dealt with more extensively in a forthcoming commentary proper. Suffice it here to note that after the thesis statement of 1:16-17, Paul goes on in the remainder of this first section (1) to lay out by means of a Jewish and Jewish Christian manner of argumentation what he and his addressees held in common regarding the sinfulness of all people, whether Gentiles or Jews, and the impartiality of God in judging all people, both Jews and Gentiles (1:18–3:20), (2) to repeat and expand on the thesis statement that heads this section of material (3:21-23), (3) to cite in support of that expanded thesis statement a portion of early Christian confessional material (allusively in chapter 2; expressly in 3:24-26), (4) to elucidate further certain primary matters that he has spoken about in his denunciations of 2:17–3:20, his expanded thesis statement of 3:21-23, and the early Christian confessional material that he quotes in 3:24-26 in support of that thesis (3:27-31), (5) to il-

15. Cf. R. N. Longenecker, *Galatians,* WBC (Dallas: Word, 1990), 80-96.

lustrate all that he has said about "righteousness" and "faith" by the example of Abraham, the prime exemplar of faith for both Jews and Christians (4:1-24), and (6) to close off this section with an early Christian confessional statement (4:25).

Much of what Paul says positively in the latter portion of this first section of the body middle of Romans can be epitomized by statements that appear in the early Christian confessional materials that he quotes in 3:24-26 — that is, (1) by the three great forensic soteriological terms in verses 24-25a: the participle δικαιούμενοι ("being justified"), the noun ἀπολύτρωσις ("redemption"), and the noun ἱλαστήριον ("propitiation," "expiation," or "sacrifice of atonement"); (2) by the emphasis in 3:25b-26a on God's δικαιοσύνη (which term incorporates nuances of both "righteousness" and "justice," with the latter evidently understood by Paul as being more to the fore); (3) by the characterization of God in 3:26b as both δίκαιον ("just") and δικαιοῦντα ("the One who justifies"), and (4) by the focus on Jesus in 3:26c as the basis for and/or object of the believer's faith. All of these motifs are distinctly Jewish Christian motifs, which Paul lauds in the latter portion of this first section of the letter's body middle and builds on thereafter in what he writes in the sections to follow.

Section II: Peace, Reconciliation, and Life "in Christ" (5–8)

In the second section of the body middle of Romans, that is, 5–8, Paul's presentation is entirely positive — as was always the second section of a "protreptic word ('speech' or 'message') of exhortation" (λόγος προτρεπτικός) in antiquity. Paul's purpose in this section, as I have proposed above, was to set out as his "spiritual gift" (1:11) for the Christians at Rome what he had been proclaiming as the Christian gospel to Gentiles in his Gentile mission — that is, "my gospel" as he calls it in 2:16 and 16:25. It is a section that moves beyond the motifs of "justification," "redemption," and "sacrifice of atonement" (or "propitiation" or "expiation") of the first section to speak of matters regarding "peace" and "reconciliation" with God, relationships "in Adam" and "in Christ," and being "in Christ" and "in the Spirit." And it closes in 8:31-39 with statements drawn from early Christian confessional materials, as did also the first section at 4:25.

The relation of this second section to the first section has been a perennial problem for interpreters. Recognizing that what Paul sets out in this second section is something of an advance over what was presented in the first, one common way of understanding that advance has been to view 1:16–4:25 as being about human sin and accountability in the first part and God's justification of the sinner in the second, whereas 5–8 deals with the believer's sanctification. Another way has been to view these two sections as setting forth somewhat parallel lines of thought, though with different emphases and differing modes of expression: the first, in 1:16–4:25, using judicial and forensic language; the second, in 5–8, using language more relational, personal, and participatory in nature. The issues are complex, but they call for some evaluation here (with more exegetical and extensive treatments to follow in a forthcoming commentary proper).

1. The Structure of the Section

There are about a dozen or so expressions that have often been identified as epistolary conventions in this second section of the body middle of Romans. These include (1) the vocative ἀδελφοί, "brothers and sisters" (7:1, 4; 8:12); (2) verbs of saying, as in τί οὖν ἐροῦμεν, "what then shall we say?" (6:1, 15; 7:7; 8:31), or of speaking, as in γινώσκουσιν γὰρ νόμου λαλῶ, "for I am speaking to those who know the law" (7:1); (3) various disclosure formulas using the verbs ἀγνοεῖτε, "you know" (6:3; 7:1), οἴδατε, "you know" (6:16), or οἴδαμεν, "we know" (7:14; 8:22, 28); and (4) the confidence formula πέπεισμαι γὰρ ὅτι, "for I am convinced that" (8:38). Most of these expressions, however, are probably to be related more to rhetorical modes of persuasion that were then in vogue than to epistolary conventions then current, and so to be seen as functioning simply to introduce a diatribal dialogue, a rhetorical question, or the citation of a biblical passage. Only the complex of expressions at the beginning of 7:1, as well as the resumptive address of 7:4 — that is, the disclosure formula ἀγνοεῖτε ("you know"), the vocative ἀδελφοί ("brothers and sisters"), and the verb of speaking in the statement γινώσκουσιν γὰρ νόμου λαλῶ ("for I am speaking to those who know the law") of 7:1, together with the possessive vocative ἀδελφοί μου ("my brothers and sisters") of 7:4 — can with reasonable certainty be identified as strictly epistolary phenomena. Nonetheless, however they are understood, it needs always to be recognized that these expressions frequently appear at breaks or turning points in the argument of the letter, and so serve to signal some type of transition of thought — either from one aspect of the argument to another aspect within the same discussion or from one major discussion to another major discussion.

More important, however, are the rhetorical conventions that are reflected in this first section of the letter's body middle, which features serve to identify and mark off the various movements in the apostle's argument. Among the more obvious examples of these rhetorical phenomena, as noted earlier (cf. Chapter VI, the section entitled "Rhetorical Analysis of Romans"), are the following:

1. *Inclusio* (i.e., similar statements, phrases, or clauses placed at the beginning and end of a relatively short unit of text that serve to frame the material presented). The repeated refrain "through our Lord Jesus Christ" (διὰ τοῦ κυρίου ἡμῶν Ἰησοῦ Χριστοῦ) that appears in 5:1, 11, 21, and 7:25, together with its synonymous expression "by our Lord Jesus Christ" in 6:23 and 8:39 (using the equivalent construction of the preposition ἐν followed by the dative), not only frames the entire section at the beginning of 5:1 and the end of 8:39 (as will be noted again below in dealing with oral conventions) but also nicely concludes four of the principal units of material within that section at 5:11; 5:21; 6:23; and 7:25.

2. *Synkrisis* (i.e., the comparison of comparable persons, objects, or things, with deficiencies and superiorities highlighted). The prominent example of *synkrisis* in Romans is in 5:12-21, where Paul sets out in striking fashion what Christ has effected through his obedience vis-à-vis what Adam brought about because of his disobedience.

3. *Enthymeme* (i.e., an imperfect or abbreviated syllogism, whose premises may involve matters of character [*ethos*], emotion [*pathos*], or reason [*logos*] but whose conclusion must be supplied by the audience or addressees). This rhetorical convention is undoubtedly involved in the questions of 6:1 ("Shall we go on sinning so that grace may increase?"), 6:2 ("How can we [who died to sin] still live in it?"), 6:15 ("Shall we sin because we are not under the law but under grace?"), and 7:7 ("Is the law sin?") — with the three questions of 6:1; 6:15; and 7:7 each highlighting a main part of the presentation and that of 6:2 amplifying the first question of 6:1.

4. *Paradeigma* (i.e., a story that provides a pattern or example to be either imitated or avoided, or an argument that is based on the use of an example, whether positive or negative). The story of sin, frustration, and inability recounted in 7:7-25, whether the "I" (ἐγώ) of the narrative is to be understood in personal terms (i.e., referring to Paul's own experience, whether past or present) or in gnomic terms (i.e., referring to the experience of humanity generally), should probably be understood rhetorically in this light.

Of significance, as well, are the oral conventions of the ancient world that seem to be present in this second section. Among the oral phenomena most discernible, as noted earlier (cf. Chapter VI, the section entitled "Oral Patterning in Romans"), are the following:

1. *Acoustical orientation* (i.e., the repetition of words and phrases that sound alike, which evidently was used as an aid to understanding and remembering what was said). A prominent example of acoustical orientation appears in 5:12-21 with the use of a series of nouns that end with the Greek letters μα: τὸ παράπτωμα ("the transgression") of Adam (vv. 15, 16, 18, and 20); τὸ χάρισμα ("the grace") effected by Jesus Christ (vv. 15 and 16); κρίμα ("depravity") brought about by Adam's sin (v. 16); κατάκριμα ("divine judgment") on sin (vv. 16 and 18); τὸ δώρημα ("the divine gift") that brought justification (v. 16; also implied in v. 15); and τὸ δικαίωμα (literally, "the righteous deed"; here used equivalently to δικαίωσις, "justification," and δικαιοσύνη, "righteousness") that leads to "life eternal" (v. 16; cf. v. 21). On a somewhat smaller scale, it needs also to be noted that each of the four clauses of 5:6-8, which passage seems to be inserted as parenthetical material into the larger section of 5:1-11, ends with a form of the verb "he [Christ] died": ἀπέθανεν . . . ἀποθανεῖται . . . ἀποθανεῖν . . . ἀπέθανεν. Such acoustical features suggest that these portions in which they are found, that is, most prominently 5:12-21 but also perhaps 5:6-8, probably (1) originated in the context of Paul's oral preaching during the course of his Gentile mission, and (2) should be viewed as having been carried over into his letter to Christians at Rome, whether consciously or unconsciously, with these particular elements of their original orality still intact.

2. *Framing statements, sentences, phrases, and/or words* (i.e., similar linguistic phenomena, whether statements, sentences, phrases, or words, that appear at the beginning and end of a relatively short unit of text and serve to frame the material presented). There are similar themes and parallel features in 5:1-11 and 8:31-39, and so many have viewed these portions as representing what ancient rhetoricians have called an *inclusio* — thereby framing what has every appearance of being a distinctive unit of material from chapters 5–8. Likewise, as noted above, throughout these four chapters there appears the repeated refrain "through [or 'by'] our Lord Jesus Christ," with only slight variations in the preposition used (διά or ἐν) and the phrase that follows the preposition (as governed by the particular preposition). This refrain appears not only at the beginning and end of the entire section at 5:1 and 8:39, thereby functioning as an *inclusio* for all of the material included within these four chapters, but also at the end of four of the principal units of material within the section, that is, at 5:11; 5:21; 6:23; and 7:25.

3. *Formulaic confessional materials* (i.e., early Christian confessional portions that were, presumably, originally oral, and that appear to have been incorporated, either whole or in part, by the authors of the NT at strategic

places in their writings). As noted above in speaking about matters pertaining to acoustical orientation, the four clauses of 5:6-8 seem to reflect early Christian confessional materials. Likewise, many of the expressions used within the lyrical and almost defiant affirmations of 8:33-39 may also be seen as having been drawn from early Christian confessional materials[16] — thereby closing off in dramatic fashion this second section of the letter's body middle, as the apostle seems to have done in closing off the first section at 4:25 (and as he will do again in closing off the third section at 11:33-36).

It is also important to observe in any discussion of the structure of this second section that the word chain shifts from the dominance in 1:16–4:25 of the nouns δικαιοσύνη ("righteousness") and πίστις ("faith"), together with the verb πιστεύειν ("to believe"), to the dominance in 5–8 of the noun ζωή ("life") and various participial forms of the verb ζάω ("living"), in contradistinction to the nouns ἁμαρτία ("sin") and θάνατος ("death") — though with δικαιοσύνη also appearing in some eight verses in this second section (see 5:17, 21; 6:13, 16, 18, 19, 20; 8:10). Further, the use of biblical quotations shifts from about eighteen citations of Scripture in eight or nine places in 1:16–4:25 to only two biblical quotations in 5–8, with the OT being used in this second section only somewhat tangentially — once in 7:7, citing in illustrative fashion the tenth commandment, "Do not covet," from Exod 20:17 and Deut 5:21; and once in 8:36, in what appears to be an early Christian confessional portion that makes use of Ps 44:22.[17] In fact, to anticipate our discussions of these matters later, this use (or non-use) of Scripture in 5–8 is not only quite different from what can be observed regarding the use of Scripture in 1:16–4:25 (where, as noted above, there are about eighteen OT quotations in eight or nine places), but is also different from the use of Scripture in 9–11 (where there are some thirty OT quotations in twenty-five or twenty-six places) and in 12:1–15:13 (where there appear an additional ten OT quotations).

Based on the rhetorical and oral conventions that appear throughout this second section of the body middle of Romans — as well as certain epistolary features that can be identified and certain patterns with respect to word chains and the use of Scripture that can be discerned — the following conclusions, it seems, can legitimately be made: (1) that 5–8 forms a discrete

---

16. Cf. R. N. Longenecker, *New Wine into Fresh Wineskins*, 19.

17. Cf. R. N. Longenecker, "Prolegomena to Paul's Use of Scripture in Romans," esp. 146-47, 158-67; see also the chapter "Paul and the Old Testament," in *idem, Biblical Exegesis in the Apostolic Period*, 2nd ed. (1999), 88-116.

unit of material in the letter to the Romans; (2) that this second section of the letter's body middle differs in many respects from the first section preceding it and the two sections that follow it; and (3) that sub-units of material within this second section can be fairly easily determined by the appearance of such rhetorical and oral conventions as framing or *inclusio* techniques, the use of vocatives, the use of verbs of saying, various disclosure formulas, and the use of rhetorical questions. Further, it can be argued that while most of 5–8 reflects a number of oral and rhetorical conventions, which suggests that at least the bulk of its material originated in an oral environment of proclamation, 7:1-6 begins in a more epistolary fashion, which suggests that this portion may have been inserted as a further illustration into what now appears as 5–8 at the time when this second section was included within the letter sent to the Christians at Rome. It may be argued that 5:6-8 is also a later parenthetical insertion into the paragraph represented by 5:1-11 (as noted above). Yet the acoustical use of the verb "he [Christ] died" in the four clauses seems to locate this portion of material in Paul's oral preaching, and so not to suggest a later epistolary inclusion.

The structure of this second section of the body middle of Romans, therefore, should probably be understood with respect to its main divisions as follows:

1. A transitional and thesis passage on "peace" and "reconciliation" (5:1-11)
2. The foundational story about what Jesus Christ effected vis-à-vis what Adam had brought about (5:12-21)
3. Three questions and an interjected illustration regarding the implications of Christ's work (6:1–7:13):

    Question 1: "Should we go on sinning so that grace may increase?" (6:1-14)

    Question 2: "Should we sin because we are not under the law but under grace?" (6:15-23)

    An interjected illustration on the extent of the authority of the Mosaic law and a statement about a Christian's freedom from the law (7:1-6); and,

    Question 3: "Is the law sin?" (7:7-13)
4. A soliloquy on the tragic plight of people who attempt to live their lives "under their own steam" (7:14-25)
5. "No condemnation" and "life" for those who are "in Christ Jesus" and therefore "in the Spirit" (8:1-17)

6. Life "in the Spirit": both personal and universal; both present and future — a life of both suffering and glory (8:18-30)
7. A triumphal affirmation of God's love in Christ, with early Christian confessional materials incorporated (8:31-39).

2. The Argument of the Section

In this second section of the body middle of Romans, that is, in 5–8, Paul shares with his addressees at Rome what he had been proclaiming as the Christian gospel in his Gentile mission — that is, his contextualization of the Christian message in a manner that resonated with pagan Gentiles who had no preparation for that message by Jewish or Jewish Christian teaching, and so did not think in Jewish categories. It was, as his missionary experience had certainly demonstrated, a way of proclaiming the "good news" that had proven to be highly significant and meaningful for Gentiles and that had resulted by God's Spirit in many Gentiles turning from paganism to personal faith in Jesus Christ.

To Jewish Christians, the foundational story of Israel's Exodus from Egypt vis-à-vis God's New Exodus through Jesus of Nazareth, together with the Jewish soteriological themes of justification, redemption, and expiation, were vitally important. For Paul in his missionary outreach to Gentiles, however, such a foundational story as the Exodus and such themes as justification, redemption, and expiation — while highly significant in a Jewish context — were, it seems, not always meaningful to Gentiles who had no Jewish or Jewish Christian background. So in proclaiming the gospel to Gentiles, Paul (1) spoke of "peace" and "reconciliation" with God "through our Lord Jesus Christ" (5:1-11), (2) told the universal, foundational story of how sin, death, and condemnation entered the world by "one man," but how grace, life, and righteousness have been brought about "through Jesus Christ our Lord" (5:12-21), (3) spelled out relationships of sin, death, and the law, on the one hand, and grace, life, and righteousness, on the other (6:1–7:13), (4) expressed the plight of all people in their attempts to live by their own insights and strength by the use of a familiar tragic soliloquy drawn from Greek literature and humanity's common experience (7:14-25), (5) highlighted the new relationships that come about when one is "in Christ" and "in the Spirit" (8:1-30), and (6) closed with a triumphal declaration of God's love and care for his own "in Christ Jesus our Lord" (8:31-39). And this type of contextualization, with many of these same features and themes, appears also in

other of his letters where Gentile believers in Jesus are addressed directly —
as, for example, in 2 Cor 5:11-21 and Eph 2.

4. Conclusions

Contrary to what has traditionally been argued, it is in the second section of
the body middle of Romans, that is, in 5–8, that, we believe, the central theological thrust of what Paul writes in Romans is to be found (see also our later
discussion in this chapter of the general exhortations of chapters 12 and 13:8-
14, which we argue represent the ethical corollary of the apostle's theological
proclamation in his Gentile mission). This second section of the letter's body
middle contains the didactic portion of Paul's "spiritual gift" that he says in
1:11 he wants to give Christians at Rome and that in 2:16 and 16:25 he calls
"my gospel." This is not to discredit what he writes in 1:16–4:25, for that is
what he held in common with his addressees. Indeed, it was on the basis of
the truths of 1:16–4:25 that both he and they originally became believers in
Jesus. In fact, it may even be postulated that Paul, on occasion, proclaimed
that message himself — particularly when addressing Jews or those who had
been influenced by Jewish or Jewish Christian thought for the better (as had
the Christians at Rome), or when addressing those who had been influenced
by Jewish or Jewish Christian thought for the worse (as had the Christians at
Galatia). But what he wanted Christians at Rome to know was the gospel
message as he had contextualized it in his preaching to purely Gentile audiences. For the Christians at Rome, too, were dominantly Gentiles ethnically,
and so he saw them as included within the orbit of his Gentile mission and
desired to strengthen them by means of his form of Christian proclamation.
Further, he wanted them to become partners with him as the sending church
in a further missionary outreach to Gentiles in the western regions of the
Roman empire, just as the church at Antioch of Syria had supported him as
the sending church to the eastern regions.

When contextualized to Gentiles, the main features of Paul's message
as set out in this second section of the body middle of Romans are as follows:

1. the proclamation of "peace" and "reconciliation" with God "through
   our Lord Jesus Christ," which is announced in the thesis paragraph of
   5:1-11;
2. the universal, foundational story of how sin, death, and condemnation
   entered the world by "one man," but how grace, life, and righteousness
   have been brought about "through Jesus Christ our Lord" in 5:12-21;

3. relations between sin, death, and the law, on the one hand, and grace, life, and righteousness, on the other, through the use of three rhetorical questions in 6:1-14; 6:15-23; and 7:7-13 — with an interjected illustration regarding the authority of the Mosaic law and a statement about a Christian's freedom from it in 7:1-6;

4. the coming to voice of the tragic soliloquy of all people in their attempts to live by their own insights and strength in 7:14-25, which consciousness of human futility is not only reflected in the Jewish Scriptures but has been known by all people of perception and has often come to expression at various places in the literature of the Greco-Roman world — with an anticipation of God's solution interjected at 7:25a: "Thanks be to God, [it is] through Jesus Christ our Lord";

5. the highlighting of new relationships that come about when a person is "in Christ" and "in the Spirit" in 8:1-30, with the impact of those new relationships being spelled out for both the present and the future *and* for both renewed people and "the whole creation"; and,

6. a triumphal declaration, which verges on being a defiant assertion, of God's love and care for his own "in Christ Jesus our Lord" in 8:31-39, with that final portion probably incorporating a number of early Christian confessional statements.

It is in this second section of the body middle of Paul's letter to the Christians at Rome that the three basic features of classical rhetoric come most fully to expression: *logos* (content or argument), *ethos* (the personal character of the speaker or writer), and *pathos* (the power to stir the emotions). Likewise, it is in this section that the themes often considered to be most distinctly Pauline are most prevalent — that is, (1) "peace" and "reconciliation" with God,[18] and (2) the believer being "in Christ" and "in the Spirit."[19] And it is in chapter 8 of Romans, using John A. T. Robinson's analogy of "a journey by canal across an isthmus" with its "series of locks" rising to and then falling away from "a central ridge," that "the heights of the epistle are reached" and there occurs "a sustained climax which takes the argument across the watershed."[20]

---

18. Cf. S. Kim, *Origin of Paul's Gospel* (1981; 2nd. ed. 1984); *idem,* "God Reconciled His Enemy to Himself," 102-24; *idem,* "2 Cor. 5:11-21 and the Origin of Paul's Concept of 'Reconciliation,'" 360-84.

19. Cf. R. N. Longenecker, "Liberty in Christ," in *Paul, Apostle of Liberty,* 156-80.

20. J. A. T. Robinson, *Wrestling with Romans,* 9.

Section III: The Christian Gospel vis-à-vis God's Promises to Israel (9–11)

The third section of the body middle of Romans, that is, 9–11, has often been viewed as a self-contained and discrete section of material. But though it is often accepted as a unified and distinguishable body of material, questions have repeatedly been asked regarding how this section is related to the two earlier theological sections and the following exhortation section. Some have theorized that it must have originally been an independent unit of material that was associated, in some manner, with the letter to the Romans in an early "copy book" of one of Paul's amanuenses — either because it appeared next to Romans in that secretarial copy book or because it exhibited similar handwriting, or both — and that it was later inserted by some undiscerning scribe into Romans itself.[21] Others have thought of it as an interpolation by Paul of a treatise he had written at some time earlier, but which in its present placement in Romans has no necessary connection with what the apostle wrote elsewhere in the letter.[22] Robin Scroggs, for example, argued that chapters 9–11, when joined with chapters 1–4, should most likely be viewed as having been at one time the latter part of an early Pauline sermon to a Jewish audience, which, for some reason, was later coupled with material that now appears as chapters 5–8 and then circulated among the various Christian communities as Paul's letter to the Romans.[23] Most interpreters, however, from patristic times to the present, have understood 9–11 as an integral part of Paul's letter to the Christians at Rome. But opinions have varied as to how its material should be understood and how what it presents is related to what has gone before and to what follows in the letter.

There have, of course, been a great many exegetical and theological treatments of 9–11. The most common ways of interpreting these three chapters today are in terms of (1) a "theological" understanding, which highlights God's sovereign grace in the salvation of people (as did many of the early Church Fathers and Augustine in his earliest comments on chapters 5–9 in the *Expositio*) coupled with an emphasis on God's predestination of "the elect" (as in Augustine's later writings and as developed by John Calvin); (2) a "salvation history" understanding, which views these chapters as Paul's un-

---

21. *A la* A. Deissmann's "copy book" thesis; see his *Light from the Ancient East*, 235-36; cf. 206, note 1.

22. So, e.g., C. H. Dodd, *Romans*, 148; J. A. T. Robinson, *Wrestling with Romans*, 108-10.

23. R. Scroggs, "Paul as Rhetorician," 271-98.

derstanding of the course of redemptive history *vis-à-vis* that of Judaism or Jewish Christianity (as proposed by Oscar Cullmann and Johannes Munck, though in differing fashion); (3) a "history of religions" or "comparative religions" understanding, which takes these chapters as proclaiming that the existence of both Judaism and Christianity is according to God's will and under his approval (as argued, for example, by Krister Stendahl); and (4) an "apologetic" understanding, which sees these chapters as Paul's vindication of God's actions (i.e., a "theodicy") in redeeming some people and condemning others (as is sometimes argued separately, but is usually worked into one or more of the other three views above).

But though there are "many commentaries, monographs and articles" on the interpretation of Romans 9–11, as Nils Dahl has pointed out in observing the obvious, it is important to note, as Dahl goes on to say, that,

> In spite of the vastness of the literature, two aspects of these chapters have not received enough attention. Scholars rarely consider Paul seriously as an interpreter of Scripture. We still have no detailed investigation of Paul's use of the Old Testament in Romans 9–11, comparing it to other Christian and Jewish interpretations of the passages quoted, and examining their wording in textual tradition and in translations. The other aspect which scholars have neglected is a formal analysis of the composition and style of Romans 9–11.[24]

And it is with respect to these two neglected matters that I would like to speak in what follows — though, admittedly, not quite in the way that Dahl has argued or would have envisioned.

Paul's argument in 9–11, I propose, is best understood when it is approached in terms of a Jewish and/or Jewish Christian "remnant theology," which combines both a distinctive use of OT texts and a distinctive type of Jewish rhetoric (cf. Chapter VII, the section entitled "Remnant Theology and Rhetoric"). It is this thesis that will guide our discussion in what follows below (and that will be exegetically elaborated in a forthcoming commentary proper). Further, my thesis includes the suggestions: (1) that an argument based on remnant theology would have been understood and meaningful not only to Jewish believers in Jesus but also to Gentile Christians who looked to the Mother Church at Jerusalem for their theological, ecclesial, and ethical guidance; and (2) that because remnant theology is foreign to a western, Gentile mentality, Paul's argument in chapters 9–11 has

24. N. Dahl, "The Future of Israel," 138.

failed to resonate with most Christian interpreters, and so they have usually failed to appreciate the significance of this section in the apostle's letter — both as to why Paul incorporated it into his letter and as to what he wanted to teach his addressees by it.

1. The Structure of the Section

Occurrences of the usual epistolary formulas of antiquity are, by comparison with the extant Greco-Roman letters of the day and Paul's other letters, somewhat limited in this third section of the body middle of Romans. The section (1) opens with an attestation statement in 9:1, ἀλήθειαν λέγω ἐν Χριστῷ, οὐ ψεύδομαι ("I am speaking the truth in Christ, I am not lying"); (2) includes verbs of saying at 9:14 and 30, τί οὖν ἐροῦμεν ("What then shall we say?"), at 11:1 and 11, λέγω οὖν ("I say then"), and at 11:13, ὑμῖν δὲ λέγω τοῖς ἔθνεσιν ("Now, I am speaking to you Gentiles"); (3) invokes a disclosure formula at 11:2, οὐκ οἴδατε ἐν Ἠλίᾳ τί λέγει ἡ γραφή ("Do you not know what Scripture says about Elijah?"); (4) uses a vocative of address at 10:1 and 11:25, ἀδελφοί ("brothers and sisters"); and (5) closes, in conjunction with that final vocative, with another disclosure formula at 11:25, οὐ γὰρ θέλω ὑμᾶς ἀγνοεῖν, ἀδελφοί ("I do not want you to be ignorant, brothers and sisters").

There are a number of other verbs of saying and transitional formulas in this third section, but these seem to be more rhetorically related than epistolary in nature — that is, related more to Paul's use of diatribal dialogue (e.g., 9:19, 20; 11:19, 24) and the citation of biblical passages (e.g., 9:9, 12, 25; 10:6, 8, 11, 16, 18, 20, 21; 11:2, 4, 8, 9). Perhaps a few of the features cited above as epistolary conventions should be understood as being more rhetorical as well. Yet, however evaluated, it needs always to be recognized, especially with respect to those forms of expression that are more obviously epistolary, that such phenomena often appear at breaks or turning points in the argument of the letter, and so serve to signal some type of transition of thought.

Likewise, the oral and rhetorical conventions often used in the Greco-Roman world must be judged — by comparison with Paul's other letters generally, but particularly by comparing this section to the other sections of Romans — to be somewhat scarce in this third section of the letter's body middle. The clearest examples of ancient oral and rhetorical conventions reflected in this section seem to be the following:

1. the framing of the major portion of this material by 9:6-8 and 11:25-32 (which passages deal with God's promises to Israel and their fulfill-

ment), and so, by means of what has been called by classical rhetoricians an *inclusio,* designating the beginning (i.e., after the introduction of 9:1-5) and the end (i.e., before the conclusion of 11:33-36) of that material;

2. the use of such rhetorical questions as "What then shall we say?" at 9:14 and 30 (cf. also "Why not?" at 9:32) and "I ask then, Did God reject his people?" at 11:1 and 11, each of which serves, in some manner, to identify the start of a section or subsection of the presentation;

3. the diatribe that appears in 9:19-21 ("One of you will say to me, 'Why . . . ? But who are you, O man, to talk back to God?" etc.) and 11:17-24 ("the natural branches broken off," "the wild branches grafted in among the others," and the inability and danger for the latter to boast);

4. the use of metaphor in speaking of Jews and Gentiles as "the natural branches" and "engrafted wild branches" in 11:17-24;

5. the retention of what appears to be chiastic features in the biblical texts quoted in 10:19 (quoting Deut 32:21), 11:3 (quoting 1 Kgs 19:10), and 11:10 (quoting Ps 69:23);

6. the possible appearance of chiasmus in 10:9-10; 11:30-31; and 11:33-35, with some of these structures apparently drawn from early Christian confessional materials; and,

7. the probable use of early Christian confessional materials at 9:5b ("Who is God over all, forever praised!"), 10:9 ("Jesus is Lord"), and 11:33-36 ("O the depth of the riches and wisdom and knowledge of God! How unsearchable are his judgments and how inscrutable his ways! . . . For from him and through him and to him are all things. To him be the glory forever. Amen").

But though the appearance of the usual Greco-Roman epistolary, rhetorical, and oral features of composition may be rather limited in this section, they still provide the interpreter with some guidance as to how the basic structure of the material should be understood. So with respect to its main divisions, it may be argued that the third section of the body middle of Romans is to be viewed as follows:

1. an introduction in which Paul speaks of his desire for his people, of Israel's heritage, and of Israel's Messiah, with a closing "Amen" (9:1-5);

2. God's promises to "the remnant" of Israel, with a number of OT texts cited in support (9:6-29);

3. Israel's failure and the Gentiles blessed, with a number of OT texts cited in support (9:30–10:21);

4. the course of God's "salvation history," which includes not just the nation Israel but more particularly the remnant of Israel, a remnant of the Gentiles, and, finally, the salvation of "all Israel" (11:1-32);

5. a conclusion that expresses rhapsodic praise to God for his wisdom and knowledge, which material was probably drawn from early Christian confessional material that incorporated biblical expressions from Isa 40:13 and Job 41:11 (11:33-36).

2. The Remnant Rhetoric of the Section

More significant than the relatively few occurrences of Greco-Roman epistolary, rhetorical, and oral conventions, however, is Paul's use of a Jewish and Jewish Christian type of rhetoric in this third major section of the body middle of Romans that appears prominently throughout 9:6–11:32 — that is, a type of rhetoric that may be called "remnant rhetoric." It is a rhetoric (1) that stems from the "remnant theology" of the OT, (2) that was used by the early Pharisees, the Dead Sea covenanters, and other Jewish sectarian groups to justify their existence, (3) that appears in a number of apocryphal and apocalyptic writings of Second Temple Judaism, (4) that was prominent in the ministry of John the Baptist in calling Jews to repentance and baptizing them (cf. Mark 1:2-6, par.), as well as in proclaiming: "Do not think you can say to yourselves, 'We have Abraham as our father'" (Matt 3:9); (5) that was present in the ministry of Jesus in inviting people to follow him (cf. Mark 1:16-20, par.), referring to his followers as his "little flock" (Luke 12:32) and calling them "my sheep" (John 10:1-30); and (6) that became, it seems, a major motif in the self-consciousness of the earliest Jewish believers in Jesus.[25] Further, it may be postulated that remnant rhetoric was a type of rhetoric that the Christians at Rome — both Jewish and Gentile believers in Jesus —

---

25. For significant treatments of "remnant theology" and "remnant rhetoric" with respect to the religion of Israel, Second Temple Judaism, John the Baptist, Jesus, and early Jewish Christianity, see F. Kattenbusch, "Der Spruch über Petrus und die Kirche bei Matthäus" (1922); K. L. Schmidt, "Die Kirche des Urchristentums" (1927); G. Gloege, *Reich Gottes und Kirche im Neuen Testament* (1929), esp. 212-19 and 241-49; A. Oepke, "Der Herrnspruch über die Kirche" (1948); J. Jeremias, "Der Gedanke des 'Heiligen Restes' im Spätjudentum und in der Verkündigung Jesu" (1949); W. G. Kümmel, "Jesus und die Anfänge der Kirche" (1953); B. F. Meyer, "Jesus and the Remnant of Israel" (1965); G. F. Hasel, *The Remnant* (1972); and B. F. Meyer, *The Aims of Jesus* (1979), esp. 118-21, 197, 220-22, and 225-29.

would have understood and appreciated, rooted as they were in the theology of the Mother Church at Jerusalem.

Remnant rhetoric is explicitly highlighted by Paul in chapters 9–11 by his use of the following OT quotations and LXX expressions:

1. the quotation in 9:27 of Isa 10:22-23, which uses the articular and intensified form τὸ ὑπόλειμμα ("though the number of the Israelites should be like the sand by the sea, only 'the remnant' will be saved");
2. the quotation in 9:29 of Isa 1:9, which uses the noun σπέρμα (literally: "seed," "posterity," or "descendant") in the figurative sense of "a few survivors" ("if the Lord of Hosts had not left us 'a few survivors,' we would have become like Sodom and been made like Gomorrah"), thereby paralleling the meaning of the terms λεῖμμα and ὑπόλειμμα;
3. the use in 9:11 and 11:5, 7, 28 of ἐκλογή ("election," "selection," or "choosing"; passive: "that which is elected," "selected," or "chosen"); and,
4. the use in 11:5 of λεῖμμα ("remnant"), even bringing λεῖμμα and ἐκλογή together in this verse in a manner not represented elsewhere in the NT ("so, too, at this present time there is a 'remnant' that is 'chosen' by grace").

There has been considerable discussion over the past century regarding the concept of "remnant" in the OT (focusing on שְׁאָר, "rest," "residue," "survivor," "remnant," and its plural שְׁאֵרִית, "survivors" or "the remnant") and in the writings of Second Temple Judaism (focusing on λεῖμμα and its intensified form ὑπόλειμμα, "remnant," as well as on the passive form of ἐκλογή ("elected," "selected," or "chosen"). Amidst all of the debate, however, it is Gottlob Schrenk and Volkmar Herntrich who have most aptly, we believe, characterized the remnant rhetoric of the OT and Second Temple Judaism in their article on λεῖμμα, ὑπόλειμμα, and cognates in *TDNT* (4.194-214), from which the following eight points are here highlighted (for a development of these points, see our Chapter VII above, the section entitled "Remnant Theology and Rhetoric"):

1. The remnant is sovereignly established by God alone.
2. The remnant may be small, but envisioned also is its greatness.
3. The remnant is both a present and a future entity.
4. The remnant is commonly associated with Zion, the city of Jerusalem.
5. While God establishes the remnant, the other side of that establishment is a response of faith and faithfulness on the part of the remnant.

6. Not only is there envisioned a remnant of Israel, but also a remnant from among the Gentiles.

7. Diverse opinions regarding the gathering of the Gentiles — whether on a proselyte basis or a missionary basis — are expressed, with that having to do with a proselyte basis being most often expressed.

8. The final goal of God is not the gathering of the remnant; rather, it is the re-adoption and salvation of all Israel.

There is much in the remnant theology of the OT and Second Temple Judaism, as well as in the remnant rhetoric of early Jewish Christianity, that needs yet to be investigated and clarified.[26] Nonetheless, the recognition of remnant rhetoric within Second Temple Judaism and early Jewish Christianity is, we believe, highly significant for an appreciation of (1) what Paul is doing in this third section of the body middle of Romans, (2) how he builds his argument, and (3) how what he argues in this section relates to what has gone before and what follows in the letter.

3. The Argument of the Section

It is not too difficult to view the addressees of Paul's letter to Rome — for whom, as we have proposed, the theology, ecclesiology, and ethics of the Mother Church at Jerusalem were foundational for their Christian faith and determinative for their continued Christian understanding (see Chapter IV, "Addressees") — as basing their own consciousness and self-identity as believers in Jesus on some form of Jewish or Jewish Christian remnant theology. They might, in fact, have embraced all of the eight points enumerated above — including even point #4, which emphasizes the importance of Zion in God's redemptive program (thereby, perhaps, providing theological justification for their understanding of the centrality of the Mother Church at Jerusalem), and point #7, which speaks of the salvation of the Gentiles as based primarily on a proselyte model of evangelism (thereby, perhaps, raising doubts in their minds about the appropriateness of Paul's missionary model of outreach to the Gentiles).

Paul, however, while honoring the Christian church at Jerusalem and its leaders, could hardly have accepted the necessity for Christian faith of either the city of Jerusalem or a proselyte model of conversion — particularly

---

26. For a highly significant study of all these matters, see M. A. Elliott, *The Survivors of Israel* (2000).

with respect to the Christian faith of Gentile believers. In Gal 4:21-31 he spoke directly against venerating "the present city of Jerusalem" (ἡ νῦν Ἰερουσαλήμ of v. 25), insisting, rather, that it is only "the Jerusalem that is above" (ἡ ἄνω Ἰερουσαλήμ of v. 26) that is important. And the thrust of what he says in Gal 1:13–2:10 about his conversion to Christ and his meeting with the "pillar" apostles of Jerusalem, as well as what he intimates about his missionary activities in many of his other letters, is all to the point of establishing the legitimacy of his missionary model of outreach to the Gentile world (what might be called a "centrifugal" model), which was certainly not the proselyte model held by Jews and Jewish Christians (what might be called a "centripetal" model). Yet Paul would have been fully supportive of the other six points set out above in the characterization of remnant theology. And in this third and final section of his theological argument to the Christians at Rome, especially in 9:6–11:32, he contextualizes that remnant theology in a Christian manner — though without any reference to points #4 and #7 cited above, which he would have vigorously debated (as he did in an earlier letter to his Gentile converts in the province of Galatia, who had been disturbed in their Christian faith by the teachings of certain Jewish Christians from the church at Jerusalem regarding precisely these two matters, that is, the central importance of Jerusalem in the redemptive plan of God and the necessity of taking on the forms and practices of a Jewish proselyte).

Various statements made earlier in Romans can generally be related to the material of chapters 9–11, and so may lend some support to the relevancy of what Paul writes in these three chapters. In the salutation of 1:1-7, for example, (1) his reference in verse 2 to the gospel as "promised beforehand through his prophets in the Holy Scriptures" may be seen as demanding a further treatment of the relation of the gospel to the hope of Israel; (2) his characterization of his ministry in verse 5 as being "to call people from among all the Gentiles to the obedience that comes from faith" may be understood as setting up questions regarding the obedience and faith within Israel; and (3) his use of the substantive adjective κλητοί ("those called") in verses 6 and 7 may suggest the need to speak more fully about God's call and about those whom he has called and will call. Likewise, Paul's denunciations of self-congratulation and boasting in 1:18–3:20 (which may be labeled "a work of deconstruction") may find an intended contrastive parallel in 11:1-32, where God's redemptive activity in human history is portrayed as now including not only the salvation of the remnant of Israel but also the salvation of the remnant of Gentiles, and will finally include, as well, the salvation of "all Israel" (which may be entitled "a work of reconstruction"). Further, the chain of affirmations in 8:29-30 about those whom God "foreknew," "predestined," "called," "justified," and "glorified" — which commentators have often dubbed "the golden chain" of human salvation — may very well be seen as setting up nicely a further exposition on these topics in chapters 9–11.

Probably more to the point, however, is the designation in 8:33 of those who believe in Jesus, whether Jews or Gentiles, as "the chosen" or "the elect of God" (ἐκλεκτοί θεοῦ). That was the title reserved for Israelites in the OT (cf., e.g., 1 Chron 16:13; Ps 105:6, 43; Isa 65:9, 22). But in bringing to a climax the second section (i.e., 5–8) of the body middle of his letter — which section, we have argued, incorporates the central theological thrust of his message to Christians at Rome — Paul concludes by ascribing this highly significant characterization to all Christians, whatever their ethnicity: that they are all, whether ethnically Jews or Gentiles, God's "chosen" or "elect" ones.

The expression with reference to believers in Jesus may have been part of an early Christian confession that Paul used in his conclusion of 8:31-39. Or, perhaps, it was drawn from portions of various early Christian confessional materials. But however it came about, the truth of the expression was of major importance for Christians generally and evidently came to be highly significant for Paul as well. So from this linguistic springboard, which encapsulates the essence of all that he had been preaching to Gentiles in the pagan world, Paul inserted a further section, that is, 9–11, between the first two theological sections and the final hortatory section of his letter — thereby expanding by this addition the usual tripartite structure of an ancient protreptic message of instruction and exhortation. And thus in this third section he sets out a remnant understanding of the story of Israel, with the purpose of that remnant rhetoric being to explain relations between the Christian gospel and the hope of Israel.

In 9:1-5, which is the introduction to this third section, Paul narrates the religious high points of the story of the nation of Israel:

> Theirs is the adoption as God's children; theirs the divine glory, the covenants, the receiving of the law, the temple worship, and the promises. Theirs are the patriarchs; and from them, according to his human ancestry, comes the Messiah. (vv. 4-5)

In 9:6-29, however, he goes on to argue that God's promises to Israel were never meant for the whole of Israel nationally; rather, they always had in mind "the remnant" of Israel. Thus in the thesis statement of this portion of material Paul declares:

> It is not as though God's word had failed. For not all who are descended from Israel are truly regarded as Israelites. Nor because they are his descendants are they all Abraham's children. On the contrary, "It is through Isaac that your offspring will come" [Gen 21:12]. In other words, it is not the natural children who are God's children, but it is the children of promise who are regarded as Abraham's offspring. (9:6-8)

And in support of such a remnant understanding, he goes on to speak of: (1) God's promise to Sarah regarding her future son (Gen 18:10, 14), (2) the prophecy to Rebekah about the supremacy of Jacob over Esau (Gen 25:23; cf. Mal 1:2-3), (3) God's word to Moses about his sovereignty in expressing mercy (Exod 33:19), (4) the biblical statement about the hardening of Pharaoh (Exod 9:7), (5) the illustration of a potter making vessels for various uses (Isa 29:16; 45:9), (6) God's words to the prophet Hosea regarding his naming of his people as "my people," "my loved one," and "children of the living God" (Hos 2:23; 1:10), (7) Isaiah's explicit statement that "though the number of the Israelites should be like the sand by the sea, only 'the remnant' will be saved" (Isa 10:22-23), and (8) Isaiah's earlier recognition that "unless the Lord of Hosts had left us 'a few survivors' [σπέρμα; lit., "seed," "posterity," or "descendants"; fig., "a few survivors," which parallels the idea of "the remnant"], we would have become like Sodom and been made like Gomorrah" (Isa 1:9).

All this leads Paul in 9:30–10:21 to raise certain important questions about Israel's failure to receive God's promised righteousness and about the Gentiles having become recipients of God's saving grace. The thesis for this passage is set out in 9:30-33, which is headed by the rhetorical question "What then shall we say?" of verse 30 (cf. also the extended question "Why not?" of v. 32a) and concludes with the cryptic statement "they stumbled over 'the stumbling stone'" (i.e., in their refusal to accept Jesus as Messiah) and a quotation from Isaiah in support (conflating Isa 8:14 and 28:16). But of even greater importance for Paul's argument, it seems, is the fact that the quotation from Isaiah concludes with God's promise: "And whoever believes in him [i.e., in Jesus, Israel's Messiah] will never be put to shame" (quoting Isa 28:16c). Thus the thesis paragraph of 9:30-33 reads as follows:

> What then shall we say? That Gentiles, who did not pursue righteousness, have obtained it, a righteousness that is by faith; but Israel, who pursued a righteousness based on the law, has not attained it. Why not? Because they pursued it not by faith, but as if it were by works. They

stumbled over "the stumbling stone." As it is written: "See, I lay in Zion a stone that causes people to stumble and a rock that makes them fall, and whoever believes in him will never be put to shame."

Paul then goes on throughout the remainder of this passage to support that thesis by the quotation of a number of OT passages having to do with (1) the "doing of the law" for righteousness on the part of Jews (Lev 18:5), (2) the nearness of God's righteousness to everyone who will respond by faith (Deut 30:12-14; Ps 19:4), (3) Israel's lack of faith in response to God (Isa 53:1; Deut 32:21), (4) God's favor on the Gentiles (Isa 65:1), and yet (5) God's continued invitation to all Israelites, "a disobedient and obstinate people" to whom God is constantly "holding out his hands" in welcome (Isa 65:2).

Following all of this, in 11:1-32 Paul sets out a Christian scenario of "salvation history" (Heilsgeschichte). It is a portrayal of the course of God's salvific activity that the apostle may have proclaimed at various times during his evangelistic outreach to Gentiles in the eastern part of the Roman empire — most likely to his own Gentile converts after their initial commitments to Jesus; perhaps also to Jews on certain specific occasions (though, of course, excluding on those occasions any direct address to Gentiles). Or such a scenario of salvation history may have been first spelled out by Paul for his addressees at Rome. But however it came about in the apostle's consciousness, preaching, and/or writing, it is meant by Paul in his letter to the Christians at Rome to be an important part of his explanation of how the gospel relates to the hope of Israel.

This section of Paul's argument begins at 11:1 with the rhetorical question, "I ask then, Did God reject his people?," with that question being repeated in slightly different words in 11:11, "Again I ask, Did they stumble so as to fall beyond recovery?" By the use of these parallel questions, Paul sets up rhetorically an extended *anaphora* (i.e., a word or expression being repeated at the resumption of a discussion that has been interrupted in some manner by other material), much as he did earlier in the first section of the body middle of the letter in stating his thesis in 1:16-17 about "righteousness" and "faith" and then restating and expanding it in 3:21-23. And in answering these questions, Paul overtly signals his use of remnant rhetoric by his explicit use of the terms λεῖμμα ("remnant") and ἐκλογή ("chosen" or "elect") in verses 5 and 7.

There is much in this "salvation history" scenario that requires careful exegetical treatment, and so it must await a more intensive and fuller exposition in a future commentary proper. Suffice it here to say that in 11:1-32 Paul is particularly interested in (1) the continued existence of the remnant of Israel (of which group he is one), (2) the responses and responsibilities of a remnant of Gentiles (to which group he has been called as an apostle), (3) not allowing attitudes of self-congratulation or boasting to arise among Gentile believers vis-à-vis their Jewish brothers and sisters (which unity he earnestly desires to preserve), and (4) having his addressees realize that God still has salvific plans and redemptive purposes for all people — both for a continued outreach to Gentiles and for the ultimate salvation of "all Israel."

Then in 11:33-36 Paul concludes his remnant rhetorical presentation regarding how the Christian gospel relates to the hope of Israel with one of the loftiest and most resounding doxologies in all of Scripture. The doxology was undoubtedly formed within the context of Jewish Christian worship, for it incorporates expressions that resonate with statements found in Isa 40:13 ("Who has known the mind of the Lord? Or who has been his counselor?") and Job 41:11 ("Who has ever given to God, that God should repay the gift?"). It was probably first used by early Jewish believers in Jesus in praise to God for all that he had done in redeeming them from sin and regenerating them to a new life. It may also be assumed that the Christians at Rome had used this doxology in their worship as well — and, further, that Paul knew that they had.

Likewise, Paul himself may have uttered these words at various times in praise to God for all he had done for humanity through the work and person of Jesus of Nazareth. Here, however, in laying out the divine scenario of salvation history, he breaks out in the words of this evidently familiar doxology in praise to God for what he has done in the past within the nation of Israel, what he is doing at the present through the remnant of Israel and a remnant of the Gentiles, and what he will yet do in the salvation of "all Israel." So he begins with the exclamation: "Oh, the depth of the riches, the wisdom and the knowledge of God! How unsearchable his judgments, and his paths beyond tracing out!" And after repeating the statements drawn from Isa 40:13 and Job 41:11, he closes with ascriptions of praise: "For from him and through him and to him are all things. To him be the glory forever! Amen."

4. Conclusions

Because 9–11 seems to be a discrete unit of structurally self-contained material, and because it reflects so few of the usual epistolary conventions of ancient letter writing, it may be conjectured that most — if not all — of its content had been preached orally by Paul at some time or times during his earlier missionary activities. If so, it would probably have been proclaimed by Paul to his Gentile converts after their initial commitments to Jesus so as to teach them regarding their place and purpose in God's overall plan of "salvation history." It may also, of course, have been orally proclaimed on particular occasions to Jewish audiences as well — though, if ever so proclaimed to a Jewish audience, with the omission of any direct address to Gentiles, as in 11:13-24.

It may further be conjectured that when Paul concluded writing the second section of the body middle of Romans, with its reference in 8:33 to all believers in Jesus as being "the chosen/elect of God" (ἐκλεκτῶν θεου), that he saw it as not only logical but also necessary to insert this earlier formed material of chapters 9–11 between the first two sections and the final section of the body middle of his letter. On the other hand, it may be that, having concluded that second major section of Romans, he took the occasion to use the significant phrase "the chosen/elect of God" of 8:33 as the linguistic springboard for a further discussion — one freshly composed for his dominantly Gentile Christian addressees at Rome — thereby "going off at a word" (as was often his practice) to give them further instruction regarding how he understood the relationship between the Christian gospel and God's promises to Israel.

But however the material of 9–11 is viewed as having come about, its authorship by Paul cannot be doubted. And although its insertion into the usual tripartite structure of an ancient "protreptic word ['speech' or 'message'] of exhortation" (λόγος προτρεπτικός) may seem somewhat unusual, Paul appears never to have been entirely bound by the conventions of his day, whether epistolary or rhetorical. Rather, as he seems to have viewed matters, this third section of his letter's body middle was absolutely necessary as a culmination of the theological arguments in 1:16–4:25 and 5–8. For here in this third major section of his letter to Rome, making use of a Jewish and Jewish Christian style of remnant rhetoric and quoting in support various OT texts that would have been meaningful to his addressees because of their theological background, he was able to answer the questions he knew would arise in their minds from the first two sections of his protreptic message to them — that is, questions regarding the relation of the Christian gospel to God's promises to Israel.

Section IV: Exhortations, General and Specific (12:1–15:13)

In the fourth and final major section of the body middle of Romans, that is, in 12:1–15:13, Paul appears to be setting out two sets of hortatory materials.

The first is a set of rather general exhortations in chapters 12 and 13:8-14 that present the Christian love ethic, which is an integral part of the Christian gospel — with a specific contextualization of that ethic in 13:1-7 on how Christians at Rome are to respond in their particular social and civic circumstances. The second is a set of exhortations in 14:1–15:13 regarding relations between "the strong" and "the weak" in the various Christian congregations of the city.

Every Pauline letter except Philemon, as we have noted above, evidences in its body middle a well-organized theological section (or sections) that is followed by a hortatory section, where in a less structured manner the message set out and developed in the theological section (or sections) is made personal by means of exhortations.[27] Likewise, ancient protreptic "words ['speeches' or 'messages'] of exhortation" (λόγοι προτρεπτικοί), while always structured in terms of first a "negative section" of censure and correction and then a "positive section" in which the author's major truth claims are presented, frequently also had a third "optional section, consisting of a personal appeal to the hearer, inviting the immediate accepting of the exhortation."[28] Thus, as was Paul's usual practice, as well as the pattern frequently found in the protreptic speeches and writings of antiquity, the body middle of Romans contains as its final section a number of exhortations — some of which are fairly general and some of which seem to be quite specific.

1. The Structure of the Section

One looks hard to find epistolary conventions in this fourth section of the body middle of Romans that are comparable to those that appear in the letter's opening sections (1:1-12) and closing sections (15:33–16:27) — or even to those in its body opening (1:13-15) and body closing (15:14-32). Such a scarcity of epistolary formulas and features was also the case, as we have noted above, in the preceding three theological sections of the letter's body middle.

There are, however, two rather standard epistolary conventions present at the start of this fourth section in 12:1: a *request formula* (παρακαλῶ οὖν ὑμᾶς, "I urge you") and a *vocative of direct address* (ἀδελφοί, "brothers and sisters"). Likewise, at the beginning of 12:3 there appears a *verb of saying* (λέγω γὰρ . . . παντὶ τῷ ὄντι ἐν ὑμῖν, "for I say . . . to every one of you"). And at the beginning of 14:14 there is a *confidence formula* (οἶδα καὶ πέπεισμαι ἐν

---

27. Paraphrasing J. L. White, *Body of the Greek Letter,* 87-88.
28. Quoting D. E. Aune, *"Mixtum compositum,"* in *Westminister Dictionary,* 385.

κυρίῳ Ἰησοῦ ὅτι, "I know and am convinced in [or 'by'] the Lord Jesus that . . ."). Each of these epistolary formulas serves to signal the start of a new section or subsection of material. But apart from these few instances, no other ancient epistolary formulas are reflected in this section.

Somewhat more prominent in 12:1–15:13 is the appearance of a few oral and rhetorical conventions of the day. One of these is the fourfold repetition in 12:3 of the infinitives ὑπερφρονεῖν . . . φρονεῖν . . . φρονεῖν . . . σωφρονεῖν ("to think" or "think with sober judgment"), which would have caught the attention of those who heard the apostle preach. Another is the almost liturgical cadence formed by the sevenfold repetition (both explicit and implied) of the particles εἴτε . . . ἐν ("if . . . in," which are set out without an expressed verb) in 12:6-8: "If prophecy, in proportion to faith; if ministry, in ministering; if teaching, in teaching; if encouragement, in encouraging; if giving, in generosity; if leadership, in diligence; if showing mercy, in cheerfulness." And in 14:4-10 there appears a clear instance of a rhetorical *diatribe*, which begins in verse 4 with the question "Who are you to judge someone else's servant?" and closes in verse 10 with the questions "You, then, why do you judge your brother or sister? Or, why do you despise your brother or sister?"

Further, it needs to be noted that twice at the close of this fourth hortatory section Paul expresses, by the use of the optative mood for the respective verbs (which mood in the NT most often expresses a wish or "prayer wish"), what have often been assumed by commentators to be doxologies or quasi-doxologies. The first is in 15:5-6, where — after speaking in verse 4 of "the steadfastness (τῆς ὑπομονῆς) and the encouragement (τῆς παρακλήσεως) that comes from the Scriptures (τῶν γραφῶν)" — Paul gives the following "prayer wish" for his addressees at Rome:

> May the God of steadfastness and encouragement (ὁ δὲ θεὸς τῆς ὑπομονῆς καὶ τῆς παρακλήσεως) give (δώῃ; optative mood) you a spirit of unity among yourselves as you follow Christ Jesus, so that with one heart you may glorify the God and Father of our Lord Jesus Christ. (vv. 5-6)

The second is in 15:13, where — after quoting in verses 9-12 passages from "the Law" (Deut 32:43), "the Prophets" (Isa 11:10), and "the Writings" (Pss 18:49; 117:1) regarding the Gentiles; and, particularly, after highlighting the fact that God's promise in Isa 11:10 includes not only that "the root of Jesse" will rule over the nations (ἐθνῶν) but also that "the Gentiles will hope in him" (ἐπ' αὐτῷ ἔθνη ἐλπιοῦσιν) — Paul goes "off at a word" to lay stress on this hope given to Gentile believers in Jesus (including, of course, the hope given to Gentile believers at Rome) in saying:

> May the God of hope (ὁ δὲ θεὸς τῆς ἐλπίδος) fill (πληρῶσαι; optative mood) you with great joy and peace as you trust in him, so that you may overflow with that hope (ἐν τῇ ἐλπίδι) by the power of the Holy Spirit. (v. 13)

These two wish statements, however, are not really doxologies — whether formal or spontaneous; whether drawn from earlier Christian confessional materials or composed by Paul himself. Rather, they should probably be classed as "prayer wishes," comparable to what can be found elsewhere in the Pauline letters at 1 Thess 3:11-13; 5:23; 2 Thess 2:16-17; 3:5; 3:16a; and 2 Tim 4:16; perhaps also 2 Cor 13:13.[29] Nonetheless, as "prayer wishes" of the apostle they serve here, as they do elsewhere in the Pauline letters, to signal the climax of their respective sections or subsections, and so function as important rhetorical features for the structuring of the material presented.

The greatest problem with regard to the structure of this fourth major section of the body middle of Romans, however, has to do with how the material of 13:1-7 relates to the rest of the exhortations in 12:1–15:13. These seven verses have appeared to many as an "independent" body of material — often as "unique" and "surprising"; perhaps even "alien" — which has somehow become incorporated into the midst of rather general exhortations that surround it in 12:9-21 and 13:8-10 (cf. Chapter V, "Purpose"). The argument of these verses (1) is specific in scope and application, whereas the exhortations that surround it in chapters 12–13 are fairly general; (2) is based on what God has established by creation, whereas Christology, eschatology, and love (ἀγάπη) are the motivational factors that appear prominently throughout the rest of chapters 12–15; and (3) seems to break the continuity of the exhortations given in 12:9-21 and 13:8-10.[30]

A number of scholars, however, as noted above, have aptly argued that 13:1-7 must be read with the realization that Paul "is addressing the church in the capital city of the empire,"[31] and therefore "it would be strange if the norm that orders the community's relationship to the state [i.e., how Chris-

29. Cf. R. N. Longenecker, "Prayer in the Pauline Letters," esp. 222-23.
30. Paraphrasing the analysis of E. Käsemann, *Romans*, 350-52, as cited earlier in Chapter V, "Purpose."
31. So, e.g., E. Käsemann, *Romans*, 350.

tians are to evaluate and relate to Caesar and his delegates] were missing in the message to the Romans."[32] And Johannes Friedrich, Wolfgang Pöhlmann, and Peter Stuhlmacher have gone further to argue that the exhortations of 13:6-7 regarding paying taxes and revenues to civil "authorities" — even offering them respect and honor — are probably to be understood against the background of unrest at Rome during the mid-50s, which came about because of the rapacious practices of those who collected the city's revenues and tolls.[33] So while on a literary basis the placement of these seven verses may seem somewhat surprising, there is much to be said historically and redactionally in favor of the passage's authenticity.

How, then, are we to understand the structure of this fourth section of the body middle of Romans? It is clear that the *request formula* (παρακαλῶ οὖν ὑμᾶς, "I urge you") and the *vocative of direct address* (ἀδελφοί, "brothers and sisters") at the beginning of 12:1 identify the hortatory section of Paul's letter as beginning at 12:1. It is also clear that the *verb of saying* (λέγω γάρ, "for I say") of 12:3 signals the start of a new subsection of material. Likewise, it may reasonably be argued that the *confidence formula* (οἶδα καὶ πέπεισμαι ἐν κυρίῳ Ἰησοῦ ὅτι, "I know and am convinced by [or 'in'] the Lord Jesus that") of 14:14 also functions as the start of a new subsection. And, further, it may be postulated that the two "prayer wishes" of 15:5-6 and 15:13 were intended by Paul to bring to a close the exhortations that precede them — whether those exhortations be understood as only the material that appears immediately before each of the two "prayer wishes," that is, in 15:1-4 and 7-12; or, more broadly, the exhortations regarding "the strong" and "the weak" in chapter 14; or even, more broadly still, all of the exhortations throughout 12–14, together with those of 15:1-4 and 7-12 — as "prayer wishes" appear elsewhere in many of Paul's other letters to close off their respective sections or subsections (as cited above).

More hypothetical are the proposals that in this fourth section of the letter's body middle are to be found (1) two sets of exhortations: the first, a set of general exhortations in chapters 12 and 13:8-14, which spell out the basic features of a Christian love ethic; the second, a set of more particular exhortations in 14:1–15:13, which exhort regarding relations between "the strong" and "the weak" in the Christian congregations of Rome, and (2) an interjected exhortation in 13:1-7 regarding the attitude and responsibilities of Christians to-

---

32. E. Käsemann, *Romans*, 240.

33. Cf. J. Friedrich, W. Pöhlmann, and P. Stuhlmacher, "Situation und Intention von Röm 13,1-7" (see also our discussion of this position in Chapter V, "Purpose").

ward the Roman emperor, the Roman state, and the civic authorities of Rome. With respect to the postulated first set of general exhortations in chapters 12 and 13:8-14, the fourfold repetition in 12:3 of the infinitives ὑπερφρονεῖν . . . φρονεῖν . . . φρονεῖν . . . σωφρονεῖν ("to think" or "think with sober judgment") and the almost liturgical cadence formed by the sevenfold repetition in 12:6-8 of the particles εἴτε . . . ἐν ("if . . . in," without an express verb) seem to suggest that much of what is written in these two chapters (with the possible exception of 13:1-7) originated in Paul's oral preaching and was incorporated into his letter to Christians at Rome as an example of what he proclaimed as part of his gospel message throughout his Gentile mission. On the other hand, with respect to the postulated second set of more particular exhortations in 14:1–15:13, the diatribal dialogue of 14:4-10, together with the specific concerns dealt with in chapter 14, seems to suggest that these hortatory materials were originally written to meet a particular problem that was then existing among the Christian congregations at Rome.

This latter observation regarding the presence of a rather lively diatribe in 14:4-10 and its possible significance for an understanding of the provenance of that portion of material in which it is found, that is, in 14:1–15:13, can be paralleled, to an extent, by the presence of diatribal dialogues in the first section of the letter's body middle, that is, in 1:16–4:25. For the diatribes of 2:1-5; 2:17-29; and (possibly) 3:1-9 also seem to suggest that the portion of material in which they appear was not written to represent the central features of Paul's preaching in his Gentile mission, and so formed in some manner his earlier oral proclamation of the Christian gospel in his Gentile mission (as we have argued for 5–8; also, as we have suggested above and will propose more formally later, for the exhortations of chs. 12 and 13:8-14), but, rather, was composed by the apostle at the time when he wrote his letter to Christians at Rome in order to meet certain objections to his message that he believed had arisen among his addressees.

Further, it needs also to be noted that some fairly significant antecedents appear in Romans for Paul's interjection of the material of 13:1-7 into the more general ethical exhortations of chapters 12–13 — that is, antecedents for what seems to be his rather common practice of inserting into more general statements an additional portion of didactic or ethical material that he evidently felt would be of special significance for the particular situation of his addressees. A major example of such an interjection is the insertion of the entire third section of the letter's body middle, that is, 9–11, which deals with the relation of the Christian gospel to the hope of Israel, into the usual tripartite structure of a protreptic speech or writing.

On a more limited scope, 7:1-6 is also probably to be viewed as an interjection of specifically addressed material into a larger body of instructional material. For in the context of answering the question "Shall we sin because we are not under the law but under grace?" (6:1), and after formally concluding that discussion with the closing formula "by/through [or 'in'] Christ Jesus our Lord" (6:23), Paul appears to have interjected additional material — which, it seems, he felt would be of particular relevance to his addressees, who were predominantly Gentile Christians ethnically but who had been influenced extensively by Jewish Christian understandings — in order to clarify and apply what he meant in chapter 6 by the use of a relevant illustration and a further hortatory statement in 7:1-6:

> Do you not know, brothers and sisters — for I am speaking to those who know the law — that the law has authority over a person only as long as that person lives. . . . So, my brothers and sisters, you also died to the law through the body of Christ, that you might belong to another.

And 11:13-24 might also be material of such a nature. For in the context of setting out a Christian understanding of the course of "salvation history," Paul seems to break into his more general presentation with a pertinent analogy and a particular word of exhortation, which he directs explicitly to the situation of his Roman addressees — who, again it needs to be pointed out, were dominantly Gentiles ethnically but who also had been heavily influenced by Jewish Christian understandings — in 11:13-24:

> I am speaking to you Gentiles. . . . Consider, therefore, the kindness and sternness of God: sternness to those who fell, but kindness to you, provided that you continue in his kindness.

These three antecedents seem to provide some rationale for believing that Paul may have also interjected the material of 13:1-7 into his more general discussion of the Christian love ethic, even though there are no explicit epistolary conventions to signal such an action. Each of these portions of material, of course, has its own purpose in the overall structure of Romans, and each of them may be somewhat differently evaluated in their particular contexts. But all of them have some bearing on the question at hand.

Therefore, drawing on what is admittedly only a handful of epistolary, rhetorical, and oral indicators and extrapolating from a few parallels of what seem to be Paul's usual practices, we propose that this fourth section of the body middle of Romans be understood in its main movements as follows:

Set I: Exhortations on the love ethic of the Christian gospel (12–13)

1. Opening statement on dedication and discernment (12:1-2)
2. The Christian attitude toward oneself vis-à-vis the Body of Christ (12:3-8)
3. Exhortations on love, non-retaliation, and peace (12:9-21)
4. Interjected exhortations on Christians and the state (13:1-7)
5. Exhortations on a Christian's debt of love (13:8-14)

Set II: Exhortations on the exercise of Christian liberty (14:1–15:13)

1. Acceptance of others in disputable matters (14:1-13)
2. Eating food and not condemning ourselves or others (14:14-23)
3. Relations between "the strong" and "the weak," with a "prayer wish" for unity (15:1-6)
4. Concluding appeal for mutual acceptance, with a "prayer wish" for joy, peace, and hope among the Christians at Rome (15:7-13).

2. The General Exhortations of Chapters 12 and 13:8-14

The exhortations of 12 and 13:8-14, apart from those of 13:1-7, comprise a series of general hortatory statements that have to do with the basic features of a Christian ethic. These exhortations deal with "dedication and discernment" on the part of a Christian (12:1-2), a Christian's attitude toward him- or herself vis-à-vis "the body of Christ" (12:3-8), new attitudes of a Christian with respect to "love," "non-retaliation," and "peace" (12:9-21), and "the debt of love" that is owed by believers in Christ (13:8-14).

A distinctive feature of these general exhortations is the extensive degree of dependence that they evidence on the teachings of Jesus. For Paul's exhortations in these statements appear not only to be based on the general teachings of Jesus but also to quote almost *verbatim* some of Jesus' specific teachings, as they were assumedly circulating within the early Christian communities and then later recorded in the Synoptic Gospels. Four of these exhortations have been seen by many to reflect quite explicitly the teachings of Jesus:

12:14: "Bless those who persecute you; bless and do not curse them" (cf. Matt 5:44; Luke 6:27-28).
12:17: "Do not repay anyone evil for evil" (cf. Matt 5:39-42; Luke 6:29-30).

12:21: "Do not be overcome by evil, but overcome evil with good" (cf. Matt 5:38-48; Luke 6:27-36).

13:8: "Owe no one anything, except to love one another; for whoever loves others has fulfilled the law" (cf. Mark 12:28-34; Matt 22:34-40; Luke 10:25-28).

There are also OT texts cited by Paul in his exhortation regarding non-retaliation in 12:19-20, with those passages being introduced by the apostle's usual introductory formula "it is written" (γέγραπται) when citing Scripture: Deut 32:35 ("Vengeance is mine [i.e., God's]; I will repay") and Prov 25:21-22 ("If your enemies are hungry, feed them; if they are thirsty, give them something to drink. In so doing, you will heap burning coals on their heads"). But these two OT quotations are sandwiched in between what appears to be more direct teachings of Jesus in 12:17 ("Do not repay anyone evil for evil") and 12:21 ("Do not be overcome by evil, but overcome evil with good"), and so should probably be viewed as being more supportive than determinative in function. Likewise, in 13:9-10 Paul cites the biblical commandments "Do not commit adultery," "Do not murder," "Do not steal," and "Do not covet" from the Decalogue, as set out in Exod 20:13-15, 17, and Deut 5:17-19, 21 — also the command "You shall love your neighbor as yourself," which is taken from Lev 19:18. While these OT passages were important in Jewish ethical teaching, they also played a significant role in Jesus' teaching (cf. Mark 12:28-34; Matt 22:34-40; Luke 10:25-28). And as a continuation of the exhortation in 13:8 ("Owe no one anything, except to love one another; for whoever loves others has fulfilled the law"), which seems to have been based on the teachings of Jesus (cf. Mark 12:28-34; Matt 22:34-40; Luke 10:25-28), these OT admonitions were probably understood — at least in the minds of the Gentile converts to whom Paul had delivered "the words of the Lord Jesus" (cf. Acts 20:35), as well as in Paul's mind when addressing Gentiles — more as teachings of Jesus that reached back to the original commandments of God than simply OT texts.

This matter regarding Paul's use of the teachings of Jesus here in his more general exhortations of chapters 12 and 13:8-14 — as well as, of course, throughout his exhortations in the remaining portions of this fourth section of the body middle of Romans (i.e., 13:1-7 and 14:1–15:13); likewise, in some of his other letters written principally to Gentile believers in Jesus (cf. 1 Corinthians *passim*, 1 Thessalonians 4–5, and Colossians 3–4; see also Acts 20:35) — is only part of a much larger question: What did Paul know about Jesus of Nazareth? It is a question that has long divided NT scholars.[34] Elsewhere I have argued that, while there is no evidence for Paul having ever met or personally known the historical Jesus, it is, nonetheless, likely (1) that he knew about Jesus of Nazareth from various Pharisaic sources during his earlier days, (2) that he thoroughly reevaluated his past understanding of Jesus and his followers after having been encountered by the risen Christ on his way to Damascus, and (3) that as a convert to the faith he once tried to destroy, he came to understand properly and more fully about Jesus' person and work through his contacts with some of Jesus' closest followers (cf., e.g., Gal 2:6-10), his awareness of the church's confessions and confessional materials (portions of which he quotes in his writings), and his knowledge of the eschatological and ethical teachings of the historical Jesus (portions of which are reflected in his writings) — with those teachings, it seems, having been first circulated in various forms in the earliest days of nascent Christianity, then collected into what scholars call a "Logia," "Sayings," or "Q" collection, and finally incorporated by the Synoptic evangelists into their Gospels.[35]

It has, of course, often been claimed that "the teaching of the historical Jesus plays no role, or practically none, in Paul."[36] On the other hand, W. D. Davies has argued that when Paul exhorts on ethical matters (as in Rom 12:1–15:13; also 1 Corinthians *passim*, 1 Thessalonians 4–5, and Colossians 3–4), in addition to various traditional materials that he used from his Jewish background, "he had also the words of Jesus to which he turned for guidance, and he makes it clear that when there is an explicit word uttered by

34. For a helpful survey of issues and stances, see V. P. Furnish, "Jesus-Paul Debate" (1965); for an analysis and significant evaluation of matters as they pertain to Rom 12:1–15:13, see D. C. Allison Jr., "Pauline Epistles and the Synoptic Gospels: The Pattern of the Parallels" (1982).

35. Cf. R. N. Longenecker, "A Realized Hope, a New Commitment, and a Developed Proclamation: Paul and Jesus" (1997), 18-42; see also *idem*, "Christological Materials within the Early Christian Communities" (2004), 90-121.

36. So R. Bultmann, *Theology of the New Testament*, 2 vols., trans. K. Grobel (New York: Scribner's, 1951, 1955 [from his 1948 German edition]), 1.35; cf. 1.187-89; for more extensive treatments, see *idem*, "Jesus and Paul," in *Existence and Faith: The Shorter Writings of Rudolf Bultmann*, ed. S. M. Ogden (New York: Meridian Books, 1960), 147-57; *idem*, "The Significance of the Historical Jesus for the Theology of Paul," in *Faith and Understanding*, trans. R. Funk (New York: Meridian Books, 1969), 220-46. And this assertion has been defended by many: e.g., W. Schmithals, "Paulus und der historische Jesus," *ZNW* 53 (1962) 145-60; G. Bornkamm, *Paul*, trans. D. M. G. Stalker (New York: Harper & Row, 1971), 109-11; cf. also N. Perrin, *The New Testament: An Introduction* (New York, Chicago: Harcourt, Brace, Jovanovich, 1974), who simply asserts: "Paul betrays no interest in anything about Jesus beyond his death and resurrection" (p. 286).

Christ on any question, that word is accepted by him as authoritative."[37] And this thesis has been supported by many others.[38] Or as Dale Allison has expressed matters in the concluding words of his article:

> The persistent conviction that Paul knew next to nothing of the teaching of Jesus must be rejected. Jesus of Nazareth was not the faceless presupposition of Pauline theology. On the contrary, the tradition stemming from Jesus well served the apostle in his roles as pastor, theologian, and missionary.[39]

And it is this thesis that I argued in my 1964 monograph *Paul, Apostle of Liberty*.[40]

What Paul seems to be doing in chapters 12 and 13:8-14 is setting out for the Christians at Rome a body of ethical material (1) that he believed was an integral part of the Christian gospel, and so must always accompany any proclamation of the Christian message, (2) that he viewed as representing the basic features of his ethical proclamation, and so he desired to inform them further regarding the nature of his ministry and message to Gentiles in the Greco-Roman world, and (3) that he wanted to share with them for their spiritual profit and growth, since they were predominantly also Gentile believers in Jesus. There is much in these admonitions that must be treated later in our forthcoming commentary proper. Suffice it here to observe that in setting out these exhortations, which he evidently wanted his addressees to understand as having been characteristic of his proclamation of the gospel to Gentiles, Paul seems also to highlight the fact that his Christian message is not only based on what Jesus Christ brought about by his "act of righteousness" and his "obedience" (cf. 5:18-21; see also the whole of chapters 5-8) but is also rooted in what Jesus taught during his earthly ministry (as he does, as

---

37. W. D. Davies, *Paul and Rabbinic Judaism*, 141; cf. 136-46 in all four editions of Davies's monograph and especially the footnote on p. 146 of his 1980 edition; see also *idem*, *The Setting of the Sermon on the Mount* (Cambridge: Cambridge University Press, 1966), 341-66.

38. E.g., X. Léon-Dufour, *The Gospels and the Jesus of History*, trans. J. McHugh (London: Collins, 1968, 1970), 59-64; C. F. D. Moule, "Jesus in New Testament Kerygma," in *Verborum Veritas* [*Festschrift* G. Stählin], ed. O. Böcher and K. Haacker (Wuppertal: Brockhaus, 1970), 15-26; repr. in his *Essays in New Testament Interpretation* (Cambridge: Cambridge University Press, 1982), 37-49; and D. C. Allison Jr., "The Pauline Epistles and the Synoptic Gospels: The Pattern of the Parallels," 1-32.

39. D. C. Allison, "The Pauline Epistles and the Synoptic Gospels," 25.

40. R. N. Longenecker, *Paul, Apostle of Liberty*, 36-38 and 187-90.

well, in 1 Corinthians *passim*, 1 Thessalonians 4–5, and Colossians 3–4; cf. Acts 20:35).

3. *The Interjected Specific Exhortations of 13:1-7*

In both their form of argumentation and content, the exhortations regarding "Christians and the state" in 13:1-7 seem — at least, at first glance — to be quite out of keeping with the general exhortations on a Christian love ethic in chapters 12 and 13:8-14. The material of these seven verses, as noted above, (1) is specific in scope and application, whereas the exhortations that surround it in chapters 12–13 are fairly general; (2) is based on what God has established by creation, whereas Christology, eschatology, and love (ἀγάπη) are the motivational factors that appear prominently throughout the rest of chapters 12–15; and (3) seems to break the continuity of the exhortations given in 12:9-21 and 13:8-10. Nevertheless, as also noted above, Paul is addressing Christians in the capital city of the Roman empire. So it would be somewhat strange if he did not somewhere in his letter speak to the question of how believers in Jesus were to evaluate and relate to their governing "authorities," that is, to the emperor, his delegates, and the officials of the city of Rome. Further, amidst conditions of civil unrest at Rome during the 50s — which, as Johannes Friedrich, Wolfgang Pöhlmann, and Peter Stuhlmacher have argued (see above; also Chapter V, "Purpose"), seem to have come about because of the rapacious practices of those who collected the city's revenues and tolls — it would be exceedingly strange if he did not speak in the letter to the issues of Christians paying taxes and revenues to a secular government and to what extent Christians should respect and honor their civic officials.

It may always be debated exactly how 13:1-7 relates to what appears both before and after it in chapters 12–13. But accepting the integrity of the passage, it may be argued that Paul viewed his inclusion of these exhortations as a contextualization of the Christian love ethic that was particularly relevant for his addressees at Rome in their specific social and civic circumstances — and that thus he exhorts them to be submissive to their governing "authorities," to pay their appointed taxes and revenues, and even to respect and honor their civic officials. Or it may be that, having based his general ethical exhortations on the teachings of Jesus in 12:14, 17, 21, and 13:8, and, further, being able to support these more specific exhortations regarding "the Christian and the State" from the teachings of Jesus as well (see below), Paul simply interjected the material of 13:1-7 into the larger context of general exhortations regarding a Christian love ethic, since they were all based in one way or another on teachings of the historical Jesus, and so concluded his exhortations of this short passage with a distillation of Jesus' teaching in verse 7: "Pay to all what is due them — taxes to whom taxes are due, revenue to whom revenue is due, respect to whom respect is due, honor to whom honor is due" (cf. Mark 12:13-17; Matt 22:34-40; Luke 10:25-28). Or it may be that Paul had proclaimed just such a message of civic responsibility elsewhere in his Gentile mission, for certainly his Gentile converts would have been faced with many of these same issues, and that he wanted to include that emphasis here in his letter to the Romans, even though in structure and content it may have been somewhat discordant with the other more general hortatory material of chapters 12–13. Or it may have been that all three of the above rationales were present, in various degrees, in Paul's mind at the time when he wrote.

But however we judge his rationale for including 13:1-7 into the larger context of chapters 12–13, it seems legitimate to believe that Paul himself interjected these rather specific exhortations into a body of more general exhortations in order to speak directly to what his addressees at Rome were facing in their social and civic responsibilities. The content of this passage may have been used elsewhere during the course of the apostle's Gentile mission. And certainly its message has relevance for all Christians in whatever social, political, or civil situation they may be located (cf. our later exegetical treatment of the passage in the commentary proper). But the material of 13:1-7 seems not to be representative of Paul's general ethical teaching that he considered part and parcel of his gospel proclamation, as we have argued for that of chapters 12 and 13:8-14. Rather, it should probably be understood as specific admonitions directed to a particular issue that faced Christians at Rome, and so to be associated more with the exhortations of 14:1–15:13.

4. The Specific Exhortations of 14:1–15:13

The exhortations of 14:1–15:13 have to do with disputes among Christians regarding the eating of various kinds of food and the veneration of certain days. It seems that those who considered themselves "the strong" were judging and despising those whom they called "the weak" because this latter group took more restrictive stances on these matters — though, as we have noted earlier (see Chapter V, "Purpose"), some have viewed the divisions as being much more complex (e.g., Paul Minear, who discerned five groups of Christians who were arguing with one another)[41] and others have understood the ex-

41. P. S. Minear, *Obedience of Faith,* 8ff.

hortations as being directed to "the weak" rather than "the strong" (e.g., Francis Watson, who views Paul as exhorting members of a Jewish Christian congregation to separate from the Jewish community and their former legal commitments and to accept and unite with the Gentile Christian congregation).[42] But whatever the precise nature of the divisions, exact delineation of the issues involved, and proper identification of those being addressed (all of which are matters that must be treated more extensively in a future commentary proper), it is obvious that Paul in his exhortations of 14:1–15:13 asks for an acceptance of others in disputable matters (14:1-13), teaches regarding the exercise of Christian liberty with respect to the eating of various foods (14:14-19), urges mutual edification among believers in Jesus, without condemning either oneself or others (14:20-23), and pleads for unity and peace (15:1-13).

Many interpreters have understood 14:1–15:13 to be hortatory material that has been abstracted by Paul from his earlier correspondence with his Corinthian converts (cf. esp. 1 Cor 8:1–11:1), and therefore not necessarily reflecting any particular situation among believers in Jesus at Rome. And on the basis of such an understanding, some have taken the exhortations of chapters 14–15 to be fairly similar in nature to the general exhortations of chapters 12–13. But references to vegetarianism in 14:2 and special holy days in 14:5-6, as well as the allusion to abstinence from wine in 14:21, find no parallel in Paul's letters to Corinth. So most scholars today view the exhortations of 14:1–15:13 as being directed to a specific situation among the Christians at Rome, not just general exhortations on Christian liberty that had been generated in Paul's mind by circumstances previously encountered during his Gentile mission (see Chapter V, "Purpose"). The majority of interpreters today, in fact, agree with Paul Minear's evaluation (as quoted earlier) regarding the nature of the exhortations in 14:1–15:13:

> It is true that Paul often incorporated into his letters didactic material which was typical of what he taught in all the churches. This catechetical material was often shaped by general practice rather than by particular situations. Chapters 12 and 13 contain material which is probably of this sort. . . . There is, however, a change in literary style between ch. 13 and 14. The apostle moves from general injunctions embodied in traditional oral forms of parenesis, to the consideration of a specific set of problems. The nearest analogy is I Corinthians (8.1-13; 9.19-23; 10.23–11.1). No

---

42. F. Watson, "Two Roman Congregations," 94-105; repr. in Donfried, ed., *Romans Debate* (1991), 203-15.

one doubts that in Corinth he was wrestling directly with a specific situation. Why then should we doubt that this was also true in Rome?[43]

And it is this understanding of the nature of the hortatory material in 14:1–15:13 that we have agreed with in our discussion of Paul's purpose in writing (see Chapter V).

Yet most scholars today have also viewed the disputes among Christians at Rome as being between a freedom-affirming type of Gentile Christianity, which may have looked to Paul as its champion, and a legalistic type of Jewish Christianity, which upheld the tenets of the church at Jerusalem. Some have gone further in attempting to identify the specific groups of disputants involved (as, e.g., P. S. Minear, who delineated five groups) or the specific congregations to which they belonged (as, e.g., F. Watson, who delineates two congregations). And others have argued for various understandings of exactly whom Paul is speaking to and what he wanted them to do (cf. Chapter V, "Purpose").

There is much in 14:1–15:13 that needs to be clarified later in a forthcoming commentary proper. Suffice it here to say that we believe that the specificity of the issues dealt with by the apostle in this passage must always be recognized. So we propose that what Paul is doing here in 14:1–15:13 is contextualizing the Christian love ethic that he proclaimed in chapters 12 and 13:8-14, and doing so with respect to a particular problem that had arisen among the Christians at Rome — much as he contextualized that same Christian ethic in 13:1-7 in a manner particularly relevant for his Roman addressees in their specific civic circumstances.

Further, it needs also to be noted that the pattern of Paul's argumentation in 14:1–15:13 is somewhat different from the pattern observable in 12–13. For whereas in the general exhortations of chapters 12–13 he bases his exhortations extensively on the ethical teachings of Jesus and cites a few OT texts in support, in chapters 14–15 he alludes to teachings of Jesus but seems to be primarily dependent on passages quoted from the OT. Allusions to the teachings of Jesus in the following three verses seem evident:

14:10: "Why do you judge your brother or sister?" (cf. Matt 7:1; Luke 6:37).

14:13: "Let us, therefore, stop passing judgment on one another. Instead, make up your mind not to put any stumbling block or obsta-

43. P. Minear, *Obedience of Faith*, 22.

cle in the way of your brother or sister" (Matt 18:7; Mark 9:42; Luke 17:1-2).

14:14: "I know and am persuaded by [or 'in'] the Lord Jesus that no food is unclean of itself" (cf. Mark 7:15; Matt 15:11).

But in 14:1–15:13, particularly in the catena of passages that refer to the Gentiles in 15:9-12, Paul's exhortations appear to be heavily dependent on quotations from the OT — with all of these quotations being introduced by his standard introductory formula γέγραπται, "it is written" (or its extension πάλιν, "again"), which signals a note of divine authority:

14:11: "'As I live,' says the Lord, 'every knee will bow before me; every tongue will confess to God'" (quoting Isa 45:23).

15:3: "The insults of those who insult you have fallen on me" (quoting Ps 69:9 [MT = 69:10; LXX = 68:10]).

15:9: "Therefore I will confess you among the Gentiles, and sing praises to your name" (quoting Ps 18:49 [MT = 18:50; LXX = 17:50]).

15:10: "Rejoice, O Gentiles, with his people" (quoting Deut 32:43).

15:11: "Praise the Lord, all you Gentiles, and let all the people praise him" (quoting Ps 117:1 [LXX = 116:1]).

15:12: "The root of Jesse will spring up, the one who will arise to rule over the nations; and the Gentiles will hope in him" (quoting Isa 11:10).

Notable in this catena of passages in 15:9-13 is the fact that these OT texts are drawn from the standard three parts of the Jewish biblical canon: the Law (Deut 32:43), the Prophets (Isa 11:10), and the Writings (Pss 18:49; 117:1). And this joining of passages in support of Paul's plea to "accept one another, just as Christ has accepted you" (15:7) — together with his thesis that "Christ has become a servant of the Jews on behalf of God's truth, to confirm the promises made to the patriarchs, so that the Gentiles may glorify God for his mercy" (15:8-9a) — would have been particularly significant for Paul's addressees at Rome, whether ethnically Jews or Gentiles, for all of them presumably (as we have argued earlier; cf. Chapter IV, "Addressees") based their understandings of the OT Scriptures and Jesus' person and work on the teachings of the Mother Church at Jerusalem.

5. Conclusions

What then can be concluded regarding the hortatory materials of 12:1–15:13? Based on the data set out above, we conclude, first of all, that the exhortations of chapters 12 and 13:8-14 should be viewed as general ethical instructions that present the basic Christian love ethic, which ethic (1) is founded primarily on the teachings of Jesus, (2) is supported by the OT Scriptures, and (3) constitutes an integral part of the Christian gospel generally and of Paul's proclamation of that gospel in his Gentile mission in particular. Further, we propose that these exhortations of 12 and 13:8-14 should be viewed as intimately associated with the theological presentation of 5–8. Thus both the didactic material of 5–8 and the hortatory material of chapters 12 and 13:8-14 should be understood as reflecting the essential nature of Paul's proclamation of the Christian gospel within the Greco-Roman world of his day, and so the essence of his distinctive message to non-Jews in his Gentile mission.

By his inclusion of both the theological affirmations of chapters 5–8 and the ethical exhortations of chapters 12 and 13:8-14 in his letter to the Christians at Rome, Paul's purpose, it seems, was to share with his addressees what he calls his "spiritual gift" to them (cf. 1:11). Here, we believe, is the essence of what Paul proclaimed in his mission to Gentiles: his gospel message in both its doctrinal affirmations (i.e., 5–8), or what may be called "the indicative of the gospel," and its ethical admonitions (i.e., 12 and 13:8-14), or what may be called "the imperative of the gospel" — that is, what he explicitly calls "my gospel" in 2:16 and 16:25.

The material of 13:1-7, however, is probably not to be seen as intended by Paul to be expressly representative of his ethical teaching to Gentiles in the Greco-Roman world. Rather, this portion of seven verses, however its location amid the general exhortations of chapters 12 and 13:8-14 may be rationalized, should probably be understood as containing specific admonitions directed to a particular civic issue that was then facing the Christians at Rome, and so to be associated more with the exhortations of 14:1–15:13.

The specificity of the last set of exhortations in 14:1–15:13 needs also always to be recognized. In these hortatory materials Paul seems to be speaking directly to a problem that had arisen within the Christian congregations at Rome. It may have been a problem between freedom-affirming Gentile Christians and more tradition-bound, legalistic Jewish Christians, as most interpreters have understood it. It seems, however, more likely — since, as we have argued, all of the Roman Christians, whatever their ethnic backgrounds, had been extensively impacted by the theology, ecclesiology, and ethics of the Mother Church at Jerusalem (cf. Chapter IV, "Addressees") — that disputes among Christians at Rome were based more on particular social circumstances and diverse doctrinal understandings than on ethnicity. Much more regarding this dispute needs to be spelled out in our exegesis in a forthcoming commentary proper. Suffice it here to say that we believe what Paul is doing in 14:1–15:13 is contextualizing the Christian love ethic, which he set out in chapters 12 and 13:8-14, with respect to a specific problem that had arisen among the Christians and the Christian congregations at Rome — much as he had contextualized that same Christian ethic in 13:1-7 in a manner that was relevant for his Roman addressees in their particular civic situation.

C. BODY CLOSING

An "Apostolic Parousia" (15:14-32)

With respect to the integrity of the material in chapter 15, it has often been argued that Romans originally consisted of only the first fourteen chapters, that is, 1–14, with or without the doxology of 16:25-27. But while there is evidence that Paul's letter to Rome did exist at some early time — particularly in North Africa, Asia Minor, and France — in a "short" form among both orthodox and heretical Christians, scholarly opinion today favors the "long" form, that is, with the inclusion of 15:1–16:23 (possibly also including 16:24), as the letter's original form, with its reduction to fourteen chapters occurring in an attempt to "catholicize" or "generalize" it (cf. Chapter II, "Integrity"). And it is this understanding of 15:1–16:23 that is adopted here and will be developed more fully in a forthcoming commentary proper.

With respect to the function of the material in 15:14-32 (with many also including verse 33), most commentators today view the body of Romans as ending at 15:13 and the final epistolary sections of the letter as beginning at 15:14.[44] We propose, however, that 15:14-32 constitutes the body closing of the letter and that the concluding epistolary sections begin with the peace bene-

---

44. E.g., J. A. Fitzmyer, "Letter to the Romans," *JBC* (1968), 2.329-30; *idem, Romans* (1993), 709-10; M. Black, *Romans* (1973), 174-86; C. E. B. Cranfield, *Romans* (1979), 2.749-814; E. Käsemann, *Romans* (1980), 389-408; J. D. G. Dunn, *Romans* (1988), 2.854-917; L. L. Morris, *Romans* (1988), 508-48; D. L. Moo, *Romans* (1996), 884-911.

diction of 15:33. And we will attempt to set out reasons for this judgment and explicate this understanding in what follows below.

In 15:14-32, which we believe is best identified as the body closing of Romans, Paul commends the Christians at Rome (v. 14), states his purpose in writing them (vv. 15-16), reviews his past ministry in the eastern part of the Roman empire (vv. 17-21), speaks about his future travel plans and proposed missionary outreach in the western part of the empire (vv. 22-29), and requests prayer (vv. 30-32). Because the section contains a number of references to Paul's past missionary journeys (cf. esp. v. 19) and future travel plans (cf. vv. 23-32), it has frequently been called a "travelogue." In 1967, however, Robert Funk coined the term "apostolic parousia" to designate a section of a Pauline letter that was particularly concerned with Paul's apostolic presence.[45] And that expression has become common today as an appropriate term for the body closing of Romans.

Funk considered 15:14-33 (including v. 33, which, as we will argue below, is better understood as the start of the concluding sections of the letter) the most complete example of an apostolic parousia in Paul's letters. He also identified other apostolic parousia sections as being 1 Thess 2:17–3:13; 1 Cor 4:14-21 (with a "secondary" apostolic parousia in 16:1-11); Phil 2:19-24 (with a "secondary" apostolic parousia in 2:25-30), Phlm 21-22, and Gal 4:12-20. Each of these latter identifications, however, is somewhat debatable, and none of them seems to be particularly relevant to our purpose here.

1. The Structure of the Section

Just as there are a number of features that reflect various epistolary conventions of the day in the beginning sections of Romans (i.e., the salutation of 1:1-7, the thanksgiving of 1:8-12, and the body opening of 1:13-15), so there can be found a number of epistolary formulas and features in the latter sections of the letter (i.e., the body closing or apostolic parousia of 15:14-32 and the concluding sections of 15:33–16:27). Those identifiable in the body closing or apostolic parousia section are:

> 15:14 — *confidence formula* and *vocative of direct address:* πέπεισμαι, ἀδελφοί, "I am convinced, brothers and sisters"
>
> 15:15 — *reminder statement:* ἔγραψα ὑμῖν . . . ὡς ἐπαναμιμνῄσκων ὑμᾶς, "I have written you . . . so as to remind you"

45. Cf. R. W. Funk, "Apostolic *Parousia*," 249-68.

15:22 — *visit wish:* ἐνεκοπτόμην τὰ πολλὰ τοῦ ἐλθεῖν πρὸς ὑμᾶς, "I have often been hindered from coming to you"

15:23-24 — *notification of a coming visit:* νυνὶ δὲ . . . ἐλπίζω . . . θεάσασθαι ὑμᾶς, "but now . . . I hope . . . to visit you"

15:29 — *confidence formula:* οἶδα δὲ ὅτι ἐρχόμενος πρὸς ὑμᾶς ἐν πληρώματι εὐλογίας Χηριστοῦ ἐλεύσομαι, "I know that when I come to you, I will come in the full measure of the blessing of Christ"

15:30 — *request formula* and *vocative of direct address:* παρακαλῶ ὑμᾶς, ἀδελφοί, "I urge you, brothers and sisters."

The presence of such a relatively large number of epistolary formulas in the space of only nineteen verses serves to distinguish 15:14-32 from the four major sections in the body middle of Romans — that is, from 1:16–4:25; 5–8; 9–11; and 12:1–15:13 — in which there is a relative paucity of such epistolary formulas. And while the four major sections of the body middle can be characterized by the prominence of a number of ancient rhetorical and oral conventions in their presentations, with only a few epistolary conventions being present (mainly a few vocatives of direct address, a few verbs of saying, and some disclosure formulas, which are located at various strategic places), the body closing or apostolic parousia section of the letter, while reflecting a number of epistolary conventions, is devoid of rhetorical or oral conventions.

The epistolary features of 15:14-32 serve to highlight the structure of the passage. And this structure in its main divisions can be set out as follows:

1. commendation of the Christians at Rome together with a statement of Paul's purpose in writing them (15:14-16), introduced by a *confidence formula* and a *vocative of direct address* in verse 14 and a *reminder statement* in verse 15;

2. review of Paul's past ministry in the eastern part of the Roman empire (15:17-21), which opens with the post-positive particle οὖν that here serves as a transitional conjunction ("therefore") in verse 17;

3. announcement of Paul's future travel plans and missionary outreach to Spain (15:22-29), which opens with a *visit wish* in verse 22 and a *notification of a coming visit* in verses 23-24 and closes with a *confidence formula* in verse 29;

4. request for prayer (15:30-32), which begins with a *request formula* and a *vocative of direct address* in verse 30.

2. The Argument of the Section

The dominance of epistolary features in the beginning sections of the letter (i.e., salutation, thanksgiving, and body opening) and its concluding sections (i.e., apostolic parousia and closing sections), with the four major sections of the letter's body middle being dominated more by rhetorical and oral features, may cause some to view Romans as simply a protreptic discourse set within an epistolary frame. To an extent, of course, that is true. Yet the materials in the epistolary frame also function to support the argument contained in the body middle of the letter. For as the beginning sections of Romans express in rather compressed or condensed fashion Paul's attitudes and concerns when writing, anticipate his primary purposes for writing, and highlight what he wants to develop more fully in the rest of the letter, so the concluding sections recapitulate and unpack many of these same attitudes, concerns, and purposes.

Thus at the beginning of the body closing or apostolic parousia section of 15:14-32, Paul speaks very well of his addressees: "I myself am convinced about you, my brothers and sisters, that you yourselves are full of goodness, complete in knowledge, and able to instruct one another" (v. 14) — which compares to what he said about them at the beginning of the thanksgiving section of 1:8-12: "First, I thank my God through Jesus Christ for all of you, because your faith is being reported all over the world" (v. 8). So as the first word before and the first word after his protreptic "message of instruction and exhortation" in 1:16–15:13, Paul speaks to his addressees in highly commendable terms — implying by both tone and expression that his purpose in writing them was not to rebuke but to encourage and strengthen them.

Then in 15:15-16 he gives one of the clearest statements in Romans regarding his purpose in writing:

> I have written to you quite boldly on some points, as if to remind you of them again, because of the grace given me by God to be a minister (λειτουργόν) of Christ Jesus to the Gentiles in the priestly service (ἱερουργοῦντα) of the gospel of God, so that the Gentiles might become an offering acceptable (ἡ προσφορά . . . εὐπρόσδεκτος) to God, sanctified by the Holy Spirit.

Here Paul directly connects what he has written to the Christians at Rome in the body middle of Romans with his apostolic responsibility to preach the gospel to the Gentiles, as he said in more compact form in 1:5b-6, 13b, and 15. Further, in these verses he claims that he has received grace from God to be a minister of Christ Jesus, which is a claim to authority that echoes the more

441

condensed statements of 1:1 and 1:5a. And he asserts that his addressees, who were dominantly Gentile believers in Jesus, should consider themselves as within the scope of his divinely mandated ministry, as suggested in his reference to "the Gentiles" in 1:5 and the inclusion of them within the scope of his ministry in 1:13b-15. In effect, what Paul is claiming in 15:15-16 is that what he has written in his letter to believers in Jesus at Rome should be viewed by them as a fulfillment of his God-given mandate to proclaim the Christian gospel to Gentiles and should be accepted by them as an authoritative contextualization of that gospel.

Likewise, in these two verses, as well as throughout 15:17-29 where he refers to his past ministries and future plans, there are hints as to how his purpose statement of 1:11-12, which has to do with his proposed visit and present writing ("I long to see you so that I may impart to you some spiritual gift to make you strong — that is, that you and I may be mutually encouraged by each other's faith"), is to be unpacked. For in writing what he has to the Christians at Rome, he wants them to be encouraged by the letter's contents and to respond by encouraging him in his planned mission to the western regions of the Roman empire — not only by their prayers, as he urges in 15:30-31, but also by their financial support, as he implies in 15:32 (so that "by God's will I can come to you with joy and together with you be refreshed").

Of some significance in his statement of purpose in 15:15-16 is the imagery that Paul uses in verse 16 with respect to his ministry — that is, (1) that his ministry to Gentiles was a priestly ministry (a λειτουργός, which is a term that he used earlier in Rom 13:6 of governmental authorities and that the author of Hebrews would use in Heb 1:7 of angels who minister on behalf of God, but in this context undoubtedly has priestly connotations); (2) that his Gentile ministry was a "priestly service of the gospel of God" (ἱερουργοῦντα τὸ εὐαγγέλιον τοῦ θεοῦ); and (3) that his desire was that through his ministry "the Gentiles might become an offering acceptable to God" (ἵνα γένηται ἡ προσφορὰ τῶν ἐθνῶν εὐπρόσδεκτος). The syntax of verse 16 is a bit difficult and requires further explication in a forthcoming commentary proper. But the priestly and sacrificial imagery is clear, and such imagery has seemed to many to be somewhat strange on the lips of the apostle to the Gentiles (or on the pen of one of his amanuenses). Some have argued from this text (and others) that Paul had a cultic understanding of his role as God's appointed apostle to the Gentiles.[46]

46. E.g., K. Weiss, "Paulus — Priester der christlichen Kultgemeinde," *TLZ* 79 (1954) 355-64.

If, however, we understand Paul to be writing to Christians at Rome who had been extensively influenced by the theology, ecclesiology, and ethics of the Mother Church at Jerusalem, whatever their ethnic backgrounds, it should come as no surprise that he would contextualize the nature of his God-given ministry to them using terms and expressions that they would appreciate — that is, using in 15:16 the metaphors of priestly service and sacrificial offering to characterize his ministry. He had earlier included the confessional material of 3:24-26, in which are found such Jewish soteriological expressions as "justification/righteousness" (δικαιοσύνη and cognates), "redemption" (ἀπολύτρωσις), and "sacrifice of atonement/expiation/propitiation" (ἱλαστήριον), as well as the phrase "in his blood" (ἐν τῷ αὐτοῦ αἵματι), when speaking in a Jewish Christian context regarding the work of Christ.

Likewise, it needs also to be pointed out that though he did not use OT quotations in the second section of the body middle of Romans, that is, in 5–8, when representing to the Christians at Rome the nature of his proclamation to Gentiles in the Greco-Roman world — for that was a portrayal to them of what he proclaimed to others who had no knowledge of the Jewish Scriptures — Paul's use in 15:21 of Isa 52:15 ("Those who were not told about him will see, and those who have not heard of him will understand") is understandable (as it was also in 1:16–4:25; 9–11; and 14:1–15:13), for in all of these passages he is speaking directly to addressees (whatever their ethnicity) who were rooted and grounded in the Jewish Scriptures. In fact, in both his use of cultic language in 15:16 (cf. also 3:24-26) and his use of the OT in 15:21 (cf. also 1:16–4:25; 9–11; 14:1–15:13) Paul gives evidence of how he contextualizes the Christian gospel to those who possess a background in and knowledge of the OT Scriptures — whereas, as we have argued earlier, when presenting to his Roman addressees in 5:1–8:39 what he has been proclaiming throughout his missionary activities to pagan Gentiles in the eastern part of the Roman empire (as well as in the corollary general exhortations of chs. 12 and 13:8-14) he shows how he contextualized that gospel message to those who possessed no such background or knowledge.

3. Conclusions

There is much in this body closing or apostolic parousia section of Romans that needs a more intensive exegetical treatment, as will be taken up in a future commentary proper. Suffice it here to say that this section is not just part of the epistolary frame for what Paul really wanted to say in the letter's body middle. More importantly, it highlights essential features regarding the apostle's attitudes, concerns, and purposes when writing to his addressees at Rome — which features were first set out in rather compressed fashion in the opening sections of the letter, then spelled out in the four major sections of the letter's body middle, and here in the letter's body closing are again highlighted and to an extent unpacked. In effect, whereas Paul's concerns and purposes mentioned in the opening sections of the letter provided something of a rough agenda for what he wrote in the letter's body middle, here in the body closing that agenda is again highlighted and now summarized. And that highlighting and summarizing, as will be seen below, is continued in the concluding sections of Romans as well.

3. The Concluding Sections

Debates regarding the integrity of the sixteenth chapter of Romans have been frequent and intensive, with a number of scholars arguing that what Paul wrote to the Christians at Rome was essentially the material of 1–15, with or without the doxology of 16:25-27 — but not including 16:1-23, with or without verse 24 (cf. Chapter II, "Integrity"). Arguments in support of the originality of a fifteen-chapter version of the letter (the so-called "intermediate" form) have been primarily internal and mostly negative. As usually stated, they are to the effect that 16:1-23 (or including v. 24) cannot originally have been part of Romans 1–15 because of (1) the different character of 16:1-23 (or including v. 24) from that of the rest of Romans; (2) the concluding peace benediction of 15:33, which reads like some of the other peace benedictions of Paul's letters that conclude their respective letters (cf. 1 Cor 16:23-24; 2 Cor 13:11; Phil 4:9); (3) the large number of persons, families, and house-church groups who are greeted in 16:3-16, often in a manner that reflects affectionate familiarity, whereas the material of chapters 1–15 seems hardly cognizant of any specific situation within the Roman church; (4) the Ephesian associations of a number of the people greeted, coupled with seeming difficulties in locating some of them at Rome; and (5) the sharp and authoritarian tone reflected in the admonitions against certain schismatics in 16:17-20, whereas the material of chapters 1–15 is more irenic and solicitous. More positively, it has been argued that the presence of a final ἀμήν ("amen"), which follows the peace benediction, reflects an earlier time when the letter ended at 15:33 (though see our proposal below regarding the affirming function of ἀμήν as strengthening the "prayer wish" of the peace benediction and not concluding the letter).

The thesis that chapter 16 is a separate letter of greetings and admonitions has been called "the Ephesian hypothesis." It usually posits that 16:1-23 (perhaps including also v. 24) was a letter originally addressed, in whole or in part, to Christians at Ephesus rather than to Christians at Rome — and only later, for some reason, was attached to Paul's letter to Rome, and so became sandwiched in between the peace benediction of 15:33 and the doxology of 16:25-27 in all of our extant Greek uncial MSS.[47] External support for the originality of a fifteen-chapter version of Romans, with a doxology possibly appended, has been seen to come principally from Chester Beatty Papyrus P[46], which dates from about A.D. 200 and contains the following arrangement of the letter's material (the first seven folios being missing): 5:17–15:33 + 16:25-27 + 16:1-23. This arrangement has suggested to a number of scholars (1) that the earliest form of Romans was either 1–15 alone or 1–15 plus the doxology of 16:25-27, and (2) that what now appears as 16:1-23 (possibly also v. 24) was probably a short letter of greetings and admonitions, whether preserved in whole or in part, that was written by Paul to converts at Ephesus — with that short letter then appended at some early time, for some reason, to Paul's much longer letter to Rome. Likewise, the originality of a fifteen-chapter version of Romans has been inferred (1) from Origen's use of only the first fifteen chapters of Romans, with his treatment of the doxology of 16:25-27 following immediately after his discussion of the peace benediction of 15:33, and (2) from certain structural affinities between 16:1-23 and a typical hellenistic letter of recommendation. But while some sort of thesis for the separate provenance of 16:1-23 (possibly including the material of v. 24) is possible, most scholars today believe that the data cited in support, both internal and external, can be understood better in some other fashion (cf. our earlier discussion of the integrity of the letter in Chapter II).

The work of Harry Gamble in his *The Textual History of the Letter to the Romans* of 1977 has not only put an end to speculations about the originality of a "short" form of Romans (i.e., 1–14, with or without the doxology of 16:25-27) but also effectively discounted theses regarding an early "intermediate" form of the letter (i.e., 1–15, with or without the doxology of 16:25-27). For as Gamble summarizes the conclusions of his research into these two postulated alternative versions of Romans: "The emergence of both the fourteen- and the fifteen-chapter forms of the text must be sought at a later point in the tradition in the letter . . . [when there was] an early effort to 'catholicize' the Roman let-

---

47. Cf., e.g., K. Lake, *Earlier Epistles of St. Paul*, 325-70.

ter."[48] In particular, his conclusion with respect to the separate existence of 16:1-23 (possibly also including v. 24) bears repeating here:

> Decisive arguments for the original unity of the sixteen-chapter text have emerged . . . through our examination of the style and structure of the Pauline epistolary conclusion. We have shown that all of the elements in ch. 16 are typically concluding elements, that without this chapter the fifteen-chapter text lacks an epistolary conclusion, and that the unusual aspects of some elements in ch. 16 find cogent explanation only on the assumption of its Roman address. Thus the unity of the sixteen-chapter text and its Roman address are established.[49]

And this is the position that we adopted earlier (see Chapter II, "Integrity") and that will be followed out both here and in a forthcoming commentary proper.

A Peace Benediction, Commendation, and Greetings (15:33–16:16)

It has often been claimed that the peace benediction and "Amen" of Rom 15:33 provide a fitting conclusion for Paul's letter to Rome (as per the thesis of an original letter of only fifteen chapters) — or, at least, provide a conclusion for the body closing or apostolic parousia section of his letter (usually citing as parallels the grace benediction of 1 Cor 16:23 and the peace and grace benedictions of 2 Cor 13:11b and 13 and of Phil 4:9b and 23). Elsewhere in his extant letters, however, Paul does not conclude either a complete letter or a section of a letter with only a peace benediction. Rather, a peace benediction, when it appears in a Pauline letter, usually begins the letter's conclusion (cf. 1 Thess 5:23; 2 Thess 3:16; Phil 4:9b), with a grace benediction then appearing either immediately after it or shortly thereafter to close off that same conclusion (cf. 1 Thess 5:28; 2 Thess 3:18; Phil 4:23).

Likewise, it may be questioned whether 16:1-2, which commends Phoebe to the Christians at Rome, is an appropriate beginning for a separate letter of introduction and greetings. For a Greek letter of introduction, unlike these first two verses of chapter 16, usually began by describing the person introduced as the "deliverer of the letter."[50] It seems best, therefore,

48. H. Gamble Jr., *Textual History,* 128.
49. H. Gamble Jr., *Textual History,* 127.
50. Cf. C. W. Keyes, "Greek Letter of Introduction," 39.

to consider 15:33–16:16 as the first unit of material in the conclusion of Romans.

1. The Structure of the Section

The peace benediction of 15:33 marks off what follows as being distinct from the body closing or apostolic parousia section before it. And that peace benediction, together with two rather standard epistolary conventions, serves to signal the beginning of the section:

> 15:33 (peace benediction): ὁ θεὸς τῆς εἰρήνης μετὰ πάντων ὑμῶν, "the God of peace be with you all";
> 16:1 (commendation of the letter carrier): συνίστημι ὑμῖν Φοίβην τὴν ἀδελφὴν ἡμῶν, "I commend to you our sister Phoebe";
> 16:3-16 (greetings sent to acquaintances at Rome): ἀσπάσασθε Πρίσκαν καὶ Ἀκύλαν, etc., "Greet Priscilla and Aquila, etc."

And the first person singular παρακαλῶ ("I appeal," "urge," "exhort," "encourage") of 16:17 separates what follows from what precedes (cf. the use of παρακαλῶ earlier in 12:1 and 15:30; see also 1 Cor 1:10; 2 Cor 2:8; Eph 4:1; Phil 4:1).

This section, therefore, can be rather straightforwardly understood as consisting of the following three parts:

1. a peace benediction (15:33);
2. commendation of Phoebe (16:1-2);
3. greetings from Paul through his addressees to acquaintances at Rome (16:3-16).

2. The Implied Arguments of the Section

A peace benediction, a commendation of a particular lady, and a set of seventeen greetings may seem, at first glance, rather standard fare for the conclusion of almost any letter written by a Christian leader during the first century, and so not particularly significant for an understanding of what is presented in the body of Paul's letter to the Christians at Rome. But intrinsic to each of these three units are certain implications that have to do with Paul's argument throughout the letter.

The peace benediction of 15:33, which appears in conjunction with the

447

grace benediction of 16:20b, should probably be viewed as included not just because it was a standard way for a Christian writer to begin a conclusion, but also, and more importantly, in order to highlight Paul's great desire for peace among the Christians at Rome who were, it seems, in dispute with one another regarding a particular matter. Probably the apostle's emphasis on peace had in mind the disputes between "the strong" and "the weak," which he referred to earlier in 14:1–15:13. Paul's use of the affirming particle ἀμήν ("so let it be," "truly," "amen") to strengthen the "prayer wish" of the peace benediction ("The God of peace be with all of you!") suggests that he viewed peace among the Christians at Rome as being of great importance. And from the facts that in the personal subscription of 16:17-23 there are (1) further references to "divisions" between believers in Jesus at Rome and to "obstacles" having been erected by some Christians against other Christians (vv. 17-18), and (2) another peace statement, "The God of peace will soon crush Satan under your feet!" (v. 20a), which appears just before the final grace benediction (v. 20b), it seems quite legitimate to infer that a concern for peace among believers at Rome weighed heavily on Paul's mind as he was writing this concluding section of his letter.

The commendation of Phoebe in 16:1-2, whom Paul identifies as "διάκονον (i.e., 'deacon,' 'servant,' or 'minister') of the church at Cenchreae," which was the port city of Corinth, is significant for (1) what is said about Phoebe herself, (2) what is suggested about the Christians at Rome, and (3) what is implied with respect to Paul's concerns when writing to the Romans. Theories regarding what status Phoebe had in the church at Cenchreae, what part she played in delivering Paul's letter to the Christians at Rome, what part she had in explaining its contents to its addressees, and what exactly Paul meant in identifying her as he does must await exegetical treatment in a future commentary proper. Suffice it here to point out that Paul takes pains in his commendation to ask the Christians at Rome "to welcome her in the Lord in a way worthy of the saints and to give her any help she may need from you" (16:2). It may be assumed that such a reception and such aid would have been natural from any Christian group for any such Christian worthy. But the fact that Paul makes a point of requesting a hospitable welcome of Phoebe suggests that he feared that the believers in Jesus at Rome might have felt somewhat distant and remained somewhat aloof from her because of her association with him and his Gentile mission. The commendation of Phoebe, therefore, seems to be intended not only to introduce Phoebe to the Christians at Rome as Paul's personal emissary, but also to break down any possible barriers between them and her. And so it should probably be understood as contributing to the establishment of a personal link between Paul and the Roman Christians.

The most noticeable features about the greetings of 16:3-16 are the large number of people greeted by Paul and the laudatory descriptions of most of those greeted, with those descriptive statements being related primarily to their association with Paul and his Gentile mission. Only in Col 4:10-14 and Phlm 23-24 are there such commendatory descriptions in a series of greetings of Paul's co-workers. In those cases, however, Paul's commendations are in the context of his conveyance of the greetings of others. Also notable in the greetings of 16:3-16 is the fact that Paul wants his greetings to be conveyed to his friends, relatives, and former associates who were then living at Rome through the Roman Christians, and not *vice versa* to the Roman believers in Jesus through his friends, relatives, and former associates. And at the end of these greetings Paul adds his usual exhortation to "greet one another with a holy kiss" (16:16a) and conveys greetings on behalf of "all the churches of Christ" (16:16b).

None of these matters, of course, taken at face value, might seem too remarkable. For after the Edict of Claudius of 49 was repealed (whether *de facto* before the emperor's death in 54 or *de jure* after his death), many of the Jewish and Gentile Christians who were known by Paul in his ministry throughout the eastern part of the Roman empire may very well have either returned to Rome or migrated to the capital city of the empire (see Chapter IV, "Addressees"). Further, it could be argued (1) that Paul believed that the Christians at Rome would profit from knowing something about the various people to whom he sends his greetings, (2) that it may not have been too unusual for him to ask his addressees to convey his greetings to his friends, relatives, and former associates living in Rome, and (3) that urging his addressees to "greet one another with a holy kiss" and to accept the greetings of "all the churches of Christ" were admonitions common to the apostle.

Yet those to whom Paul sends his greetings, whom he asks his addressees to greet on his behalf, were people who were already part of the Christian community at Rome, not just visitors or outsiders — and so, presumably, were well known to most of Paul's addressees, not strangers who needed to be introduced. It seems, therefore, not ingenuous to understand that a principal function of the list of greetings in verses 3-15 was to promote Paul's credibility with the Christians at Rome, and that he does so by highlighting the personal relationships he has had with several of the people of their community. Or as Harry Gamble has observed and stated with regard to these greetings:

It is especially striking how, in the descriptive phrases, a heavy emphasis is placed on the relationship between the individuals and Paul himself. He ties them to himself, and himself to them. From these features it can be seen that Paul's commendatory greetings to specific individuals serve to place those individuals in a position of respect vis-à-vis the community, but also, by linking the Apostle so closely to them, place Paul in the same position.[51]

Likewise, it seems reasonable to infer from the final greeting of verse 16 that Paul himself sends to his addressees, as well as from the greetings he conveys to them from "all the churches of Christ," that his purpose in so doing involved (1) an affirmation of his authority as God's apostle to the Gentiles to send such greetings, for he had been ordained by God to proclaim the gospel message to the Gentile world, (2) a recognition of his relationship with Gentile Christians throughout the eastern portion of the Greco-Roman world, for he had sustained such a particularly significant position with them that he could speak on their behalf, and (3) an invitation to his addressees at Rome to join with these other churches in acknowledging the appropriateness of his Gentile ministry and the validity of his contextualization of the Christian gospel to pagan Gentiles. As Jeffrey Weima points out and argues with respect to the greetings conveyed in 16:16b:

> Nowhere else does Paul speak so broadly ("all the churches") in passing on the greetings of others. So here, it seems, Paul presents himself to the Romans as one who has the official backing of all the churches in Achaia, Macedonia, Asia, Galatia, Syria and elsewhere in the eastern part of the empire. Furthermore, their support demonstrates that his gospel has a proven track record among believers throughout the Mediterranean world. Consequently, there is in this greeting an implied challenge to believers in Rome that they join these other churches in recognizing the author of Paul's apostleship and his gospel.[52]

Or as James Dunn has stated matters more concisely and a bit more mundanely: "The greeting thus has a 'political' overtone: Paul speaks for all these churches, and they are behind him in his mission."[53]

---

51. H. Gamble Jr., *Textual History*, 92.
52. J. A. D. Weima, *Neglected Endings*, 227.
53. J. D. G. Dunn, *Romans*, 2.899.

Personal Subscription: Additional Admonitions, a Grace Benediction, Further Greetings, and a Doxology (16:17-27)

Paul usually concluded his letters with a personal subscription or postscript that (1) frequently included further greetings and/or additional admonitions, (2) sometimes incorporated both a peace benediction and a grace benediction, but always ended in some fashion with a grace benediction, and (3) was written in his own hand.[54] And the material of 16:17-27 (minus v. 24, as we will argue below) appears to be such a subscription.

Some scholars have viewed the personal subscription of Romans as being all of chapter 16, others as starting at 16:21, directly after what they believe to be a peace benediction at 16:20a and then the grace benediction of 16:20b. We believe, however, that the letter's subscription should be seen as beginning at 16:17 with the request formula παρακαλῶ ὑμᾶς ("I urge you") and the vocative of direct address ἀδελφοί ("brothers and sisters") and ending with the doxology of 16:25-27. Here in this final section of the letter Paul seems to have taken the pen from Tertius, one of his associates who served as his amanuensis, and added a postscript in his own handwriting.

The personal subscriptions of Paul have generally been treated in a rather cursory fashion, largely because of (1) the natural tendency of commentators to focus on the weightier matters found in the thanksgiving sections and body sections of the apostle's letters, and (2) the supposition that the opening salutations and closing subscriptions of the apostle's letters are purely conventional in nature and function only to establish or maintain contact with their addressees. But as Adolf Deissmann long ago argued (with particular reference to the personal subscription of Gal 6:11-18, though with application to all of the subscriptions of Paul's letters): "More attention ought to be paid to the concluding words of the letters generally; they are of the highest importance if we are ever to understand the Apostle."[55] And this thesis has been significantly developed by Ann Jervis[56] and by Jeffrey Weima.[57]

What it appears Paul wanted to do in this personal subscription of 16:17-27 (minus the inclusion of v. 24, which is weakly attested) was (1) to re-

---

54. Cf. Gal 6:11-18; 2 Thess 3:16-18; 1 Cor 16:19-24; Col 4:18; and Philem 19-25; see R. N. Longenecker, "Ancient Amanuenses and the Pauline Epistles," 282-92.

55. A. Deissmann, *Bible Studies,* 347; see also G. Milligan, *The New Testament Documents: Their Origin and Early History* (London: Macmillan, 1913), 21-28.

56. L. A. Jervis, *Purpose of Romans,* 132-57.

57. J. A. D. Weima, *Neglected Endings,* 215-30; *idem,* "Preaching the Gospel in Rome," 358-66.

inforce the few personal connections he had with his addressees at Rome, (2) to validate all he had written in the letter, whatever sources were used and however the letter was finally produced, (3) to express some concerns he had about his Roman addressees, (4) to send the greetings of those who were associated with him at Corinth and Cenchreae, and (5) to summarize the major thrust of what he wrote in his letter to the Christians at Rome, which he characterized as being "my gospel."

1. The Structure of the Section

The section contains in only seven verses a relatively substantial number of rather common epistolary formulas and conventions of the day:

16:17 (*request formula* and *vocative of direct address*): παρακαλῶ ὑμᾶς, ἀδελφοί, "I urge you, brothers and sisters"

16:19 (*expression of joy*): ἐφ᾽ ὑμῖν χαίρω, "I rejoice over you"

16:21 (*conveyance of the greetings of others*): ἀσπάζεται ὑμᾶς Τιμόθεος ὁ συνεργός μου καὶ Λούκιος καὶ Ἰάσων καὶ Σωσίπατρος οἱ συγγενεῖς μου, "Timothy, my co-worker, greets you, as do also Lucius, Jason, and Sosipater, my relatives"

16:22 (*inserted greeting*): ἀσπάζομαι ὑμᾶς ἐγὼ Τέρτιος ὁ γράψας τὴν ἐπιστολήν, "I, Tertius, who wrote [down] this epistle greet you"

16:23 (*conveyance of further greetings of others*): ἀσπάζεται ὑμᾶς Γάιος. ἀσπάζεται ὑμᾶς Ἔραστος . . . καὶ Κούαρτος, "Gaius greets you, Erastus greets you, . . . as does also Quartus."

The section also includes a grace benediction in 16:20b, which follows a peace statement in 16:20a. The peace statement of 16:20a, however, is not strictly a peace benediction (as in 15:33), but rather should be seen as a promise of peace that God will bring about with respect to the situation alluded to in 16:17-19.

A second grace benediction at what has traditionally been versified as verse 24 is highly doubtful. Some have wanted to retain it, particularly when the integrity of the doxology of 16:25-27 is questioned, so as to close off the entire letter with a final grace benediction, as Paul does elsewhere in his other letters.[58] But evidence for a second grace benediction at 16:24 is lacking in the

---

58. So, e.g., H. Gamble Jr., *Textual History,* 122-24; L. A. Jervis, *Purpose of Romans,* 138-39.

Greek textual tradition, with no major papyrus or uncial manuscripts in support. Further, farewell wishes in ancient Greek letters — which usually begin with ἔρρωσο or ἔρρωσθε, "farewell," but at times begin with εὐτύχει or its intensified form διευτύχει, "good luck" or "best wishes" — evidence a rather standard pattern: the first farewell appearing somewhere in the first part of a letter's conclusion, in material written down on behalf of an author by an amanuensis or secretary; the second farewell appearing in the personal subscription of a letter, written by an author himself in his own handwriting. And this is the pattern in the concluding sections of Romans: (1) the peace benediction at the beginning of the letter's concluding sections at 15:33, with the first section of that conclusion, that is, 15:33–16:16, written down by Tertius at Paul's direction; (2) the grace benediction in the personal subscription section at 16:20b, with the second section of that conclusion, that is, 16:17-27 (minus v. 24), evidently written by Paul himself in his own handwriting.

In the personal subscription of Romans, however, there is also a further set of greetings in 16:21-23, which appears immediately after the grace benediction of 16:20b. This latter set in 16:21-23 is different from the first set in 16:3-16. For whereas in the first set Paul sends his own greetings to friends, relatives, and former associates living in Rome, which he asks his addressees to convey (16:3-15) — as well as requesting the Christians at Rome to "greet one another with a holy kiss" and conveying greetings from "all the churches of Christ" (16:16) — in this latter set he sends the greetings of seven of his co-workers, relatives, and friends at Corinth and Cenchreae to the Christians at Rome (16:21 and 23). And, interestingly, included within this latter set of greetings is the inclusion of a greeting from Tertius (16:22), who served as Paul's amanuensis in the writing of Romans and actually describes himself as "the one who wrote [down] this letter 'in the Lord'" (ὁ γράψας τὴν ἐπιστολὴν ἐν κυρίῳ) — whatever the expression "in the Lord" in this context may mean.

A grace benediction is normally the last item in the personal subscriptions of the Pauline corpus of letters. But personal subscriptions in Paul's letters, as well as in the extant letters of antiquity generally, vary considerably in format. And it may be presumed that the variations that appear in the subscriptions of both ancient letters generally and Paul's letters in particular are the result of, and therefore reflect, the particular situations that then existed when those respective letters were written.

Here in Romans it may be postulated that after Paul had written his final grace benediction at 16:20b, some of his co-workers, relatives, and friends at Corinth and Cenchreae had gathered — or, perhaps, were called together by Paul himself — to hear the apostle's letter read to them (whether by Paul himself, or by Tertius, or by a combination of readers from the group itself), before entrusting it to Phoebe to be carried on to Rome. Likewise, it may also reasonably be conjectured that after the letter was read, those who had gathered asked that their greetings also be sent with the letter — not only as an act of cordiality, but probably, and more importantly, to lend their support to what Paul had written. Tertius, too, who was Paul's amanuensis at the time, evidently wanted to be included and to express his support as well, and so took back the pen from Paul to include his greeting. And it may be further conjectured that, after having appended that set of rather spontaneous and supportive greetings, Paul then — desiring to emphasize again his primary purpose for writing and to highlight what he considered to be the major thrust of what he had written — closed off his letter to the Christians at Rome with the more formal, rather eloquent, and summarizing doxology of 16:25-27.

The individual items in Paul's personal subscription of Romans can, therefore, be set out as follows:

1. additional admonitions (16:17-20a), which begin with a *request formula* (παρακαλῶ ὑμᾶς, "I urge you") and a *vocative of direct address* (ἀδελφοί, "brothers and sisters") in verse 17, but interject also a note of confidence with an epistolary expression of joy (ἐφ᾽ ὑμῖν χαίρω, "I rejoice over you") in verse 19;
2. a grace benediction (16:20b);
3. further greetings sent to Rome by Paul from his co-workers, friends, and relatives associated with him at Corinth and Cenchreae (16:21-23);
4. a concluding doxology (16:25-27).

2. The Implied Arguments of the Section

Jeffrey Weima has observed with respect to the function of a Pauline conclusion, which in the letter to the Romans he rightly identifies as being the materials of 15:33–16:27 (minus v. 24), that

> Paul commonly shapes and adapts this epistolary unit in such a way that it relates directly to — sometimes, in fact, even summarizes — the major concerns and themes taken up in the bodies of their respective letters. Thus the letter closing functions a lot like the thanksgiving, but in reverse. For as the thanksgiving foreshadows and points ahead to the major concerns to be addressed in the body of the letter, so the closing serves to highlight and encapsulate the main points previously taken up

in the body. This recapitulating function of Paul's letter closings suggests that the letter closing of Romans is likewise significant for revealing the central concern(s) of Paul at work in the rest of the letter.[59]

And this we believe to be true not only for the first section of Paul's conclusion in 15:33–16:16, which Tertius wrote down at Paul's direction (i.e., the peace benediction, a commendation of Phoebe, and a long list of personal greetings), but also for the second section or personal subscription of 16:17-27 (minus v. 24), which Paul evidently wrote in his own handwriting (i.e., additional admonitions; the grace benediction; further greetings conveyed by the apostle from his co-workers, friends, and relatives at Corinth and Cenchreae; and a concluding doxology).

The admonitions of 16:17-20a seem to have in mind the disruptions referred to in 14:1 15:13, which had to do with conflicts between "the strong" and "the weak." For here in this additional set of admonitions Paul alludes to "divisions," "obstacles," and those who "by smooth talk and flattery deceive the minds of naive people," characterizing what was taking place as "contrary to the teaching you have learned," and urging the Roman Christians to "keep away from them" (16:17-18). His admonitions, however, are not rebukes of his addressees. For even when speaking of divisions and obstacles within the Christian congregations at Rome, he refers to his addressees as "brothers and sisters" (v. 17a), acknowledges that they had received proper teaching (v. 17b), and distinguishes them from those who were causing trouble in the Christian congregations at Rome by "not serving our Lord Christ but their own appetites" (v. 18). In fact, Paul goes on to praise the Christians at Rome for their "obedience" (16:19a), urges them in a rather nonjudgmental manner to be "wise about what is good and innocent about what is evil" (16:19b), and assures them that "the God of peace will shortly crush Satan under your feet" (συντρίψει τὸν Σατανᾶν ὑπὸ τοὺς πόδας ὑμῶν ἐν τάχει).

This matter of relations between "the strong" and "the weak" within the community of Christians at Rome seems to have been one of great concern to Paul. It was a situation that he had evidently heard about from others and that he dealt with in a rather direct manner in 14:1–15:13. Here in 16:17-20a, however, at the very beginning of his personal subscription, he raises it again — though not so much to suggest that it was of major importance on his own agenda, but to acknowledge that it was a major concern on his ad-

59. J. A. D. Weima, "Preaching the Gospel in Rome," 359.

dressees' agenda and to use that situation within the various congregations at Rome as another opportunity to build relations with his addressees.

Paul's major concerns when writing, as we have argued (see Chapter V, "Purpose"), had to do with (1) the Christians at Rome understanding and appreciating his distinctive manner of contextualizing the Christian message in his Gentile mission (i.e., his "spiritual gift" to them, as referred to in 1:11 of the thanksgiving section; cf. also "my gospel" of 2:16 and 16:25) and (2) the mutual benefit that they and he could derive from each other (as alluded to in 1:12 of the thanksgiving section; cf. also 15:24 and 32 of the apostolic parousia section). Here in 16:17-20a, however, he seems to be aligning himself with his addressees in their particular situation and with one of their major concerns — speaking affectionately of them as "brothers and sisters" (v. 17a), affirming their proper grounding in the Christian faith (v. 17b), placing them in an entirely different category from certain divisive persons in their midst (vv. 18-19a), praising them for their obedience (v. 19a), urging them in a non-judgmental manner to be "wise about what is good and innocent about what is evil" (v. 19b), and assuring them that "the God of peace will shortly crush Satan under your feet" (v. 20a) — all of this in order to build relations with them.

The set of greetings in 16:21-23, however, as noted above in positing a probable scenario for their inclusion, also serves to build relations with Paul's Roman addressees. It is not just a further set of greetings, in competition with the earlier set of greetings in 16:3-16, but a complementary set to that of 16:3-16. For just as the greetings of the earlier set in 16:3-16 (esp. vv. 3-15) to friends, relatives, and former associates who were at that time living in Rome, which Paul asks his addressees to convey, should be seen as functioning principally to promote the apostle's credibility among the believers in Jesus at Rome by highlighting the personal relationships that he had with several of the people of their community, so this second set of greetings in 16:21-23, which he sends from seven of his friends, relatives, and associates at Corinth and Cenchreae (and to which Tertius, who acted as his amanuensis, attaches his greetings), should be seen as having been included primarily to support Paul's apostolic authority and to enhance the acceptability of his contextualization of the gospel among the Christians at Rome.

The authenticity of the doxology of 16:25-27 has been, as noted earlier (cf. Chapter II, "Integrity"), rather hotly contested, on both textual and literary grounds. The textual tradition exhibits various understandings of its placement: (1) after 14:23 (i.e., at the end of the "short" form of the letter); (2) after 15:33 (i.e., at the end of the "intermediate" form of the letter); (3) after 16:23/24 (i.e., at the end of the "long" form of the letter); (4) after both 14:23 and 16:23/24 (e.g., in uncial codices A [02] of the fifth century and P [025] of the ninth century); (5) after both 14:23 and 15:33, with 16:1-23/24 being omitted (i.e., in minuscule 1506); or (6) omitted altogether (e.g., in uncial codices F [010] and G [012] of the ninth century). The language and style of the doxology have also been seen by many to be non-Pauline. The majority of NT scholars today, therefore, have viewed the doxology of 16:25-27 as a post-Pauline addition to Romans — with many also postulating that it probably originated in the mid-second century during the time of Marcion, who, it is argued, was the one who excised chapters 15–16, and whose followers would then have composed the doxology as a fitting conclusion to chapters 1–14.

Paul's usual style, as many have observed, was not to finish off a letter with a doxology, but, rather, to conclude with a grace benediction. One exception is the love wish of 1 Cor 16:24, which should probably be viewed as a postscript penned by Paul himself, that appears after the grace benediction of 1 Cor 16:23, and so may be seen as something of a parallel to the concluding phenomena in Romans where further greetings in 16:21-23 and a doxology in 16:25-27 appear after the grace benediction of 16:20b. A further problem is that the language of 16:25-27 is quite formal, perhaps even liturgical, being more like the so-called deutero-Pauline letters, particularly Ephesians and the Pastorals. But if these later letters are accepted as being in some sense written by Paul — whether as an encyclical letter (as possibly Ephesians) and/or with an amanuensis having been given greater freedom (as possibly the Pastorals) — then this particular phenomenon loses much of its adverse critical value. So while the above cited observations regarding the placement and language of the doxology of 16:25-27 are pertinent, conclusions often drawn from them against the authenticity of these three verses are not overly convincing.

Some of what can be said regarding the concluding doxology of Romans has already been said earlier in Chapter II, "Integrity," and much of what needs to be said by way of exegesis can only be explicated in a forthcoming commentary treatment. Suffice it here (1) to remind readers that there are a number of good scholars, both of a previous generation and today, who hold to the authenticity of the doxology and its placement as the final feature of Paul's letter to Rome, and (2) to declare our openness to Paul as the author of the doxology and its original placement at the end of chapter 16, reserving a more extended exegetical treatment for the commentary to follow.

The doxology of 16:25-27, as Jeffrey Weima points out, is "striking for the way in which it recapitulates the concern of Paul" as expressed throughout his letter to the Christians at Rome.[60] In particular, as Weima goes on to note:

> The reference to "*my* gospel" recalls well Paul's concern in the letter opening, thanksgiving, letter body and apostolic parousia to share his gospel with the Roman believers. The doxology claims that Paul's gospel will be used by God "to strengthen" (στηρίξαι) the believers in Rome — the same point that was made in the thanksgiving section (1.11, "in order that you may be strengthened" [στηριχθῆναι]). The doxology further highlights the continuity of Paul's gospel with the message of the OT — a matter also stressed in the letter opening (1.2-4). More specifically, the phrase "through the prophetic writings" (16.26, διὰ γραφῶν προφητικῶν) is a deliberate allusion to the opening words of the letter, "through his prophets in the holy writings" (1.2, διὰ τῶν προφητῶν αὐτοῦ ἐν γραφαῖς ἁγίαις). The goal or purpose of making the mystery of the gospel known is "to bring about the obedience of faith for all the Gentiles" (16.26, εἰς ὑπακοὴν πίστεως εἰς πάντα τὰ ἔθνα). This phrase from the doxology provides yet another direct verbal link with the letter opening: "to bring about the obedience of faith for all the Gentiles" (1.5, εἰς ὑπακοὴν πίστεως ἐν πᾶσιν τοῖς ἔθνεσιν). It also recalls Paul's point in the apostolic parousia that Christ is working through him "to bring about the obedience of the Gentiles (15.18, εἰς ὑπακοὴν ἐθνῶν).[61]

And as Weima additionally observes: "The strong recapitulating character of the doxology serves as yet a further means by which Paul seeks to establish the authority and acceptability of his gospel among the Roman believers."[62]

Supplemental Bibliography

See also "Bibliography of Selected Commentaries." All references in the footnotes to works included in this list are by the authors' names and abbreviated titles.

Aageson, James W. "Scripture and Structure in the Development of the Argument in Romans 9–11," *CBQ* 48 (1968) 265-89.

Achtemeier, Paul J. "*Omne Verbum Sonat:* The New Testament and the Oral Environment of Late Western Antiquity," *JBL* 109 (1990) 3-27.

---

60. J. A. D. Weima, *Neglected Endings*, 229.
61. J. A. D. Weima, *Neglected Endings*, 229.
62. J. A. D. Weima, *Neglected Endings*, 229.

Aletti, Jean-Noël. "The Rhetoric of Romans 5–8," in *The Rhetorical Analysis of Scripture: Essays from the 1995 London Conference,* ed. S. E. Porter and T. H. Olbricht. JSNT.SS 146. Sheffield: Sheffield Academic Press, 1997, 294-308.

Allison, Dale C., Jr. "The Pauline Epistles and the Synoptic Gospels: The Pattern of the Parallels," *NTS* 28 (1982) 1-32.

Anderson, R. Dean, Jr. *Ancient Rhetorical Theory and Paul.* Kampen: Kok Pharos, 1996; rev. ed. Leuven: Peeters, 1998, esp. 169-219.

Aune, David E. *The New Testament in Its Literary Environment.* Philadelphia: Westminster, 1987, 183-225.

————. "Romans as a *Logos Protreptikos* in the Context of Ancient Religious and Philosophical Propaganda," in *Paulus als Missionar und Theologe und das antike Judentum,* ed. M. Hengel and U. Heckel. WUNT 58. Tübingen: Mohr-Siebeck, 1991, 91-124; abbreviated version: "Romans as a *Logos Protrepikos*," in Donfried, ed., *Romans Debate* (1991), 278-96.

————. *The Westminster Dictionary of New Testament and Early Christian Literature and Rhetoric.* Louisville: Westminster/John Knox, 2003.

————, ed. *Greco-Roman Literature and the New Testament: Selected Forms and Genres.* SBL.SBS 21. Atlanta: Scholars, 1988.

Baird, William R. "On Reading Romans Today," *Int* 34 (1980) 45-58.

Bassler, Jouette M. *Divine Impartiality: Paul and a Theological Axiom.* SBL.DS 59. Chico: Scholars, 1982.

————. "Divine Impartiality in Paul's Letter to the Romans," *NovT* 26 (1984) 43-58.

Beker, J. Christiaan. *Paul the Apostle: The Triumph of God in Life and Thought.* Edinburgh: T&T Clark; Philadelphia: Fortress, 1980, 59-93.

————. "The Faithfulness of God and the Priority of Israel in Paul's Letter to the Romans," in *Christians among Jews and Gentiles,* ed. G. W. E. Nickelsburg and G. W. MacRae. Philadelphia: Fortress, 1986, 10-16.

Berger, Klaus. "Abraham in den paulinischen Hauptbriefen," *MTZ* 17 (1966) 47-89.

Bjerkelund, Carl J. *Parakalō: Form, Funktion und Sinn der parakalō-Sätze in den paulinischen Briefen.* BTN 1. Oslo: Universitetsforlaget, 1967.

Boers, Hendrikus W. "The Problem of Jews and Gentiles in the Macro-structure of Romans," *Neot* 15 (1981) 1-11.

————. "The Foundation of Paul's Thought: A Methodological Investigation — The Problem of the Coherent Center of Paul's Thought," *ST* 42 (1988) 55-68.

————. *The Justification of the Gentiles: Paul's Letter to the Galatians and Romans.* Peabody: Hendrickson, 1994.

Brown, Raymond E. "Not Jewish Christianity and Gentile Christianity, but Types of Jewish/Gentile Christianity," *CBQ* 45 (1983) 74-79.

————. "The Beginnings of Christianity at Rome" and "The Roman Church near the End of the First Christian Generation (A.D. 58 — Paul to the Romans)," in R. E. Brown and J. P. Meier, *Antioch and Rome: New Testament Cradles of Catholic Christianity.* New York: Paulist, 1983, 92-127.

459

————. "Further Reflections on the Origins of the Church of Rome," in *The Conversation Continues: Studies in Paul and John in Honor of J. L. Martyn*, ed. R. T. Fortna and B. R. Gaventa. Nashville: Abingdon, 1990, 98-115.

Campbell, William S. "Romans III as a Key to the Structure and Thought of Romans," *NovT* 23 (1981) 22-40; repr. in Donfried, ed., *The Romans Debate* (1991), 251-64.

————. "Paul's Strategy in Writing Romans," in *Paul's Gospel in an Intercultural Context: Jew and Gentile in the Letter to the Romans*. New York: Peter Lang, 1991, 132-60.

————. "A Theme for Romans?" in *Paul's Gospel in an Intercultural Context: Jew and Gentile in the Letter to the Romans*. New York: Peter Lang, 1991, 161-99.

Carras, George P. "Romans 2,1-29: A Dialogue on Jewish Ideals," *Bib* 73 (1992) 183-207.

Dahl, Nils A. "The Missionary Theology in the Epistle to the Romans," in *Studies in Paul: Theology for the Early Christian Mission*. Minneapolis: Augsburg, 1977, 70-94.

————. "The Future of Israel," in *Studies in Paul: Theology for the Early Christian Mission*. Minneapolis: Augsburg, 1977, 137-58.

Davies, W. D. *Paul and Rabbinic Judaism: Some Rabbinic Elements in Pauline Theology*. London: SPCK, 1948[1], 1955[2], 1970[3]; Philadelphia: Fortress, 1980[4]; see pages 136-46 in all four editions and the footnote at page 146 in the 1980 edition.

Deissmann, Adolf. *Bible Studies: Contributions Chiefly from Papyri and Inscriptions to the History of the Language, Literature, and the Religion of Hellenistic Judaism and Primitive Christianity*, trans. A. Grieve. Edinburgh: T&T Clark, 1901.

————. *Light from the Ancient East: The New Testament Illustrated by Recently Discovered Texts of the Graeco-Roman World*, trans. L. R. M. Strachan. London: Hodder & Stoughton, 1927 (from "fourth, completely revised" German 1923 ed.).

Donfried, K. P., ed. *The Romans Debate*. Minneapolis: Augsburg, 1977; revised and expanded edition. Peabody: Hendrickson, 1991.

Doty, William G. *Letters in Primitive Christianity*. Philadelphia: Fortress, 1973.

Dunn, James D. G. "The New Perspective on Paul," *BJRL* 65 (1983) 95-122; repr. in *idem, Jesus, Paul and the Law: Studies in Mark and Galatians*. London: SPCK; Louisville: Westminster, 1990, 183-214.

————. "Paul's Epistle to the Romans: An Analysis of Structure and Argument," in *ANRW* II.25.4, ed. W. Haase and H. Temporini. New York: de Gruyter, 1987, 2845-90.

————. *The Partings of the Ways between Christianity and Judaism*. London: SCM; Philadelphia: Trinity Press International, 1991, 117-39.

————. "The Formal and Theological Coherence of Romans," in Donfried, ed., *The Romans Debate* (1991), 245-50.

————. "How New Was Paul's Gospel? The Problem of Continuity and Discontinuity," in *Gospel in Paul: Studies on Corinthians, Galatians and Romans for Richard N. Longenecker*, ed. L. A. Jervis and P. Richardson. Sheffield: Sheffield Academic Press, 1994, 367-88.

————. "Paul and Justification by Faith," in *The Road from Damascus: The Impact of Paul's Conversion on His Life, Thought, and Ministry*, ed. R. N. Longenecker. MNTS. Grand Rapids: Eerdmans, 1997, 85-101.

————. *The New Perspective on Paul: Collected Essays*. WUNT 185. Tübingen: Mohr-Siebeck, 2005.

Dupont, Jacques J. "Le problème de la structure littéraire de l'Epître aux Romains," *RB* 62 (1955) 365-97.

————. "Appel aux faibles et aux forts dans la communauté romaine (Rom. 14,1–15,13)," in *Studiorum Paulinorum Congressus Internationalis Catholicus 1961*. Rome: Pontificio Instituto Biblico, 1963, 257-66.

Elliott, Mark A. "Romans 9–11 and Jewish Remnant Theology." Th.M. Dissertation, Wycliffe College — Toronto School of Theology, University of Toronto, 1986.

————. *The Survivors of Israel: A Reconsideration of the Theology of Pre-Christian Judaism*. Grand Rapids: Eerdmans, 2000.

Feuillet, André. "Le plan salvifique de Dieu d'après l'Epître aux Romains," *RB* 57 (1950) 336-87 and 489-506.

————. "Les attaches bibliques des antitheses pauliniennes dans la première partie de l'épître aux Romains (1-8)," in *Mélanges bibliques*, ed. B. Rigaux. Gembleux: Duculot, 1970, 33-349.

Friedrich, Johannes, Wolfgang Pöhlmann, and Peter Stuhlmacher. "Zur historischen Situation und Intention von Röm 13,1-7," *ZTK* 73 (1976) 131-66.

Funk, Robert W. *Language, Hermeneutic, and Word of God: The Problem of Language in the New Testament and Contemporary Theology*. New York: Harper & Row, 1966, 250-74.

————. "The Apostolic *Parousia*: Form and Significance," in *Christian History and Interpretation: Studies Presented to John Knox*, ed. W. R. Farmer, C. F. D. Moule, and R. R. Niebuhr. Cambridge: Cambridge University Press, 1967, 249-68.

Furnish, Victor Paul. "The Jesus-Paul Debate: From Baur to Bultmann," *BJRL* 47 (1965) 342-81.

Gamble, Harry, Jr. *The Textual History of the Letter to the Romans: A Study in Textual and Literary Criticism*. SD 42. Grand Rapids: Eerdmans, 1977.

Gloege, Gerhard. *Reich Gottes und Kirche im Neuen Testament*. Gütersloh: C. Bertelsmann, 1929, esp. 212-19 and 241-49.

Goodspeed, Edgar J. "Phoebe's Letter of Introduction," *HTR* 44 (1951) 55-57.

Grayston, Kenneth. "'I Am Not Ashamed of the Gospel': Romans 1:16a and the Structure of the Epistle," in *Studia Evangelica* 2. TU 87. Berlin, 1964, 569-73.

Grobel, Kendrick. "A Chiastic Retribution-Formula in Romans 2," in *Zeit und Geschichte. Dankesgabe an R. Bultmann*, ed. E. Dinkler. Tübingen: Mohr-Siebeck, 1964, 255-61.

Guerra, Anthony J. "Romans: Paul's Purpose and Audience with Special Attention to Romans 9–11," *RevistB* 97 (1990) 219-37.

————. *Romans and the Apologetic Tradition: The Purpose, Genre and Audience of Paul's Letter*. SNTS.MS 81. Cambridge: Cambridge University Press, 1995.

Hall, David R. "Romans 3.1-8 Reconsidered," *NTS* 29 (1983) 183-97.

Harvey, John D. *Listening to the Text: Oral Patterning in Paul's Letters.* Grand Rapids: Baker, 1998.

Hasel, G. F. *The Remnant: The History and Theology of the Remnant Idea from Genesis to Isaiah.* Berrien Springs, MI: Andrews University Press, 1972.

Hays, Richard B. "Psalm 143 and the Logic of Romans 3," *JBL* 99 (1980) 107-15.

Hillebrand, Bruno. *Zur Struktur des Romans.* Darmstadt: Wissenschaftliche Buchgesellschaft, 1978.

Hommel, H. "Das 7 Kapitel des Römerbriefs im Licht antiker Überlieferung," *TV* 8 (1961) 90-116.

Hooker, Morna D. "Adam in Romans 1," *NTS* 6 (1960) 297-306.

————. "A Further Note on Romans 1," *NTS* 13 (1966) 181-83.

Hurtado, Larry W. "The Doxology at the End of Romans," in *New Testament Textual Criticism: Its Significance for Exegesis (Essays in Honour of Bruce M. Metzger),* ed. E. J. Epp and G. D. Fee. Oxford: Clarendon, 1981, 185-99.

Jeremias, Joachim. "Der Gedanke des 'Heiligen Restes' im Spätjudentum und in der Verkündigung Jesu," *ZNW* 42 (1949) 184-94.

————. "Chiasmus in den Paulusbriefen," *ZNW* 49 (1958) 145-56.

————. "Die Gedankenfügung in den paulinischen Briefen," in *The Law of the Spirit in Rom 7 and 8,* ed. L. de Lorenzi. Rome: St. Paul's Abbey, 1976, 129-46.

Jervis, L. Ann. *The Purpose of Romans: A Comparative Letter Structure Investigation.* JSNT.SS 55. Sheffield: Sheffield Academic Press, 1991.

Jewett, Robert L. "Following the Argument of Romans," *WW* 6 (1986) 382-89; adapted and expanded in Donfried, ed., *The Romans Debate* (1991), 265-77.

————. "Paul, Phoebe, and the Spanish Mission," in *The Social World of Formative Christianity and Judaism,* ed. J. Neusner, E. S. Frerichs, P. Borgen, and R. Horsley. Philadelphia: Fortress, 1988, 148-55.

Kattenbusch, Ferdinand. "Der Spruch über Petrus und die Kirche bei Matthäus," *TSK* 94 (1922) 96-121.

Keck, Leander E. "The Function of Romans 3.10-18," in *God's Christ and His People: Studies in Honor of N. A. Dahl,* ed. J. Jervell *et al.* Oslo, 1977, 141-57.

————. "What Makes Romans Tick?" in *Pauline Theology,* vol. 3: *Romans,* ed. D. M. Hay and E. E. Johnson. Minneapolis: Fortress, 1995, 3-29.

Kennedy, George A. *New Testament Interpretation through Rhetorical Criticism.* Chapel Hill: University of North Carolina Press, 1984, esp. 152-56.

Keyes, C. W. "The Greek Letter of Introduction," *AJP* 56 (1935) 28-44.

Kim, Seyoon. *The Origin of Paul's Gospel.* Tübingen: Mohr-Siebeck, 1981; Grand Rapids: Eerdmans, 1982; 2nd ed. Tübingen: Mohr-Siebeck, 1984.

————. "God Reconciled His Enemy to Himself: The Origin of Paul's Concept of Reconciliation," in *The Road from Damascus: The Impact of Paul's Conversion on His Life, Thought, and Ministry,* ed. R. N. Longenecker. MNTS. Grand Rapids: Eerdmans, 1997, 102-24.

————. "2 Cor 5:11-21 and the Origin of Paul's Concept of 'Reconciliation,'" *NovT* 39 (1997) 360-84.

————. *Paul and the New Perspective: Second Thoughts on the Origin of Paul's Gospel.* Grand Rapids: Eerdmans, 2002.

Kinoshita, Junji. "Romans — Two Writings Combined: A New Interpretation of the Body of Romans," *NovT* 7 (1965) 258-77.

Kümmel, Werner Georg. "Jesus und die Anfänge der Kirche," *ST* 7 (1953) 1-27.

Lake, Kirsopp. *The Earlier Epistles of St. Paul: Their Motive and Origin.* London: Rivingtons, 1927².

Léon-Dufour, X. "Situation littéraire de Rom 5," *RSR* 51 (1963) 83-95.

Lincoln, Andrew T. "From Wrath to Justification: Tradition, Gospel, and Audience in the Theology of Romans 1:18–4:25," in *Pauline Theology,* vol. 3: *Romans,* ed. D. M. Hay and E. E. Johnson. Minneapolis: Fortress, 1995, 130-59.

Lohse, Eduard. "Zur Analyse und Interpretation von Röm 8.1-17," in *The Law of the Spirit in Rom 7 und 8,* ed. L. de Lorenzi. Rome: St. Paul's Abbey, 1976, 129-46.

Longenecker, Bruce W. "Different Answers to Different Issues: Israel, the Gentiles, and Salvation History in Romans 9–11," *JSNT* 36 (1989) 95-123.

————. *Eschatology and the Covenant: A Comparison of 4 Ezra and Romans 1–11.* JSNT.SS 57. Sheffield: JSOT, 1991.

————, ed. *Narrative Dynamics in Paul: A Critical Assessment.* Louisville: Westminster/John Knox, 2002.

Longenecker, Richard N. *Paul, Apostle of Liberty.* New York: Harper & Row, 1964; repr. Grand Rapids: Baker, 1976; repr. Vancouver: Regent College, 2003.

————. "Ancient Amanuenses and the Pauline Epistles," in *New Dimensions in New Testament Study,* ed. R. N. Longenecker and M. C. Tenney. Grand Rapids: Zondervan, 1974, 281-97.

————. "Three Ways of Understanding Relations between the Testaments — Historically and Today," in *Tradition and Interpretation in the New Testament* (*Festschrift* for E. Earle Ellis), ed. G. F. Hawthorne with O. Betz. Tübingen: Mohr; Grand Rapids: Eerdmans, 1987, 22-32.

————. "Prolegomena to Paul's Use of Scripture in Romans," *BBR* 7 (1997) 145-68.

————. "A Realized Hope, a New Commitment, and a Developed Proclamation: Paul and Jesus," in *The Road from Damascus: The Impact of Paul's Conversion on His Life, Thought, and Ministry,* ed. R. N. Longenecker. MNTS. Grand Rapids: Eerdmans, 1997, 18-42.

————. "The Focus of Romans: The Central Role of 5:1–8:39 in the Argument of the Letter," in *Romans and the People of God* (Essays in Honor of Gordon D. Fee on the Occasion of His 65th Birthday), ed. S. K. Soderlund and N. T. Wright. Grand Rapids: Eerdmans, 1999, 49-69; repr. in *Studies in Paul, Exegetical and Theological.* Sheffield: Phoenix Press, 2006, 96-121.

————. *Biblical Exegesis in the Apostolic Period.* Grand Rapids: Eerdmans, 1975; 2nd ed., 1999.

463

―――. *New Wine into Fresh Wineskins: Contextualizing the Early Christian Confessions*. Peabody: Hendrickson, 1999.

―――. "Prayer in the Pauline Letters," in *Into God's Presence: Prayer in the New Testament*, ed. R. N. Longenecker. MNTS. Grand Rapids: Eerdmans, 2001, 203-27.

―――. "Christological Materials within the Early Christian Communities," in *Contours of Christology in the New Testament*, ed. R. N. Longenecker. MNTS. Grand Rapids: Eerdmans, 2004, 47-76; repr. in *Studies in Hermeneutics, Christology and Discipleship*. Sheffield: Phoenix, 2004, 90-121.

Luz, Ulrich. "Zum Aufbau von Röm 1–8," *TZ* 25 (1969) 161-81.

Lyonnet, Stanislaus. "Note sur le plan de l'Épître aux Romains," *RSR* 39 (1952) 301-16.

Manson, William. "Notes on the Argument of Romans (ch. 1-8)," in *New Testament Essays: Studies in Memory of Thomas Walter Manson*, ed. A. J. B. Higgins. Manchester: Manchester University Press, 1959, 150-64.

Martin, James P. "The Kerygma of Romans," *Int* 25 (1971) 303-28.

Martin, Ralph P. *Reconciliation: A Study of Paul's Theology*, rev. ed. Grand Rapids: Zondervan, 1990.

Meyer, Ben F. "Jesus and the Remnant of Israel," *JBL* 84 (1965) 123-30.

―――. *The Aims of Jesus*. London: SCM, 1979, esp. 118-21, 197, 220-22, and 225-29.

―――. "The Pre-Pauline Formula in Rom 3.25-26a," *NTS* 29 (1983) 198-208.

Minear, Paul S. *The Obedience of Faith: The Purposes of Paul in the Epistle to the Romans*. SBT 2.19. London: SCM, 1971.

Moiser, Jeremy. "Rethinking Romans 12–15," *NTS* 36 (1990) 571-82.

Morris, Leon. "The Theme of Romans," in *Apostolic History and the Gospel: Biblical and Historical Essays Presented to F. F. Bruce on His 60th Birthday*, ed. W. W. Gasque and R. P. Martin. Exeter: Paternoster; Grand Rapids: Eerdmans, 1970, 249-63.

Munck, Johannes. *Paul and the Salvation of Mankind*, trans. F. Clarke. London: SCM; Richmond: John Knox, 1959, 196-209.

―――. *Christ and Israel: An Interpretation of Romans 9–11*, trans. I. Nixon. Philadelphia: Fortress, 1967.

Mussner, Franz. "Heil für Alle: Der Grundgedanke des Römerbriefes," *Kairos* 23 (1981) 207-14.

Noack, Bent W. "Current and Backwater in the Epistle to the Romans," *ST* 19 (1965) 155-66.

O'Brien, Peter T. "Thanksgiving and the Gospel in Paul," *NTS* 21 (1974) 144-55; repr. in *Introductory Thanksgivings in the Letters of Paul*. NovTSup 49. Leiden: Brill, 1977, esp. 197-230.

Oepke, Albrecht. "Der Herrnspruch über die Kirche, Mt 16,17-19 in der neuesten Forschung," *ST* 2 (1948) 110-65.

Patte, Daniel. *Paul's Faith and the Power of the Gospel: A Structural Introduction to the Pauline Letters*. Philadelphia: Fortress, 1983, 232-96.

Plevnik, Joseph. "The Center of Paul's Theology," *CBQ* 51 (1989) 460-78.

Prümm, Karl. "Zur Struktur des Römerbriefes. Begriffsreihen als Einheitsband," *ZKT* 72 (1950) 333-49.

Räisänen, Heikki. "Zum Verständnis von Röm 3.1-8," in his *The Torah and Christ: Essays in German and English on the Problem of the Law in Early Christianity.* Helsinki: PFES, 1986, 185-205.

Sanders, E. P. *Paul and Palestinian Judaism: A Comparison of Patterns of Religion.* Philadelphia: Fortress, 1977.

Schmidt, Karl L. "Die Kirche des Urchristentums," in *Festgabe für Adolf Deissmann zum 60. Geburtstag.* Tübingen: Mohr (Siebeck), 1927, 258-319 (esp. 290-92).

————. ἐκκλησία, *TDNT* 3.501-36 (esp. 525-26).

Schrenk, Gottlob, and Volkmar Herntrich. "λεῖμμα, ὑπόλειμμα, κτλ," *TDNT* 4.194-214.

Schubert, Paul. *Form and Function of the Pauline Thanksgivings.* BZNTW 20. Berlin: Töpelmann, 1939.

Scroggs, Robin. "Paul as Rhetorician: Two Homilies in Romans 1-11, in *Jews, Greeks, and Christians (Festschrift* for W. D. Davies), ed. R. Hammerton-Kelly and R. Scroggs. Leiden: Brill, 1976, 271-98.

Siegert, Folker. *Argumentation bei Paulus. Gezeigt an Röm 9-11.* WUNT 34. Tübingen: Mohr-Siebeck, 1985.

Stegner, William R. "Romans 9.6-29 — A Midrash," *JSNT* 29 (1984) 37-52.

Stirewalt, M. Luther, Jr. "The Form and Function of the Greek Letter-Essay," in Donfried, ed., *Romans Debate* (1977), 175-206; (1991), 147-71.

————. *Paul, the Letter Writer.* Grand Rapids: Eerdmans, 2003.

Stowers, Stanley K. *The Diatribe and Paul's Letter to the Romans.* SBL.DS 57. Chico: Scholars, 1981.

————. "Paul's Dialogue with a Fellow Jew in Romans 3:1-9," *CBQ* 46 (1984) 707-22.

————. *Letter Writing in Greco-Roman Antiquity.* Philadelphia: Westminster, 1986.

————. "The Diatribe," in *Greco-Roman Literature and the New Testament,* ed. D. E. Aune. SBL.SBS 21. Atlanta: Scholars, 1988, 71-83.

————. "Diatribe," in *Anchor Bible Dictionary,* 6 vols., ed. D. N. Freedman. New York: Doubleday, 1992, 2.190-93.

————. *A Rereading of Romans: Justice, Jews, and Gentiles.* New Haven: Yale University Press, 1994.

Theissen, Gerd. *Psychological Aspects of Pauline Theology.* Philadelphia: Fortress, 1987.

Thielman, Frank S. "The Story of Israel and the Theology of Romans 5-8," in *Pauline Theology,* vol. 3: *Romans,* ed. D. M. Hay and E. E. Johnson. Minneapolis: Fortress, 1995, 169-95.

Thompson, Michael B. *Clothed with Christ: The Example and Teaching of Jesus in Romans 12.1-15.13.* JSNT.SS 59. Sheffield: JSOT, 1991.

Watson, Francis. "The Two Roman Congregations: Romans 14:1-15:13," in *Paul, Judaism and the Gentiles: A Sociological Approach.* SNTS.MS 56. Cambridge: Cambridge University Press, 1986, 94-105; repr. in Donfried, ed., *Romans Debate* (1991), 203-15.

Wedderburn, Alexander J. M. "Adam in Paul's Letter to the Romans," *Studia Biblica* 3, ed. E. A. Livingstone. Sheffield: JSOT, 1980, 413-30.

Weima, Jeffrey A. D. *Neglected Endings: The Significance of the Pauline Letter Closings.* Sheffield: Sheffield Academic Press, 1994.

—————. "Preaching the Gospel in Rome: A Study of the Epistolary Framework of Romans," in *Gospel in Paul: Studies on Corinthians, Galatians and Romans for Richard N. Longenecker,* ed. L. A. Jervis and P. Richardson. Sheffield: Sheffield Academic Press, 1994, 337-66.

White, John L. "Introductory Formulae in the Body of the Pauline Letter," *JBL* 90 (1971) 91-97.

—————. *The Form and Function of the Body of the Greek Letter: A Study of the Letter-Body in the Non-Literary Papyri and in Paul the Apostle.* SBL.DS 5. 2nd ed. Missoula: Scholars, 1972.

—————. "Saint Paul and the Apostolic Letter Tradition," *CBQ* 45 (1983) 433-44.

—————. "Ancient Greek Letters," in *Greco-Roman Literature and the New Testament: Selected Forms and Genres,* ed. D. E. Aune. SBL.SBS 21. Atlanta: Scholars, 1988, 85-106.

Wiefel, Wolfgang. "The Jewish Community in Ancient Rome and the Origins of Roman Christianity," in Donfried, ed., *Romans Debate* (1977), 100-119; (1991), 85-101 (trans. of "Die jüdische Gemeinschaft im antiken Rom und die Anfänge des römischen Christentums. Bemerkungen zu Anlass und Zweck des Römerbriefs," *Jud* 26 [1970] 65-88).

Williams, Sam K. "The 'Righteousness of God' in Romans," *JBL* 99 (1980) 241-90.

Wolter, Michael. *Rechtfertigung und zukünftiges Heil: Untersuchungen zu Röm 5,1-11.* BZNTW 43. Berlin, New York: de Gruyter, 1978.

Wuellner, Wilhelm. "Paul's Rhetoric of Argumentation in Romans: An Alternative to the Donfried-Karris Debate over Romans," *CBQ* 38 (1976) 330-51; repr. in Donfried, ed., *Romans Debate* (1977), 152-74; (1991), 128-46.

Postscript

All of the critical issues discussed in the eleven chapters of this book are important in a scholarly study of Romans. Other scholars will deal with many of these matters differently than we have, and that is to be expected. For the interpretation of Scripture is a human endeavor, and everything human expresses human frailties, inabilities, and errors that need to be corrected and dealt with more accurately and effectively. Nonetheless, most (if not all) of the issues presented above need to be taken into consideration in every scholarly treatment of Paul's letter to Rome. So we present to serious readers of Romans what we have set out in this book, trusting that, under the direction of God's Spirit, it will (1) give guidance with respect to many of the thorny critical issues in the letter, (2) enliven interaction with Paul's most famous letter, and (3) aid in the understanding of the letter's contents — with all of these purposes coming to fruition, through the ministry of God's Spirit, in a growth of intellectual understanding, a greater response to God and his love, mercy, and grace, a better appreciation of the person and work of Christ, and a heightened commitment to the Christian gospel ("the Good News") and its implications for one's own life, for the ministry of the Christian church, and for society generally.

What needs now to be done is to use our treatments of the critical issues in the study of Romans as a basis for a truly exegetical commentary on Paul's letter to the Christians at Rome — not only providing (1) a new translation of the letter, but also, and more importantly, presenting for each unit of material in the letter (2) a series of text-critical notes and evaluations for the "establishment" of the original Greek text; (3) a summary of matters regarding the form, structure, and setting of the passage in question; (4) an in-depth exegesis of what is written in each particular unit of material; (5) a drawing together of matters in each of the passages into an elementary Christian biblical theology; and (6) a suggestive treatment of how each of the units in the letter functions as a paradigm for believers in Jesus and for the church at large in contextualizing the "Good News" of the Christian gospel today. And it is such an exegetical commentary on Romans that we are preparing today and hope to publish in the very near future.

Index of Authors

Index of Scripture and Other Ancient Writings